PRAISE FOR *THE PRICE OF PEACE*

"Zachary D. Carter's outstanding new intellectual biography of John Maynard Keynes offers a resonant guide to our current moment, even if he finished writing it in the time before Covid-19. It's rare for a 600-page economic history to move swiftly along currents of lucidity and wit, and this happens to be one of them. . . . Carter begins with a love story, and ends with an elegant explanation of a credit default swap; even readers without a background in high finance will learn how to appreciate the drama of both. . . . Carter's explications of macroeconomic theory are so seamlessly woven into his narrative that they're almost imperceptible; you only notice how substantive they are once you get to his chapter on Keynes's notoriously dense 1936 book, *The General Theory of Employment, Interest and Money,* and realize that you're riveted by a passage on fluctuations in liquidity preference because you somehow know exactly what it is that Carter is talking about. . . . [A] brilliantly incisive book."

—Jennifer Szalai, *The New York Times*

"When we worry that uncertainty and fear will turn a momentary downturn into a prolonged recession, we are channeling John Maynard Keynes. It is our good fortune, then, that at this most Keynesian of moments, Zachary Carter has produced a spectacular new biography that paints a rich and textured portrait of the great economist and locates his ideas within the broad sweep of economic and intellectual history. Although Carter is known for his reporting on economic policy for *HuffPost,* he has found an even higher calling as a writer who can explain economic concepts with such clarity and simplicity that we digest them with the same ease and satisfaction as a plump oyster sliding down our gullet. With his first book, Carter establishes himself as the rare writer who can weave compelling narrative, insightful analysis and explication of complex phenomena in prose that is accessible, elegant, almost lyrical at times. *The Price of Peace* should be required reading for every economics major and anyone who struggles to understand the interplay of money, markets and economic policy."

—Steven Pearlstein, *The Washington Post*

"Timing, paradoxically, can be critical to a history book, and *The Price of Peace: Money, Democracy, and the Life of John Maynard Keynes* couldn't have appeared at a more opportune moment. Journalist Zachary Carter has crafted a timely, lucid and compelling portrait of a man whose enduring relevance is always heightened when crisis strikes. . . . Mr. Carter has, with this fresh reappraisal, made an outstanding authorial debut. The financial and economic questions with which Keynes wrestled, both as scholar and adviser, were complex, and it is tempting for an author writing for a wide audience to gloss superficially over the more difficult ones. But whether the subject is war reparations or interest-rate policy, Mr. Carter leaves no reader behind, and he writes with wit and clarity. . . . The best single-volume biography of this intellectual giant."

—Benn Steil, *The Wall Street Journal*

"Astoundingly well-written . . . an extraordinary achievement . . . a phenomenal book . . . enjoyable, entertaining, enriching."

—Chris Hayes, host of MSNBC's *All In with Chris Hayes*

"[Shows] brilliantly how Keynes was vastly more important to modern social thought and today's politics than the 'Keynesian models' of aggregate demand conventionally associated with Keynes today . . . Zachary Carter's brilliant book enables us to watch the unfolding of Keynes's insights and the development of his practical wisdom, against the backdrop of history and Keynes's personal life. . . . Carter wonderfully describes the well-known story of how Keynes became a leading public intellectual. . . . Carter's book is wonderful for taking Keynes's story across the ocean after World War II as it played out in the United States, which succeeded Britain as the apex of the global economy."

—Jeffrey Sachs, *The American Prospect*

"Ingenious . . . an entertaining summary of twentieth-century economic history that will appeal to the general reader."

—*The Economist*

"The book that swept me away this summer, though, is . . . *The Price of Peace*, by Zachary D. Carter. . . . Carter shows how Keynes's economic weapons have played out in the long drama circling social justice. . . . Carter's book soars."

—Taylor Beck, *Los Angeles Review of Books*

THE
PRICE
OF
PEACE

THE
PRICE
OF
PEACE

$\diamond$

Money, Democracy, and the Life of John Maynard Keynes

ZACHARY D. CARTER

RANDOM HOUSE
NEW YORK

Published in the United States by Random House, an imprint and
division of Penguin Random House LLC, New York.

RANDOM HOUSE and the HOUSE colophon are registered
trademarks of Penguin Random House LLC.

Originally published in hardcover in the United States by Random House,
an imprint and division of Penguin Random House LLC, in 2020.

Library of Congress Cataloging-in-Publication Data
Names: Carter, Zachary D., author.
Title: The price of peace: money, democracy, and the life of
John Maynard Keynes / Zachary D. Carter.
Description: First edition. | New York: Random House, 2020 | Includes
bibliographical references and index.
Identifiers: LCCN 2019037057 (print) | LCCN 2019037058 (ebook) |
ISBN 9780525509059 (trade paperback) | ISBN 9780525509042 (ebook)
Subjects: LCSH: Keynes, John Maynard, 1883–1946. | Economists—Great Britain—
Biography. | Economics—History—20th century. | Bloomsbury group.
Classification: LCC HB103.K47 .C376 2020 (print) | LCC HB103.K47 (ebook) |
DDC 330.15/7092 [B]—dc23
LC record available at https://lccn.loc.gov/2019037057

Printed in the United States of America on acid-free paper

randomhousebooks.com

4 6 8 9 7 5 3

Book design by Caroline Cunningham

For Ming

In the long run, we are all dead.

—John Maynard Keynes, December 1923

In the long run almost anything is possible.

—John Maynard Keynes, April 1942

CONTENTS

————————◇————————

INTRODUCTION

———————◇———————

I N THE SPRING OF 1922, John Maynard Keynes was in love. He was terrified.

Ever since boarding school, Maynard, as his friends called him, had been almost exclusively interested in men. Suddenly at age thirty-eight, he was besotted with a woman nearly a decade his junior: Russian ballet starlet Lydia Lopokova. "I'm entangled—a dreadful business—and barely fit to speak to," he wrote to his friend Lytton Strachey.[1]

To Maynard's confidants in London's cultured enclave of Bloomsbury, the infatuation made no sense. "What are we all coming to, pray?" Lytton wondered. "The Universe totters."[2] Virginia Woolf was appalled by the thought of Maynard being "controlled" by a lover.[3] His days of wild romance were supposed to be long buried in the past. As he had told Lytton two years earlier, in matters of the heart, he could be drawn only into "shallow waters." "Up to the middle, not head over ears at my age."[4] He preferred dispassionate, on-again-off-again affairs, like his relationship with the psychologist Sebastian Sprott, whom he was still seeing when he found himself abruptly overwhelmed by Lydia.

Gender and passion accounted for only part of the shock. Maynard was a man of the world. A respected economist and former Treasury official, he had garnered great fame and not a little fortune for the precise clarity of his mind. The august bankers in the City of London and titled aristocrats who followed his work in the financial pages could not believe their ears when they heard that the great Keynes had fallen for, in the words of one earl, "a chorus girl."[5] Even Virginia's sister, Vanessa Bell, an artist of middle-class stock, was annoyed by the way Lydia chatted up household servants as though they were social equals.

But Lydia dazzled Maynard. Her wit was as nimble as her limbs. He had watched her perform night after night as the Lilac Fairy in the Ballets Russes rendition of Tchaikovsky's *Sleeping Beauty*. He had visited with her backstage, invited her to lunch, stayed out into the small hours of the morning laughing at her jokes, and rented her a flat in the same London square as his own—all within the span of a few short weeks. To Maynard, she was not merely a dancer but an artist, fluent in the high cultural lexicon that linked St. Petersburg, Paris, London, and New York. Though a pending jaunt to India with a British cabinet minister presented him with an opportunity to cool his fevered passions, Maynard found himself unable to break away. He canceled the trip and took Lydia sightseeing around London in a hired car instead. "I'm in a terribly bad plight," he confessed to Vanessa. "She seems to me perfect in every way."[6]

Perfect, but very different. As a child, Lydia had shared a cramped St. Petersburg apartment with four siblings before an audition with an imperial dance academy had rescued her from poverty. Maynard came from a comfortable academic household in Cambridge and made his international reputation working in British government. "Is there any resemblance between you and me?" Lydia asked. "No! So different it becomes attractive."[7] And to Maynard, the enchanting Russian ballerina was more than a talented, talkative artist; she was the living embodiment of an ideal he thought he had lost eight years earlier at the outbreak of the Great War.

Bloomsbury had always been a tiny, insular haven for artists and intellectuals, but paradoxically, it had connected Maynard to a wider, vibrant world beyond London and across oceans. Before the war, Vanessa had visited Pablo Picasso's studio in Montparnasse; Maynard's friend and sometime lover Duncan Grant had stayed with Gertrude Stein in Paris.[8] Maynard himself had been good friends with the Austrian philosopher Ludwig Wittgenstein, and Bloomsbury's art openings, garden parties, and evenings of debate had helped him appreciate other cultural movements whose power transcended language and nationality, from French Postimpressionism to German romanticism and the novels of the Russian pacifist Leo Tolstoy. Through Bloomsbury, Keynes joined an international community of progressive intellectuals who believed themselves to be breaking down the crude medieval barriers between peoples through the power of love and beauty.

The war had shattered that collective illusion. And its fractured, bitter aftermath seemed to show that the golden years of Maynard's youth had been little more than the trivial diversions of the British leisure class at the apex of British colonial hegemony. Now, for the first time in years, Lydia offered Maynard hope—not the abstract, probabilistic optimism he typically carried, but a powerful, almost religious *hope*—that the dream he had lived as a young man could be realized once again. Whatever vendettas Europe's leaders might pursue, the wild, impossible love between Lydia and Maynard was proof that the world was filled with beautiful potential. Beneath the ugly, cynical empires of money and politics lay a deeper, more powerful empire of ideas waiting to unite humanity across borders and languages.

The life of John Maynard Keynes was filled with turning points. Few citizens of the twentieth century reinvented themselves with the regularity that Keynes did over the course of his nearly sixty-three years. But the unexpected blossoming of his romance with Lydia Lopokova was the decisive juncture that made him a force in the history of ideas. When Keynes finally did break away from Lydia for a few weeks in April and May of 1922, it was to embark on a new project that, in a turn nearly as surprising as his recent outbreak of love, would establish him as the most important economic thinker of his day.

Keynes was off to the Italian city of Genoa that spring. He did not leave intending to write his first great work of economic theory. He was hoping to make his name as a journalist and perhaps reestablish a place for himself as an adviser to the power brokers of Europe. It was a career experiment born of necessity. Less than three years earlier, Keynes had been exiled from Whitehall and Parliament over the publication of *The Economic Consequences of the Peace*—his devastating attack on the Treaty of Versailles, the compact which had set the terms of peace at the close of the Great War. His book had exposed the underhanded machinations of Keynes' own government at the 1919 peace conference and predicted that the treaty's financial arrangements would march Europe to economic ruin, dictatorship, and war.

To the surprise of both Keynes and his publisher, this grim tract had been an international bestseller, vaulting Keynes to the celebrity status of European nobility and American motion picture stars. Over the ensuing three years, his reputation soared to still greater heights as his predictions began to take on the aura of prophecy: ruthless unemployment fueled labor strikes in Britain, riots across Italy, and a wave of political assassinations in Germany. And now newspaper publishers from Vienna to New York were betting that he could repeat the success of his famous book.

Central bankers, treasury officials, and heads of state were gathering in Genoa for what was to be the most important financial conference since the end of the war—the first meeting of the victorious Allies and the vanquished Germans since Versailles. It was to be European diplomacy on the grandest scale. Even the deviant new socialist government of Russia would be sending a delegation. Newspapers in New York, Manchester, and Vienna offered Keynes the astounding sum of £675—over $45,000 in today's money—to cover the conference; his transcontinental audience would number in the millions.[9] This was not merely a contract offered to a talented reporter; his publishers hoped that Keynes would infuse his dispatches with the detailed flair and ferocity that had made his book a sensation.

Keynes did not share his publishers' confidence in his abilities. He was still new to popular writing and worried that *Economic Consequences* had been a fluke. As a young man, he had fired off academic articles with carefree confidence; as he entered middle age, he struggled to translate his complex ideas into something ordinary people might actually understand. It was a frustrating, degrading experience for someone who had long been celebrated for his brilliance. "Journalism eats one up; leaves no energy for higher matters," he once wrote to Lydia.[10] And the stratospheric paychecks for his work in Genoa only intensified his anxieties. It was too much money to turn down, but it established impossibly high expectations. If he couldn't deliver the goods, his name might never recover.

But as Keynes walked Genoa's corridors of power, his new love helped embolden his self-confidence. Maynard and Lydia exchanged a daily correspondence bursting with sexual and intellectual energy, infused with Lydia's gift for metaphor and the unusual cadences of a woman still finding her bearings in English. "I blend my mouth and heart to yours," she wrote.[11] His dispatches from the conference were "like clear compact buildings." Although she found it "annoying that financial experts do not want stabilization" of the world's major currencies, she insisted that her new lover's keen analysis would bring them around: "To-days article on the reparation problem is very energetic, when the conference experts read it they will adopt the right course."[12]

Most important, her letters reminded Keynes what he was in Genoa to achieve. This was not merely a gathering of banking experts assembled to debate interest and principal; it was Europe's last, best hope to save itself from an authoritarian future. And it was Keynes' chance to show that the little world of art, beauty, and cross-cultural understanding he and Lydia had created could be replicated in economic diplomacy.

Armed with his massive audience, Keynes found himself newly appreciated by the men of power who surrounded him. His ideas were serious, his proposals important. The British delegation even gave brief consideration to an overhaul of the international currency system Keynes had devised to ameliorate the monetary mayhem of inflation, deflation, and devaluation that had taken hold since the end of the war.

But the conference was not going well. "Under the surface, amidst dark intrigue, the European diplomatists are playing their old games," Keynes warned in the pages of *The Manchester Guardian.* "Combinations are being tentatively formed . . . which may, left to themselves, produce as inflammable a Europe as in 1914. The old political ideas, which for a thousand years have periodically devastated Europe, are not dead."[13]

British diplomats did not conceal their contempt for their German counterparts. One British official called Weimar foreign minister Walther Rathenau a "bald-headed Jewish degenerate," while Soviet commissar for foreign affairs Georgy Chicherin was ridiculed as "the degenerate he is"—Chicherin was gay—"and of course except for himself and Krassin . . . the [Russian delegates] are all Jews."[14]

These poisonous sentiments infected debate over the astronomical debts that had arisen out of the Great War. To Keynes, the debts were not merely an economic problem but a political wildfire waiting to ignite. Europe's war-ravaged economy, he believed, was too weak to support massive payments to war creditors. The fact that the debts were owed to foreign banks and governments was inflaming old rivalries, setting peoples against each other. Money shipped to creditors overseas could not be spent on reconstruction projects or public aid at home, and people knew it. A nationalist backlash was already in motion, sowing the seeds of another war. To Keynes, the purpose of the conference was to get past the debts or at least create a new framework for cooperation that might lead to their elimination. "I will be no party to the continuation of a European blood-feud, however great the past guilt," he had written to a friend a year earlier.[15]

But for France and Great Britain, war debts were both a burden and a source of income.[16] Both nations had borrowed enormous amounts from the United States, but both had also loaned extraordinary sums to the tsarist regime in Russia during the early years of the war. Now Vladimir Lenin's Bolshevik government had repudiated those debts. And so once all of the grandees had assembled in Genoa, Britain and France announced that the Soviet government would be required to acknowledge the legitimacy of the tsar's financial contracts as a pre-condition for participation in the talks. The Bolsheviks might do what they liked with their internal economic program, but in matters of international diplomacy, the customs of nineteenth-century capital-ism would have to be observed. Debts must be honored, revolution or no.

Keynes was outraged. Russia was in the middle of a famine that would eventually claim five million lives. It was both a humanitarian crime and a monetary delusion to believe it could hand over the equivalent of billions of dollars to France and Britain. The money would never be paid, whatever arrangement might end up on paper. "We act as high priests, not as debt collectors," he wrote. "It is a reli-gious ceremony we are demanding at Genoa. . . . instead of trying to disentangle the endless coil of impossible debt, [the conference] merely proposes to confuse it further."[17]

The conference had descended into a referendum on socialism. To Keynes, it was the wrong problem. Socialism was a practical question to be resolved among people of goodwill—a dispute within the broad family of Enlightenment liberalism. The real danger was from those who rejected international harmony for national glory—the violent ultranationalist movements rising across the continent. "Many appre-hend the issue of the near future as between the forces of Bolshevism and those of the bourgeois states of the nineteenth-century type," Keynes wrote from Genoa. "I do not agree. The real struggle of today . . . is between that view of the world, termed liberalism or radicalism, for which the primary object of government and of foreign policy is peace, freedom of trade and intercourse, and economic wealth, and that other view, militarist, or, rather, diplomatic, which thinks in terms of power, prestige, national or personal glory, the imposition of a culture, and hereditary or racial prejudice."

If militarists were to prevail, Keynes told his readers, "sooner or later an economic disease spreads which ends in some variant of the *delirium tremens* of revolution." The great threat facing liberalism was not socialism but the thirst for military domination. "Soldiers and diplomatists—*they* are the permanent, the immortal foe."[18]

Keynes underestimated the Soviet government's potential for paranoid brutality. But his warnings about the momentum for revolution on the right were prescient. His impassioned dispatches from Genoa were published six months before Benito Mussolini's Blackshirts would march on Rome, nine months before the French invasion of the Ruhr, and nineteen months before Adolf Hitler's Beer Hall Putsch in Munich. And yet Keynes' words at the conference fell on deaf ears. He had reestablished himself among the power elite, but the elite were not yet ready to accept his advice.

Keynes' work did not end when the diplomats packed their bags and retreated to their various corners of Europe. Reunited with Lydia in London, he assembled his favorite dispatches from Genoa and spent weeks revising and supplementing them with masses of new material. By the time he was finished, what had begun as an intimidating foray into popular journalism had transformed into his first major work of economic theory. Published in December 1923, *A Tract on Monetary Reform* was, like its predecessor, a deceptively technical title filled with shocking ideas.[19] It was not merely the sanctity of international debt contracts that must be abandoned, Keynes informed his readers, but the entire global financial system that had established the foundation of free exchange between nations. The gold standard, the benchmark of economic sanity for as long as anyone could remember, had become a barrier to peace and prosperity—a "barbarous relic" incompatible with "the spirit and the requirements of the age."[20] One by one, Keynes was taking aim at the sacred tenets of nineteenth-century capitalism. The world was about to change.

Today, Keynes is remembered as an economist because it was through the field of economics that his ideas exercised their greatest influence.

College students are taught that he urged governments to accept budget deficits in a recession and spend money when the private sector cannot. But his economic agenda was always deployed in service of a broader, more ambitious social project. Keynes was a philosopher of war and peace, the last of the Enlightenment intellectuals who pursued political theory, economics, and ethics as a unified design. He was a man whose chief project was not taxation or government spending but the survival of what he called "civilisation"—the international cultural milieu that connected a British Treasury man to a Russian ballerina.[21] A decade after Genoa, when a reporter asked him if the world had ever seen anything like the unfolding Great Depression, Keynes replied in perfect sincerity: "Yes. It was called the Dark Ages, and it lasted 400 years."[22]

Keynes first saw the darkness encroaching at the outbreak of war in 1914. He gave his opponents different names—"militarists" and "imperialists" in the years before the Second World War, "brigand powers" and even "enemies of the human race" in those that followed.[23] Any idea or tactic was fair game so long as it protected his community of art, letters, and fine living from the march of authoritarianism. At different stages of his career, he embraced everything from free trade to stiff tariffs as potential remedies. His best-known work, *The General Theory of Employment, Interest and Money,* was not just an effort to provide theoretical justification for public works projects but a frontal assault in his crusade against militarism—a book he hoped would be used as kind of tool kit for anti-imperialist policy making. "If nations can learn to provide themselves with full employment by their domestic policy," he wrote in the book's conclusion, "there need be no important economic forces calculated to set the interest of one country against that of its neighbours."[24]

To his students at the University of Cambridge in the 1930s, many of whom would go on to implement his ideas around the world, the book contained an entire philosophy of life. In the words of one such student, David Bensusan-Butt, "The *General Theory* was to us less a work of economics theory than a Manifesto for Reason and Cheerfulness, the literary embodiment of a man who, to those who ever saw him, remains the very genius of intellect and enjoyment. It gave a rational basis and moral appeal for a faith in the possible health and sanity of contemporary mankind."[25]

That was not an easy belief to sustain amid the rise of fascism in the 1930s. Nor is it easy to maintain in our own time, as new bastions of authoritarian extremism consolidate power across Europe, the United States, Latin America, the Middle East, and Asia. But it is an essential faith for any who hope to address the world's problems through persuasion and the written word—and a conviction fundamental to the practice of democracy itself. As democratic institutions again find themselves under assault in the early twenty-first century, there is no intellectual from the twentieth century whose thought—its triumphs, its failures, and its fragilities—is more relevant than that of John Maynard Keynes.

Keynes was a tangle of paradoxes: a bureaucrat who married a dancer; a gay man whose greatest love was a woman; a loyal servant of the British Empire who railed against imperialism; a pacifist who helped finance two world wars; an internationalist who assembled the intellectual architecture for the modern nation-state; an economist who challenged the foundations of economics. But embedded in all of these seeming contradictions is a coherent vision of human freedom and political salvation. Keynes died before he could systematize those ideas into a singular, definitive philosophical statement—even the heights of ambition on display in *The General Theory* formed only one piece of the broader Keynesian project. This book is an effort to assemble it from the essays, pamphlets, letters, and books he left to posterity—and to show its still transformative implications for our own time.

It is also an attempt to chart the history of what became known as Keynesianism as it crossed the Atlantic and metamorphosed into a distinctly American political ethos. Here, too, there is no shortage of irony. Keynes never liked America—the weather was always too hot and there weren't enough birds in the countryside—or Americans, who were at once too brash and too sensitive. Yet without the political support his ideas won in the United States, Keynes and his work would be a minor curiosity for professional intellectuals.

Unlike his eventual marriage to Lydia, the union between Keynes and the United States was always difficult and unhappy. Leaders of the emerging hegemon had little interest in the anti-imperialist dimensions of Keynesian thought as they adapted *The General Theory* to the task of erecting a new global order around U.S. power. Influential American economists, more than their peers across the pond, were eager to view their work as politically neutral, an expert mathematical science far removed from the speculative ruminations of the Enlightenment philosophers Keynes had venerated. Even had they wished to act on such ideas, his more philosophically inclined successors—most notably John Kenneth Galbraith—found their work constrained by the political horizons of the American empire even as they sought to deploy Keynesian thought as a tool against empire itself.

And so the history of Keynesianism is an intellectual history of American power, both its promise and its abuse. Keynesianism took on a life of its own Keynes himself could scarcely have predicted. It is a history in which battles over textbooks on college campuses play as prominent a role as military deployments, election results, and stock market crashes—a history of numbers and equations but also of ballerinas and animal spirits.

In the spring of 1934, Virginia Woolf sketched an affectionate three-page "biographical fantasy" of her great friend, attempting to encompass no less than twenty-five themes, which she jotted down at its opening: "Politics. Art. Dancing. Letters. Economics. Youth. The Future. Glands. Genealogies. Atlantis. Mortality. Religion. Cambridge. Eton. The Drama. Society. Truth. Pigs. Sussex. The History of England. America. Optimism. Stammer. Old Books. Hume." Like the life Woolf imitated, her narrative jaunted from a farm in East Sussex to King's College, Cambridge, to the opera at Covent Garden to a rare bookshop before reaching her final, intimate homage: "He heard them crying the news in the street. And shrugging his shoulders applied himself to the great green board on which were pinned sheets of symbols: a frolic of xs controlled by ys and embraced by more cryptic symbols still: which, if juggled together would eventually, he was sure, positive, produce the one word, the simple, the sufficient the comprehensive word which will solve all problems forever. It was time to begin. He began."[26]

THE
PRICE
OF
PEACE

ONE

◇

AFTER THE GOLD RUSH

J OHN MAYNARD KEYNES WAS not an athletic man. Though a spirited debater, he had always suffered from fragile health. Overworked by choice and underexercised out of habit, he had acclimated himself to living in the constant shadow of head colds and influenza attacks. He was thirty-one years old on the first Sunday of August 1914 and had lived nearly all of those years at Cambridge, where, like his father before him, he held a minor academic post. His friend and mentor Bertrand Russell was accustomed to seeing the younger man reviewing figures or buried in papers on weekend afternoons. A King's College man, Keynes might, in moments of extreme restlessness, calm himself with a walk through the Great Court of Russell's Trinity College, taking in the turreted medieval towers of King's Gate, the soaring gothic windows of the chapel built during the reign of Queen Elizabeth, and the steady waters of the fountain designed when William Shakespeare had composed *Hamlet*. Keynes was a man who savored tradition and contemplation. He was perfectly suited for a life at the timeworn university.

But there was Keynes, hustling down the weathered flagstones that afternoon, tearing past the lush, closely cropped green lawns. Russell stopped his young friend to ask what was wrong. Keynes, with a brusque flutter of words, told him he needed to get to London. "Why don't you go by train?" the philosopher asked.

"There isn't time," Keynes replied to the baffled Russell and hurried along.

There were more curiosities to come. Keynes left the court and approached a motorcycle belonging to his brother-in-law, Vivian Hill. Keynes—who was nearly six feet seven—folded his long legs into the sidecar, and the two proceeded to putter and jostle their way sixty miles to the capital.[1] Their odd, frantic journey would change the fate of the British Empire.

England was in the fifth day of the most violent financial crisis it had ever experienced—one that threatened to tear its economy apart even as the nation's leaders wrestled over the most momentous diplomatic question of their generation: whether to enter the war breaking out on the European continent. Though none of the foreign policy experts and financial engineers huddled in London recognized it at the time, the economic system that had fed and fueled Europe for the past half century had just come to a sudden, cataclysmic end.

Since the close of the Franco-Prussian War in 1871, the world's great powers—and many of its minor players—had grown to depend on complex international trade arrangements to provide their citizens with everything from basic foodstuffs to heavy machinery. It was an era of ostentatious prosperity for both the aristocracy and an expanding, increasingly powerful middle class, a period future generations would romanticize with names like "La Belle Époque" and "The Gilded Age."[2] In England, factory workers spun Egyptian cotton and New Zealand wool into fineries that decorated homes all over the continent. The well-to-do and the up-and-coming adorned themselves with diamonds and ivory from South Africa embedded in settings crafted from gold mined in Australia. In Paris, the Hôtel Ritz served afternoon tea from India, while a new mode of haute cuisine spread through the luxury hotels of Europe, combining ingredients from the New World with what had once been regional specialties of France, Italy, and Germany.[3]

"In this economic Eldorado, in this economic Utopia," Keynes would later recall, "life offered, at a low cost and with the least trouble, conveniences, comforts, and amenities beyond the compass of the richest and most powerful monarchs of other ages."[4]

The cultural explosion was the product of empire. England, Spain, France, Germany, Russia, Belgium, the Netherlands, the Ottoman Empire, and even the adolescent United States all deployed military force to cultivate power over the people and resources of other continents. Keynes was aware of the brutalities that accompanied British imperialism, once earning a rebuke from a top official at the India Office for issuing a report that depicted a "coldblooded" British response to a plague that had "terribly ravaged" India.[5] But Keynes did not consider such events an integral element of the world's economic structure. They were instead unfortunate impurities, flaws that would eventually be distilled away by the engines of progress. "The projects and politics of militarism and imperialism, of racial and cultural rivalries, of monopolies, restrictions, and exclusion, which were to play the serpent to this paradise, were little more than the amusements of [the] daily newspaper, and appeared to exercise almost no influence at all on the ordinary course of social and economic life."[6]

What fascinated Keynes as a young economist was not the manner in which this new material abundance was extracted by European powers but the "the easy flow of capital and trade" among them. All across the continent new financial contracts had been woven into the patterns of global commerce. Companies were accustomed to borrowing money in one country, selling their products in another, and purchasing insurance in yet another. The proud, beating heart of this order was the City of London, the financial district of the British capital, where fully half of the world's business affairs were financed.[7] Whatever their nationality, the storied banking dynasties of the age—the transcontinental Rothschilds, the French Lazards, the Schröders of Hamburg and the American House of Morgan—all set up critical operations in London, where more than a billion dollars in foreign bonds were issued every year to private enterprise and sovereign governments alike.[8] This financial power had transformed London into the thickest bustling metropolis on the planet, with a population of more than six million, nearly double that of 1861.[9]

For all its complexity, the system London oversaw had enjoyed a remarkable stability. Trading accounts between nations were balanced, capital flows were steady and predictable, and financial disruptions in the Old World were brief affairs, always quickly corrected. Measured against such fabulous symmetries, most members of the leisure class considered even the underbelly of this system—domestic industrial poverty, a twenty-year agricultural depression in America—to be inconsequential. "The inhabitant of London could order by telephone, sipping his morning tea in bed, the various products of the whole earth, in such quantity as he might see fit, and reasonably expect their early delivery upon his doorstep," Keynes wrote. "Most important of all, he regarded this state of affairs as normal, certain, and permanent, except in the direction of further improvement."[10]

The new financial reality had spawned its own political ideology. In 1910, the British journalist Norman Angell published *The Great Illusion,* a book claiming to demonstrate that the international commercial entanglements of the twentieth century had made war economically irrational. No nation, Angell argued, could profit by subjugating another through military conquest. Even the victors would suffer financial harm, whatever the spoils might be.[11]

Angell was wrong—and, worse, misunderstood. His book sold millions of copies, developing a cult following of influential public officials who came to believe that because war was financially counterproductive, it was now a problem of the past. That was not what Angell himself actually preached; "irrational" did not mean "impossible." But in an age possessed by an ideal of enlightened, rational government, many political leaders came to believe that the prospect of war was becoming "more difficult and improbable" by the day.[12] It was an early version of the doctrine *New York Times* columnist Thomas L. Friedman would eventually formulate in a bestseller of his own a century later, when he declared that "no two countries that are both part of a major global supply chain . . . will ever fight a war."[13]

But the unthinkable event had in fact arrived. On June 28, 1914, a teenage Yugoslav nationalist murdered Archduke Franz Ferdinand, the heir to the throne of the Austro-Hungarian Empire, during a visit to Sarajevo, and the empire retaliated by declaring war on Serbia. Armies were now mobilizing from France all the way to Russia. As the thicket of political alliances appeared certain to draw empire upon empire into the looming conflict, the seemingly impregnable payment system that had made London the center of the economic universe abruptly collapsed.

The chaos began in the Vienna stock market and spread to every European capital within days. When banks and investors suffered heavy losses in one city, they withdrew money from others, forcing further liquidations abroad. By Thursday, July 30, London and Paris were the only trading centers open in Europe, as governments tried to stop the sudden plunge in securities prices by shutting down stock exchanges entirely. That only intensified the pressure on the French and British markets as foreign investors placed orders in London to sell off securities at almost any price, sending stock values into free fall.

This was bad enough—but the bigger problem was the sudden halt to the flow of payments the City typically received from overseas. Millions of pounds' worth of debts were due in London every day, and the war declarations suddenly made it impossible for even solvent foreign debtors to pay their obligations in London. Countries on one side of the budding conflict forbade investors to pay firms on the other side. The cost of insuring international gold shipments exploded, making it impossible to move money abroad. Shipping routes were interrupted, and world trade began to break down. Paris withdrew £4 million in gold from the Bank of England in an effort to shore up French banks.[14] Money was going out, but it wasn't coming in. Great Britain was under financial bombardment.[15]

That placed the entire international monetary system—the gold standard—in peril. "The influence of London on credit conditions throughout the world was so predominant that the Bank of England could almost have claimed to be the conductor of the international orchestra," Keynes later wrote.[16] If London were to go down, global finance would go down with it.

The Bank of England was not a bank in the traditional sense. It didn't accept deposits from workers, issue mortgages to families, or lend money to shopkeepers. Instead, it managed the British currency system by setting interest rates—a powerful tool that determined the price of credit in the economy, which, in turn, dictated the pace of economic growth, overall wage levels, and, critically, the flow of imports and exports. It was the world's most prominent central bank and served as a model for the Federal Reserve, which President Woodrow Wilson had recently established in the United States.

The Bank of England managed all of this by transacting with the ordinary banks that did business with customers, who, in turn, performed the real commercial activity of society. Its most important resource for those transactions was gold, the ultimate measure of economic might in the Gilded Age. The currencies of major countries were issued in gold coin or in paper notes that could be exchanged for a specific amount of gold. This was the Bank of England's only major obligation to consumers. Anyone who presented the Bank with legitimate paper money had to be paid in gold, on demand.

The more currency a country circulated, the more economic activity it could support—so long as there was a corresponding amount of gold stored away in bank vaults to back up its bills. The financial thinkers of the day believed that without gold to give money some value independent of a government's say-so, issuing fresh currency could not ultimately boost the economy. Instead, it would cause inflation, an overall increase in prices that would devalue the savings people had previously accumulated and eat away at the purchasing power of their paychecks.

Britain's vast political empire gave the Bank of England advantages that other central banks couldn't access. It could purchase raw gold directly from mines in South Africa at favorable prices to bolster its reserves.[17] That often came in handy, but it was a slow and clumsy process that couldn't respond to the daily demands of global commerce, much less the rapid currents of a financial crisis.

In fact, though gold anchored the international currency regime, relatively little was shipped back and forth between nations to balance trading accounts. Instead, central banks regulated their gold hoards with interest rates. If its gold reserves were decreasing, the Bank of England would raise interest rates, encouraging people to keep their money in British currency by increasing the return on everything from bank deposits to the corporate bonds of British businesses. Gold did not earn interest; its value was permanently fixed at a specific unit of currency. But the prospect of higher interest rates on the pound could convince skittish investors to keep their money in London instead of cashing it out for gold that could be reinvested in francs or dollars.

Raising interest rates also levied a toll on the domestic economy by making it more expensive for retailers and manufacturers to borrow money, increasing their costs. But as the Bank of England's gold position strengthened due to higher rates, it could relax the rates, easing the pressure on domestic business. Those maneuvers enabled central banks to deal with many everyday international payments by keeping accounts for foreign central banks in their own vaults, literally pushing gold across the room to keep track of transactions. International gold shipments were reserved for settling large, long-term balances between nations—or for unseen emergencies.

What terrified policy makers in August 1914, however, was the fact that high interest rates weren't working. The Bank of England had more than tripled the interest rate over the final week of July to an astronomical 10 percent, but nothing, it seemed, would stop the outflow of gold.

The sudden halt in foreign payments to London created an immediate crisis for the City's "acceptance houses"—entities that specialized in helping foreigners move their money into the British banking system. The acceptance houses had large accounts with stockbrokerages, firms that bought and sold stocks on the exchange for their investor clients. The brokerages, in turn, had significant debts to the major banks. The system had to keep money moving in order for everyone to stay in business; each institution depended on payments from others to make good on its liabilities to other firms. If the acceptance houses collapsed, it could trigger a chain reaction that would bring down the entire London financial complex—a calamity that a nation on the verge of war quite literally could not afford.

The dominoes were already falling. Foreign bank branches headquartered in the City began selling off their assets to send money—gold—home.[18] To save their own skins, City stockbrokers were forced to dump valuable long-term securities in order to get their hands on quick cash. Six brokerage firms failed in the span of just a few days, and the rush to sell at some price, any price, sent the market into free fall. That made stocks a bargain—but any businessman with the luxury to think beyond the immediate chaos was confronted with vast knots of commerce tying together six continents. It was simply impossible to untangle them and calculate the potential risks the war might pose to any particular firm or sector. In less than a week, the predictable and prosperous global economy had dissolved into a swamp of uncertainty.

So the British money men did what any other reasonable people would have done: They panicked. The Bank of England lost two-thirds of its gold reserves in just three days as financiers cashed in anything they could for gold, hoping to replace their suddenly unstable paper with the one asset universally recognized across national boundaries. Fearing for their own solvency, the banks hoarded gold and began refusing to advance funds to stockbrokers seeking short-term cash to weather the storm.[19] Clients who had been trusted for decades were turned away. The banks even stopped paying out gold coins to local depositors hoping to make withdrawals for daily shopping—a maneuver the titans of Lombard Street had, until that day, viewed as a disgrace to their personal character and moral integrity.[20]

The Bank of England enjoyed no such discretion. In an unmistakable sign of imminent catastrophe, hundreds of anxious customers formed a long line outside the central bank's doors, clogging pedestrian traffic throughout the day as they waited to receive their coinage.[21]

The British Treasury responded to the mayhem by shutting down the stock market and declaring a four-day bank holiday—the longest in the nation's history. The top Treasury official, Chancellor of the Exchequer David Lloyd George, imposed a one-month stay of any financial claims against the quaking acceptance houses. But the emergency maneuver that would eventually carry the weightiest consequences was a seemingly random personnel decision: enlisting an unrenowned thirty-one-year-old academic to fight the panic.

Keynes was an unlikely character to be drawn into the high strategy sessions of the Great War. His Cambridge degree was in mathematics, not economics, and he preferred the company of artists to that of bureaucrats. His social engagements were typically organized around highbrow debates over aesthetics, conversations among friends who swapped lovers and opened their marriages, insisting to others in their tight community that such romantic chaos was itself an act of social progress, a purge of the Victorian prudery that had strangled England's creative souls at the turn of the century. This society of novelists, painters, philosophers, poets, and art critics referred to itself as the Bloomsbury set, named for the London neighborhood where its central figures lived together, exchanging ideas and sharpening personal rivalries in an endless cycle of tea and dinner parties. In time they would become notorious for their outrageous personalities, collectively impressing the famed American journalist Walter Lippmann as, in the words of his biographer, "mad and perverse, given to wearing strange costumes, practicing elaborate jokes, and speaking in riddles."[22]

But for all their sexual and intellectual fecundity, the members of this whirlwind collective had accomplished very little as they approached middle age. One of Maynard's closest friends, Virginia Woolf, fancied herself a writer but had never published a book. Lytton Strachey, his most influential companion since their days in an undergraduate secret society, still depended on a financial lifeline from his widowed mother. Keynes himself had endured a brief and uneventful tenure at the British government's India Office, a bureaucratic post that had never required him to leave London.

He summarized what he'd learned on the job in his first book, *Indian Currency and Finance.* Published in early 1913, it was a technical work of modest ambition. Over the course of 260 pages, he argued that India's currency didn't need to be convertible into gold within India to support everyday commerce. The ability to cash in money for gold was important only for international trade, where merchants needed some objective measurement of value that could be applied consistently across different currencies.[23] As a young man, Keynes accepted the empire as a fact rather than a moral dilemma. He believed he had a responsibility to improve the quality of British governance and respect local authorities, but he did not question Great Britain's right to rule. He was interested in the details of Indian commercial exchange, not the power relations or human rights questions underlying those economic arrangements. The book had sold just 946 copies, and Keynes had slipped back to his alma mater, where he was now working on an abstract treatise about mathematical probability, receiving comments and advice from Russell, a versatile intellectual eleven years his senior.[24]

In the summer of 1914, Keynes was an obscurity. He was also a genius. "Keynes's intellect was the sharpest and clearest that I have ever known," Russell wrote.[25] "When I argued with him, I felt that I took my life in my hands, and I seldom emerged without feeling something of a fool."

The sheer power of his mind impressed itself on everyone he came into close contact with, from Cambridge to the India Office. Basil Blackett had been working at the British Treasury for a decade when the war broke out and had served with Keynes for a few months on a royal commission dealing with Indian finance. He was sufficiently impressed with his colleague to write him on Saturday, August 1, as the financial meltdown threatened to overwhelm a bureaucracy that had never experienced anything approaching its speed and intensity.

"I wanted to pick your brains for your country's benefit and thought you might enjoy the process," Blackett wrote. "If by chance you could spare time to see me on Monday I should be grateful, but I fear the decisions will all have been taken by then."[26]

Keynes divined the ultimatum in Blackett's polite note. It was an opportunity that would not come again. David Lloyd George was seeking the advice of the leading lights in British finance, Bank of England governor Walter Cunliffe and Baron Nathan Mayer Rothschild among them.[27] Keynes would have the chance to prove himself in a crisis. The policy choices made in the next few days would shape the empire's war economy, perhaps even determine the outcome of the war itself. "A mistake," Lloyd George observed, "might injure the credit and confidence so essential to full strength and use of 'the sinews of war.'" And so Keynes, who could neither drive nor afford the extravagance of an automobile, hitched a ride to London on a motorcycle.

He arrived at a city in thrall to bankers possessed by the fiercest of financial demons. "These three [bank] holidays were some of the busiest and most anxious days I ever spent," Lloyd George recalled long after the war. "Financiers in a fright do not make an heroic picture."[28]

The major banks had established a secret joint committee to devise a rescue plan and submit it to the Treasury. The strategy was simple: Cut off all gold payments to foreign customers, banks, and governments, hoarding it in England, where it would be available to stabilize the banks.

A string of bank failures would have ravaged the stock market and every commercial enterprise that borrowed money in its regular course of business, from farms to department stores. But the most frightening prospect of the crash was the potential for the Bank of England to exhaust its gold reserves—a devastating blow to both British political prestige and the management of the international monetary system.

The bankers' emergency plan reflected their understanding of the crisis: They weren't getting paid, and they needed to stay alive. Their proposed solution carried significant wartime appeal to Lloyd George and the Treasury. Hoarding gold domestically would do more than help save the banks; it would bolster the empire's financial position for the conflict ahead. More gold in Britain, according to proponents of the bankers' plan, would mean greater economic power for Britain over its enemies and greater influence among its allies.

Those considerations weighed all the more heavily on Lloyd George by Monday, August 3, when Germany declared war on France, radically escalating the scope of the conflict. That afternoon, British foreign secretary Sir Edward Grey addressed the House of Commons, calling on Parliament to follow through on a treaty to defend France against invasion. It was a tough sell for Grey, whose own Liberal Party had long harbored a strong pacifist wing. Many legislators opposed injecting Great Britain into the violent entanglements of other powers, and even some more militant members of the Conservative Party were reluctant to automatically approve a war declaration triggered by a treaty signed long ago by other men. Grey appealed primarily to their sense of moral outrage. Germany would soon invade Belgium, a country that had remained neutral as great alliances had crisscrossed the continent over the past two decades. Belgium posed no military threat to Germany. The assault was purely instrumental. The Germans were merely seeking a way through to France, which in turn was being invaded for no reason beyond Kaiser Wilhelm II's urge to expand German territory.

"Could this country stand by and witness the direst crime that ever stained the pages of history and thus become participators in the sin?" Grey intoned. But he also invoked what he saw as a colder, more concrete result of British inaction: the effect on his nation's bottom line. By degrading its international reputation for reliability, he argued, Great Britain would "not escape the most serious and grave economic consequences."[29] He did not, however, emphasize that his country was at that very moment on the brink of financial ruin.

As the foreign secretary addressed Parliament, Lloyd George and the Treasury debated in Whitehall, and Keynes, newly arrived on the scene, drew up his own plan to staunch London's monetary bleeding.

Its key points were the exact opposite of the bankers' agenda. Any foreigner who asked to redeem his bills for gold, Keynes wrote, should be paid in full. But domestic needs—including those of the banks themselves—could be met with a new, alternative paper currency that would allow the Bank of England to preserve British gold for obligations abroad.

The bankers were aghast. But they had, Keynes believed, misjudged the crisis by viewing it principally as a matter of their own survival, rather than a question of what their survival was meant to accomplish. The chief matter for the Bank of England was not gold but economic power, just as the chief question for the war to come was not how many rifles to fire but how to secure Great Britain's political dominion. Gold was a tool, and perhaps a weapon, but not an end in itself. "It is useless to accumulate gold reserves in times of peace unless it is intended to utilise them in time of danger," Keynes wrote to Lloyd George. The moment of peril had arrived.[30]

To Keynes, London's real financial might rested not on its holdings of a relatively useless, shiny metal but on its international reputation for reliability. If the Bank of England continued paying foreign men of affairs on demand, at any time, in whatever denomination they desired, London's preeminence as *the* global financial center would be preserved and with it Great Britain's economic power over other nations. The fears and demands of local bankers, by contrast, were relatively unimportant. It was true that every other country in Europe was pursuing a domestic hoarding strategy, but those countries were not the premier banking center of the day. That status carried tremendous power for the British Empire, but it was delicate. If London broke the perception that its commitments were ironclad certainties, a new power might rise to replace it, forever diminishing Great Britain's position in global affairs.

And it was the banks themselves that were responsible for nearly the entirety of the threat facing the Bank of England. Though policy makers had been alarmed by the early withdrawals of French funds, it was clear to both the Bank and the Treasury that only a small portion of the run was directly tied to foreign demands. The vast majority was the result of simple panic on the part of domestic bankers. Fearing that the Bank of England's vaults would soon be empty, the banks were drawing gold even when they had no immediate need for it, just to ensure they would not come away empty-handed if they should need it in a few days' time. As the panic drained the central bank's reserves, the prophecy was beginning to fulfill itself. The day before the bank holiday, the central bank informed the Treasury that domestic banks alone had withdrawn more than £27 million from its gold reserves in the past few days—nearly seven times the outflow to France—and it expected to have less than £10 million on hand by the close of business.[31]

"The bankers completely lost their heads and have been simply dazed and unable to think two consecutive thoughts," Keynes wrote to his father on August 6.[32]

He stopped short of calling to abandon the domestic connection between gold and British currency. Citizens would technically retain the right to trade in their new paper notes for gold—but that right would be guaranteed by the thinnest of legal veneers, one with the explicit aim of preserving gold for foreign payments. The functional result would be much like the arrangement Keynes had advocated for India in his book. "Gold should only be available at the head office of the Bank of England," Keynes wrote to Lloyd George. "The only way in which the ordinary man, who had no real need for it, would be able to obtain gold would be by going to the Bank of England in person."[33] For a man living in Cornwall or Scotland, multiple days of travel to withdraw gold would be out of the question.

Keynes would spend decades wrestling with the gold standard, and his labors would shape the future course of politics on both sides of the Atlantic. At the moment, however, he was an obscure academic with no official Treasury position and no record of government achievement who was attempting to turn the chancellor of the Exchequer against the official consensus of London's banking elite. He recognized the economic damage that would result if his plan didn't work. But his daring advice was the result of months of thinking about the role governments should play in managing national economies. And Keynes knew he had allies in both the Bank of England and the Treasury who agreed with him. They had, after all, invited him to London. Resolving a run on the Bank of England, he had written to Blackett earlier in the summer, wasn't just a question of restoring gold reserves; it was "really about a much more important question—namely, as to where in the future the centre of power and responsibility in the London money market is to lie."[34] Was Treasury in charge—or the big banks?

After witnessing the bankers' relentless pursuit of their own narrow concerns during the crisis, Keynes was becoming even more wary of their political influence. In a letter to his economics mentor Alfred Marshall, Keynes excoriated the work of two bank leaders during the crisis negotiations: "The one was cowardly and the other selfish. They unquestionably behaved badly."[35] Consumed by "panic and despair," he later wrote, the bankers focused on their own short-term "pecuniary profit," abandoning all thought of "the honour of our old traditions or future good name."[36] Some kind of political oversight was needed to protect the national interest.

On Tuesday, August 4, German troops moved into Belgium. Within hours, the British government retaliated by declaring war on Germany. David Lloyd George agreed to the basic tenets of Keynes' financial rescue, converted by the persuasive force of a memo written in Keynes' own hand.[37] The Treasury scrambled to print its new currency before the bank holiday lifted on Friday, August 7. On Thursday, Parliament approved legislation legalizing the new paper money. The public nervously awaited news reports from the battlefront, and the financial world held its breath for the opening of the markets. The morning would bring rescue or ruin.

It worked. The British public accepted the new paper currency. The Bank of England stabilized. Prices didn't skyrocket. People even began making deposits at their local banks instead of withdrawing money.[38] Although the stock market would remain shuttered for another five months, the most dangerous, acute phase of the crisis was over.[39]

And it had ended with London's financial power fully intact. As nation after nation announced that it would suspend international gold payments, Great Britain was the only major country to maintain its foreign gold commitments in full.[40]

The experience left a deep impression on Keynes. Financial markets, he had discovered, were very different from the clean, ordered entities economists presented in textbooks. The fluctuations of market prices did not express the accumulated wisdom of rational actors pursuing their own self-interest but the judgments of flawed men attempting to navigate an uncertain future. Market stability depended not so much on supply and demand finding an equilibrium as it did on political power maintaining order, legitimacy, and confidence.

Twenty-two years later, those observations would become central tenets of the economic theory presented in Keynes' magnum opus, *The General Theory of Employment, Interest and Money:*

> A large proportion of our positive activities depend on spontaneous optimism rather than on a mathematical expectation, whether moral or hedonistic or economic. Most, probably, of our decisions to do something positive . . . can only be taken as a result of animal spirits—of a spontaneous urge to action rather than inaction, and not as the outcome of a weighted average of quantitative benefits multiplied by quantitative probabilities. Enterprise only pretends itself to be mainly actuated by the statements in its own prospectus. . . . Only a little more than an expedition to the South Pole, is it based on an exact calculation of benefits to come. Thus if the animal spirits are dimmed and the spontaneous optimism falters, leaving us to depend on nothing but a mathematical expectation, enterprise will fade and die;—though fears of loss may have a basis no more reasonable than hope of profit had before.[41]

The lesson was not confined to periods of acute crisis. Markets, Keynes concluded, were social, not mathematical, phenomena. Their study—economics—was not a hard science bound by iron laws, like physics, but a flexible field of custom, rule of thumb, and adjustment, like politics. Market signals—the price of a good or the interest rate on a security—were not a reliable guide to consumer preferences or corporate risks in the real world. At best, they were approximations, always subject to change based on new attitudes about an uncertain future.

The 1914 crisis made Keynes' career. No longer a minor, cloistered scholar, he secured a job at Treasury as a top adviser on British war finance—one of the most important and influential positions in the entire government during the Great War. He went from dissecting mathematical abstractions with Russell and other Cambridge figures to hobnobbing with top politicians, traveling to France and the United States to negotiate loans and make arrangements for armaments and foodstuffs. He was now "a coming man," in the words of Virginia Woolf's nephew Quentin Bell, "although nobody at that time could foresee how conspicuously and how scandalously he would arrive."[42]

"I *am* going to Paris, and we start Sunday or Monday," Keynes gushed to his father in late January 1915. "It's a most select party; Lloyd George, Montagu, the Governor of the Bank of England, and me, together with a private secretary. We are to be the guests of the French government."[43]

The treatise on probability would have to wait.

TWO

———◇———

BLOOD MONEY

THE PARTIES ON THURSDAY evenings, Virginia Woolf recalled, were "full of smoke; buns, coffee and whisky."[1] Her brother's friends from Cambridge would arrive at her home at 46 Gordon Square, infusing it with argument and absurdity until all hours of the morning. There was Lytton Strachey—waifish and cheerfully ridiculous—flanked by Leonard Woolf, a trembling pessimist. The poet Saxon Sydney-Turner would sit by Duncan Grant, a gifted and penniless artist who was often as interested in the hors d'oeuvres as he was in the conversation. Other young Edwardians drifted in and out, some of them famous, some of them rich: the poet W. B. Yeats, the novelist E. M. Forster, an aristocrat named Lady Ottoline Morrell in lace and pearls, always with a new lover in tow. And of course the "formidable" John Maynard Keynes, "able to rend any argument that came his way with a blow of his paw," who concealed "a kind and even simple heart under that immensely impressive armour of intellect."[2]

During the ten years before the Great War, Virginia and her closest friends came to love Gordon Square as "the most beautiful, the most exciting, the most romantic place in the world."[3] Together, they made the four-story home the site of a relentless assault on the astringent

Victorian culture in which they had all been raised. "Customs and beliefs were revised,"[4] Virginia wrote, as they sat and debated *everything*—art and poetry, good and evil, love and sex, all the way down to the mechanics of each. They pursued, in Leonard's words, a "complete freedom of thought and speech," a "sweeping away of formalities and barriers," that every one of them found "so new and so exhilarating."[5]

For Virginia and her sister, Vanessa, it was an intellectual awakening. "The young men had no 'manners.' . . . They criticized our arguments as severely as their own. They never seemed to notice how we were dressed or if we were nice looking or not. All that tremendous encumbrance of appearance and behavior which . . . had piled on our first years vanished completely. One had no longer to endure that terrible inquisition after a party—and be told, 'You looked lovely.' Or, 'You did look plain.' Or, 'You must really learn to do your hair.' "[6] For the first time, Virginia and her sister were appreciated for their talents. In Bloomsbury, Vanessa was as serious a painter as Pablo Picasso or Henri Matisse (whom she visited on a trip to Paris). Virginia's essays were evaluated with the same enthusiasm as Forster's novels.

Soon the revelry expanded beyond Thursday evenings. "All sorts of parties at all hours of the day or night happened constantly," Vanessa wrote. Bloomsbury's luminaries invited each other over to redecorate rooms and sit for morning portraits, drinking champagne to pass the time.[7]

Word began to spread through London. According to the rigid formalities of the day, it was generally a breach of decorum for men to address each other by their first names. For men to call *women* by their first names was simply unthinkable.[8] Yet at Gordon Square, *unmarried* men and women lived together! Sometimes men dressed *as women* for private comedic routines. The whole Bloomsbury entourage once ventured to the medieval monument of Crosby Hall costumed as scantily clad characters from Paul Gauguin's Tahitian paintings. Rumors began to circulate that they sometimes wore nothing at all at their parties, that Keynes had once made love to Vanessa on a couch right in front of everyone. Even young people were offended. Vanessa later recalled being questioned sharply about her evenings with "a tone of disapproval."[9]

Bloomsbury was refining a radical and subversive code of conduct, seeking total sexual and intellectual liberation. Under this new ethic, all of the old familial norms were dismissed as religious superstition, and religion itself became a subject of mockery. No one was entitled to possessive emotions. Any embrace was fine and proper so long as everyone involved remained honest about her feelings. Men could love men, and married women could carry on as many affairs as they liked with whomever they wanted of whatever gender they fancied. Every arrangement imaginable was fair game except dishonesty. And anyone who objected on grounds of fidelity was an iconoclast, a barrier to moral progress.

It was an impossible standard to meet, and the group was continuously riven with jealousy. Vanessa married her brother's friend Clive Bell in 1907, a union that soon fizzled as Clive pursued other partners and flirted shamelessly with Virginia. But Vanessa had no shortage of suitors as she considered her future. The mathematician Harry Norton fell for her during the months when an art critic named Roger Fry was snapping stylized photographs of her nude on a rocky beach in Dorset. She eventually settled down with Duncan Grant, winning him away from Maynard, who had maintained a passionate romance with the artist for years. Soon Duncan was wandering into dalliances with other men, particularly the talented young writer David "Bunny" Garnett, who also occasionally found himself in Maynard's arms. It was a dizzying, complicated web of romantic attentions. But it was also an impressively stable community. The bonds that connected Bloomsbury were built of genuine affection, strengthened by openness and sincerity. Whatever the outside world might say, Bloomsbury was its own self-contained and self-sustaining universe, a model of progress which, its members were certain, the world would eventually come to emulate. As late as 1913, according to one art historian, the collective believed that all of European society was on the precipice of a new "enlightened order, in which disinterested love and cooperation between individuals would dismantle government and domestic hierarchies."[10]

The war exploded everything. The parties, the ideas, the code of ethics were revealed to be, in Virginia's words, so much "lustre and illusion."[11] In all their conversations about sex and truth, Bloomsbury had never really confronted questions of power, violence, or imperialism. "How could we be interested in such matters," Vanessa wrote, "when beauty was springing up under one's feet so vividly?"[12] As armies marched across Europe and empires shuddered, Bloomsbury's romanticism suddenly appeared trivial, its new morality an indulgent distraction.

Maynard's work on the 1914 banking crisis swept him into the diplomatic currents of the conflict. At Treasury, he was charged with analyzing the financial position of Great Britain's allies and helping negotiate the terms of British support for other nations. "I was in the Treasury throughout the war and all the money we either lent or borrowed passed through my hands," he later wrote.[13] Within just a few months, he found himself dispatched to summits all over the world, called to parliamentary debates in the House of Commons, and welcomed into the social circles of the British political elite. Like all of Bloomsbury, Keynes experienced the war as a personal tragedy. He held his breath when friends were dispatched to the trenches and cried when he learned they would not return. But the war was also the defining event of his professional life; it transformed him from an inconspicuous, content academic into one of the most influential figures of his generation.

With one of its own thrust onto the world stage, Bloomsbury had to confront ideas and moral dilemmas it had never considered. The group would never be quite the same. One evening in the spring of 1918, Maynard arrived home to Gordon Square after a grueling day at Whitehall. It was well past dinner time, and as he entered he found Vanessa, Duncan, David, Harry, and the classicist J. T. Sheppard relaxing in conversation after their meal. Where once they had debated the atmosphere of Postimpressionist paintings and the meter of obscure English poets, they now tackled the news of the day: a failed peace overture from Austro-Hungarian emperor Karl I. Beleaguered and exhausted, Keynes was in no mood for political speculation from a crowd of painters and poets. He "treated their views with the utmost contempt," according to David, and, as the conversation soured, provoked his friends with an attack on their integrity. It was impossible for anyone to be a "genuine" conscientious objector to the war effort, Maynard declared, knowing full well that almost everyone in Bloomsbury was a CO, many of them listed on official government ledgers. No one had an obligation to sign up for military duty, he suggested, but it was silly to conflate such impulses with high moral principles. A storm of outrage ensued. Vanessa and Harry took turns denouncing Maynard, who refused to recant or even debate the matter. "Go to bed," he repeated. "Go to bed."

"Maynard," Sheppard warned, "you will find it is a mistake to despise your old friends."[14]

Before they called themselves the Bloomsbury set, Keynes and his tight social circle referred to themselves as Apostles—the name of an all-male secret society of Cambridge undergraduates. By the time Keynes arrived on campus in October 1902, the Apostles had been around for eighty years and boasted a few semilegendary alumni, including the philosophers Henry Sidgwick and Alfred North Whitehead. Leonard Woolf and his friend Lytton Strachey recruited Maynard for the group when he was just a freshman—unusually young for the group, but the upperclassmen recognized a prodigy.

"His conversation is extraordinarily alert and very amusing," Strachey wrote to Woolf in February 1905. "He analyses with amazing persistence and brilliance. I never met so active a brain (I believe it's more *active* than either Moore's or Russell's). . . . he perpetually frightens me."[15]

This was the highest possible praise in the social microcosm the Apostles had created. Though Bertrand Russell was still a few years away from publishing *Principia Mathematica*, the philosophical treatise that would establish his international reputation, he had been accepted into the club during the waning years of the nineteenth century and carried with him the aura of a respected elder statesman at its events and debates. G. E. Moore, another Apostle from Russell's generation, had published his masterpiece, *Principia Ethica,* in 1903. Still regarded today as one of the most important works of moral philosophy to emerge from the twentieth century, Moore's book was a sensation among Keynes and his cohorts, who deployed it as political manifesto, self-help guide, and declaration of intellectual war against the entire Victorian generation.[16]

"We were at an age when our beliefs influenced our behavior, a characteristic of the young which it is easy for the middle-aged to forget," Keynes recalled in 1938. "It was exciting, exhilarating, the beginning of a renaissance, the opening of a new heaven on a new earth, we were the forerunners of a new dispensation, we were not afraid of anything."[17]

Principia Ethica was a sophisticated attack on the moral and political philosophy that had dominated English thought since the late eighteenth century—a doctrine that went by the name "utilitarianism." Developed by Jeremy Bentham and John Stuart Mill, utilitarianism declared that pleasure was the basis of all morality. A good or right action would produce pleasure. The more pleasure a good deed produced for the more people, the more righteous it was. And so the aim of all government was to produce more pleasure. The best society was the happiest society.

Intellectual descendants of Enlightenment philosophers, Bentham and Mill had attempted to apply the principles of empirical science to moral analysis, to demystify the divine into something that could be observed and measured. Goodness wasn't a mystical abstraction or the ancient edict of church authorities; it was part of the natural world. Bentham even believed there could be a moral "calculus" tabulating the precise amount of pleasure that resulted from various laws and actions.

Moore and the Apostles hoped to overturn utilitarianism without reverting back to the moral authority of the Church, which was quickly falling out of fashion in English culture. Things were not good because they produced pleasure, Moore argued. They were good because they were *good*. Pleasure itself could be either good or bad. People enjoyed all kinds of terrible things, and the pleasure they derived from them was not good but perverse. A good horse, a good piece of music, and a good person, meanwhile, all had something ineffable but vitally important in common: they were all *good*. But you could not find this goodness under a microscope. It could not be measured or derived from some set of facts about the natural world; it was a fundamental property, "simple, indefinable, unanalysable,"[18] that could only be intuited directly by human reason. There were objective facts about value just as there were facts about colors; it wasn't a matter of opinion whether the sky was blue or Goethe was a great poet. But good things could be understood solely in their "organic unity"; they could not be intellectually broken up into smaller components.

Moore believed that his philosophy had serious implications for how to live. The aim of a good life was to enjoy the highest goods, not simply to maximize pleasure or satisfaction. Reading a tragic play might make you sad, but a full life required a little Shakespeare. People should strive to cultivate "certain states of consciousness, which may be roughly described as the pleasures of human intercourse and the enjoyment of beautiful objects."[19]

Keynes and Strachey quickly developed Moore's work into a personal ethos, elevating youthful romantic excursions and sophomoric debates over art and society into the highest of ethical pursuits. For the enlightened Apostle, art and love towered over all other human experience. The profound truths were pure "states of mind" achieved in moments of mutual understanding between lovers or afternoons spent contemplating great works of art. The political arena, by contrast, was petty and debased—a confusion of means with ends. The grotesqueries of money, the illusions of social prestige, and the compromises necessitated by public affairs were anathema to those moments of clarity that gave life its meaning.

Moore's attack on utilitarianism was a formative intellectual experience for Keynes. Utilitarianism and classical economics had developed alongside each other in English-language thought and shared important conceptual foundations. Both were concerned with efficiency. Economists following Adam Smith focused on the efficiency of agricultural and industrial production; utilitarian philosophers mused about the efficient production of pleasure. Both utilitarianism and the economics discipline were oriented around simple mathematical conceptual schemes: more was better and getting more with less better still. But after reading *Principia Ethica*, Keynes rejected the idea that efficiency could be the central organizing principle of a good society. No simple equation could approximate the best way to live.

But although these philosophical concerns would eventually make Keynes into a unique economist, they also led him as an undergraduate to assemble a code of personal conduct that celebrated aristocratic escapism. It unsettled members of the Apostolic old guard. "The tone of the generation some ten years junior to my own was set mainly by Lytton Strachey and Keynes," Russell wrote in 1967. "It is surprising how great a change in mental climate those ten years had brought. We were still Victorian; they were Edwardian. We believed in ordered progress by means of politics and free discussion. The more self-confident among us may have hoped to be leaders of the multitude, but none of us wished to be divorced from it. The generation of Keynes and Lytton did not seek to preserve any kinship with the Philistine. They aimed rather at a life of retirement among fine shades and nice feelings, and conceived of the good as consisting in the passionate mutual admirations of a clique of the elite."[20]

Regular gatherings of the Apostles were a sort of hybrid between a graduate seminar and a dinner party. One Apostle would present a paper before the others, who would stay up late into the evening in enraptured discussion, debating its implications, connecting their comrades' ideas to events at Cambridge, movements in art, and, at times, for all its unclean corruptions, even the political world.

There was an obnoxious stuffiness to the Apostles, and their pretensions were exacerbated by the club's secret status. Apostles saw themselves not merely as clever young men but as members of an undetectable elect whose greatness could be fully appreciated only from within. Not every great mind at Cambridge found that self-

importance alluring. Keynes' lifelong friend Ludwig Wittgenstein re-
coiled from their meetings, which he saw as "a mere waste of time."[21]

But Keynes took immediate comfort from the society. He had
learned to navigate the currents of the British upper class at Eton
boarding school, but his quickness of mind had separated him from
his peers even as it won their admiration. Keynes felt the social distance between himself and the aristocracy, a discomfort that registered
in letters home mocking everyone from Kaiser Wilhelm II to Queen
Victoria. Not that Maynard had grown up poor. The financial remains
of his grandfather's flower business had been good for a middle-class
home staffed with a few domestic servants. But the family lived at the
fringes of class respectability, and Maynard had cut his path into both
Eton and Cambridge with merit scholarships rather than inherited
prestige.[22] At Eton, he had something to prove. In the Apostles, he
discovered an alternative elite that rewarded his strengths and celebrated his interests. He would yearn for the society's atmosphere for
the rest of his life, creating and leading exclusive intellectual sects all
the way through World War II.

The secrecy the Apostles surrounded themselves with tightened the
social bonds among them and created a space for activities much more
radical than philosophical snobbery. Keynes and Strachey oversaw a
sexual revolution among the Apostles, persuading its membership of
the moral legitimacy of gay love. Though wrapped in the intellectual
skin of their creed—sexual liberation was an aesthetic necessity, the
ultimate organic unity!—Keynes was creating a safe haven for young
men whose desires were regarded by public morality as a grievous sin.
Less than a decade after Oscar Wilde's internationally notorious sodomy conviction, open homosexuality remained grounds for imprisonment. Among the Apostles, one could speak freely. The community
closely guarded its secrets, even as youthful promiscuities fomented
unacknowledged romantic competitions.

The Apostles not only allowed Keynes to express his sexuality, they
helped him grapple with a deep insecurity about his appearance. "I
have always suffered and I suppose I always will from a most unalter-
able obsession that I am so physically repulsive that I've no business to

hurl my body on anyone else's," Keynes wrote to Strachey in 1906.[23] It was a common sentiment among the group; Virginia Woolf once noted the lack of "physical splendour" and even "shabbiness" among the Apostles, one of whom she eventually married.[24] But Keynes always knew the Apostles admired his intellect, and that awareness emboldened his sexual confidence.

All of this liberation carried a distinctly misogynist edge. Keynes, Strachey, and their closest confidants celebrated their sexual doctrine as a "higher sodomy." Women were intellectually inferior to men, they reasoned, so love between two men must involve a deeper, more profound connection than anything mere heterosexuality could offer. Cambridge at the turn of the century was institutionally hostile to women. There were so few women among the undergraduates that Keynes could write about his encounters with them as a zoological perturbance. "I seem to hate every movement of their minds," he once wrote to Duncan. "The minds of the men even when they themselves are stupid and ugly, never appear to me so repellant."[25]

According to Bloomsbury chronicler Frances Spalding, at least some of the group's sexism reflected a distaste for the norms of behavior Victorian society demanded of women. Women who spoke frankly about their sexuality, ideas, or even interests were considered unfit for high society, but the restrictions placed on women also made their conversation seem dull to Keynes, who was accustomed to passionate debate and assertive opinions. After graduation, when he encountered bold, radical women such as Vanessa Bell and Lydia Lopokova who were willing to pay the high social price for discarding Victorian etiquette, Keynes found them "lovely," "beautiful," and "amusing." Though he would not go so far as to think them truly brilliant until his late twenties, Keynes respected women who behaved like gifted men.[26]

For a while Keynes and Strachey were lovers, but as Keynes began to rival his patron for dominance among the club's leadership, the two drifted apart, frequently vying with each other for the affections of other students. It was a volatile friendship. Though they often lived and traveled together, for most of the years leading up to the Great War, Strachey could establish a relaxed connection with Keynes only during periods of his younger friend's vulnerability, when his intellect did not appear quite so threatening and his amorous achievements seemed less intimidating. "Poor Keynes!" Strachey wrote. "It's only when he's shattered by a crisis that I seem to be able to care for him."[27]

Keynes made a habit of stealing Strachey's lovers. At Cambridge, he began an affair with Arthur Hobhouse, whom Strachey had coveted, and in 1908, at the age of twenty-five, he won the affections of Duncan Grant, wounding Strachey so deeply that their entire social circle nearly broke apart. Though Keynes long considered Duncan the great love of his life, the significance of the relationship was inseparable from his original connection to Strachey. Throughout Keynes' life, the young man who had recruited him into the Apostles was one of only a tiny handful of people from whom Keynes would readily accept intellectual criticism. He craved Strachey's approval and could imagine no better way to demonstrate his own excellence than to win a lover away from the man he most admired.

Despite his self-doubts, Keynes was a prolific lover. In his papers at King's College there is a table penciled on a note card tallying what appear to be dozens of sexual encounters between 1901 and 1916. The list is accompanied by four columns of mysterious statistics assigned to the rendezvous. He described his anonymous partners on an accompanying note card with names that read like the cast of characters from a spy movie: "The Soldier of the Baths," "The Shoemaker of the Hague," "The Young American near the British Museum," "The Clergyman."[28] And he was indeed living a clandestine, double life. He could be open about his sexuality with the Apostles or in Bloomsbury, but he strictly guarded any hint of his romantic entanglements from heads of state, Treasury officials, and diplomats.

The Apostles had thus ordered their lives into a paradox: Deeply committed to a radical individualist code of conduct, they nevertheless required the cooperation and protection of a community to practice their freedom to the fullest. They may have rejected public office, but they were living not merely in contempt of general society but in covert rebellion against it, their very way of life a secret act of political defiance.

And even in these deepest days of what Russell deplored as the Apostles' "stuffy girls-school sentimentalising,"[29] Keynes infuriated Strachey with lapses in his devotion to their apolitical ideal. Strachey and Woolf were not the only Cambridge students to take note of the talented young student when he enrolled in 1902. Edwin Montagu, a young politician from the Liberal Party, had invited Keynes to address the Cambridge Union debating society. It was a breach with Strachey, but it was also an opportunity for Keynes to prove his mettle among the young elite and in doing so advance himself beyond the social position he had inherited from his parents. Soon he was being celebrated for his eloquent denunciations of the Conservative Party. Keynes associated the Liberal Party with rational inquiry and Conservatives with suffocating traditionalism. He supported modest expansions of British social welfare programs, but his speeches to the Union from 1903 reflect a preoccupation with the Church—which he considered a source of sexual and intellectual tyranny—and unfettered trade. "I hate all priests and protectionists," he declared in December 1903. "Free trade and free thought! Down with pontiffs and tariffs. Down with those who declare we are dumped and damned. Away with all schemes of redemption or retaliation!"[30]

This enthusiasm for free trade was not derived from any sophisticated economic theory. In 1903, Keynes hadn't studied economics. It reflected instead a particular vision of the British Empire and British power. To Keynes, free trade was part of a benevolent, open approach to the broader world. It acknowledged the "interdependence and connexion of material well being" between different peoples. And it reflected the highest ideals of the British Empire, uniting the world in paternalistic goodwill. "We who are imperialists," he told the Union in January 1903, "believe . . . that British rule brings with it an increase of justice, liberty, and prosperity; and we administer our Empire not with a view to our pecuniary aggrandizement . . . but looking rather towards the fortunes of those who are fellow citizens and to their prosperity." The British, in this telling, didn't conquer for glory or pillage; they spread wealth and democracy around the globe. "When a country becomes part of the Empire it is free to pursue its own destiny," Keynes insisted to the Cambridge Union in November 1903, "under freedom and justice and without molestation from abroad." In his "ideal" and "democratic" global future, the world would be made up of "self governing states having the same sort of relation to one another that the parts of the British Empire have"— "friendly" and "free of jealousy."

The war would force Keynes to confront uglier truths, but as an undergraduate he was concerned not with the moral implications of imperialism as such but with the Conservative variant of imperialism. The central economic proposal of the Tories was the tariff, which Keynes found incompatible with his own lofty internationalist ideals. Tariffs created barriers between peoples, seeking British profit at the expense of foreigners. The Conservative imperial ideal, Keynes said, was "a forced, unreal, and worthless unity" derived from sheer power. Tariffs projected a "Spirit of Nationalism," which was "one of the most considerable hindrances to the progress of Civilisation"—"a feeling that anyone else's prosperity is your damage, a feeling of jealousy, of hatred."

Keynes was simultaneously naive about the historical violence of British conquest and sharply critical of contemporary failures to live up to his sanitized ideal. When the president of Venezuela repudiated his country's large foreign debt in 1902, the British government joined Germany and Italy in a military blockade against Venezuelan ports to demand payment on behalf of British investors. Keynes told the Cambridge Union the attack was an outrageous abuse of power. "An investor in South American stock invests with his eyes open," he said in January 1903. "It is not for his government to support his demands with gunboats and to subsidize the holder of foreign bonds." The blockade was the kind of brute-force imperialism Keynes would expect from "Bismarck"—not the civilized British Empire.[31]

It is a mistake to invest collegiate debates with great historical significance. Keynes' economic ideas and political convictions would change dramatically over the course of the war and the subsequent depression. In time, he would become disillusioned with both free trade and Great Britain's role on the world stage. But his life among the Apostles was a formative experience for his conception of human freedom. He became skeptical of simple rules of conduct, sexual or otherwise, and distrusted edicts of the ruling elite—even as he celebrated elite habits by becoming a champion of the fine artist, committed to the defense of creativity and experimentation. That individualism was universal and international; the British did not have a monopoly on artistic genius. The rational, enlightened Apostle could intuit truth and beauty whatever their origin. Where other Apostles turned their backs on politics, Keynes believed the Liberal Party was the best vehicle for their beliefs in global affairs. Accommodating this individualist ethos to the world stage and the often brutal realities of a faltering imperial order would prove the defining intellectual challenge of his life.

And so Bloomsbury was born. A group of Apostles—Maynard Keynes, Leonard Woolf, Lytton Strachey, E. M. Forster, J. T. Sheppard, Gerald Shove, Saxon Sydney-Turner, Clive Bell, and Adrian Stephen—moved from Cambridge to London, establishing group homes at 46 Gordon Square and nearby 38 Brunswick Square, adding Duncan Grant and "Bunny" Garnett along the way. Soon their ties were solidified by marriage. Clive married Adrian's beautiful, provocative sister Vanessa, prompting Lytton Strachey to make an abortive, embarrassed proposal to Adrian's other sister, Virginia. No sooner had Virginia refused him than Lytton began encouraging Leonard Woolf—a committed heterosexual—to pursue Virginia. Bloomsbury would last as long as their marriage.

Unlike nearly every other member of this society, Keynes was not himself an artist, a fact that at times made him feel keenly inferior to his companions, an attitude encouraged by sneering criticism of his aesthetic judgment by Strachey and Clive Bell, in particular. These weren't just matters of taste in Bloomsbury—the "states of mind" so sacred to all Apostles were at stake.

But for all their strange internal competitions, Bloomsberries, as Virginia Woolf dubbed them, shared a deep affection for one another.

"What a bad taste he's got," Lytton once mused to Leonard about Maynard. "And what a good heart."[32] When war broke out in 1914, those sensitivities were not prepared for the anguish ahead. Most members of the British leisure class, including Keynes himself, expected the conflict to end quickly, taking an Angell-ian view that the sheer financial insanity of the violence would prevent it from dragging on. "We are bound to win—& in great style too" thanks to "all our brains & all our wealth," Virginia wrote in her diary after dining with Keynes in January 1915.[33] Keynes had an ease with the economic nuances of the conflict that made him seem to Virginia "like quicksilver on a sloping board—a little inhuman, but very kindly." At the same dinner, Keynes urged Leonard to turn down a £100 offer from the Fabian Society to write a book on the causes of war and its prevention. Wars, Keynes argued, were fading from history; serious twentieth-century intellectuals like the Woolfs should concern themselves with weightier matters.

Keynes was voicing the Bloomsbury consensus. "It looked for a moment as if militarism, imperialism, and antisemitism were on the run," Leonard Woolf later recalled. "For the first time in the history of the world the rights of Jews, cobblers, and coloured men not to be beaten, hanged, or judicially murdered by officers, Junkers, or white men were publicly admitted."[34] As Bloomsbury's only Jewish member, ethnic discrimination was not an abstraction to Leonard.

And then came the war. Though he projected confidence with the Woolfs, by the autumn of 1914 Keynes' letters to Strachey reveal a man already racked with guilt. "I am absolutely and completely desolated," he wrote. "It is utterly unbearable to see day by day the youths going away first to boredom and discomfort and then to slaughter."[35] Not long after accepting his position at Treasury, Keynes wrote to Duncan Grant, "Yesterday came news that two of our undergraduates were killed, both of whom I knew, though not very well, and was fond of. . . . It is too horrible, a nightmare to be stopt anyhow. May no other generation live under the cloud we have to live under."[36]

When Keynes had rushed to London in the summer of 1914 to salvage the empire's finances, he had considered his actions patriotic.

The violence in which the financial crisis was embedded was an abstraction, foreign and remote. Now he was watching his government spend its money on a project that sent his friends and students to die.

In the early months of fighting, Keynes had the moral luxury of an intentionally brutal enemy. The atrocities committed by the German army in the early months of the war were gruesome and politically dire enough to give even committed nonviolence advocates pause. German military leaders had meticulously devised a war strategy requiring very public demonstrations of extreme inhumanity. Those displays, they hoped, would encourage swift surrenders, allowing the army to march through on its business to win the war quickly with a minimum of bloodshed. Commanders ordered mass executions of civilians. In the small town of Aarschot on August 19, the German army killed 150 residents. At Dinant, they massacred 664. Medieval cultural monuments were destroyed and whole towns burned to the ground. Proclamations posted by the German army in Belgian villages declared that entire communities would receive violent punishment for the misconduct of individuals. As Barbara Tuchman has chronicled, "The method was to assemble the inhabitants in the main square, women usually on one side and men on the other, select every tenth man or every second man or all on one side, according to the whim of the individual officer, march them to a nearby field or empty lot behind the railroad station and shoot them."[37]

Collective punishment for civilians had been explicitly barred by the Hague Conventions of 1899[38] and 1907.[39] Advocates of British intervention argued that Germany was shredding the standards of civilized conduct, making war not merely upon Belgium and France but upon human progress itself.

To believe that, of course, required ignoring what imperial governments had grown accustomed to doing around the globe. Tens of thousands of South Africans had died in what the British had called "concentration camps" during the Boer War at the turn of the century, and the British had slaughtered well over 100,000 Indian civilians (by conservative estimates) during an uprising only a few decades earlier. Yet it was common for leading European minds of the day to discount

what went on in the colonies. Leonard Woolf summarized Bloomsbury's own prewar attitude decades later: "There were, of course, wars,
but they were either colonial wars, in which white men slaughtered
yellow men, or brown men, or black men, or wars between second-rate
white men or second-rate white men's states in the Balkans or South
America."[40] When forced to confront the reality of imperial violence
within Europe itself, many intellectuals were shaken. Virginia Woolf
became a committed pacifist and Leonard an outspoken critic of imperialism. If this was the way occupying powers treated other Europeans, imagine the horrors elsewhere.

The war crimes committed in Belgium faded from public attention
as casualties on both sides escalated into the hundreds of thousands.
In the east, Britain's Russian allies killed hundreds of Jewish civilians
in pogroms during their occupation of Galicia as early as mid-August.
"Robbery and rape were commonplace," notes one historian. "Jewish
villages were burnt down." More than a thousand were taken prisoner
and tens of thousands deported to the Russian hinterlands.[41] The war
entered a grotesque stalemate, with millions of young soldiers dug
into trenches across France, where endless shelling, machine-gun fire,
and poison gas attacks were decimating an entire generation. Images
of bodies piled up in fields, strung lifelessly along barbed wire, were
burned into the public consciousness. The pacifists seemed to have a
point: The war was going nowhere.

Maynard's career, however, was ascending to dizzying new heights. In
the spring of 1915, Prime Minister Herbert Henry Asquith formed a
new coalition government, making Lloyd George minister of munitions and replacing him at Treasury with fellow Liberal Reginald
McKenna. Keynes, already considered indispensable, was promoted to
the team responsible for war finance. No sooner had he landed the job
than he was dispatched to the French city of Nice, where his delegation would work out the terms of a British loan to Italy, which had just
joined the Allies.

"I am overwhelmed with work (and naturally much excited)," he wrote to his father on June 1. "As usual they have given me just 24 hours to get up and write memoranda on a more or less new subject."[42] McKenna was delighted with his new pupil, whom he began inviting along on family holidays and introduced to Asquith himself. Keynes tended to work himself to the point of physical collapse. Shortly after the trip to Nice, he was rushed to the hospital with appendicitis and then came down with pneumonia only ten days after his emergency surgery. Just over a month later, he was back at full speed, setting off for Bologna to negotiate with the French about how to approach U.S. banks for a loan.

The technical terms of inter-ally finance were daunting. The economics of everything from agriculture to heavy machinery had been thrown into chaos by the conflict. Each nation needed to coordinate the trade of food and raw materials without relying on goods from enemy countries that had only recently been trading partners. If any one nation consumed too much of any particular good—wheat, iron, coal, anything—it could jeopardize the position of its allies, who also needed the same raw materials.

Under traditional economic theory, markets were supposed to clear these problems by themselves. Prices would rise and fall according to supply and demand, encouraging goods to flow to where they were most needed. A country that produced too much iron could trade it to a country that produced too much wheat and vice versa. Keynes didn't dispute the idea in principle, but he and other Allied policy makers recognized that battalions could run out of ammunition and cities could starve while everyone waited for markets to adjust. Free markets were a luxury that a nation at war could not afford.

The term *macroeconomics* wouldn't exist until after World War II, when American economists began disseminating Keynes' later work. But during his time at the India Office, Keynes had already become accustomed to analyzing economic systems as a whole, looking at the way different arrangements fit together—or didn't. He had studied Indian currency in its relationship with the currencies of Great Britain and Europe, not just the markets for wheat or tea. At Treasury he was again analyzing economic patterns from the perspective of an imperial manager. His new boss, McKenna, began to deploy him as a kind of in-house theorist, writing memos to shape the way the cabinet understood the economic problems of the war. Lloyd George, who had ushered Keynes into the top tier of the British civil service during the financial crisis, now found himself frequently at odds with his diamond in the rough. McKenna had elevated Keynes "into the rocking chair of a pundit, and it was thought that his very signature appended to a financial document would carry weight," Lloyd George later complained.[43]

In September 1915, Keynes authored two memoranda on inflation that serve as some of the earliest demonstrations of his potential as an economic theorist. Economists had long been aware that inflation was a common problem during wartime. When cash-strapped governments printed money to pay their bills, prices rose, reflecting, according to the theory, the higher quantity of money in circulation. In a nationally self-sufficient economy like that of Germany, Keynes argued, inflation functioned as "a concealed tax." Wages couldn't increase evenly with the prices of goods, because the German government had frozen workers' pay rates for the duration of the war. So although the German people were taking home the same paychecks they had received in 1913, those paychecks didn't have the same purchasing power they had once carried. Printing notes gave governments more money to spend on the war as it reduced the standard of living for the citizenry—transferring wealth from the public to the government, just as taxation might have done. That system might be attacked on grounds of "social justice"—why, after all, were "the working classes" being required to pay for the war instead of the very rich?—but there was no risk in Germany that inflation would lead to a runaway disaster during the war. When the German government stopped printing extra currency to pay its military bills, the price increases would stop. Higher prices were a hardship for the public, but they would not interfere with the government's ability to fund the men and materials it needed.

German self-sufficiency was a recent development. Prior to the war, Germany had been a free-trading superpower, competing head to head with Great Britain for dominance in the world's export markets. Keynes' memo did not dwell on how the change had occurred. The Allies imposed a naval blockade against Germany, shutting down its ability to access international shipments of everything from armaments to foodstuffs. Germany became self-sufficient out of necessity. And that self-sufficiency would not last forever. In time, the blockade would claim hundreds of thousands of civilian lives.

But inflation would function much differently in the British economy. Because Britain relied so heavily on international trade, Keynes argued, inflation could serve only as a very temporary expedient. When British prices increased, it affected not only household budgets but also the prices the British paid for imports. At the same time, the prices British producers received for their exports did not increase; the amount they could fetch in foreign markets depended on the prevailing market prices abroad, not on the going rate at home. As a result, inflation had the effect of exacerbating the British trade deficit—the British were paying more to consume goods from abroad than they received from the sale of exports. And since foreign suppliers wanted to be paid in either foreign currency or gold, the British could inflate themselves into bankruptcy. A sustained trade deficit would deplete Great Britain's gold reserves. Once those were gone, the government would be unable to purchase the food, munitions, and raw materials from abroad that it required to prosecute the war.

This was an important theoretical point in Keynes' intellectual development. Money wasn't just a passive force that people used to keep track of the value of goods and services; it was an active power in its own right. A problem in the monetary system could create unexpected trouble in the realm of what Keynes called "real resources"—the equipment, commercial products, and savings of a community.[44]

So far as the war effort was concerned, all of this high theory pointed to efficiency as the overriding economic concern. "The industrial capacity of the country" must be "fully employed," Keynes wrote. Everyone must work as much as possible to produce as much stuff as possible. Ordinary families would have to cut back on expenditures to help fight inflation. There were only so many resources to go around once the economy was running at full tilt, and as many of those as possible had to be directed into the hands of the government: cotton and wool for uniforms, wheat and cattle for field rations, iron and dynamite for munitions. Keynes collaborated with his mother, Florence, on a pamphlet printed by the Cambridge War Thrift Committee, urging families to be stingy shoppers and expect higher taxes. "If the allies are to win this war the money *must* be raised 'in the form of tax or of loan.'" If that sounded bad, the alternative was worse: "If the allies do *not* win, most assuredly shall we suffer still more seriously in pocket."[45] The chief economic problem of the war was one of scarcity: There weren't enough goods for everyone to use as they pleased. Keynes' job was to help the British war economy produce more with less.

Keynes and the British Treasury sought to eliminate waste in the Allied financial arrangements by centralizing as much decision making as possible within the British government. The British would extend loans to France, Italy, Russia, and Belgium and oversee international purchases from each nation, ensuring that nobody wasted the funds on reckless purchases that would undercut other Allies. Italy, for instance, had once bought up an entire year's supply of North American wheat, driving up prices for Britain and Russia. Since Italy was dependent on Great Britain for the very money it used to buy the wheat, Keynes intervened, convincing the Italian government to at least consult the British on its international purchases to avoid accidentally undermining its military allies.

Keynes described the centralization effort in terms of efficiency, but it was also a power grab. Every country wanted as much autonomy as possible in the conduct of its own wartime affairs, and, as Keynes quickly learned, the nation that held the purse strings was able to exercise a unique level of political control over its friends and neighbors.

But most of Keynes' day-to-day work involved mundane number crunching rather than grand strategy. He pored over data on wheat stores, iron ores, and gold positions, considering the best way to make payments to different allies—in gold, goods, or currencies?—and the surest way to remove waste from the international system. He was good with numbers and enjoyed the work. It seemed practical, useful, and far removed from the death being doled out in trenches. It was one thing to develop an abstract interest in pacifism, quite another to just let Great Britain lose a war to foreign aggressors. Sending British soldiers off to battle without proper equipment wouldn't bring back Rupert Brooke.

By the end of 1915, Bloomsbury's artistic output had taken a subversive turn. Vanessa titled a still life featuring a lamp, a bottle of wine, and a gin decanter *Triple Alliance,* mocking the pretensions of imperial strategists. In letters to friends, her sister Virginia dismissed patriotism as "a base emotion" and assailed war as "a preposterous masculine fiction."[46] The Omega Workshops—art installations and events organized by Vanessa, Duncan, and Roger Fry—became showcases for pacifist works and gatherings for antiwar intellectuals including Lytton and the playwright George Bernard Shaw. In this suddenly political art scene, a Treasury man raising money for the war was a target for ridicule.

In November 1915, Duncan was harassed by an English policeman for failing to join the army, leading Bunny to lash out at Keynes,

> *What are you? Only an intelligence that they need in their*
> *extremity . . . a genie taken out of a bottle by savages to serve them*
> *dutifully for their savage ends, and then—back you go into the bottle.*
> *Probably you won't make any difficulty about that—you probably*
> *long to be back in it—but don't be too good natured. Don't believe the*
> *savages are anything but savages. . . . You pull the strings and the idol*
> *Juggernaut opens its mouth & shuts its eyes.*[47]

Of course there was more to the rift than ethical principle. Keynes was now a man of affairs, enmeshed in the great problem of the day, while his Bloomsbury friends remained merely difficult people with complicated romantic lives. They were bright enough to understand the chasm of social status that had opened between Maynard and themselves and insecure enough to envy his professional advancement.

Less than a month after denouncing Maynard, Bunny wrote him again: "My parents cannot now support me in Paris or any where else. . . . I shall have to come back to do what? . . . Live upon my friends in one way or another."[48] In another letter, Bunny asked to borrow £1 from Keynes,[49] a sum that soon swelled to "very near £20."[50] Within a few months, he had developed an almost criminal dependency.

Dear Maynard,

I suppose you know in your absence Duncan and I made free with your house.

This was done on the grounds of my suffering from influenza which happily was cured the day after I got it.

I enjoyed my breakfasts, and Miss Chapman did not seem to dislike our being there.

Thank you very much for your hospitality.

Yours affectionately, David Garnett

We also drank about a noggin of whiskey.[51]

But the howls of the pacifists were sincere. To Keynes, they carried a deep emotional resonance. These were decrees from the ultimate authority in his ethical hierarchy: the struggling artist, the great source of so many Apostolic organic unities and good states of mind.

By the time Bunny wrote his fierce letter, Keynes couldn't pretend to be a mere functionary, taking orders and improving shipping costs. Financing the war had become a fundamental element of combat strategy, with the potential to shape the postwar balance of power around the globe. Keynes and his boss, McKenna, were regularly in conflict with Lloyd George and Secretary of State for War Horatio Herbert Kitchener. The military men wanted to land a "knock-out blow" against the Germans—a single massive discharge of power that would crush the enemy and bring a quick finish to the war, a mirror image of what the Germans had tried and failed to achieve against civilians in August 1914. Keynes insisted that this project was unaffordable, urging the government to pursue a strategy of bleeding the German economy instead. "It is certain that our present scale of expenditure is only possible as a violent temporary spurt," he wrote in a Treasury memo. "The limitations of our resources are in sight."[52]

Keynes and McKenna believed that the strongest weapon in the British arsenal was its economy. Great Britain was the richest nation in the conflict, providing money to Russia, France, Italy, and everyone else on the Allied side. The ultimate source of wealth in this war chest was the country's formidable industrial sector, fueled by the resources of its vast global empire and its dominating navy. If Britain was to support its own soldiers, much less the entire Allied project, it would also need men on the home front running machines, harvesting fields, and performing essential economic work. A surge of troops would deplete essential manpower at home.

It was a matter of both production and payment. The British needed men in factories to manufacture the weapons used on the front lines. But they also needed men to produce exports that could be sold abroad, particularly in the United States. When the British bought supplies from America, their U.S. trading partners had to be paid in dollars. And the most reliable way for the British to get dollars was to sell products to Americans. The government could sell off imperial assets for dollars—stocks, bonds, royal treasure—but a fire sale during wartime would probably yield disappointing prices and would permanently reduce the wealth of the empire.

A far more efficient course of action was to simply expand exports of consumer goods and raw materials to the United States. But Great Britain couldn't magnify its exports if all of its factory workers were off fighting in France. The plan for the knockout blow, Keynes thought, was economically self-defeating. As his political patron Edwin Montagu put it in a war cabinet meeting, the British needed to "stop this recruiting of men that we cannot arm."[53] Where Kitchener wanted more than 1.6 million new recruits from the civilian population, Board of Trade president Walter Runciman, an ally of Keynes, argued that the economy could spare only 840,000.[54]

Keynes and his faction had a powerful ally in Prime Minister Asquith. The two men not only saw eye to eye on war strategy, they shared a genuine affection for each other and were frequent guests in each other's households. And they were right that an endless open-ended commitment to war spending would eventually weaken the British Empire. But they were often wrong about the week-to-week or month-to-month constraints, and the effects on domestic production proved very difficult to predict. Though overall British economic output fell in 1914 and 1915 as trade routes were disrupted and the economy shifted to war production, by 1916 the government was orchestrating massive economic growth. By the end of the war, the British economy had expanded by nearly 15 percent, even after accounting for the effects of inflation.[55] Keynes, Asquith, and McKenna would learn from the experience. After the war, all three men advocated activist government policies to boost the economy, believing that what had worked during the war could succeed during peacetime.

In the fall of 1915, however, the British army was bent on delivering a program of immediate and overwhelming force against Germany. It launched a massive joint offensive against the Germans near the town of Loos in northern France. The disastrous result is memorialized at Pas de Calais, where more than twenty thousand headstones commemorate the lives of British soldiers whose final resting place remains unknown.[56] It was the first battle in which the British army deployed poison gas as a weapon. They lost the battle, and the war ground on.

For Lloyd George and Kitchener, the problem wasn't just money but manpower. The architects of the knockout blow thought it was now obvious that a volunteer force could not meet the demands of the French and British generals, and began talking about conscription. They called for all single men to register for the draft to replenish the soldiers the Allies were losing in the trenches.

The conscription proposal inflamed a fierce pacifist opposition among Keynes' peers. Russell embarked on speaking tours, giving passionate lectures against the war and publishing pamphlets denouncing it. He was eventually imprisoned for his activism. Clive Bell published two antiwar pamphlets, one of them considered so subversive that the mayor of London ordered all copies of it to be burned.[57]

In December 1915, Keynes had told his friends that he, McKenna, and Runciman were considering resigning together in protest—a move intended to strengthen Asquith's hand in his battle within the war cabinet against Lloyd George and Kitchener. In January, Keynes published a vehement letter to the editor in the *Daily Chronicle* under the pseudonym "Politicus" in which he denounced "compulsory military service" as "a new weapon for the subjugation of labour to the will of the governing classes." The "military megalomania" of conscription, he argued, would damage Great Britain's economy and jeopardize an otherwise certain Allied victory.[58]

Within Treasury, he worked to amend the bill to provide various protections and exemptions to the draft. When the final legislation passed, single men between the ages of eighteen and forty-one became eligible for conscription, but those who performed work of "national importance" could avoid the draft, as could citizens who demonstrated a true "conscientious objection" to the war. Keynes was disappointed in the final product—it was, after all, still conscription—but not enough to quit his job. "Things drift on, and I shall stay now, I expect, until they begin to torture one of my friends," he wrote to his mother.[59]

Bloomsbury was growing impatient. Lytton regarded Maynard's failure to resign as a personal betrayal. When he saw Keynes dining one evening in February 1916, he dropped an envelope onto his friend's dinner plate (he had come prepared). Enclosed was a newspaper clipping of a warmongering speech by Montagu—and a curt note: "Dear Maynard, Why are you still in the Treasury? Yours, Lytton."[60]

Lytton was taking aim at Maynard's soul, attacking the political side of his personality that Lytton had reproached since their college days. It was Montagu who shepherded Keynes into the Cambridge

Union political debate society, where he rose to secretary and then president before graduation. Montagu had helped Keynes secure a post at the India Office, gone to bat for him in the English bureaucracy, and landed him the post on the royal commission where he met Blackett, the man who invited him to London to work on the 1914 financial crisis. Montagu had even pulled strings to get Keynes a permanent position in Treasury after the crisis. "I owed . . . nearly all of my steps up in life to him," Keynes later wrote his wife.[61] Everything Keynes had devoted himself to professionally, Lytton implied, had been a violent lie.

The newspaper clipping—which affected Keynes so deeply that he preserved it for posterity in his personal papers—quoted Montagu saying that "war was deeply ingrained in the people of the Germanic nation" and that "she must be taught a lesson."[62] This was not the story Keynes told himself about the war. He'd read too much Goethe to believe there was anything innately wrong with German society. He viewed the war as a colossal mistake, not an inevitable clash. He even had close friends in the opposing army. In 1914, Wittgenstein had hurried home from Cambridge to Vienna and volunteered as an infantryman for the Central Powers, going so far as to send letters to Keynes from the front trying to keep up with Russell's theoretical work and Keynes' ideas on probability.[63] Though Keynes hoped the war would end with a happy harmony of European goodwill, his own political patrons were now pressing jingoistic British superiority. It was embarrassing.

Shortly after the conscription bill passed, the government granted Keynes an exemption from the draft, citing his work at Treasury as work of national importance, making it obvious that he would never be sent to the battlefront. But he still feared losing his Bloomsbury salvation. Just days after Lytton's dinner stunt, he formally applied for status as a conscientious objector:

> I claim complete exemption because I have a conscientious objection to surrendering my liberty of judgement on so vital a question as undertaking military service. I do not say that there are not

conceivable circumstances in which I should voluntarily offer my-self for military service. But after having regard to all the actually existing circumstances, I am certain that it is not my duty so to offer myself, and I solemnly assert to the Tribunal that my objec-tion to submit to authority in this matter is truly conscientious. I am not prepared on such an issue as this to surrender my right of decision, as to what is or is not my duty, to any other person, and I should think it morally wrong to do so.[64]

Keynes never bothered to attend the official hearing to consider his conscientious objector status, which, after all, was irrelevant. But the futility of the gesture speaks to how deeply he was affected.

The Bloomsbury taunts finally quieted when Keynes used his influ-ence in government to keep his friends away from the front. Since novel-writing and portrait-painting were not considered to be work of "national importance," he urged Duncan and Bunny to obtain work on a fruit farm and helped them apply for an exemption to the draft as essential agricultural laborers. When the government rejected their application, Keynes testified on their behalf at their conscientious ob-jection hearings. They were granted noncombatant status, meaning they would not have to carry weapons, but that was no guarantee of safety. Keynes' brother, Geoffrey, was a noncombatant medic, and his family was frequently gripped by anxiety when he dropped out of con-tact after a particularly gruesome battle (Geoffrey survived the war and went on to a career as a famous surgeon). So Keynes continued to press the conscientious objector cases for Duncan and Bunny until both men were officially granted total reprieve from any role in the war. It was not an isolated incident. "I spend half of my time on the boring business of testifying to the sincerity, virtue and truthfulness of my friends," he wrote in June 1916.[65]

It was an extraordinary tangle of convictions. Keynes raised money for the war effort even as he sought to deprive the British army of its soldiers. He was disgusted by the nationalist chauvinism of British politicians, but he was helping those same leaders win a war for impe-rial territory. Keynes was at war with himself.

Death was everywhere, even on the home front. "As I write, zeppelin bombs are dropping all round, about one every minute and a half I should say, and the flashes and explosions are most terrifying," Keynes wrote to his mother from his Bloomsbury flat. "I am much more frightened than I thought I should be."[66] His diplomatic duties required frequent travel through contested seas. If not for a last-minute administrative switch, he would have been killed in the summer of 1916. He had been scheduled to travel to Russia on a ship carrying Secretary of State for War Kitchener. But shortly before departure, Whitehall ordered Keynes to stay put in London. They couldn't spare him for the span of weeks the Russian expedition would require. Only hours after departure, the ship hit a German naval mine and sank, killing Kitchener and all but a dozen on board. "It is a most dreadful shock," Keynes wrote.[67] "I've been working intimately for the last week or two with all of them." His mother was shaken. "My darling son," she wrote. "To know that you missed it by so little! I could hardly breathe when I realized."[68]

In 1916, the internal politics of the war cabinet had become volatile. The showdown over conscription had demonstrated that Kitchener and Lloyd George were the dominant personas in the war cabinet. Now Kitchener was gone, and Lloyd George didn't miss his political moment. Though he and Asquith hailed from the same Liberal Party, in December 1916 Lloyd George led a bloodless coup against Asquith with support from rank-and-file members of the Conservative Party. When Asquith was forced out, he and his wife, Margot, dined with Keynes as they tried to recover their political wits. The former prime minister was "quite unmoved and magnanimous," Keynes told Virginia Woolf, but "Margot started to cry with the soup, sent for cigarettes, and dropped tears and ashes together into her plate—utterly overcome."[69]

As an Asquith ally, Keynes found his political stature diminished even as his responsibilities at Treasury grew more stressful by the day. Consumed by questions of combat strategy, war ministers had blinded themselves to the decaying financial support for their machinations. And as with the financial crisis of August 1914, Keynes believed the question of money had become a question of power. Much of the British Empire's economic might over the previous half century had been derived from its status as a creditor nation. When other countries needed funds, they turned to London, which gave the British a unique ability to influence how that money was spent and whom it would benefit. But the war had forced Great Britain to look abroad for its own financing needs, and Keynes recognized that as the empire became increasingly dependent on foreign help, it ceded geopolitical influence.

The United States was the only plausible source of funds for the British war machine, but President Woodrow Wilson and his secretary of state, William Jennings Bryan, refused to allow the U.S. government to lend money to any nation involved in the conflict. So the British Treasury turned to private American investors. Here, too, there were limits to the prospective largesse. The war was unpopular in the United States, and lines of allegiance were not uniform among its supporters. German immigrants and their descendants throughout the Midwest complicated British hopes for U.S. support, as did the significant Irish populations in New York, Boston, and Philadelphia. Ultimately, financial relief would come from a relatively narrow community on Wall Street, as American banks connected the British to wealthy individuals for loan subscriptions. But the aid proved essential. By mid-1916, Keynes calculated that 40 percent of the £5 million a day the United Kingdom was spending on the war was coming from the United States, nearly all of it organized by a few leading men of finance.[70]

The most prominent beneficiary of this arrangement was the banking house of J.P. Morgan, whose president, John Pierpont Morgan, Jr., was an Anglophile who had inherited from his father a knack for converting money into political power. He and his bank secured an exclusive deal to act as Great Britain's purchasing agent in America. Roughly half of all goods the British Empire obtained from the United States during the war were obtained by J.P. Morgan and transferred to the British for a finder's fee of 1 percent. Even with America officially neutral, Morgan was able to profit twice from the war: first by lending money to the British and again by taking a cut of what the British spent their funds on in the United States. As British purchases of American goods swelled, J.P. Morgan netted $30 million from its purchasing operations alone. It was an unheard-of deal in early-twentieth-century finance, widely viewed as the most important in the bank's formidable history.[71] The arrangement won Morgan political influence on both sides of the Atlantic, transforming his bank into an unofficial organ of U.S. diplomacy with bipartisan clout. Though his devout Republicanism rendered him a political foe of the Wilson administration, Morgan himself landed a role as an adviser to the Fed, and one of his top deputies, Thomas W. Lamont, would be dispatched to Paris in 1919 to help negotiate the peace treaty at war's end. In the short term, Morgan effectively mobilized much of the U.S. economy for war, whether Wilson and Bryan liked it or not, creating a web of economic constituents with an interest in both Allied victory and American intervention.[72]

Much of Morgan's enthusiasm was owed to the family's uniquely close relationship with British royalty. But many investment houses on Wall Street kept at least a few personnel in London, the world's financial capital. Wall Street was still a rising locus of economic power in 1914, emulating the customs and institutions of the British banking center. There was a shared sense of elite status between the City and Wall Street—an international class solidarity distinct from but related to Bloomsbury's international aestheticism.

But as the war dragged on, it became clear that the British were ceding not only economic power but political influence to their American rescuers. Keynes foresaw a postwar international realignment in which Americans and Wall Street financial power would dominate the future course of Western affairs, with France and Great Britain fading into history as client states of the New World.

Between October 3 and October 10, 1916, a joint delegation of French and British diplomats, including Keynes, held six meetings with the top men from J.P. Morgan to consider their options for mobilizing more American money into the war effort. The financiers included Jack Morgan himself; Henry Davison, who had helped secure the contract to serve as Britain's purchasing agent; John Harjes, a top partner at Morgan's Paris affiliate; and Edward Grenfell, the head of Morgan's London office. When the British informed the Morgan clan that they would need an additional $1.5 billion over the coming months, the Morgan team "did not conceal their dismay," Keynes recorded in a Treasury memo. Davison called the revelation "staggering." "The money required," he said, "is more than or as much as, exists." But by the fall of 1916, Morgan knew his firm was invested too heavily in the British war effort to back out. By the end of the negotiating sessions, he conceded that if his team couldn't get Britain everything it needed by March 31, "payments will be sufficiently postponed" on the empire's existing loans until they could. If it came to it, Morgan would let Britain slip into default on what it owed the bank for a time.[73] He was prepared to be lenient with his clients, but it was clear who held the keys to Britain's destiny.

On October 10, Keynes fired off a memo to the Foreign Office titled "The Financial Dependence of the United Kingdom on the United States of America," noting that Wilson and the Fed could, at a whim, make further British military efforts "a practical impossibility" by simply discouraging the U.S. financial sector from buying British bonds, leading to "a situation of the utmost gravity" on the western front. The government was not in a position to bargain with America on matters of diplomacy. It was time to beg.

"The sums which this country will require to borrow in the United States of America in the next six or nine months are so enormous, amounting to several times the entire national debt of that country, that it will be necessary to appeal to every class and section of the investing public," Keynes wrote. "It is hardly an exaggeration to say that in a few months time the American executive and the American public will be in a position to dictate to this country on matters that affect us more nearly than them. It is, therefore, the view of the Treasury, having regard to their special responsibilities, that the policy of this country towards the U.S.A. should be so directed as not only to avoid any form of reprisal or active irritation but also to conciliate and to please."[74]

The war had already nearly cost Woodrow Wilson the presidency.[75] His secretary of state, Bryan, had resigned in protest, worried that economic entanglements would eventually draw the United States into the conflict. Even running for reelection on the antiwar slogan "He kept us out of war" hadn't prevented the 1916 presidential race from tightening into one of the closest electoral contests in U.S. history, with the final result hinging on California, which Wilson carried by just 3,806 votes—less than four-tenths of a single percentage point of more than 1 million cast.

The son of a Presbyterian minister, Wilson viewed nearly every aspect of his presidency as a matter of grave moral urgency. He considered his domestic "New Freedom" agenda a frontal assault on unearned privilege and aristocratic power. By establishing the Federal Trade Commission, he empowered the federal government to fight monopolists. Creating the Federal Reserve was an attack on "the Money Trust." He believed American democracy to be a unique and sacred thing and was reluctant to risk it on a foreign battlefield.

But Wilson had been revising his ideas about Europe and Europeans over the course of his political career, undergoing an intellectual transformation that carried dramatic implications for the conflict overseas. In *A History of the American People,* which Wilson published in 1902, he had written disparagingly of immigrants from eastern and southern Europe, claiming that they had "neither skill nor energy nor any initiative of quick intelligence."[76] Desperate for immigrant votes on the presidential campaign trail in 1912, however, he had been forced to change his tune, proclaiming that "the country should be divested of all prejudices" and welcome people from all corners of Europe.[77] He didn't really mean *all* prejudices. Wilson consistently excluded black America from his reform agenda and even sought to segregate racially integrated departments of the federal workforce. But he made good on his promises to the immigrant communities of New York as president, and in 1915 he vetoed a bill to restrict European immigration.[78] Even eastern and southern Europe, Wilson now believed, were capable of producing men who could shoulder the responsibilities of self-government.

That changed his views about America's responsibilities to the people of Europe in an age of imperialism. To Wilson, the United States existed on its own high moral plane, and he became eager to assert its enlightened influence as a force against imperialist abuse. The great empires prevented fair diplomatic play among peoples and fought meaningless, unnecessary wars. With the violence of the Great War deepening, America's duty to lead the world out of darkness and into the light was quickly becoming the great moral imperative of Wilson's time in office. But Wilson was also a shrewd politician who was reluctant to jeopardize his shaky electoral fortunes by entering the war. He hoped instead that diplomatic pressure could force both sides to withdraw from the conflict and agree to a peace agreement mediated by the United States. As Keynes had worried he would do, Wilson decided to use finance to force the issue.

On November 28, 1916, less than two months after Keynes' meeting with Morgan, Wilson's Fed chairman, William Gibbs McAdoo, issued a decree formally advising all American investors to exercise caution with short-term loans to England and France. Though not an outright ban, McAdoo's notice was both an official expression of government disapproval and a warning about the Allies' creditworthiness. Its impact was immediate, effectively cutting off the flow of American money to the British. Even Morgan pulled back in the face of federal pressure. Wilson was strangling the European war machines in pursuit of what he called a "peace without victory" for either side.

By early 1917, the Fed memo had created a full-blown financial crisis in England. Without access to fresh credit from J.P. Morgan and other U.S. investors, the British had to pay their international obligations in gold. On March 17, Keynes informed the chancellor of the Exchequer that the Treasury had only weeks before its gold reserves would be completely exhausted. London's prowess as a financial center was on the brink of annihilation. Without access to American money, the British war machine would collapse.

Keynes distrusted American motives and feared for his country's diminishing stature on the world stage. But he couldn't fault Wilson's tactics. He, too, wanted the war to end, and he recognized that staunching the flow of American money was the most efficient way to end it—even more effective than the mobilization of an American army might prove.

But the kaiser couldn't leave well enough alone. Convinced that it was mere weeks from a total victory, Germany escalated its submarine attacks on civilian boats from the United States, some of which carried shipments of war supplies for the Allies. It was an act of retaliation against the British, whose naval blockade against Germany was causing widespread malnourishment and even starvation in German and Austrian cities. But to most Americans, the attacks seemed unprovoked acts of brutality against a neutral country, and the resulting civilian deaths were politically intolerable stateside. McAdoo reopened the money spigot, rescinding the Fed's warning about European loans, and private banks resumed writing loans to the British government. On April 6, Congress declared war, only a week before Keynes had believed the British Treasury would run dry. Public money soon followed private: Congress approved a $3 billion loan to France and England, placing the full faith and credit of the U.S. government behind the Allies for the first time.

The second British financial crisis of the war was over. The Allies had been rescued. Ironically, though the American entry guaranteed that the war would slog on, it assuaged for a time much of Keynes' personal anguish. The Americans were now responsible for prolonging the carnage, as Keynes saw it. His daily efforts to keep the Treasury solvent for an additional week or fortnight had become morally immaterial. So he stayed on, earning a reputation within the Treasury as a figure of prowess, or at least grudging respect. In May, he was named a companion of the Order of the Bath, a high honor in the British bureaucracy close to knighthood, for his general contributions to the war effort at the Treasury.

But he chafed at the new constraints imposed by his American paymasters. After buying into the war, Wilson and McAdoo could not believe its cost and were perpetually convinced that the British were overcharging them or secretly deploying funds for domestic frivolities. Keynes wrote a memo to McAdoo insisting that his government was not prioritizing debts to J.P. Morgan over its obligations on the battlefield. The biggest war the world had ever known, he emphasized, was simply a very expensive endeavor. Since America's entry, total British assistance to France, Russia, Italy, and Belgium had more than doubled the U.S. commitment to those same allies.[79] The Americans were financing the British, but the British had continued financing the rest of Europe.

The British government got away with at least one splurge instigated by Bloomsbury. When the French art dealer Georges Petit announced that his gallery would be auctioning off everything from Edgar Degas' studio following his death in September 1917, Duncan urged Maynard to get in on the bidding.[80] In his plea to Chancellor of the Exchequer Bonar Law, Keynes did his best to dress the scheme up in some kind of economic logic. Degas had died only a few months earlier, and the value of his paintings would probably go up over time as they influenced future artists. Demand for the paintings would be low with the fighting so near to Paris literally scaring off bidders. There would probably never be another chance to acquire these masterpieces at so low a price.

It was a strong effort but total nonsense. Nobody could predict the future value of Postimpressionist works, and the British government had no obligation to feature works from every great French artist in British museums. But the conservative Treasury chief was "very much amused at my wanting to buy pictures and eventually let me have my way as a sort of joke," Keynes wrote to Vanessa.[81] Keynes was dispatched to Paris with the director of the National Gallery, Charles Holmes, and £20,000, which was spent acquiring more than twenty paintings. He picked up four others for his private collection for a little under £500 of his own money.[82]

This "great picture coup," as Keynes called it,[83] was a rare cause for wartime celebration in Bloomsbury. Back at 46 Gordon Square, Keynes revealed one of his conquests—a still life of six apples painted by Paul Cézanne—to Vanessa, Virginia, J. T. Sheppard, and Roger Fry. "Roger very nearly lost his senses," Virginia wrote. "I've never seen such a sight of intoxication. He was like a bee on a sunflower."[84]

"Nessa and Duncan are very proud of you," Bunny wrote to Keynes. "You have been given complete absolution and future crimes also forgiven."[85]

Bloomsbury had not completely abandoned merrymaking during the war years. Keynes was still throwing the occasional dinner party, and Vanessa had taken over Charleston Farmhouse near Lewes in Sussex, which became the favorite country getaway of the entire set. Duncan soon moved in with her, and Keynes—despite hints of romantic rivalry—found the rural atmosphere a refuge from both the grind of London and the moral reproach of his other friends. While Virginia started attending speeches by suffragettes and Leonard took on paid work with the Labour Party, Vanessa remained sincerely and ardently apolitical. Seated next to Prime Minister Asquith at a dinner party early in the war, she had asked him without a trace of irony, "Are you interested in politics?"[86] She alone among the entire crowd could listen to Keynes spin stories of the absurd eccentricities of his life in public affairs and laugh along without harboring or suppressing some unspoken outrage over his compromised moral standing. Politics for Vanessa was just another site for human drama, a field of literary aesthetics rather than a test of sin and salvation. Maynard became infused with, in Virginia's words, a "doglike affection"[87] for Vanessa.

As his tensions with Bloomsbury eased, his frictions with the Americans intensified. Keynes described the Inter-Ally Council for War as a "monkey house"[88] whose meetings were a "farce"[89] of bureaucratic incompetence. According to his friend Basil Blackett, Keynes "made a terrible reputation for his rudeness out here"[90] when he was dispatched stateside for a diplomatic mission in the fall.

American money had not brought about a speedy victory, and U.S. troops would not arrive on the battlefield until the summer of 1918. In the meantime, the bloodshed only intensified. The Americans were being so tightfisted about the expense that the British were forced to ration food domestically. The Allies might well win the war, but both the global order and the domestic culture Keynes had been raised in had already disappeared. It left Keynes disillusioned and depressed.

"My Christmas thoughts are that a further prolongation of the war, with the turn things have now taken, probably means the disappearance of the social order we have known hitherto," he wrote to his mother. "With some regrets I think I am on the whole not sorry. The abolition of the rich will be rather a comfort and serve them right anyhow. What frightens me more is the prospect of *general* impoverishment. In another year's time we shall have forfeited the claim we had staked out in the New World and in exchange this country will be mortgaged to America.

"Well, the only course open to me is to be buoyantly bolshevik; and as I lie in bed in the morning I reflect with a good deal of satisfaction that, because our rulers are as incompetent as they are mad and wicked, one particular era of a particular kind of civilization is very nearly over."[91] He did not spare himself from culpability. Writing to Duncan, he confessed, "I work for a government I despise for ends I think criminal."[92]

Keynes' sense of competition with the United States and his disdain for American culture would continue throughout his life. During World War II, he belittled the beauty of the U.S. countryside and dismissed U.S. intellectuals as incapable of "intuition." But it was in the United States that the economic ideas that would make him famous would first gain a foothold. And it would be an American who would resolve Keynes' final crisis of conscience during the First World War.

On January 8, 1918, Wilson gave the most important speech of his life. A month earlier, he had delivered his fifth State of the Union address, asking Congress to expand the U.S. state of war to include the Austro-Hungarian Empire. After receiving approval a few days later, he called lawmakers back to Capitol Hill for yet another talk—a major inconvenience for men who were accustomed to being home on recess during the winter months. In the days before hourly shuttle flights, a trip to Washington could prevent congressmen from seeing family, friends, and constituents for weeks. But Wilson had a powerful vision to offer, one that he hoped would redefine not only his presidency but America's role in world affairs. With the nation's lawmakers assembled, he laid out what became known as the Fourteen Points—terms that all parties in the Great War must adhere to if they wanted any eventual peace treaty to last. Though there were fourteen points, the speech was dedicated to a broad concept that became known as "self-determination," the right of all peoples to live under a government of their own choosing, free from foreign pressure.

Some points were general principles. The First Point called for an end to secret diplomatic pacts, while the Fourth Point demanded disarmament "to the lowest point consistent with domestic safety." The Third Point invoked economic fairness, calling for "the removal, so far as possible, of all economic barriers and the establishment of an equality of trade conditions." This trade would be facilitated by the Second Point, which guaranteed "freedom of the seas."

Fully half of the points Wilson outlined were explicitly territorial. He wanted to draw new national boundaries granting ethnic groups a right to autonomous development independent of the great European empires—a more benevolent expression of the same biological racism that he deployed domestically. The Eighth Point called for an independent Belgium, the Tenth Point for an "autonomous" Austria-Hungary. Under the Eleventh Point, all troops would be required to evacuate Romania, Serbia, and Montenegro, while Turkey and Poland were to be granted independence under points Twelve and Thirteen. Even Bolshevik Russia—which frightened Central Power and Allied leaders alike—should be granted "an unhampered and unembarrassed opportunity for the independent determination of her own political development and national policy and assure her of a sincere welcome into the society of free nations." He was presenting a detailed rejection of European territorial conquest as an acceptable outcome to the war and demanding that new buffer states be created between the great empires to preserve a lasting peace.

The Fourteen Points were much more than a set of instructions for winding down the conflict; they were a moral guide to a postwar global order—an attempt to forge something lasting and good out of a catastrophe that had been arbitrary and cruel. Wilson's conception of global justice was rooted in nineteenth-century ideas of nationalism and identity, rather than ideas about individual rights. The only human right Wilson presented was the right to be a member of an independent nation. But his call for all nations, large and small, victorious and vanquished, to enjoy an equal seat at the table of international governance—this was a radical idea with the power to bring centuries of empire to an end. Wilson, the priestly Presbyterian, was offering Europe an opportunity to redeem itself.

As with all of Wilson's grand visions, he never applied the same logic to the United States. If ethnic groups were to be granted their own governments, then surely African Americans would qualify for a new nation. To Wilson, America was an ethnically unique amalgam of enlightened democracy. He could find no place for African Americans in that racial formula for political success, but he also denied them their right to self-determination. For the United States to be a hero that could liberate Europe from the injustice of its backward medieval factionalism, it would have to ignore its own internal oppressions.

Yet to Keynes, Wilson's promise of absolution came as a relief. The Fourteen Points offered to bestow a broader moral significance on his work during the war. At Wilson's decree, the war had transformed from a meaningless scramble for territory into a crusade to end imperialism for all time. In a letter to his mother, Keynes praised Wilson's ideas as "fourteen commandments."[93] The message resonated with all of Bloomsbury, which became steadfast devotees of Wilson's Fourteenth Point, the establishment of a new League of Nations to adjudicate future diplomatic quarrels. And they noticed a change in their friend at Treasury. Less than a week after Wilson's speech, Virginia Woolf recorded in her diary that Maynard had become "the chief fount of the magic spirit"[94] that collectively animated their artistic community.

Almost nine months after giving his Fourteen Points address, Wilson pressed further in an address at the Metropolitan Opera House in New

York, dedicating an entire speech to the League. By October 6—eighteen months to the day from the U.S. declaration of war—Germany decided to take Wilson up on the idea. The German citizenry had been backed into a corner economically. The British Treasury had been resuscitated by American credit, and the Allied naval blockade against food shipments to Germany, Austria, and Turkey had never relented. Independent experts would later estimate that this policy had resulted in the starvation deaths of more than 400,000 civilians. The German government, which only a few months earlier had believed itself on the brink of total victory, had seen enough. Prince Maximilian of Baden sent a public note saying Germany would withdraw from conflict if the Allies would abide by Wilson's principles for peace. The official armistice came down a few weeks later—on the eleventh hour of the eleventh day of the eleventh month. The war was over.

"What an astonishing fortnight this has been in the history of the world!" Keynes wrote to his mother, overflowing with optimism. "I feel real confidence now that it's all over and the govts of the world, whatever the newspapers may say, genuinely, I am sure, want to make peace."[95]

THREE

——◇——

PARIS AND ITS DISCONTENTS

On December 16, 1918, scores of military cavalrymen paraded through the streets of Paris atop well-groomed black horses, their polished sabers and brass helmets gleaming in the pale sunlight. The soldiers heralded a procession of carriages filled with the world's most powerful leaders, including French prime minister Georges Clemenceau and his British counterpart, David Lloyd George. Infantrymen lined the streets, their bayonets pointing to the sky as the convoy rolled through. The dignitaries were trailed by an expensive display of technological prowess: a retinue of automobiles. The Great War was over, and its victors streamed down the Champs-Élysées toward the Arc de Triomphe, a grand display that upstaged even Napoleon Bonaparte, who had been forced to settle for a wooden model of the unfinished monument when he had entered the city a century earlier.

A screaming, exultant crowd pushed into the streets, waved on rooftops, cheered from windows, and clamored into city squares. One million people lived in Paris at the time, but two million admirers had braved the frigid, windy afternoon hoping to steal a glimpse of American president Woodrow Wilson. "Every inch was covered with cheering, shouting humanity," according to his wife, Edith. "Flowers rained upon us until we were nearly buried."[1]

By the conflict's end, Wilson was the most celebrated man on the Continent. U.S. military might had turned the tide for the Allies after years of bloody stalemate. But Wilson also enraptured the European public for another reason: He had arrived in the French capital for a peace conference that would set the terms of international politics for the next generation. Alone among the leading men of the Great War's victors, Wilson had laid out a vision of a new global order in which a new League of Nations would use diplomacy to prevent the type of mayhem Europe had just inflicted upon itself. To the war-wearied masses, he seemed more a prophet than a politician. Crowds in Rome, according to one Secret Service agent, "literally hailed the president as a god—The God of Peace.'"[2] His dream captivated the millions of French, Italian, and British families who had lost fathers, sons, and livelihoods to the ghastly carnage of war. His popularity transcended political faction, language, and nationality. In Paris, the Communist newspaper *L'Humanité* sang Wilson's praises,[3] while Jan Smuts, a future prime minister of South Africa, declared Wilson "the noblest figure—perhaps the only noble figure in the history of the war."[4]

"What a place the President held in the hearts and hopes of the world when he sailed to us in the *George Washington!*" wrote Keynes. "What a great man came to Europe in those early days of our victory!"[5]

As the parade crossed the Seine, more than 100,000 cheering Parisians crowded into the Place de la Concorde.[6] On the Rue Royale, the procession passed under a banner of electric lights that spanned the entire street, declaring VIVE WILSON as onlookers hailed him with cries of "Wilson *le juste!*" The elderly president grinned like a schoolboy, waving his top hat in appreciation.

There were no parades for John Maynard Keynes when he arrived in Paris on January 10, 1919. He had informed the Treasury that the conference would be his final act as a British government official— "when it is over I am a free man."[7] He left home optimistic, the existential turmoil between his Bloomsbury code of ethics and his ambitions on the world stage at last coming to an end. He told his mother that the prospects for a stable and lasting peace were "good" and to expect him back home within a month, with all the affairs of the conference complete. He had already started vetting job offers, cheerfully fantasizing about a postwar lifestyle of abundant pay and extensive leisure.[8]

But the peace conference shocked him back to the present. "There is an enormous crowd here and as you may imagine a perpetual buzz of chatter, gossip and intrigue," he reported home.[9] Negotiations were already in full swing. The British delegation was spread across four hotels, but the choice rooms were in the Hôtel Majestic on the Champs-Élysées, which became a kind of "universal rendezvous place" since meals for British delegates in the hotel dining room were free and prepared by British cooks. Keynes tried to take his lunches with other sophisticates at the pricier restaurants around town. It was a way to flaunt his social status, but the off-site meals also helped him maintain a reputation as a man with more worldly priorities than those of his provincial colleagues, as he rubbed elbows with foreign journalists and other influential figures.[10]

It was a chaotic and haphazard scene. Wall Street attorney Paul Cravath told Keynes that the U.S. outpost at the Hôtel Crillon on the Place de la Concorde was "like a rabbit warren,"[11] and security was so tight that Clemenceau himself was once held up by wary U.S. guards on his way to a meeting inside.[12] There had not even been a formal opening of negotiations. In the weeks following the armistice, diplomats from all over the world had simply filtered into the city's luxury hotels, hosting dinners and strategizing over drinks, taking limousine rides to and from meetings on the Quai d'Orsay along the bank of the Seine. There was an abundance of official inter-ally committees from the war, many of which had transferred their operations to Paris and began drafting proposals and counterproposals, haggling over territorial boundaries, verbs, and currencies long before Wilson and Clemenceau presided over an introductory plenary session on January 18. The conference published a slate of regulations to guide negotiations on January 21, but even the terms of procedure would remain a diplomatic battleground until March, when the conference was reorganized around a Council of Four: Wilson, Clemenceau, Lloyd George, and Italian prime minister Vittorio Orlando.[13]

Keynes kept a grueling personal schedule. In a letter home written four days after his arrival, he described a single workday that included separate meetings of the Armistice Commission, the Supreme War Council, and the Supreme Council of Supply and Relief, independent briefings with Chancellor of the Exchequer Bonar Law and Lord Reading (a powerful figure in the British judiciary), a strategy session with American delegates, and an after-dinner confab with other delegates from the British Treasury to compare notes and plan for the following day.[14]

The Germans and other Central Powers had not been invited to the proceedings. The Allies, everyone believed, would determine their own terms for the treaty, which would then be presented to the German leaders to open the real negotiations that would shape the future of Europe. The delegates assembled in Paris felt their vanquished enemy's presence only through a steady stream of reports from diplomats stationed abroad, which painted vivid, horrifying scenes of enemy cities. Berlin was in the throes of a violent revolution. Foreign officers were counting the ribs on starving children in the streets of Vienna. After the armistice had been signed, according to a U.S. delegate named Herbert Hoover, "The danger to civilization from militarism was at once replaced by the imminent danger from economic collapse."[15] The collective relief that had accompanied the armistice and the ecstasy that had surrounded Wilson's arrival a month earlier had given way to an atmosphere of anxiety, foreboding, even disease in Paris. A devastating influenza pandemic had been taking lives all over the world for the past two years, and with the world gathered in Paris, the conference became a vector for contagion. One British diplomat, William Stang, had already died of the flu in Paris, and Lloyd George, Wilson, Clemenceau, and Keynes himself would all grapple with the illness over the course of the conference.[16]

"Paris was a nightmare, and every one there was morbid," Keynes wrote. "A sense of impending catastrophe overhung the frivolous scene; the futility and smallness of man before the great events confronting him; the mingled significance and unreality of the decisions; levity, blindness, insolence, confused cries from without,—all the elements of ancient tragedy were there."[17]

In the early days of the conference, Keynes' greatest source of frustration came from within his own government. The Majestic, he told Bloomsbury, was a "hellish place," where bureaucrats and politicians radiated "self-importance and bored excitement."[18] His own position at Paris had been upended by a British election held on December 14, 1918. Lloyd George, recognizing the moment of Allied victory as a rare political moment, had exercised his authority as prime minister to call a parliamentary election almost as soon as the armistice had been signed. The Liberal Party and the Conservative Party had controlled Great Britain during the war under a coalition government, and Lloyd George hoped not only to expand his coalition majority but to oust some of his political rivals within his own Liberal Party. On election day, all of Keynes' most powerful allies lost their seats in Parliament: McKenna, Runciman, even Asquith himself. It left Keynes furious—he later publicly accused Lloyd George of "political immorality" fueled by "private ambition" for calling the election.[19]

And so although Keynes arrived in Paris with prestigious titles—the Treasury designated him its top delegate, and he had been named the British Empire's representative on the Supreme Economic Council—his reliable political patrons in Whitehall were gone.[20] And his wartime feud with Lloyd George had not ended with the armistice. They now clashed over reparations—the amount of money Germany would be required to pay the victors in compensation for the economic destruction caused by the war.

Even before hostilities had formally ended, the Treasury had asked Keynes to calculate precisely the amount Germany could afford to pay. Keynes identified a maximum of £2 billion—half paid up front, the other half spread out over the next three decades.[21] The actual costs of the war, of course, had been vastly higher, but a more exacting indemnity would prove counterproductive. To generate the wealth needed to make reparation payments, Germany would have to boost its exports, taking international market share from British producers and thus ultimately undercutting British wealth. If the Allies tried instead to seize German gold, German mines, or German factories, they would only undermine Germany's ability to generate future wealth that could be devoted to tribute. "If Germany is to be milked," Keynes wrote in a report for the British delegation, "she must not first of all be ruined."[22]

But during the 1918 election campaign, Lloyd George had commissioned former Bank of England governor Walter Cunliffe and a judge named Lord Sumner to make a reparations report of their own, promising the British public the largest possible indemnity that could be secured from their defeated enemy. Sumner and Cunliffe suggested that Germany could afford £24 billion (which translated to $120 billion at the time)—an amount they had arrived at because it happened to be the entire cost of the war.[23] At over five times the size of Germany's prewar economy,[24] the number was so preposterous that U.S. diplomats initially laughed it off, even as Lloyd George pointed to it solemnly on the stump. "A perfectly absurd figure," noted Wilson adviser and Paris delegate Thomas Lamont.[25]

The result was a British government simultaneously negotiating for different aims. Keynes, dispatched by the Treasury to work out a realistic indemnity, was already deep into reparation talks with American financial experts, including Paul Cravath and Norman Davis, a representative of the Wilson Treasury Department and an old friend of J.P. Morgan partner Henry Davison. Yet Lloyd George named the hardliners Sumner and Cunliffe to the official Reparations Committee at the peace conference.

And like so many other thickets of money and numbers that Keynes encountered in his life, the battle over reparations wasn't really a quarrel over arithmetic; it raised fundamental questions about the meaning of the war, the limits of political progress, and the nature of human freedom. "The subject of reparations caused more trouble, contention, hard feeling, and delay at the Peace Conference than any other point of the Treaty of Versailles," according to Lamont[26]—quite an achievement for a pact that also redrew national boundaries across Europe,

Asia, Africa, and the Middle East. Keynes had become the flash point of a profound ideological clash.

Wilson had staked his presidency on the idea that European imperialism could be cured. The domestic achievements of his first term in office—creating the Federal Reserve and the Federal Trade Commission, reinvigorating a crusade against monopoly—had already secured him a legacy as an accomplished reformer before his reelection in 1916. Though cynics accused him of joining the Great War to line the pockets of American businessmen, Wilson saw the United States as an objective party that had been forced to take sides in a dispute between imperfect foreign rivals. Wilson had been an academic before entering politics; he was a respected political theorist and historian who had helped elevate Princeton University to the top tier of American research institutions. He believed that the Great War was the result not merely of avarice and ambition but of the decrepit political system in the Old World. Germany and the Ottoman Empire were autocracies that were destined for instability because their systems of government were themselves illegitimate—they relied on pure dominance to sustain their power over ethnic groups that ought to govern themselves as independent nations. The French and British empires were somewhat better due to their democratic domestic governments, though Wilson believed they were still polluted by the legacy of monarchism. He was cautiously optimistic about the new Bolshevik government that had seized power in Russia in 1917. Whatever the Communists' flaws, the old tsarist regime had been despotic and illegitimate.

Like everyone else at Paris, Wilson blamed Germany for the war. Unlike many, however, he did not blame the German *people*. Indeed, to Wilson's mind, German citizens had been victims of the kaiser's autocratic excess before the peoples of Belgium, France, Russia, and Great Britain had been, as he told Congress in April 1917: "We have no quarrel with the German people. We have no feeling towards them but one of sympathy and friendship. It was not upon their impulse that their Government acted in entering this war. It was not with their previous knowledge or approval. It was a war determined upon as wars used to be determined upon in the old, unhappy days when peoples were nowhere consulted by their rulers and wars were provoked and waged in the interest of dynasties or of little groups of ambitious men who were accustomed to use their fellow men as pawns and tools."[27]

In short, he believed that the war had been caused by autocracy—an idea bound up inexorably with empire, since conquered peoples were denied their own government. Its solution was democracy—and by implication, the end of imperialism. "A steadfast concert for peace can never be maintained except by a partnership of democratic nations. No autocratic government could be trusted to keep faith within it or observe its covenants. . . . Only free peoples can hold their purpose and their honour steady to a common end and prefer the interests of mankind to any narrow interest of their own."[28] Great empires had led Europe to cataclysm; its salvation would be found in a new order of smaller, nation-state democracies, with a League of Nations empowered to settle international conflicts without the need for war. In Wilson's mind, the United States would be playing not for territory or tribute at the peace conference but to stake a claim as the moral leader of a new era. America would seek no new lands and demand no reparations. The economics of the treaty would be a secondary consideration to the needs of the League, which would advance the interests not of the United States but of the world.

Despite its American origin, Wilson's vision entranced Keynes. "The President played a nobler part at Paris than any of his colleagues," he wrote a friend, Allyn Young,[29] telling Norman Davis after the conference that Wilson "was the one member of the Four who was *trying* to do right."[30] No sooner had Keynes arrived in Paris than Davis and the U.S. delegation had charmed him with a gesture of goodwill. Great Britain was dependent on American money at the end of the war and would continue to be so until its domestic economy had transitioned back to peacetime operation. Technically, congressional authorization for British financial support had expired with the end of hostilities in November. But Davis quietly assured Keynes that the real U.S. priority was to coordinate Wilson's grand diplomatic agenda with the British. "The last thing . . . they want to do is quarrel with us prematurely over money," Keynes reported back to the Treasury.[31]

Wilson's high idealism was sincere, but he issued his disavowal of reparation from a privileged economic position. The 116,708 soldiers the United States had lost seemed staggering on the American home front, but they constituted just 2 percent of Allied military deaths—less than half the fatalities suffered by Romanian forces alone.[32] Four and a half years of Allied war orders had been a tremendous source of wealth for American farms and factories, while the Allied demand for American money had transformed Wall Street into the world's dominant financial power. And the U.S. delegates were unsparing creditors. Wilson adviser Oscar T. Crosby told Keynes before he arrived that any talk of reducing or voiding Allied war debt was not "a proper subject of discussion by the Peace Conference."[33] It was not hard to understand why. By the end of the war, the European allies owed the U.S. government more than $7 billion and another $3.5 billion to American banks.[34] It was easy for Wilson to talk about sweeping global change when the war had transformed the United States from an industrializing young nation into a global superpower in the span of a few short years.

The situation was starkly different in France, which had lost 1.4 million soldiers and 300,000 civilians,[35] not including deaths from the flu pandemic. Total industrial production in France had declined by nearly one-third over the course of the war.[36] In northern France, six thousand square miles of territory had been ravaged, and with it, some of the most fruitful assets of the French economy. The ruined region had produced 20 percent of French crops, 70 percent of French coal, 90 percent of French iron, and 65 percent of French steel. At least 250,000 buildings had been "completely destroyed" and another 250,000 "damaged," while 1.2 million acres of forest had been "laid waste."[37] The country owed $3 billion to the U.S. government, $2 billion to the British government, and still more to British and American investors.

French economic conditions were so dire that the French government hosted Keynes for what was billed as a "holiday" in northern France, hoping to impress upon him the magnitude of the devastation with personal tours of scarred battlefields at Lille, Reims, and the Somme.[38] The French urgently needed resources and capital, and their delegation at Paris looked on the defeated Germans as a just source of economic spoils.

French prime minister Clemenceau quickly became Keynes' chief ideological adversary at the conference. Nicknamed "The Tiger," the French prime minister had spent his entire adult life embroiled in nearly uninterrupted political turmoil. As a young man, he had worked as a radical newspaperman, was jailed for writing articles criticizing Emperor Napoleon III, and fled France for New York City, where he came to admire the Radical Republicans who briefly held power in Washington during the years immediately following the Civil War. He returned to Paris during the Franco-Prussian War and was eventually elected to the French National Assembly after the fall of the Napoleonic regime. During the anti-Semitic panic of the Dreyfus Affair, Clemenceau had defended the French military captain Alfred Dreyfus, who had been wrongly accused of spying for the Germans, and had published Émile Zola's internationally famed "J'Accuse . . . !" essay on the front page of his daily newspaper, L'Aurore, in January 1898. By 1902, he was back in parliamentary politics, an elected member of the Senate.

But his idealism had faded with age. He had devoted much of his first stint as prime minister, from 1906 to 1909, to breaking strikes, diminishing his stature in left-wing circles, where his dueling habit (Clemenceau fought in twenty-two duels) tainted him as a decadent aristocrat.[39] His aggressive temperament was not confined to politics. Clemenceau had managed to get his American wife jailed for adultery while he was serving in the National Assembly, stripped of her French citizenship, and packed off to New York.[40] Now seventy-seven, Clemenceau had come to see politics as an eternal quest for dominance. "Life is only a struggle," he told a French member of Parliament in 1919. "This struggle, you will not suppress it."[41] He was indifferent to Wilson's League of Nations and paid lip service to the Fourteen Points only as a legal formality that had secured a German surrender. When Wilson insisted at a private meeting of prime ministers that the use of force in diplomacy was a "failure," Clemenceau retorted that "The U.S.A. was founded by force and consolidated by force. You must admit that!"[42] Writing later in *The Economic Consequences of the Peace*, Keynes observed, "He felt about France what Pericles felt of Athens— unique value in her, nothing else mattering; but his theory of politics was Bismarck's. He had one illusion—France; and one disillusion— mankind."[43]

Keynes intended the passage as a personal insult. Prince Otto von Bismarck, the Prussian militarist who forged the German Empire, had been one of Clemenceau's most bitter foreign enemies in the late nineteenth century. As a member of the French National Assembly, Clemenceau had voted against the 1871 peace treaty between France and Germany, preferring to prolong a war that France was losing badly rather than submit to his international foe.[44]

To Clemenceau, there was no use trying to strike balances or prevent future conflicts at the peace conference. Europe would eventually come to blows again over some pretext or other, and when the moment came, he wanted France to be strong and its enemies to be weak. There was little room in his worldview for human progress or the prospect of a more peaceful future. "I take men as they are, the facts as they are: humanity will not change so soon,"[45] he said. It was a hard doctrine born of a hard world. "One could not despise Clemenceau or dislike him, but only take a different view as to the nature of civilized man, or indulge, at least, a different hope," Keynes wrote.[46]

On many of the thorny issues debated at Paris, Wilson and Clemenceau differed over technical or strategic questions. Which peoples within the old empires had a right to a new state of their own? How should a people be defined? Where would national boundaries be drawn? But on reparations, their worldviews met in a head-on collision. Clemenceau and the French delegation supported nearly any statistical maneuver that would elevate the calculations of how much damage Germany had caused in the war or raise the estimates of Germany's capacity to pay for that damage. The Americans, by contrast, wanted lower numbers, seeking a sustainable economic balance between the European combatants.

Between those two poles stood Lloyd George. Like Clemenceau, Lloyd George had been a radical in his youth. As a member of the House of Commons, he had helped create a government pension program for the elderly. As chancellor of the Exchequer, he had devised new taxes on wealthy landowners under a prewar domestic project of "raising money to wage implacable warfare against poverty and squalidness."[47] On foreign policy, he made a name for himself by assailing Great Britain's war against the Boers in South Africa as a humanitarian crime.

But his opposition to the Boer War had accompanied grandiose, unabashed imperial ambitions. For Clemenceau, negotiating with Wilson and Lloyd George was like being caught "between Jesus Christ on the one hand, and Napoleon Bonaparte on the other."[48] Several territorial questions had been settled in Great Britain's favor by the time the armistice was signed. The Allied capture of German colonies, including German East Africa, gave the British an unbroken chain of dominion stretching from Egypt all the way to South Africa. The fall of the tsars had assuaged long-standing British fears of a Russian threat to India by way of central Asia. And the German navy, the only serious rival to British sea power on the globe, had surrendered its ships and submarines.

With those victories already in hand, punishing Germany became a top priority. Lloyd George did not blame imperialism for the Great War, only the unique recklessness of the German Empire. He told his war cabinet that "Germany had committed a great crime" and that the world had a responsibility to "make it impossible that anyone should be tempted to repeat that offence."[49] His early support for the Sumner and Cunliffe report and its ludicrously high reparation figure was part of this effort. But Lloyd George had no deep passion for any particular reparation number or even for the use of reparation itself as the chief form of punishment. He could be persuaded to accept other methods if they better suited British interests.

And Britain did face economic challenges. The country had lost a million soldiers and civilians to the war. But its deepest problem as a global power was not about natural resources or manpower but finance. British banking, the source of so much of the empire's prewar influence, had been exhausted by the war effort. And because the British money borrowed abroad had been spent on destruction rather than productive new European enterprise, there were serious questions about the ability of Britain's allies—especially France—to repay what they owed. Where Clemenceau saw himself fighting to preserve the basis of French production and security, Lloyd George was more concerned with maintaining the City's prominence as a center of financial power alongside Wall Street. The war had vanquished Germany and Russia as serious rivals to British power. At Paris, Lloyd George wanted to ensure that the British Empire would not lose ground among the victorious Allies.

All three men could cite lofty principles to defend their positions. Even Clemenceau at times chalked up his disputes with Wilson's "Utopian" thinking to personal experience, rather than a difference of fundamental values. "Mr. Wilson has lived in a world that has been fairly safe for Democracy," he told Wilson's translator at Paris. "I have lived in a world where it is good form to shoot a democrat."[50]

The Paris Peace Conference was fundamentally a struggle for dominance among three rival powers who happened to have been allies in the Great War. But it was also a moment of intellectual crisis for Enlightenment liberalism. Prior to the war, most Europeans had seen nothing shameful about imperialism. It was simply the way things were. But the havoc the war had wreaked on European society had inspired European intellectuals to grapple with questions that had long been obvious in imperial colonies. Could the progressive ideals that Lloyd George, Clemenceau, Wilson, and Keynes defended at home be reconciled with imperial dominance abroad? What kind of political order would—or could—replace the imperial milieu that had brought the world to war? Neither the economic structure of the postwar era nor the ideological fate of liberal imperialism could be resolved without grappling with the problem of German reparations. And so German reparations became the central, iconic drama of the peace conference.

But before the Allies could settle questions about the coming global order, they had to resolve a humanitarian crisis. The Allies had maintained the British naval blockade against trade to Germany and Austria after the armistice had been signed on November 11, 1918. As it had during the war, the blockade prevented the Central Powers from accessing international food shipments. It was part of a starvation strategy aimed at decimating both enemy morale and population. Estimates of the total humanitarian cost of the blockade over the course of the war vary, but it claimed a quarter of a million civilian lives in Germany during the months after the shooting had stopped.[51] As the Allies took their time initiating the peace talks, they also exploited the monthly renewal of the armistice as an opportunity to extract concessions from Germany before the terms of the peace treaty had been finalized.

The French began armistice renewal talks with the Germans alone, hoping to seize German gold, securities, and even the printing presses for German marks.[52] They were not interested in lifting the blockade—not because they opposed feeding the Germans, they insisted, but because they objected to Germany actually paying anyone for food. Whatever the Germans spent on domestic nutrition, after all, could not be turned over to France in reparation.

Herbert Hoover, the director of the U.S. Food Administration, was apoplectic about the blockade, decrying it as a humanitarian disaster that would foment revolution. "The whole mass of urban humanity formerly under enemy domination seemed headed directly for Bolshevism, or anarchy—from which there could be no hope of peace,"[53] he later wrote. Keynes agreed: "I hardly know why we, the English, decided to promote its continuance."[54] Yet when the British and Americans caught wind of the French talks, they dispatched Keynes to oversee British interests during negotiations in Trier in Germany. There, for the first time, he came face-to-face with defeated enemy officials. "A sad lot they were in those early days, with drawn, dejected faces and tired staring eyes, like men who had been hammered on the Stock Exchange,"[55] he later recalled.

Like Hoover, Keynes recognized the moral urgency of the situation. But although he believed in Hoover's good intentions, Keynes noted that the Americans planned not only to supply the Germans with food but to overcharge them for it. Hoover, as part of his duties in the United States, just happened to be saddled with a massive surplus of American pork in need of a buyer. The U.S. government had guaranteed its farmers high prices during the war to encourage production, and since France and England had been willing to pay top dollar for whatever they could get, it had been easy to pass those costs on to France and England. But with the fighting done and German submarine warfare at an end, the French could now buy food at much lower prices from South America.[56] Hoover had an enormous supply of freshly slaughtered American pork and no buyer to take it off his hands at the elevated price he required. He had the same problem with wheat as Italians attempted to duck out of an order of 100 million bushels.[57]

"The situation is a curious one," Keynes wrote in a January 14 memo to Sir John Bradbury, a top Treasury official.

Germany is to receive fat supplies on a very generous scale. Bolshevism is to be defeated and the new era to begin. At the Supreme War Council President Wilson was very eloquent on the subject of instant action on these lines. But really the under-lying motive of the whole thing is Mr. Hoover's abundant stocks of low-grade pig products at high prices which must at all costs be unloaded on someone, enemies failing Allies. When Mr. Hoover sleeps at night visions of pigs float across his bedclothes and he frankly admits that at all hazards the nightmare must be dissipated.[58]

Nor were the Americans the only party with ulterior motives. The British wanted Keynes to get control of the German commercial shipping fleet—a valuable economic asset for the British Empire. Ultimately Keynes and Hoover beat back the French and got the Germans fed. But they also made the Germans pay for their overpriced rations with ships and gold. As Keynes later acknowledged to Bloomsbury, "Our relations with them were partly in good faith and partly in bad."[59]

The food crisis was a microcosm of the peace conference writ large. The Germans didn't have food. The Americans had food they didn't want. While dressing up their diplomacy in the language of freedom, progress, and selflessness, the Americans were engaging in subtle financial ruthlessness. The British, likewise, testified to American altruism and assailed Clemenceau and his finance minister for inhumanity—as Keynes himself capitalized on an opportunity to secure a source of wealth for the British Empire.

To Lloyd George, once Keynes had secured the German commercial fleet, the most critical British interests at Paris had been taken care of. "The truth is that we have got our way," he said. "We have got most of the things we set out to get. If you had told the British people twelve months ago that they would have secured what they have, they would have laughed you to scorn. The German Navy has been handed over; the German mercantile shipping has been handed over, and the German colonies have been given up. One of our chief trade competitors has been most seriously crippled and our Allies are about to become her biggest creditors. That is no small achievement."[60]

Keynes began to feel unwell on the journey back from Trier. Two days after returning to Paris, he was bedridden with a fever and body chills that left him in a "nearly delirious" state, frightened by the decor of his hotel suite. "The image of the raised pattern of the *nouveau art* wall-paper so preyed on my sensibilities in the dark that it was a relief to switch on the light and, by perceiving the reality, to be relieved for a moment form the yet more hideous pressure of its imagined outlines."[61] After three days in bed he was transferred to the conference sick bay—the top floor of the Majestic had been converted into a hospital to deal with the flu pandemic[62]—reporting to his mother that while he still felt "miserably weak," the fever had at last broken. "Contrary to my belief the Doctor declares this is *not* influenza, but some special poisonous infection acquired in Germany. Two other members of the party (at least) are down with the same thing, including my American financial colleague;—so financial affairs are pretty well at a standstill for the time being! and Germany is famished by further delays before she gets her food!"[63]

Keynes was likely suffering from both the flu and a secondary bacterial infection—an often lethal combination in the days before antibiotics. His friends in Bloomsbury—some of whom feared leaving the house at the height of the pandemic[64]—knew enough to be worried. "I was very glad, I say, to find a letter from you in your own hand," Clive Bell wrote to Keynes on February 2, nearly two weeks after his friend had fallen ill. "The accounts that were dripping through into Gordon Square were really beginning to alarm me . . . you have such a habit of almost dying, my dear Maynard, that one of these days one fears you will do it tout de bon."[65]

The food blockade was at last lifted in March, and Keynes dived headlong back into the reparations problem. "I have no private life and attend to affairs of state from morning to night including Sunday," he reported home. "It's a great mixture of boredom and excitement and altogether an extraordinary affair. . . . I suppose [I] shall lapse into insanity sooner or later."[66] Still, there were some reasons for optimism. The German relief negotiations had boosted Keynes' status with both Wilson and Lloyd George—the prime minister had personally pressed Keynes' case to world leaders with dramatic rhetorical force.[67] It was a considerable improvement over his situation in the informal hierarchy of the delegation before the peace talks had begun. It was also exactly the diplomatic alliance between Britain and America that Keynes believed would need to emerge to secure the foundations of European prosperity.

But the British delegates Sumner and Cunliffe on the Reparations Commission remained a problem. They stuck to their $120 billion estimate of Germany's capacity to pay—a figure so ludicrously high that the French could sit back and watch the Americans fight with the British, offering occasional support for the British, whose figures were always closer to French goals. Keynes, who did not have a seat on the commission, began supplying figures to Davis and Lamont to counter the work of his own delegation. Lloyd George agreed that the figures offered by "the Heavenly Twins,"[68] as Keynes began derisively referring to Sumner and Cunliffe, were not credible, but he continued to fret over the domestic political implications of a plausible figure. He had, after all, just campaigned on an implied promise of $120 billion. By the end of March, Sumner and Cunliffe were creating so much trouble that Davis and Lamont had given up hope on the commission's work and shifted their attention to direct talks with the Council of Four: Clemenceau, Wilson, Lloyd George, and Orlando.

"If we can quiet down the Heavenly Twins by agreeing [to] any fool report for the time and then get rid of them by winding up the Commission," Davis told Keynes, "we can get around with some human beings and start quite afresh."[69] Keynes wasn't on the Reparations Commission, but he did have a spot on the Supreme Economic Council—and, after the blockade negotiations, a direct line to Lloyd George. It might be best to cave in to Sumner and Cunliffe on the Reparations Committee and then try to have the Reparations Committee's work thrown out by another, more clear-eyed negotiating body with greater authority.

Clemenceau's economic adviser Louis Loucheur, meanwhile, began to make noises about how the spoils would be divided. Whatever reparation number the commission arrived at, Loucheur told Keynes privately, France would never be satisfied by any share less than triple the size of what the United Kingdom received.[70]

When the subject of reparations came before the Council of Four, other members of the British delegation were piling on in bad faith. General Jan Smuts of South Africa agreed with Keynes' diagnosis of the treaty. But when Lloyd George pressed his subordinates for figures that would inflate the cost of the war damage, Smuts complied. He submitted a memo to the heads of state arguing that Germany should be held responsible for any pensions the Allied governments paid to soldiers who had fought in the war, as well as any separation allowances paid to their families while they were away on duty. That doubled the costs Germany would be held liable for, and none of Wilson's legal advisers believed the move was consistent with the logic of the Fourteen Points. But the barrage of figures was becoming too much for Wilson, who erupted at his lawyers during the council session: "Logic! Logic!" he roared. "I don't give a damn for logic. I am going to include pensions."[71] This account, recorded by Lamont, is confirmed by a glum April 1 memo from U.S. delegate John Foster Dulles: "The President stated that he did not feel bound by considerations of logic."[72]

Though the president's team was embarrassed by his outburst, the substance of Wilson's frustration was essentially correct. Neither the British nor the French were treating the reparations question as a legal or economic matter bound by the constraints of logic or reason. The negotiations had become a purely political charade. Even the preposterous numbers generated by the legal contortions over pensions proved insufficient for Clemenceau, who began calling to simply remove any mention of a final reparations number in the treaty at all. French opinion was so stridently in favor of German punishment, Clemenceau insisted, that he would be removed from office if the public got wind of the figures currently under discussion—an event that would in turn require all other work on the treaty to be renegotiated. After months of technical back-and-forth, Clemenceau proposed punting the issue to a new Reparations Commission to be formed under the League of Nations, which could work on the issue after the treaty with Germany was signed.

It was terrible economic policy that would delay any project of rebuilding for months, leaving a major financing question unanswered. But it was clever politics, allowing every leader at Paris to give his constituents whatever assurances he wanted about the eventual reparation bill. "Mr. Lloyd George, who never lent a deaf ear to political considerations, readily fell in with this point of view," Lamont recorded.[73]

There had been no meaningful discussion about how to address the long-term economic rehabilitation of the European economy. Keynes believed that France and Belgium would simply not be able to repair the war damage without foreign financial help, and he had watched Britain's economy stretch to its financial breaking point during the war. The only country in any condition to offer aid was the United States. Its factories had been running at full tilt, its workers' wages had soared, its farmers were receiving better than top dollar for their produce, and its bank vaults were flush with European gold.

Debt relief was the simplest form of aid. If the Americans would write down the war debts of Great Britain and France, it would give both countries financial space to devote their resources toward rebuilding. The U.S. delegation had been pouring cold water on the idea of debt reduction since before Keynes had arrived in Paris,[74] but he gave it another stab in March. If the United States would cancel all of its war debts, Keynes proposed, so would Great Britain. It would be a greater financial sacrifice for America, but the bulk of the direct benefits would flow not to the British but to France, Italy, Russia, and Belgium. And though the U.S. government (not to mention J.P. Morgan) would be forgoing interest payments, American farmers and manufacturers would see their economic position improve when a financially stabilized Europe spent its money on American exports.

But the chief argument Keynes advanced in the proposal wasn't about profits and losses; it was a political point about human psychology. The war debts of Allies and enemies alike were so massive that they would be stirring up social turmoil for years to come. Governments would have to curb services to their citizens in order to meet foreign interest payments. Taxes would need to be raised in order to ship money overseas. The notion that this was a fair return for America's help in the war might resonate with financiers and government officials, but it would make little sense to citizens. A farmer who had lost his son and half his acreage would not feel a rush of gratitude at the prospect of diverting a huge portion of his labor to the enrichment of American bankers. The austerity required by debt repayment would breed resentment and invite demagoguery from opportunists looking to blame a country's problems on outsiders.

"The existence of the great war debts is a menace to financial stability everywhere. There is no European country in which [debt] repudiation may not soon become an important political issue," Keynes wrote in a confidential memo shared with Wilson. "Will the discontented peoples of Europe be willing for a generation to come to so order their lives that an appreciable part of their daily produce may be available to meet a foreign payment, the reason of which . . . does not spring compellingly from their sense of justice or duty? . . . I do not believe that any of these tributes will continue to be paid, at the best, for more than a very few years. They do not square with human nature or march with the spirit of the age."[75]

But as with many of Keynes' theoretical breakthroughs, that flash of insight was accompanied by naiveté. Keynes had convinced himself that Wilson might come to see that a bit of American financial sacrifice was only fair—the other Allies had already devoted far more of their own blood and treasure to the collective cause than the United States had. Instead, Wilson was personally offended by the suggestion that America was being stingy. He had risked his political neck to bail out Great Britain and France in 1917, and the United States had sent its sons to die in a foreign war. The least the Allies could do in return was pay back the money America had loaned them. "From start to finish of the Peace Conference President Wilson and his advisers, without exception, opposed vigorously and finally any such suggestion or proposition of cancellation," wrote Lamont in 1921. "The question in one form or another constantly arose. It was always 'stepped on' by the American delegates."[76]

Nothing was working. In a desperate bid to salvage the economic terms of the treaty, Keynes began work on an alternative economic proposal that would, if adopted, replace all of the financial conditions being kicked around in Paris. The "Scheme for the Rehabilitation of European Credit and for Financing Relief and Reconstruction," as he elegantly titled it, was an overly complex invention born of political necessity. But the convoluted contraption should, he believed, satisfy the interests of every stubborn mind at the negotiating table. Under the plan, Germany would raise the money to pay its reparation bill and rebuild its economy by issuing new bonds. In order to attract investors wary of Germany's word, those bonds would be guaranteed against default by the Allied governments. That guarantee would allow Germany to raise an otherwise impossibly large sum, which in turn would allow the Allied governments to impose a larger reparations penalty. England, France, and Belgium would use their reparation money to rebuild domestically and to pay down their debts to the United States. The whole project would be administered by the League of Nations to ensure fair play among all involved, and there would be enough money to go around to ensure that no nation, no matter how extravagant their claims, would be shortchanged.

It was a brilliant mechanism. But Keynes knew he was attempting to shoot the moon. If he were to have any hope of convincing the Council of Four to jettison proposals and compromises that had taken months to be hammered out, he would need the enthusiastic support of Lloyd George. But the prime minister was getting tired of adjudicating what were now thoroughly predictable disputes between Keynes and the Heavenly Twins and was leaning toward Clemenceau's proposal to postpone reparation questions until after the peace conference. Keynes needed new political allies.

So he took a radical step: He left Paris. Returning to London, he huddled with members of the war cabinet and explained the virtues of his brainchild. The contrast between the cities was jarring. "The state of Europe is very desperate,—the economic system jammed and the peoples without hope," Keynes wrote to his mother. "But here in England everything seems very normal and everyone very comfortable,—and certainly very oblivious of what is going on the other side of the curtain."[77] His meetings with the war cabinet went well. Chancellor of the Exchequer Austen Chamberlain took up the Keynes plan as a personal cause and made a direct appeal to Lloyd George, which won over the prime minister. Reviewing the "Grand Scheme," as it was becoming known, Lloyd George immediately recognized its value. Keynes' financial Rube Goldberg device would provide all the long-term economic benefits of a war debt write-off and a minimal reparation penalty without provoking any of the public opinion troubles that such proposals might arouse. There would be no need for onerous new taxes. Lloyd George presented the plan directly to Wilson, together with an explanatory note signed by the prime minister that had in fact been written by Keynes. This time, he lavished the Americans with praise. Hoover's relief work was saving lives. But that heroic rescue only revealed how thoroughly dependent Europe remained on outside help. "In short," Keynes wrote, "the economic mechanism of Europe is jammed" and only U.S. leadership could solve "the greatest financial problem ever set to the modern world."[78]

And although the Grand Scheme was described as a shared commitment between Allies to forge a better future, it was entirely dependent on American magnanimity. A successful bond issue would require subscriptions from U.S. investors—the United States, after all, was where the money was. The terms of the loan issue might state very clearly that every Allied nation would stand behind the German bonds in case of a default, but only the American commitment would matter to investors. Everyone else was bankrupt. Keynes was, in essence, asking the United States to trade in the debt it was owed by the Allies for new debt owed by defeated Germany—to accept a similar return on its investment while taking on the greater risk of lending to a defeated enemy. In a May 3 letter to Lloyd George, Wilson rejected the entire scheme outright. The barrage of abuse that French and British delegates had directed at Americans seeking more moderate indemnities had not been forgotten.

"Throughout the reparations discussions the American delegation has steadily pointed out to the other delegations that the plans proposed would surely deprive Germany of the means of making any appreciable reparation payments. I myself, as you know, have frequently made the same observation. But whenever any of us was urgent on this point, he was accused of being pro-German," Wilson wrote. If the great problem of the day was to relieve Germany from the threat of Bolshevism, why were the British proposing a plan to raise money for Germany, only to take most of it away in reparation? The British were, in effect, using the threat of political crisis in Germany to secure a cheap source of funding for themselves. "America, has in my judgment, always been ready and always will stand ready to do her full share financially to assist the general situation. But America has grave difficulties of her own. . . . You have suggested that we all address ourselves to the problem of helping to put Germany on her feet, but how can your experts or ours be expected to work out a *new* plan to furnish working capital to Germany when we deliberately start out by taking away all Germany's *present* capital? How can anyone expect America to turn over to Germany in any considerable measure new working capital to take the place of that which the European nations have determined to take from her?"[79]

Keynes couldn't find much fault with the president's technical objections. The Grand Scheme was, after all, an attempt to make the best of a bad situation. But he was infuriated by Wilson's refusal to connect his high-minded ideals about international cooperation and support for democracy to the financial realities being debated at Paris. Perhaps Europe had no right to expect help from America, but Wilson never hesitated to remind anyone at Paris that the United States was forgoing any claim whatsoever to reparation under the treaty—evidence of his good faith and strong moral principle. Keynes' Grand Scheme was exactly the sort of thing Wilson insisted he was focused on securing under the treaty: an ambitious act of international diplomacy secured by U.S. money and goodwill. Yet Wilson had thrown the plan back in his face without even suggesting so much as a starting point for further negotiation. Four months of frustration boiled over. Keynes wrote a letter to Duncan Grant, raging against the president: "Wilson, of whom I've seen a good deal more lately, is the greatest fraud on earth."[80]

With time, Keynes would soften the severity of this judgment. He would come to see Wilson not as a fraud but as a fool who had been "bamboozled" by wily European leaders. Though Keynes did not know it at the time, Wilson had privately exhibited a series of strange and erratic behaviors during his stay in Paris. Historians continue to debate the exact cause of his mental lapses—a minor stroke and cognitive damage from a bout of the flu in early April have both been floated as possible explanations—but it seems clear that the president's mind was not always at its keenest during the later months of the peace conference.

Still, his rejection of the Grand Scheme can't be chalked up to confusion alone. Nobody on the American side wanted to write down the Allied war debt. Much of the U.S. delegation—Davis, Lamont, and Bernard Baruch, among others—had enjoyed distinguished careers in finance before joining the government, and like most bankers they were ideologically averse to revising the terms of loan contracts—especially loans with favorable terms for creditors.

Two members of the delegation—Davis and Lamont—were intertwined with J.P. Morgan itself. A decade later after the stock market crash of 1929, Davis would be revealed as a beneficiary of the bank's secret insider trading ring.[81] Lamont was perhaps the most influential partner at the bank. When he had embarked for Paris, Lamont had hoped to establish a new Anglo-American financial cartel. In June meetings with Keynes and the British banker R. H. Brand a month after Wilson's rejection of the Keynes plan, Lamont floated the idea of having a Morgan-directed consortium of American banks take a 50 percent stake in the largest British banks. By joining forces, all parties involved would be liberated from the profit-diminishing pressures of competition. American capital and British business contacts could establish a private financial empire linking the American railways to Persian oil and the Indian spice trade. Where Keynes' Grand Scheme would have put the League of Nations in charge of Europe's financial future, Lamont envisioned J.P. Morgan at the helm.

The transcontinental banking monopoly never materialized, but the House of Morgan would continue to play a dominant role in European politics after the war, when Lamont became a trusted adviser to Benito Mussolini, easing the dictator's relationship with the U.S. government and extending him a $100 million loan from J.P. Morgan in 1926.[82] Lamont would describe himself as "something like a missionary" for Italian fascism, which had become a fount of "sound ideas" led by "a very upstanding chap."[83] Mussolini was just one of Lamont's unsavory political clients. In 1931, Imperial Japan invaded the Chinese province of Manchuria, a clear violation of the League of Nations Covenant that was condemned by President Hoover as "an act of rank aggression." Japan's Ministry of Finance issued a statement papering over the abuses committed by its fifteen thousand troops as acts of "self defense" that the world had misunderstood, insisting that Japan had "no intention whatsoever of making war on China" and entertained "the friendliest feelings towards the Chinese." Japan had, in fact, initiated a cycle of military conquest that would culminate in Pearl Harbor. Not a word of the propaganda—printed in *The New York Times*—was true. It had been written by Thomas Lamont.[84]

Keynes never comprehended the chasm between his own views on Allied war debts and those of his American friends. Since they agreed with him on reparations, he chalked up their obstinacy to "inexperience[] in public affairs."[85] After Wilson's dismissal of the Grand Scheme, he had tried to sway Davis and Lamont to open some line of negotiation with the president and for a short time believed he had made headway, unaware that Lamont himself had been the actual author of the rejection letter signed by Wilson.[86]

Keynes, meanwhile, had finally been broken by Paris. He wrote to his mother on May 14:

> It must be weeks since I've written a letter to anyone:—but I've been utterly worn out, partly by work partly by depression at the evil round me. I've never been so miserable as for the last two or three weeks; the Peace is outrageous and impossible and can bring nothing but misfortune behind it. Personally I do not believe the Germans will sign, though the general view is to the contrary (i.e. that after a few moans and complaints they will sign anything). But if they do sign this will be in many ways the worse alternative; for it is out of the question that they should keep the terms (which are incapable of being kept) and nothing but general disorder and unrest could result. Certainly if I was in the Germans' place I'd rather die than sign such a Peace.
>
> Well, I suppose I've been an accomplice in all this wickedness and folly, but the end is now at hand. I am writing to the Treasury to be

released of my duties by June 1 if possible and not later than June 15 in any event.[87]

He bade farewell to Norman Davis on June 5: "I am slipping away on Saturday from this scene of nightmare. I can do no more good here. You Americans are broken reeds, and I have no anticipation of any real improvement in the state of affairs."[88]

In a similarly worded letter to David Lloyd George written the same day, Keynes formally resigned his position. He would not return to the British government for more than a decade.

Dear Prime Minister, I ought to let you know that on Saturday I am slipping away from this scene of nightmare. I can do no more good here. I've gone on hoping even through these last dreadful weeks that you'd find some way to make of the treaty a just and expedient document. But now it's apparently too late. The battle is lost. I leave the twins to gloat over the devastation of Europe and to assess to taste what remains for the British taxpayer.[89]

The peace conference had failed to deliver Keynes the salvation he had hoped to realize after devoting four years of his life to war finance. His friends in Bloomsbury had been right: he had taken part in an atrocity. He returned to England angry, ashamed, and exhausted.

But the war and the months in Paris had changed the way Keynes understood money and power. Before the conflict, he had agreed with economists who believed that governments should generally keep out of markets. After helping the British government run the British economy for four years, he wasn't so sure. German reparations and Allied war debts were the most important economic issues of the day—and there was no escaping the fact that those critical financial issues were, at their heart, political. Market economies were not a distinct realm, independent of the state, operating according to their own principles. The rhythms of trade, their logic and mechanisms, had to be defined and supported by political authority. His battle over repara-

tions and inter-ally debt had made him a lifelong enemy of austerity—
the doctrine that governments can best heal troubled economies by
slashing government spending and paying down debt. When a government was burdened with too much debt, Keynes had come to believe, it was generally better to swear off the debt than to pay it off by
burdening the public with a lower standard of living.

Keynes was only beginning to process the implications of his
changing worldview. But in a few short months he would present its
first fruits to the public. They would shock the world.

FOUR

◇

CONSEQUENCES

T HE SUN HAD BROKEN through in the afternoon, setting the crystal chandeliers sparkling, their bright dazzle reflected in the great mirrors that give the grandest room in the Palace of Versailles its name. World leaders seated themselves at three long tables in the Hall of Mirrors as journalists and photographers filled almost every inch of standing room between the walls paneled in richly veined marble and fine gold detail. Biblical prophets and heroes of great battles overlooked the crowd from baroque scenes painted across the high vaulted ceiling as Woodrow Wilson, his hand trembling with the energy of the moment, signed the treaty that brought an end to the War to End All Wars.[1]

"It is much more than a treaty of peace with Germany," he declared in a statement provided to the American press. "It liberates great peoples who have never before been able to find the way to liberty. It ends, once and for all, an old and intolerable order under which small groups of selfish men could use the peoples of great empires to serve their ambition for power and domination. . . . [It is] a great charter for a new order of affairs."[2]

The crowd outside offered their final tribute to the man who had come to Paris seven months earlier, once again hailing him with shouts of "*Vive Wilson!*" Women rushed forward, declaring they just wanted to touch the man who had, five years to the day after the assassination of Archduke Franz Ferdinand, made peace a reality.

There was no denying that the treaty was transformational. The empires of the Central Powers were cut to pieces. The Austro-Hungarian Empire was divided into the new nations of Austria, Czechoslovakia, Yugoslavia, Hungary, and an expanded Romania. The British took control of Palestine and modern-day Iraq from the fallen Ottoman Empire, while the French acquired modern Syria and Lebanon. Fifteen long months earlier, Germany had carved Finland, Estonia, Latvia, and Lithuania from the new Bolshevik government in Russia. It now lost all of those vassal states to independence, with backing from the League of Nations. On Germany's western border, the region of Alsace-Lorraine went to France, along with mining rights to the coal-rich Saar Basin, while the long strip of territory along the Rhine River—loaded with iron, copper, and other industrial ores—would be occupied by French forces for years to come. In the east, the city of Danzig and the Memel region became independent, while parts of the German province of Prussia were ceded to the new state of Poland. German colonies in Liberia, Cameroon, East Africa (modern-day Tanzania, Rwanda, and Burundi), and South Africa fell under the authority of the League, which quickly distributed them among France and Great Britain, as the litany of Pacific islands under German control eventually went to Japan, New Zealand, and Australia. German railroads would turn over 5,000 locomotives and 150,000 railway cars to the Allies, and major German river transportation would become the domain of the League. Germany would be required to eliminate tariffs on Allied goods, but the Allies would be free to put up their own tariffs against German products. There were no definite terms on reparations. The great bugbear of Paris would be settled by a special commission at the League of Nations, as Clemenceau had advocated. In the meantime, Germany would pay 20 billion gold marks (about $5 billion) to the Allies by May 1, 1921, while the Reparations Commission got to work. Whatever the final bill might come to, Germany had already paid a substantial economic price.

Not everyone shared Wilson's sense of euphoria at Versailles. Jan Smuts, Keynes' confidant from South Africa, affixed his signature to the treaty but filed an additional statement detailing objections to the severity of the terms against Germany. Smuts revered Wilson, believing him to be a figure surpassing even Abraham Lincoln among American statesmen.[3] But Wilson's principle of self-determination seemed to apply only to the defeated empires. Wilson ignored pressure from the black socialist W.E.B. Du Bois to use the treaty as an opportunity to empower African Americans. Neither France nor Britain relinquished any colonies or protectorates. The treaty was even silent on the cause of Irish nationalists, who were actively engaged in revolutionary guerrilla combat with British authorities. The very setting of the signing ceremony embodied a connection with the imperial order Wilson hoped to transcend. Forty-eight years prior, Otto von Bismarck and the Prussian military elite had gathered in the Hall of Mirrors to declare Wilhelm Friedrich Ludwig of Hohenzollern the first kaiser of a unified Germany at the close of the Franco-Prussian War. The Allies of the Great War now used the same location to humiliate the German delegation. The bitter rivalries of long-dead monarchs were an inescapable element of the scene. In the gardens of the château built for King Louis XIV, a volley of cannon fire sounded—a celebration and a sign of days to come.[4]

Three hundred miles to the northwest, across the English Channel, John Maynard Keynes was in a very different garden.[5] He spent his afternoons at Duncan and Vanessa's farmhouse protecting his knees with a scrap of carpet, as he weeded the gravel path through the fruit trees and vegetable patches with a pocketknife, working with such regularity that Bunny Garnett would measure the length of Keynes' visits by the condition of the path.[6] But before getting down to gardening, Keynes liked to read the papers, making the occasional keepsake of articles that mentioned the British Treasury's head of war finance. In his papers at King's College in Cambridge, there is still a small cutting from the June 11, 1919, edition of *The Manchester Guard-*

ian titled "Mr. Maynard Keynes's Resignation" that lent more than a
hint of mystery and intrigue to the event:

> Various rumors have appeared in the London press about Mr.
> Maynard Keynes, the British financial adviser at the Paris Confer-
> ence. It has been said that he has resigned because of a breakdown
> in health. I am told by a friend of Mr. Keynes that it is true that he
> has resigned, but not on account of ill-heath, and that he is about
> to resume his work at Cambridge University.
>
> The reason for his resignation is understood to be the rejection
> by the Government of his financial advice. He had devised the
> lines of a general scheme for the basis of the indemnity settlement,
> but it was not accepted, and this, with his general disagreement
> about the character of the economic terms as tending to financial
> disaster, has led to his resignation.[7]

"Tending to financial disaster" was not the consensus opinion in
Great Britain during the early weeks that followed Keynes' angry departure from Paris. Most subjects of the Crown were eager to see the document as Wilson did—a victory for the Fourteen Points and the coming
Age of Democracy. Those with a greater thirst for vengeance could take
comfort in the dejected displays of frustration from the new German
government. There seemed to be something in the peace for everyone.

The general contentment left many conference delegates uneasy.
Parsing Wilson's statements about the final pact revealed that beneath
his gauzy rhetoric, even the president believed that years of delicate
diplomacy at the League of Nations would be needed to make the
peace treaty work. The political will to unwind some of the most troubling terms would be hard to conjure if the public understood the
document as a triumph.

Nobody who remained in office, however, was interested in jeopar-
dizing his own position by speaking out against a document that had
taken more than half a year to negotiate. But a few of Keynes' allies
from Paris began suggesting that the newly unemployed economist
might be the right man for the job—nothing too inflammatory, of

course; an excessively stringent critique by a former British official might interfere with the League's work or even convince the United States to reject the treaty outright. But there did seem to be a need for a responsible critic to seed a few doubts in the minds of thinking men. "If you had the time to write a brilliant article," Undersecretary of State for Foreign Affairs Lord Robert Cecil suggested to Keynes, "exposing from a strictly economic point of view the dangers of the Treaty, it might do a great deal of good."[8]

There was a great deal of money to be made from keeping quiet, however. Before he left for Paris, Keynes was already fielding job offers from the financial sector, turning down a position as chairman of a London bank for around £5,000 a year—well over $350,000 in today's money and more than triple his final Treasury salary of £1,500 (he had started in 1914 at £700). It was the kind of work offered to well-connected men of affairs, not controversial muckrakers who publicly criticized their government. After the first bank offer, Keynes told his mother that he was not interested in "any work of that kind," but it was the prospective workload that offended his sensibilities, rather than any scruples about moving through the revolving door between the Treasury and the City. "In the way of directorships which meant no work, I should give way to Mammon,"[9] he admitted. Shortly after the conference, however, he turned down a £2,000-a-year offer to work one day a week for a Scandinavian bank. He couldn't bring himself to lobby the British government for a foreign enterprise.[10] The peace conference left him disillusioned with his country's leadership, but it had not broken his sense of allegiance.

Life at Charleston Farmhouse, in the meantime, was serene and pleasant, particularly after the mad rush of Paris. After coming inside from the garden for afternoon tea, Keynes typically fielded his correspondence. A letter from Smuts may have pushed him over the edge and back into the public arena. Smuts suggested something to help the "plain man" understand what had happened at Paris: "The Treaty will in any case emerge as a rotten thing, of which we shall all be heartily ashamed in due course." Keynes should "help the public virtually to scrap this monstrous document."[11]

The Economic Consequences of the Peace is a provincial, shortsighted, vicious, and in many respects deeply unfair polemic. It is also a masterpiece and very likely the most influential work Keynes ever put his name to.

Written in a passionate burst of activity, Keynes intended it as a work for a narrow audience of British experts. He was taking sides in a dispute within the British government and hoped to make an informed statistical case that would aid members of his faction much as he had done in his first book, *Indian Currency and Finance.* That slim tract had enhanced his prestige within the British civil service but had brought him neither fame nor fortune.

But this time the narrow audience Keynes had in mind included Bloomsbury. *Economic Consequences* was Keynes' first literary attempt to come to terms with his trampled ideal of the British Empire. Right up to 1914, he had envisioned his country as a beacon of democracy and an engine of global prosperity through wise imperial rule. The war and the peace conference had exposed a more mundane reality: The empire's leaders were every bit as enamored with conquest and domination for their own sake as the kaiser and Clemenceau were. Keynes' own Liberal Party had proved incapable of meeting the moral standard set by brash *Americans.* He had to atone for his folly but had no Church to hear his prayers. Only Bloomsbury could redeem him.

The war had changed Bloomsbury nearly as much as it had changed Keynes. The aesthetic escapism that had pervaded the set had been replaced by an almost desperate sense of elite responsibility. "I am convinced," Lytton told his conscientious objection tribunal in March 1916, "that the whole system by which it is sought to settle international disputes by force is profoundly evil."[12] And Lytton, perhaps most improbably of all Bloomsberries, had set about to right such wrongs through his art. In 1918, he published *Eminent Victorians,* a quartet of biographical portraits that sent shock waves through the London literary world, not only for its dizzying prose but for its treatment of his subjects.[13] In Lytton's hands, revered heroes of the Victo-

rian generation became false idols of a corrupt order marching the
world to destruction. He attacked English boarding schools, the
Church of England, and British colonialism with equal verve, and
the result had transformed Keynes' eccentric friend into Bloomsbury's
first celebrity. For Keynes, who had once sought to demonstrate his
own self-worth by stealing Lytton's lovers, it would not be enough to
merely prostrate himself in remorse before his friends; he would have
to prove himself on their terms, as an artist.

The product of his labors, *Economic Consequences,* still stands today
as both a landmark of political theory and one of the most emotionally compelling works of economic literature ever written. Like all of
Keynes' best work, it is not fundamentally a work of economics at all,
but a treatment of the great political problem of the twentieth century—a furious tirade against autocracy, war, and weak politicians. It
is at once a howl of rage directed against the most powerful men in the
world and an ominous prophecy of the violence that would again
sweep the continent in the years to come.

The book opens with a sunny portrait of the global financial order
that persisted between the close of the Franco-Prussian War and the
summer of 1914, describing the free international trade system as an
engine of prosperity unparalleled in human history. Economic inequality had been the essential ingredient of that social progress, creating large personal fortunes that the rich could invest in new
enterprises that addressed society's needs and advanced the progress
of "civilisation." Though the mechanisms of growth were inherently
unfair, with capitalists at the top reaping far more economic fruit than
workers at the bottom, the gains improved the lives of all who participated: better food, nicer fineries, all the extravagances of La Belle
Époque that could be purchased at ever-declining prices by an ever-
expanding middle class. "Society was working not for the small pleasures of to-day but for the future security and improvement of the
race,—in fact for 'progress.' "[14]

The steady piling up of material riches over the decades had created
the impression of a strong and resilient system. But Keynes believed
the arrangement was a fragile historical anomaly. It depended on "a

double bluff or deception": the system would only work if workers believed in it, and workers would not believe in it unless it worked. Break the collective faith in a better tomorrow, and workers would walk off the job, riot in protest, or worse.

The war had shattered the illusion of certainty and predictability that the system required to function. The economic threads connecting different nations and cultures had broken easily in 1914, and economic life had instead been sustained by wartime patriotism and fear of foreign domination. The prewar economic engine could not simply be restarted as if nothing had happened. Why would anyone accept the unprecedented inequality of the Gilded Age if everything could go to ruin in war a few months or years down the line? Life was too short.

"The principle of accumulation based on inequality was a vital part of the pre-war order of Society and of progress as we then understood it," Keynes wrote. "This principle depended on unstable psychological conditions, which it may be impossible to recreate. It was not natural for a population, of whom so few enjoyed the comforts of life, to accumulate so hugely. The war has disclosed the possibility of consumption to all and the vanity of abstinence to many."[15]

Nor could Europe turn to "the natural wealth and virgin potentialities" of the "New World" in the twentieth century as it had in the nineteenth. Colonialism had granted Europe access to cheap foreign resources. But the "abundance" of the New World was no longer cheap due to population changes and "a steady increase of real costs." He didn't detail the causes of those costs, but the price of labor had increased since the abolition of slavery.

The peace conference had offered world leaders an opportunity to revive the public faith in progress that capitalism required to function. It would have to begin with a down payment on the public welfare among victor and vanquished alike. All over Europe there were trenches to be filled, factories to be rebuilt, barbed wire tangles to be scoured from the earth. It was foolish to pretend that communities could be rebuilt while shouldering the massive war debts and reparation payments demanded under the treaty, and still more foolish to believe that citizens of the world would accept such a fate without a fight. Keynes held fast to his belief that the war debts had to be written off, reparation claims moderated, and some method of international cooperation established in which the needs of the people, not the creditors, would be paramount. Prosperity could not be secured by wise investments and hard work alone; only political leadership could provide the certainty and predictability that progress required.

Keynes understood this program as a defensive maneuver intended to salvage the cultural achievements of La Belle Époque from more radical alternatives. Bolshevism, offering one alternative social vision, was already on the march, and the uncertainty unleashed by the collapse of the old order would lead the public to support any doctrine promising stability and predictability. All over Europe—but particularly in the defeated German Empire—conditions were ripe for the rise of a strongman. Without food, jobs, a sense of purpose, and confidence in a better tomorrow, Europe was already on the path to another war.

"If we aim deliberately at the impoverishment of Central Europe, vengeance, I dare predict, will not limp. Nothing can then delay for very long that final civil war between the forces of Reaction and the despairing convulsions of Revolution, before which the horrors of the late German war will fade into nothing, and which will destroy, whoever is victor, the civilization and the progress of our generation."[16]

Herbert Hoover had impressed this grim vision upon Keynes at the peace conference, when the two men had worked to provide food relief to Germany. It had been a moment when, in Hoover's words, there was "real danger of a revolution on one side from the militarists and on the other from the . . . Communists." Both groups, he emphasized, had been "working on the emotions of the hungry people."[17] Food relief had eventually arrived, and the situation in Germany was not so dire in the autumn of 1919, when Keynes finished his book, as it had been when he arrived in Paris. But the prospect of years of economic deprivation could not be borne on a continent already at the end of its psychological rope. And the fact that this deprivation would be entwined with steep financial obligations to foreigners would present demagogues with convenient scapegoats. Economic frustration could be channeled into ethnic animosity.

One of the great rhetorical tricks of *Economic Consequences* is the ease with which Keynes moves from images of "terrible exhaustion" in Austria and Germany to the prospect of continent-wide economic crisis. The "oppressive interest payments to England and America" still on the books would soon reduce France, Italy, and Belgium to the same condition as Germany. The economic fate of Europe, Keynes insisted, was already indivisible, and that economic union would write its political future.

Governments burdened with heavy debts, Keynes predicted, would resort to inflation to ease the burden, just as they had during the war—a situation that would quickly prove politically destabilizing. Inflation had unequal effects. People with substantial savings—a small minority of the population in 1919—were hit hardest, as the value of their nest egg was eroded; it was a "hidden tax" on a particular economic demographic. Such a morally arbitrary "rearrangement of riches" would fuel anger at the "capitalist classes." "Lenin was certainly right," Keynes wrote. "There is no subtler, no surer means of overturning the existing basis of society than to debauch the currency."[18] (Though this has become one of the Marxist leader's most popular aphorisms over the years, the prose is pure Keynes; he was paraphrasing an interview Lenin had given to a New York newspaper.)[19]

After taking power, the Bolsheviks had repudiated the Russian debt incurred by the tsars. Keynes was in effect calling for all of Europe to follow Lenin's lead by wiping out the debts incurred during the war. As a result, his book was infused with more than a touch of radicalism. Debt, economic inequality, even the investment process of capitalism itself were not the sacred foundations of civilization, he argued, but mere conventions. They had been adopted to improve the lot of humanity as a whole and could be revised to meet its changing needs.

But references to Lenin or no, Keynes was not issuing a Marxist assault on unearned bourgeois privilege; he was presenting a fundamentally conservative political vision inspired by Edmund Burke. In his 1790 masterpiece *Reflections on the Revolution in France,* the Irish philosopher had castigated the revolutionaries for attacking the foundations of the existing French social order. Whatever the philosophical merit their paeans to human rights and democracy might hold, Burke had predicted, their overthrow of the French monarchy would destroy the social bonds of custom and tradition that enabled peaceful rule, empowering a "popular general" who would make order out of chaos through violent repression.[20] That militarism would do far more damage to the ideals the revolutionaries cherished than the old monarchy had. The subsequent Reign of Terror and Napoleon's early-nineteenth-century rampages gave Burke's psychological analysis a certain historical sting. Keynes made his radical propositions in an effort to preserve what could be saved of the status quo, which he believed to be facing an existential threat.

Keynes' admiration for Burke was unusual in Bloomsbury. The group understood the French Revolution as the fundamental juncture in modern politics—the great barrier separating conservatism and their own progressive liberalism. According to Leonard Woolf, "The world is still deeply divided between those who . . . agree with Pericles and the French revolution and those who consciously or unconsciously accept the political postulates of Xerxes, Sparta, Louis XIV, Charles I, Queen Victoria, and all modern authoritarians."[21] Keynes, too, saw authoritarianism as a great evil—the greatest evil of his time. But he placed a higher priority on stability than most of his friends did.

His Burkean commitments predated Bloomsbury. Keynes had fallen under the sway of the Irish philosopher during his undergraduate days, when he had won an essay contest for an eighty-page thesis on Burke's political theory. He agreed with Burke that governments were justified not by inalienable individual rights but by their results—their ability to achieve social stability and public happiness—and he shared with his predecessor a profound fear of social upheaval. But though he agreed with Burke's aims and his mode of analysis, he rejected many of his methods. Burke, like the population theorist Thomas Malthus, had seen economic scarcity as an inescapable fact of human life. There just wasn't enough wealth to go around, and if humanity was to realize any abiding cultural achievements, mitigating inequality could not be a function of government. Democracy, to Burke, would lead to collective poverty and the end of all fine living. A monarchy that protected the rights of private property was the only way to secure a decent society.

Keynes, too, feared overpopulation as a menace to prosperity, but he had come of age in an era of increasing abundance, and believed—in contrast to Burke—that democracy had fostered a more luxurious society; its customs and traditions had protected a flowering of art and ideas. As he wrote in his thesis: "Democracy is still on its trial, but so far it has not disgraced itself."[22]

Keynes had crafted an innovative philosophical cocktail. Like Burke, he feared revolution and social upheaval. Like Karl Marx, he envisioned a great crisis on the horizon for capitalism. And like Lenin, he believed that the imperialist world order had reached its final limit. But alone among these thinkers, Keynes believed all that was needed to solve the crisis was a little goodwill and cooperation. The calamity he foresaw in 1919 was not something inevitable, hardwired into the fundamental logic of economics, capitalism, or humanity. It was merely a political failure, one that could be overcome with the right leadership. Whereas Marx had called for revolution against a broken, irrational capitalist order, Keynes was content to denounce the leaders at Versailles and called for treaty revisions. As with Burke, it was revolution itself that Keynes hoped to avert. But he was optimistic, blaming capitalist instability and inequality as the fuel for social upheaval rather than democracy.

The warnings Keynes issued in the pages of *The Economic Consequences of the Peace* would reverberate through European history as militant demagogues rose across Europe, exploiting inequality, austerity budgeting, inflation, and uncertainty to take power by preaching vengeance and hate. Benito Mussolini would march on Rome in three years' time. In Germany, hyperinflation and Adolf Hitler's Beer Hall Putsch would follow soon after, the rise of Josef Stalin a short time after that. Keynes' slim masterpiece remains essential today not because of its statistical prowess or its analytical detail but because the mass psychology he presented would prove so integral to the great tragedies of the twentieth century. And the explanatory power of his narrative can be applied with only modest revisions to the great problems of the twenty-first century. Substitute the financial crisis of 2008 for the Great War, swap European austerity budgets and the American foreclosure crisis for war debts and reparations, and the result is a modern recipe for militant far-right nationalism.

There is a deeply personal tone to the exultations and denunciations woven through *Economic Consequences*. Keynes' fury over the darkness to come is fused with a naive nostalgia for prewar politics that sidesteps nineteenth-century colonial outrages to meditate on his own leisure-class experience. "What an extraordinary episode in the economic progress of man that age was which came to an end in August, 1914!" he declared. Even the working class had been "to all appearances, reasonably contented" with their lot; for those who were not, "escape was possible, for any man of capacity or character at all exceeding the average, into the middle and upper classes."[23] It is not only Europe Keynes mourns for but the happy innocence of elite life. The war, as he told Bloomsbury's Memoir Club, had provided him his first inkling that "civilisation was a thin and precarious crust erected by the personality and the will of a very few, and only maintained by rules and conventions skillfully put across and guilefully preserved."[24] As with Burke, it was elite culture that Keynes ultimately sought to preserve. For Keynes, the true horror of the starvation and bloodshed to come would not be measured by body counts but in the collapse of art, literature, and learning. Bloomsbury's good states of mind would not survive a world of rioting masses in thrall to a demagogue or a regime of militant strongmen bent on war and ethnic persecution. In this peculiar democratic ideal, the well-being of the masses is a convenience that raises cultural standards for elites, while the masses themselves are a danger that must be defused.

The Economic Consequences of the Peace is about Europe. Keynes breezed past Great Britain's relationship with India, suggesting only that it be included in a new free trade union with Europe and the United States. For all his admiration for the Fourteen Points, free trade remained for Keynes a still more fundamental principle than self-determination, a path to progress and global harmony that could be applied to an array of political arrangements. He similarly demonstrated no interest in economic conditions in the Middle East, Africa, or Japan, where some of the most politically destructive terms of the treaty were imposed. He mentioned the word *petroleum* just once, as a line item in a table documenting prewar German imports, while "oil" is referenced as something that comes from seeds. He did not grasp the importance of the commodity to the future of world politics or ruminate on the fact that Lloyd George, Wilson, and Clemenceau had divided up much of the world in pursuit of its control.

Keynes had not been included in territorial debates at Paris, of course, and much of the emotional force of his presentation is a result of his intimate involvement with the elements of the treaty he assaults. But there is more to his omission of the oil problem than expertise or even European chauvinism, though there is surely much of both. In the twentieth century, Keynes believed, it was debt, not oil, that made the world go round. New technologies and specialization were making it easier for societies to mass-produce the goods they needed to sustain themselves, while the problem of *paying* for that process was creating new difficulties. Already at Paris, world leaders had convinced themselves that a large number on paper would conjure resources and labor that were, in truth, impossible to summon. There was something unusual and illusory about the realm of money and its connection to the world of production. When Keynes developed these insights about money and scarcity, he would become the most important economist to emerge from the Depression.

The Economic Consequences of the Peace was Keynes' first manifesto. Over the following two decades, he would refine his views about democracy, reason, and passion as he came to believe that the material possibilities of the twentieth century were far greater than those Europe had enjoyed before the war. Far from representing the apex of human achievement, the economic arrangements of the Victorian era would come to represent unscientific superstition to Keynes. His belief in a greater, increasing economic abundance would allow him to embrace political views he would have considered obscenely radical during the war. But he would never fully abandon Burke. It was the finer things in life that mattered most to Keynes. The task for economics was to determine how many people could enjoy them.

As Keynes put the finishing touches on his manuscript, he solicited critiques from friends and family. Virtually everyone outside of Bloomsbury was mortified. It was not Keynes' political vision they found unsettling but his bracing attack on the leaders he held responsible for the peace treaty's faults. He described Wilson as a "blind and deaf Don Quixote."[25] Lloyd George was "this syren, this goat-footed bard, this half-human visitor to our age from the hag-ridden magic and enchanted woods of Celtic antiquity." Paris was "a nightmare."

The biting mockery that pervades Keynes' book was directly influenced by the ironic prose of *Eminent Victorians*. Keynes' portraits are more vivid than Strachey's for their brevity, achieving a level of characterization that inspired high praise from Virginia Woolf but that even Strachey—a champion of the outrageous—thought should be toned down. "I seem to gather from the scant remarks in the newspapers that your friend the President has gone mad," Strachey wrote to Keynes on October 4, 1919. "Is it possible that it should gradually have been borne in upon him what an appalling failure he was, and that when at last he fully realized it his mind collapsed? Very dramatic, if so. But won't it make some of your remarks almost too cruel?— Especially if he should go and die. Awkward! I pray for his recovery."[26]

Keynes' parents, meanwhile, warned that one attack on Lord Sumner was libelous and insisted that the sketch of Lloyd George be struck. "You owe some loyalty to your Chief, even if you don't agree with him."[27] Both passages were removed, but the tone of the book remained annihilatory. "The moderate people can do good and perhaps the extremist can also do good; but it is no use for a member of the latter class to pretend that he belongs to the former," Keynes wrote to Arthur Salter, who had been secretary at the Supreme Economic Council in Paris. "Besides, it is much a hopeless business trying to calculate the psychological effect of one's actions; and I have come to feel that the best thing in all the circumstances is to speak the truth as bluntly as one can."[28]

No one was going to mistake him for a defender of the treaty. Keynes' old friend Daniel Macmillan agreed to publish the book, but after a few administrative headaches, Keynes took the unusual step of fronting the printing costs himself—a decision that put him in total control of publishing choices and dramatically escalated the royalties he would receive from any sales. Though its name would be printed on the binding, Macmillan was functionally reduced to the role of a very hands-on distributor, taking only 10 percent of the proceeds and leaving the rest to Keynes and the booksellers.[29]

The arrangement proved a financial windfall for Keynes. When it was published on December 12, 1919, *The Economic Consequences of the Peace* quickly sold out of its original British printing of five thousand copies. Macmillan dutifully ordered up another printing—a more than respectable showing, particularly for a text littered with tables of debts and shipping tonnages. The sales of Virginia Woolf's first novel, *The Voyage Out,* for example, had not yet justified a second printing beyond its initial run of two thousand in March 1915.[30]

The effect on conventional wisdom was immediate. Woodrow Wilson had been awarded the Nobel Peace Prize two days before the book was published. All of a sudden, the treaty became toxic. Within just a few months, the Liberal Party—whose own Lloyd George remained prime minister—had published an excerpt of Keynes' book as an official party pamphlet denouncing Lloyd George's 1918 election campaign.[31] "No single individual," remarked Adam Tooze, a leading economic historian of twentieth-century Europe, "did more to undermine the political legitimacy of the Versailles peace than Keynes with his devastating book."[32]

Though Chancellor of the Exchequer Austen Chamberlain "chortled with joy," taking "malicious pleasure" from "the Conference chapter," he scolded his former underling for the damage he had done to his colleagues' efforts. However frustrated Keynes might have been with the treaty, the book undercut the sustained argument by British Liberals that the war had been a righteous endeavor to save civilization from autocratic aggression. "Frankly I am sorry that one who occupied a position of so much trust and consequence in the British Delegation in Paris should feel impelled to write in such a strain of the part that this country played in the Peace negotiations. . . . I cannot help fearing that our international cause will not be made easier by such comments from a late public servant."[33]

That was, of course, the point. Keynes had not written the book to highlight numbers in need of adjustment. The treaty terms had put the lie to the entire Anglo-American narrative of a just war. He had gone on with the charade long enough. "The policy of humbugging with the Americans has been given a good trial and has not been a brilliant success," Keynes replied to Chamberlain. A "candid expression of views" would do more good than "oceans of semi-sincere platform sentiment."[34]

His old boss Reginald McKenna agreed: "I have only heard one adverse comment and that was in sorrow from Reading, because 'of the harm it would do in America.' Fudge! It will do nothing but good everywhere. Until we get back to the truth there is no hope for the world."[35]

But neither Keynes nor his admirers could control the behemoth he had unleashed across the Atlantic, where the book was becoming a sensation. "It is a magnificent and courageous achievement," declared Cornell economist Allyn Young, who had been a member of the American delegation at Paris.[36] "Everybody is reading it," gushed Paul Cravath.[37] Excerpts had been read into the *Congressional Record*. "Our Senators are feeding hungrily upon the strong meat you have offered to the world," reported Oscar T. Crosby, an American financial bureaucrat who had worked with Keynes on the Inter-Ally Council for War. "Here, as in England, the book will have a profound effect upon official and public sentiment. You have performed a service which, I regret to say, could not have been performed here. The enlightened English liberal is still the worlds' best spokesman for great causes."[38]

The book owed much of its stateside success to Walter Lippmann, a founding writer at *The New Republic* who had helped cultivate enthusiasm for Wilson among various elements of the American Left. Lippmann had met Keynes in Paris—the beginning of a lifelong friendship—and had been profoundly disillusioned by the peace treaty, which he denounced in the pages of his magazine. Though his critique lost *The New Republic* roughly ten thousand subscribers who proved more devoted to the president than the publication, it remained a powerful force among liberal-minded intellectuals.[39] American book sales soon skyrocketed into six figures, though Keynes groused about the 15 percent royalty he received on foreign sales (very reasonable by publishing standards then and now but a pittance compared to his British cut).

It was not the power of Keynes' argument that propelled the book to such wild success. It was the vicious, detailed personal portraits of the Great Men he lambasted. In America, the book reinforced the prevailing sentiment among every faction of the public that had been critical of the Great War, which had fallen to the nadir of its popularity as the production boom of 1916 and 1917 had given way to inflation and a deep recession.

Though Keynes was ignorant of the politics, Wilson had undermined his own frequent appeals to the glories of democracy during the war years with a crackdown on American dissent. He had rammed through the Espionage and Sedition Acts and used them as a weapon against antiwar advocates, jailing critics and pacifists, censoring antiwar newspapers and magazines. To a public that had grown disenchanted with the war, the depictions of a cold, ruthless Clemenceau and the disingenuous opportunism of Lloyd George confirmed American suspicions that Europe was an incorrigible backwater. Keynes' cruel depiction of a "bamboozled" Wilson stirred the hearts of nationalists who thought the treaty didn't secure enough spoils for the United States. Keynes was at least as gifted a polemicist as he was an economist. A reader did not need a background in Adam Smith and David Ricardo to be swept away by his power to set a scene:

My last and most vivid impression is of . . . the President and the Prime Minister as the center of a surging mob and a babel of sound, a welter of eager, impromptu compromises and counter-compromises, all sound and fury signifying nothing, on what was an unreal question anyhow, the great issues of the morning's meeting forgotten and neglected; and Clemenceau silent and aloof . . . throned, in his gray gloves, on the brocade chair, dry in soul and empty of hope, very old and tired, but surveying the scene with a cynical and almost impish air.[40]

Human beings often inflict deeper wounds on their friends than on their enemies, and Keynes reserved the harshest of his abuse for Wilson, whom he painted as weak and pathetic:

The President was not a hero or a prophet; he was not even a philosopher; but a generously intentioned man, with many of the weaknesses of other human beings, and lacking that dominating intellectual equipment which would have been necessary to cope with the subtle and dangerous spellbinders whom a tremendous clash of forces and personalities had brought to the top as triumphant masters in the swift game of give and take . . . the Old World's heart of stone might blunt the sharpest blade of the bravest knight-errant. But this blind and deaf Don Quixote was entering a cavern where the swift and glittering blade was in the hands of the adversary.[41]

Keynes had addressed his book chiefly to the British government. But *The Economic Consequences of the Peace* became powerful ammunition for advocates of America's withdrawal from the world stage and its repudiation of the League of Nations—something Keynes had never for an instant desired. The Republican leaders and self-described "irreconcilables" who opposed the treaty in the United States did not really agree with Keynes—few cared about financial arrangements in Europe—but they trumpeted his criticism in an effort to discredit the treaty and with it the League. "Our Republican statesmen do not seriously urge that the Treaty deals too harshly with Germany," Young reported to Keynes. "As against the President most of them would support the French position."[42]

By the time the book was released, Wilson was unable to defend himself. He had not gone mad in October 1919, as Strachey had implied; he had suffered a massive stroke that left him permanently debilitated. Though he would live for another four and a half years, the remainder of Wilson's presidency was a chaotic administrative jumble as cabinet officials and family members attempted to shoulder various presidential duties to keep the government running. In a distinctly somber letter from March 1920, Norman Davis, who had considered Keynes a friend at the peace conference, accused his old ally of demeaning himself by unfairly abusing the president. "It is quite true that he is not a master of sinister diplomacy," he wrote of Wilson, "but he is a master of something else much more valuable."[43]

The rebuke stung. Keynes respected Davis. "People much prefer to be thought wicked than stupid, and hence my account of the President is taken as much more hostile than it really is," Keynes fired back on April 18. "The president, for me, was a fallen hero. I describe the others as very clever and very wicked; the President as sincere, well-intentioned and determined to do what was right, but perplexed, muddleheaded and a self-deceiver."[44] But the damage was done. Smuts, who had encouraged Keynes to write a critique of the treaty, now regretted his advice. "I did not expect [Keynes] to turn Wilson into a figure of fun."[45]

Bernard Baruch and John Foster Dulles provided the response from Wilsonian officialdom. In 1920, they published *The Making of the Reparation and Economic Sections of the Treaty* under Baruch's name. One of several southern financiers who had supported Wilson since his 1912 campaign, Baruch had served as an American economic adviser at Paris, while Dulles had been a legal expert.[46] The defense the book mounted was remarkable for how much it conceded to Keynes. Baruch didn't deny that the treaty's economic terms were untenable—only that Woodrow Wilson and the U.S. delegation were to blame.

"The Treaty was made in the still smouldering furnace of human pas-sion," he wrote. "I believe that every fair-minded man who can speak familiarly on the subject will agree that the repression and minimizing of the vengeful elements in the treaty were due in largest measure to Woodrow Wilson and the high purposes he set."[47]

The United States never ratified the Treaty of Versailles, and its refusal to do so doomed the League of Nations. But the Senate's rejec-tion of the treaty had much more to do with American sentiment and partisan intransigence than it did with Keynes' polemic or even Wil-son's stubborn refusal to make legislative concessions. Against that opposition, the ailing Wilson and his League stood no chance.

The French government, meanwhile, reacted to the book with sput-tering outrage. André Tardieu, one of Clemenceau's closest political advisers, wrote a long essay for *Everybody's Magazine* declaring that Keynes "did not occupy a prominent seat at the Conference."[48] Clem-enceau's interpreter at Paris, Paul Mantoux, went so far as to claim that Keynes had never attended a regular session of the Council of Four at Paris—an accusation that, if true, would have undermined Keynes' credibility, revealing his expressive character sketches to be little more than one bureaucrat's flights of fancy.[49] But Mantoux wasn't telling the truth. Minutes from several Council of Four meet-ings record Keynes' participation, and the French interpreter walked back his claim during a 1924 investigation by the Norwegian Nobel Committee,[50] which was considering awarding Keynes the Nobel Peace Prize five years after the publication of his famous book.

The Committee decided not to present any award that year, but the fact that Keynes became a serious contender demonstrates the pro-found influence of *The Economic Consequences of the Peace* on global opinion.

The book's impact on Keynes' own career would be transforma-tional. It was a victory for Bloomsbury idealism on the world stage, but one that strained friendships and ended opportunities for Keynes in British government. For the first time in years, Keynes had to de-cide what to do with his life.

FIVE

— ◇ —

FROM METAPHYSICS TO MONEY

As an undergraduate, John Maynard Keynes' highest ambition had been to secure a position for himself in the British Treasury. When he was forced to settle for a job in the India Office, it had been one of the harshest disappointments of his overachieving young life, and he spent much of the next seven years angling for some way to make the leap to the Treasury. He had agreed to teach economics at Cambridge in 1908 for the lowly stipend of £100 a year—something like $12,500 today—hoping to develop his résumé as a serious mind fit for serious Treasury work, and began publishing academic articles to bolster his qualifications.[1] When he finally received a call to the Treasury in the early days of the war, he had been so overjoyed at the fulfillment of a dream that he had thrown a lavish party at the Café Royal, inviting all of Bloomsbury to celebrate his appointment.[2]

Five years later, he had grown accustomed to his own formidable reputation and a life among the international financial elite. Even before *Economic Consequences* had added to his aura, he was invited to a private meeting in Amsterdam with the governor of the Bank of the Netherlands and the American investment banking icon Paul Warburg as they drew up plans for an American loan to rescue Europe.[3] The project failed, but not over any qualms about Keynes' bona fides.

Sir Charles Addis, a director of the Bank of England, regarded him as "intelligence personified," and he was understood in Whitehall to be "the ablest theorist on finance in England."[4]

The Economic Consequences of the Peace destroyed this promising career path through British government, even as it sent Keynes' reputation as an intellectual soaring. The book was too venomous, too popular, too brilliant. No politician could risk hiring an adviser who might publicly humiliate him after a policy dispute—especially in the combative arena of Liberal Party politics as Asquith and Lloyd George plotted against each other.

And so despite his unexpected new fame, Keynes began the postwar years in a state of deep professional disappointment. He had made up his mind to leave the Treasury before the peace conference at Paris had started—after four grueling years in wartime, he was ready for a break—but he had never intended to exile himself from power. His life now seemed to rewind to 1913, with the optimism and energy of youth replaced by a tangle of frustrated middle-aged ambitions. At thirty-six, he was once again a philosopher with a minor perch in the economics department at the University of Cambridge. Nobody who knew Keynes in 1920 would have guessed that over the next few years, he would transform himself into the most important economic theorist of his generation—much less that he would successfully leverage that reputation to claw his way back to political influence.

But first he would have to suffer another professional setback. Since 1908, his official position at Cambridge had been in the economics department, and he had earned some distinction as the editor of *The Economic Journal,* one of the founding academic publications in the discipline. But the field itself was still young, small, and eccentric. Its major practitioners in the previous century had been wealthy men of influence such as Thomas Malthus, David Ricardo, and John Stuart Mill, but they hadn't derived their prestige from their economics; their economic work had been taken seriously because they were prestigious men. Cambridge hadn't established an independent economics department until 1903, and most of Keynes' original academic work as an economist had been derived from his experience as a policy maker at the Treasury. His reputation on campus as a high-powered intellectual was a result of his social connection with the Cambridge philosophy department, where Apostles including Bertrand Russell, G. E. Moore, and others had built prestigious careers. And as Keynes settled back into life in Cambridge after the war, his career as a philosopher was about to implode.

The war had spun placid Cambridge into turmoil. In 1916, the university had stripped Bertrand Russell of his teaching position and expelled him from his on-campus lodging over his persistent antiwar activism. Outraged by the university's mistreatment of Russell, other faculty members organized protests in the name of academic freedom, and by 1919, Russell had his job back, despite having served six months in prison for criminal pacifism.

Other Apostles, however, would never return to the university. The poet Rupert Brooke had died in the early days of the war; the Battle of the Somme had claimed the life of the young Apostle Francis Kennard Bliss, another poet, a year later. Keynes lost friends on both sides of the conflict. Ferenc Békássy, a Hungarian poet who had fallen in with the Apostles while studying history at King's College, was killed fighting for the Austro-Hungarian army in 1915. Wittgenstein had also rushed off to enlist with the Central Powers, but Keynes had heard nothing from him since the young philosopher had somehow managed to get a letter through to Great Britain from the battlefront in 1915 (Keynes had responded with a note of his own: "I hope you have safely been taken prisoner by now."[5]).

In March 1919, as Keynes was finally putting the German food relief debacle behind him at the Paris peace conference, he received an unexpected note from Russell. Wittgenstein, Russell relayed, had been taken prisoner by the Allies and was holed up at a POW camp near Cassino, Italy. Russell enclosed a recent note he had received from their mutual friend and asked Keynes to pull whatever strings he could with the Allied governments on their friend's behalf—if Keynes couldn't get him sent to England outright, might he be able to allow

Wittgenstein to correspond more freely with Russell? The moody Austrian was forbidden to ship anything other than two short post-cards a week from the prison camp, which made it impossible for the two men to exchange any serious philosophical ideas.[6]

But Keynes was drawn to something else in the correspondence, a brief passage that would set in motion a chain of events that would ultimately prove the undoing of Keynes' philosophical career and turn loose one of the most influential works of the twentieth century. Wittgenstein told Russell that he had written a book during the war and kept the manuscript with him when he had been taken prisoner. The *campo concentramento* was not an ideal environment for discussion or critique, and Wittgenstein's excitement about what he referred to as his life's work leaped off the pages of his letters. "I believe I've solved our problems finally," he wrote. "This may sound arrogant but I can't help believing it." It was all in his little book, although Wittgenstein was confident that Russell "would not understand it without a previ-ous explanation as it's written in quite short remarks. This of course means that *nobody* will understand it; although I believe it's all clear as crystall [sic]. But it upsets all our theory of truth, of classes, of numbers and all the rest."[7]

Wittgenstein could overpower even Keynes with his arrogance. After one particularly colorful Wittgenstein visit, Keynes had dead-panned, "Well, God has arrived. I met him on the 5.15 train."[8] But Wittgenstein wasn't overstating the importance of the strange manu-script stashed away with his belongings in Italy. Writing from Paris, Keynes pressured the British government to guarantee the secure shipment of Wittgenstein's work to himself.[9] He may have been on his way out the door, but Keynes was still the top Treasury man in charge of British war finance. By the end of June, he had the book. On the day the peace treaty was signed, he wrote Wittgenstein—who was still in Italy—from Duncan and Vanessa's farmhouse to say he was sending the manuscript along to Russell.[10]

With help from Russell and a young Cambridge philosopher named Frank Ramsey, Wittgenstein's manuscript was eventually pub-lished in 1922 as the *Tractatus Logico-Philosophicus,* setting off a revolution in philosophy throughout the English-speaking world with its unique distillation of the relationships among language, logic, and ultimate truth. The book was, Wittgenstein wrote, an attempt to "draw a limit to thinking." On one side of the limit would be matters of genuine knowledge, while "what lies on the other side of the limit will be simply nonsense."[11]

In Wittgenstein's view, there are some truths that can be investigated, discussed, and debated meaningfully—things that can be "said" intelligibly. That realm is essentially the world of facts which can be uncovered by empirical science. But nearly everything that philosophers concern themselves with—the good, rationality, logic—is *outside* the territory of meaningful linguistic expression. Even logic is part of the internal architecture of language itself. No one can speak meaningfully about anything *without* logic, but there is nothing meaningful that philosophers can say *about* how logic itself works; that is ultimately mystical.

For Keynes, the implications of Wittgenstein's work were not mere abstractions; they carried a deep and troublingly personal significance. As an undergraduate, Keynes, together with Lytton Strachey, had been inspired by G. E. Moore's philosophical treatise *Principia Ethica*. In the years leading up the war, Keynes and Russell had been hard at work attempting to expand Moore's ideas into an entire school of thought encompassing rationality, the nature of knowledge, ethics, and even political theory. As he settled back into Cambridge in 1920, Keynes resumed his chief contribution to that project, *A Treatise on Probability*. Expectations for the book could not have been higher among the thinkers who mattered. Russell had even put some of his own work on the nature of cause and effect on hold, hoping to build on whatever Keynes came up with on probability.[12] When he at last sent the manuscript off to his publisher, Daniel Macmillan, in May 1921—several months before Wittgenstein's *Tractatus* would be published—Keynes believed he had completed his magnum opus. "I feel a little sentimental," he wrote Macmillan, "at writing the last words of what has occupied me for fifteen years and, apart from the five years interlude of war, has been a pretty constant companion. I shall never attempt anything again on so large a scale."[13]

It was true in a sense. Keynes had written a comprehensive theory of rationality and human action by considering the problems posed by uncertainty about the future. How, he asked, can people make rational decisions in the present based on beliefs about the future when those beliefs may or may not be vindicated by events? Since we do not know the future, how can we rationally decide what to do in the present? We must, he concluded, be capable of judging sophisticated probabilities.

Keynes argued that there is a difference between probabilities and statistical frequencies. To say that some state of affairs is probable, according to Keynes, is not to simply state that mathematically, it will occur a certain percentage of times in a simulation (that is, if fifty of the one hundred coins in a bag are quarters, I have a 50 percent probability of drawing a quarter every time I reach in). Mathematical data might be *useful* in a person's assessment of probability, but it cannot *be* probability itself.

Keynes positioned himself firmly in G. E. Moore's rationalist tradition. True probabilities, he argued, are not mere hunches or matters of opinion—they are objective realities, which can be assessed *before* events take their course. In Keynes' thinking, an event could be objectively probable in 1920, even if, looking back from 1922, it never actually came to pass. And it is the objective probability—not the subsequent course of events—that matters for human reason. There is a difference between being rational and being right.

Like many other theorists of ethical reasoning, Keynes was trying to construct an authoritative definition of rationality that would justify his own habits and preferences.[14] After sketching his ideas about probability, he moved on to suggest that it is more rational for people—and society itself—to pursue small goods with a high probability of attainment than it is to strive for grand utopias with minute probabilities of attainment.

Keynes intended *A Treatise on Probability* to be the climax of his intellectual career. Thanks to Wittgenstein, it became instead a transitional work—the place where some of the most important concepts he would later develop as an economist were first expressed. Its preoccupation with uncertainty, its distrust of mathematics as a reliable guide to human reasoning, and its skepticism about the wisdom of difficult, long-term endeavors would all become hallmarks of Keynesian economics.

At its heart, *A Treatise on Probability* was an attempt to apply the scientific rationalism of the Enlightenment to probability and uncertainty, hoping to reveal deep truths about rationality itself. Wittgenstein, by contrast, argued that this entire enterprise was nonsense—literally *non*-sense—an effort to express something with words that language could not in fact express. Keynes, according to Wittgenstein, was attempting to provide rigor and precision to realms that were fundamentally mystical. "Whereof one cannot speak," Wittgenstein wrote, "thereof one must be silent."[15] Keynes could examine patterns of human behavior and study trends in the way people actually made decisions; that was science, a subject of meaningful inquiry. But he could not investigate rationality itself. Rationality simply was—or was not.

And so the manuscript Keynes had helped salvage from a POW camp in Cassino, Italy, pushed Keynes out of the philosophy business. *A Treatise on Probability* was debated avidly by the leading lights of Cambridge philosophy but quickly fell out of favor. Wittgenstein's work, meanwhile, became the foundational text of analytic philosophy—a school of thought that still dominates English-speaking philosophy departments, in which language itself is understood to be the source of all truths that philosophers can uncover.

For the second time in two years, Keynes was professionally at sea. Paradoxically, he found himself fabulously rich. He had been supplementing his income by dabbling in the stock exchange since 1905 and by 1910 had built up a nest egg of £539 (about $70,000 today). One thing led to another, and by the end of 1914, his investments had snowballed to £4,617 (more than $500,000 today).[16]

Keynes enjoyed gambling, and did not see a substantive distinction between playing the ponies at the racetrack and betting on stock prices. Both provided a "fun and mild excitement" that he likened to alcohol consumption—typically pleasant, only occasionally ruinous. "I think it would add to the cheerfulness of life if practically everyone in the country was to wake up each Sunday morning stretching out for the Sunday paper with just a possibility that they had won a small fortune," he once told an official committee of Parliament. "It is agreeable to be habitually in the state of imagining all sorts of things are possible."[17]

Agreeable perhaps, but ethically dubious for a man with access to the most sensitive economic secrets of the British government. Keynes continued bidding on stocks and commodities throughout the war— a flagrant conflict of interest given the nature of his Treasury work, which required him to make personal decisions affecting the total price and supply of all kinds of commodities. He didn't advise the government to make strategic decisions that would maximize his own profits; when he'd urged the government not to break with gold in 1914, for instance, the result had cost him hundreds of pounds. But the arrangement would be scandalous today. It was simply impossible for him to make careful investments that were *not* informed by the privileged knowledge he acquired just by walking through Whitehall. By war's end, he had more than tripled his securities holdings to £14,453.

After the war he put his financial mind to work betting on currency values—a new frontier for investors that had opened as nation after nation had suspended the gold standard during the war. Since currencies were no longer directly anchored to a specific amount of gold, they now fluctuated in value against one another, presenting new profit opportunities for quick-thinking traders. After six months, he had secured a profit of £6,154 on currency speculation alone. His reputation as a master investor had grown so powerful that King's College set aside £30,000 for him to speculate with on behalf of the school. He started a new investment partnership with friends and family with an initial capital of £30,000—half supplied by Keynes, the other half by friends, family, and an investor named Oswald Toynbee Falk. Keynes agreed to pay any losses to his friends out of his own pocket—so long as he could—but would let any gains accrue to them proportionally. Given his very long run of success in the markets, it seemed a safe bet to Duncan, Lytton, and Vanessa.

He nearly lost everything. Keynes bet that the dollar would strengthen and most European currencies would soften—a reasonable expectation given the relative strength of the U.S. economy. But a fit of arbitrary optimism had temporarily thrown currency values in the opposite directions—leaving Keynes holding the bag. By April 1920, he had lost a staggering £22,575—millions of dollars in today's money. Not for the last time, Keynes had become a victim of the market's irrationality.

Undeterred, he sought out a new partnership with Cologne banker Sir Ernest Cassel, promising "very substantial profits" for anyone "prepared to stand the racket." His political contacts made him "practically certain" that no international loan was in the works that could reverse the general trends in currency values that were just around the corner. If Cassel would provide just £190,000 in working capital for Keynes to gamble with, Keynes would accept whatever cut of the profits the banker deemed acceptable. After losing a fortune for himself and his friends, he was now proposing that Cassel provide him with what would amount to about $25 million in today's money to right the ship.

He got a £5,000 loan instead. And after a few weeks, Keynes' wild predictions began to bear fruit. By the end of 1922, his joint project with friends and family was debt free and back up to £21,000. By 1924, he enjoyed a personal net worth of £63,797. And by the mid-1940s, his fund for King's had tripled the performance of the college's other investments.

Soon he was parading his wealth around town, playing the part of an ostentatious aristocrat. Amid so many professional setbacks, Keynes had a reputation to maintain. The author of *The Economic Consequences of the Peace* should be a rich man, and Keynes was determined to act like one—even if he occasionally made a fool of himself in the process.

"Well my first hunt is over," he reported from the Crown Hotel in Exford.

I saw the prey start running but I never saw it again. It ran for between 4 and 5 hours. . . . I had no idea a horse could go on so long. After that time I was up with the hounds and the huntsmen. Then

soon after I found myself (the horse being tired and going slowly)
almost alone on a tract of open moor with the hounds some way
ahead. . . . Soon after I lost myself in the bottom of a deep valley and
then found that my horse had lost one of its shoes and could do little
more. . . . I rode slowly but the horse's foot got more and more tender,
until finally, to spare him, I got off and walked. After some miles I
came to an inn, stopped my horse and left him there, got a pint of beer
from a rascally innkeeper and motored home. . . . It all seemed quite
an adventure—but wasn't really![18]

He fared better with a different horse on another hunt later in the week, but the second fox ultimately escaped.[19]

When he wasn't out foxhunting, Keynes was hosting dinner parties and frequenting the ballet, taking conspicuous seats for himself and his guests among members of the "kid gloves and tiara set."[20] And in the winter of 1921, he saw Lydia Lopokova dance a dual role as Aurora and the Lilac Fairy in an adaptation of Tchaikovsky's *Sleeping Beauty*.

He had seen Lydia dance before, years earlier—but this was something different. Captivated, he found himself returning night after night, mesmerized by Lydia's movements.

Lydia had joined Sergei Diaghilev's groundbreaking Ballets Russes in 1911, and by 1921, she was one of its biggest stars. When the avant-garde troupe came to London, the British press celebrated her as a "London sparrow" of "exquisite plebian beauty."[21] The company even sold "Lydia dolls" to adoring crowds who packed the halls in European capitals.

The performances of the Ballets Russes were lavish enough to rival the grand productions of nineteenth-century imperial operas, but with an artistic dedication to experimentation, confrontation, and the outrageous. Diaghilev commissioned Pablo Picasso, Henri Matisse, Jean Cocteau, and other internationally renowned artists to design his sets, and Claude Debussy was just one of the musical innovators corralled into writing the accompaniments. In May 1913, Diaghilev premiered a new symphonic ballet he had written with a young composer named Igor Stravinsky and so shocked the Paris audience with their impassioned aural and visual avant-garde that it broke into a riot. *The Rite of Spring* became an instant, controversial classic.

Lydia was more than a little romantically entangled in late 1921. Nearly six years earlier, she had married Diaghilev's business manager, Randolfo Barocchi, during an American tour. Barocchi, unbeknownst to Lydia, was already married to a woman named Mary Hargreaves when he signed his marriage certificate to the acclaimed ballerina. Lydia's relationship with Barocchi had broken down in 1919, but its legal status remained in full force until she could challenge it in court.

Just four months after marrying Barocchi, moreover, Lydia had started a secret affair with Stravinsky, himself a married man.[22] Igor and Lydia drifted apart over the years as he returned to his family and her performance schedule sent her around Europe and across the Atlantic. The couple rekindled their romance in the spring of 1921 during a production of *Petrushka* in Madrid, but the Parisian actress Vera Sudeykina caught his roving eye over the summer and accepted a small role in the ballet company to be near her new lover. When the troupe arrived in London, a smoldering love triangle had formed.[23]

Stravinsky returned to France with Vera in December, leaving Lydia frustrated just as Keynes began to show interest. Keynes purchased some of the most expensive seats to *Sleeping Beauty* to get close to the action on stage, and she had not missed his devoted attendance. He inquired after her backstage and asked her to lunch on December 18. Five days later they dined together and stayed up talking together until 1:00 in the morning.[24] She invited him to tea on December 26, and it was clear that both were already smitten.[25] Lydia, according to her biographer, was "mesmerised by his astonishing mind," just as he was "hypnotised by Lydia's energy and talent."[26]

Lydia had been raised to revere intellectuals. Her father had worked as usher for the Alexandrinsky Theater in St. Petersburg and impressed upon his children an appreciation for both dance and the elite intelligentsia who frequented his place of work.[27] Her interests had always roved beyond the rigors of her craft, and she longed to be accepted as a "serious woman" without abandoning the joie de vivre that had made her a star.[28] In Bloomsbury, of course, Keynes had come to worship artists as almost supernatural beings. By April, they were exchanging erotic updates by mail. Lydia was self-conscious about her English, but her nonnative flair for metaphor entranced her suitor. "I gobble you my dear Maynard," she wrote.[29] "I place melodious strokes all over you."[30] She was "full of electricity towards your thoughts and yourself."[31]

The Sleeping Princess was a rare commercial flop for Lydia and Diaghilev—too lush and earnest for the cynical postwar mood. At the end of its disappointing run in London, Keynes established Lydia in an apartment at 50 Gordon Square and set her up with a bank account (she had been trusting her payments to the care of the porter at the Waldorf Hotel).[32] When Lydia was away performing, Keynes sent along newspaper clippings of his articles and updates on his research. Their sexual correspondence would continue for years. After a spell of digging through ancient Babylonian currency in 1926, Keynes came across what he believed to be the oldest "love poem" yet uncovered, quoting it to the delighted Lydia: "Come to me my Ishtavar and show your virile strength/ Push out your member and touch with it my little place."[33]

Her letters show almost as much interest in his articles on economic policy. "Only this morning I have received 'Reconstruction in Europe.' It does look well, there lies strength in it because it is your production . . . after reading your article they must stabilise money."[34] "When I read what you write somehow I feel bigger than I am. It is very nice for me. I blend my mouth and heart to yours."[35]

During the early months of their courtship, Lydia, an artist herself, seemed to fit in with Keynes' literary friends, exchanging letters with them, joining shopping expeditions, or hosting them for tea. Years of experience with the Ballets Russes had prepared her for the love triangles and jealousies that defined much of social life in Bloomsbury. An undated note, likely from late October or early November 1922, shows Lydia and the gang reveling in one another's company without any guidance from Keynes:

Dearest Maynard,
  we are w [indecipherable scrawl]
  crazy drunk

We are slightly tipsy
Duncan invited Vanessa and me to a big jug of beer. . . . We all
drank your health and we kiss you, and I too more than anybody:
Lydia.[36]

But as it dawned on Bloomsbury that Lopokova wasn't just another of Keynes' note card conquests to be statistically analyzed, his old friends began to see the young Russian as a threat. Her fame trivialized their own achievements, and she was dominating the attentions of their most famous member (not to mention benefactor). Virginia, Vanessa, and Lytton bad-mouthed Lydia in private letters, taking malicious joy in imitating her accent and belittling her efforts to familiarize herself with English literature and politics. "Lydia came over here the other day and said 'Please Leonard tell me about Mr Ramsay Macdonald. I am seerious—very serious,'" Virginia wrote to the French painter Jacques Raverat. "However then she caught a frog and put it in an apple tree; and thats whats so enchanting about her; but can one go through life catching frogs?"[37]

Though Maynard and Lydia were vacationing with Leonard and Virginia as early as September 1923, some of that secret disdain must have come through. Despite her financial and artistic success, Lydia was about a decade younger than the original Bloomsberries, whom Maynard considered paragons of English respectability. She craved their intellectual approval but did not receive it. "I assure you its tragic to see her sitting down to King Lear," Virginia wrote. "Nobody can take her seriously: every nice young man kisses her. Then she flies into a rage and says she is like Vanessa, like Virginia, like Alix Sargent Florence, or Ka Cox—a seerious wooman."[38]

By December 1922, Virginia was urging her sister to talk sense into their love-struck economist before he did something irreversible:

Seriously, I think you ought to prevent Maynard before it is too late. I can't believe that he realizes what the effects would be. I can foresee only too well Lydia stout, charming, exacting; Maynard in the Cabinet; 46 [Gordon Square] the resort of the dukes and prime minis-

ters. M. being a simple man, not analytic as we are, would sink be-
yond recall long before he realised his state. Then he would awake, to
find 3 children, and his life entirely and for ever controlled.

That is how it appears to me, without considering my own griev-
ances. If you dont put your view before him, he will have a case
against you when the catastrophe arrives. Moreover, Lydia is far bet-
ter as a Bohemian unattached, hungry, and expectant, than as a ma-
tron with nothing to hope, and all her rights secure.[39]

Lopokova quit the Diaghilev scene in 1922. Hailed as a genius throughout his life, the director remained notorious for his intense, overbearing personality for decades after his death. The character of Boris Lermontov in Michael Powell and Emeric Pressburger's spell-binding 1948 film *The Red Shoes* was based largely on Lydia's taskmaster. Lopokova had enough financial freedom with Keynes to take dance work where and when she wanted it, no longer dependent on the company to sustain her lifestyle. (Like Keynes, Lydia was not above ostentatious displays of wealth.)

She also enjoyed the public clamor that surrounded her new love's work. "You are very famous, Maynard,"[40] she praised, a sincere refrain she repeated in her early letters: "So very famous"[41] or simply "Very famous!"[42] When he felt disheartened by efforts to translate his ideas into publicly digestible op-eds or magazine features, Lydia offered encouragement: "Do not speak against your articles in journalism—just think how many peoples read, understand and remember it, and when you go to bed have the feeling of the work you have done with mind and inspiration."[43]

This was of course a radical shift in Maynard's sexual outlook. He had been enthusiastically gay for as long as he could remember being attracted to anyone. Here he was head over heels for a *woman.* Bloomsbury had grown accustomed to gay men settling down with lady companions; Duncan and Vanessa shared a farmhouse, Lytton had moved in with the painter Dora Carrington, and Bunny had married the illustrator Ray Marshall in 1921. These were all unconventional arrangements that generally allowed the men to continue pursuing male

lovers. Keynes was fully enraptured by Lydia, but his transition to heterosexual monogamy took time. Lydia knew of Maynard's background
and didn't hesitate to establish a bridge to new desires for him during
the early days of their relationship. She bought a pair of men's pajamas
and teased him about seducing him in a golf outfit. Various efforts
with fingers and mouths proved successful for both partners.[44] Still,
Maynard continued his dalliances with Sebastian Sprott for two years
after falling for Lydia, finally relenting to her pleas for fidelity in late
winter of 1923.[45] It was his last serious relationship with a man. His
letters make clear that he was satisfied by Lydia. He longed to be
"foxed and gobbled abundantly."[46]

Keynes still had a career to tend to when he wasn't busy seducing ballerinas. With his philosophical career dried up, he devoted most of his
writing energy to fielding critiques of *The Economic Consequences of the
Peace* in newspapers and magazines, responding in letters to the editor
and essays of his own. *The Manchester Guardian* recruited him as a columnist on international financial affairs, and he wrote long features
surrounding efforts to revise the Treaty of Versailles and reach a final
reparations figure. To his surprise, what had begun as an exercise in reputation management had flowered into a prominent journalistic career.

He had closed *Economic Consequences* with a call to harness "those
forces of instruction and imagination which change *opinion*," and for
new intellectual leaders to find "the true voice of the new generation,"
which had "not yet spoken."[47] At the time, he had imagined himself
playing a role behind the scenes in the formation of that new consensus, working as he had before the war in academic journals and writing books for high-minded experts. The art of public persuasion was a
different skill set, a little plebian, too close to politics and propaganda
to be the proper endeavor of a former Apostle. But after several well-
received articles on the peace treaty for *The Manchester Guardian*,
Keynes secured a £300 contract to cover the spring 1922 financial
conference at Genoa, which he quickly supplemented with another
£375 to syndicate that same work among publications in Vienna and

New York. Combined, it came to upward of $45,000 in today's money, a better rate word-for-word than even the windfall he had received from his international bestseller.[48]

The conference assignment meant much more to Keynes than money or even the prestige provided by transatlantic bylines. Genoa was full of British Treasury veterans; Basil Blackett was there, along with Charles Addis from the Bank of England. Genoa seemed a good opportunity for Keynes to embed himself back within political society, where he might leverage his growing reputation as a public intellectual to ingratiate himself with men of power. By the spring of 1922, he was armed with an ambitious new policy idea aimed at overhauling the postwar international monetary order.

Great Britain had never formally abandoned the gold standard during the war. It had adopted a host of convoluted measures to prevent British subjects from trading in paper money for bullion at home, and it had used similar tricks abroad. When France, Germany, Russia, and Austria-Hungary abandoned the gold standard in 1914, dealers in the London gold market had refused to export British gold to them as payment for goods. It was a way for Britain to maintain the gold standard on a technicality: It would honor the gold standard when dealing with other nations that also honored the gold standard. Since almost everyone except the United States had broken with gold, Britain was effectively breaking with it as well.[49]

Those emergency measures allowed the government to print its way through much of the war's costs. By the end of the conflict, the total money supply in Great Britain had swelled from about $5 billion in 1913 to a whopping $12 billion, while the nation's gold reserves had remained steady. That was a recipe for inflation, an across-the-board increase in consumer prices. By 1920, the cost of standard consumer goods had more than doubled since the beginning of the conflict.[50]

Inflation was everywhere in the early days of the peace. The United States, France, and Germany had all printed huge sums of money to help cope with war costs. The French money supply had more than tripled over the course of the war, while Germany's currency supply had more than quadrupled.[51] Exchange rates, once predictable and stable, now swung this way and that. Great Britain had fixed the pound at \$4.86 before the war; it averaged just \$3.66 over the course of 1920, plunging as low as \$3.40.[52] Trade became suddenly unpredictable; international contracts might transform into either bargains or ripoffs due to unexpected currency swings. As prices surged and foreign exchange markets were rocked by a volatility unheard of during Gilded Age finance, a nearly unanimous call went out from the global financial world to restore order: bring back gold.

Before the war, inflation, deflation, and foreign exchange had been governed by the gold standard. The amount of money in circulation was restricted by a nation's gold reserves, and since every major currency could be converted into a certain weight in gold, international trade benefited from stable, fixed exchange rates that enabled predictable patterns of commerce between nations. International prices had been easily discerned, as currencies essentially served as names for different weights of gold.

To its champions, the gold standard represented much more than price stability. It secured a particular vision of free trade in which governments would not interfere with the exchange of goods across international boundaries. The whole point of fixing a specific gold value to a currency, after all, was to prevent governments from manipulating patterns of trade by meddling with currency values. The gold standard, economists believed, left commerce free to take its own natural course.

This free trade ideal was entwined with a humanitarian sentiment in which the exchange of goods was inseparable from the exchange of goodwill. International trade, in this thinking, led to mutual understanding, helping different peoples appreciate each others' customs and ideas. For Keynes, the benevolent power of free trade was a foundational belief, the central conviction with which all other political views and proposals had to either find harmony or be discarded.

The notion that commerce served as a pacifying force in political affairs was in fact much older than the heyday of the gold standard, having been popularized by the French thinker Montesquieu in the mid-1700s.[53] But precisely because it expressed this older principle of Enlightenment liberalism, the gold standard carried a profound social meaning. Gold represented a normal state of affairs in which the world was gliding inexorably to peace, prosperity, and progress. And since the prewar system had collapsed at its zenith, a return to the gold standard was viewed as an opportunity to revive a lost glory, to prove that there were some things even the Great War could not destroy. For prominent bankers, Keynes noted, restoring the gold value of the pound was a question of "national prestige"—of ensuring a "more glorious" Great Britain.

Keynes saw that in the minds of most financial thinkers, the idea of returning to the gold standard was "hopelessly entangled" with what were in fact different issues—the inflations and currency depreciations that had taken root during and after the war. The leading men of Lombard Street wanted not only to get Britain back on gold but to get back at precisely the same weights and exchange rates that had prevailed before the war. Though they called this plan a program of "stabilization," it was in fact a new round of monetary disruption—a deliberate policy of strengthening the pound against the dollar through deflation.[54]

There was more to such thinking than pure confusion or fetishization of the old ways. More sophisticated City grandees believed that if London hoped to recover the financial power it had ceded to Wall Street during the war, it would have to prove that investing in Great Britain was a better bet than investing in the United States. That meant demonstrating to the global financial markets that the British government would not allow anything to devalue their investments in British money or British debt—not even war.

Keynes had used a similar argument during the financial crisis of 1914, when he had urged London to keep paying foreigners, no matter what the drain on gold. But he believed the economic world had fundamentally changed over the ensuing years. The nations of Europe, he argued in a dispatch from Genoa, were now all massively indebted, facing totally different resource constraints than they had a decade prior. Borders had been redrawn; fields, mines, and factories had been destroyed. It was foolish to believe that the financial arrangements of 1913 would meet the needs of 1922.

More important, Keynes was experiencing a fundamental crisis of confidence in the classical economic theory he had studied at Cambridge. Under the accepted textbook dogma, a problem such as deflation wasn't supposed to cause sustained economic damage. As prices fell, so would paychecks, leaving workers about where they had been beforehand. There would be a brief disruption, but market forces would quickly return the world to its normal state of affairs: a stable, prosperous equilibrium between buyers and sellers, supply and demand. The cure for economic turmoil was always the same: Let the market do its work.

The test of this doctrine began in February 1920, when all the world's countries seemed to embark on a race to outdeflate their neighbors. France, Italy, Sweden, Norway, Denmark, and crucially, the United States, all aggressively brought down their domestic prices. This effort was partly a product of the collective belief in the virtue of lower prices. But it was also a result of American stubbornness. When the Fed raised interest rates to bring down American prices, gold flowed from the rest of the world to the United States. If the rest of the world didn't want to run out of gold, it would have to raise interest rates in response. With the largest gold hoard and the largest economy at its command, America could now orchestrate the terms of international finance the way the Bank of England once had.

In Great Britain, prices fell by half.[55] The social costs were shocking. Farms were foreclosed and businesses failed, throwing millions of people out of work. British unemployment soared to over 23 percent in 1921 and averaged 14.3 percent over the course of 1922.[56] Wages plummeted, prompting fierce agitation from organized labor, especially among coal miners. In April 1921, when coal barons demanded pay cuts from rank-and-file miners, the British government called in eleven infantry battalions, three cavalry regiments, and military tanks over fears of a massive strike by miners, railwaymen, and transport workers.[57] The country, it seemed, was waiting to catch fire.

For many socialists in the burgeoning Labour Party, the sudden depression confirmed what they had long suspected: Capitalism was not only unfair and unjust, it simply couldn't work. Keynes had never studied Marxism with any serious rigor, but even if he had, the emotional break that would have been required for him to abandon his faith in the virtues of capitalism was simply too great.

Maybe the problem was money itself. "The individualistic capitalism of today . . . *presumes* a stable measuring-rod of value, and cannot be efficient—perhaps cannot survive—without one,"[58] Keynes wrote in *The Manchester Guardian*. Monetary disruptions—inflation and deflation—had disparate effects on different segments of society. If inflation took hold over the life of a loan, the debtor got a good deal out of it; he could pay back exactly the dollar amount that he owed, but the real value of those dollars would have been inflated away. Under deflation, the exact opposite took place: the burden of debts became heavier through no fault of the borrower's.

Debtors fared differently from creditors; workers fared differently from bosses; citizens fared differently from foreigners. The level playing field that capitalist exchange required was distorted. The solution, Keynes thought, was not to abandon supply and demand or free trade and free thought, but to stabilize the monetary system so that those forces could work their magic.

Keynes began a public campaign at Genoa and in the pages of *The Manchester Guardian* to stabilize prices around the world. Price instability undermined the public's faith in its government and its institutions; failing to control it would, Keynes told the Treasury, "strike at the whole basis of contract, of security, and of the capitalist system generally."[59] The cure for wartime inflation was stability on a new plateau, not the tumble back downhill advocated in the City.

Under Keynes' plan, countries that had already deflated their way near to the prewar gold price were welcome to follow through, but none should try to hit the 1914 mark by deflating its currency by more than 6 percent a year. Currencies that had lost at least 20 percent of their 1914 value would be spared the misery of a further deflationary push altogether.

Politically, the plan was breathtakingly audacious—an agenda that would require a level of peacetime financial coordination by the world's great powers that the Allies had only partially achieved during the war. Writing from her new Bloomsbury flat, Lydia counseled her new lover to be bold. "You produce every day new works and they ought to be known to the whole world," she wrote. "You must stay there till the conference lasts. Do you not see how they need you. Perhaps you don't see, but I as an outside person observe clearly how necessary you are."[60]

But Keynes' plan was doomed. There could be no meaningful progress on the international values of the pound, the franc, or the mark if the dollar was not part of the discussion. And the United States was sitting out the Genoa conference, ostensibly to protest France's refusal to consider reducing German reparations. Without U.S. participation, the British delegation at Genoa was afraid to stick its neck out for Keynes' new idea. Lydia, supportive as ever, blamed the shortsightedness of the other delegates. "It is annoying that financial experts do not want stabilisation but I also understand they cannot be Maynards (there is only *one* Maynard),"[61] she wrote. In time, the United States would come around. "A little later I see U.S. stepping into it by your idea," she consoled him. "You are very famous, Maynard."[62]

It would take more than two decades. Not until the 1944 conference at Bretton Woods, New Hampshire, would Keynes and the American leadership at last find common ground on the international monetary system—and even then only after a head-to-head struggle for power.

Yet in developing the plan, Keynes had waded into new theoretical waters. Something was happening in the British economy that economics declared to be impossible: prolonged, agonizingly high unemployment. In 1922, Keynes attributed that evil and the social unrest that accompanied it to monetary instability. The solution was for governments and their central banks to begin directly regulating the value of money, raising or lowering interest rates in order to secure a stable price level. That doctrine—that managing the overall supply of money was the best way for governments to achieve economic growth and stability—became known as monetarism.

It was a radical rethinking of the way central banks should operate.[63] The Bank of England typically managed its gold reserves with an eye to fluctuations in international trade, ensuring that Great Britain didn't run out of gold due to too many imports or a shortage of exports. If Britain was running a trade deficit, then money—gold—would be flowing out of the country, because Britain was effectively purchasing more goods from abroad than it was selling to foreigners. In that situation, the Bank would raise interest rates, effectively lowering the price of British goods on the international market until trade levels were balanced. The idea was to have the real terms of trade determining the price level. Keynes was suggesting the opposite, regulating prices to ensure stability—a strategy that would have implications for the course of trade. It was a step away from the laissez-faire doctrine that public officials should not meddle in economic affairs. Governments would find themselves forced to choose between maintaining a stable exchange rate and a stable price level. When the choice came, Keynes argued, there should be no hesitation: Keep prices stable, and adjust exchange rates. It might be true that "over the long run," rashes of inflation and deflation would burn themselves out. "But this long run is a misleading guide to current affairs," Keynes observed. "*In the long run,* we are all dead. Economists set themselves too easy, too useless a task if in tempestuous seasons they can only tell us that when the storm is long past the ocean is flat again."[64] A lot could happen while governments waited for inflation to calm down: unemployment, hunger, riots—even revolution. As he had argued in *A Treatise on Probability,* short-term, easily realized improvements in social welfare had a higher priority than long-term reforms that might never be realized.

"*In the long run,* we are all dead" was more than a clever turn of phrase. It distinguished Keynes from other contemporary monetarists, and those in the years to come who would affiliate themselves with right-wing politics. Like the monetarist Milton Friedman, Keynes looked to price stability as a way to shore up classical economic thinking. For the most part, he believed, laissez-faire economics worked. Supply and demand *did* bring society to a prosperous equilibrium. They just needed a few pieces of basic economic architecture to work: property rights, the rule of law, and price stability. But unlike Friedman, Keynes had arrived at monetarism as a creative way to expand the power of the state to fight the uncertainties and anxieties of postwar life. If monetarism would not deliver the goods—if it did not actually bring about short-term economic and *political* stability—Keynes would be happy to try something else.

Keynes assembled these insights—many of them first published in the pages of *The Manchester Guardian* in 1922—into a new book, titled *A Tract on Monetary Reform*. It was his first major and controversial work of economic theory. Wall Street and the City were aghast, recognizing that Keynes was in effect calling to rob the gold standard of its meaning. Though he didn't propose to officially sever the connection between paper money and gold, allowing governments to revalue their currency in a pinch amounted to the same thing. His critics asked: What was the point in fixing the pound to a certain weight of gold if that weight could be changed on a whim? Keynes countered: What good was the gold standard if it could function only by creating social unrest?

"To close the mind to the idea of revolutionary improvements in our control of money and credit is to sow the seeds of the downfall of individualistic capitalism," he warned Charles Addis at the Bank of England. "Do not be the Louis XVI of the monetary revolution."[65]

If Keynes' new economic theory did not inspire quite the same public uproar that *The Economic Consequences of the Peace* had produced, he was nevertheless flooded with attention and criticism from the leading lights of the City. The pushback served as a badge of honor for him in Bloomsbury, demonstrating that he had not stopped challenging revered figures and sacred doctrines. And Keynes found that the work he had done as a public intellectual gave his theoretical work much greater urgency than that of a typical academic. Keynesian ideas inspired letters to the editor, meetings with central bankers, even the occasional invitation from Whitehall. And so after a few good years with *The Manchester Guardian*, Keynes decided to magnify his public persona by purchasing a newspaper of his own.

The Nation and Athenaeum was a longtime organ of Liberal opinion whose editor, Henry Massingham, had fallen under the sway of the Labour Party and was now in the habit of commissioning articles to younger Labour writers—including Leonard Woolf—that attacked the Liberal Party from the left. In January 1923, Keynes assembled a consortium of investors and took it over, making himself the chairman of a new board of directors and forcing Massingham out.

The Woolfs were dismayed. Keynes' Liberal commitments spelled trouble for the steady stream of income from their Labour breadwinner.[66] Both now in their early forties, the Woolfs lived comfortably, but the couple had never been financially secure. Virginia's books didn't sell, and her unstable mental health required extensive and expensive treatment, including lengthy hospitalizations, in the days before the National Health Service. After weak sales of her first two books, the Woolfs had self-published Virginia's third novel, *Jacob's Room*, on their own Hogarth Press in October 1922. It finally brought her the critical adulation she craved, but good reviews didn't pay the bills. In 1924, her combined revenue from three novels and a book of short stories amounted to just £37, including American sales (Hogarth managed to turn a £3 profit that year).[67] With *The Nation* changing hands, it appeared that Leonard would have to start looking for work.

Still, having a friend in charge of a weekly paper might afford *some* perks. Toward the end of 1922, Virginia had set about organizing financial support for a very promising poet friend whose creative energy, she feared, was being stymied by his career at Lloyds Bank. She'd solicited subscriptions for a fund that would allow the poor man to end his lucrative day job and focus on writing poetry full-time but hadn't been able to secure more than a few hundred pounds for her cause. If Keynes could find some work for him in the range of "£3 to £400 a year,"[68] Virginia pleaded, her poet friend could finally quit the bank.

Keynes had a job open for a literary editor, but there was a problem: None of the other directors of *The Nation* had heard of Virginia's friend. In fact, very few people in England had. His most noteworthy

effort to date had been a very long poem he had published in the first
issue of his own literary magazine just a few months before Keynes
had taken over *The Nation*. Keynes liked the poem, as indeed he should
have—it was a reimagining in free verse metaphor and abstraction of
the themes and ideas Keynes had presented in *The Economic Consequences of the Peace*. Like Keynes' masterpiece, the poem was a violent
eulogy for an idealized continent that would never come again and a
condemnation of the leaders who had destroyed it.[69] It even included
an image of Carthage "Burning burning burning burning"—an invo-
cation of a central metaphor Keynes had deployed for the Treaty of
Versailles. The final peace document, Keynes had warned, was a "Car-
thaginian Peace" that would cast Germany out of Europe, destroying
its people and traditions as Rome had ended Carthage's time among
the great cultures of the ancient Mediterranean. Virginia was so enthusiastic about the poem that she and Leonard published it as a
stand-alone book in September—but the first U.K. edition of *The
Waste Land* by T. S. Eliot had a run of only 450 copies.[70]

Virginia helped Keynes go to work on the other directors. She
asked Lytton Strachey to write a letter promising to write for *The Nation* if it would hire Eliot as literary editor, vowing that "Maynard is
going to pay his contributors highly."[71] After two weeks of drama
with the board, Keynes offered Eliot the job.

Suddenly the poet had reservations. He would need to take a holiday first. And he would need to give three months' notice at the
bank—his work was highly specialized. Editors at *The Times* were
signing five-year contracts—could he get that kind of guarantee?
Maybe two years?[72] As the negotiations dragged on for weeks, the
Eliot project became, in Keynes' words, "a fiasco."[73]

So he abandoned it. On March 23, 1923, he offered the literary
editor position to an "astonished" Leonard Woolf.[74] The job paid £500
a year for two and a half days a week in the office. "It was very good of
you to take so much trouble" over Eliot, Virginia wrote to Maynard
semiapologetically that afternoon. "Nevertheless, I can't help feeling
he was not the right person for the job."

Keynes' weekly paper served as the Woolfs' financial anchor until

Virginia's career finally caught traction with the publication of *Orlando* in 1928 (she made £1,434 that year—over $100,000 today—and enjoyed steady returns on her writing for the remainder of her life).[75] The job was much more than a lifeline to Virginia. As editor, Leonard commissioned work from Lytton, Clive Bell, Roger Fry, Bunny Garnett, and other old friends, converting *The Nation* into the voice of Bloomsbury. The part-time nature of Leonard's job allowed the Woolfs to devote more time and resources to Hogarth, which expanded its output from a handful of titles a year to dozens, publishing Roger, Clive, and E. M. Forster alongside new friends including Robert Graves and better-known writers such as Gertrude Stein, H. G. Wells, and even Sigmund Freud. Some of Hogarth's most reliable bestsellers were political pamphlets written by Keynes.[76] Keynes was using *The Nation* and his celebrity to underwrite all of Bloomsbury. In doing so, he gave his friends a platform for their ideas and helped fuel their later fame and fortune. His own life had become a microcosm of his ideal state, an economic engine supporting the true aims of human achievement: art and letters.

It also liberated him from a lingering insecurity over his aesthetic bona fides. Whatever Clive and Lytton might say about his taste in art, he was running the journal that let them say it. He might never produce a work as beautiful or complete as the various modernist masterpieces that began pouring out of Bloomsbury in the 1920s, but he no longer needed to rescue Cézannes to prove that he belonged in their world. T. S. Eliot had even written a poem based on his book. Not that he stopped caring what Bloomsbury thought. His place among them solidified, Bloomsbury continued to serve as his lodestar. "Cabinet Ministers and *The Times* might praise, but if he had an uneasy suspicion that Lytton Strachey, Duncan Grant, Virginia Woolf and Vanessa Bell did not share their enthusiasm, public flattery might appear something to be ashamed of," according to Clive Bell.[77]

But Keynes was also using *The Nation* to stake out new ideological territory for his Liberals amid the rise of the Labour Party as a progressive force. In the eight years before the war, Herbert Asquith and David Lloyd George had moved liberalism away from strict laissez-faire policies to embrace the modest beginnings of the welfare state. Where once only market justice had reigned, now old-age pensions and unemployment benefits helped improve the quality of life for people who could not work. Lloyd George and Asquith had split over how to prosecute the war, and Lloyd George's victory in the struggle had subjugated the Liberal domestic social welfare agenda to the interests of his broader imperial project, which had tied the Liberal leader and his party to their traditional political enemy—the Conservatives—to establish a governing coalition. The result was a political party that had reeled off a string of victories—from pensions to the Great War—and lost its ideological direction. In the editorial for his first issue of *The Nation* on May 5, 1923, Keynes presented a new manifesto for the party. The great problems of the day—war, peace, and economics—had been scrambled by the war. "The ideas of all of us are so confused and incomplete that the real points of controversy have scarcely begun to emerge," he declared. The prewar Liberal agenda of free trade and a progressive income tax that funded modest programs for the poor had "been shattered by the war debt." Securing prosperity meant grappling with new conceptions of economic structure and "industrial control" that had not yet been formulated—ideas like the monetarism he had explored in the pages of *The Manchester Guardian.*

But Keynes did not imagine his ideas about central banking to be the end of the debate. *The Nation* would present new ideas as they sprang to life and sharpen them into tools policy makers could use. "Our own sympathies are for a Liberal party which has its centre well to the left, a party definitely of change and progress, discontented with the world, striving after many things; but with bolder, freer, more disinterested minds than Labour has, and quit of their out-of-date dogmas."[78]

By the end of 1923, *The Economic Consequences of the Peace, A Tract on Monetary Reform,* and his commentary in *The Nation* had transformed Keynes into one of the most influential figures in Liberal politics.

Even if nobody wanted to hire him as an adviser, nearly every British politician now wanted Keynes in his corner at election time—a remarkable transformation from his position as a brilliant pariah only a few years earlier. And the economic upheaval of the interwar years was creating plenty of partisan turmoil. The British held a national election in each of three consecutive years from 1922 to 1924. Though David Lloyd George had won a convincing victory for his coalition government in the December 1918 election. The campaign had been a profound disappointment for the Labour Party, which had hoped to capitalize on the postwar expansion of the franchise to secure its first-ever majority in Parliament. Never before had women been allowed to vote in Great Britain (even then, only those over the age of thirty were permitted), and voting restrictions on all men over the age of twenty-one had been removed. Labour's poor showing in 1918 meant that the Lloyd George coalition depended heavily on the Conservative Party for its majority. By 1922, that was a strong position for the Conservatives to be in. As prime minister, Lloyd George took the blame for the postwar inflation and deflation yo-yo, and the Tories took full control of the government, breaking their alliance with the Liberals. But the Conservative Bonar Law—yet another prime minister who had previously served as Keynes' boss at the Treasury—would head the government for little longer than six months before falling seriously ill with throat cancer, which would quickly claim his life. When their own prime minister stepped down, the Conservatives called another election.

Liberals dispatched Keynes to the countryside to help take advantage of the crisis. He was not a natural political orator. Awkwardly tall with a slight stoop, he viewed the delivery of lectures as among the most unpleasant of his academic responsibilities. By his own admission, he spoke too fast in political settings—a serious flaw for a man whose area of expertise was both technical and abstract.[79] But Keynes was a famous man whom people would come to see, whatever their interest in politics. In Blackpool on the coast of the Irish Sea, Keynes addressed an audience of three thousand people.[80] "The interest of the public is remarkable," he told Lydia of a rally the following evening. "I have never seen a theatre so packed (the whole of the stage behind me was full of people as well as the auditorium crammed to the roof, and they stood in queues to get in an hour before the doors were opened)."[81] His speeches were written up in *The Manchester Guardian* and in the local press, and locals wished him luck at the train station.

The 1923 election was a referendum on the Conservative plan to boost the economy by imposing protective tariffs on foreign imports. Since the election was all about economic policy, having the support of the world's most famous economist gave the Liberals a significant boost. Keynes happily preached the long-standing Liberal orthodoxy that government meddling in the form of tariffs would be counterproductive. Raising tariffs against foreign products would only increase costs for domestic consumers, he argued, which would lower the standard of living for many households. Free trade was more efficient. By enabling every nation to enjoy the specialties of other nations, everyone would enjoy a more abundant world.

Keynes did not, in this presentation, linger on the implications of his new monetary theory. By allowing countries to revalue their currencies to fight domestic deflation (or inflation), he was effectively calling to rearrange international trade flows in the name of British prosperity. A "stronger" pound value relative to the dollar would make British goods more expensive—and less popular—in the U.S. market, while a "weaker" pound would make them cheaper—and more popular. So far as free trade was concerned, revaluing the currency did the same work a tariff would.

Few members of Keynes' audience were attuned to that inconsistency. The politics of trade policy—then as now—were governed more by rallying slogans than by careful analysis. And for the Liberals, Keynes' position was politically convenient. Party leaders could present him as an innovative expert who knew how to fix the dysfunctional, high-unemployment status quo with his revolutionary monetary ideas, while simultaneously trotting him out to insist that their old free trade policy had been right all along.

Keynes was helping the Liberals—who just a year earlier had been officially allied with the Conservatives—forge a new alliance with the openly socialist Labour Party. He was sent to Barrow-in-Furness in northwest England, where both he and party leaders knew that the Liberal candidate for Parliament was doomed. His job was to peel away enough Conservative votes to let a Labour candidate get through.[82] That was how the national election turned out. Though the Conservatives finished with more seats than any other individual party, both Labour and the Liberals made significant gains, and the two minority parties banded together to form a majority, making Ramsay MacDonald the first Labour prime minister of Great Britain. When the results were in, Keynes was ecstatic about the new opportunity for his party. "Politics is a big confusion," he wrote to Lydia on December 9, 1923. "I want to get to London and hear the gossip. Liberals must move towards Labour and not in the other direction."[83]

For Asquith, the alliance seemed a safe experiment: Liberals could bend Labour to their will on important issues, because Conservatives would never ally with a socialist party. (Winston Churchill called the very idea of a Labour government "a national misfortune" comparable only to defeat in war).[84] Any bad press for the Liberal-Labour coalition, meanwhile, could be pinned squarely on MacDonald and his socialist neophytes. "It is we, if we really understand our business, who really control the situation," Asquith told his Liberal compatriots.[85]

Deflation and unemployment were the most pressing domestic issues facing the new government, but the new regime took office as the international economic arrangements of the Treaty of Versailles gave way to international crisis. Germany had not paid its reparations bills. Of the initial installment of 20 billion marks assessed by the treaty in 1919, only 8 billion had made their way into Allied coffers by the May 1921 deadline.[86] That shortfall was rolled into the final indemnity established by the Reparation Commission at the League of Nations. Germany was now required to pay a total of 132 billion marks, in installments that began at about 3 billion marks every year. Keynes reassessed the peace treaty given those final terms and concluded, to no one's surprise, that it remained too stringent. The most Germany could afford was about 1.25 billion marks a year, spread out over thirty years.

Reparations alone did not cause the ensuing German financial turmoil, but they were a powerful catalyst for calamity. The young Weimar Republic was in a state of near-constant upheaval. While the
Allies had been working out the terms of the treaty in Paris, the German military had been putting down a Communist uprising and mur-
dering its leaders (including, most famously, the Marxist intellectual
Rosa Luxemburg). The German Right, meanwhile, was hostile to the
new democratic constitution, which gave ultimate authority to the
Reichstag, not the monarchy or the military. With the postwar economy in shambles and mass starvation a very recent memory, the leaders of the young democracy tried to establish their public legitimacy
by approving new social benefits. In 1920, the Reichstag made war
victims eligible for welfare payments and began drawing up plans for
youth assistance and a more generous unemployment relief program.

Weimar politicians were extremely wary about imposing new taxes
on the war-battered public to fund these new initiatives, let alone reparation payments abroad. "Lives," argued the conservative Reichstag
member and coal industrialist Hugo Stinnes, "were worth more than
money."[87] So Germany closed its budget gap by pursuing a deliberate
policy of double-digit inflation. Foreign Minister Walther Rathenau
defended the tactic in a June 1922 meeting with the U.S. ambassador
in Berlin, comparing his country's economy to "an army which is completely surrounded, and which to preserve its existence must break
through, however great its losses, so as to get air and a chance at life
for the whole."[88] Ten hours later, Rathenau was murdered by a squad
of right-wing terrorists, one of hundreds of political murders carried
out by an enraged far Right in the aftermath of Versailles.

For a while, the inflationist strategy seemed to work. Though prices
rose fortyfold over the course of 1922, wages generally kept pace,
and—in sharp contrast to the situation in Britain—jobs were not hard
to find. But in November 1922, the German government failed to
make a reparations payment to France, and on January 11, 1923, the
new conservative French prime minister, Raymond Poincaré, ordered
an invasion of the Ruhr Valley. It was a simple profit calculation. Con-

trol of the Ruhr coal mines, he believed, would more than compensate France for the costs of military occupation.

He was right. But France would pay a steep price in the court of public opinion. "I regard the present operations of the French government with violent disapproval," Keynes wrote to Reichsbank chancellor Rudolf Havenstein on January 17. "I think their action is wrong on law, and on morals, and on expediency."[89] Ramsay MacDonald denounced the French occupation as "evil."[90] The swiftness with which British and American diplomats came to side with their recently vanquished enemy over their wartime ally underscored the lasting influence of Keynes' 1919 polemic. Germany had, after all, failed to pay its reparation obligations due under the peace treaty. The fact that world leaders considered the French military campaign an illegitimate act of aggression revealed the fact that few in power outside France believed the reparations arrangement to be just or practical.

With global attitudes sympathetic to its situation and its nationalist political factions whipped into a state of total frenzy, the government in Berlin guaranteed financial support for the popular resistance in the Ruhr. Though not a formal military response, German citizens refused to work in the mines, sabotaged railway cars, and embroiled themselves in the occasional violent altercation with French troops. Roughly 120 citizens were killed during the occupation, and the French forced 147,000 other Germans to leave the valley.

"Hyperinflation," according to conservative economic historian Niall Ferguson, "is always and everywhere a *political* phenomenon,"[91] and the political turmoil of the French occupation sparked a swift and terrible reaction in currency markets. International confidence in the mark collapsed. In January, one U.S. dollar could buy 7,260 German marks. In August, it bought an unfathomable 6 million.[92] By 1924, one prewar gold mark could be exchanged for upward of *one trillion* postwar paper marks. As the money became meaningless, the system of commerce broke down, and unemployment skyrocketed to 20 percent.

The political consequences were still more catastrophic. Dozens were killed in a Communist uprising in Hamburg, as radicals attempted to secede from the state. In Munich, Adolf Hitler and the archnationalist general Erich Ludendorff attempted their infamous Beer Hall Putsch. Though their leader was jailed, the Nazis exploited the anger and despair brought on by the twin hyperinflation and occupation crises to secure a foothold in legitimate German politics, winning thirty-two Reichstag seats and nearly two million votes in the May 1924 election.

The international financial order that had been codified at Versailles was falling apart. The war debts owed to the United States suffered the same ultimate fate as all unpayable debts: They were not paid. Wilson was forced to put a two-year moratorium on repayment in 1919, and in 1923 the Warren Harding administration eased the pressure by extending the payment schedule for more than sixty years to reduce annual payments. Even that limited relief was "bitterly resented in London," as the annual payments remained more expensive than the interest on all the national debt Great Britain had carried in 1913 combined.[93]

The unfolding political crisis in Germany managed to shake the Calvin Coolidge administration from its diplomatic torpor. Coolidge deputized the House of Morgan as the unofficial agent of U.S. foreign policy, and the terms of the plan would make clear the scope of State Department pressure on the bank. Jack Morgan's antipathy toward Germany was known across both continents, and his bank was about to come to Germany's aid. The ensuing project became known as the Dawes Plan, named for Charles Dawes, a Morgan-allied Chicago banker who would be elected the American vice president in the fall. Its chief architects, however, were Morgan partner Thomas Lamont and Owen D. Young, the head of Morgan vassals General Electric and Radio Corporation of America.

The Dawes Plan was ambitious. It aimed to ease the weight of German reparations, get France out of the Ruhr, and restart European trade, which had ground to a halt during the German hyperinflation. It would pursue those goals with a very limited set of tools. Coolidge insisted that Dawes not discuss war debts owed to the United States, while France demanded that Germany's total reparations burden be maintained. The Morgan men thus decided to reduce Germany's annual reparations payments by extending the period over which it would pay by several decades. Instead of fixing the annual payment amount based on some estimate of Germany's "capacity to pay," it would index reparations to the tax burden borne by the British and French. This was a clever rhetorical excuse to justify a new round of diplomacy, but it relied on circular reasoning. The British and French based their tax rates in part on the amount of money they owed to the United States and the amount they could expect to receive in reparations. The tax burden was therefore not a static, independent phenomenon. Lamont, Young, and Dawes were setting reparations based on a figure that depended on whatever amount was paid in reparations. But the gambit was accompanied by other attractive items for both Germany and France. J.P. Morgan arranged a $200 million loan that would allow Germany to meet its new obligations and get its commerce moving again. France would withdraw from the Ruhr in exchange for a $100 million loan of its own. It was a start.

The drafters of the plan were terrified of a public denunciation from Keynes, who was now perhaps the most powerful public intellectual in the world. They leaked him a copy before the terms were made public. "Everyone in France is saying—What will Keynes say?'" wrote Josiah Stamp, a British official on the committee in a letter to Keynes. "So go easy on the vials of your wrath at present."[94]

Despite reservations, Keynes complied in the name of progress. "The report is the finest contribution hitherto to this impossible problem," he wrote in *The Nation and Athenaeum* in April 1924. "Though the language seems at times the language of a sane man who, finding himself in a madhouse, must accommodate himself to the inmates, it never loses its sanity. Though it compromises with the impossible and even contemplates the impossible, it never prescribes the impossible. This façade and these designs may never be realised in an edifice raised up in the light of day. But it is an honourable document and opens a new chapter."[95]

With Keynes' blessing secured, the Allies convened a conference in

London to formally revise the Treaty of Versailles to implement the deal. But the French government seemed even less enthusiastic about the Dawes proposal than Keynes did. According to MacDonald's diary from the conference, French diplomats were "obsessed with "will-o-the-wisps in armed power, tricky diplomacy," and "stupid economics."[96] Talks dragged on for weeks, but France eventually relented. The $100 million loan from Morgan would provide France with immediate funds to attend to its own still pressing reconstruction needs, which had always been the most persuasive justification for heavy German reparations.

The Dawes Plan was strong enough to buy Europe time to work out a better solution. It was forced to function, however, as the foundation of European and transatlantic trade. The United States, through J.P. Morgan, loaned money to Germany, which turned it over to France and Great Britain in the form of reparations, which sent it back to the United States in payments on war debts, enabling the cycle to begin again. It was a fragile system, but it worked—as long as Germany could keep getting foreign loans.

"Nothing real passes—no one is a penny the worse. The engravers' dies, the printers' formes are busier. But no one eats less, no one works more," Keynes wrote. "The sums written on paper mount up, of course, at compound interest. . . . How long can the game go on? The answer lies with the American investor."[97]

It was essentially a delayed, expensive caricature of the system Keynes had urged at Paris. American capital was at last reluctantly being deployed to rebuild the continent. But in this convoluted version, governments downplayed their involvement and worked through strange diplomatic channels with agents of private finance. As it would time and again over the coming decades, the world had at last hit upon a distorted rendition of a Keynesian solution after succumbing to the catastrophe it had been designed to prevent.

SIX

◇

PROLEGOMENA TO A
NEW SOCIALISM

I F THE GREAT WAR had ended the political dominance of a fading
European nobility, nobody told Queen Marie of Romania. A grand-
daughter of both Queen Victoria and Tsar Alexander II, cousin to
Kaiser Wilhelm and King George V, she had been married off to
Prince Ferdinand when she was just seventeen. Though her husband
was ten years her senior, it was Marie who wielded real power in the
Romanian court, pushing her adopted homeland to the Allied cause
during the war and personally securing a vast expansion of Romanian
territory at the peace conference. Considered a great beauty all over
Europe, she was prone to extravagance, adorning herself with long
strings of pearls that were as iconic in the early twentieth century as
the mustache on Charlie Chaplin's tramp. Once, when seen on the
streets of Paris, her mere presence so impassioned a crowd of admirers
that they swarmed her car and lifted it into the air.[1]

When she traveled to London, Marie was feted in the most rarefied
social circles. On May 27, 1924, the British power elite attended a lavish dinner party in her honor. David Lloyd George and the Conservative leader, Stanley Baldwin, were there, along with King Alfonso XIII
of Spain and the archbishop of Canterbury, resplendent in his formal
violet robes. John Maynard Keynes donned his Order of the Bath

medallion and was seated two places down from Lloyd George. Having lost the backing of the Conservatives in 1922, Lloyd George was now making very public attempts at reconciliation with his former Liberal rivals. At dinner, he even praised the renegade economist who had caused him so many headaches during the war. "I approve Keynes, because, whether he is right or wrong, he is always dealing with realities." Baldwin, confident that Keynes would never convert to the Conservative cause, was less gracious, gently mocking Keynes' royal decoration: "You look such good dog with the collar round your neck."[2]

Keynes wrote two breathless letters to Lydia detailing the evening's decadent intrigue. "It was a terrific party," he gushed. "Oh what a day!"[3] King Alfonso had "said that of everyone I was the person in London he wanted most to speak with, that he read my books with greatest care."[4]

By 1924, Keynes was firmly embedded in the most exclusive echelons of European society, relishing the attentions of politicians and international royalty. But he was embarrassed when Lydia relayed such events to friends. "To *you* I can make boasting and not fear to be misunderstood—it is an internal boasting," he scolded his lover. "But to others it is not so well."[5] The thrill of elite acceptance was not a Bloomsbury value—at least, not officially.

Bloomsbury had always walked a fine line between the celebration of aristocratic habits and participation in the aristocracy itself. Its members insisted that their love of art, literature, and learning was not merely an expression of class privilege but a deep appreciation for truth and beauty. Keynes drew that distinction himself over years of personal correspondence, essay drafts, and speeches on "love of money" and "the curse of Midas"—the mythical king whose touch turned everything to gold. The tragedy of Midas was his inability to actually enjoy the things wealth was supposed to confer. Money existed to be spent on finer things: the pursuit of Apostolic "good states of mind." From his undergraduate days to his deathbed, Keynes believed that these were not exclusive goods. One man living a good life did not detract from another's ability to live well any more than one person's enjoyment of a painting would ruin another's ability to appreciate it.

That was not the way most members of the elite deployed their wealth. They acquired paintings like awards and read the right books, if they read them, to broadcast their cultural superiority. Money was a tool to enforce distinctions of social rank—something that could help you gain entrance, say, to a party with the queen of Romania. And the value of that, as Virginia Woolf wrote in a review of Marie's 1934 biography, was exclusivity for its own sake. "Royalty is no longer quite royal," Woolf wrote, when it has "sauntered out into the street."[6]

There is an unresolved tension running throughout Keynes' work between his desire to democratize the trappings of ruling-class life and his own reverence for that same ruling class. "The great trouble with Keynes was that he was an idealist," his colleague and collaborator Joan Robinson once wrote.[7] His faith that "an intelligent theory would prevail over a stupid one"[8] was hard to square with a world in which "vested interests" often rejected reforms that carried broad benefits for all, preferring even a dysfunctional status quo as long as it maintained their place at the top of the social pecking order.

But that tension made Keynes a politically potent character. As European royalty discovered Keynes, so, too, did leaders of the socialist Left, who recognized that his intellectual aura carried the power to legitimize some egalitarian ideas among an influential audience—if not among actual members of the nobility, then perhaps among Treasury officials and members of Parliament.

Keynes and the Left had shown little interest in each other before the publication of *The Economic Consequences of the Peace*. His partisan commitments fell to the Liberals rather than Labour, and his economic loyalties were thoroughly mainstream, as he championed free trade and the gold standard. During the war, his closest friends had understood him to be a symbol of the English political establishment: Cambridge traditionalism and the financial power of Treasury combined in a single self-important persona. But his famous book had presented a different figure to the world: a man of peace, unafraid to speak hard truths to the same powers that were targeted by socialists. Over the second half of the 1920s, Keynes became one of the most important figures in British left-wing politics—even as his own lifestyle became increasingly divorced from the everyday concerns of working people.

On November 12, 1925, the British journalist Henry Noel Brailsford sent Keynes a copy of his latest book, *Socialism for Today*. As a member of a Carnegie Endowment for International Peace commission, Brailsford had documented unspeakable horrors perpetrated by various nationalist sects during the Balkan wars of 1913.[9] Now a committed labor activist, he was trying to work out a policy agenda for a workers' party, seeking input on imaginative uses for the state—which socialists had historically viewed as a tool of the rich—to instead transfer wealth and power from the well-off to the poorly paid. In a remarkable response written on December 3, Keynes offered two brief paragraphs that contain a sprawling universe of high theory:

Dear Mr. Brailsford,

Very many thanks for sending me your book. I have read it, as I do everything you write, with a good deal of pleasure. Partly I agree with it, but partly I am still confused in my own mind. At present I am busy on a technical treatise about the theory of money and credit. Once I am through with this I want to give myself up to getting quite clear in my own mind as to where I stand in relation to the ideal future of society. At present, my feeling is that this has to be attacked in the first instance from the ethical side rather than from the standpoint of technical economic efficiency. What we need is a form of society which shall be ethically tolerable and economically not intolerable.

My opinions on a good many matters are shifting, but I do not yet clearly see where I am being led to. When it comes to politics, I hate trade unions.

Yours sincerely,

JMK[10]

To find merit in a socialist policy agenda while dismissing the underlying source of socialist power—trade unions—is a classic distillation of Keynes' politics. We also get a snapshot of Keynes' view of economics in the hierarchy of intellectual pursuits. Ethics—by which Keynes meant the elements that made up a good life—were a more important consideration for public policy than economics, the field that had made Keynes famous. The remains of his early reverence for Edmund Burke is evident in the note's distinct modesty of ambition. Even when imagining the "ideal future of society," Keynes could only envision striking a balance between what was "tolerable" and what was "not intolerable."

Keynes had in truth already been working on his political theory project for some time. In the archives of King's College at Cambridge, there is a single page of notes from June 8, 1924, penciled in Keynes' spidery handwriting. Though he would eventually discard the working title of this outline in favor of something more accessible, the original captures the sense of innovation and excitement he felt about his initiative. He was forging a new set of philosophical foundations for twentieth-century society. He announced the program across the top of the page: "Prolegomena to a New Socialism—The Origins and End of Laissez-Faire."

Keynes had an ambiguous relationship with the word *socialism.* Sometimes he deployed it as an epithet; in other moods, he used it to describe a progressive ideal. As he told readers of *The Nation and Athenaeum* in 1923, " 'socialism,' whatever that may mean . . . is merely a word, only useful so long as it cloaks decently the nakedness of Labour policy"[11]—more a label than a doctrine or set of principles. In *The End of Laissez-Faire*—as Keynes titled the final version of his "Prolegomena"—he attempted to sketch a critique of the conventional philosophical wisdom and chart a path forward. He agreed with the socialists that the prevailing order had failed. It was time to experiment with new forms of political organization. But his critique differed markedly from the standard Marxist analysis. Marx saw capitalism as an inevitable historical phase building toward an equally inevitable final crisis. Keynes understood laissez-faire capitalism as a historical

accident, which had wrongly left the most important elements of social management without a manager. It was time for capitalism not to
be overthrown but to be "wisely managed." Exactly how, he wasn't
quite sure. "Our problem," he wrote, "is to work out a social organization which shall be as efficient as possible without offending our no-
tions of a satisfactory way of life"—language that echoes his letter to
Brailsford.[12]

The doctrine of laissez-faire, he argued, had captured the public
imagination by finding a harmonious tone between several otherwise
discordant intellectual traditions. It took the conservative defense of
individual property rights developed by Burke, John Locke, and David
Hume, and melded it with the "democratic egalitarianism" of Jean-
Jacques Rousseau and the "utilitarian socialism" of Jeremy Bentham.
At the same time, it satisfied the logic of both Social Darwinism
(competition would ensure the advancement of the best and strongest) and variants of Christian theology in which God guided human
affairs according to a divine plan (winners were chosen by God).

Keynes rejected those last two doctrines as inhumane and simply
wrong. But the deeper point he wanted to make was about conservatism and socialism. Burke and Hume were fathers of modern conservatism, while Rousseau had bequeathed the French Revolution and
heavily influenced the socialist tradition. Burke had sought to protect
the property of the wealthy—that is, to defend economic inequality.
Rousseau had viewed equality as both the origin of humanity and its
ultimate ideal, one that could be achieved not via commercial exchange but through "the General Will" of a democracy.[13] Yet devotees
of both thinkers could celebrate laissez-faire if defending the property
rights of the wealthy resulted, through the magic of commerce, in a
more equal division of power and wealth than governments could secure through more ambitious state planning.

Quite by accident, Keynes argued, laissez-faire had become a wildly
popular doctrine because it reconciled otherwise incompatible ideas.
But if laissez-faire didn't deliver the goods—if it didn't generate
broadly shared prosperity—then the ideological coalition it bound together would become unstable. Laissez-faire had seemed to work in

the seventeenth and eighteenth centuries, Keynes argued, because the corrupt favoritism of European monarchs had been so dysfunctional that stripping them of economic authority had been an improvement. But with monarchs out of the way, society now faced problems that could not be solved by individuals acting alone and uncoordinated in a market. "Many of the greatest economic evils of our time are the fruits of risk, uncertainty, and ignorance. It is because particular individuals, fortunate in situation or in abilities, are able to take advantage of uncertainty and ignorance, and also because for the same reason big business is often a lottery, that great inequalities of wealth come about; and these same factors are also the cause of the unemployment of labour, or the disappointment of reasonable business expectations, and of the impairment of efficiency and production. Yet the cure lies outside the operations of individuals; it may even be to the interest of individuals to aggravate the disease."[14]

Keynes believed it was now only a matter of time before other ideas supplanted laissez-faire. People were not attached to laissez-faire because it worked; it had simply hardened into an unthinking dogma. "To suggest social action for the public good to the City of London is like discussing the *Origin of Species* with a bishop sixty years ago. The first reaction is not intellectual, but moral. An orthodoxy is in question, and the more persuasive the arguments, the graver the offence."[15]

By the time he presented *The End of Laissez-Faire* to a lecture audience at Oxford in November 1924, British unemployment had been in double digits for nearly five consecutive years. Instead of creating equality and harmony, laissez-faire had generated vast inequality and social unrest, so much of each that all the splendid things liberal individualism was supposed to foster—fresh thinking, great art, fine wine, exciting conversation—were now threatened by social instability. It was time to move on.

"It is *not* true that individuals possess a prescriptive 'natural liberty' in their economic activities," Keynes wrote. "There is *no* 'compact' conferring perpetual rights on those who Have or on those who Acquire. The world is *not* so governed from above that private and social interests always coincide. It is not a correct deduction from the principles of economics that enlightened self-interest always operates in the public interest."[16]

In *A Tract on Monetary Reform,* Keynes had argued that state regulation of the price level would cure the malaise of the postwar economy. At the time, he had believed that the persistent unemployment in Great Britain was the result of capitalism being denied one of its basic building blocks: stable prices. There was nothing wrong, he had believed, with the general idea that a free market would reach a prosperous equilibrium for all.

Now, only a few years later, he believed the problem with the British economy was more fundamental. His new agenda for the state, however, was remarkably vague: "The important thing for government is not to do things which individuals are doing already, and to do them a little better or a little worse; but to do those things which at present are not done at all."[17] Keynes envisioned "semi-autonomous corporations" and "semi-autonomous bodies within the State" taking the place of a competitive marketplace in key areas where the private sector couldn't fulfill some basic social need.[18] The Bank of England, for instance, was technically a private enterprise, but it functioned for all intents and purposes as a wing of the British government. The question of whether the government would need to formally nationalize major industries like the coal business or the railroads was, Keynes insisted, a diversion prompted only by dogmatic fealty to an outdated nineteenth-century vision of "State Socialism." "One of the most interesting and unnoticed developments of recent decades," he wrote, "has been the tendency of big enterprise to socialise itself"[19] by responding to public need rather than private profit.

This was an excessively optimistic view of big business, inspired by Keynes' rosy view of prewar imperial capitalism. But the vision of a "semi-socialised" arena of activity would indeed become central to the modern nation-state over the coming decades, as governments took a more aggressive role in regulating different avenues of commerce, from electrical utilities to banks to airlines. The independent agencies created under Franklin Delano Roosevelt's New Deal—from the Tennessee Valley Authority to the Federal Deposit Insurance

Corporation—were assigned duties that the private sector in the 1930s either would not or could not shoulder. *The End of Laissez-Faire* is too imprecise to be called a blueprint for the New Deal; Keynes simply didn't think of rural electrification or deposit insurance in 1924. But it did provide a philosophical grounding for what was to come.

The moral and ethical commitments Keynes expressed in *The End of Laissez-Faire* ultimately share much more with the "democratic egalitarianism" of Rousseau than the property rights advocacy of his undergraduate hero, Burke. "I criticize doctrinaire State Socialism, not because it seeks to engage men's altruistic impulses in the service of society, or because it departs from *laissez-faire,* or because it takes away from man's natural liberty to make a million, or because it has courage for bold experiments. All these things I applaud. I criticise it because it misses the significance of what is actually happening."[20]

Yet Keynes still found room to quote Burke approvingly. Like Burke, he believed that the question of "what the State ought to take upon itself to direct by the public wisdom, and what it ought to leave, with as little interference as possible, to individual exertion" would turn on the empirical economic facts in society: how the world actually worked and what actually produced prosperity, rather than abstract principles about rights and obligations.[21] In the more productive economic world of the 1920s, there was greater room for more egalitarian state economic management than Burke had been able to imagine in the eighteenth century.[22]

This was the remarkable synthesis Keynes tried to formulate throughout his career: how to make the practical, risk-averse, antirevolutionary conservatism of Burke fit the radical democratic ideals advanced by Rousseau. He was, in short, attempting to unify two traditions of political theory that philosophers had understood to be polar opposites ever since the French Revolution.

It was a difficult task, beyond Keynes' abilities in the mid-1920s. He had demonstrated that laissez-faire was an economic theory incapable of bringing together Burkean conservatism and Rousseau's egalitarianism. He would spend the rest of his life working out an economic theory that could.

On August 4, 1925, John Maynard Keynes married Lydia Lopokova in a simple ceremony at the St. Pancras Registry Office in central London. He was forty-two years old, his bride a few months shy of thirty-three. They had been living together for two years and finally wedded after a protracted international legal ordeal to annul her prior marriage to Randolfo Barocchi. Lydia was only slightly past the apex of her dancing career; the couple were international celebrities, and photographs of the event were splashed across newspapers from Newcastle in northern England as far abroad as Burma.[23] "The marriage of the most brilliant of English economists with the most popular of Russian dancers makes a delightful symbol of the mutual dependence upon each other of art and science," mused *Vogue*.[24] Outside the courthouse, a throng of enthusiastic admirers had gathered, and Maynard tried to calm the chaotic scene to give the newspaper photographers a chance to snap their images, but the crowd soon became overpowering. When a crazed stranger threw confetti in Lydia's face and then attempted to stuff a bag down her wedding suit, Maynard steered her away into a taxi back to Gordon Square.[25]

Like most weddings, it was a rearrangement of priorities. The tension between Bloomsbury and Lydia had never fully abated, and Maynard had planted his flag for love. Duncan Grant was his only friend to attend the ceremony. Keynes had atoned for his role in the war with *The Economic Consequences of the Peace*, but the "worldliness" of his soul, as Virginia Woolf described it, appeared to be incurable. As the crowd of photographers at the otherwise spartan event attested, his marriage to a celebrity ballerina was a full embrace of a life in the public eye, and those close to him took note of a change in his demeanor. Both his Cambridge pupil Richard Kahn and Mary Paley, the widow of his first economics teacher, Alfred Marshall, declared the marriage "the best thing that Maynard ever did." Keynes, according to Kahn, "became far less a member of the Bloomsbury intelligentsia, and far more devoted to serious creative work."[26]

His old friends rebelled against their demotion with public tantrums and private gossip. Lytton, Virginia, and Vanessa wrote letters complaining of the meager hospitality at the Keynes household. The birds they cooked were too small, and there was never enough wine. But though they served little to their friends, Virginia noted, Maynard himself was getting "portentious," the bulk of his person expanding with his personal fortune.

Art, once a glue that had bound the group together, could now sow division. Vanessa and Maynard both claimed ownership of a particular painting by Duncan—a dispute that carried deep emotional significance, given the romantic history involved. Functionally, the matter was mooted by the fact that Duncan and Vanessa kept a room at Maynard's home at 46 Gordon Square, but when they decided to move out their belongings, Vanessa planned to quietly abscond with the painting. She discovered to her frustration that Maynard had anticipated the caper and screwed the artwork firmly into the wall of his bathroom. "Determined not to be outwitted," the "furious" Vanessa feigned defeat and invited Maynard down to Charleston Farmhouse for a weekend getaway. While he was on his way, she hurried up to Gordon Square, armed with a spare key to number 46 and a screwdriver. She stole the painting and returned to Charleston without saying a word of her covert operation.[27]

All of this backbiting occurred while Keynes was financially supporting most of the set either directly or indirectly. In addition to running *The Nation and Athenaeum*—where Leonard Woolf remained employed and Virginia, Clive Bell, Bunny Garnett, E. M. Forster, and even Duncan were being published—he had been managing some of his friends' personal investments. In 1923 alone, he secured hundreds of pounds' worth of profit for Vanessa and Duncan by speculating on lead prices.[28] He had negotiated Lytton's American publishing deal for his book *Queen Victoria* and protected the deal against a subsequent plunge in the value of the dollar, which Lytton considered an act of "extreme cleverness and unexpected benevolence."[29] There were, it appeared, limits to the credibility money could buy in Bloomsbury—not that anyone thought to return the checks. In private letters after the wedding, Virginia began badmouthing her own husband's paper, encouraging friends to cancel their subscriptions. Leonard did not quit.

In time, Keynes' friends adjusted to the new social equilibrium. The marriage was not a complete break with the past. The Keyneses leased a farmhouse in Tilton near Charleston Farmhouse and the Woolfs' country retreat, and the couples continued to host each other into the 1940s (though Vanessa initially considered moving to escape the intolerable proximity of "the Tiltonians"). Virginia and Leonard celebrated Christmas with the Keyneses every year, a tradition they honored until Virginia's death. Jack Sheppard, the classicist with whom Keynes had quarreled about conscientious objectors during the war, championed Lydia's wit and energy early on. Duncan—another creative spirit whose intellect Bloomsbury routinely underrated—defended Lydia against attacks on her intelligence.

Leonard was particularly close to Lydia. He had spent decades enduring casual anti-Semitic barbs from his friends and even his own wife. Bloomsbury did in fact accept Leonard as one of its own, but members of the set also believed their high-mindedness excused the occasional joke about Jewish accents or Jewish clothes.[30] Simultaneously a pillar of their community and a misfit, Leonard quickly reached an understanding with the Russian immigrant Lydia—an irony, given that Lydia, despite her appreciation for Leonard, was no more self-conscious about the anti-Semitic current in her sense of humor than was her husband or his friends.[31]

As Bloomsbury adapted, the Tiltonians busied themselves with new friends. H. G. Wells, George Bernard Shaw, and the Fabian Socialists Beatrice and Sidney Webb became frequent guests at their country house and considered Lydia a charming intellectual peer. Though Charleston Farmhouse was just down the road, Lydia and Maynard had created their own social center of gravity. "It dawns on me that they are no more anxious to see us than we to see them," Vanessa acknowledged to Duncan in 1926.[32]

Lydia grew on Bloomsbury with time (and distance). The old friends, especially Virginia, would come to regret the animosity they directed toward her. As Keynes spent more of his time at Cambridge, Vanessa, Duncan, and Lytton traveled up to visit him, staying overnight for concerts and attending dinners and other celebrations. Even in the months immediately following the wedding there were moments of tenderness. Though Virginia was often critical of Maynard in her letters—particularly when corresponding with her sister—her diary entries are more sympathetic.

> Maynard & Lydia came here yesterday—M. in Tolstoi's blouse & Russian cap of black astrachan—A fair sight, both of them, to meet on the high road! An immense good will & vigour pervades him. She hums in his wake, the great mans wife. But though one could carp, one can also find them very good company, & my heart, in this autumn of my age, slightly warms to him, whom I've known all these years.[33]

After their wedding, Maynard took Lydia on a long, luxurious honeymoon by train to Leningrad, where they celebrated their new life together with Lydia's mother, Karlusha, and two of her siblings, Fedor and Evgenia. Travel to and from Russia was still heavily restricted by the Soviet government, and Keynes had secured passage for the two of them by accepting an invitation to speak at a conference in Moscow. Maynard had never met Lydia's family. Lydia herself had not returned to Russia since leaving as a teenager. In the intervening fifteen years, her father had died young, his body giving out after years of heavy drinking. Her mother still kept Lydia's childhood keepsakes around the house and had struggled emotionally to "live so far away from my child" for so long. But the reunion was a joyous occasion. The whole family approved of the match, and Karlusha urged Lydia "to be a good woman" to her prestigious new husband.[34]

The imperial St. Petersburg of Lydia's youth was now Soviet Leningrad, but she had missed some of the most disruptive years of
hunger and deprivation and was surprised by how much of the city
remained as she remembered—the same cakes at a favorite restaurant,
the ballet still an institution of national pride. The most troubling
changes were subtle things—differences of attitudes and atmosphere.

Keynes found himself at once repulsed and rejuvenated by Russia.
He recorded his impressions of the Soviet project in a series of essays
for *The Nation and Athenaeum*, which were reprinted as a pamphlet for
Leonard and Virginia's press.[35] He was enthralled by the excitement
of a new social experiment but bemoaned "the mood of oppression"[36]
filled with "cruelty and stupidity."[37] Whatever its economic methods,
the way of life the Soviet government was fostering was just no fun:

> Comfort and habits let us be ready to forgo, but I am not ready for
> a creed which does not care how much it destroys the liberty and
> security of daily life, which uses deliberately the weapons of perse-
> cution, destruction, and international strife. How can I admire a
> policy which finds a characteristic expression in spending millions
> to suborn spies in every family and group at home, and to stir up
> trouble abroad? . . . How can I accept a doctrine which sets up as
> its bible, above and beyond criticism, an obsolete economic text-
> book which I know to be not only scientifically erroneous but
> without interest or application for the modern world? How can I
> adopt a creed which, preferring the mud to the fish, exalts the
> boorish proletariat above the bourgeois and the intelligentsia who,
> with whatever faults, are the quality in life and surely carry the
> seeds of all human advancement?[38]

Clearly, Vanessa and Virginia were not the only snobs in Bloomsbury. But the experience of a few weeks under a different economic
regime gave him a new perspective on a British system he had already
come to see as moribund and outdated. If he had lived in Russia,
Keynes wrote, "I should detest the actions of the new tyrants not less
than those of the old. But I should feel that my eyes were turned to-

wards, and no longer away from, the possibilities of things."[39] At least the Soviets were trying something original.

Great Britain, he was now sure, was not just enduring the material suffering of mass unemployment; there was a sickness in his country's soul. Over the past half century, the British public had largely abandoned Christianity as its guiding moral doctrine. Church attendance was down; atheism was no longer considered shocking or perverse. The British had filled the void with a godless, capitalist "love of money" that cultivated no sense of shared responsibility or community, and provided no lasting satisfaction. Only a "continuing crescendo" of extravagance on extravagance could distract his countrymen from the emotional emptiness that surrounded them.[40] "We used to believe that modern capitalism was capable, not merely of maintaining the existing standards of life, but of leading us gradually into an economic paradise where we should be comparatively free from economic cares. Now we doubt whether the business man is leading us to a destination far better than our present place. Regarded as a means he is tolerable; regarded as an end he is not so satisfactory."[41] Keynes could not stomach the Soviet experiment. But neither could he tolerate the cultural stagnation he found when he returned to Britain. His country was addicted to an era that had ended a dozen years earlier, incapable of embracing the present.

Keynes was even beginning to question the partisan loyalties that had been the bedrock of his political identity since childhood. It was time to "invent new wisdom for a new age," to be "troublesome, dangerous, disobedient to them that begat us"[42]—and this was not the disposition of the Liberal Party, which was preaching the same doctrine it had advanced in 1906: free trade and a modest progressive income tax to fund old-age pensions and unemployment benefits. The Liberals were so attached to their own party dogma that they cheered a return to the gold standard, a decision that allied them with the Conservatives.

The Labour Party's commitment to the working class, Keynes believed, made it too susceptible to demagoguery, too narrow in its conception of righteousness, and too eager to tear down the nation's cultural achievements. "I can be influenced by what seems to me to be justice and good sense; but the *class* war will find me on the side of the educated *bourgeoisie.*"[43] But Labour possessed an "unselfish and enthusiastic spirit." "The political problem of mankind is to combine three things: economic efficiency, social justice, and individual liberty," Keynes wrote. "The second ingredient is the best possession of the great party of the proletariat."[44] Those were not the words of a man trying to stake out intellectual territory in the political center; he wanted to reshape liberalism into a more aggressive, more effective vehicle for the moral goals of Labour. "The republic of my imagination lies on the extreme left of celestial space,"[45] Keynes told readers of *The Nation and Athenaeum.* "The Liberal Party should be not less progressive than Labour, not less open to new ideas, not behindhand in constructing the new world."[46]

Keynes was not the only great man in Great Britain who was rethinking his political allegiances. With the Liberals wiped out in the 1924 election, Winston Churchill shamelessly switched parties to land a post as chancellor of the Exchequer in the new Conservative cabinet under Prime Minister Stanley Baldwin. By 1925, Britain had been functionally off the gold standard for a decade, and the clamor within the City of London to return had reached a fever pitch. Well over a million men had been unemployed across the country for the entire period since the war, with the unemployment level dipping below 10 percent for just five months in 1924, when it had dropped only as low as 9.3 percent. This was a new kind of crisis for most working people in Britain. The country had known poverty and severe economic inequality before the war, but it had not seen double-digit unemployment since 1887, and even then, the crisis had lasted just three years. Britain was now entering its sixth year of economic depression.[47] British exports were still 25 percent below their prewar levels—a devastating gap for the nation most dependent on international trade of all the world's major economies.[48] To many, it seemed that the hard times were a result of Britain's departure from the monetary good sense of the gold standard. Bringing it back would resurrect the days of high profits, high employment, and high imperial glory.

Keynes was not exactly enthusiastic about that view. "Those who think that a return to the gold standard means a return to these conditions are fools and blind," he wrote in *The Nation and Athenaeum*.[49]

Much of his frustration with political ideology and cultural stagnation was connected to his impotence on British monetary affairs. Ever since the publication of *A Tract on Monetary Reform*, he had been calling for the Bank of England to stabilize the price level in the name of predictable commerce and social stability. These entreaties had been ignored. Since the inflationary spike of 1920, the Bank of England had steadily deflated the value of the pound by almost 30 percent. By raising interest rates, the Bank forced down domestic prices, making the pound more valuable relative to foreign currencies in a quest to restore the exchange rates that had prevailed in 1913.

Lower wages were in a very real sense the point of deflationary policy; the idea was to bring down the price of everything, including labor. Under classical economic theory, this cost cutting did not have to result in mass layoffs. "Unemployment is a problem of wages, not of work," Keynes' Austrian contemporary Ludwig von Mises wrote in 1927.[50] As high interest rates imposed higher costs of credit on employers—or reduced demand for their goods—companies could reduce labor costs by cutting pay all around. Lower wages wouldn't really hurt workers, the thinking went, because with the price of goods falling, workers wouldn't need as much money as they had before. Based on this reasoning, Conservatives, bankers, and even Liberal politicians blamed the British jobs crisis on trade unions. People had to be laid off, these critics insisted, because companies had signed collective bargaining contracts that required them to keep wages artificially high. Since wages couldn't be lowered, firms had no other choice but to fire people to bring down their costs. Firms that couldn't fire people had to close. Keynes lampooned what he called the "orthodox" explanation: "Blame it on the working man for working too little and getting too much."[51]

All of that might make sense on paper, Keynes argued, but it was totally divorced from what happened in the real world. "Deflation does not reduce wages 'automatically,'" he observed in the *Evening Standard*. "It reduces them by causing unemployment."[52] Keynes had little enthusiasm for unions, but by 1925 he believed that steep deflation could never be accomplished without mass layoffs unless the government became deeply involved in managing the affairs of the business world. It was not only collective bargaining that stood in the way of uniform wage reductions; it was human psychology. No sane worker negotiating with his boss would accept a pay cut in the name of broader social welfare without some guarantee that other workers would take the same deal. He could easily find himself shortchanged for nothing. "Those who are attacked first are faced with a depression of their standard of life, because the cost of living will not fall until all the others have been successfully attacked too," Keynes wrote. "Nor can the classes, which are first subjected to a reduction of money wages, be guaranteed that this will be compensated later by a corresponding fall in the cost of living, and will not accrue to the benefit of some other class. Therefore they are bound to resist so long as they can; and it must be a war, until those who are economically weakest are beaten to the ground."[53] Contrary to the conventional wisdom, then, it was not the departure from gold that was causing Great Britain's economic malaise, it was the country's enthusiasm to return to gold at the exchange rates that had prevailed before the war.

The gold problem was not simply a question of unemployment but of international power. Before the war, Great Britain had overseen the most respected financial system on the planet. But now that status belonged to the United States. And thanks to the enormous war debts the Allies still owed, conditions were already in place for gold to keep flowing from Europe to America to meet those obligations. Its vast gold reserves gave the United States enormous freedom of action in the international economy; whatever it decided to do, it would be almost impossible for it to run out of gold. If Britain returned to the gold standard, locking in its exchange rates with its trading partners, it would effectively be relegated to second-class status in the international financial order, forced to comply with whatever actions the U.S.

Federal Reserve demanded. If America deflated its currency, Britain would have to deflate as well. If the United States inflated, Britain would have to follow suit.

"Are you quite sure that the rigid linking up of the London and New York money markets is all honey?" Keynes wrote to Charles Addis. "It means that we should become, without any power of helping ourselves, the victim of every inflationary boom that America may indulge in."[54]

It was a lonely crusade. Almost nobody, it seemed, wanted to hear Keynes tell them that a return to 1913 was not only impossible but foolish. At the Treasury, Sir John Bradbury said that a return to gold would make the economy "knaveproof," revive British exports, and protect the economy from the "fool's paradise of false prosperity" in an inflationary boom.[55] The leaders of every major bank in London but one continued to believe that restoring the gold standard at the 1913 exchange rate of $4.86 to the pound was the most important economic policy Great Britain could pursue. As Churchill put it in a speech to Parliament: "A return to an effective gold standard has long been the settled and declared policy of this country. Every Expert Conference since the War—Brussels, Genoa—every expert Committee in this country, has urged the principle of a return to the gold standard. No responsible authority has advocated any other policy. No British Government—and every party has held office—no political party, no previous holder of the Office of Chancellor of the Exchequer has challenged, or so far as I am aware is now challenging, the principle of a reversion to the gold standard in international affairs at the earliest possible moment."[56]

Keynes' prowess as an economic theorist and political commentator, however, would at least give him a seat at the table to make his case. As deflation steadily pushed the pound closer to $4.86, Churchill invited Keynes to dinner to discuss whether Britain should now return to gold and make the exchange rate permanent. Keynes was joined by his old Treasury boss Reginald McKenna, who was now the chairman of Midland Bank and one of Keynes' only intellectual allies in the London financial scene. Sir John Bradbury argued against them, and by the end of the evening, even McKenna conceded that Churchill had no political alternative, given the force of public opinion: "There is no escape; you have got to go back. But it will be hell."[57]

On April 28, 1925, Churchill announced that the monetary embarrassments of the Great War had at last been erased. Great Britain was back on the gold standard, with the pound fixed at its prewar level of $4.86. Newspaper headlines celebrated a new era of international stability and cooperation.

Disaster ensued almost immediately. The problem was not just gold but the $4.86 exchange rate. Even after years of grinding deflation, the pound was still only trading at about $4.40 on the eve of the return to gold, a difference of more than 10 percent. By overvaluing the pound at $4.86, Great Britain had increased the dollar price of its exports to the United States by more than 10 percent. This caused the U.S. demand for British goods—particularly coal—to collapse, as American buyers turned to cheaper domestic alternatives. In response, British mine owners demanded steep wage cuts for miners to make up for their new price disadvantage against American coal. Mine workers and trade unions rejected those demands, and tensions escalated until Prime Minister Baldwin agreed to subsidize wages at current levels to paper over the dispute.

Keynes' class sympathies may not have been proletarian, but stupidity transcended class. He sided with the workers. "Why should coal miners suffer a lower standard of life than other classes of labour?" he wrote in *The Nation and Athenaeum*. "They may be lazy, good-for-nothing fellows who do not work so hard or so long as they should. But is there any evidence that they are more lazy or more good-for-nothing than other people? On grounds of social justice no case can be made out for reducing the wages of the miners. They are the victims of the economic juggernaut. They represent in the flesh the 'fundamental adjustments' engineered by the Treasury and the Bank of England to satisfy the impatience of the City fathers to bridge the 'moderate gap' between $4.40 and $4.86."[58]

When the mine subsidy expired in May 1926, all hell broke loose. Mine owners locked workers out of their jobs in an effort to force concessions on the union contract. In response, British labor unions organized a general strike of all workers, bringing the whole of British industry to a standstill. Labor leaders didn't like their odds in a direct standoff with the government and had tried to prevent the strike, but the passions unleashed by the Tory administration's decision to side with employers could not be controlled. The government called in the military to secure food shipments.

This was more than a clash over wages. When railwaymen and dockworkers, electricians, and gas and chemical employees declared support for the beleaguered coal miners, they were making a statement about British identity and citizenship. The government had prioritized the interests of the City in setting economic policy, making industrial workers into collateral damage for the stronger pound. That was no way to treat citizens of a civilized democracy.

Baldwin recognized the symbolic nature of the dispute immediately and began printing a propaganda outlet edited by Churchill called *The British Gazette*. In its pages, Baldwin declared the Tory government the champion of the Magna Carta and rule of law. "Constitutional Government is being attacked," he wrote. "The laws are in your keeping. You have made Parliament their guardian. The General Strike is a challenge to Parliament and is the road to anarchy and ruin."[59]

Keynes abhorred the government's military crackdown and called for further negotiations to resolve the dispute without ramming a steep wage cut down the throats of the mine workers. Keynes and Leonard Woolf fought about whether workers would be best served by pro-worker articles or a suspension of operations at *The Nation and Athenaeum*. Anyone who sympathized with the striking labor unions was not supposed to go to work, thereby intensifying the impact of the strike on the general economy and increasing workers' leverage with the government. Keynes wanted to keep defending the workers in print, but Woolf actually controlled the printing presses, which were owned by Hogarth, and won the argument.[60]

The strike ended after just nine working days, with workers getting nothing. Coal miners remained locked out for months to come and could return to work only after accepting brutal wage reductions. The mine owners and the Baldwin government had won. But what kind of victory? What self-proclaimed conservative would prefer tanks in the street and the "war atmosphere" of the strike to a reduced exchange rate? Baldwin and Churchill had jeopardized "the future peace and prosperity of this country" to defend "old-fashioned orthodoxies," Keynes wrote.[61]

Keynes subjected Churchill to the same public flogging he had once administered to Lloyd George, publishing a withering attack on Whitehall's mismanagement of the return to gold under the title "The Economic Consequences of Mr Churchill." A Hogarth pamphlet under the same title sold out its initial run of seven thousand "at once."[62]

Keynes believed the strike to be a social disaster caused not by some historically inevitable conflict between the working class and the capitalist regime but by straightforward intellectual error. Churchill and the Bank of England had simply been wrong and refused to listen to reason. Keynes had offered what was becoming his classic policy formulation: pursuing a conservative aim of avoiding a class revolt by implementing an unorthodox, left-wing reform—breaking with the gold standard. And Churchill had rejected him, not because he was corrupted by vested interests or class solidarity with the wealthy but because he just didn't think straight. He could have been convinced otherwise. There was more than a touch of naiveté in Keynes' faith in the power of ideas and persuasion, but he rested his hopes for intellectual progress on reasonable men in government, rather than the executive suite. If large industrial corporations were developing a sense of social responsibility, as Keynes had argued in *The End of Laissez-Faire,* they were developing it very slowly. "Business men," he told an audience at the University of Berlin, had been "narrow and ignorant, unable to adapt themselves"—much as he had found them during the financial crisis of 1914.[63]

Churchill, for his part, did soon come to see the return to gold as the gravest mistake of his public career. "Everybody said that I was the worst Chancellor of the Exchequer that ever was," he said in 1930.

Portrait of John Maynard Keynes by Duncan Grant, 1908.

Portrait of Keynes by Gwen Raverat, circa 1908.

© *National Portrait Gallery, London.*

Keynes with Bertrand Russell (left) and Lytton Strachey (right), 1915.

Photograph by Ottoline Morrell. © National Portrait Gallery, London.

Above: A note card that appears to tally years of sexual encounters between Keynes and various lovers. Below: An accompanying note describing many of those lovers.

King's College Library, Cambridge, JMK/PP/20A/1–4.

Keynes and Lydia
Lopokova in the 1920s.

*Photograph by Walter Benington
for Elliott & Fry. © National
Portrait Gallery, London.*

Lydia Lopokova, 1915.

*Photograph by Bain News Service.
© National Portrait Gallery, London.*

Lydia and Maynard outside the St. Pancras Registry
Office in London on their wedding day, 1925.

Bettmann Archive via Getty Images.

Keynes at work on an economic recovery plan for Germany at a conference with Bank of the Netherlands director Gerard Vissering and others, 1922.

Courtesy of ullstein bild via Getty Images.

Keynes addressing the Bretton Woods conference, 1944.

Universal History Archive via Getty Images.

Keynes with Harry Dexter White at the inaugural meeting of the International Monetary Fund's board of directors in Savannah, Georgia, 1946.

Public domain, courtesy of the IMF archives.

John Kenneth Galbraith (left) with John F. Kennedy, Lyndon B. Johnson, and Indian Prime Minister Jawaharlal Nehru at Andrews Air Force Base, 1961.

Photograph by Bob Gomel/LIFE Images Collection via Getty Images.

Galbraith with Jacqueline Kennedy in New York, 1965.

Bettmann Archive via Getty Images.

Galbraith testifies before Congress alongside Alan Greenspan in October 1979 to commemorate the fiftieth anniversary of the stock market crash of 1929.

Bettmann Archive via Getty Images.

"And now I'm inclined to agree with them. So now the world's unanimous."[64]

The coal debacle furthered Keynes' breach with the Liberal political establishment, ending one of his oldest friendships in politics. Keynes and H. H. Asquith had not only seen eye to eye on matters of public interest, they had moved in the same social circles since the early days of the war. Asquith's wife, Margot, was one of the few political personalities welcome at Bloomsbury dinner parties.

In the turmoil of the general strike, however, the Liberal leader had been swept away by the currents of authoritarian nationalism every bit as thoroughly as Baldwin had been. Lloyd George had not exactly been a hero, but he had at least supported further negotiations as an alternative to Baldwin's outright militarism, while Asquith had roared for law and order. Sensing another coup attempt by Lloyd George, the Asquiths rashly imposed a loyalty test on the party, assuming that their supporters would overpower whatever faction Lloyd George might have assembled. "It comes to this Ll.G. or H?" Margot wrote to Keynes. "Those who prefer the former will not want to retain as a friend yours sincerely."[65]

Keynes had staked his professional reputation in the battles over gold and coal and suffered too much abuse to abandon his intellectual cause over another man's mistake. His attacks on the gold standard had cost him credibility in the eyes of the London banking establishment. His attacks on Churchill and Baldwin had cost him whatever truck he had earned with the Tories during the war. If Keynes backed his old friend Asquith, he would be defending the brutal enforcers of the very overvalued gold standard he had crusaded against. In letters to Margot, Keynes refused to give the couple the public show of support they demanded: "I know what Ll. G. is like and so do most of those who feel as I do over this affair—we are under no illusions. But the split has come in such a way that any radical, who is not ready to subordinate his political ideas entirely to personalities, has absolutely no choice."[66] In the pages of *The Nation and Athenaeum*, he cautiously defended Lloyd George's "radical" credentials, describing him as a Liberal who was now determined to work with Labour rather than the Tories.[67]

The Asquiths were furious. Margot denounced Keynes' "savage and spiteful" coverage of the strike and uninvited him from a weekend retreat at the family's country house in Oxfordshire. Keynes tried to talk her down, but Margot would not hear it. "My peaceful words have done no good," he mourned to Lydia.[68] The breach would never be repaired. The former prime minister suffered a stroke less than two weeks after Margot sent her kiss-off to Keynes. He resigned as head of the party in October. Another stroke in January impaired his ability to walk, and his mind deteriorated rapidly after a third stroke at the end of 1927. He died in February 1928, his final twenty months a tragedy of physical and political impotence after a life as one of Great Britain's most formidable statesmen.

Keynes found himself in the unforeseeable position of becoming an honored member of Lloyd George's inner circle for the first time in his political life. Whatever the bankers and brokers said about Keynes on Lombard Street, Lloyd George viewed a consistently outspoken critic of British financial policy as a useful ally in an era of sustained economic dislocation. If their alliance was built on tactical convenience, Lloyd George nevertheless made good on it, treating Keynes as one of the party's chief ideological standard-bearers. For Keynes, it was a significant promotion within the Liberal ranks. Asquith had taken his allegiance for granted and in recent years had run roughshod over the policy pronouncements Keynes had offered in the pages of *The Nation*. Lloyd George knew from experience that Keynes' loyalty was not unconditional and so relied on him to help develop and promote the party's economic platform, the dominant issue in British politics.

It seemed to Keynes like the culmination of the long project he had begun with *The Economic Consequences of the Peace*. In 1919, he had rejected the connections of an insider and pursued influence as a brutally honest outsider assailing the political establishment. As a way to effect government policy, it had seemed the best play available to him at the time. Over the ensuing decade, his books, pamphlets, and newspaper had embedded his ideas deep in the public consciousness, but City bankers had mocked his theoretical innovations and politicians had ignored his policy advice. Now his goat-footed nemesis from the Great War was presenting an opportunity for his long shot to strike home.

It was also a chance to put into practice the themes Keynes had outlined in his *Prolegomena* five years earlier. Working with the economist Hubert Henderson, Keynes compiled the pamphlet *Can Lloyd George Do It?*, presenting an ambitious program that previewed many of the initiatives Franklin Delano Roosevelt would implement under the New Deal in the United States. The core policy was a massive roadbuilding project to create one of the great engineering marvels of the modern world, revolutionizing Great Britain's transportation infrastructure for the automobile. It was not a patchwork effort to expand the existing road network at the margins but a call for new highways, beltways, bridges, and tunnels that would connect disparate regions of the country and bring paved development deep into the rural countryside. It would cost £145 million over two years, directly putting at least three hundred fifty thousand men to work in the first year of the program alone.

It was a direct attack on the unemployment crisis that continued to plague Britain after the gold debacle. With the pound fixed at a high exchange rate to the dollar, the Bank of England had to impose crushingly high interest rates on the British economy in order to keep the price of British goods down in international markets. It was a successful strategy—but the lower prices were secured by throwing people out of work. As a result, a full decade after the Great War, more than a million men were still looking for a job.

But although there seemed to be plenty of idle manpower, Keynes was proposing a tremendous undertaking. Mobilizing a workforce on that scale was something the government had previously achieved only through military conscription.

The three hundred fifty thousand jobs created by roadbuilding in year one only accounted for a fraction of the full job impact Keynes and the Liberals anticipated. For every man put to work on roadways and bridges, the private economy would create new jobs to manufacture and ship his materials. The wages that roadbuilders spent, moreover, would support jobs in retail shops and restaurants. And so every pound the government spent on roads would generate much more than one pound of economic activity. This was the first Keynesian expression of a concept known as "the multiplier"—the idea that government spending can reverberate through the economy, creating indirect growth well in excess of an initial investment. Based on Keynes' estimates, the total direct and indirect employment from the roadbuilding program alone would result in 850,000 new jobs over the first year.[69]

But Keynes and Lloyd George weren't content with refashioning Great Britain as an automotive society. They also included a plan to build a million homes as a replacement for the infamous slums of London—work that would directly or indirectly require another 150,000 men for ten years of work. Yet another 150,000 would be needed for telephone development and rural electrification.[70] Still more would be needed to take "decisive, national action to preserve the downs, moors, lakes, woods, hills and commons of the countryside, and to conserve their beauties and their amenities for future generations."[71] It was a full-scale attack on unemployment, intended to eliminate joblessness outright in every region of the country.

The project would be financed for the most part with borrowed money. Paying people to work would not be as expensive as it looked, as the Treasury would be able to stop cutting unemployment checks as people accepted government jobs. The remaining debt could be paid back as tax revenues from a growing economy swelled the Treasury coffers over the coming years.

It was a wholesale rejection of laissez-faire individualism as an engine of social progress. The private derring-do of entrepreneurs would not be sufficient to lead Britain into the next phase of its history. Great men had invented the automobile, the telephone, and alternating current, but it would take the collective work of a great society to realize their potential.

Keynes knew the plan was radical. Six years earlier, the City orthodoxy had been horrified by his proposal to regulate price stability. Now he was proposing military-scale government mobilization of resources to reshape the very landscape of life in Britain. Keynes was not just talking about the monetary system anymore, he was reimagining the structural underpinnings of British commerce and planning a social transformation from the far reaches of the countryside to the slums of London. His politics had been drifting leftward throughout the 1920s, but with the publication of *Can Lloyd George Do It?*, he fundamentally redefined what it meant to be a Liberal. The party of free trade and the gold standard had become the party of massive government investment programs and deficit spending.

But the inherent radicalism of the proposal floated along a strong current of conservatism that runs throughout the pamphlet. To Keynes, it was far riskier to leave the unemployed idle and accept the economic misery of the past decade as the new, normal course of life.[72] "The idea that it represents a desperate risk to cure a moderate evil is the reverse of the truth. It is a negligible risk to cure a monstrous anomaly."[73] There was work to be done and workers available to do it. Putting the two together was just common sense. Leaving them idle and angry was a recipe for upheaval.

Indeed, it required some bizarre intellectual acrobatics to convince people that it was really impossible and foolish to pay people to do useful work. Apologists for the status quo were arguing that public works would rob future generations of the chance to get a job. All of the work, they claimed, would already be done. "Our main task," Keynes said of his pamphlet, "will be to confirm the reader's instinct that what *seems* sensible *is* sensible, and what *seems* nonsense *is* nonsense."[74]

Was it socialism? Keynes asked the question, then sidestepped it. "It is not a question of choosing between private and public enterprise in these matters. The choice has been already made. In many directions—though not in all—it is a question of the state putting its hand to the job or of its not being done at all."[75]

That svelte rhetoric was intended to assuage the very human fear of the tremendous changes Keynes and Lloyd George were proposing. Even a departure from misery would be accompanied by at least some fear of an uncertain future. But however calming it might have been for his readers, the presentation of a government merely filling the gaps in a patchwork private economy was not an accurate reflection of the ideological shift Keynes was trying to enact. His concerns about the preservation of the natural world gave away the game. Rivers, streams, and mountains did not require active human work to be preserved; nature took care of that on its own. Something had to be done to protect nature precisely because human beings, acting as uncoordinated individuals, were doing too much, not too little. Undirected commercial life was making the world an ugly, depleted place to live in. Keynes was calling for a new government role in the economy that would replace private industry with public action—and he had not worked out a principled limit to the government's sphere of activity.

The fundamental reform Keynes pursued in *Can Lloyd George Do It?* was psychological, not mathematical. In important ways, his country had proved more resilient than he had predicted at the end of the war. As Italy had succumbed to fascism and Germany was grappling with the politics of National Socialism, authoritarianism had only briefly reared its head in Great Britain during the general strike, despite a decade of economic depression. But it had been a close thing. The collective faith of the citizenry in the ability of the nation's economic system to deliver steady, predictable gains had collapsed. Millions of British workers had joined together in an attempt to shut down the entirety of the nation's commercial life. People—*most people*—had actively harmed their own society in order to make a political point. The unrest had extended well beyond the ranks of the unemployed; only people who had jobs could go on strike, after all. There was clearly no sense among the public that their welfare rested on secure foundations.

It was as if the "double bluff" of the prewar years had been reversed, creating a downward spiral of doubt and decay. People had once accepted an unequal system because it had improved their lives; because they had embraced it, the system had been able to generate prosperity. Now everyone from the coal miner to the investment house magnate had come to believe in a bleak, limited future (whatever the bankers said about the virtues of the gold standard, the paucity of actual investment in the economy was a more telling measure of their true feelings). That collective doom and gloom could not be broken by individual acts of courage. A worker running through the city proclaiming himself ready and willing to take on any task needed an actual job offer to do any good. A lone investor striking into the economic wilds with confidence and gusto would watch his money sink into a sea of public pessimism.

For the thing to work, Keynes recognized, everyone would have to take the plunge together. Just as friends and family come to the rescue of a loved one in need to preserve the bonds of their community, so society would need to support its citizens to establish the foundations of prosperity. That would require economic coordination and direction.

Over the course of a decade, the project Keynes began in *The Economic Consequences of the Peace* to wipe out war debts had flowered into an ambitious reimagining of the state itself, replete with a vast array of new administrative machinery and government responsibilities. Keynes was still inspired by Burke—the general strike had made clear to him that the social cohesion between the government and the public was breaking down, with potentially explosive results. But he had become convinced not only that the risks of inaction were great but that the potential for prosperity and social transformation was enormous.

"There is no reason why we should not feel ourselves free to be bold, to be open, to experiment, to take action, to try the possibilities of things," he wrote. "And over against us, standing in the path, there is nothing but a few old gentlemen tightly buttoned-up in their frock coats, who only need to be treated with a little friendly disrespect and bowled over like ninepins." He concluded the pamphlet with a smirk: "Quite likely they will enjoy it themselves, when once they have got over the shock."[76]

Can Lloyd George Do It? was a sprightly manifesto that presented many of the groundbreaking theoretical insights that Keynes would eventually formalize in *The General Theory of Employment, Interest and Money* in a brief, accessible package. Together with *The End of Laissez-Faire* and *A Short View of Russia*, it forms the core of a unique, practical political theory that the United States would put to work on a vast scale in just a few years. Even Bloomsbury loved it. Writing to Vanessa's son Quentin, Virginia talked about the "more congenial" Maynard who had written "a pamphlet which is to turn the scale at the elections."[77]

But it was the wrong manifesto for Great Britain in May 1929. The public no longer needed to be convinced that laissez-faire was a dead end. They had decided for themselves in 1926 and taken to the streets. The cool, buoyant prose of the Keynes pamphlet—though perfect for the early days of FDR's "Happy Days Are Here Again" administration—simply could not get any purchase in a political environment that had been defined so starkly by class conflict. After the general strike, people were either with the working class and the Labour Party or the government tanks and the Conservatives. The Tories didn't hide from the showdown, campaigning on a slogan of "Safety first," hoping to make the election a choice between law and order and mob rule by the rabble.

Conservatives underestimated the degree to which a decade of economic depression had swelled the ranks of the dispossessed. In the 1929 election, the Labour Party gained 136 seats, nearly doubling its previous number of 151 and putting it just 21 shy of an outright majority. The Liberals gained 19 seats—a dramatic improvement from the 118-seat hemorrhage of 1924 but nothing close to what was necessary to make the party a dominant force in British politics. Only a dozen years removed from its heyday, the Liberal Party had been permanently transformed by the postwar economy into a minor faction. Asquith's great gamble of 1923, in which the Liberals would serve as the power behind the Labour throne, had backfired. Its 59 seats se-cured government control for Labour but exercised limited influence, accounting for less than one-fifth of the seats in the new majority. Keynes had predicted a 190-seat Liberal triumph.[78]

"I have relapsed into rather a depressed state about the Election," he wrote to Lydia. "I can't see that anything satisfactory can possibly result from it."[79]

He could not have imagined the calamity just around the corner.

SEVEN

———— ◊ ————

THE GREAT CRASH

FINANCIAL DISASTER FOLLOWED WINSTON Churchill everywhere in the 1920s. Forced out of office as chancellor of the Exchequer by the 1929 elections, he accepted an invitation from former
Wilson adviser Bernard Baruch for a dinner in his honor in New
York.[1] Wall Street's greatest banking barons would be in attendance,
and Churchill rarely shied away from high-society bacchanalia—his
scotch consumption and fondness for Pol Roger champagne were already the stuff of legend. He needed no encouragement to embark on
a trip to shore up his credentials with American power brokers after
yet another political downfall as a member of yet another political
party. With Labour's Ramsay MacDonald once again established at
10 Downing Street, it seemed an appropriate time for Churchill to
take a break from a British political scene where he now found himself devoid of influence.

The morning before the private gala at Baruch's Fifth Avenue
home, Churchill paid a visit to the New York Stock Exchange.[2] The
Dawes Plan had established a steady if precarious flow of war debt
interest from Europe to the United States, and England's overvalued
pound had given American manufacturers a competitive edge that
had both elevated the value of U.S. stocks and made lending to Amer-

ican exporters an easy profit opportunity. By keeping interest rates relatively low during the middle of the decade, the Federal Reserve had made it cheaper for firms to expand their operations with borrowed money, encouraging them to invest in new technologies and production. In 1924, the discount rate—the amount the Fed charged for ordinary banks to borrow money that they in turn could lend out to businesses—touched a low point of 3 percent. The international economy had showered Wall Street with more money than it knew what to do with. A stock market that seemed to increase inexorably seemed as good a place as any to put it, particularly when economists as esteemed as Yale theorist Irving Fisher insisted that the gains had reached "a permanently high plateau" and indeed might well rise still further.[3]

By the time Churchill ascended to the visitors' gallery at the NYSE, the Fed had been raising interest rates for three months from levels that were already elevated by historical standards. But even high interest rates couldn't curb the enthusiasm for what had become one of the sweetest returns on capital in the New York banking world. At a draconian 6 percent, the Fed's discount rate was still easily drowned by the rate lenders received on loans to stockbrokers, which could now soar as high as 12 percent—room for a very profitable spread. What's more, the stockbrokers offered the banks collateral for those loans in the form of stocks, which, of course, just kept rising in value. It all seemed like a very healthy and safe line of business, and everyone wanted in on it. By 1929, the volume of brokers' loans outstanding had more than quadrupled since the early 1920s to over $6 billion.[4]

Alas, the stock market could not bear Winston Churchill's company very long. Trading volume from the 10:00 A.M. bell was tremendous, as brokers stamped to and from the trading posts, placing orders for massive blocks of shares. Prices initially held steady, but eventually the dam gave way. Values began to fall, then to plunge. As the numbers descended, stunned speculators panicked at the once unthinkable prospect of recording a loss. Many were playing with borrowed money. If stock prices increased, they would be rich. But if they fell they might have to sell their car, maybe their house. Better to get out before things got bad. Best to get out right now. Immediately. Across the trading floor, according to one historian, "the instinct to unload threatened to turn into a frenzy."[5] The stock ticker, recording the price of each trade, was overwhelmed, falling far behind the activity of the overwhelmed brokers. Uncertain investors rushed to sell still more. Stop-loss orders—safety measures that speculators had set up ahead of time requiring brokers to sell if stocks fell below a certain price—were triggered en masse, forcing a flood of additional sales that drove prices down still further with shocking speed. The calamity fed on its own momentum, and by 11:30 A.M., the market had "surrendered to blind, relentless fear."[6] The visitors' gallery was closed, and even the prestigious Mr. Churchill was forced to leave.[7] Rumor of the disaster spread through the city, and a crowd gathered six deep outside the doors of the stock exchange at the corner of Wall Street and Broad. Businessmen packed into the boardrooms of stockbrokerages and speculators surrounded their offices. "Some cried out their astonishment at the unfamiliar prices they saw," recorded one journalist. "Others laughed in disbelief."[8] A dark and peculiar sound began reverberating down the towers and canyons of lower Manhattan as thousands gasped, moaned, and screamed at the shock. "Violence was in the air,"[9] and police were dispatched to keep the peace. When a man began doing repair work atop one of the skyscrapers, the crowd below assumed that he was preparing to take his own life and "waited impatiently for him to jump."[10]

As Churchill departed from the scene, another of Keynes' old sparring partners was gathering his forces in the offices next door. Of all his friends and enemies from the debacle at Paris in 1919, none had fared better from the war and its aftermath than Thomas Lamont. A onetime journalist, Lamont had befriended the investment banker Henry Davison during a chance encounter on a New York commuter train, joined his firm, and traveled with him to the offices of J.P. Morgan in 1911.[11] The Morgan job had made Lamont extraordinarily wealthy. Every Morgan partner received a $1 million bonus in 1928 (equivalent to about $15 million today), and Lamont was much more than a typical partner.[12] He was routinely dispatched by the U.S. government for quasi-official diplomatic purposes, and he prided himself on what he considered a progressive internationalist worldview un-common among his Republican peers, cultivating friendships with the likes of H. G. Wells and Walter Lippmann.[13] He tended not to advertise the coolheaded ruthlessness with which he pursued power and profit as an agent of both Benito Mussolini and Imperial Japan. Though John Pierpont's son Jack was still officially the head of the bank, by 1929, everyone knew it was Lamont's operation. Appropri-ately, Jack was traveling in Europe when the crash came, while Lamont was encamped at Morgan's office at 23 Wall Street.[14] "There has been," he remarked coolly to reporters later that day, "a little distress selling on the Stock Exchange."[15]

In truth, Lamont had been blindsided by the crash. Only five days earlier, he had written to another former Keynes confidant, President Herbert Hoover, dismissing concerns that excessive speculation might pose some danger to the stock market or the broader economy. "We must remember that there is a great deal of exaggeration in current gossip about speculation," Lamont wrote. "Since the war the country has embarked on a remarkable period of healthy prosperity. . . . The future appears brilliant."[16]

Hoover had spent decades as a public servant, cultivating a reputa-tion as a sincere humanitarian whose work during and after the war had saved more lives than anyone could count. That legacy was about to be erased. By 1952, when he published his memoirs, Hoover was known simply as the man who botched the Great Depression. Like millions of other Americans, he blamed Wall Street for his misfor-tune. "The New York bankers all scoffed at the idea that the market was not 'sound,'" he recalled, remarking icily that Lamont's "long memorandum" from October 1929 "makes curious reading today."[17] The memo itself, preserved in his presidential library, is emblazoned with Hoover's sardonic handwriting: "This document is fairly amaz-ing."[18] Hoover also claimed in his memoir to have implored the acting president of the New York Stock Exchange, a Morgan broker named Richard Whitney, to take some kind of action against excessive specu-lation, but alas, Whitney had declined. Hoover even reserved some wrath for the local authorities: "There was some doubt as to the con-

stitutionality of Federal control of the stock exchanges but I hoped
that at least, when we had exposed the situation, the Governor of New
York would recognize his fundamental responsibility and act accord-
ingly. That hope, however, proved to be little more than wishful thinking."[19] The governor of New York at the time was a Democrat named
Franklin D. Roosevelt, who would soon challenge Hoover for the
presidency.

Lamont had been telling Hoover what he wanted to hear. At the
height of the Jazz Age on Wall Street, nobody wanted the music to
stop. Hoover did not believe in an activist federal government and
simply could not conceive of the administrative architecture his suc-
cessor would construct. Even if he had been able to, by October 1929
the situation was already well out of hand. There existed, moreover, a
storied tradition of American bankers banding together to perform
heroic rescues in moments of extreme financial duress. In 1907, John
Pierpont Morgan himself had assembled the leading men of New
York in his personal library to orchestrate the salvation of the Trust
Company of America and one of the largest stockbrokers in New
York, pooling the money of the biggest U.S. banks. Lamont was well
aware of the institutional heritage he represented as he assembled the
great bankers of his own generation at his office across the street from
the stock exchange: National City Bank president and chairman
Charles Mitchell, Albert Wiggin of Chase National Bank, Seward
Prosser of Bankers Trust, and William Potter of Guaranty Trust.

The group quickly decided on a plan of action: They would rig the
market.

The operation would be modeled on a manipulation technique
made popular during the recent boom. The bankers would combine a
portion of their vast resources—together, they controlled an astounding $6 billion in assets[20]—and buy up stocks at optimistic prices.
Speculators, observing the sudden increases—not to mention the
prestigious names behind the purchases—would expect a further rise
in prices (and perhaps further support from the Morgan cabal) and
begin buying with a renewed sense of confidence. In 1927 and 1928,
this had been a surefire way to make a stock pop. It was also classic

anticompetitive behavior, but few worried about the inconveniencies of free competition when everyone was making money on the market's skyward ascent—or when the market appeared to be on the verge of collapse.

There were obvious risks. Lamont and his friends were not trying to make a quick buck but to reverse an avalanche. If the gambit failed, the banks would have squandered resources that everyone knew would become much more precious in the gloomy days that would inevitably follow. The alternative, however, appeared to be a mindless destruction of American wealth. The bankers committed $240 million to the rescue. At 1:30, Whitney—rising to the occasion a few days later than Hoover might have preferred—strolled across the floor of the exchange and bid 205 for 20,000 shares of U.S. Steel, well above the price of the prior sale.

The signal to traders was unmistakable. Whitney was Morgan's broker, and U.S. Steel was a monopoly that had been created by Morgan-approved mergers in 1901. The cavalry had arrived. "There was a roar of cheers, as on a battlefield after a successful charge."[21] Prices suddenly soared. "Fear vanished and gave way to concern lest the new advance be missed." By the close of trading, most of the terrifying losses of the morning had been recovered. U.S. Steel even recorded a net gain on the day.[22] *The Wall Street Journal* splashed a triumphant headline, in its excitement more than quadrupling the actual commitment from the rescue committee (only a fraction of which was ever spent): "BANKERS HALT STOCK DEBACLE: 2-Hour Selling Deluge Stopped After Conference at Morgan Offices: $1,000,000,000 FOR SUPPORT."[23] The market—not to mention the bank chairmen's dinner with Winston—had been saved.

Of course it was not to last. Black Thursday was followed by Black Tuesday and Black Tuesday by four years of relentlessly deepening depression. John Maynard Keynes—though no stranger to the erratic swings of financial markets—was shocked. "Wall Street *did* have a go yesterday," he wrote to Lydia that Friday. "Did you read about it? The biggest crash ever recorded. . . . I have been in a thoroughly financial and disgusting state of mind all day."[24]

Over the summer there had been clear signs that the U.S. economy was entering a rough patch: Residential construction had fallen from the previous year, while consumer spending growth had slackened considerably.[25] Hoover and other respectable voices in the months leading up to the crash had expressed concerns that the wild activity on Wall Street had become unglued from conditions in the broader economy. Paul Warburg, a conservative banker who had helped establish the Federal Reserve in 1913, had warned about "orgies of unrestrained speculation" as early as March.[26] And to Keynes, the precrash situation had become a source of significant anxiety due to his concerns about the policy response of the American central bank.

The international gold standard, as he understood it, was essentially a dollar standard. The United States had accumulated such vast quantities of gold during and after the war that it could dictate the currency management of other nations. When the Federal Reserve raised interest rates to combat a stock market bubble, the British had to raise rates, too—or watch the Bank of England's gold dwindle away as investors cashed out pounds and bought dollars. The British central bank had lost 20 percent of its gold reserves over the summer before the crash, and in August 1929, Bank of England governor Montagu Norman had warned the Fed that its high rates might well force Great Britain and much of Europe off the gold standard altogether.[27] Though they did little to curb stock speculation in New York, the Fed's high interest rates wreaked havoc abroad.

So the crash eased Keynes' mind. It meant that an obvious problem festering in American finance would not get any worse. And it gave U.S. policy makers room to take action that would alleviate global unemployment. The Keynes statement published in the *New-York Evening Post* the day after Black Thursday, however, has aged only slightly better than Lamont's cheerful letter to Hoover:

> *We in Great Britain can't help heaving a big sigh of relief at what seems like the removal of an incubus which has been lying heavily on*

the business life of the whole world outside America. . . . The extraor-
dinary speculation on Wall Street in past months has driven up the
rate of interest to an unprecedented level. Since the gold standard en-
sures a high degree of mobility of international lending, this meant
dear money everywhere. But nothing has happened to enable industry
and enterprise outside America to support a higher rate than before.
The result is that new enterprise has been damped down in countries
thousands of miles from Wall Street and commodity prices have been
falling. And this was due to a wholly artificial cause. If the recent high
rate of interest had lasted another six months, it would have been a
real disaster.

But now, after the drastic and even terrible events of the last few
weeks, we see daylight again. There seems a chance of an epoch of cheap
money ahead. This will be in the real interests of business all over the
world. Money in America has already become very cheap indeed. The
Federal Reserve Bank of New York will probably take the first oppor-
tunity of putting its rate even lower. If so, I am sure that the Bank of
England and the other European central banks will not be slow to
follow suit. And then perhaps enterprise throughout the world can get
going again. Incidentally commodity prices will recover and farmers
will find themselves in better shape.

I may be a bad prophet in speaking this way. But I am sure that I
am reflecting the instinctive reaction of English financial opinion to
the immediate situation. There will be no serious direct consequences
in London resulting from the Wall Street slump except to the limited
number of Anglo-American securities which are actively dealt in both
here and in New York. On the other hand we find the longer look
ahead decidedly encouraging.[28]

The era of "dear money"—high interest rates and deflation—would
give way to a period of "cheap money"—low interest rates and stable,
perhaps even modestly rising prices. The crash, though bad for many
stock market investors, would ultimately enable policy makers to get
business moving again not only in the United States but around the
world.

Keynes was right on every point—at first. In the immediate after-math of the crash, Federal Reserve Bank of New York president George Harrison provided nearly unlimited emergency funds to the Manhattan banks, and at his urging, the Fed slashed the discount in-terest rate from 6.0 percent to 2.5 percent—moves that would sub-stantially alleviate the deflationary pressure sparked by the collapse in stock values. But Keynes' sanguine outlook would prove to be entirely wrong based on one factor that he had not considered and another that he misjudged: The faltering American banking system was too weak to salvage Europe on its own, and the Federal Reserve's commit-ment to fighting deflation was weak and short-lived.

The crash decimated the market for brokers' loans, with the volume collapsing by $4.4 billion—more than half the pre–Black Thursday peak.[29] The New York banks, bolstered by the New York Fed, rushed in to prevent a total collapse of the stock market, but that effort could ensure only a relatively orderly sell-off. A lot of money that had been loaned to buy stocks was plainly not going to be repaid. And the col-lateral that the banks had accepted for the loans—stocks—was con-tinuing to plunge in value. This put enormous pressure on bank balance sheets, making bankers more cautious about issuing new loans and encouraging them to call in loans they already had outstanding. The higher cost of credit and its decreasing availability forced U.S. manu-facturers to cut production, and businesses that had a hard time fi-nancing their operations began laying off workers. Those workers, in turn, lost their incomes, which prevented them from buying goods and services, which in turn made it more difficult for firms that sold things to employ other workers. Commodity prices began to plummet in November, as tight credit conditions caused a collapse in demand, with the price of corn falling 15 percent by the end of the year and that of coffee declining by a third. A vicious cycle had begun.[30]

Internationally, the consequences of this banking instability were if anything still more dire. Ever since the hyperinflation crisis of 1923, the German and Austrian economies had been completely dependent on American loans to function. When the flow of credit from across the Atlantic began to dry up, their own banking systems began to crumble. The process had already begun when the Fed raised interest rates over the summer of 1929. It accelerated after the stock market crash in October as U.S. banks restricted lending in order to shore up their balance sheets. Europe and the United States were chained together by the gold standard and the cycle of credit established by the Dawes Plan; they would fall as one.

For Keynes, the calamity offered both opportunity and inspiration. With the old order crumbling around him, new ideas might, he hoped, build a better world.

It would take eighteen months for everything to come apart. In the meantime, Keynes found himself in an unfamiliar position: political influence. After studiously ignoring his advice during a decade in which he had been right about nearly every important economic issue facing the world, the British government had decided to hire him immediately following the worst prediction of his career.

In November 1929, Ramsay MacDonald appointed Keynes to the new Committee on Finance and Industry—better known as the Macmillan Committee, so dubbed for its chairman, a judge named Hugh Pattison Macmillan. The Labour government was determined not to squander its second chance at power and made a very public show about soliciting expert economic advice, eager to prove that the rabble could govern by reason. In addition to the Macmillan Committee, MacDonald established the Economic Advisory Council, where Keynes was also installed. The prime minister invited him to lunch and trumpeted the meeting to the press. Keynes could not have been more pleased. "I am becoming more fashionable again," he crowed to Lydia on November 25.[31]

Neither post had formal policy-making power. Keynes couldn't write regulations, lend money, or broker trade agreements. But as the global economy shuddered, both panels became critical forums for debate. The Macmillan Committee, in particular, became the world's foremost official body tasked with processing the mechanics of "The Slump" and explaining both its causes and potential remedies to the public. Macmillan hearings became a focal point of British politics, and though Keynes was not technically in charge, he was far and away the leading personality, savoring every minute of his star turn in the political limelight as he cross-examined some of the most illustrious personalities in British finance, from top Treasury officials to Bank of England governor Montagu Norman.

The Macmillan Committee gave Keynes a platform to present and refine the ideas he had been assembling in *A Treatise on Money*—the "technical treatise" he had mentioned in his 1925 letter to the journalist Henry Noel Brailsford. When it was finally published in 1930 after seven agonizing years of writing, rethinking, and revision, Keynes once again believed he had delivered the great work of his life—just as he'd thought when he completed *A Treatise on Probability* nearly a decade earlier.

Released in two sprawling volumes, *A Treatise on Money* is more than twice as long as *The General Theory* and in many respects a more ambitious work, jammed with equations, tables, definitions, and arguments about everything from Shakespeare to proposals for a new international currency union. "Artistically it is a failure," Keynes conceded. "I have changed my mind too much during the course of writing it for it to be a proper unity."[32] But for those willing to persevere through its 787 intimidating pages, the *Treatise* can be a joyful, exuberant mess, packed with moments of genuine comedy and dazzling intellectual showmanship, studded with aphorisms that rival Friedrich Nietzsche: "There is nothing worse than a moderate evil! If wasps and rats were hornets and tigers, we should have exterminated them before now. So with Great Britain's obligations to her *rentiers* arising out of the war."[33]

In truth, the *Treatise* was two separate projects: an economic history of the world from prehistory to 1930 and a unique diagnosis of the Great Depression culminating in what had become Keynes' preferred treatment for economic ailments. When a slump was truly dire, "the government must itself promote a programme of domestic investment"—public works projects.[34] Though Keynes' theory of the Depression was what captured the attention of economists and policy makers in 1930, his history is more critical to economic thought today.

Over the course of the 1920s, Keynes was periodically gripped by an obsession with ancient currencies. As he reported to Lydia in January 1924:

I feel little better than lunatic this evening. It is just like three years ago—the same thing has happened. Feeling rather leisurely, I re-opened to my old essay on Babylonian and Greek weights. It is purely absurd and quite useless. But just as before, I became absorbed in it to the point of frenzy. Last night I went on working at it up to 2 o'clock; and to-day I went on continuously from the time I got up until dinner time. Extraordinary! Anyone else would think the subject very dull. Some charm must have been cast on it by a Babylonian magician. The result is I feel quite mad and silly.[35]

In November 1925, he was at it again, writing on Babylonian money "until I was dizzy and the fire was out."[36] The following night, he found that "the old currency has become an uncontrollable madness," overwhelming him all afternoon and evening and into early morning. "The time flashed by. I have made a vow not to do it to-night" in the name of rest and sanity.[37] But within a few days he was testing the addiction once again. "My evening letters are finished," he informed Lydia. "Shall I creep back to the old currency?"[38] Three days later he was eager to cancel plans to attend a party and a concert so he could "retire here to Babylonia."[39]

Keynes had discovered an ancient history that upended some basic tenets of economics going back to Adam Smith and undermined nearly three centuries of Enlightenment political theory. Ever since Thomas Hobbes had published *Leviathan* in 1651, most European philosophers had imagined government as an artificial imposition on what Hobbes called "the state of nature." For Hobbes, the state of nature was a nightmare of violent disorder where life was "nasty, brutish and short,"[40] making government—specifically monarchy—a source of human salvation. Even thinkers who rejected Hobbes' politics accepted his history. In *The Wealth of Nations*, Smith had presented markets for trade as a primordial force that came into being long before the development of the political state. Commercial life had started with people bartering goods, trading goats for wheat or cloth for buttons. They eventually adopted money as a medium of exchange, since passing tokens to each other proved to be more convenient than toting wagonloads of cumbersome goods. All of this activity had taken place among free individuals undisturbed by the machinations of capricious, meddling sovereigns, who entered the scene much later. The market was natural, while the state was a relatively recent artifice that intervened in or distorted the independent rhythms of trade.

Studying Athens, Babylon, Assyria, Persia, and Rome, Keynes concluded that this history was all wrong. Capitalism itself was an ancient creation of government, dating back at least as far as the Babylonian Empire of the third millennium B.C. "Individualistic capitalism and the economic practices pertaining to that system were undoubtedly invented in Babylonia and carried to a high degree of development in epochs more distant than the archaeologists have yet explored,"[41] he wrote—one of several startling observations recorded in seventy pages of unpublished notes and fragmentary argument from his 1920s research. Money, moreover, was not a custom developed by local traders for convenience but a sophisticated tool of rulership that had emerged simultaneously with other developments of the state, including written language and standardized weights and measures.

Smith and other thinkers had been led astray by confusing the development of coinage with the invention of money. Coinage, according to Keynes, was "just a piece of bold vanity . . . with no far-reaching importance";[42] money had existed in "representative" form much longer. Its real significance was as a "unit of account"—the demarcation of debt and "the legal discharge of obligations,"[43] which governments had been maintaining in ledger books, scrolls, or clay tablets for millennia. Powerful, economically sophisticated empires had developed without using coinage at all.

States, moreover, had always maintained a policy of active monetary management as a basic condition of rulership. They created and abolished debts as reward or punishment and reformed units of measurement, depreciating or debasing their currency not merely as a trick on unsophisticated subjects but to stimulate trade and ease social tension. Inflation—viewed by orthodox economists of the 1920s as an underhanded sovereign's subversion of the natural order—had instead been a near-constant condition "throughout almost all periods of recorded history."[44]

Keynes eventually refined these observations into a state-centered theory of money that formed the foundation of the *Treatise*. Money, he argued, was an inherently political tool. It was the state that determined what substance—gold, paper, whatever—actually counted as money—what "thing" people and the government would accept as valid payment. The state thus created money and had always regulated its value. "This right is claimed by all modern states and has been so claimed for some four thousand years at least."[45] The significance of gold to economic history was both relatively recent—it had only really mattered in the past few decades—and arbitrary. The true source of monetary stability was the public legitimacy of the political authority that happened to *choose* gold as its preferred medium of exchange. Money had no meaning absent political authority.[46]

Keynes thus came to see economic history as a fundamentally political story—the tale of riches conquered and surrendered by political powers as empires rose and fell. Economics, by extension, could not be a bloodless scientific investigation into unshakable laws of nature but only a set of observations about trends in human political arrangements. Economics as a field of study had to adjust to the social behavior of human beings, which might very well change over time. As Keynes explained before the Macmillan Committee, "I do not think it is any more economic law that wages should go down easily than that they should not. It is a question of facts. Economic law does not lay down the facts, it tells you what the consequences are."[47]

The development of the modern economy, moreover, was inextricably linked with the rise of European colonialism. When the Spanish conquistadors began shipping silver from the Americas back to Europe, they had sparked a rapid price inflation, causing prices to quintuple over the following eight decades.[48] "In these golden years," he wrote, "modern capitalism was born."[49] The flood of new money sparked a rush of new economic projects and investments, as enterprising folks saw prices and profits increase and bet on new endeavors. The inflation caused by New World precious metal soon spread to France and then to England, where it brought about an artistic awakening as producers of all varieties ramped up production, chasing the opportunity to profit from an increase in prices before wages caught up. "We were just in a position to afford Shakespeare at the moment when he presented himself!"[50] Keynes wrote. The British had compounded that development with "the booty brought back by Drake in the *Golden Hind*," which could "fairly be considered the fountain and origin of British Foreign Investment." "Economic factors" had been responsible for "moulding the Elizabethan age and making possible its greatness."[51] Though Keynes cheerfully breezed past the implications of his analysis, he had presented a history in which the intricacies of the modern economy were the by-products of intercontinental pillage.

There is plenty in the *Treatise* for economic historians to argue over. It is not clear, for instance, that the growth of the European silver supply can be credited with the surge in European political power that began in the sixteenth century, much less with the work of Shakespeare. But the basic story of money as a creature of the state has withstood decades of further historical research. The idea that modern financial systems were developed to meet the demands of warring states is widely accepted even among economic historians hostile to Keynes. "In the beginning was war," Niall Ferguson concluded in 2001.[52]

The *Treatise*, then, was an all-out assault on the intellectual foundations of laissez-faire. There was no such thing as a free market devoid of government interference. The very idea of capitalism *required* active state economic management—the regulation of money and debt. Keynes had also defined the aim of economic policy: to set the foundations of an exciting intellectual culture. His rubric for determining economic success or failure was not growth or productivity but "greatness." There were objective aesthetic cultural achievements—Shakespeare, for instance—that economic policy was supposed to support. This was a conception of human freedom diametrically opposed to the ideas that free-market economists would develop in the decades to come.

Keynes believed there were practical contemporary lessons to be learned from all of that historical material. Deflation brought social unrest and national decline. "My reading of history is that for centuries there has existed an intense social resistance to any matters of reduction in the level of money incomes," he told the committee on February 20, 1930. "There has never been in modern or ancient history a community that has been prepared to accept without immense struggle a reduction in the general level of money income."[53]

It was no use, then, to demand wage concessions from trade union leaders, on the belief that lower pay might bring more jobs. That was simply not how the world worked. Keynes argued that both the source of trouble and the primary source of its solution lay in the monetary system. Banks and other financial intermediaries existed to link up people who wanted to save their money with others who needed money to invest in new projects. When things were running smoothly, the money that one person saved would swiftly flow into productive research or a factory expansion. A society's total savings would be equal to its total amount of investment. By "investment," Keynes was not referring to personal decisions to invest money in stocks or bonds but to a type of business spending: purchases of new equipment or research that would eventually enable an expansion of overall production.

Ideally, according to Keynes, the savings of the people would equal the investments of the business world. But things could go haywire; there was no process by which savings were automatically converted into investment. The impetus to save and the impetus to build were different motivations. "It has been usual to think of the accumulated wealth of the world as having been painfully built up out of that voluntary abstinence of individuals from the immediate enjoyment of consumption which we call thrift," he wrote in the *Treatise*. "But it should be obvious that mere abstinence is not enough by itself to build cities. . . . It is enterprise which builds and improves the world's possessions. . . . If enterprise is afoot, wealth accumulates whatever may be happening to thrift."[54]

The role of the banking system was to ensure that the savings of society were perfectly tuned to society's capacity for investment. If the interest rates lenders offered were set correctly, savings would equal investment and society would operate happily at full employment. But if total investment exceeded the total amount that a society wanted to save, the result would be inflation. And if the reverse occurred—if a society saved more than it invested—the result would be a "slump."

Keynes was throwing out an economic idea he had proffered in *The Economic Consequences of the Peace*. In 1919, he had viewed thrift and abstinence as Victorian virtues that enabled the creation of capital hoards that could be invested in great projects. By 1930, he recognized that—as with other Victorian pruderies—too much thrift could take the fun out of life. It sapped societies of their energy and strangled their development. "Were the Seven Wonders of the world built by Thrift? I deem it doubtful."[55] Excessive thrift—otherwise described as underconsumption—could cause economic trouble.

As with his rejection of the gold standard seven years prior, Keynes was making a technical observation that carried radical political implications. Banks, he claimed, were both tremendously powerful and unreliable. Nothing guaranteed that they would operate with prescience or perfection. No invisible hand would correct an imbalance of over- or underinvestment. Bankers might just get it wrong and do so without revealing any significant deterioration in their own profits or balance sheets. Indeed, banks did not see themselves as the regulatory supervisors of the national economy. They were out to make a profit—or at least avoid losing their shirts in reckless investments.

But someone had to steer the ship. The most obvious choice of commander was a central banker who could control interest rates and thus find the magic number that would tune the public's desire to save to the needs of business for investment.

This was a more radical step than Keynes had taken in *A Tract on*

Monetary Reform. In that book, he had called for a central bank to deliberately pursue a policy of price stability, adjusting interest rates to keep inflation or deflation from disrupting the normal course of commerce. Now he was arguing that a central bank should deliberately cause inflation or deflation to treat other, more important economic troubles. The goal was no longer price stability but sustained investment and unemployment. If necessary, central banks could pursue inflation in order to alleviate unemployment.

It was a new idea. But it is important not to overstate Keynes' breach with the conventional academic wisdom of the day. He continued to view unemployment as a basic supply and demand problem, just as Ludwig von Mises and his conservative Austrian disciples did. Keynes merely rejected the view that markets could resolve the problem on their own or that states could speed up the project by curbing the power of labor unions to set unrealistically high wages. Inflation, ultimately, was a roundabout way of cutting everyone's pay. Rising prices reduced the purchasing power of workers' paychecks. With pay reduced, employers would then be able to hire more people. A policy of deliberate inflation was not only politically easier than an attack on organized labor, it ensured that particular industries would not be unfairly singled out. "The method of raising prices throws the burden over a much wider area," he told the Economic Advisory Council in a September memo. "In particular, it throws a due share on the *rentier* class and other recipients of fixed money incomes. Thus, from the point of view of both justice and self-interest, the trade union leaders are right in preferring a rise of prices to a reduction of money wages."[56]

But the *Treatise* appears incremental only by comparison with the ideas Keynes would put forward years later. In 1930, the financial establishment considered his new theory to be terribly dangerous. It was a sustained assault on nearly every precept of sound City finance. To Keynes, a little inflation was normal; an occasional heavy dose was good policy. Gold was not a source of centuries of economic good sense but merely "part of the apparatus of conservatism,"[57] fostering dangerous superstitions about laissez-faire and prosperity. Central bankers should be responsible for much more than maintaining a steady balance of international trade; they must regulate not only the price level but total employment.

The *Treatise* grew more radical still. There was no way for a central bank, Keynes argued, to guarantee that the right interest rate would lead to the right amount of domestic investment. Under some conditions, lowering interest rates might only serve to encourage investment in *foreign* projects. Keynes argued that Great Britain was now in precisely that position because of its overvalued $4.86 pound, which priced British goods out of the international market. Under such conditions, lower interest rates just encouraged capital to go where it could back more competitive investment projects: overseas, especially to the United States. Keynes noted that the situation could be remedied by devaluing the pound to a more sustainable level. But doing so would mean suspending the gold standard. It was hard to predict how the global economy would respond to such a shock in 1930, so Keynes offered another policy alternative: since the ultimate problem facing the British economy was a shortage of investment spending, just have the state spend money on public works, putting people to work directly.[58] Great Britain, he said, had three choices: It could embrace a large-scale public works agenda, breach the gold standard through devaluation, or be guided by the gold standard and laissez-faire into "revolution."[59] "As I have already indicated, this is my own favourite remedy," he told the Macmillan Committee in March 1930.[60] "We must look to a bold Government programme to lift us out of the rut."[61]

A Treatise on Money hit the economics profession like an earthquake. Across the Atlantic, young students who read it were inspired to make pilgrimages to Cambridge to hear the great author's words, and many of them would go on to rank among the most influential policy makers of the next generation. In academic circles, the *Treatise* prompted fascination and controversy. Everyone had an opinion of Keynes' big, strange book, and Keynes began to eclipse the American economist Irving Fisher as the most argued-over thinker in the profession. The most important critique came from a young Austrian economist named Friedrich von Hayek. Sensing the emergence of a serious intellectual threat to laissez-faire, Hayek penned a scorching two-part indictment of the *Treatise* for the academic journal *Economica*. He mocked the "almost unbelievable" density of Keynes' writing and attacked his technical definitions of "profits" and "investment" in service of an assault on Keynes' policy regime. Hayek was not only hostile to public works as a remedy for depression; he also rejected "any attempt to combat the crisis by credit expansion."[62]

Despite its energetic language, there was not much theoretical heft to Hayek's critique. By insisting that any attempt to correct a downturn with fresh currency was inflationary and counterproductive, he condemned not only public works spending by the government but essentially any efforts by central banks to alleviate a crisis via monetary policy. Milton Friedman, Hayek's most famous ideological ally in the latter half of the twentieth century, believed Hayek encouraged a "do-nothing policy" that "did harm" by insisting that "you just have to let the bottom drop out of the world."[63]

But the sheer intensity of Hayek's attack—he raged that Keynes did not understand the great ideas of the more sophisticated Austrian economists Hayek himself had studied under—drew enough blood to inspire a barbed response in *Economica* from Keynes himself ("one of the most frightful muddles I have ever read"[64]). As Hayek became an increasingly influential figure on the American political Right in the second half of the twentieth century, his early exchange with Keynes would take on a near-mythic status as a great clash of economic titans.[65]

It was not. But it *was* the opening salvo in a very serious, multigenerational struggle over political theory. The great battles in that struggle, however, were still decades away.

As economists processed Keynes' latest theory, the Great Depression deepened all over the world. In the United States, between August 1929 and August 1930, total production plunged by 27 percent, wholesale prices dropped by more than 13 percent, and personal income fell by 17 percent. Hundreds of banks failed across Missouri, Indiana, Illinois, Iowa, Arkansas, and North Carolina, while in New York, the Bank of the United States—a private commercial bank that catered largely to immigrants—became the largest bank to fail in U.S. history.[66] Millions of people were thrown out of work as factories slowed or shut down altogether. Breadlines and soup kitchens tried to feed the hungry, but soon charities were strained to their limits. Nothing like it had ever happened before. "The funds we have are altogether inadequate to meet the situation," reported Arthur Burns, the head of the Association of Community Chests and Councils of America. In an era before federal unemployment benefits, only eight states offered financial aid to the out-of-work, none of it sufficient to meet the accelerating social emergency. In rural America, according to the historian Robert S. McElvaine, "hungry people sometimes turned to eating weeds," while in American cities "scenes of men digging through garbage cans and city dumps" became commonplace. In March 1930, hundreds of New Yorkers waiting in a breadline attacked a pair of trucks making a bakery delivery, scattering pastries into the street.[67]

In Great Britain, the unemployment rate soared over the course of 1930 from 12.4 percent to 19.9 percent.[68] British exports, already struggling due to the overvalued pound, fell by nearly 40 percent from their 1929 peak.[69]

The perils in the United States and Great Britain were moderate compared to the disaster unfolding in Germany. On September 14, Adolf Hitler's Nazi Party shocked the world by securing 6.4 million votes and 107 seats in the German Reichstag, making it the second-most-popular political party in that fracturing country. In October, Hjalmar Schacht, the financial alchemist who had orchestrated Germany's revival after the hyperinflation disaster of 1923, embarked on a speaking tour of the United States in which he blamed Hitler's rise on Germany's abuse under the Treaty of Versailles, explicitly linking Nazi popularity to the severity of the reparation demands. By 1930, reparations were just one of several factors crushing the German economy—tight lending from America and the collapse of world markets for German exports were at least as onerous—but reparations became the scapegoat. "If the German people are going to starve, there are going to be many more Hitlers," Schacht told *The New York Times*.[70]

Amid so much darkness, Keynes retained a buoyant spirit. There was no denying things were bad. But he was convinced that they would not always be so. "Both of the two opposed errors of pessimism which now make so much noise in the world will be proved wrong in our own time," he told readers of *The Nation*, "the pessimism of the revolutionaries who think that things are so bad that nothing can save us but violent change, and the pessimism of the reactionaries who consider the balance of our economic and social life so precarious that we must risk no experiments."[71]

Part of this sunny demeanor was just Keynes being Keynes. His optimism was deeply ingrained, a matter almost of moral conviction, and was encouraged by his personal joy at finding himself back at the center of things. Everyone was talking about what he had to say. He was not only being asked to write for publications and advise the prime minister but to prepare broadcasts for a new and powerful medium in British politics, the radio—operated by the British Broadcasting Company, founded in 1922. "Therefore, O patriotic housewives, sally out tomorrow early into the streets and go to the wonderful sales which are everywhere advertised," he advised listeners in January 1931. "You will do yourselves good—for never were things so cheap, cheap beyond your dreams. Lay in a stock of household linen, of sheets and blankets to satisfy all your needs. And have the added joy that you are increasing employment, adding to the wealth of the country because you are setting on foot useful activities. . . . For what we need now is not to button up our waistcoats tight, but to be in a mood of expansion, of activity—to do things, to buy things, to make things."[72] The broadcast was published as an essay in *The Listener*, and Keynes found himself deluged with fan mail.

But much of Keynes' enthusiastic disposition came from his enduring faith in the power of ideas. He had been thinking about the economic miseries of the postwar world for a decade and had come to the conclusion that global calamity was a result of simple intellectual error. The problems were great, but they had straightforward and essentially painless solutions.

In October 1930, Keynes published an essay entitled "Economic Possibilities for Our Grandchildren," an unapologetically utopian portrait of a near future in which people worked "three-hour shifts or a fifteen-hour week"[73] and enjoyed an eightfold increase in their standard of living. Technological advance and the power of compound interest[74] would soon lead to unheard-of economic productivity— new machines that rendered human labor increasingly obsolete. The process had already begun, and would reach fruition within a century. "In our own lifetimes . . . we may be able to perform all the operations of agriculture, mining, and manufacture with a quarter of the human effort to which we have been accustomed."[75]

Such massive changes were a cause for celebration rather than alarm. "This means that the economic problem is not—if we look into the future—*the permanent problem of the human race.*"[76] The era of history in which human beings struggled to secure food, housing, clothing, and—if they were lucky—the occasional luxury was coming to an end. Not only would citizens be liberated from dull jobs and the anxiety of low bank balances; a revolution in cultural values was just over the horizon. "When the accumulation of wealth is no longer of high social importance, there will be great changes in the code of morals," Keynes wrote. "The love of money as a possession—as distinguished from the love of money as a means to the enjoyments and realities of life—will be recognized for what it is, a somewhat disgusting morbidity, one of those semi-criminal, semi-pathological propensities which one hands over with a shudder to the specialists in mental disease."[77]

The era of scarce resources was coming to an end and with it, the need to sacrifice moral and ethical concerns to the needs of efficiency. "I see us free, therefore, to return to some of the most sure and certain principles of religion and traditional virtue—that avarice is a vice, that the exaction of usury is a misdemeanor, and the love of money is detestable, that those walk most truly in the paths of virtue and sane wisdom who take least thought for the morrow. We shall once more

value ends above means and prefer the good to the useful."[78] Bloomsbury would triumph over Wall Street, as citizens savored good states
of mind and the joys of creative life. It would happen within eighty
years. All we had to do was avoid major wars and population booms,
while keeping an eye on capital accumulation and distribution. In the
depths of the worst depression in living memory, Keynes declared that
the permanent end of all economic woe was in sight.

Robert Skidelsky and other historians have noted the similarity in
Keynes' vision to that presented by the young Karl Marx in *The German Ideology*, one of the only sketches Marx ever presented of what he
believed life after the Communist revolution might look like. Under
capitalism, he wrote, "man's own deed becomes an alien power opposed to him, which enslaves him instead of being controlled by him.
For as soon as the distribution of labour comes into being, each man
has a particular, exclusive sphere of activity, which is forced upon him
and from which he cannot escape. He is a hunter, a fisherman, a shepherd, or a critical critic, and must remain so if he does not want to lose
his means of livelihood; while in communist society, where nobody
has one exclusive sphere of activity but each can become accomplished
in any branch he wishes, society regulates the general production and
thus makes it possible for me to do one thing today and another tomorrow, to hunt in the morning, fish in the afternoon, rear cattle in
the evening, criticise after dinner, just as I have a mind, without ever
becoming hunter, fisherman, shepherd or critic."[79]

Keynes had not read the Marx essay. It had been suppressed during
Marx's lifetime and was not published until 1932.[80] And Keynesian
utopia was more conservative than the Marxist vision. It would be the
peaceful end product of capitalism, not the result of its violent overthrow. But the social vision—the good society toward which both
men strived—was remarkably similar. Both yearned for a world in
which the daily interests and ideas of citizens would be able to take
priority over the requirements of material sustenance and the drudg-
ery of mindless wage work.

Keynes and Marx also shared the unfortunate fate of being right
about the revolutions to come and wrong about their social implica-

tions. As Marx predicted, Communists overthrew capitalists all over the world in the twentieth century. Keynes, for his part, got his math about right. If anything, he was overly pessimistic about the economic potential about to be unleashed. By 2008, the Nobel laureate economist Joseph Stiglitz has noted, global economic output reached a level sufficient to raise every man, woman, and child on the face of the earth above the U.S. poverty line—a very great improvement for the domestic poor and an astounding achievement for the global poor.[81] According to a recent analysis by Harvard University economist Benjamin M. Friedman, we are, moreover, on track for an eightfold increase in the standard of living in the United States by 2029—if standard of living is taken to mean the total economic output per person.[82] "The numbers hang together," observed another Nobel laureate, Robert Solow[83]—even though the world did not, in fact, escape several catastrophic wars in the decades since Keynes' essay.

But the age of farmer-critic-fishermen is not yet upon us. We do not live in a utopia where all people work fifteen hours a week, reserving the rest of their time for painting, literature, and walks in the park. What went wrong? In his essay, Keynes distinguished between human needs essential to survival and semi-needs whose "satisfaction lifts us above, makes us feel superior to, our fellows. Needs of the second class, those which satisfy the desire for superiority, may indeed be insatiable."[84] This effort to keep up with the Joneses has no doubt played a role in lengthening the workweek. But the primary culprit is simple inequality. The tremendous expansion of output and productivity over the past ninety years has been harvested for the most part by a very small section of society. For everyone else, economic prospects are roughly where they were in the mid-1920s (although a decline in the overall workweek from 1930 to 1970 suggests very clearly that people are not really eager to work the hours they do). As any working family can attest, they work because they have to.

Keynes, in short, overlooked the need to regulate economic distribution—either through the structures of markets themselves or through activist tax policy. Living up to "Economic Possibilities for Our Grandchildren" would have required hefty taxes on the wealthy, a mechanism to guarantee that workers shared proportionally in corporate gains, and a political process that prevented powerful entities from hijacking the spoils.

"Economic Possibilities for Our Grandchildren" was not a light-hearted flight of fancy; it was a serious work that helps place Keynes' other economic theory in philosophical context. Keynes did not see economics as a foundational science upon which politics must be carefully constructed—it was a passing phase, almost past its period of relevance. Without the constraints of resource scarcity, economics as a discipline wouldn't matter much at all. In the classless society of the near future, economists would be like "dentists"—respectable, professional, and politically irrelevant.

"Economic Possibilities for Our Grandchildren" was the last major essay Keynes would publish in *The Nation and Athenaeum*. The Liberal Party's fate as a second-tier organization in British politics had been sealed by the 1929 election, rendering the effort to shape its agenda increasingly unnecessary. *The New Statesman* was a like-minded publication looking for a new editor, and Leonard Woolf, enjoying the financial security provided by the success of his wife's recent novels, was ready to leave the hectic demands of a thinly staffed weekly publication.[85] *The New Statesman* agreed to a merger in which Keynes named Kingsley Martin as the new editor and was himself named chairman. The combined paper was renamed *The New Statesman and Nation*. But Keynes' days as a minor media mogul were over. His columns and commentary would be the only elements of his old paper's identity that would survive the deal. For the remainder of his life, his professional attention would be focused on academic research and his duties in public office.

He did not lose many readers in the merger. The sheer awfulness of the Depression was helping him build a wider audience for his various calls to break with financial orthodoxy. Whatever merits the City doctrine might have had before the war, everyone could see that things were not working anymore. Keynes might be giving strange advice, but he had very publicly lost every serious policy battle since 1919. At the very least, he could not be blamed for the current state of affairs.

For Keynes, the only pleasure greater than the joy of being right was being right when everyone of respectability was wrong. And the most politically shocking turn in his thought after the Wall Street crash wasn't his theory of money or his case for public works or even his vision of unlimited prosperity a few decades around the corner; it was his call for a tariff.

His friends were among the first to learn of his conversion. "Maynard has become a Protectionist," Virginia wrote to a friend in September 1930. "Which horrified me so that I promptly fainted."[86]

In March 1931, Keynes told the world in the second issue of *The New Statesman and Nation,* prompting a flurry of editorial cartoons and newspaper attention. Economically, the proposal fit neatly with his call for low interest rates and public works. By overvaluing the pound in 1925, Great Britain had made its products too expensive on the international market and given foreign products a pricing edge in its home market. It could ameliorate this position by forcing down its domestic wages to reduce the price of its exports, but six years of that project had not done the trick. Devaluing the currency—going off the gold standard—would also work, but, as Keynes had noted in *A Treatise on Money,* doing so would be a dramatic change that could lead to unpredictable disruptions. Instead, Britain could level the playing field in its domestic market by imposing a tariff on foreign goods. That wouldn't help it export more, but it would help boost sales within the country for British manufacturers, who were currently forced to compete with artificially cheap imports. It would raise the cost of living by increasing prices for domestic consumers, but not by much—and a modest cost of living bump would bring a significant increase in new jobs. Since the trade position was already out of kilter, the boost to incomes created by those jobs would even help the British buy more imports. Best of all, any tax revenue generated by the tariff could be spent on public works.

In principle, none of this was any more radical than what Keynes had outlined in the pages of *The Manchester Guardian* in the early 1920s, when he had called for flexible exchange rates. Both tariffs and monetary adjustments were efforts to alter the flow of trade, thus expanding domestic production and employment. One functioned by changing the price of goods, the other by changing the price of money, but the effect was the same.

Great Britain's free-trading economy, moreover, was more dependent on exports than it was on imports. Food and the basics of heavy industry—coal and iron—it had in abundance, and what the island lacked, the empire could provide. It would take a hit on efficiency—but only relative to a free-trading ideal. And Keynes knew that the world of 1931 was not an ideal one. The monetary malpractice of the 1920s meant that trade had not really been free for some time. Britain was already suffering the worst that it could expect from a trade war; it had little to risk from escalation.

But in interwar England, the tariff was a political bombshell. Here was Keynes, champion of the Liberal-Labour alliance, endorsing the central plank of the Conservative economic platform. Since the turn of the century, the Conservative vision for the British Empire had been based on the notion that domestic prosperity would be secured through a tariff, which would protect local industry from foreign competition as it raised money to be spent on small social welfare measures. Even in the election of 1923, when exchange rate questions and the gold standard had first come to the forefront of Keynes' theoretical endeavors, he himself had not been able to stomach a call for tariffs on the campaign trail. His old undergraduate cry of "Free trade and free thought!" had still been too central to his understanding of what it meant to be a right-minded Liberal. Even Labour socialists believed in free trade. It was heresy, not against "the maxims of City pundits" but against the foundation of liberalism itself, and Keynes knew it. So he tried to give the minds he would shock a way to accept the policy without renouncing their doctrine in full.

"Free traders may, consistently with their faith, regard a revenue tariff as our iron ration, which can be used once only in emergency," he wrote. "The emergency has arrived. Under cover of the breathing space and the margin of financial strength thus afforded us, we could frame a policy and a plan, both domestic and international, for marching to the assault against the spirit of contractionism and fear."[87]

It did little good. Nearly all of his economic allies in the intelligent-sia either turned away in horror or returned fire in outrage. Keynes' own paper, *The New Statesman and Nation,* published a barrage of criticism from nearly a dozen prominent writers, including his Cam-bridge colleague Lionel Robbins and William Beveridge, who would later author Britain's National Health Service and post–World War II welfare state hand in hand with Keynes.[88] The wife of Philip Snowden, Labour's chancellor of the exchequer, wrote to Keynes on March 7, 1931, "I have read your article, and will tell him the contents when he is able to listen. I dare say he will feel as sad as I do that you should think it necessary to take this line, for we are as strongly convinced that it is wrong . . . as you are that it is right."[89]

Indeed, many economic thinkers who had been open to reforms during the 1920s now reacted to the deteriorating international em-ployment and trade conditions by clinging—however implausibly—to whatever remnants of intellectual normalcy they could. Perhaps *some-thing* was wrong, but surely not *everything* they had believed in had to be thrown out. If Keynes was now calling for a tariff, maybe his other ideas weren't as promising as reformers had believed. Hubert Hender-son, the *Nation* editor who had enthusiastically coauthored *Can Lloyd George Do It?* with Keynes in 1929, now scolded his friend for profli-gacy:

> My complaint against the tenor of all your public writings or utter-ances in the last year or so is that in not a single one of them has there been a trace of a suggestion that the Budget situation is one which is really very serious and must be treated seriously. On the contrary, over and over again you have implied that it doesn't matter a bit, that ex-penditure is a thing you want to press on with, whether by the Gov-ernment or by anybody else, and that the question of whether it involves a Budget charge is a minor matter which is hardly worth considering. . . . The effect is to convey the impression to all people, however intelligent and open-minded, who have some appreciation of the financial difficulties, that you have gone completely crazy.[90]

Henderson was right that Great Britain's budgetary position was not good. Under the gold standard, overspending governments could literally run out of money. If a government ran out of gold, the nation would be bankrupt—forced to pick and choose which obligations to meet and which to default upon. And after a decade of weak economic performance and an ugly balance of trade, that limit was not far off. The Bank of England had raised interest rates right into 1931 in an attempt to attract more gold to Britain, even though doing so had slowed the British economy. Even the Labour government was running a budget surplus—taxing more than it spent—to maintain investor confidence in the pound and discourage pound holders from cashing out their notes for gold. But Britain risked running out of money precisely because it spent more on imports at home than it received from exports abroad. The tariff Keynes advocated would attempt to stop that outflow by discouraging imports and, where they could not be blocked altogether, collecting a tax.

Keynes was unsparing with his critics, accusing them of empty "parrot talk from the past."[91] He attacked Beveridge for "pure intellectual error . . . shared, I fancy, by a multitude of less eminent free traders."[92] Consciously or not, his critics were all insisting that they lived in a self-correcting international economy, when the global economy had been stubbornly refusing to correct itself for a decade.

"The ideal of the free play of natural forces simply cannot be pursued today—the contrary forces are too strong,"[93] Keynes wrote in a follow-up for *The New Statesman*. "My critics have not taken any notice of, or shown the slightest interest in, the analysis of our present state, which occupied most of my original article and led up to my tariff proposal. . . . Is it the fault of the *odium theologicum* attaching to free trade? Is it that economics is a queer subject or in a queer state? Whatever may be the reason, new paths of thought have no appeal to the fundamentalists of free trade. They have been forcing me to chew over again a lot of stale mutton, dragging me along a route I have known all about as long as I have known anything, which cannot, as I have discovered by many attempts, lead one to a solution of our present difficulties—a peregrination of the catacombs with a guttering candle."[94]

Calling for the tariff had been an attempt to reckon with a mathematical error Churchill had made on the return to gold, but it forced Keynes to reevaluate his beliefs about the connection between free trade and international harmony. He retained his faith in the power of trade to connect cultures and enable disparate peoples to appreciate one another. But the cultural exports that actually fostered mutual understanding between nations were becoming a vanishingly small part of the modern economic mix. When the economist David Ricardo had made the classical argument for free trade in the early nineteenth century, scarcity had been the paramount economic problem.[95] Free trade, Ricardo had explained, allowed countries to specialize in what they did best, enabling the world economy to produce more than if each individual country tried to supply itself with homegrown goods. But technology had eliminated many of the advantages of national specialization. International trade was dominated by heavy manufacturing products that could now be made for the same price just about anywhere. Wherever they came from, coal was coal, steel was steel, and cars were cars. "Experience accumulates to prove that most modern mass-production processes can be performed in most countries and climates with almost equal efficiency," Keynes wrote in 1933.

There would be costs for any nation that wished to make the lion's share of its economy a domestic concern. But innovation had dramatically reduced those costs. National self-sufficiency, he wrote, was fast "becoming a luxury which we can afford if we happen to want it."[96]

And he believed that there might very well be reasons to want it. The hyper-financialization of the global economy had separated business owners from the social impact of their ownership decisions. Shareholders on Wall Street didn't lose much sleep over profits generated from polluting a river in Pennsylvania or laying off workers in Minnesota; they didn't swim in the rivers or spend Christmas with the jobless. When that kind of abuse took place across international borders, however, it sowed resentments. Hot speculative money could flow into currencies and industries one day, then draw out the next without any concern for what would happen to the people who lived in the communities where those funds were flooded and withdrawn. "The remoteness between ownership and operation is an evil in the relations between men, likely or certain in the long run to set up strains and enmities," he observed. But at least within national boundaries there was a political body that could set rules about the way the financial sector could behave, and police abuses. Across national borders, there was no social accountability. "It does not now seem obvious," Keynes wrote, "that the penetration of a country's economic structure by the resources and the influence of foreign capitalists, that a close dependence of our own economic life on the fluctuating economic policies of foreign countries, are safeguards and assurances of international peace." "Ideas, knowledge, art, hospitality, travel—these are the things which should of their nature be international," he wrote. "But let goods be homespun whenever it is reasonably and conveniently possible; and, above all, let finance be primarily national."[97] It was a total repudiation of his prewar view of the world.

As it happened, global currency flows and the realpolitik of Parliament would determine the fate of the tariff, rather than debates in a liberal magazine. On May 11, 1931, the Austrian economy ran out of international rope. Creditanstalt, by far the largest bank in Vienna with fully half of the country's total deposits, collapsed. It was a devastating psychological blow to the Austrian banking system. Creditanstalt was the most prestigious bank in the country. Its board of directors included Baron Louis de Rothschild along with men from the Bank of England and the German banking house of M.M. Warburg—the same banking dynasty that included Paul Warburg, a founder of the Federal Reserve.[98] If Creditanstalt was going down, Austrian depositors wondered, imagine the condition of the other Austrian banking houses.

The run on Austrian banks quickly escalated into a run on the schilling itself, as anxious investors and opportunistic speculators began to believe that the Bank of Austria might run out of gold, too. They began cashing out their schilling notes en masse, which of course only accelerated the drain on the government's gold reserves. In London, Bank of England governor Montagu Norman pledged emergency funds to try to salvage the Austrian currency—and with it Austria's standing as a nation pegged to the gold standard. It was a heroic maneuver from Norman, who knew perfectly well that the Bank of England's own position was far from secure. But he didn't get much help. A broader coalition including the United States, France, and Belgium provided just $14 million in relief—almost imperceptible in the face of Creditanstalt's $100 million in short-term foreign obligations.[99]

The international aid to Austria was too little, too late. Vienna had no choice but to suspend its commitment to the gold standard. And the contagion had already spread to Germany, where funds were now flowing out at an alarming rate. For the United States, the German crisis had enormous potential consequences, thanks to the international cycle of credit that had been established by the Dawes Plan.

Keynes had set off to the States during the Austrian crisis to give a series of lectures in Chicago and meet with President Hoover and Fed chairman Eugene Meyer in Washington.[100] Along the way, he discovered the flaw in his sanguine analysis of the 1929 stock market debacle. "The anxiety of many banks and of many depositors throughout the country is a dominating factor, the importance of which I had not fully estimated before visiting the United States," he wrote to the Economic Advisory Council in London. "It is, I think one of the biggest obstacles overhanging the situation."[101]

Under the Dawes Plan, U.S. banks loaned money to Germany, which paid it to France and England in reparations, which in turn paid the United States and U.S. banks interest on war debts. Europe's finances would break down if American banks did not restart the cycle by providing fresh international credit to Germany. And after the stock market crash of 1929, the funds available to U.S. banks that might have gone to Germany began to be squandered in bank failures. In the final two months of 1930 alone, 608 American banks control-

ling $550 million in deposits had failed.[102] But just as Berlin was de-
pendent on loans from New York for its financial survival, so too were
New York banks dependent on German repayment for their own solvency. Berlin, Keynes learned, now owed £200 million to New York
lenders, including an average of over £20 million to each of the five
largest banks in Manhattan. Those were "sums far larger than they
could afford to see in jeopardy on the top of their other troubles."[103] If
Berlin fell, everyone feared, so would New York, and with it the dollar
and the whole global economic order that had been chained to it by
the gold standard. The global economy stood at the edge of a precipice.

In New York, Thomas Lamont called Herbert Hoover. Now that all
else had failed, it was time to face up to the problem established in
1919: unpayable war debts and reparations. As an emergency measure,
Hoover could impose a one-year moratorium on all war loans and
reparation dues. The political gesture might be enough to quell the
panic and buy the world time to save the international banking system
from a catastrophic collapse. Lamont promised to give Hoover credit
for the idea and subtly vowed to clear the Republican presidential
field of any primary challengers in the 1932 presidential election, now
only a year away. "These days you hear a lot of people whispering
about sidetracking the Administration in the 1932 Convention," he
told Hoover. "If you were to come out with such a plan as this, these
whisperings would be silenced overnight."[104]

Hoover did it. The French were enraged by the leniency to Germany, but the accelerating currency crisis forced them to come to an
agreement by July. It should have been a moment of glory for Keynes.
The very same American diplomats who had stymied him on the
question of war debts at Paris had finally acknowledged, in deed if not
in word, that he had been right all along. But the triumph came too
late.

While the French negotiated with Hoover, German banks began to
fail. Germany pleaded first with England and then—as an almost inconceivable last resort—with France for an emergency loan to stabilize the mark. The French, recognizing that Germany was not in a
position to refuse, demanded that a set of political conditions be in-

cluded in any aid package: Germany would have to abandon a planned
trading union with Austria, halt the construction of two battleships,
and ban nationalist street demonstrations. They were mild terms, but
the German government could not bear to submit to political demands from the French, whose army had been in the Ruhr just six
years prior. Germany rejected the offer, preferring to risk financial
death over international dishonor. It then implemented a desperate
slate of restrictions to rebuild the country's once again decimated
monetary position, a last-ditch effort to fend off what everyone worried would be a disaster on par with 1923. The Reichsbank raised interest rates to a shocking 15 percent. The Treasury suspended interest
payments on foreign debts and began limiting the withdrawal of
capital from the country.[105] It was the end of the gold standard in
Germany. If foreign creditors could not move money in and out of
Germany, the reichsmark was no longer really exchangeable for gold.

The German debt default and capital controls only intensified the
anxiety of international investors and currency speculators with commitments in other shaky countries. The panic now spread not, as
Lamont and Hoover had feared, to the United States, but rather to
the even more fragile British financial system.

On July 13, the Macmillan Committee issued its final report on the
British banking system and its role in the economy. It had been, on the
whole, a satisfying experience for Keynes. The hearings had provided
him direct access to the leading financial minds of his country for the
first time since the war, and his public questioning had embarrassed
some of his old nemeses, particularly Norman. Though he had dominated the proceedings, he referred to the committee's report as a
"compromise" he was "rather happy about" despite its flaws as a "long-
winded" "composite" of different views.[106] Sadly for Keynes, nobody
cared about the theoretical work or policy advice it contained. Instead,
investors focused on a set of statistics buried within the report. London banks owed £407 million in short-term funds to other countries.[107] But that was not the most important side of the balance sheet.

London banks also had about £100 million in assets that were now tied up in Germany.[108] With such large debts and frozen assets, investors suddenly worried that the British banking system was insolvent. When German chancellor Heinrich Brüning announced the German debt default on July 15, the run on British banks began. The Bank of England lost about £2.5 million in gold every day until August 1, when it obtained a total of £50 million in funding from the Banque de France and the Federal Reserve Bank of New York.[109]

In the subsequent calm, Prime Minister MacDonald wrote to Keynes, asking for thoughts on an austerity package the Labour government was considering as part of a plan to balance the budget—a gambit intended to boost investor confidence with the British.

Keynes was horrified. He told MacDonald that the package of government spending cuts and tax increases would be "both futile and disastrous." It was an affront to "social justice" to ask teachers and the unemployed to carry the burden of deflating a doomed currency in the name of balanced budgets. "It is now nearly *certain* that we shall go off the existing gold parity at no distant date. Whatever may have been the case some time ago, it is now too late to avoid this. We can put off the date for a time. . . . But when doubts as to the prosperity of a currency, such as now exist about sterling, have come into existence, the game's up."[110] Instead, he argued, the British should pursue a new global currency union along with an international public works campaign to rebuild their own economy and that of continental Europe.

The French and American loan bought the British about a week of relief before the run on the pound began again. Forced to abandon a vacation, MacDonald took a midnight train to London to begin negotiations for yet another loan to defend the British currency. He reached out to the unofficial agent of U.S. foreign policy, the House of Morgan, to raise a loan from Wall Street investors. Morgan wanted political concessions as a demonstration of the British willingness to repay. High priests of the dying orthodoxy, they called for the government to deflate its currency by balancing the budget. It was another battle between Keynes and the austerians, a replay of the struggle in 1919.

Morgan partner Edward Grenfell made clear to MacDonald that there would be no loan without a serious attack on government spending and British wages. "We are all getting tired of promises," he told the prime minister.[111] Privately, Grenfell doubted the Labour leader's willingness to slash salaries and social services. He had always had a low opinion of MacDonald, once telling Lamont "The only white thing about him is his liver, and the only portion of him that is not red is his blood,"[112] a double-barreled insult that succinctly encapsulated the Morgan clan's racial and economic worldview.

On August 12, Keynes revised his dour prediction—slightly. It might be possible to preserve the gold standard in England, he wrote to MacDonald, but only if the government undertook a comprehensive program rejecting deflation: a tariff, massive public works, slashing interest rates. But it would have to be a big, go-for-broke program, something to shock the system. "The impressions I have collected today persuade me that there will be a crisis within a month unless the most drastic and sensational action is taken."[113]

The chaos in the money markets was becoming a cultural event. Just as in the days before the general strike, economic turmoil was taking over dinner conversations and street corners. The nation pulsed with a sense of foreboding, while the prospect of devaluing the currency or going off gold was becoming an insult to "national pride" in some quarters.[114] "The country is in the throes of a crisis," Virginia Woolf recorded in her diary on August 15. "Great events are brewing. Maynard visits Downing Street & spreads sensational rumours . . . will future ages, as they say, behold our predicament (financial) with horror?"[115]

MacDonald and his chancellor of the Exchequer, Philip Snowden, were no cowards. Both men had made tremendous personal sacrifices for their beliefs and taken daring political stands on the world stage. An ardent pacifist, Snowden had nearly destroyed his political career by opposing the war. MacDonald's indignation over the Ruhr invasion had finally forced the Americans to get involved in the European postwar crisis. But after a series of covert cables among Morgan, the New York Fed, the Bank of England, and MacDonald, the prime minister rejected the Keynes plan. It was simply too radical even for the socialist prime minister.

Instead, MacDonald and Snowden threw their weight behind a Morgan-approved program to raise taxes by £60 million and cut spending by £70 million, including a 10 percent reduction in unemployment benefits.[116] It was a political thunderbolt. The idea of attacking unemployment benefits with over a million men still out of work was abhorrent to the rest of the Labour government. The bedrock social justice commitments of a British socialist administration were being held hostage by a team of American bankers. As negotiations reached their climax on the evening of Sunday, August 23, the Labour government descended into "pandemonium," its ministers "hot and tired" and consumed by "bickering." At 10:20 P.M., an exhausted MacDonald presented his resignation to the king.[117]

But the austerians were not finished. The next day, MacDonald was renamed prime minister as the head of a new coalition of all the opposition parties allied against Labour, making him a left-wing figurehead for a Tory government. The budget cuts were approved and Morgan kept its promise, organizing a $200 million loan for the British government from the United States, coupled with another $200 million from France.[118]

Keynes was despondent. "The country has been stampeded into an attempt to make this deflation effective, and heaven knows how it will end,"[119] he wrote to his mother. To New York banker Walter Case he reported being "utterly depressed. . . . To read the newspapers just now is to see Bedlam let loose."[120]

Publicly, he denounced the deal. It wouldn't work. Great Britain couldn't deflate its way to salvation. The Morgan loans would be water down the drain. The gold standard had broken Europe. As he had warned in 1925, it had chained British policy to the priorities of an unreliable Federal Reserve, which had hoarded gold while Europe burned. There was, Keynes saw, a remarkable difference between the Fed's crisis management in 1931 and the British response to the financial crisis of 1914. As Great Britain kept money flowing on demand to where it was wanted, the Fed had protected the American stockpile, fearing a U.S. default. More than half of the world's gold reserves were now in the United States, where they sat useless in vaults, instead of being loaned out to countries in financial distress or even to faltering American banks on the brink of collapse. Neither the British budget nor the cash infusion would fix that underlying problem.

"The government's policy is, in truth, no policy at all," Keynes told readers of *The New Statesman and Nation*. "They have submitted to the conditions of foreign lenders as to the manner in which we should balance our budget, in order to obtain a short-term loan expressed in foreign currencies which will enable us to repay short-term loans expressed in sterling. . . . The whole world is heartily sick of the selfishness and folly with which the international gold standard is being worked. Instead of being a means of facilitating international trade, the gold standard has become a curse laid upon the economic life of the world."[121]

The attack on the pound continued, revealing the folly of the Morgan-MacDonald plan. On September 16, members of the House of Commons called in Keynes to discuss the crisis. In blunt terms, he told them the country was headed for disaster. "The Budget fails on every test," the notes of his speech read. "In my opinion the Govt.'s programme is one of the most wrong and foolish things which Parliament has deliberately perpetrated in my lifetime."[122] It would increase unemployment by 10 percent by Christmas alone and probably cost 400,000 jobs by the time it had finished working its course. It might improve the balance of trade, but only because people would spend less on food imports after being thrown out of work. "What an extraordinarily roundabout and extravagant way of reducing our imports of food!"

His policy advice was by now familiar: tariffs and subsidies for British producers to improve the trade situation; an international agreement to cancel all war debts and reparations; international funding of the other external debts of all debtor countries for three years; a massive new pool of international credit to finance improvements to government infrastructure; "cheap money everywhere"; and "every govt. to undertake large public works programme."[123]

Both the spirit and the letter of the proposal were strikingly similar to the international prescription Keynes had written in 1919. The cocktail had been strengthened with tariffs and public works, but he was fundamentally concerned with the same problem: The private interests of the major players in the global financial system were either unwilling to or incapable of addressing the social challenges faced by Europe. The problems were too big, the cost of failure too high. However difficult it might be to forge, there was simply no alternative to a state-backed system.

"During the last 12 years I have had very little influence, if any, on policy," he told the lawmakers. "But in the role of a Cassandra, I have had a considerable success as a prophet. I declare to you, and I will stake on it any reputation I have, that we have been making in the last few weeks as dreadful errors of policy as deluded statesmen have ever been guilty of."[124]

The austerian victory was pyrrhic. By September 18, the Morgan loan had been exhausted in a fruitless effort to support the British currency. Its back to the wall and all other options exhausted, the government at last severed ties with the gold standard on September 21, 1931. Keynes spent the morning not at Whitehall or in Parliament but in Bloomsbury, sitting with Virginia Woolf and Richard Kahn. They were "like people in the war," Virginia recalled. "Guards out: Tower defended" as they talked economics and politics.[125] It was an appropriate description. The demise of the gold standard was the final battle in an economic struggle Keynes had been fighting since he had scrambled to London in the sidecar of Vivian Hill's motorcycle in August 1914. And his experience with the Labour government carried echoes of his role with Lloyd George at Paris in 1919. Once again, his influence as an adviser to his own government had been overwhelmed by American financial intransigence. And once again his advice had proved tragically correct. For Great Britain and the United States, the price would be another war.

EIGHT

◇

PHOENIX

IN EARLY JANUARY 1932, Keynes made a brief, quiet trip to Berlin—no public announcement, no newspaper fanfare, not even an entry in his appointment book. He was beloved in Germany for his attack on the Treaty of Versailles and his persistent calls for international leniency on reparations, but he and conservative chancellor Heinrich Brüning were not kindred spirits. During a long meeting with Keynes, Brüning maintained that his country had been too scarred by the hyperinflation of 1923 to consider tactics that might prove inflationary. Absent some form of international aid, he would balance the country's books the old-fashioned way—through continued, grinding deflation.

"I am just back from a short visit to Germany," Keynes wrote to Bank of England director Alexander Shaw on January 13, 1932. "The position there is really appalling."[1] In the pages of *The New Statesman and Nation* he was more specific: "Germany today is in the grip of the most terrible deflation that any nation had experienced. . . . The result reaches, or goes beyond, the limit of what is endurable. . . . Too many people in Germany have nothing to look forward to—nothing except a 'change,' something wholly vague and wholly undefined, but a *change*. And it is now more than seventeen years since the outbreak of war."[2]

Ruefully, Keynes attacked the "experts" who had led Germany to a state in which a third of the population was out of work and the standard of living "cruelly curtailed" for everyone else. The public psychology of austerity was generating extreme resentment toward the authors of that austerity both at home and abroad. "The reparations problem has become a matter of human feelings of deep popular gusts of passion, and, consequently, of very simple reactions and decisions," he wrote. "Although it is scientifically true" that Germany's situation "was created by a complex of events of which reparations and war debts have been only one, the common man cannot be expected to see it this way. If he is to think and feel about it at all, as today he must, he has to simplify it. And if he is determined on a 'change,' he can only demand what is concrete and appears to him to be within his mere power to effect."[3]

It was the same political warning against providing fuel for a strongman that Keynes had offered in 1919, and he repeated his now-tired call to eliminate war debts and reparations while moving forward with an international reconstruction plan. But the tone of solemnity that permeates the brief article suggests Keynes recognized the game was up. The piece has no rhetorical fire, no biting invective or witticism to distinguish it as one of his great essays. It is haunted by the recognition that a great project—the cause that brought him international renown—was headed for a defeat too sinister to be measured on balance sheets.

Six months later, the German electorate forced Brüning from power. The young man whose Beer Hall Putsch had been the subject of international mockery after the disasters of 1923 became chancellor of Germany. His rise to official power tempted many in the press to moderate their judgments of the Führer and his Nazi Party. "The sharp edges of many of its views are becoming blunt," *The New York Times* calmed its readers, while *The Brooklyn Daily Eagle* soon concluded that Hitler was striking a "conciliatory note" that made him "barely recognizable" as the demagogue on the stump.[4] Even Walter Lippmann, the most prominent syndicated columnist in America, declared him "the authentic voice of a genuinely civilized people."[5] But

Keynes recognized Hitler's election as the unmitigated tragedy it was. "The Germans, broken in body and spirit, seek escape in a return backwards to the modes and manners of the Middle Ages, if not of Odin," he told readers of the *Daily Mail*.[6]

When he returned to the British government in the early 1930s, Keynes had grounds for optimism about the power of economic policy to improve the lives of his countrymen. His thinking over the previous decade had led him to believe that economic policy might be used not only to prevent many bad things but to actively promote something good, and elected officials had decided to give him not one but two official perches of influence on economic committees. But they had squandered his advice. And by 1932, it was not only Germany that appeared bleak. A second visit to Lydia's family in Leningrad had left Keynes "very depressed about the Bolshies." He did not write about it publicly, in an effort to spare his wife's family from potential Soviet retribution, but he confided his horrors to friends and family: "It is impossible to remember, until one gets in the country, how mad they are and that they care about their experiment more than about making things work."[7] In England, a young member of Parliament named Oswald Mosley had resigned when the MacDonald government had rebuffed Keynes' economic ideas during the 1931 crisis. He went on to found the British Union of Fascists. The economic problem, as Keynes feared, was festering into political instability, a public yearning for authoritarian solutions.

Meanwhile, Marxism was winning converts within Bloomsbury itself. The intellectual dance at Cambridge now moved to the beat set by Lytton's cousin John Strachey, who published a blistering Marxist-Leninist tract called *The Coming Struggle for Power* in 1932 that quickly became "the Bible for Cambridge students," according to Lorie Tarshis, a prominent Canadian economist who studied with Keynes in the 1930s.[8] Strachey did not deny that it was scientifically possible for capitalism to operate in a more humane fashion than it had since the war. But he and many other British Marxists believed that such reforms were politically impossible. The capitalist class that wielded power in Europe and the United States would never make the necessary concessions to working people absent a violent revolution.[9] And indeed, there were plenty of men on Wall Street and in the City of London who seemed to be trying to prove Strachey's point. Even when the Labour Party had been able to win elections, it had failed spectacularly in its economic efforts while taking financial marching orders from J.P. Morgan. The socialists had won over Vanessa's son Julian, now a Cambridge undergraduate, who reported home that "It would be difficult to find anyone of any intellectual pretensions who would not accept the general Marxist analysis of the present crisis."[10]

Still, Bloomsbury continued to follow the turns of Keynes' economic thought closely. But the question Bertrand Russell's wife, Dora, asked in a letter to *The New Statesman and Nation* was on everyone's mind: If Keynes' ideas were so good and entrenched class interests were not blocking their implementation, why hadn't anybody picked them up?

"Because I have not yet succeeded in convincing either the expert or the ordinary man that I am right," Keynes replied. "The class-war faction believe that it is well known what ought to be done; that we are divided between the poor and good who would like to do it, and the rich and wicked who, for reasons of self-interest, wish to prevent it; that the wicked have power; and that a revolution is required to depose them from their seats. I view the matter otherwise. I think it extremely difficult to know what ought to be done, and extremely difficult for those who know (or think they know) to persuade others that they are right—though theories, which are difficult and obscure when they are new and undigested, grow easier by the mere passage of time." Compared to the persuasive power of good ideas, he insisted, "the power of self-interested capitalists to stand in their way is negligible."[11]

This was quite a departure from the cheerful author of *Can Lloyd George Do It?*, who had assured the public that an ambitious public works agenda was the obvious and intuitive solution to Great Britain's recent troubles. *Everyone* could see it was the right way to go, Keynes had declared in 1929—at least, when they weren't being frightened out of their senses by the ravings of City pundits.

There was more to this reorientation than a rearguard action against historical materialism. Keynes was overhauling his approach to the art of persuasion. The arc of his public life from the outbreak of war to the British financial crisis of 1931 had been one long, fruitless attempt to bend European policy to his brilliance. As a member of the Treasury, he had failed to convince the war cabinet that financial pressures precluded a knockout blow or conscription. As a delegate to the Paris Peace Conference, he had failed to persuade world leaders that a lasting peace in Europe required a collaborative public commitment to rebuilding the continent. Ineffective as an insider, he had tried his hand as an outside agitator, pressuring the government as a journalist, public intellectual, and media mogul. By 1932, it was clear that in this, too, he had failed. He had conquered the Liberal Party just in time for the Liberals to become irrelevant. Though his proclamations in *The Economic Consequences of the Peace* and *The Economic Consequences of Mr. Churchill* were now conventional wisdom for the man on the street, the fulfillment of his prophecies had driven his political allies from power. Now the party he had opposed since childhood reigned, and imposed a tariff not out of any deference to Keynesian arguments but for the simple reason that Tories had been advocating tariffs for fifty years. Great Britain's break with the gold standard had given the country plenty of leeway to undertake a public works program, but none had made the governing agenda. Everyone agreed the Treaty of Versailles to be a debacle, but nobody had fixed it in time to prevent disaster in Germany.

When a 1933 conference tasked with overhauling the international monetary order collapsed without any plan or process for future cooperation, Keynes despaired of European leadership, predicting that the inability to overcome financial orthodoxy would spread the political disease already festering in Germany. "It is now evident that there was no cat in the bag, no rabbits in the hat—no brains in the head," he wrote. "The fiasco of the Conference merely increases the general cynicism and the lack of respect toward those in power. This growing lack of respect is, as recent examples elsewhere have shown, one of the most serious things which can befall a democracy."[12]

Keynes had fashioned an extraordinary career for himself over the course of this nightmare. By demystifying high finance for the general public, he had transformed himself into the world's foremost public intellectual. Economic ideas, he maintained, were not really all that complex; people were simply intimidated by the technical jargon financiers deployed and by the prestige of their affluent personas. Surely rich men must know something about money—how else would they have acquired so much of it? There was, it turned out, a tremendous market for anyone with credibility who could translate City babble into everyday English and knock down the arguments defending policies that everyone could see were not working.

His ability as a public intellectual brought him personal rewards beyond money. At age fifty, he was socially unrecognizable from the clever, promiscuous obscurity who had puttered off to Whitehall on his brother-in-law's motorcycle. He had a country estate, an open door at the offices of book publishers on every continent, invitations to parties with European royalty, and an internationally acclaimed ballerina as his wife. He was the chief patron of Bloomsbury, an art movement that had spawned at least one true genius in Virginia Woolf, whose work was celebrated on both sides of the Atlantic. A man of limited aesthetic talent himself, his fame and fortune had enabled him to thrive among the people he most wanted to emulate—the great artists of his day.

He seemed destined to be mentioned by writers compiling histories of the greater events he had lived through: the war, the Depression, modernism. But he was not a man whose life transcended the confines of his own era, because he had been unable to convert his fame into political power. The world forgot most of the celebrities from the interwar era decades ago. Keynes would be just another famous man in the footnotes had he not found a way to shape the future.

Keynes had built quite an audience as a man of letters, but the audience had not moved its leaders. Whatever they said during election season, once in power, prime ministers and cabinet officials turned to the same cult of financial mystics who issued their incantations, venerated their sacred equations, and inevitably divined that a balanced budget and high interest rates were the only true path to salvation. That priesthood, Keynes at last recognized, distilled much of its power from the separation it created between its own economic doctrines and the vulgar opinions of the general public. The more laymen Keynes persuaded, the easier it was for City prophets to convince politicians that they alone understood the true secrets drifting in the financial mists. Surely no sane prime minister would put a man off the street in charge of the Treasury; the more clamorous the calls for reform, the more important it was to have a reliable expert steering the ship. If Keynes wanted to reach the sovereigns, he would first have to convert the priesthood.

And so Keynes decided to become a mystic himself. He changed the way he described economic problems. No longer were financial dilemmas simple matters with easy solutions anyone could understand. They were hard, complex—the territory of brilliant gladiator-intellectuals questing after great truths. He stopped needling and mocking his adversaries in the popular press and began focusing his energy on technical arguments in academic journals. He cast himself not as a debunker of myths but as an economic Albert Einstein at work on the grand new theory that would revolutionize the old ways of thinking. It was a form of flattery directed against his academic opponents: they might be wrong, but they were not stupid or deluded; indeed, their views were so secure that only an intellectual sea change could be expected to move them at all. To his adversaries in public affairs, he avoided confrontation or even explanation. He was too busy with theoretical wonders beyond their comprehension to make time for their inquiries. When the banker R. H. Brand asked for help understanding the new "problems of demand" Keynes had mentioned in a radio address, Keynes brushed him away. "I am afraid there is nothing which I can yet refer you to," Keynes said before informing Brand that the opinions of bankers were not, at this moment of intellectual history, terribly important. Only economists mattered. "I am working hard at my new book. . . . When it appears, it will be on extremely academic lines; since I feel, rather definitely, that my object must first of all be to try and convince my economic colleagues."[13]

With his Marxist friends, Keynes began gesturing at vague vistas of thought he would soon unlock. "I believe myself to be writing a book on economic theory which will largely revolutionise—not, I suppose, at once but in the course of the next ten years—the way the world thinks about economic problems," he wrote to the socialist playwright George Bernard Shaw. "When my new theory has been duly assimilated and mixed with politics and feelings and passions, I can't predict what the final upshot will be in its effect on action and affairs. But there will be a great change, and, in particular, the Ricardian foundations of Marxism will be knocked away.

"I can't expect you, or anyone else, to believe this at the present stage. But for myself I don't merely hope what I say, in my own mind I'm quite sure."[14]

Such occult grandiosity must have baffled the English elite. Across the Atlantic, however, in a country Keynes did not like, whose government he had never trusted, events were conspiring to give economic heretics a chance at real power.

A week before the U.S. presidential election of 1932, Nevada governor Fred Balzar put in a call to his lieutenant governor, Morley Griswold. Balzar had spent the past few days in Washington negotiating—pleading, really—with officials in Herbert Hoover's administration for a $2 million emergency loan. A chain of Nevada banks owned by the western finance titan George Wingfield had been burning through cash all year, and the state's top political brass was convinced that the little empire was doomed without federal aid. Wingfield controlled thirteen of the thirty-two banks in the still thinly populated state and had grown accustomed to a cozy relationship with Nevada's power elite. Five years earlier, when more than half a million dollars in public funds had mysteriously disappeared from a Wingfield bank, the people of Nevada had generously offered—through their elected representatives, of course—to shoulder two-thirds of the loss in the form of a special tax rather than force their financial steward to pay back the money himself. Over the course of the Depression, a torrent of de-

faults on loans to cattle and sheep herders had combined to put the
Wingfield operation in jeopardy—and with it the entire state economy. More than 57 percent of all the bank deposits in Nevada were
tied up in Wingfield banks, nearly all of which would evaporate if the
banks failed.[15]

In 1932 alone, Wingfield had gone through $4 million in support
from the new Reconstruction Finance Corporation (RFC) and nearly
$1 million from the Federal Reserve Bank of San Francisco. Governor
Balzar was calling his second in command with bad news: The Hoover
team in Washington had rejected his entreaties. Wingfield didn't have
the collateral to cover another $2 million advance from the RFC, and
the feds had decided not to throw in good money after bad. So Balzar
ordered his lieutenant governor to try something radical in American
politics: close down all of the state's banks through November 12 (a
timeline that just happened to run through the election) to prevent
depositors from pulling any additional funds from Wingfield and give
the state government time to salvage the situation.

Griswold pored over the statutes but couldn't find the authority to
impose a statewide bank holiday. Instead, he declared a general business holiday, during which "the payment of all debts and obligations
of every nature and description except the payment of taxes and obligations prescribed by statute shall be suspended." Even that, Griswold
had to allow, would be voluntary. He didn't have the power to force
businesses to close up shop.

It didn't work. When every Wingfield bank shut down and its
healthy competitor, the First National Bank of Reno, remained open,
everyone in the state recognized where the trouble was. Wingfield was
finished. His banks never reopened.

The resulting commercial chaos "destroyed the financial and industrial life of the State of Nevada," future senator Pat McCarran later
recounted to his daughter. "The Wingfield banks, by reason of political affiliation, and by reason of political power had in their custody
some one million, two hundred thousand dollars of public funds. This
crippled every form of life. School moneys were involved. The funds of
the University were tied up. . . . The San Francisco wholesalers issued

an order that no credit would be extended for shipment of goods at wholesale to the merchants of Nevada."[16]

Wall Street is a long way from Nevada, and the road was even longer in the 1930s. The state had legalized gambling only a year before its banking crisis, hoping to generate new attractions targeting young men who had signed on for a dam project on the Colorado River. Wingfield hadn't even bothered to set up shop in the small, dusty outpost where they congregated after work, a town called Las Vegas. Nevada's effort to save the Wingfield machine was followed by a similar experiment in another notoriously corrupt state far from the halls of federal power. In February, the indomitable southern demagogue Huey Long informed his citizens that the banks of Louisiana would close—ostensibly in honor of the sixteenth anniversary of Woodrow Wilson's decision to sever diplomatic ties with Germany.

These separate events on opposite ends of the country were politically connected. The crisis unfolding in the backwaters and frontiers of U.S. commerce was inseparable from the Great Crash of 1929, the financial mayhem in Europe, and the response from the Federal Reserve and Washington. Banks weakened by years of corruption were only the first to fall. And their corruption fueled skepticism about the wisdom of any potential federal action to rescue banks anywhere. By February, Union Guardian Trust, the largest bank in Michigan, the nation's roaring industrial core, was seeking $50 million in emergency RFC funds. The Hoover administration tried to work out a rescue deal in which Henry Ford would waive certain payments Union Guardian owed to him, but Ford refused to play ball. "There isn't any reason why I, the largest individual taxpayer in the country, should bail the government out of its loans to banks," he declared. "Let the crash come."[17] Michigan closed its banks.

Ford was channeling the attitude of Hoover's recently reassigned Treasury secretary, Andrew Mellon, who had advocated a response to the Depression that amounted to financial nihilism: "Liquidate labor, liquidate stocks, liquidate farmers, liquidate real estate," he told Hoover. "It will purge the rottenness from the system . . . people will work harder, live a more moral life."[18] That had been Hayek's position in his attack on *A Treatise on Money*. A bust was the inevitable consequence of a reckless boom, and any government sugarcoating of the necessary losses would only make matters worse.

All of Keynes' instincts and assumptions were wired against that school of thought. He loved Burke too much to invite change through the disorder of institutional collapse. And the puritanical glorification of punishment as a cleansing exercise held no attraction to a man whose sexuality had divorced him from the Church. When he had breathed a sigh of relief after the stock market crash, it was precisely because he expected the mess to spur leaders into adopting aggressive financial rescue operations.

But the Fed seemed to agree more with Hayek than with Keynes. There had been a quick rush of relief funding after Black Tuesday thanks to the efforts of New York Fed president George Harrison, and the central bank had indeed cut rates until 1931. But even the historically low level of 2.5 percent was less than heroic after the stock market crash. At a meeting of the Fed board of governors in September 1930, Adolph Miller told his fellow financial stewards that "money is not really cheap nor easy" despite the low rates; the rapidly deflating currency was making small economic numbers feel very big.[19] And the emergency aid to New York banks that had followed the crash had not been extended to the rest of the banking system. As the New Deal economist Lauchlin Currie argued (in an analysis later echoed by Milton Friedman), the Fed could have bolstered bank reserves and protected rural and small-town banks from failure by purchasing securities from them at reasonable prices, giving them cash to meet demands for withdrawals or even lend to local businesses.[20] Instead, central bankers and leading economists seemed to view the struggles of weak banks as a sign that the overall system was being strengthened. When the weak were killed off, what remained would be strong. Any help for the banks, the Harvard economist Joseph Schumpeter believed, "which is merely due to artificial stimulus leaves part of the work of depressions undone."[21]

In the fall of 1931, as speculative raids targeted central bank after central bank following the collapse of Creditanstalt in Austria, the

Fed raised interest rates to discourage investors from cashing out dollars for gold. Those higher rates increased costs for American businesses that relied on borrowed money, prompting a cascade of defaults, particularly in agriculture, where farmers were simultaneously contending with a fall in demand as laid-off workers in other industries cut their household budgets. When farmers failed to pay back their loans en masse, their banks began to falter. That meant serious trouble for rural states like Nevada and Louisiana. When combined with problems at urban banks from European lending, the result was a second wave of nationwide financial collapse. By the end of 1932, an incredible 42 percent of all the bank deposits in the country had been obliterated—not including losses from the 1929 crash.[22] This in turn pulled money out of the economy, deflating the currency even further. The rot was indeed being purged, along with everything else.

Hoover himself had been more committed to supporting the system than some of his advisers were. Hoover had resisted efforts to establish the RFC for months and relented only in the face of popular pressure and insider maneuvering from the Fed's Eugene Meyer.[23] Like all of Hoover's recovery efforts, the RFC was a small program limited in scope by strict rules. He didn't really believe in it. In an address to Congress in late 1930, Hoover had argued that "economic depressions cannot be cured by legislative action."[24] He instead relied predominantly on rosy predictions and declarations of soundness in an effort to bolster public confidence. As unemployment surged in the months following the stock market crash, quickly overtaking more than a fourth of the national workforce, his optimism served only to convince the public that the president was in over his head. Few were surprised, then, when a few days after the Nevada banks closed, the governor of New York—an unpredictable New York aristocrat named Franklin Delano Roosevelt—bested Hoover in the presidential election by a margin of nearly 18 percent, carrying all but six states.

But Hoover was not going to sacrifice his economic principles over something so fleeting and contingent as an electoral wipeout. As the Michigan governor was forced to declare a bank holiday, the president wrote a letter to FDR asking the president-elect to issue a joint proclamation with him on national finance. "It would steady the country greatly," he wrote, "if there could be prompt assurance that there will be no tampering or inflation of the currency; that the budget will be unquestionably balanced, even if further taxation is necessary; that the Government credit will be maintained by refusal to exhaust it in the issue of securities."[25] Though Hoover crowed in his memoir about attempting to come to a bipartisan accommodation with FDR to stabilize the banking system, in a letter to Pennsylvania senator David Reed he admitted that he was asking FDR to approve "the whole major program of the Republican administration" and the "abandonment of 90% of the so-called new deal" on which Roosevelt had campaigned.[26]

FDR had no intention of endorsing the agenda that had led the country to its present calamity, much less before taking office. With state after state closing *every* bank within its own borders, meanwhile, the public decided to take their deposits into their own hands. As Arthur M. Schlesinger, Jr., observed, "Everyone determined to play it safe—to place their money, if they had a little, in a sock, or if they had a lot, in a foreign country."[27] A nationwide panic had begun.

And as with every American banking crisis, the truly massive bank runs were concentrated in New York. In February 1933 alone, banks in New York city lost $760 million in deposits and liquidated $260 million worth of U.S. government bonds to get the cash they needed to pay depositors.[28] The Manhattan banks held funds for smaller banks all over the country, which were all suddenly forced to call this money in to meet customer withdrawals of their own. For the same reason, a collapse of the major New York banks would have meant the annihilation of the country's financial system; local banks all over the country would have been destroyed almost immediately if their deposits in New York had been wiped out. New York governor Herbert Lehman, only a few weeks into his new job, began to prepare for an unprecedented shutdown of the New York banking system. Fearing the damage to Wall Street's international reputation, Thomas Lamont pressured Lehman to keep the banks open, even as Fed chairman Eugene Meyer began urging Hoover to take a truly radical step.

An obscure clause from the 1917 Trading with the Enemy Act seemed to give the president authority to close *all* of the nation's banks as a matter of national security. But Hoover demurred. The statute was unclear, he said. Such sweeping federal action might well do more harm than good. Bank regulation was really a matter for individual states to work out. He would support providing emergency federal funding to the banks—but not a full-fledged closure—if the president-elect would issue a joint proclamation with him.[29] Finally, at 4:20 A.M. on Saturday, March 4, Lehman decided he could wait no longer. He issued an emergency edict closing every bank in the state of New York. With the financial capital of the world suddenly offline, states all around the country quickly followed suit. "As dawn broke over America, the banks of the nation seemed in *rigor mortis.*"[30] It was inauguration day.

Roosevelt had campaigned as an exuberant optimist eager to break with the dreary status quo. In the months between election day and the inauguration, he and his most trusted advisers had packed the coming administration with reformers of every stripe: Bryanite populists, Wilsonian liberals, Brandeisian trust busters, and more than a few outright Communists. In the winter of 1933, Roosevelt didn't have a sophisticated scientific understanding of economics, but he had a very clear idea of what he wanted to do, and the collective output of his ideologically eclectic team would make him the world leader who at last gave political life to Keynesian ideas.[31] The New Deal would prove that Keynesian policies could work and *The General Theory*—the heady academic book Keynes was working on—would explain why the New Deal made sense—at least, those elements of it that did make sense.

It was to be an awkward intellectual courtship, but Keynes immediately recognized a kindred spirit upon FDR's inauguration speech: here was a man who was as comfortable mingling among the social elite as he was uncomfortable with its bad ideas, even if he wasn't always quite sure what his own ideas were. He began his administration by addressing a central object of Keynesian thinking dating back to 1914: the instability of private finance. FDR's first inaugural address was a bold assertion of public authority over the banking sector and a nakedly populist attack on the titans of high finance. "Plenty is at our doorstep, but a generous use of it languishes in the very sight of the supply," Roosevelt said. "Primarily this is because the rulers of the exchange of mankind's goods have failed, through their own stubbornness and their own incompetence, have admitted their failure, and abdicated. Practices of the unscrupulous money changers stand indicted in the court of public opinion, rejected by the hearts and minds of men. . . . They know only the rules of a generation of self-seekers. They have no vision, and when there is no vision the people perish." Lest there be any doubt about who was responsible for the mess, the president continued: "The money changers have fled from their high seats in the temple of our civilization. We may now restore that temple to the ancient truths. The measure of the restoration lies in the extent to which we apply social values more noble than mere monetary profit."[32] It remains a radical idea today: the private profit motive cannot serve as the foundation of a prosperous economic order, whatever role it might play within such a system.

FDR had a remarkable capacity to show different faces of his political persona to different audiences when it suited him, and his rhetoric didn't always match his policy agenda. But over the coming years, he would show that he meant what he said on his first day in office. The abandonment of laissez-faire in banking didn't happen all at once, but it proved to be extremely thorough. Roosevelt would leave the gold standard, socialize the deposit system, nationalize the Federal Reserve System, synchronize monetary policy with fiscal policy by placing the Fed under Treasury oversight, and force the nation's biggest banks to break up into smaller institutions with narrower lines of business. In sum, he broke the political back of the American financial sector and began using it as an instrument of economic recovery, directed by the federal government.

It would prove a triumph of Keynesian policy more comprehensive than Keynes had ever imagined possible in the United States—a fundamental change in the relationship among the state, society, and money. But Roosevelt's ideological alignment with Keynes in 1933 was inconsistent. "Our greatest primary task is to put people to work," FDR said in his inaugural address. "This is no unsolvable problem if we face it wisely and courageously. It can be accomplished in part by direct recruiting by the Government itself, treating the task as we would treat the emergency of a war." That was, of course, precisely what Keynes had been advocating in Britain, to no avail. But this was not: "Federal, State, and local governments [must] act forthwith on the demand that their cost be drastically reduced." Nor was FDR's fervor for "putting our own national house in order and making income balance outgo."

FDR's first inaugural address is best remembered today for its opening: "First of all, let me assert my firm belief that the only thing we have to fear is fear itself—nameless, unreasoning, unjustified terror which paralyzes needed efforts to convert retreat into advance." These words were not only a call for a renewal of national faith; they were a direct plea for calm in the middle of a banking panic Roosevelt would have to attack immediately after issuing his brief address.

Herbert Lehman's bank holiday had effectively shut down the U.S. financial system for Saturday, March 4. Banks were also closed the following Sunday. At 1:00 A.M. on Monday, March 6, FDR declared a national bank holiday. For the next week, the banks remained closed as federal examiners inspected their books and determined the fate of every bank in the country, while Congress rushed through legislation authorizing broader rescue powers for the federal government and the Federal Reserve. More than two thousand of the more than seventeen thousand banks shuttered on March 4 would never reopen.[33] But every bank that survived did so with an implicit government guarantee that the government would pay the liabilities of any bank that got into trouble. The banks that closed were unsound. The banks that survived were not—and FDR would not let panicked withdrawals sink otherwise healthy enterprises.

That was the substance of his first "fireside chat," a radio address to the entire nation broadcast on March 12, 1933, shortly before the banks reopened. Radio had gradually become a staple of entertainment in middle-class households during the 1920s, but Roosevelt was the first American politician to fully exploit the new medium's potential for mass political communications. And his first message was an attempt to calm the worst bank run the country had ever seen. Over the course of thirteen brisk minutes, FDR explained the basic operations of a typical bank to the American public and detailed the government's plan for responding to the crisis. "The banks that reopen will be able to meet every legitimate call. The new currency is being sent out by the Bureau of Engraving and Printing in large volume to every part of the country. It is sound currency because it is backed by actual, good assets. . . . I can assure you that it is safer to keep your money in a reopened bank than under the mattress."[34]

By presenting the psychology of banking panics and the dynamics of a run in plain language, Roosevelt hoped to assuage fears and prevent another run when the banks reopened. He was projecting a bravura facade of total confidence, but unlike his predecessor, he backed up that public disposition with dramatic policy changes. People were not being asked to believe something they knew to be false; they were being asked to put their faith in something new. "There is an element in the readjustment of our financial system more important than currency, more important than gold, and that is the confidence of the people. Confidence and courage are the essentials of success in carrying out our plan. You people must have faith; you must not be stampeded by rumors or guesses. Let us unite in banishing fear. We have provided the machinery to restore our financial system; it is up to you to support and make it work.

"It is your problem no less than it is mine. Together we cannot fail."[35]

To the surprise of everyone on Wall Street, Roosevelt's banking gambit worked. Banks reopened over the course of the following week without being poisoned by national panic. The financial system survived, protected by new federal rules and directed by new federal standards. Even the bankers at J.P. Morgan exulted in the achievement in a cable to London: "The whole country is filled with admiration for

President Roosevelt's actions. The record of his accomplishment in just one week seems incredible because we have never experienced anything like it before."[36]

The honeymoon didn't last long. When Roosevelt took the United States off gold a month later, the orthodoxy struck back. *The New York Times* declared in a front-page headline that the new president had made himself the nation's "MONETARY DICTATOR."[37] And the president was, in fact, exercising an unprecedented level of executive control over the nation's currency. He ordered all gold coins and gold certificates in the country to be turned over to the Federal Reserve at the exchange price of $20.67 per ounce. Shortly afterward, he ended domestic convertibility; the Fed would no longer pay out gold to Americans in exchange for paper notes.

It was the first step in FDR's plan to deliberately raise prices— inflationism, a practice Keynes had advocated in *A Treatise on Money* but which FDR would pursue in a distinctive way. FDR did think that raising prices would be good for industry, but he was chiefly concerned with rescuing the American farm. During the Great Depression, more than half of the country's population still lived on farms or in the small towns that served as local hubs for agricultural trade (today, about 80 percent of Americans live in cities). And a staggering one-half of all farm loans were in default when FDR came into office.[38] The crushing deflation of the Depression had done what it always did to farmers: Though the prices for their produce fell, the loan balances farmers had taken on to seed and harvest their fields remained high. When farmers were forced to sell their crops for less, their debts became overwhelming.

FDR established an array of programs to get farmers more attractive loans. But lower rates on mortgages could help only at the margins if the president couldn't stop the relentless decline of commodity prices. In the summer of 1933, he dispatched his economic adviser, George Warren, to Europe to survey monetary strategies abroad. Warren returned with a grim political assessment. "Hitler is a product of deflation," he wrote to Roosevelt. "It seems to be a choice between a rise in prices or a rise in dictators."[39]

Events at home, meanwhile, had already convinced Roosevelt of the need to take drastic measures. Three weeks after the president had ordered citizens to turn over their gold coins, Judge Charles C. Bradley had taken up a slate of foreclosure cases in Le Mars, Iowa. A total of fifteen farms were at risk of being repossessed when 250 angry farmers descended on Bradley's courtroom and demanded that he impose a countywide moratorium on foreclosures. The agitators stormed the bench, threw a rope around Bradley's neck, and dragged him to a country crossroads, where they "nearly lynched him."[40] Roosevelt had prevented a financial collapse on inauguration day, but rural America remained on the verge of revolution.

With half of the country living off the land, somewhat higher grocery bills resulting from higher crop prices would have been worth the sacrifice. But Roosevelt decided to bring crop prices up primarily by bringing the value of the dollar down. If it worked, the price of *everything*, including wages, would effectively go up, easing the effect of higher food costs on household budgets. "It is simply inevitable that we must inflate," FDR wrote to Woodrow Wilson's old aide, Colonel Edward M. House. "Though my banker friends may be horrified."[41]

Roosevelt had not wholly severed the dollar's connection to gold, even though ordinary citizens could no longer cash in their notes for precious metal. The value of the dollar was still technically pegged to the price of gold. By having the Treasury purchase gold at gradually escalating prices, FDR could induce speculators to buy at higher prices in the anticipation that the government would buy at still higher levels, thus elevating the market price of gold. A higher price for gold, in turn, was just another way of saying that the dollar had been functionally devalued against gold—instead of paying $20.67 for an ounce of gold, the government was paying more. The value of the dollar would fall. That, Warren believed, would result in higher prices across the board. The much-hoped-for inflation would begin.

Things did not quite work out that way. Keynes remarked that Warren's program "looked more to me like the gold standard on the booze than the ideal managed currency of my dreams."[42] Crop prices bounced around during the gold-buying experiment and, in late 1933, briefly fell. Part of the trouble was that when FDR had seized all of the country's gold, he had also seized the gold held by banks, meaning that even though the number of dollars that could be received for an ounce of gold was increasing, banks didn't have any gold to trade for more dollars to lend out. And banks were the key mechanism of the plan, since the money would get into the economy in the form of new bank loans.[43]

The gold-buying program was not a total bust, however. It devalued the dollar against international currencies, giving U.S. products an advantage in international trade, which enabled farmers and other American producers to sell more overseas. FDR had also psychologically prepared the country for a more formal devaluation of the dollar and acclimated the world to the idea that the U.S. government would be actively managing its monetary policy for the sake of raising prices, something the Federal Reserve had never done.

After six months of experimentation, FDR fixed the price of gold at $35, an official devaluation of nearly 60 percent from the $20.67 when he had taken office. That did not just create an advantage for U.S. exports; it caused a lot of gold to flow into the United States. The government was, in effect, offering international investors more dollars for the same amount of gold. If you wanted dollars, it was a good deal. This inflow of gold went to the Federal Reserve and from the Federal Reserve to the banking system. After steadily falling by 27 percent since the stock market crash, consumer prices climbed more than 5 percent over the course of FDR's first year in office.[44] It was a start.

Ferdinand Pecora was a Sicilian immigrant who became the top lawyer for the Senate Committee on Banking and Currency in the waning days of the Hoover administration. His job was to investigate the causes of the 1929 stock market crash. What he did, over the course of several hearings in the first fifteen months of the FDR presidency, was present the public with the most infuriating show on Earth.

Wall Street derived much of its political power from the prestige
that surrounded secretive men of means and the close-knit institutions they forged with one another. In the days before mandatory financial disclosures, firms lived, died, and excelled on their reputations
alone—which they cultivated through an elaborate performance
aimed at other elites, in which direct financial considerations were
often only an afterthought. The clients they accepted, the rates they
charged, the lines of business they supported, even the way they
dressed during their forays to the stock exchange—all were elements
of a complex dance, intended to communicate specific ideas about the
kind of bank they operated. Top partners at Morgan were renowned
for their financial discipline, though the firm had never once published a balance sheet. The great leaders from Kuhn, Loeb and Company, Chase National Bank, and First National City Bank were, in
Pecora's words, "demigods . . . men whose names were household
words, but whose personalities and affairs were frequently shrouded in
deep, aristocratic mystery."[45]

Pecora obliterated that facade. Beginning with National City Bank,
he exposed nearly every major financial house in New York as a den of
corruption or reckless excess. National City Bank president Charles
Mitchell had evaded federal income taxes by setting up a series of
sham transactions with his wife and was arrested shortly after his testimony to Pecora. Chase chairman Albert Wiggin had established six
private companies to speculate on the stock exchange, including three
incorporated in Canada to avoid taxes, and had made a $4 million
profit shorting his own company's stock during the crash.[46] Most
scandalous of all was the House of Morgan, which had been shower-
ing favors on a secret list of "preferred" clients. When Morgan agreed
to underwrite a stock offering, it would accept its fee in shares of stock
of the new company. Some of those shares would end up in the hands
of its favorite friends at below-market prices, allowing them to cash in
when the stock officially hit the market. A Morgan client would be
issued shares of a new railroad at $20 and sell a few days later at, say,
$35, booking an enormous instant profit. These special friends in-

cluded both business titans and leading politicians. The architect of
the Dawes Plan, Owen D. Young, was on the list, as was Bernard
Baruch, an adviser to Woodrow Wilson at the Paris Peace Conference. So were former President Calvin Coolidge, Democratic senator
and former Wilson Treasury secretary William Gibbs McAdoo,
Hoover's secretary of the navy, and the chairmen of both the Republican and Democratic National Committees.[47] It was insider trading
with a helping of political corruption.

Even after just a few hearings, Pecora was generating enormous
public pressure for the most sweeping structural reforms to the banking sector ever contemplated by an American legislature. Newspapers
had grown accustomed to covering trials as arenas for sensation and
scandal, and Pecora's daily interrogations made for powerful headlines. Congress was deluged with letters from constituents calling for
the government to guarantee their banking deposits. The fresh currency pumped into the banks in March 1933 had saved thousands of
institutions, but depositors wanted a stronger government commitment that their money would never disappear. Millions had already
seen their savings evaporate in bank failures, and Pecora's hearings
made clear that additional funds were being jeopardized by extravagant and reckless stock market speculation.

Neither Roosevelt himself nor Senate Banking Committee chairman Carter Glass was enthusiastic about having the government provide deposit insurance, a guarantee from the government that
depositors would keep their money, even when a bank failed. Like
much of the banking world, FDR worried that the practice would
encourage bad banking practices. Depositors were really creditors to
banks—deposits were loans paying interest—and by guaranteeing
their money, the government would eliminate market incentives for
creditors to discipline the management of the banks. But there was
simply no way to circumvent the public demand. Dozens of House
Democrats had signed a petition calling for deposit insurance, and
Glass bluntly informed FDR that if he didn't put the program in a
new banking bill himself, someone else in Congress would.[48] "Wash-

ington does not remember any issue on which sentiment of the country has been so undivided or emphatically expressed as this," reported *Business Week*.[49]

If taxpayers were going to be on the hook for deposits, Glass didn't want them to be backstopping speculation and corruption in the securities markets. It was one thing for banks to lend out money to businesses, but buying and selling stocks and bonds for quick profits was a risky operation. So in addition to guaranteeing deposits, the new Glass-sponsored banking bill required all commercial banks that accepted deposits to get out of the securities business. This could not, of course, entirely prevent a speculative wildfire; respectable private investment houses had proved themselves perfectly willing to gamble their clients' money in 1929. But it seemed better than putting taxpayer guarantees behind what amounted to gambling—or worse, theft.

It would require a tremendous reorganization on Wall Street. As recently as 1932, the Investment Bankers Association had insisted that the combination of securities dealing and commercial banking was "necessary" for all "corporate finance."[50] But after just a few Pecora hearings, both Chase and National City had publicly committed to shedding their securities affiliates. Though Glass-Steagall, as the provision breaking up the banks came to be known, was never popular on Wall Street, it was not the prominent source of banker discontent with the 1933 Banking Act. Rather, it was deposit insurance that generated the most unrest among bankers. Jack Morgan called it "absurd," while the president of the South Carolina Bankers Association even warned it would force another banking panic by convincing the public that the system was unsound.[51] To Glass, the opposite was true: without real reforms, Roosevelt would be risking another collapse.

Glass proved to be closest to the truth. When the Banking Act was approved, it set off, as the economist John Kenneth Galbraith later observed, a "revolution" in finance. Bank runs were effectively ended within the United States for decades. When citizens knew their money was safe, they did not exacerbate whatever other problems might exist by withdrawing their deposits in a state of panic. "With this one piece of legislation the fear which operated so efficiently to transmit weakness was dissolved. As a result the grievous defect of the old system, by which failure begot failure, was cured. Rarely has so much been accomplished by a single law."[52] Drawing a bright line between the high-flying world of securities trading and the relatively mundane, clerical business of commercial banking would carry lasting consequences, as well. Not only did it limit the size and scope of speculative bubbles, it mitigated contagion between different types of financial business. No stock market chaos, however calamitous, would ever threaten the integrity of the banking system while the law remained on the books.

Keynes monitored these developments from across the pond, looking for ways to show support for FDR's efforts and bring the president further into his intellectual orbit. But he was aware of the tendency for his words to backfire in the United States. He had hoped that his book on the Treaty of Versailles would inspire Americans to improve it. They had abandoned it instead. "It is frightfully difficult to know how to influence American opinion," he wrote to the Bank of England's Alexander Shaw in 1933.[53] So he started with flattery. When Roosevelt pulled the United States out of an international financial conference in 1933, Keynes applauded him in an article headlined "PRESIDENT ROOSEVELT IS MAGNIFICENTLY RIGHT" and proceeded to insert his own agenda into Roosevelt's vague and abrupt action, hoping the administration would take the hint.

"The President's message has an importance which transcends its origins. . . . The United States of America invites us to see whether without uprooting the order of society which we have inherited we cannot, by the employment of common sense in alliance with scientific thought, achieve something better than the miserable confusion and unutterable waste of opportunity in which an obstinate adherence to ancient rules of thumb has engulfed us. . . . We are offered, indeed, the only possible means by which the structure of contract can be preserved and confidence in a monetary economy restored."[54]

Keynes was an outlier in his enthusiasm. A crop of Roosevelt advisers quit the administration in fury when FDR backed out of the conference, and both Great Britain's socialist prime minister, Ramsay MacDonald, and Fascist Italy's minister of finance, Guido Jung, cabled their frustration to the American president.[55]

In December 1933, Keynes hosted Felix Frankfurter as his guest at the King's College Founder's Feast, where the two men conspired about how to turn Keynesian ideas into American policies.[56] Keynes had met Frankfurter at Paris in 1919, before the American attorney had gone on to form the American Civil Liberties Union. Frankfurter and FDR were close, but the academic preferred to maintain his post at Harvard, recruiting intellectual soldiers for the New Deal rather than joining the president in Washington as an official member of the administration. Frankfurter arranged to have Keynes write an open letter to FDR, which Frankfurter delivered to the president ahead of its publication in *The New York Times*—a strong signal to Roosevelt about the import his Harvard talent scout felt Keynes carried.

The resulting column was an arrogant lecture that misread a great deal of the U.S. political situation and nevertheless offered very good practical advice while casually presenting a revolutionary new conception of a national economy.

Keynes told FDR that the world viewed the president as engaged in "a double task, recovery and reform." Both elements were important, but Keynes argued that the reform efforts depended on Roosevelt's ability to achieve a recovery. Since the old guard didn't want the reforms, they would blame them for the bad economy if Roosevelt could not turn the Depression around. Keynes' policy prescription was the same as it ever was: plenty of cheap credit and a robust public works regimen. What was new in his letter was the rationale supporting that now-familiar remedy. No longer was he discussing how banks could bring savings into equilibrium with investment, as he had in *A Treatise on Money*. Now he was talking about bypassing the financial system entirely. The government, he argued, should act directly to expand economic "output" and consumer "purchasing power" through deficit-financed expansion. Whatever else FDR might do in office, the fundamental imperative was to spend, spend, spend: "I lay overwhelming emphasis on the increase of national purchasing power resulting from governmental expenditure which is financed by loans and is not merely a transfer through taxation, from existing incomes. Nothing else counts in comparison with this."[57]

Cheap credit and an expanded money supply were not enough. The government would have to actually spend that new money it created in order to get the economy moving again. Relying on monetary policy alone, Keynes argued, was "like trying to get fat by buying a larger belt. In the United States today your belt is plenty big enough for your belly. It is a most misleading thing to stress the quantity of money, which is only a limiting factor, rather than the volume of expenditure, which is the operative factor."[58]

Keynes was explaining why FDR's gold-buying program had generated such modest results: Deflation could be prevented by flushing banks with cash, but neither inflation nor economic growth could begin until creditworthy borrowers actually showed up to borrow that money and put it to work in the real world. Keynes argued that the ideal borrower of the moment was the federal government.

This remains the popular understanding of Keynesian economics to this day: in a slump, governments should borrow money and spend it on useful projects to kick-start a recovery. When the government spends this money, it goes into the pockets of its citizens, who in turn can spend it on other wants and needs, expanding the total size of the economy and ensuring a prosperous recovery rather than a downward spiral in which retrenched spending feeds unemployment and further reductions in spending. Keynes presented the idea to Americans in the pages of *The New York Times* on December 31, 1933, nearly three years before the publication of *The General Theory of Employment, Interest and Money*.

It was a political vision as much as an economic doctrine, an antidote to the militarism and resentment being pursued in Russia, Italy, and Germany. FDR, Keynes felt, did not need to intimidate other countries or terrorize his minorities to prove his mettle; he just needed to spend more money. "You remain for me the ruler whose general

outlook and attitude to the tasks of government are the most sympathetic in the world," he wrote to Roosevelt. "You are the only one who
sees the necessity of a profound change of methods and is attempting
it without intolerance, tyranny or destruction."[59]

In important respects Keynes believed Roosevelt's banking overhaul had set the stage for a breakthrough. He would later rank FDR's
early efforts to bring order to the financial system as among the most
important acts of his presidency.[60] The financial doctrine Keynes
began preaching in 1914 was at last finding political purchase.

Keynes' open letter to Roosevelt matters historically not for its influence on policy making but as the first clear, public presentation of the
economic idea he would refine into *The General Theory*. He offered no
technical or theoretical explanation for his new focus on "purchasing
power" beyond the belt metaphor. The details of his conceptual terrain
were still in flux, and FDR was not quite convinced by his presentation. When Walter Lippmann wrote Keynes a few weeks later relay-
ing the influence his letter had had on the president, he reported that
Keynes had inspired a new front in the administration's war for lower
interest rates, rather than a consensus about deficits or public works.[61]

Roosevelt was running a deficit, of course, but he was trying not to.
Though he believed in public works—he had quickly established both
the Public Works Administration and the Civilian Conservation
Corps to put people to work on everything from environmental projects to building schools—he believed in paying for them with higher
taxes. Deficit-financed recovery, he had once written in a private note,
was "Too good to be true—You can't get something for nothing."[62] He
viewed budget gaps as unfortunate imperfections—something he
would have to deal with to achieve a greater good. Though spending
would accelerate over the next few years, very little money was in fact
going out the door in Roosevelt's first year in office, which had
prompted Keynes to emphasize spending in his letter. It took time to
get projects off the ground and insulate them from charges of corruption. Much of the country was governed by spoils systems and patron-

age regimes. In Nevada, for instance, one senator even monitored the appointment of post office janitors as an opportunity to dole out rewards.[63] Though FDR's reform agenda was ambitious—he created the FDIC, the Securities and Exchange Commission, the Agricultural Adjustment Administration, and the Tennessee Valley Authority within his first hundred days in office—the new agencies weren't up and running yet. His early deficits were due largely to the continued collapse in income tax receipts caused by unemployment. If you didn't get a paycheck, you weren't paying taxes on it, either.

But Frankfurter wasn't done. Everyone Roosevelt had hired believed the government needed to be more aggressive in fighting the Depression, but they didn't agree on how or why to do it. After delivering Keynes' letter, Frankfurter identified several members of the administration who were sympathetic—or at least not hostile—to the new ideas Keynes had discussed with him at Cambridge, and he arranged a series of meetings between Keynes and those figures for late May 1934, a trip culminating in a private audience with the president himself. Agricultural Adjustment Administration Director Rexford Tugwell was advocating for a barrage of government farm production and housing programs and needed intellectual backup. Frances Perkins, the secretary of labor, was eyeing various mechanisms aimed at raising worker pay. Treasury Secretary Henry Morgenthau, Jr., who operated a farm in upstate New York and had the good fortune to have landed the Roosevelts as neighbors, was enthusiastic about public works but terrified of budget deficits.

When he preached to the converted, Keynes came away a great success. Perkins, for instance, already believed that the New Deal "constituted an effective demonstration of the theories which John Maynard Keynes had been preaching and urging upon the English government." When he came to Washington, she recalled, Keynes "pointed out that the combination of relief, public works, raising wages by NRA codes, distributing moneys to farmers under agricultural adjustment, was doing exactly what his theory would indicate as correct procedure." She immediately grasped key concepts including the multiplier when Keynes explained them, and was charmed by his "faith that we in the United States would prove to the world that this was the answer."[64]

But to the president, who was "unfamiliar" with Keynes' theoretical academic work, Keynes was an impractical mystic. Though he insisted to Frankfurter that he and Keynes had a "grand talk" together and that he "liked" the British economist "immensely,"[65] the truth was that FDR had been annoyed by the haze of high theory in which Keynes had enshrouded their conversation.

"I saw your friend Keynes," Roosevelt told Perkins afterward. "He left a whole rigamarole of figures. He must be a mathematician rather than a political economist."

In particular, FDR thought Keynes politically naive about the president's relationship with Wall Street. He believed that a banking industry hostile to his reform program was driving up the interest rates on government debt by sitting out Treasury bill auctions. "There is a practical limit to what the Government can borrow—especially because the banks are offering passive resistance in most of the large centers."[66]

Keynes did make progress on monetary policy. FDR's Fed chairman, Marriner Eccles, and his top aide, Lauchlin Currie, had both worked out rough-and-ready economic rationales for deficit spending that approximated Keynes' ideas. The Fed didn't have power over spending, but both men agreed with Keynes that looser monetary policy—lower interest rates—could help the government spend its way out of the Depression by keeping the financing costs of government borrowing down—if Roosevelt summoned the will to intentionally run big deficits.

And so Eccles and Currie wrote a bill that would overhaul the governance of the central bank, giving the Federal Reserve Board in Washington the power to purchase government bonds to move interest rates up or down. Under the Fed's unusual regional structure, that power had long been held by individual Fed branches, particularly the New York Fed, whose president was in practice more powerful than the Fed chairman in Washington. Those branches were in turn influenced heavily by the major banks in each region, which appointed top officials to the local Fed branch. This was of course undemocratic, but it was also an avenue through which conservative financial orthodoxy infected national and international economic policy making.

Wall Street immediately recognized the Eccles-Currie legislation as an attack on its influence. James Warburg, a rare Roosevelt adviser to hail from an international banking dynasty—his father had helped establish the Fed in 1913—decried the idea before Congress. "I am not one who sees a Communist under every bed," he warned, "but I sometimes wonder if the authors of these bills realize whose game they are playing"—adding that whenever "the long arm of the Treasury reaches out into the control of the credit machinery" disaster had soon followed.[67] Such dark intimations about Soviet influence would wreak havoc on Currie's reputation after World War II, but during the Roosevelt presidency, he tended to get his way. The legislation passed, establishing far greater public control over interest rates and the movement of money in the American economy.

It was a Keynesian victory: unifying monetary and fiscal policy would ensure that the two worked in harmony. But Keynes, Currie, and Eccles could not overcome FDR's deficit hawks. Morgenthau remained firmly committed to balanced budgets. Even among New Dealers in America, in whom Keynes placed his greatest hope for economic progress, clever arguments and patient conversation could only help sympathetic departments defend plans they had already sketched out. Keynes needed much more to sway the whole administration into coordinated action. He needed an intellectual movement, a united class of experts deploying their prestige and influence against the edifice of government. He couldn't win the war for ideas one meeting at a time. He needed a great work—something intellectually powerful enough to bring in converts and culturally shocking enough to force the experts to pay attention. "It takes a theory," as the Harvard economist Alvin Hansen would later claim, "to kill a theory."[68] And so Keynes devoted nearly all of his energy to his last, best effort to save the world: converting the priesthood of academic economists to his new doctrine.

NINE

◇

THE END OF SCARCITY

WHEN JOAN ROBINSON RETURNED to Cambridge in 1929, she did not expect to take part in an intellectual revolution. She had earned an economics degree from the university four years earlier, then promptly married "a dashing young man"[1] and sailed with him for India. While her new husband, Austin, served as a tutor to the child maharajah, Jivajirao Scindia, Joan had spent her days in the city of Gwalior without any official duties, living in a mansion near the royal palace, where a retinue of servants attended to her needs.

Joan was young, brilliant, and full of ambition. She befriended local Indian officials, including Colonel Kailash Narain Haksar, and returned to London to advocate for local Gwalior interests before the British government. But she quickly learned that highbrow English society made little room for intellectually serious women. It was a continuation of a lesson that began back at Cambridge. The university's still young Economics department had developed in the shadow of its first department chair, Alfred Marshall, a man who had married the first woman to lecture at Cambridge in economics, Mary Paley, and then set about sabotaging her career, leaning on a publisher to keep her book out of print and advocating the abolition of mixed-gender education altogether. As an undergraduate, Joan was enraged to see the old man treat his wife like "a housekeeper and a secretary."[2] Joan, too, had married an economist and, for a time, subsumed her ambitions to his.

But the department had changed while the Robinsons had been away. Marshall was dead, and Cambridge economics now followed the lead of John Maynard Keynes. Arrogant, impatient, and difficult to please, Keynes was an imposing figure—one of the few men at Cambridge who lent prestige to the university rather than relying on the university to bestow it upon him. And his friendships with Virginia Woolf and her sister Vanessa had long since acclimated him to the idea that women could be important thinkers. When Joan returned to Cambridge with Austin, she did not have an official position or even a master's degree. But as her husband began lecturing in economics, Robinson did the same—she was paid almost nothing—and set about publishing her own academic research, hoping to win a faculty job of her own. Austin didn't mind, but it was hard to make an impression on Keynes.

Between the Great Depression and Keynes' persona, Cambridge economics was becoming a radical space—far more adventurous than the political and financial circles where Keynes had been spending most of his time since the war. With social breakdown evident all around, many students who might otherwise have pursued literature, politics, or history were drawn to the study of money and resources. "To be reading economics at a university was to be an intellectual— possibly a radical intellectual—and did not at all suggest the image of a student at an American business school,"[3] recalled the economist Vivian Walsh years later.

"Keynes's General Theory was the most important and exciting intellectual development of the time,"[4] according to Michael Straight, who joined the Apostles when studying at Cambridge in the 1930s. "The largest lecture hall in Cambridge was crowded when Keynes, in a series of talks, set forth the principles of his General Theory. It was as if we were listening to Charles Darwin or Isaac Newton. The audience sat in hushed silence as Keynes spoke. Then, in small circles, he was passionately defended and furiously attacked."[5]

Much of Keynes' old secret society had become a hotbed for Communist efforts linked directly to the Kremlin. After identifying as a Communist during his Cambridge years, Straight would go on to serve in the Roosevelt administration, where, Straight later confessed, he passed U.S. government documents to Soviet agents.[6]

Whatever insults Keynes might hurl at *Das Kapital*, there was simply no way for him to avoid attracting radicals to his lectures—not when he was trumpeting his economic ideas as a wholly new innovation that would demolish the theoretical underpinnings of the political status quo. Besides, however much Keynes might have hated communism, he liked many of the young Communists. "There is no one in politics today worth sixpence outside the ranks of liberals except the post-war generation of intellectual Communists under thirty five," Keynes told *New Statesman and Nation* editor Kingsley Martin in a conversation published in 1939. "Them, too, I like and respect. . . . With them in their ultimate maturity lies the future, and not with the old jossers."[7]

The most striking of these radicals was Joan Robinson. "She was," in the words of her Hungarian classmate Tibor Scitovsky, "a charming and beautiful young woman" "who chain-smoked cigarettes, wore a long scarf and was visibly . . . in love" with her husband.[8] Her impact on the field was almost immediate. Had Keynes not already established himself as the Great Man of the department, she might well have sent the entire course of Cambridge research off in a direction all her own, as indeed she would in the decades to come, after Keynes was gone.

Most economists in the early 1930s assumed that markets were competitive. Producers could outperform one another based on either quality or price. To get a competitive edge, they would either improve the quality of their goods or charge a lower price than their competitors'. Given a competitive market, economists could proceed to analyze a host of other phenomena. Without competition, even basic concepts such as supply and demand would fall out of kilter, eliminating the incentive for producers to respond to consumer preferences.

The exception to a competitive market was monopoly, in which one producer could dictate prices without regard to consumer response, because it had cornered the market. Some classical economists believed that the state had to constrain monopolists—either through regulation or by breaking them up into smaller firms—but most believed that monopoly, in which a single firm dictated pricing for an entire sector or market, was a rare, obvious departure from the competitive market, which was the normal state of economic affairs.

Robinson demolished that paradigm. She developed a new concept of "imperfect competition" in which markets could regularly exhibit the flaws associated with monopoly power even when large firms controlled much less of the market than a formal monopoly position, where a single firm quite literally dictated the terms for an entire market. The competitive landscape wasn't an on/off switch between competition and monopoly; it was a spectrum in which perfect competition—the condition assumed by economists—was a "special case" that almost never existed in real-world commercial activity. The markets for most products were at least a little monopolistic; even if a company didn't literally control *all* production of, say, tennis shoes, it might control enough of the market that other tennis shoe makers set their prices based on whatever that company did. As Robinson put it, monopoly wasn't a "special case" deviating from the normal, real world of perfect competition. Instead, perfect competition was the "special case" deviating from monopoly-esque conditions that persisted throughout the economy to varying degrees.[9] And it wasn't just large producers that could dictate anticompetitive prices in the market; major buyers could as well. No matter how many producers of a given product existed, if there were only a handful of customers available to purchase their wares, the customers could effectively dictate lower prices. This idea, which Robinson called "monopsony," became an essential concept for understanding supply chains and wholesalers.[10]

Robinson knew that her theory had important implications for economic inequality. All you had to do was apply her reasoning to the labor market. Under the competitive market paradigm, economists had been able to argue that workers were paid a wage equal to the true value they added to the business. With competition whittling away waste and excess, workers would end up receiving what economists called the "marginal productivity" of their work. Each worker would be paid an amount exactly equal to how much more productive he or she made the operation. That meant, particularly for the Austrian economists Hayek and Mises, that complaints about low wages were really complaints about worker productivity. If workers wanted better pay, the only sustainable way to get it was by working harder.

But that argument would fall apart if it could be shown that labor markets were not perfectly competitive—if, instead, they exhibited some of the features of monopoly. If the only jobs in town were at the coal mine, then the mine owners wouldn't have to compete with other employers by offering better pay. When Robinson showed that markets were almost always at least somewhat anticompetitive, she believed she had "hacked through" a "prop to *laisser-faire* ideology."[11] Capitalists, according to Robinson, were chronically underpaying their staff.

It was a tremendous breakthrough, and her book *The Economics of Imperfect Competition* was immediately recognized in academia as a major work. The deeply moved Mary Paley Marshall sent Robinson a letter of gratitude: "Thank you for helping to lift off the reproach cast on the Economic Woman."[12] But Robinson was just getting started. By the time she finished her career, Robinson would be the most accomplished economist of any gender ever passed over for a Nobel Prize.

In the early 1930s, she was drawn to the flurry of activity surrounding Keynes that followed the publication of *A Treatise on Money.* As Keynes workshopped the ideas that would become *The General Theory of Employment, Interest and Money,* a small group of faculty members that began calling themselves the Cambridge Circus became his sounding board and supplied him with important innovations of their own. Composed of Richard Kahn, Piero Sraffa, James Meade, and the Robinsons, this tiny circle—but especially Joan Robinson and Kahn—helped Keynes deliver *The General Theory* to the world after a complicated and often difficult gestation.

They were all eccentrics, nearly as strange and controversial as

Keynes himself. Sraffa was a friend of the Italian Marxist Antonio Gramsci and had infuriated Benito Mussolini with two articles on the Italian banking system, both written for publications edited by Keynes. Sraffa had experience in the banking sector, and he criticized the reliability of financial data reported by Italian banks, a disclosure which Mussolini considered an attack on the Italian nation itself. With Keynes' help, Sraffa fled Italy for a post at Cambridge.

He was a shy lecturer but an effective tutor and teammate whom Keynes relied on throughout his feud with Hayek. When the Austrian published a book of his own—*Prices and Production*—attempting to topple *A Treatise on Money,* Sraffa agreed to deliver a scholarly takedown of the book, publishing a vicious attack in an academic journal Keynes edited accusing Hayek of circular reasoning. This not only helped expand Sraffa's publishing oeuvre, it allowed Keynes to get in his punches while presenting himself to the academic community as a man above the fray, too absorbed in important theoretical matters to concern himself with the buzzing of a comparatively small man like Hayek.

While Sraffa led the offensive, Joan Robinson played defense, responding to Hayek's criticisms of *A Treatise on Money* with clarifications, counterpoints, and the occasional rhetorical jab. She and Kahn, meanwhile, were working out new ideas of their own and integrating them into the intellectual frame Keynes was constructing.

By the mid-1930s, Keynes was writing self-aggrandizing letters to famous friends describing his coming work as a comprehensive revolution in economic ideas. But he wasn't always so sure. It was Robinson who convinced Keynes that he was orchestrating an earthquake. "Keynes was himself not aware of the fact; certainly not fully aware of the fact, that he was leading an intellectual revolution," recalled Lorie Tarshis, a Canadian student who made the pilgrimage to Cambridge after reading *A Treatise.* "He backed into it. Richard Kahn and Joan Robinson took a lot of time and effort to persuade him that what he was doing had a significance."[13] "There were moments when we had some trouble in getting Maynard to see what the point of his revolution really was," according to Robinson.[14]

Keynes began to realize that his theoretical breakthrough could have political consequences far broader than the development of a few public works projects—a thought that frequently made him uncomfortable. "Keynes was really making a bigger revolution than he was willing to admit to himself," recalled Abba Lerner, one of the earliest converts to the new doctrine. "He was, in fact, saying that the market doesn't work. He only half recognized it."[15] For all his grand optimism and ecstatic visions of a fifteen-hour workweek, Keynes remained a Burkean conservative, anxious about actually implementing the changes he believed possible, even those he thought necessary to the preservation of democracy. "I find it hard to judge whether my ultimate policy would strike the ordinary person as violently drastic or evolutionary," he wrote to former Labour MP Susan Lawrence.[16]

As Keynes grew more distant from Bloomsbury, Kahn and Robinson began to fill the roles once played by Virginia and Lytton—the rare, respected confidants whom Keynes would allow to change his mind. Kahn had been one of Keynes' favorite pupils as an undergraduate, before Keynes hired him as something of a personal assistant he often took along to Tilton or London on nonacademic business. "He is a marvelous critic and suggester and improver," Keynes wrote to Joan of Kahn's services. "There never was anyone in the history of the world to whom it was so helpful to submit one's stuff."[17]

The collaborative atmosphere makes it difficult to discern who was responsible for which developments. Years later, the economic historian Lawrence Klein would pinpoint a 1933 journal article by Robinson as the first exposition of the basic thesis of *The General Theory*.[18] Kahn, meanwhile, published work under his own name developing the concept of the multiplier, the idea that government spending could "multiply" through the economy, creating greater economic output than the initial outlay. Keynes had presented the basic concept in *Can Lloyd George Do It?*, but Kahn made a science of it, converting the idea into a measurable quantitative tool that remains part of the stock-in-trade of macroeconomists today. Kahn hashed out his multiplier with help from James Meade, the youngest member of the Circus.

Though Meade would go on to win a Nobel Prize in 1977, within this select circle he self-effacingly described himself as a second-class intellect. "From the point of view of a humble mortal like myself Keynes seemed to play the role of God in a morality play; He dominated the play but rarely appeared himself on the stage. Kahn was the Messenger Angel who brought messages and problems from Keynes to the 'Circus' and who went back to Heaven with the result of our deliberations."[19]

Such "evangelical metaphors" became common parlance around Cambridge, used both in jest and with "ominous seriousness" as Keynesian ideas became, in the words of Robinson's biographers, "a gospel."[20] Austin Robinson joked that members of the Circus "went about asking: Brother, are you saved?" as they discussed their new doctrine.[21] The Circus operated very much like a small religious sect, with the primary insiders recruiting a few promising graduate students or undergraduates to help them workshop their ideas, slowly expanding the circle of trusted confidants. To those living outside the cult, the activity of its believers appeared increasingly strange. By April 1932, Robinson and Keynes were already corresponding about material that would form the heart of *The General Theory*.[22] Their letters eventually swelled to hundreds of pages as Keynes passed along draft sections of the book, and their repartee seemed to devolve into obscure mesmerism as they attempted to define the parameters of entirely new economic concepts. When he reached a dead end trying to convert the economist Ralph Hawtrey, Keynes asked Robinson to review the "voluminous correspondence" between the two men and see if he had gone awry. She concluded that Hawtrey, not Keynes, was to blame for failing to see the light: "I certainly don't think an archangel could have taken more trouble to be fair and to be clear."[23] When disciples met with top young minds from the London School of Economics to present their revelations, the LSE students left bewildered by the Cambridge set, who seemed to be speaking their own private language. These were new ideas that Keynes had never presented in his public writings.

Like any cult worth its salt, the Circus was riven by private ambitions and sexual intrigue. Keynes first began to imagine that something was amiss in early 1932. Dropping in unannounced on Kahn one afternoon—a liberty he had a habit of taking in moments of intellectual excitement—he stumbled into an awkward scene. As he reported to Lydia, "His outer room was in darkness, but there closeted in his inner room were he and Joan alone, she reclining on the floor on cushions. We were all embarrassed—they were so much like lovers surprised, though I expect the conversation was only The Pure Theory of Monopoly."[24] A few weeks later, when Kahn threw a small party, Joan and Austin arrived together, but Joan, according to Keynes, seemed "rather white, silent and sad"—that is, until Austin left early "without even asking Joan to come with him."[25]

"I feel it is a drama," he continued, "but a concealed one, and having (has it?) no solution."[26] What was a shepherd to do about such troubles within his flock? Joan was the intellectual heavyweight in her marriage. She and Austin shared interests, but her husband's real academic gifts were in administration, not high theory. Her relationship with Austin was the only thing keeping her at Cambridge and her only meaningful source of income. By the time of Kahn's party, Joan had no official position at Cambridge and had given only one set of lectures for just £25. Keynes did advocate for talented women in his life—he published Virginia's writing, publicized Vanessa's painting, and eventually managed a theater to bolster Lydia's acting career. But there was no chance he could secure a job for Joan in the economics department if she divorced a full-time member of the faculty.

And what had he really witnessed? Whatever was going on, Keynes reasoned, the tension couldn't last long. The Rockefeller Foundation had awarded Kahn a grant for a research project that would soon take him away to the United States. Keynes had been a little apprehensive about being forced to operate without his right-hand man for a few months, but he had made do without Kahn in the past, and it was slowly dawning on him that many of the young man's best ideas were coming from Joan anyway. But in May, Kahn abruptly informed

Keynes that he wanted to delay the trip. "Two days ago he rang me up to say he thought he would like to stay at Cambridge next term to finish some theory he is at, and go to America after Christmas," he wrote to Lydia. "When I get back I hear that Austin is to go to Africa on a mission for five months and will be *away* from Cambridge all next term. The human heart! To finish something he is at!"[27] With Austin out of the picture, Kahn wanted to stay in Cambridge with Joan.

Keynes decided there was nothing to be done about the affair. But he couldn't avoid it—at least, not without improving his manners. "I went to see [Kahn] this morning and found him lying on the inner floor of his inner room with Joan—no socks on and unshaven," he told Lydia in October 1933. "But you musn't suppose wrongly. They were on the floor because that is the only convenient way of examining mathematical diagrams, and there is a Jewish Feast on to-day during which to wear socks or to shave is against the law of Moses."[28]

The affair between Kahn and Robinson lasted for years, surviving the birth of her two children with Austin, multiple transatlantic separations, and personal crises. In the autumn of 1938, Keynes began to notice a manic quality to Robinson's letters, some of them strange, others nearly indecipherable. Once, with Austin, she was overcome by a mysterious "frenzy." After being unable to sleep for more than a week, medical professionals intervened, dosing her with a powerful sedative and hospitalizing her for several months. Though the psychiatrists were mystified by her condition, she eventually recovered. By the time she returned to work, Great Britain was again at war; both Austin and Kahn had been called to London to assist the government, and their lives fell into a rhythm that allowed her to make time for both men when they came down to Cambridge. "I am very proud of it," she wrote to Kahn in November 1940. "You know I like such odd combinations much more than commonplace success."[29]

It was a team that enjoyed flying close to the sun, if not the edge of their own sanity. This odd furnace of adultery, ambition, and academic warfare, embedded within a darkening backdrop of international conflict, would, against all odds, produce the most influential work by an economist in 160 years. The continuous recycling of ideas, language, and energy among these companions would transform Keynes from a social critic into a controversial visionary.

The General Theory of Employment, Interest and Money is one of the great works of Western letters, a masterpiece of social and political thought that belongs with the monuments left by Aristotle, Thomas Hobbes, Edmund Burke, and Karl Marx. It is a theory of democracy and power, of psychology and historical change, a love letter to the power of ideas. *The General Theory* is a dangerous book because it demonstrates the necessity of power. It is a liberating book because it reframed the central problem at the heart of modern economics as the alleviation of inequality, pivoting away from the demands of production and the incentives facing the rich and powerful that had occupied economists for centuries. It is a frustrating book because it is written in novel abstractions, argued in convoluted sentences and dense equations. And it is a work of genius because it proves a simple truth that, once offered, seems obvious: Prosperity is not hard-wired into human beings; it must be orchestrated and sustained by political leadership.

It is remembered as a work of economics because it is, as Keynes wrote, "chiefly addressed" to economists, ensuring that the economics profession would become the book's primary interpreters and guardians of its legacy. In its ostentatious preface, Keynes presents economists— not prime ministers, emperors, bankers, or generals—as the privileged elect who, armed with obscure truths, can alone free the world from unnecessary misery. "The matters at issue are of an importance which cannot be exaggerated. But, if my explanations are right, it is my fellow economists, not the general public, whom I must first convince. At this stage of the argument the general public, though welcome at the debate, are only eavesdroppers."[30]

The transformational influence of *The General Theory* can be measured by the sudden and dramatic upgrade in the political status of the economist that followed its publication. In the years between the wars, economists were intellectuals rather than power brokers, viewed by the ruling elite much the way academic philosophers are perceived today. Even in the economist-friendly Roosevelt administration, an economics degree was not a particularly salient qualification for policy work. During the 1920s, an Ivy League education had been useful for anyone seeking a career in the upper echelons of American power, but a man who had studied economics at Harvard carried no more prestige than one who had studied poetry. A brilliant publishing record in the academic journals didn't carry nearly as much weight with leaders trying to fill a Treasury position as a few years of experience at the right bank. Nobody had built a dazzling career sorting out detailed statistics on GDP and productivity, because such numbers simply did not exist. The term *macroeconomics* hadn't even been coined yet; it would flower as a field of study only as people began digesting and interpreting *The General Theory*. Keynes was not only inventing modern economics, he was helping invent the modern economist and placing him at the apex of a new intellectual power structure.

Sections of *The General Theory* are beautiful and profound. But much of it is nearly incomprehensible. Taken as a whole, it is very likely the worst-written book of its significance ever published in the English language. Still, bad writing can make a career in academia just as surely as exceptional writing can. Readers who encounter dense and unclear prose often conclude that it is a work of great import accessible only to the very brilliant. *The General Theory* is indeed a work of great import, but it need not have been accessible only to the very brilliant. Keynes was one of the best writers who ever referred to himself as an economist. His career as a popular journalist demonstrated that he knew how to make himself understood, and he had come to the central ideas of *The General Theory* years before its publication. He had plenty of time to make it presentable. The book is difficult and obscure because he wanted it to be. And its sheer ugliness created a small industry of interpreters, some of whom enjoyed distinguished careers and won Nobel Prizes just by simplifying or interpreting sections of the book. This prestige industry helped credential Keynesian economists to politicians, opening doors to corridors of power that had previously been reserved to generals, bankers, and their heirs.

Prior to *The General Theory*, economics was almost exclusively concerned with scarcity and efficiency. The very word for the productive output of society—economy—was a metaphor for making do with less. The root cause of human suffering was understood to be a shortage of resources to meet human needs. Social reformers might protest the extravagances of the rich, but poverty and squalor were driven not by inequality but by the hard fact that there weren't enough resources to go around. Only by creating more goods more efficiently could the material ills of society be cured—or, more likely, tempered—over the long haul.

The economic system was understood to be apolitical and self-correcting, akin to population dynamics in the natural world. Everything—wages, commodity prices, interest rates, profits—responded automatically to any unexpected change in other areas, quickly bringing the system to an equilibrium in which the maximum amount of goods was being produced and consumed, so that social needs were met to the greatest extent possible.

Labor was just another input in the productive system. Like any other commodity, it had a price that changed according to its real value to society. If there were too many steelworkers and not enough farmers, factory wages would fall and field hands would get raises. Though everybody wanted a bigger paycheck, the enlightened economist recognized that high wages were dangerous. They raised the cost of doing business, which not only crimped profits for the entrepreneur but resulted in lower productivity and the production of fewer goods, which meant more squalor in society at large. The price of labor adjusted automatically to supply and demand, just as the price of fruit or finished steel did, and workers could only find themselves out of a job if they insisted on artificially high wages. Politicians who wanted to look after the poor by meddling with pay or profit were like naturalists who tried to protect a favored species of rabbit in the wild: Their efforts might promote more cuddly animals for a while, but those would soon deplete the surrounding vegetation, forcing both rabbits and other creatures to starve, doing more harm than good, an exercise in futility.

It was a harsh vision of the social order, but most of human existence had in fact been hard, particularly when the eighteenth- and nineteenth-century theorists who invented the doctrine had been writing. As the great economist Thomas Malthus had demonstrated, population nearly always expanded to the absolute limit of productive capacity, ensuring that the vast majority of people throughout history lived at the ragged edge of subsistence. Progress was a function of increased production through greater efficiency.

This was the worldview of what Keynes called the "classical economists." He included just about everyone in the economics profession who wasn't either a Marxist or a crank in that category, but he listed David Ricardo, James Mill, John Stuart Mill, and the Cambridge luminaries Alfred Marshall and Arthur Cecil Pigou as some of the classical school's most prominent theorists.[31] Keynes had a great deal of admiration for their picture of the economy, and he believed it had once been an accurate understanding of how social needs could best be met. But the sheer productive power of modern capitalism and the "miracle of compound interest" had rendered the portrait obsolete. Technological advances now allowed people to produce so much more with so much less effort than they had in the past that scarcity was no longer the overriding problem of humanity. Economists, he believed, were now lost in the distant past fighting a war that had ended long ago. As early as *The Economic Consequences of the Peace,* Keynes had been battling economic problems that were not principally matters of physical resource constraints. The greatest threats to harvest yields were not a lack of labor, fertilizer, or rainfall but insufficient investment and the mismanagement of money and credit.

The material abundance of the Gilded Age had sown doubts in Keynes about the supposed scarcity of resources, but it was the ravages of the Depression that made him certain the old order had it wrong. Clearly the trouble was not a shortage of production. Crops were rotting in the fields while children went hungry in the streets. Producers were not cutting back because they couldn't afford to meet the high wage demands of workers; laborers were roaming from town to town, desperate for any work at all. As he wrote in the opening chapter, "It is not very plausible to assert that unemployment in the United States in 1932 was due either to labour obstinately refusing to accept a reduction of money-wages or to its obstinately demanding a real wage beyond what the productivity of the economic machine was capable of furnishing."[32]

For Keynes, the empirical fact of the Depression proved that the classical theory was wrong. The economy was not self-correcting. Even if politicians were messing things up with bad policy, the system should at some point between 1919 and 1936 have been able to sort itself out. A bad level for gold in 1925 or a wrong-headed tariff in 1931 should have been no different than a bad harvest or a fire, something quickly remedied by the automated magic of supply, demand, and the price mechanism. But *The General Theory* didn't just list the various problems then facing society and declare the argument settled. Almost nothing in the book is empirical. There are no case studies or statistical regressions. It is instead an attempt to explain *why* the classical system could not account for the facts facing the world in 1936. It is a conceptual reordering accompanied by an alternative account of human motivation in post-scarcity society that only occasionally gestures at its own practical implications for policy makers.

Keynes had been trying to explain the problem of unemployment since 1919. In *The Economic Consequences of the Peace,* he had argued that unmanageable war debts and reparations would strip Europe of its capacity to yield sufficient bounty from its fields and factories. In *A Tract on Monetary Reform,* he had argued that price instability was making the capitalist mechanism erratic and dysfunctional. And in *A Treatise on Money,* he had argued that a fear of inflation was preventing the labor market from adjusting to unexpected shocks.

Those early theories had assumed that there was nothing fundamentally wrong with the way classical economists understood the world—only with the way their ideas were applied to contemporary circumstances. For the most part, Keynes had assumed, along with his classical predecessors, that markets were indeed self-adjusting and would eventually reach a prosperous equilibrium. It was just a question of figuring out how to *allow* them to adjust, given the political and social realities of the twentieth century. But by reaching back to ancient history, *A Treatise on Money* had opened the door to new thinking. If societies had always needed to actively manage their monetary systems to secure prosperity, then maybe markets didn't work the way economists believed they did.

For Keynes, the soft underbelly of the classical theory was Say's Law, which he summarized as the maxim that "supply creates its own demand." Postulated by Jean-Baptiste Say, a French contemporary of Adam Smith, it linked together three problems Keynes saw in the classical story: the outdated focus on scarcity, the notion that markets self-correct, and the idea that involuntary unemployment is impossible. Classical theorists recognized its importance, too. Adherence to Say's Law was "a litmus by which the reputable economist was separated from the crackpot,"[33] noted John Kenneth Galbraith, who was already a practicing economist when *The General Theory* was released.

Say's Law meant that there could not be unspent income in a society. Because the supply of new products created its own demand for them, increased production automatically brought the economic system of payment and consumption into equilibrium at a higher level of activity. When the producer of a good accepted its purchase price and passed that income on to workers in the form of wages (enjoying some himself in the form of profits), he created a new source of demand in society exactly equal to the value of what he had produced. That money would be spent on other goods, ensuring that there could be no deficiency of total demand in the economy. Even the money that people set aside as savings was just another form of spending: spending on the future. Say acknowledged that overproduction might occasionally arise in particular industries but insisted that such problems were "only a passing evil" that couldn't apply to the economy as a whole for any meaningful period of time. "I do not see how the products of a nation in general can ever be too abundant, for each such product provides the means for purchasing another."[34] The upshot: Depressions are impossible. The very act of producing forecloses the possibility that a society will be unable to afford the fruits of production. The overall standard of living might be high or low, but it depends on how efficiently the society makes use of its resources. Unemployment cannot be a significant factor.

But depressions are real, and Say's Law is wrong. People don't spend all of their incomes, and what they save is not automatically converted into other spending by anyone, now or later. In the classical worldview, banking was supposed to ensure that savings aligned with investment through the establishment of interest rates ensuring that the money people wanted to save would be profitably invested in new projects. *A Treatise on Money* had tasked central banks with handling this duty. By cutting interest rates, central banks could make it more attractive for firms to borrow the money needed to expand production and discourage people from putting money in the bank, where it would earn a lousy return. Keynes argued that although this might work—he remained to the end of his days an advocate of low interest rates and cheap money—it very well might not.

First, there was a limit to how far central banks could reduce the interest rate: zero. But more important, Keynes believed, economists had created "an optical illusion" for themselves around banking. Commercial bankers might approve loan applications, and central bankers might set interest rates, but bankers did not ultimately control investment. There is no "nexus which unites decisions to abstain from present consumption with decisions to provide for future consumption; whereas the motives which determine the latter are not linked in any simple way with the motives which determine the former."[35] Investment was driven not by banks but by firms making the decision to upgrade equipment or devote resources to new research. Workers didn't decide to save or spend based on sophisticated considerations about maximizing the utility of their money over the course of several years; they saved when they could *afford* to save, not when interest rates reached an attractively high level. Particularly during hard times, people exhibited a powerful "liquidity preference"—the desire to hold cash on hand rather than tie up their money in investment vehicles. Even bankers, eyeing the economic landscape, could be reluctant to approve longer-term loans, instead opting to either hold on to cash or devote it to quick projects that would return the money fast. Titans of industry, surveying a world of depression, would be cautious about dumping money into new projects that would take years to pay off. Interest rates didn't find the equilibrium between savings and investment; they just measured the price at which people were willing to forgo the convenience or certainty of cash.

None of that behavior was irrational, but it could be counterproductive. Long ago, during his days debating philosophy of language with Bertrand Russell and Ludwig Wittgenstein, Keynes had put great stock in the fact that people had to make decisions without knowing what the future would bring. The rationality of a decision could not be assessed by its outcome, since the future is always uncertain at the moment we make our choices. Keynes had tried and, most of his philosophical peers believed, failed to formulate a theory of rationality based on probabilities. But in his role as an economic theorist, uncertainty became the central psychological insight of his work. Uncertainty couldn't be measured statistically. Just because events had proceeded in a certain way in the past did not mean they would continue to proceed that way in the future. People had different levels of confidence about the future, but nobody could calculate it. I feel very confident that the sun will rise tomorrow. I feel slightly less confident than this that I will have a job tomorrow. I feel slightly less confident that it will be the same job I have today and slightly less that I will earn the same income. But circumstances can be arranged in which my confidence will be damaged or depleted. And in such circumstances, it will be perfectly rational for me not to spend my money but to hoard it. This is particularly true during, say, an economic depression, when the sad state of the economy makes people worry about their economic future. The same is true for people managing firms surveying the possibility of expanding operations or upgrading equipment. If things don't look very good, investing seems like a bad bet. Central bankers could try to affect those judgments by manipulating interest rates, but there were real limits. Savings very well might—and do—go unspent, lying idle and useless.

The possibility of excessive savings carried tremendous consequences. Capitalism would be in a state of *overproduction*. The supply
of goods and services would exceed the demand for those goods and
services because money—savings—was not being spent. Producers
would respond by cutting production and laying people off. That
would bring supply and demand into equilibrium, but it would be a
bad equilibrium in which nobody made the investments necessary to
hire people and expand production. Unemployment could creep in as
a permanent part of a low-functioning economy.

Keynes was conceding, in this analysis, a feud he had been engaged
in with Friedrich von Hayek since 1931. Hayek had insisted that the
total savings of society must *always* equal the total investments of society, that the idea of savings and investment getting out of kilter that
had been so central to *A Treatise on Money* was wrong. Keynes now
agreed with Hayek. But this only radicalized Keynes further. Savings
and investment were forced into equivalence by changes in the total
output of the economy. When one declined, the other would fall along
with total production. The economy would shrink and prosperity
would be diminished—not for lack of resources but simply because
people were reluctant to spend money.

Indeed, it was money itself that had made the Depression possible.
"A monetary economy," Keynes wrote, "is essentially one in which
changing views about the future are capable of influencing the quantity of employment."[36] Classical economists had considered money as
a facilitator or lubricant, something that eased the exchange of different goods. Trading goats for automobiles was awkward and inefficient;
money made it easy. But Keynes recognized that money was not only
a mechanism for transmitting information about the relative values of
different goods; it was also a store of value, which enabled people to
make and express judgments about their own material security *through
time*. Classical economics saw money as something static, like a painting. Keynes saw it as creating narratives of economic possibility, more
like a film or a novel. "The importance of money essentially flows from
its being a link between the present and the future."[37]

Keynes had long ago recognized the moral implications of money's function as a store of value. In "Economic Possibilities for Our Grand-children," he had emphasized that people were capable of confusing means with ends, of being consumed by "love of money" rather than a pursuit of the good life. Instead of enjoying great art and beautiful evenings, they would take satisfaction from contemplating the size of their bank accounts or from purchasing items that were not really beautiful or excellent but merely served as ostentatious displays of wealth.

In *The General Theory,* Keynes showed how this same property of money could lead not only to personal character flaws but to the breakdown of the economic system. "Consumption," he wrote, "is the sole end and object of all economic activity."[38] But money enables us to put off consumption to another day and another day and another indefinitely without losing our ability to consume *at some point.* We may substitute holding money for realizing actual material satisfaction not out of vice or confusion but out of simple fear for our future prospects. But when we refuse to consume, we deny others their income. This not only forces society to live with less—it risks making our fear into a contagion, realized in the form of decreased production, layoffs, and suffering amid surplus.

And modern financial systems powerfully amplified the ability of money to transform fear into suffering. Financial markets and stock exchanges had enabled disparate individuals to pool their resources and knowledge to support enterprises that had been inconceivable only a century or so before. Classical theorists believed that the more liquid those markets were, the better. More money and more investors enabled the market to settle on the right price of various companies and securities, the odd judgments of a few evened out by the level heads of the many.

But that wasn't the way it worked in practice, as Keynes had observed over the course of nearly two decades as a speculator. People didn't actually bet on the value of different enterprises; they bet on the judgments of other speculators. As Keynes put it in one of the few accessible passages from *The General Theory*: "Professional investment may be likened to those newspaper competitions in which the com-

petitors have to pick out the six prettiest faces from a hundred photographs, the prize being awarded to the competitor whose choice most
nearly corresponds to the average preferences of the competitors as a
whole; so that each competitor has to pick, not those faces which he
himself finds prettiest, but those which he thinks likeliest to catch the
fancy of the other competitors, all of whom are looking at the problem
from the same point of view. It is not a case of choosing those which,
to the best of one's judgment, are really the prettiest, nor even those
which average opinion genuinely thinks the prettiest."[39]

This didn't just mean that financial markets were prone to panic and
instability, as excitement and emotion overtook cool reasoning; it
meant there was no reason to believe that markets *ever* accurately
gauged the value of various investments. Wall Street and the City
were perfectly capable of turning extraordinary profits for themselves
without doing much for the greater good—indeed, they could do active social harm without intending to. "There is no clear evidence from
experience that the investment policy which is socially advantageous
coincides with that which is most profitable."[40]

That was not a result of irrationality or malevolence. Like the rest of
us, speculators and investors have to make their judgments under conditions of uncertainty about the future. "If we speak frankly, we have
to admit that our basis of knowledge for estimating the yield ten years
hence of a railway, a copper mine, a textile factory, the goodwill of a
patent medicine, an Atlantic liner, a building in the City of London
amounts to little and sometimes to nothing."[41] Stock exchanges didn't
actually shed any light on this problem. "The social object of skilled
investment should be to defeat the dark forces of time and ignorance
which envelop our future. The actual, private object of the most skilled
investment to-day is 'to beat the gun,' as the Americans so well express
it, to outwit the crowd, and to pass the bad, or depreciating, half-
crown to the other fellow."[42]

At best, capital markets could only magnify the hunches and dispo-
sitions of their participants. But the market prices of stocks, bonds,
and other assets created an illusory sense of mathematical certainty
about prospective investments. Though the numbers on tickers and

exchanges only approximated the temperament of the investment mob, they appeared to be the precise, scientific conclusions of prestigious experts—and bankers, politicians, and the public mistakenly took them to be just that. When speculators were in a dour mood—or even when they simply believed that other speculators were feeling pessimistic—they would underprice securities. Seeing the low valuations, other investors would be reluctant to put money behind similar projects, noting that the seemingly objective market had rendered an unfavorable judgment. This was what Keynes believed had happened across the entire global economy during the Depression. Humanity had not suffered some mass collapse of creative energy or business acumen any more than it had been engulfed by a sudden international unwillingness to work for a reasonable wage. Economic underperformance, whatever its original cause, had created an investment market that now assumed chronic underperformance to be the norm—and was perfectly capable of fulfilling its own prophecy.

Keynes' analysis of the investment process thus paralleled his understanding of democracy. Uncertainty about the future—not irrationality or stupidity—makes crowds prone to calamity in both finance and politics, particularly under conditions of significant anxiety. Markets are no more self-correcting than a mob hailing a demagogue. To work at all, they must be structured, guided, and managed. They might even have to be replaced. In *A Treatise on Money*, Keynes had argued that money was inherently political—the creation of the state. He was now extending that observation to markets themselves.

The General Theory only briefly touches on policy solutions to the problems of the 1930s. Uncertainty challenged the very idea of a rational market by attacking the idea of rational investors or workers pursuing their own self-interest. Under conditions of substantial uncertainty, self-interest was impossible to determine. If we took seriously the way investors and entrepreneurs behaved, it was clear that how much money someone stood to gain from a new endeavor was only one factor in the decision to embark upon it. Keynes suggested that governments might need to resort to various political embarrassments to boost the confidence of the business class and reanimate the primal urge to activity that a financialized economy can sedate, but he believed other remedies might prove more reliable, including his old policy standby, public works—a direct investment by the government in social improvement.

If governments refused to build, however, any activity that directly enhanced the purchasing power of the public would probably help. By putting money in the hands of workers by hiring the unemployed, reducing their taxes, or offering other direct material benefits, governments could increase the aggregate demand in society. When an economy faced an excess of supply, the normal business response would be to cut production, creating unemployment. To prevent that outcome, a government could boost demand, allowing businesses to maintain high levels of production by enabling consumers to buy more products. With more money in their pockets, citizens could buy more goods. Businessmen and investors, seeing those encouraging signs, would get their confidence back, resume taking the risks necessary for economic growth, and put money behind useful projects. This was the way out of the Depression.

It had profound and counterintuitive implications for the monetary system. Because if conditions were serious enough—and they had never been more serious than they were during the Depression—it didn't really matter exactly *how* consumption was stimulated, so long as the government did *something*. "Pyramid-building, earthquakes, even wars may serve to increase wealth" so long as the government spent money on them. Borrowing money or running a deficit to do so, moreover, was not inherently risky. It was, after all, creating new wealth by furthering new enterprise and activity. Each dollar the government spent could multiply on its way through the economy: a dollar spent on construction would be paid to a steel plant, which in turn would pay a mining operation, ultimately putting money in many pockets and generating more than one dollar in total economic activity. But the same could be true of a dollar spent on nothing at all, as long as the people who received it actually went out and spent it. "If the Treasury were to fill old bottles with banknotes, bury them at suitable depths in disused coalmines which are then filled up to the surface with town rubbish, and leave it to private enterprise on well-tried principles of *laissez-faire* to dig the notes up again (the right to do so being obtained, of course, by tendering for leases of the note-bearing territory), there need be no more unemployment and, with the help of the repercussions, the real income of the community, and its capital wealth also, would probably become a good deal greater than it actually is. It would, indeed, be more sensible to build houses and the like; but if there are political and practical difficulties in the way of this, the above would be better than nothing."[43]

This is one of the most enduring and outrageous images from *The General Theory*. Conservative critics of the book often point to the anecdote as a *reductio ad absurdum* of the entire Keynesian enterprise. Surely anyone who believes such nonsense to be a good idea must have gone off track somewhere. The proposal is fundamentally at odds with our basic intuitions about the nature of economic problems. It turns economic activity into a meaningless ritual—a trick we collectively play on one another to make sure we keep an arbitrary machine running smoothly. Most of us understand work as something functional. Our paychecks are essential to our survival, and we invest our labors with a sense of personal identity and emotional significance. We want to believe that our economic status, even if shaded by luck and circumstance, has at least *something* to do with our contribution to society. We like to believe that we can get more for ourselves by doing better for society—a farmer should grow more crops, a writer should write better books. Keynes was laying bare the idea that in a monetary economy, improving society did not necessarily require virtuous or even useful work.

He was attacking not only the sense of self-worth we derive from our labor but the meaning of suffering in the Depression. It is terribly deflating to learn that the horrors and deprivations of seventeen years are only a malfunction in the ad hoc bookkeeping system of modern finance. It was not the cruelty and greed of the capitalists or the sloth of the masses that had created so much social rot—only a technical problem, easily remedied. The Depression was a mistake, not a titanic clash between good and evil.

Such a message was, no doubt, a lot to swallow. But in a postscarcity economy, the very meaning of work was a technicality, something people just have to do because it keeps the system running, not because it is truly essential to clothing and feeding the public. Keynes had come to terms with this idea in "Economic Possibilities for Our Grandchildren." Much of what we imagine ourselves to be contributing to society through our work is in fact an accounting trick to enable consumption. Particularly today, nearly eighty years after the essay's publication, we could in fact prosper while working less if we managed the system intelligently and ensured that its fruits were distributed widely.

That observation robbed the Depression of its moral significance, but it opened up radical political possibilities. Our problem was not a scarcity of goods and resources. There was more than enough stuff, food, clothing, shelter, music, and dancing to go around. Too much, in fact—society was almost perpetually in a state of chronic oversupply.

The chief economic question facing each society, Keynes believed, was no longer what it could *afford* but how its members would like to live. A titan of industry could not shrug off poverty as an inevitable element of every society. Democracies could choose different paths.

Keynes was no longer telling a story about adjusting a machine that generally tended toward a functional, prosperous equilibrium. *The General Theory* did not prove that governments may need to intervene in the operations of a free market from time to time to correct excesses or imbalances. It showed, instead, that the very idea of a free market independent of government structure and supervision was incoherent. For markets to function, governments had to provide demand. Eras of laissez-faire prosperity like the British golden age before the war were very rare—a "special case" resulting from unique psychological and material circumstances that were impossible to replicate with any regularity through speculative financial markets, in which "the capital development of a country becomes a by-product of the activities of a casino."[44]

Keynes argued that "a somewhat comprehensive socialisation of investment will prove the only means of securing an approximation to full employment."[45] Though there was no need, he believed, for the state to take over the direct "instruments of production," applying *The General Theory* "would mean the euthanasia of the rentier, and, consequently, the euthanasia of the cumulative oppressive power of the capitalist to exploit the scarcity-value of capital."[46] Capitalists made their money by providing something rare—capital—that others needed. If the government could create and provide investment capital itself, capitalists would lose their choke hold on the development of society. Clearly, Keynes was contemplating a much broader role for the government than tax policy and interest rate adjustments. "I expect to see the State, which is in a position to calculate the marginal efficiency of capital goods on long views and on the basis of the general social advantage, taking an ever greater responsibility for directly organising investment."[47]

Keynes had, he believed, destroyed "one of the chief social justifications of great inequality of wealth."[48] In his youth, he had understood saving as a virtue that benefited society at large. The fortunes of the rich, accumulated over generations, created a source of investment capital that could be deployed for the benefit of all. With *The General Theory*, Keynes demonstrated that capital growth was not the result of virtuous saving by the affluent; it was a by-product of the income growth of the masses. Creating large amounts of savings at the top of society did not bring about higher levels of investment. The causal arrow pointed the other way: Creating large amounts of investment caused higher levels of savings. And so "the removal of very great disparities of wealth and income" would improve social harmony and economic functionality.

Keynes remained frightened of sudden changes in the structure of society. He anticipated a slow transition to a better future and offered few suggestions for its implementation. "The euthanasia of the rentier, of the functionless investor, will be nothing sudden, merely a gradual but prolonged continuance . . . and will need no revolution."[49] And he insisted that none of his ideas required any utopian fantasies about human goodness or the efficiency of governments. "The task of transmuting human nature must not be confused with the task of managing it."[50] He was taking people as he believed they were: a little selfish, more than a little afraid, interested in social progress, capable of stymieing their own talents.

A few months before *The General Theory* was released, Keynes published an essay in *The Listener* titled "Art and the State." Ostensibly concerned with encouraging the production of art, the piece swiftly morphed into an ambitious call for social rejuvenation from an activist government. Keynes argued that the utilitarian moral philosophers of the eighteenth and nineteenth centuries had popularized "a perverted theory of the state" guided by "business arithmetic" in which the final judgment on the social value of any activity was to be found in whether it turned a profit.[51] But the market, he argued, was not a reliable statement of society's preferences, and it could not invisibly guide a polity to salvation. The market simply failed to deliver a host of real social goods that the public enjoyed, particularly art. The things that make life meaningful—beauty, community, a vibrant and multifaceted culture—all required collective, coordinated action. "Our experience has demonstrated plainly that these things cannot be successfully carried on if they depend on the motive of profit and financial success. The exploitation and incidental destruction of the divine gift of the public entertainer by prostituting it to the purposes of financial gain is one of the worser crimes of present-day capitalism."[52]

The economics of *The General Theory* are inextricably linked to Keynes' conception of the good life. He believed that strict adherence to the arbitrary tides of high finance during the Depression had acclimated the British to a sterile, ugly existence, when they might instead have enjoyed "parks, squares and playgrounds, with lakes, pleasure gardens and boulevards, and every delight which skill and fancy can devise. Why should not all London be the equal of St James's Park and its surroundings? The river front might become one of the sights of the world with a range of terraces and buildings rising from the river. The schools of South London should have the dignity of universities with courts, colonnades, and fountains, libraries, galleries, dining-halls, cinemas, and theatres for their own use."[53] With *The*

General Theory, Keynes showed how the very construction of those wonders could create the wealth with which they would be paid for.

The General Theory proved that the condition and organization of society were not the inevitable, dispassionate requirements of tragically insufficient resources. They were, instead, political choices that societies could not avoid. Keynes did not pursue how those choices ought to be made, evaluated, or held to account. He offered no metric for economic success other than "full employment"—and even that he kept vague. He spent almost no time discussing how, exactly, governments should go about managing aggregate demand or purchasing power or socializing investment. He had instead opened the door to a new world of political possibilities that both the financial establishment and its Marxist critics had believed to be impossible. It meant that society could look very different than it currently did—but also that the prevailing order did not need to be destroyed or overthrown to be improved. It carried the seeds of radical transformation through the preservation of the existing social order and its institutions.

Keynes explicitly connected this doctrine of domestic prosperity to a program of international peace. The gold standard and laissez-faire had foreclosed every option available to an economy in distress except a competitive trade war with other countries. Since governments couldn't spend or inflate their way out of trouble, they had to find ways to dump their goods in foreign markets and block the entry of foreign goods into their own. That meant that the free-trade ideal Keynes had grown up with—in which different peoples exchanged different goods and benefited from one another's expertise—was, in practice, a zero-sum struggle for survival. Trade, he now believed, exercised "a less benign influence" on foreign affairs than economists had assumed. People began to view the citizens of other countries with suspicion and enmity, while their statesmen began to see other nations—as French leaders had understood Germany after the war—as mere economic prey. That economic competition fueled militarist nationalism at home and made trade a source of international tension, rather than an avenue for mutual understanding. Keynes believed he had discovered a way to relieve the pressure:

If nations can learn to provide themselves with full employment by their domestic policy . . . there need be no important economic forces calculated to set the interest of one country against that of its neighbours. . . . International trade would cease to be what it is, namely, a desperate expedient to maintain employment at home by forcing sales on foreign markets and restricting purchases, which, if successful, will merely shift the problem of unemployment to the neighbor which is worsted in the struggle, but a willing and unimpeded exchange of goods and services in conditions of mutual advantage.[54]

There is a steady acceleration of ambition over the course of *The General Theory*. The book opens with an appeal to the economics profession, asking its members to rethink the underlying tenets of the classical doctrine that then dominated the field. But by its close, Keynes has largely left his fellow professional economists behind, believing he has settled the facts of the case beyond serious question. He closes with an appeal to Marxists: Do not discount the power of ideas to triumph over the economic interests of the ruling class. The vested interests of the capitalists, he argued, did not reign sovereign over the great gears of human history; the beliefs and ideas of the people did. They could choose to shrug off the suffering and dysfunction of the past two decades without resorting to violent revolutionary upheaval. All they needed was to be convinced by an idea.

Is the fulfillment of these ideas a visionary hope? . . . The ideas of economists and political philosophers, both when they are right and when they are wrong, are more powerful than is commonly understood. Indeed the world is ruled by little else. Practical men, who believe themselves to be quite exempt from any intellectual influences, are usually the slaves of some defunct economist. Madmen in authority, who hear voices in the air, are distilling their frenzy from some academic scribbler of a few years back. I am sure that the power of vested interests is vastly exaggerated compared with the gradual encroachment of ideas. Not, indeed, immediately, but after a certain interval; for in the field of economic and political philosophy there are not many who are influenced by new theories after they are twenty-five or thirty years of age, so that the ideas which civil servants and politicians and even agitators apply to current events are not likely to be the newest. But, soon or late, it is ideas, not vested interests, which are dangerous for good or evil.[55]

For his students and their allies in Cambridge, Keynes had presented a powerful, almost intoxicating vision. To Paul Sweezy, *The General Theory* "opened up new vistas and new pathways to a whole generation of economists," infusing them with "a sense of liberation and intellectual stimulus."[56] It was about much more than economics. As Lorie Tarshis recalled years later, "What Keynes supplied was *hope:* hope that prosperity could be restored and maintained without the support of prison camps, executions and bestial interrogations . . . many of us felt that by following Keynes . . . each one of us could become a doctor to the whole world."[57]

TEN

◇

CAME THE REVOLUTION

As Keynes secured his place in the pantheon of great Western thinkers, the once illustrious crowd of Bloomsbury intellectuals he had surrounded himself with as a young man was slowly dying, literally and metaphorically. The tight circle had channeled the tragedy of the Great War into an aesthetic movement encompassing portraiture, literature, ballet, and even economics. But the world had moved on to other calamities. Bloomsbury, so enraged and exhausted by the war, did not have the strength to fight the Depression, much less Adolf Hitler. Only Keynes would continue to cast a light for the world as it fell deeper into darkness.

On January 21, 1932, at the age of fifty-one, Lytton died of stomach cancer at his farmhouse in Wiltshire. The eminent Edwardian had struggled from his bed for more than two months with severe bowel problems and intermittent fevers, encouraged by a steady stream of visitors and an overly optimistic medical team that at one point had included six doctors and three nurses.[1] Lytton proved as unconventional in death as he had been in life, scribbling private poems in his final days, passing away surrounded by his longtime lover, Dora Carrington, and her husband, Ralph Partridge. He was cremated without a funeral. It was a terrible emotional blow to his friends. Though they were scattered across various country homes and tied down in marriages, every member of Bloomsbury still regarded Lytton as a central organizing figure in their lives; they cherished his wit and craved his approval, though many refused to acknowledge it in the heat of argument. Without him, the group lost both its sense of professional focus and its social direction. Virginia was particularly wounded. She recounted the final evening of his life in her diary:

> Lytton died yesterday morning. I see him coming along the street, muffled up with his beard resting on his tie: how we should stop: his eyes glow. Now I am too numb with all the emotion yesterday to do more than think thoughts like this. Well, as I know, the pain will soon begin. One toys about with this & that. How queer it was last night at the party, the tightness round everyone's lips—ours I mean. Duncan Nessa & I sobbing together in the studio—the man looking out the mews window—a sense of something spent, gone: that is to me so intolerable: the impoverishment: then the sudden vividness. Duncan said "One misses people more & more. It comes over one suddenly that one will tell them something. Then the pang comes over one, after years." . . . Yes, 20 years of Lytton lost to us, stupidly: the thing we shall never have again.[2]

Virginia's own career began to reflect the toll the Depression had taken on Bloomsbury's intellectual reserves. Over the previous dozen years, she had published a major work in all but two, and the list of her achievements staggered even her talented friends. *Mrs. Dalloway, To the Lighthouse, Orlando,* and *A Room of One's Own* had all electrified literary critics within a span of just four years and had been followed swiftly by another experimental triumph, *The Waves.* But it would be five years after Lytton's death before she would release another masterpiece, *The Years.* In 1933, she found time to write *Flush,* a light comedy written from the perspective of a cocker spaniel, which, Leonard maintained, "cannot seriously be compared with her major novels."[3] Overwhelmed by the political tide, Virginia was treading water.

Of all the founding members of Bloomsbury, Keynes had drifted

furthest from Lytton, his onetime lover and rival, as their careers had
taken flight. But their relationship had remained warm since the end
of the war, though with each passing year it had depended more on
correspondence and less upon social gatherings. Lytton had been one
of the few Bloomsberries to accept Lydia without raising an emotional clamor and had remained to the end one of the few people in
the world who could convince Keynes that his thinking was morally
or intellectually unsound. Keynes was shaken by the death of his
friend, telling Virginia he was especially upset there had been "no
mark to say This is over"[4] without a memorial service. But he wanted
the intimate details of their lives together to remain private. When
Lytton's brother James asked for advice on how to handle his correspondence, Keynes made an urgent plea for discretion. "The letters?—
for God's sake lock them up for years yet." Keynes' sexuality remained
a dangerous secret.[5]

Socially, he dug himself deeper into the Cambridge milieu with
Kahn and Robinson, distancing himself further from the old Gordon
Square gang. Though Lydia had aged past her dancing prime, Keynes
put up the funds for a new theater in Cambridge, which became a
venue for his wife's acting career as the couple attempted to transform
the university town into a major European performing arts hub. By
the mid-1930s, Lydia was no longer the darling of the international
art world, but she could still draw a crowd, particularly as she developed an unlikely broadcasting career with the BBC, hosting music
and ballet specials and once narrating Hans Christian Andersen's
dance fable "The Red Shoes."

But Keynes' health could not withstand the demands he was now
placing on himself. Writing a book of economic theory, teaching
courses, managing a theater, advising the British government, and
writing popular articles on politics and finance were too potent a combination for a man now in his midfifties. In the final months of 1936,
he began feeling persistently weak, his frequent colds lasting too long,
his breath short even when sitting. He became unable to walk even
modest distances, overwhelmed after as little as a quarter of a mile.
When Lydia attempted to enforce some relaxation with a trip to

Cannes in March 1937, her husband experienced an alarming series of spasms in his chest. On their return to Cambridge, his mother compelled him to see the family doctor, her brother Walter Langdon-Brown, whom Keynes affectionately referred to as "Uncle Walrus."

After some correspondence, a physical exam, and a chest X-ray, Uncle Walrus concluded that a recent bout of the flu had inflicted "a slightly poisonous effect" on his heart. He prescribed bed rest and a "heart tonic" that elicited strong complaints from Keynes for interfering with his work by leaving him foggy-headed. That was, of course, partly the intent.[6] Everyone around Keynes worried he was working himself to death.

His ill health spurred Keynes to put his some of his financial affairs in order. His college friends were now well into middle age, and the pure artists among them were long past the zenith of their earning potential. Duncan could no longer hope to find a market for edgy works of good taste—the fireplace mantels of middle-class shoppers or foxhunting families were now more likely to win him a decent sale. And so Keynes provided his old flame with a handsome annuity to free him from his aesthetic prison. Duncan, whatever he chose to paint, however he carried on with or without Vanessa, would be taken care of.

"I do not know how to thank you for what you are doing for me," the painter wrote Keynes in April 1937. "I have never been able to save any money and this seems an odd sort of punishment for my thriftlessness. . . . I am only telling my mother and Vanessa about it at the moment because I think if it gets about that I am a moneyed man no-one will buy any more pictures."[7]

In the meantime, Keynes' health was not improving. Bed rest and heart tonic were not going to counter decades of heavy smoking, high stress, an unpoliced diet, and a life spent chained to desks and typewriters that all but ignored exercise. On May 16, he collapsed on his way to lunch with his parents at their Cambridge house on Harvey Road. Lydia rushed over upon hearing the news, fearing she would miss the final moments of her husband's life. But though he had suffered a severe heart attack, he survived. Lydia canceled her acting commitments and spent the next month nursing her husband, who was too weak to leave the bed in his parents' home. Finally, on June 19, an ambulance carried him away to Ruthin Castle, a hospital and rehabilitation center in Wales for ailing members of the British elite.

The news rocked Bloomsbury, leaving Virginia "anxious about Maynard to the extent of dreading post or buying a paper."[8] The gloomy setting of the clinic, meanwhile, depressed Lydia. And though she befriended a few other women who were staying in the area to attend their sick husbands, her nickname for the crew—a "hen party of Castle widows"[9]—reflected her low spirits. Her husband was desperately ill. Keynes, who was still sneaking letters and notes under the bedcovers when his nurses weren't looking, shot off a word to his brother, Geoffrey, himself a physician, reporting that the specialists at Ruthin had found his tonsils in "shocking condition, covered with pus to the naked eye and creeping apparently with animals called fusillaria."[10] Swabs of his throat bloomed "at once into an orchard,"[11] according to Lydia. Uncle Walrus had completely overlooked a streptococcal infection in Keynes' respiratory system, which had lodged itself in his heart and arteries, which had in turn been weakened by his smoking habit—though doctors at the time were not aware of the link between tobacco and heart disease.

Penicillin, the world's first mass-produced antibiotic, would not become widely available until 1945. Though the Ruthin doctors swabbed Keynes' throat with "organic arsenic"[12] treatments, they could do little for him other than monitor his status and force him to rest.

In the meantime, tragedy struck Bloomsbury again. Vanessa's son Julian had sharpened his Marxist thinking in debates with his uncle Maynard over the course of his twenties. By 1937, the young man had come to see international class solidarity as the only effective means of putting an end to the Fascist thundering from Hitler, Mussolini, and General Francisco Franco. Following, as Keynes later wrote, a "duty of fearless individual judgment" which "impelled him past all dissuasions," Julian volunteered as an ambulance driver for the socialist Republican forces battling Franco in the Spanish Civil War.[13] He was killed by a bomb on July 18 during the Battle of Brunete. Virginia and

Leonard rushed to Charleston to join Duncan, Quentin, Vanessa, and their teenage daughter, Angelica, in mourning.[14] Despite their philosophical differences and Julian's frequent charges that Keynes was naive or sentimental about the prospects for political change, the old economist had loved the young poet all the same for his intellectual daring and admired his courage. Confined to his hospital bed, Keynes did his best to console his bereaved friends.

"My Dearest Nessa," he wrote on June 29, "A line of sympathy and love from both of us on the loss of your dear and beautiful boy with his pure and honourable feelings. It was fated that he should make his protest, as he was entitled to do, with his life, and one can say nothing."[15]

Keynes wrote an obituary for Julian in a Cambridge publication, praising him as a young man of intellectual integrity who had followed through on his deepest moral convictions. He could offer no higher praise. When the article reached Vanessa, she sent Keynes a long, tender letter musing on family, war, and adulthood, detouring into the significance of a trip by Julian to China and reflections on the time Keynes had spent with Julian and his brother, Quentin, when the two were growing up. Vanessa used the occasion of a thank-you note to plead for contact with one of her oldest friends, who remained bedridden. "I like what you have written so much," Vanessa wrote. "I've really only written all this because I should have liked to talk to you."[16] Julian's death catalyzed a long overdue reconciliation between Keynes and Vanessa. The years of feuding over trifles that began with Lydia's introduction to Bloomsbury were finally ended, and the two at last returned to the warm sincerity that had united them during the war years.

The tragedy also focused Keynes' attention on the Spanish conflict and his disagreements with the younger generation of peace-loving progressives whose worldview had not been shaped by the experience of the Great War. Whatever the protests of doctors, friends, and family, Keynes could not bear to observe the world's steady march to annihilation from his hospital bed without at least putting pen to paper. Just three weeks after being admitted to Ruthin, he published an essay on British foreign policy in *The New Statesman and Nation* calling for cool heads as the continent teetered on the brink of destruction. The piece was framed as a response to W. H. Auden's poem "Spain," but Julian's ghost haunts every sentence. Like Julian, Auden had volunteered as an ambulance driver for the Republican forces. His poem grieved over the brutality unleashed by Franco's army, issuing a mournful call for international solidarity in "the struggle," including the "conscious acceptance of guilt in the necessary murder"—war as a tragic but inescapable means to liberation. It was, quite literally, a call to arms. Julian had advanced the same view in 1935 for an introduction to a book on conscientious objectors to the Great War: "The war-resistance movements of my generation will in the end succeed in putting down war—by force if necessary."[17]

Across Europe and the United States, idealistic young men were going to Spain to fight fascism, convinced that violence was required to beat back the rising authoritarian threat. It was an ideological conflict with obvious implications for Germany and Italy. But Keynes remained so deeply scarred by the First World War that he viewed the possibility of a second as a nearly unthinkable disaster to be avoided at—almost—any cost. Spain's future must be left for Spain to decide. He could respect the consciences of the young volunteers, but escalating local conflicts into global war was for Leninist revolutionaries, not right-thinking lovers of peace:

> I maintain that the claims of peace are paramount; though this seems an out-of-date view in what used to be pacifist circles. It is our duty to prolong peace, hour by hour, day by day, for as long as we can. We do not know what the future will bring, except that it will be quite different from anything we could predict. I have said in another context that it is a disadvantage of "the long run" that in the long run we are all dead. But I could have said equally well that it is a great advantage of "the short run" that in the short run we are still alive. Life and history are made up of short runs. If we are at peace in the short run, that is something. The best we can do

is put off disaster, if only in the hope, which is not necessarily a remote one, that something will turn up.[18]

Keynes acknowledged that there might be cause to revise that judgment in the future. "There are circumstances when war on our part, whether defensible or not, is unavoidable." But he did not yet see Germany or Italy as an imminent threat; they were too belligerent and incompetent for their own good. If Great Britain was eventually forced into war against "the brigand powers," it wouldn't have trouble finding allies when the time came. "One of them is busily engaged in outrageing every creed in turn. If they could find another institution or another community to insult or injure, they would do so. Both of them are spending a lot of money on an intensive propaganda to persuade the rest of the world that they are the enemies of the human race. It is having the desired result, not least in the United States. No one trusts or respects their word. . . . And if, indeed, the thieves were to have a little more success, nothing is likelier than that they would fall out amongst themselves."[19]

As a matter of military history, the point is essentially moot. The British had neither the manpower nor the equipment to risk a global conflict by engaging directly with Germany and Italy over Spain in 1937. The Americans would not be supplying armaments or other wartime aid for years to come, and there simply were not enough soldiers ready to be mobilized. But the essay reveals a great deal about Keynes' own thinking about war and peace. Though he had spent his entire postwar career warning of the potential for economic mismanagement to bring the Fascists to power, as late as 1937 he underestimated the threat they posed. Despite all of the international dysfunction he had witnessed over reparations and war debts, he continued to assume a much greater capacity for European diplomatic collaboration against Germany than in fact existed. Though his persistent optimism frequently enabled him to find solutions his contemporaries never imagined, it was just as often reckless, even delusional.

The rise of the Nazis posed other problems for Keynes' worldview.

In his letters to Lydia, Keynes at times used "Jewish" and "circumcised" as synonyms for "greedy." The economist Robert Solow has even suggested that Keynes' attacks on "love of money" in "Economic Possibilities for Our Grandchildren" reflect a "polite anti-semitism."[20] Solow presses his case too far, but Keynes' jokes with Lydia do represent more than some unfortunate, outdated terminology. In 1926, he had written a brief sketch of Albert Einstein, one of his intellectual heroes, after meeting him in Berlin. Einstein, according to Keynes, was one of the *good* Jews—"a sweet imp" who had "not sublimated immortality into compound interest." Keynes knew many such good Jews in Germany. There was a Berlin banker named Fuerstenberg "who Lydia liked so much" and the "mystical" German economist Kurt Singer and even his "dear" friend Carl Melchior, whom he had met at the Paris Peace Conference. "Yet if I lived there, I felt I might turn anti-Semite. For the poor Prussian is too slow and heavy on his legs for the other kind of Jews, the ones who are not imps but serving devils, with small horns, pitch forks, and oily tails. It is not agreeable to see a civilisation so under the ugly thumbs of its impure Jews who have all the money and the power and the brains."[21]

The sketch was rancid even by the standards of his own time. Keynes may have realized it. The piece was not published until after his death. After the Nazis came to power, Keynes became more considerate with his vocabulary. In August 1933, he told the German economist Arthur Spiethoff, who was helping to publish a German translation of some of Keynes' work, that he could not avoid using the term "barbarism" in the text because "that word rightly indicates the effect of recent events in Germany. . . . It is many generations in our judgement since such disgraceful events have occurred in any country pretending to call itself civilised."[22] When Melchior died after an anti-Semitic attack in 1933, Keynes rejected a personal invitation from the mayor of Hamburg to give an economics lecture, as an act of protest. "After the death of my friend . . . there is nothing left that could attract me to Hamburg."[23]

His friend Ludwig Wittgenstein had bounced all over Europe after the war, working as a gardener in a monastery, designing an austere

CAME THE REVOLUTION 285

modernist house in Vienna, securing a PhD from Cambridge, living in Norway and then Dublin. When Germany annexed Austria in March 1938, Wittgenstein wrote to Keynes asking for help. He could not go back to Austria. Three of his grandparents had been born Jewish, setting his very wealthy family up for persecution. Keynes, still convalescing under Lydia's care, helped establish his old colleague with a job at Cambridge, where he would be safe from Nazi pursuit.[24] "Thanks for all the trouble you've gone to," Wittgenstein wrote him afterward. "I *hope* I'll be a decent prof."[25] In April 1938, Keynes wrote to Archibald Sinclair, the head of the Liberal Party, urging him "to be active" on "the refugee problem," noting that President Roosevelt's effectiveness seemed to be stymied by political obstacles.[26] "The least we can do is to be more generous and constructive."[27]

Keynes would be more aggressive in 1939 and 1940, after the British Home Office began rounding up over eighty thousand people living in England who had been born in Germany, Austria, or Italy and sending thousands to internment camps on the Isle of Man as suspected subversives or enemy sympathizers. These included Jewish refugees who had fled Nazi aggression. Keynes was infuriated. "Our behavior towards refugees is the most disgraceful and humiliating thing which has happened for a long time," he wrote to one friend. To another: "I can remember nothing equal to what is going on for stupidity and callousness." Just as he had tasked himself in World War I with securing conscientious objector cards for his friends, so now he worked his connections with the British government to guarantee the freedom of his German Jewish economist friends Eduard Rosenbaum, Erwin Rothbarth, and Hans Singer.[28] It was a long process. Rothbarth was ultimately interned along with Piero Sraffa for the summer of 1940, but after Keynes secured the release of both men, Rothbarth volunteered for the British army. He was killed in action in November 1944.[29]

In the fall of 1937, however, Keynes was still slowly recovering his health. Lydia at last brought him home to Tilton, and they even managed a few weeks at Gordon Square around Christmas to be reunited with Bloomsbury. "We put Maynard to bed on 2 chairs," wrote Vir-

ginia Woolf, "and talked and talked until he worked himself into such
a fury about politics, that Lydia called the car and off they drove."[30]
But most of their days were spent resting, listening to radio broadcasts
together, or taking slow walks around their country home. His spirits,
despite the state of the world and his heart, remained as odd and energetic as ever. When Lydia scolded him for walking too fast during a
visit from Quentin Bell, Keynes turned to a nearby shepherd in his
employ and asked, "What would you do if an old sheep looked at you
as Lydia is looking at me now?" It was a question, Quentin later recorded, that "anyone might have found . . . difficult to answer.' "[31]

His strength had improved so much by early 1938 that he ventured
to correspond not only with old friends like Wittgenstein but with the
president of the United States.

In his first term in office, Franklin Delano Roosevelt had overseen the
most profound transformation of American government since the
Civil War. The more than two dozen new federal agencies he had established were now busy revamping American life. The Rural Electrification Administration and the Tennessee Valley Authority brought
entire regions of the country into the twentieth century. The National
Labor Relations Board and the Department of Labor overhauled the
relationship between workers and their bosses. The Home Owners'
Loan Corporation refinanced mortgages for borrowers in trouble, and
the Federal Housing Administration introduced a new kind of home
loan that made home ownership feasible for millions of families who
had never dreamed of it. The Public Works Administration and the
Civil Works Administration were revolutionizing the nation's infrastructure, building dams, bridges, and power plants, while the Works
Progress Administration was invigorating local life with new schools,
theaters, museums, playgrounds, and hospitals. The Securities and Exchange Commission was policing Wall Street, and the Banking Act
had at last stabilized the nation's system of credit.

But someone had to do all of this administering. The economics
profession in the early 1930s was almost exclusively an academic af-

fair, supplemented by little more than a few positions at the Fed and
the Treasury. Graduate students nearing the completion of a dissertation routinely found inexplicable new problems to explore or suffered
strange, overpowering cases of writer's block that prevented them
from finishing their work for at least another semester. The job market
for bona fide PhD economists was so thin that many students preferred to maintain their lowly employment status rather than risk receiving a degree. But with new agency after new agency opening in
Washington, suddenly "a nearly unlimited number of jobs were open
for economists at unbelievably high pay in the federal government,"
according to John Kenneth Galbraith, himself one of those eager
young economists. This "new gold rush"[32] not only transformed the
discipline, it attracted younger, more ideologically flexible economists
to the government, since older conservatives were not eager to leave
their prestigious, hard-won jobs at major universities.

The New Dealers were scrambling to fill all of these new posts as
quickly as possible. When Galbraith arrived in Washington in 1934,
he was just twenty-six years old, with a fresh PhD in agricultural economics from Berkeley, where he had written a dissertation about bees.
Born in rural Canada, he'd received an undergraduate degree in animal husbandry from the Ontario Agricultural College. And though
he hadn't yet applied for U.S. citizenship, he already revered FDR.
"Only after Roosevelt's death did I realize that a President could be
wrong,"[33] he later joked. Galbraith's first stint in the Roosevelt administration proved inconsequential: a few months of well-compensated
work that he used to pay off all of his student debts before taking a
minor post at Harvard. But it did provide him with an early political
education he would eventually put to use in four different Democratic
administrations. Like Keynes, Galbraith would spend his early career
as a brilliant, underappreciated government functionary. And like
Keynes, he would in time become one of the most important English-
speaking public intellectuals of his generation.

"When F.D.R. came to office in March 1933, so desperate was the
economic position that for the business and financial community he
was an angel of rescue," he later wrote. "By 1934, things were enough

better so that his efforts on behalf of farmers and the unemployed, his tendency to make light of economic orthodoxy, could be disliked and even feared. Roosevelt had become 'that man in the White House' and 'the traitor to his class.' "[34]

The ill will between Roosevelt and the rich was a matter of power, not results. No peacetime U.S. president in the years since has matched the economic growth achieved during the first three full years of FDR's administration. Adjusted for inflation, the economy grew by a monumental 10.8 percent, 8.9 percent, and 12.9 percent during 1934, 1935, and 1936, respectively.[35] Over the course of his first term, the unemployment rate plunged from over 20 percent to less than 10 percent, as the ranks of the unemployed were thinned by more than half, from roughly 11.5 million to 4.9 million (there were about 1.4 million unemployed prior to the stock market crash).[36] Only once has a U.S. *wartime* economy matched Roosevelt's initial economic miracle— a few years later, during the mobilization for World War II. Though FDR had to wrestle with Congress, the Supreme Court, and even himself over spending, taxes, regulations, budget deficits, and everything else that made up the New Deal, he was in fact spending a lot of money, nearly doubling the expenditures of the federal government from $4.6 billion to $8.2 billion as the deficit surged from $2.6 billion to $4.3 billion—though he offset some of the deficit impact of his new programs by increasing taxes on the wealthy.

Those figures were modest compared to what Keynes had advocated and indeed compared to what was to come. In his 1934 trip to the United States, Keynes had advocated annual deficits of $4.8 billion to members of the administration. In 1936, federal outlays still accounted for less than one-tenth of the total U.S. economy. By the end of the war, government projects would total $92.7 billion a year and account for more than 40 percent of all U.S. economic activity (since the beginning of Ronald Reagan's presidency, spending has fluctuated by a few percentage points around 20 percent of gross domestic product).[37]

All of this offended the policy sensibilities of the elite, who hated progressive taxation, deficits, and devaluation as much as the British banking establishment did. But there was more at stake than Wall Street's bottom line. The New Deal did not, in fact, crimp legitimate business on Wall Street; Roosevelt just reorganized it. In 1935, with the United States off gold and onto Glass-Steagall, and with the SEC policing traders and the federal government incurring unheard-of deficits, the amount of securities offerings underwritten by investment banks expanded to four times the level of the previous year.[38] With the economy growing rapidly, brokers and traders had more work to do.

Everybody did. But the rich, as a group of Harvard economists observed, continued to "complain bitterly" of their tax burden, which they perceived as a violation of "divine right"—even though "the additions to their incomes, resulting from the government's activities, are far greater in amount than the additional taxes they pay."[39] Jack Morgan, according to one chronicler of the family, viewed the New Deal "less as a set of economic reforms than as a direct, malicious assault on the social order."[40]

Which, of course, it was. Morgan was only the most obvious, iconic embodiment of what was quickly becoming a hereditary American nobility. Close friends with King George V, adored by the king's infant granddaughter who would one day become the second Queen Elizabeth, Jack enjoyed traditional aristocratic recreations, shooting pheasant when the affairs of his firm overtaxed his nerves. But whereas the landed European gentry of the nineteenth century had understood themselves as a chosen elect, Morgan and his elite countrymen believed they had won their place in society through business acumen and the sound stewardship of a grateful society. That was an incredible idea for a man who had been handed the most powerful post in American finance from his father, who in turn had inherited the banking house from his father before him. It was nevertheless sincere. Even the great scourge of Wall Street, Ferdinand Pecora, commended Morgan for his "deeply genuine" testimony before his Senate committee, in which Jack stated it was impossible for a "private banker" to "become too powerful," because such status was attained "not from the possession of large means, but from the confidence of the people" and the "respect and esteem of the community."[41] This self-conception was fed by the energy both Jack and his father had devoted to philanthropy, paying hundreds of thousands of dollars a year in salaries for Episcopalian clergy and underwriting social services offered by the church. Jack even opened his father's study and art collection to the public as a museum. That was standard social stewardship for the Carnegies, Mellons, and Fricks who dominated the U.S. economy.

The New Deal dynamited the whole worldview. Not only had FDR shackled families like the Morgans with new taxes, regulations, auditors, and overlords, his system actually worked. It was not the great genius of financial patricians that made the economy grow at unheard-of rates; it was, as Keynes had argued, the purchasing power of the masses.

It sent Morgan into paroxysms of fury. Even the mention of *Teddy* Roosevelt prompted him to scream "God damn all Roosevelts!"[42] As his sense of self-worth and place in society collapsed, he retreated to the safety of his banking fief, discarding his former sense of noblesse oblige. "I just want you to know," he shouted to Dawes Plan architect Owen Young, "that I don't care a damn what happens to you or anybody else. I don't care what happens to the country. . . . All I care about is this business! If I could help it by going out of this country and establishing myself somewhere else I'd do it—I'd do anything."[43]

"Regardless of party and regardless of region, today, with few exceptions," wrote *Time*, "members of the so-called Upper Class frankly hate Franklin Roosevelt."[44] The president returned the favor. Subjected to relentless attacks from "the Wall Street bankers" throughout his first term, he denounced them as "economic royalists" in a fiery speech to the Democratic National Convention in 1936. "They had begun to consider the Government of the United States as a mere appendage to their own affairs," he roared from the podium. "We know now that Government by organized money is just as dangerous as Government by organized mob. Never before in all our history have these forces been so united against one candidate as they stand today. They are unanimous in their hate for me—and I welcome their hatred!"[45]

There was at least as much political calculation in FDR's posture as genuine outrage. His inner circle still included a few baffled but pragmatic bankers, typically from outsider firms or those allied with new industries. Sidney Weinberg, head of the then-minor investment bank Goldman Sachs, was an FDR confidant from the 1932 campaign until the president's death.[46] And FDR studiously courted advice from and sought avenues for agreement with Morgan partner Owen D. Young. A conservative Democrat, Young tried his best to cooperate, though in moments of weakness he wondered if a "totalitarian state" might not be better equipped than Roosevelt's version of democracy to administer "economically desirable" "self-discipline"—particularly corporate tax cuts.[47]

But Roosevelt's counterpunches against the elite had a powerful effect on public opinion. The financiers who denounced him were not going to vote Democrat, but attacks raining down onto Roosevelt from such prestigious men could erode support among voters who were genuinely on the fence. Roosevelt called into question the legitimacy of his opponents and rallied his own supporters against them. Anti-FDR fervor was no longer a reasoned critique from learned men but merely the kind of thing you could expect from people who didn't like democracy. "When Roosevelt countered, a whole generation joined on his side," Galbraith observed. "If the privileged were against Roosevelt, we obviously must be against privilege. If Roosevelt found the moral posture of big business unconvincing or fraudulent, it must be so."[48]

Whatever confidence, respect, and esteem the masses had given to the oligarchs of the Gilded Age, they rescinded it in 1936. Almost anyone could have defeated Hoover soundly in the depths of the 1932 Depression, and Roosevelt did. But his margin of victory in 1936 stunned even seasoned political operatives. He lost just two states in the Electoral College and secured 60.8 percent of the popular vote. No candidate has matched FDR's electoral vote margin in the years since, and only Lyndon B. Johnson has improved on his share of the popular vote. Not since 1820 had any president won so overwhelming a victory. Though Jim Crow kept black voters in the South from casting ballots, Roosevelt had even managed to wrest the black vote in the North away from the Party of Lincoln.

And then, with the political wind at his back and the economy charging ahead, Roosevelt nearly blew his entire presidency. He had always been anxious about his deficits. His Treasury secretary, Henry Morgenthau, Jr., was simply terrified of them. Convinced that the administration had been pressing its luck for much too long, Morgenthau urged Roosevelt to pursue a balanced budget to improve the confidence of businessmen in his leadership. The president accepted the advice and curbed WPA and PWA public works spending as unemployment relief payments were trimmed.

A new element of the president's reform agenda, moreover, had created a new tax. With fully half of the elderly population living in poverty,[49] FDR had approved the new Social Security program to provide what he called "social insurance" payments for those who could not work due to old age or disability. Social Security would revolutionize life for the elderly, eventually combining with Medicare and a few smaller programs to drive the elderly poverty rate down to its current rate of about 10 percent. But the first benefit check would not go out the door until 1940. In the meantime, Congress and FDR had decided to raise funds for the program through payroll taxes on workers, which began taking effect in 1937. That took $2 billion out of American paychecks. By the summer of 1937, the federal government had all but eliminated the deficit.[50]

As Keynes had predicted, disaster ensued. With nearly 8 million people still looking for a job, the hit to demand resulting from reduced spending and new taxes threw the country back into depression. Corporate profits plunged by four-fifths, the stock market nose-dived, and manufacturing ground to a halt.[51] More than 2.5 million citizens were thrown out of work, erasing more than half of the job gains secured during FDR's first term.[52]

Critics pounced. The sudden collapse showed that the president was out of his depth or that the reform agenda had crippled businessmen. Republicans began referring to the "Roosevelt recession" or the "Democratic depression." Advertising executive Bruce Barton, who had written a best-selling book in the 1920s portraying Jesus as a hard-charging business tycoon, won a special congressional election in Manhattan by blaming "politics and the threat of more politics" for the sudden downturn. "There is no possible explanation of the present fear and loss except one: too many politicians monkeying too much."[53] Not all of the attacks came from myopic opportunists. Chemical magnate Lammot du Pont II, hailing from a dynasty of conservative Democrats, bemoaned the "uncertainty" the administration had created. "Are taxes to go higher, lower, or stay where they are? . . . Are we to have inflation or deflation, more government spending, or less?"[54] Even some trusted FDR confidants agreed. "Practically no business group in the country has escaped investigation or other attack in the last five years," observed one adviser, Adolf Berle. "Irrespective of their deserts, the result has been shattered morale."[55] But everyone in his inner circle agreed on one point: If FDR and his Democratic Party could not turn the economy around, the ambitious reforms of the past five years would be short-lived. "We are headed right into another depression," warned Morgenthau.[56]

In 1934, the president had told Keynes that the bankers who invested in government debt were pushing up interest rates with a campaign of "passive resistance" by refusing to purchase Treasury bonds. He now believed that the "economic royalists" he had maligned in 1936 were deliberately sabotaging the economy to undermine his presidency. "I know who's responsible," he told a cabinet meeting. "Business, particularly the banking industry, has ganged up on me."[57] He told Morgenthau that a "wise old bird" had informed him that there was a corporate conspiracy afoot, but—tellingly—declined to give up his source.[58]

There really had been anti-Roosevelt conspiracies that involved figures from Wall Street. In 1934, a bond broker named Gerald McGuire approached retired Marine general Smedley Butler about leading a coup d'état against FDR, backed by $6 million to install a Fascist regime modeled on that of Mussolini. The scheme had collapsed when Butler reported it to a congressional committee.[59]

But conspiracies weren't responsible for the recession. Stingy fiscal policy had rendered it inevitable. Recuperating from his Tilton farm-house, Keynes wrote to the president urging him to block out the noise and consider what had worked during his first term. The over-haul of the banking system and low interest rates from the Fed had given enterprise a fighting chance, but public works and relief pay-ments to the unemployed had done the heavy lifting during the recov-ery. There could be no return to "prosperity," he argued, "without a large-scale recourse" to public investments, particularly in "durable goods such as housing, public utilities and transport." If the political situation would allow it, FDR should nationalize the railroads and utilities to guarantee equipment upgrades, line expansions, and a bus-ier train schedule. But if not, new housing offered tremendous benefits on its own: it would create construction jobs all over the country and increase demand for raw materials, while cutting costs for low-income households. Keynes, with characteristic modesty, admonished the president for having done "next to nothing" on this "obvious" eco-nomic front since their last meeting. And even as he urged national-ization of the railroads, Keynes faulted FDR for taking too hard a rhetorical line with business interests, courting unnecessary conflict. They were not "wolves and tigers" but "domestic animals" who "have been badly brought up and not trained as you would wish."[60]

Throughout his life, Keynes projected his own intellectual flexibility (he had transformed from a free-trading gold standard advocate into a public works–supporting protectionist) onto people he did not know or understand. This was a dangerously naive habit, especially in the United States, where political support for the New Deal was always more complex and fragile than FDR's electoral margins implied. Pub-lic polling showed that most Americans approved of Roosevelt and did not blame him for the recession. But the public also wanted a bal-anced budget, and voters were starting to replace Democrats in Con-gress with Republicans.[61] The personal hardship of the Depression and the sheer ambition of the New Deal had, moreover, fueled a re-alignment in partisan politics. The Republican Party, which had once welcomed antislavery radicals, prairie populists, and elite liberal social reformers, had effectively purged all but die-hard Roosevelt haters from its ranks. Republican National Committee chairman Henry Fletcher now publicly likened FDR to "Mussolini and Hitler." Rich Democrats and Republicans formed the American Liberty League, a steadfastly "nonpartisan" organization devoted to ousting Roosevelt and his allies from power. Wall Street, according to *The New York Times*, regarded the new group as "little short of an answer to a prayer."[62] This was not a moment when shrewd businessmen might suddenly support the president's recovery plan out of respect for a change in tone from FDR and the prospect of a higher national income.

But Keynes also misunderstood the sea change Roosevelt was overseeing in expertise and legitimacy—a process that, whether or not FDR consciously intended it, furthered the Keynesian agenda by empowering the economist's disciples. By challenging the good faith and credibility of men like Morgan to pass judgment on public policy, FDR created room for the rise of the academic economist—not only within his own administration but as the dominant intellectual figure in American politics, the expert adjudicator of government effectiveness. As Keynesian thinking took over the economics profession, the ascent of the economist would establish variants of Keynesian thinking as a new policy orthodoxy.

Keynes ended his letter with a message of encouragement: "Forgive the candour of these remarks. They come from an enthusiastic well-wisher of you and your policies. I accept the view that durable investment must come increasingly under state direction. I sympathise with Mr Wallace's agricultural policies. I believe that the SEC is doing splendid work. I regard the growth of collective bargaining as essential. I approve minimum wage and hours regulation. . . . But I am terrified lest progressive causes in all the democratic countries should suffer injury, because you have taken too lightly the risk to their prestige which would result from a failure measured in terms of immediate prosperity."[63] The fate of democracy around the world rested on Roosevelt's ability to combat unemployment in the United States.

Roosevelt had Morgenthau dispatch a noncommittal response declaring the housing ideas "interesting." But he seemed to take Keynes' words about the fate of democratic government to heart. "The course of democracy and world peace is of deep concern to me. Domestic prosperity, you will agree, is one of the most effective contributions the United States can make to their maintenance."[64] A few weeks later, in a fireside chat addressed to the nation, his rhetoric was even stronger: "Democracy has disappeared in several other great nations not because the people of those nations disliked democracy, but because they had grown tired of unemployment and insecurity, of seeing their children hungry while they sat helpless in the face of government confusion. . . . The very soundness of our democratic institutions depends on the determination of our government to give employment to idle men. . . . Your government, seeking to protect democracy, must prove that government is stronger than the forces of business depression."[65] In the same address, he called for $3 billion in additional public works spending, including $300 million for the United States Housing Authority.

Keynes' true influence with FDR was indirect. It came through *The General Theory of Employment, Interest and Money*.

The book was not a publishing success. No American paperback edition would be issued until the 1960s. Though academic journals fulminated with discussion and debate almost immediately, the general public didn't stop to take note that Keynes had radically challenged the economics profession. Early reviews, addressed almost exclusively to experts, were mixed. The book baffled or infuriated most trained economists who grappled with it, and even some Keynes enthusiasts who had cheerfully endured both volumes of *A Treatise on Money* found the ideas strange and confusing. But the new concepts made sense to people who had spent time around Keynes and his Cambridge Circus. And *The General Theory* was a dense work. Even sympathetic Americans needed missionaries who had been indoctrinated abroad to guide them through such a difficult and unusual text.

It would depend on a few precocious graduate students. Back in

1932, Lorie Tarshis had applied for a Rhodes Scholarship. He was, the judges later told him, the leading candidate among three finalists. But he was passed over for the coveted award at the urging of his economics professor from the University of Toronto, Wynne Plumptre. A Rhodes Scholarship would have sent Lorie to Oxford, and Plumptre had arranged to send his star pupil to Cambridge, where he could study with Keynes. And so Tarshis settled into "the worst stateroom of the oldest ship that still went across the Atlantic" to make the journey. He was joined by his friend Robert Bryce, an engineering student who was foundering for direction in the Depression.[66]

Neither man took to Cambridge at first. Even Tarshis was lost in the early Keynes lectures. He had spent years studying *A Treatise on Money*—"I thought it was the greatest thing on earth," he later told an interviewer—but Keynes had obviously moved on to other ideas. He spent hours defining new terms in front of the blackboard and changed the subject of his class from the theory of money to what he called "the theory of output as a whole," developing what would become *The General Theory*. It was a depressing setting. English days were short, cold, and "gloomy," and winter set in early. Tarshis considered switching to anthropology or simply moving away. He wrote to Plumptre, asking to have his scholarship rearranged so that he and Bryce could study in Paris. "We felt that Paris and French girls had something to offer that we couldn't match in Cambridge," he said decades later. "I think we were right, but we neither one of us were allowed to do it."[67]

Plumptre resorted to desperate measures. He contacted Keynes, who had taught Plumptre himself just a few years prior, and secured invitations for Bryce and Tarshis to the secretive Political Economy Club that Keynes hosted on Monday nights. It was a ritualistic theater for intellectual debate, modeled on the old meetings of the Apostles. Every attendee was required to wear his formal Cambridge gown to get in the door (Joan Robinson was the only woman permitted), and young acolytes approached each meeting with a mixture of anxiety and exhilaration. "It was a memorable feeling," Tarshis said. "We'd walk up to King's and the church bells would be tolling evensong . . . it was often raining and windy and godawful." Once in the door, Kahn would hand each young acolyte a slip of paper. "You didn't look at it immediately because you wanted to be sitting when you looked." A blank slip was a relief—anybody holding one had only to listen to the proceedings in silence. But anyone holding a paper with a number on it would be required to respond to the presentation and debate its ideas, a high-stakes performance often judged from the sidelines by Kahn, Robinson, Sraffa, and Keynes himself.

Bryce and Tarshis adapted to this cultish arena. Before long, both had graduated from acolytes to evangelists. In the early 1930s, Robinson was already the most energetic missionary for Keynesian ideas, recruiting converts while Keynes himself was locked away in his study workshopping drafts of *The General Theory*. She brought Bryce, Tarshis, and other enthusiastic young Keynesians to meetings with students from the London School of Economics, then a temple of laissez-faire orthodoxy dominated by Hayek. These were ostensibly debate sessions between students of Hayek and students of Keynes, but functionally, they served to spread the Keynesian gospel to a new institution. Sharp-tongued, Robinson enjoyed intellectual combat as much as she enjoyed coaching her new recruits. Her politics were unapologetically radical—"she was far to the left of many of the Marxists," one friend observed[68]—and she had some of her greatest successes with LSE students who couldn't stomach the conservative implications of the LSE framework. The budding socialist Abba Lerner became interested in Keynes after talking with Robinson and fully converted during lunch debates with Tarshis. He soon left the LSE for a six-month stint at Cambridge and in time would help develop ideas for market socialism and Keynesian government budgeting that would prove influential in both the United States and Europe.

The new sect also won over Lerner's LSE comrade Paul Sweezy. On paper, Sweezy was an unlikely Robinson ally. He had been born into a wealthy New York family, the son of a banker in the Morgan orbit who had amassed a large enough fortune to remain comfortably rich even after losing most of it in the stock market crash. Paul and his older brother Alan had both attended Exeter Academy, one of the most exclusive American prep schools, before decamping to Harvard.

Paul began his economics education as a hard-liner for the orthodoxy, attracted to the LSE by the opportunity to study with Hayek. But the British intellectual scene was far more adventurous than anything he had encountered during his cloistered New England adolescence, and eventually a copy of Leon Trotsky's *History of the Russian Revolution* broke his faith in the doctrine his father had passed down to him. But Marxist economics at the time, Paul observed, "wasn't terribly useful" for describing the problems that were ravaging the United States and Europe.[69] Capitalism was irrational, exploitative, and headed for collapse—all of that he could accept. But he couldn't see what any of it had to do with a sudden and persistent global decline in commodity prices. In the Keynesian ideas Robinson presented to him, Sweezy found a set of precepts with radical political potential that could also make sense of the specific forces at work in the Depression. Armed with Keynesian insights, he was destined to become one of the most important Marxist economists of the twentieth century.

Not all of the early Keynesians were headed for careers as professional socialists. Bryce would eventually spend decades as one of the most powerful economists in the Canadian government. Walter Salant, whom Bryce and Tarshis befriended at Cambridge, later went on to become the top economist at the ultra-establishment Brookings Institution think tank in Washington. But before any of these young men made names for themselves in public affairs, they would make a name for Keynes in the United States.

Sweezy, Bryce, and Salant soon traded one Cambridge for another, heading to Harvard to complete their doctorates, while Tarshis followed in the fall of 1936, taking a job as an instructor at nearby Tufts University. This was all hostile ideological territory. Harvard's economics department had been founded expressly to enforce laissez-faire purity. In the 1870s, Harvard philosopher Francis Bowen had written a textbook declaring that where economic matters were concerned, "God regulated them by his general laws, which always, in the long run, work to good," obviating any need for government interference with the divine order.[70] But even Bowen proved too radical for a group of leading Boston merchants, who pressured university administrators to move him into a different job teaching Christian ethics and paid to establish a new department "filled only by men known for their sound money views."[71] It was the first economics department at an American university, soon to be emulated at Yale, Johns Hopkins, and Columbia.

In the years that followed, the defense of right-wing monetary doctrines became a Harvard tradition, setting a standard for the entire American academic economics industry. In 1932, the department made its splashiest hire to date, luring Joseph Schumpeter, a conservative Austrian aristocrat who wore riding gloves during his lectures, to the United States. Within two years, Schumpeter and six of his colleagues had published *The Economics of the Recovery Program*, purporting to provide a "scientific" debunking of the New Deal.[72] Those were not simply the grumblings of stubborn old men. Coauthors Edward Chamberlin, Edward Mason, and Seymour Edwin Harris were in their thirties, while Wassily Leontief was still in his twenties. Even Schumpeter was just fifty-one. Department chair Harold Hitchings Burbank was grooming the next generation of conservative thought leaders.

But Bryce, Sweezy, and Tarshis had other plans. "Keynes is Allah," Schumpeter bemoaned, "and Bryce is his prophet."[73] Bryce and Sweezy began hosting an informal evening seminar on Keynes before *The General Theory* had even been published, using a paper from Bryce to lay out the basic ideas for other students. When the British edition of the book was released, Bryce arranged to have dozens of copies shipped to Harvard, which the two economists used as a textbook until an American edition was at last issued. As Keynes had hoped, something profound was happening among the younger generation of economic minds. Though Schumpeter remained impervious to the siren's call, Harvard man after Harvard man succumbed. Seymour Harris became a devoted Keynesian. So did John Kenneth Galbraith, who had returned to Harvard from his first stint in the Roosevelt administration. "The old economics was still taught by day," he later recalled. "But in the evening, and almost every evening from 1936 on, almost everyone discussed Keynes."[74] Galbraith was so enthusiastic that he shipped off to Cambridge, England, to study directly with the master himself, only to find Keynes on leave after his heart attack. He studied instead under Joan Robinson, forging an intellectual partnership that would span four decades. As Galbraith came into his own as a major American intellectual in the 1950s and '60s, he would serve as a powerful, popular international conduit for Robinson's ideas. She was, he wrote in the final year of her life, "my friend, critic and conscience."[75]

After some initial hostility to Keynes' book, Harvard professor Alvin Hansen made Keynesian economics the core tenet of his official seminar in the new Harvard Graduate School of Public Administration, which began to draw guests from Washington on a regular basis. Within a few years, Harvard had unleashed yet another generation of Keynesian academics who would eventually prove to be wildly influential in their own right, including future Nobel laureates James Tobin and Paul Samuelson.

Nearly all of them found their way into government in the late 1930s and early 1940s. One convert, Richard Gilbert, became an aide to WPA Director Harry Hopkins. Salant landed a job at the Treasury, and then the SEC. His brother William became an aide to Lauchlin Currie, a top official at the Federal Reserve who became FDR's personal economic adviser in 1939. Currie, himself a former Harvard man who had flirted with some early Keynesian monetary ideas before joining the government, became a convert once *The General Theory* was published and took great care to recruit top Harvard Keynesians to federal posts, eventually calling up Galbraith for a job at the National Defense Advisory Commission. From positions like these, early Keynesians could see how blindsided the Roosevelt administration had been by the sudden recession in 1937. "The New Deal government was in a state of total shock," observed Sweezy, who would work for the Roosevelt administration during World War II. "They didn't know what to make of this."[76]

In 1938, Sweezy and his wife, Maxine, joined Tarshis, Richard Gilbert, William Salant, and a handful of other Cambridge Keynesians to write *An Economic Program for American Democracy*. Published in the fall of 1938, the slim book distilled *The General Theory* into a brief, publicly digestible explanation of what had gone wrong in the 1930s and what to do about it. Their work was Keynesian in both its policy recommendations and its geopolitical outlook. Sweezy and company called to begin making Social Security payments immediately; to provide federal medical care; to build schools, parks, playgrounds, and hospitals; to nationalize the railroads and raise the minimum wage. Everything should be paid for with borrowing, and the deficit should be of no concern; with the economy growing and people back to work, the debt would take care of itself in time, they argued, and only deficit finance could make the necessary growth a reality. But it was essential that New Dealers act quickly. "The conception of government as the organized expression of the collective strength and aspirations of the great mass of the people has come to stay. The New Deal has not failed. Rather its great weakness has been a wavering adherence to its own principles."[77] The great political threat facing the country was not government spending but Wall Street cynicism. "The danger exists that businessmen, obsessed with a devil theory of government, will attempt to use their economic power to suppress democracy and place in its stead a dictatorship supposedly dedicated to their desires."[78]

Unlike *The General Theory*, *An Economic Program for American Democracy* sold remarkably well, particularly in Washington, where Currie made sure to present it to FDR himself. The president was delighted, telling some of his closest advisers that the book was a perfect summary of the philosophy behind the New Deal.[79] And by the spring of 1939, it was. The economic collapse in 1938 and rebound in 1939 had even persuaded Morgenthau of the necessity for Keynesian measures. As he told the House Ways and Means Committee: "In a depression it is inevitable that there will be deficits . . . the sequel to deficits in emergencies should be surpluses during years of prosperity."[80]

The economics profession, in short, was developing much as Keynes had hoped it would in the final pages of *The General Theory*, while the status and influence of economists within the government was rapidly expanding. All of that had been made possible by the nature of the New Deal government and the antipathy between Roosevelt and Wall Street.

But as was so often the case with the British genius and his American audience, political currents were already flowing which Keynes could neither predict nor navigate. They would profoundly shape not only the public understanding of his ideas but their future development as a technical field in academia.

In the late 1930s, the conservative Harvard administration had become decidedly uncomfortable with the sudden left turn its economics department had taken. Alan Sweezy and a left-wing labor economist, J. Raymond Walsh, were denied tenure and fired, ostensibly due to their poor "teaching capacity" and supposedly inferior "scholarly ability."[81] Both men were highly regarded by colleagues and students alike, and their termination created a national scandal over academic freedom, invoking outrage from the American Federation of Labor and the American Civil Liberties Union. After a prolonged internal investigation and public relations struggle, the university prevailed in dismissing the two men, and John Kenneth Galbraith's mentor at Harvard, the agricultural economist John Black, privately urged his disciple to look for work elsewhere. There was no chance that a man with Galbraith's political commitments could now find a place among the tenured faculty at Harvard.

Galbraith would land on his feet. A job offer soon arrived from Princeton, and Currie brought him back to Washington not long afterward. But the Red Scare that would dominate Washington during the early decades of the Cold War had in fact already begun, years before the election of Senator Joseph McCarthy or even the bombing of Pearl Harbor. Indeed, outside Harvard Yard and Washington, the intellectual tide was turning against the New Dealers.

By 1938, Walter Lippmann was perhaps the most influential American man of letters. His column for the *New York Herald Tribune* was syndicated nationwide, and though his employer was a bastion of Wall Street Republicanism, the fluidity of his ideological commitments had earned him a reputation for objectivity and open-mindedness. As a young writer, he had transitioned smoothly from a socialist to a Wilsonian to a staunch critic of the Treaty of Versailles. But the ease with which he assimilated new ideas had become chaotic during the Great Depression as he struggled to come to terms with social breakdown and new forms of authoritarian government rising around the globe. He had initially celebrated FDR's policy agenda, going so far as to publicly advocate temporary dictatorial powers for the president, and touted *The General Theory* as the theoretical breakthrough key to conquering the Depression. But he had since grown uncomfortable with the power FDR's government wielded, a concern inflamed by discussions with Hayek and Mises. He had half-heartedly voted for Republican Alf Landon in 1936 but by 1938 was ready to present a systematized attack on the Roosevelt administration with his book *The Good Society.* In it, he denounced the New Deal as a form of "gradual collectivism" that had accomplished nothing but "the conferring of privileges upon selected interests." Like Stalinism and fascism, Lippmann claimed, the New Deal was a species of "absolutism" that existed "in rebellion against the moral heritage of western society" and threatened a "relapse into barbarism." "There are . . . important differences between lions and tigers, even between African and Indian lions. But from the point of view of, let us say, a goat or a lamb, the common characteristics of all the great carnivores are more significant than their differences."[82] So, too, with the New Deal, fascism, and communism.

In his introduction, Lippmann acknowledged the influence of Hayek and Mises, economists who remained, for the moment, all but unknown outside academic circles. But even as Lippmann railed against Roosevelt's agenda, he proposed a set of policy prescriptions that seemed perfectly compatible with Keynesian and New Deal sensibilities: public works, a social safety net, progressive taxation to limit excessive wealth, and a sustained attack on corporate monopoly power. He even praised Keynes by name next to Hayek and Mises. However bad the New Deal might be, a return to the "corporate collectivism" of "Old Guard Republicanism" would not do. The result, as Lippmann's biographer Ronald Steel observed, is a "perplexing" work of "confusion" that merely "tacked on" a popular policy agenda to a totally in-compatible intellectual argument.[83]

Or so it seemed looking backward from the 1980s. In the 1930s, Lippmann saw himself participating in an ideological project to rede-fine liberalism for an age of political and economic turmoil—the same project that Keynes had attempted a dozen years earlier in *The End of Laissez-Faire*. And it made sense to group Hayek, Mises, and Keynes together. They all still called themselves liberals and considered them-selves inheritors of the same Enlightenment intellectual tradition. They were all anti-Nazi and anti-Soviet and had come of age believing that free trade and the gold standard were essential to the preservation of individual liberty. But this shared tradition had been fracturing for years, and with Roosevelt the breach became irreparable.

Lippmann's own enthusiasm for individual liberty was inconstant. When Lytton Strachey's brother John was deported from the United States for giving lectures arguing that capitalism was a form of fas-cism, Lippmann wrote that Communists were not entitled to free speech protections. After Pearl Harbor, he visited California, declared the entire West Coast to be in "imminent danger of a combined attack from within and without," and supported the federal removal of any-one who might inflict "organized sabotage" against the country. It was a full-throated support for the mass internment of Japanese Ameri-cans in what FDR would call "concentration camps"—one of the most notorious civil rights violations in U.S. history.[84] Lippmann also criti-cized Roosevelt for being, he claimed, too hard on the Jim Crow South.

Lippmann did not consider himself a man of the political Right, but the practical effect of his book in 1938 was to breathe new intel-lectual life into complaints about Roosevelt that Wall Street had been repeating for years. It wasn't true, as Lippmann claimed, that "collec-tivist" economics had brought the Nazis to power. Hitler had ascended with deflation and mass unemployment and had implemented cen-trally planned deficit spending and loose monetary policy only *after* taking power. But Lippmann was popularizing the idea that Nazi economics and Nazi politics were inseparable. For that, he became a cause célèbre for Hayek and Mises, who hosted a grand meeting of antigovernment conservatives and FDR skeptics in Paris. Dubbed the "Colloque Walter Lippmann," the event became the blueprint for Hayek's Mont Pelerin Society, one of the most important institutions in the development of twentieth-century right-wing politics. Though they themselves weren't quite sure what they were founding, the philosophical tradition known as neoliberalism had been born.

Roosevelt was perfectly aware of the momentum building on the right. In June 1938, he signed into law the Fair Labor Standards Act, mandating a forty-hour workweek and a minimum wage as benchmarks in U.S. employment law. It was another landmark for the New Deal, but it would be one of the last. For the first time, Roosevelt had been forced to pass a major bill without the support of conservative southern Democrats. Partisan loyalties had persuaded this electoral faction to work with the president on prior reforms, but their participation had always come at a price. FDR's agenda often accepted ugly compromises with his Southern allies that excluded African Americans, Jews, southern and eastern European immigrants, and women from enjoying the fruits of important reforms. But after the recession of 1937 and 1938, conservative Democrats were no longer interested in compromise. They abandoned urban New Dealers in the North for a functional alliance with Wall Street Republicans, preferring policies that rewarded the wealthy and the white to what the northern Democrats were cooking up. Over the ensuing decades, that cooperation would become more explicit, steadily converting the South into an electoral bulwark for the GOP.

The shift began with the elections of 1938, which brought a streak of four consecutive Democratic Party electoral triumphs to an end. FDR's party lost seven Senate seats in November 1938, including populist and progressive redoubts in Ohio, Wisconsin, Nebraska, and South Dakota, as business-class Republicans defeated liberal Democrats in New Jersey, New Hampshire, and Connecticut. In the House of Representatives, Democrats shed seventy-two seats. Though Democrats continued to hold comfortable majorities in both chambers, the ideological split within the party meant that the Roosevelt presidency had slipped into a stalemate on domestic policy. Liberal northern Democrats lost to Republicans, while conservative southern Democrats remained in power. Ambitious reforms gave way to battles over funding, though here FDR was generally able to carry the day, running a $2.9 billion deficit in 1939, proof that Keynes had at last triumphed in the ideological war within the administration. The unemployment rate, which had jumped from 9.2 percent to 12.5 percent during the Roosevelt recession, began to abate, falling to 11.3 percent in 1939 on its way back to 9.5 percent in 1940 and 6.0 percent in 1941.[85]

The New Deal did not save capitalism in the sense that it restored some idyllic state of affairs that had prevailed before the stock market crash of 1929; it created an entirely new and untested form of government. *The General Theory* provided these reformers with intellectual legitimacy—the scientific assurance that a more egalitarian, democratic reorganization of society was not only economically possible but necessary for the attainment of widely shared prosperity. The success of the New Deal, moreover, reinforced Keynes' prestige around the world, proving to the world that Keynesian ideas could actually work—without resorting to the totalitarian methods spreading through Europe.

ELEVEN

———— ◇ ————

WAR AND COUNTERREVOLUTION

N 1938, AMERICAN KEYNESIANS had been overwhelmingly confident about the prospects for economic recovery. Despite its title, *An Economic Program for American Democracy,* the influential book by Paul Sweezy, Lorie Tarshis, and other Harvard economic heretics, had been chiefly concerned not with growth, productivity, or unemployment but with political power. The Roosevelt administration could spend its way to recovery, the writers had argued, or it would be replaced by a dictatorship imposed by intemperate men of "business." This American strongman, they emphasized, would spend his way to recovery. People who needed work would get jobs. But they would find themselves engaged not in the building of houses, dams, and hospitals but in the mass production of "weapons of death and destruction which must sooner or later be used to plunge the country into a holocaust of slaughter and bloodshed."[1] Absent Keynes' conception of the good life, the basic governing tools of Keynesian economics—deficit spending and activist government—could be instruments of brutality.

Keynes, of course, had recognized this for years. He had lived through the economic boom of World War I and knew that borrowing money and spending it was a surefire way to get many different kinds of factories running. "War," he had written to Roosevelt in 1934, "has always caused intense industrial activity," noting that even conservative bankers regarded war as a "legitimate excuse for creating employment by government expenditure."[2]

Keynesian economics were formulated as a defense against fascism, so it is appropriate that Keynes and every author of *An Economic Program for American Democracy* would join the war effort against Nazi Germany and Fascist Italy. But Keynesianism was also developed to prevent war, and it remains one of the great tragic ironies of intellectual history that the very catastrophe Keynes had attempted to avert for nearly two decades would be the event that finally demonstrated the viability of his economic ideas on the world stage. Both *The General Theory of Employment, Interest and Money* and *The Economic Consequences of the Peace* achieved their political apotheosis in the same calamity.

The Second World War transformed Keynesian economics as a profession, winning the doctrine an unexpected set of institutional allies in what Dwight D. Eisenhower would eventually label the "military-industrial complex." Keynesian ideas, which had been developed explicitly to combat "militarism," became essential to the maintenance of a permanently militarized world. This new doctrine of what John Kenneth Galbraith would eventually label Reactionary Keynesianism would dominate the governing philosophies of Harry Truman, Eisenhower, Lyndon B. Johnson, Richard Nixon, and Ronald Reagan and inform successive campaigns of mass death that would outlast even the Cold War.

The Keynesians themselves, of course, did not believe they were signing up for this project when they went to work for the U.S. and British governments in the early 1940s. They understood the war as a defensive effort against an unprecedented evil and accepted a new role for the American military largely out of necessity. But they were also captivated by a new human rights vision in foreign policy that Roosevelt formulated to make his case for the war. In this new doctrine, the idealized humanitarian aims of liberal imperialism that Keynes had admired as a young man were refitted for an era of U.S. hegemony.

Roosevelt began talking about the United States as an "arsenal of democracy" in a fireside chat on December 29, 1940, and presented the
full, breathtakingly ambitious doctrine to Congress a week later in his
1941 State of the Union address. Though it has always been overshadowed by his remarks after Pearl Harbor—which was still some eleven
months away—what became known as the "Four Freedoms" speech
would be his most important public address of the war.

By 1941, Woodrow Wilson's international project appeared to have
been a comprehensive debacle. More than 116,000 U.S. soldiers had
died in the First World War, double the number of fatal American
military casualties that would eventually be registered in Vietnam, at
a time when the population was half the size it would be in the 1970s.
The scar that World War I left on the American imagination was if
anything deeper than those left upon future generations by the conflicts in Vietnam and Iraq. Almost as bad as the carnage itself was the
perception that it had been a waste.[3] Wilson and other proponents of
U.S. intervention had believed, in the words of Walter Lippmann's
biographer, that "an imperialist war could be transformed into a democratic crusade."[4] It had not. And the League of Nations had seemed
useless in the face of the various calamities that followed. The French
invasion of the Ruhr, Italy's attack on Ethiopia, and even Hitler's military advance only proved to millions of Americans that Europe was
an incorrigible backwater where American virtue could accomplish
nothing. That the United States had technically been on the winning
side in The Great War—indeed, that its involvement had almost certainly been the factor distinguishing victor from vanquished—had
only served to inflame the sense of futility. Even military success had
resulted in moral failure.

Wilson had made his case for war by pledging to end imperialism
and usher in a new era of international democracy. He had relied on
basic assumptions about ethnic nationalism. Imperialism, he had believed, imposed unnatural foreign rulers on naturally developing ethnic nation-states. Democracy, by contrast, was the process by which

free "peoples"—ethnic nationalities—governed themselves. His Fourteen Points were not a human rights doctrine. A free people was to be
left to its own devices to sort out what policies and prerogatives it
deemed appropriate for its own governance—it was silent on what
rights and responsibilities a free people must afford to individuals. The
role of the United States, and for international diplomacy more
broadly, was to protect the rights of these communities to find their
own course, free of foreign coercion or belligerence.

Roosevelt's task was to revive the idea of vigorous U.S. international
leadership in a manner that clearly distinguished American values and
ambitions from those of Germany, Italy, and Japan. Why was it
acceptable—even imperative—for the United States to assert its will
violently in far corners of the world, when it was outrageous for other
nations to do the same? The answer, to Roosevelt, was an international
law founded on free people rather than free peoples. What distinguished America from the dictatorships was not its unique ethnic
makeup or a distinctive combination of nutrients in its soil. It was the
guarantee of basic freedoms to every individual, regardless of nationality or ethnicity. Like Wilson, FDR looked forward to "the cooperation
of free countries, working together in a friendly, civilized society." Unlike Wilson, he declared governments that failed to respect what became known as "the Four Freedoms" *within their own borders* to be
illegitimate bastions of "tyranny." And he reserved for the United
States the right to liberate all people who had been forced—through
violence or threat of violence—to live under such "domination." "Freedom," he said, "means the supremacy of human rights everywhere."
Though he nodded to the problems created by the Treaty of Versailles
and postwar diplomacy, FDR was presenting a metric by which those
failures—and the far worse "new order of tyranny" that was now
sweeping the world—could be gauged. The trouble with Versailles, he
suggested, was not that it had been an inevitable debacle forged by wily
Europeans but rather that it had failed to secure both economic and
military security for the people of Europe. Consciously or not, FDR
was taking the ideas of *The Economic Consequences of the Peace* and expanding them into a foreign policy doctrine of breathtaking ambition:

In the future days, which we seek to make secure, we look forward to a world founded upon four essential human freedoms. The first is freedom of speech and expression—everywhere in the world. The second is freedom of every person to worship God in his own way—everywhere in the world. The third is freedom from want—which, translated into world terms, means economic understandings which will secure to every nation a healthy peacetime life for its inhabitants—everywhere in the world. The fourth is freedom from fear—which, translated into world terms, means a world-wide reduction of armaments to such a point and in such a thorough fashion that no nation will be in a position to commit an act of physical aggression against any neighbor—anywhere in the world.

That is no vision of a distant millennium. It is a definite basis for a kind of world attainable in our own time and generation. That kind of world is the very antithesis of the so-called new order of tyranny which the dictators seek to create with the crash of a bomb.[5]

Roosevelt knew this was a fundamental break with prior U.S. policy. These were not merely claims to national security or national interest. The president of the United States was declaring a right to pass moral judgment on the affairs of other sovereigns. When Roosevelt was drafting the speech, his aide Harry Hopkins had immediately objected to the persistent refrain of "everywhere in the world."

"That covers an awful lot of territory, Mr. President," Hopkins said. "I don't know how interested Americans are going to be in the people of Java." Roosevelt was undeterred. "I'm afraid they'll have to be some day, Harry," he said. "The world is getting so small that even the people in Java are getting to be our neighbors now."[6]

The expansiveness of his vision is underscored by the fact that at least two of Roosevelt's freedoms—freedom from want and freedom from fear—were not respected in the United States itself, while the boundaries of freedom of speech were nearly always being contested and redefined. The culture and institutions of the Jim Crow South were openly based on the domination of African Americans by whites, while northern cities were segregated into neighborhoods that condemned blacks, immigrants, and their descendants to substandard schools and public services and often violent squalor. Unemployment and poverty remained rampant throughout the country. Southerners vehemently rejected the parallels Hitler drew between Nazi racism and Jim Crow, but the Four Freedoms offered no shelter for the codified racism of the American South. FDR denounced Nazism in terms that applied to America's own demons:

> Certainly this is no time for any of us to stop thinking about the social and economic problems which are the root cause of the social revolution which is today a supreme factor in the world. For there is nothing mysterious about the foundations of a healthy and strong democracy. The basic things expected by our people of their political and economic systems are simple. They are: Equality of opportunity for youth and for others. Jobs for those who can work. Security for those who need it. The ending of special privilege for the few. The preservation of civil liberties for all.[7]

The Four Freedoms, then, were aspirational, political, and profoundly radical—a rallying cry for righteous war that lumped in opponents of FDR's domestic reforms as moral cousins of the enemy abroad. Liberation from poverty was a *human right*—not a mathematical problem that might someday be solved if resources and growth rates permitted. The idea had seemed impossible under the scarcity economics of the nineteenth century. But under the Keynesian formulations of "Economic Possibilities for Our Grandchildren" and *The General Theory* that Roosevelt was now implementing, it was a scientifically plausible way of life.

Keynes had never framed his ideas with anything like the language Roosevelt deployed in his Four Freedoms address. The two men shared a reformist zeal, but Keynes lacked FDR's Christian sense of principle. His major works had emphasized possibilities and consequences, not political rights. Rights were ironclad, inviolable commitments, and the world was not an ironclad place. Keynes was about finding the balance between "tolerable" and "not intolerable" and making the best of what the world presented. His idea of the good life involved securing as many good states of mind as possible, and his ideal society enabled as many people as possible to share in the good life. But it was a problem that depended on material reality, not fundamental rights. Governments that ignored his ideas were foolish, ungenerous, and petty. That was surely bad enough—but he did not consider them to be violating anybody's basic rights.

But the practical meaning and viability of Keynesian ideas had always been dependent on the ability of New Dealers to reformulate and accommodate them to American political reality. By accelerating the transfer of international power from Great Britain to the United States, the war would also deepen the Americanization of Keynesian thinking—with both triumphant and disastrous results.

U.S. efforts to realize freedom from fear and freedom from want would be arduous, complex, and incomplete. But as a guide to international diplomacy, the Four Freedoms address was among the most influential speeches of the twentieth century. It formed the basis of the Atlantic Charter issued by Churchill and FDR a few months later, which declared an Anglo-American alliance to establish a peace "which will afford assurance that all the men in all the lands may live out their lives in freedom from fear and want." It was the moral backbone behind the establishment of the United Nations, and it informed the creation of both the European Union and NATO. If the New Deal was, as the historian Ira Katznelson has suggested, a project comparable only to the French Revolution in its enduring political significance, then the Four Freedoms address was its Declaration of the Rights of Man and Citizen. And Roosevelt intentionally fostered this idea in future press conferences, comparing the ideals of the Four Freedoms and the Atlantic Charter to the Magna Carta and—false modesty be damned—the Ten Commandments.[8]

There was a dark side to this crusader enthusiasm. Subsequent American war advocates have invariably cited the protection of human rights abroad as an overriding moral concern, often attesting to high ideals to divert attention from less benign motivations: claims on resources, imperial strategy, or simple belligerence. The pattern began in World War II. While FDR pitched the conflict to Americans as a fight for human rights "anywhere in the world," the U.S. State Department—the chief organ of American diplomacy—repeatedly refused aid to Jewish refugees. On the West Coast, more than 100,000 Japanese Americans were forced from their homes and ordered to report to internment camps, a policy that originated in Roosevelt's War Department. It was not only conservatives who found themselves able to look the other way. "As the military influence grew, numerous liberals, attracted by the style or persuaded that the soldiers were neutral or indifferent on domestic policy and fully committed on the war, joined them," John Kenneth Galbraith observed, forging a "partnership" that shifted the balance of power within the Roosevelt administration away from new agencies headed by liberal reformers to older, more conservative—and often paranoid—wings of the federal bureaucracy.[9] As military spending skyrocketed, public works became more important than ever—but only public works for war aims. The WPA and CCC dwindled away as the federal government converted the domestic economy into a munitions juggernaut. Some of the best minds among the reformers became leading lights of the war machine.[10]

But the ideals FDR espoused in the Four Freedoms address were not empty promises. They profoundly shaped the future course of American liberalism, a change that began almost immediately. Six months after he gave the Four Freedoms speech, Roosevelt signed Executive Order 8802, banning racial discrimination in the defense industries and establishing the Fair Employment Practices Committee to investigate abuses targeting black workers. The order didn't materialize on its own—Roosevelt had been pressured to sign it by the black labor leader A. Philip Randolph, president of the Brotherhood of Sleeping Car Porters, who was threatening to send more than 100,000 protesters to the National Mall if FDR didn't do something for black workers in the war economy. But Roosevelt was also boxed in by his own rhetoric in the Four Freedoms address.[11] If this was to be a war for everyone, everywhere, then surely it must also be a war for black workers in the United States.

The FEPC had a small budget and was largely ineffective in combating racism among southern employers committed to segregation. But in northern industry, the new legal protections were significant, particularly in combination with other New Deal reforms such as the Wagner Act, which had empowered labor unions. The international ideals FDR put forward in the Four Freedoms speech spurred American liberals to commit themselves to domestic reforms even when the conservative control of Congress had foreclosed the possibility of new reform legislation. "We cannot fight fascism abroad while ignoring fascism at home," *The Nation* editorialized in 1943. "We cannot inscribe on our banners: For democracy and a caste system." The war, in the words of historian Alan Brinkley, cemented the "identification of liberalism with the effort to secure civil rights for African Americans, and later, many other groups," building momentum for postwar reforms that "few progressives or New Dealers had ever seriously contemplated."[12]

In the meantime, Keynes was at last in good health again. He owed his new energy in part to Hitler's aggression. In 1939, Keynes had hired János Plesch, a Hungarian Jewish doctor who had relocated to London after fleeing Nazi persecution. Plesch had assembled an impressive list of patients, including Keynes' friends Albert Einstein and George Bernard Shaw. Keynes regarded Plesch as "something between a genius and a quack"—a reputation earned by the unorthodox treatments he prescribed for Keynes, including the application of ice packs to his chest for three hours at a time, a regimen of opium pills, and the elimination of salt from his diet.[13] But the creative physician also prescribed Keynes Prontosil, a new drug derived from red dye developed in German labs by Bayer before the war. Though it had the unfortunate effect of turning its patients' skin pink—and made Keynes miserably ill immediately after injections—Prontosil made him feel like a new man within days. It was, in fact, one of the earliest antibiotics. Though modern science has since declared the treatment useless against bacterial infections of the heart, Keynes nevertheless found his energy level nearly back to where it had been before his collapse. His persistent throat infections were cured.

After two decades of depression, however, the British economy was entering the fight of its life in ragged condition. The shipbuilding industry's output in 1937 was less than two-thirds what it had been in 1930.[14] By 1939, Keynes believed his country was running 10 percent below its capacity and would have to completely overhaul not only its industrial processes but their relationship to the government if the war was to be prosecuted effectively. In the United States, Roosevelt had made government regulation and technological improvement a normal part of the economic landscape. The same could not be said for Great Britain's Conservative government, whose tariff-protected heavy industries had improved their output over the course of the 1930s but lagged in productivity. On the eve of war, worker productivity was 125 percent higher in the United States than it was in Britain.[15] Great Britain had entered World War I as the most powerful economy on the planet; it entered World War II as a limping, wounded animal needing every kind of economic aid available, from food to textiles to weaponry to money. "If, indeed, it ever comes to war, this lack of preparation may prove disastrous," Keynes warned readers of *The New Statesman and Nation* in January 1939. "Our plans and preparations are ludicrously feeble."[16]

Though the United States had not fully recovered from the Depression, its industrial energy had been reinvigorated by the New Deal. The war now fueled an economic frenzy. As in World War I, the United States began producing armaments and other essential supplies for British defenses long before America itself committed any soldiers to the fight. Beginning in 1939, the United States began selling armaments and essential war materiel to Britain on a "cash-and-carry" basis. In doing so, Roosevelt was overturning very recent congressional actions. In 1935, 1936, and 1937, Congress had passed a series of Neutrality Acts that restricted U.S. trade with nations in-

volved in a war. The idea was to prevent the United States from becoming entangled in another bloody foreign conflict. But after Hitler's
invasion of Poland in 1939, Roosevelt was able to chip away at those
restrictions. Under the new cash-and-carry program approved by
Congress, the United States could sell armaments to Great Britain, so
long as it paid in cash and transported the material in British ships;
there would be no *Lusitania*s in 1939. But by 1940, it was clear that
Great Britain didn't have the funds to sustain the program for very
long. "Well boys, Britain's broke," announced British ambassador
Philip Kerr in November 1940. "It's your money we want."[17]

In response, FDR concocted the Lend-Lease program, in which
the United States allowed Britain to "borrow" American war materiel
if the administration believed that doing so was essential to the defense of U.S. interests. Congress didn't specify the terms of these loans,
however, and even within the Roosevelt administration there was a
great deal of disagreement over how the arrangement should work.
The promised aid was slow to materialize.

In the meantime, Germany had shifted its offensive focus to London. The Blitz, though relatively ineffective at shutting down British
production, had a powerful impact on daily life and public morale.
Leonard and Virginia Woolf lost not one but two homes to German
bombs. Virginia recorded her first experience of the bombers outside
her home in Rodmell in August 1940:

> They came very close. We lay down under the tree. The sound was
> like someone sawing in the air just above us. We lay flat on our
> faces, hands behind head. Dont close yr teeth said L. They seemed
> to be sawing at something stationary. Bombs shook the windows
> of my lodge. Will it drop I asked? If so, we shall be broken to-
> gether. I thought, I think, of nothingness—flatness, my mood
> being flat. Some fear I suppose. . . . Hum & saw & buzz all round
> us. A horse neighed on the marsh. Very sultry. Is it thunder? I said.
> No guns, said L. from Ringmer, from Charleston way. Then slowly
> the sound lessened. Mabel in kitchen said the windows shook. Air
> raid still on, distant planes.[18]

British diplomats didn't have time to waste. After trying everything else, they brought in Keynes.

Everyone in Whitehall remembered the disastrous attempts Keynes had made at U.S. diplomacy during World War I, including Keynes himself—though he preferred to blame the selfishness of Americans, rather than his own rudeness, for his failures with the Wilson administration. In truth, Keynes' indelicate personal touch had been far less important than the different ideological and strategic priorities between Wilson and Lloyd George. There would be similar differences between Roosevelt and Churchill, though Keynes would not fully appreciate them until the end of the war. And at fifty-eight, Keynes was a changed man from the fussy, impatient Treasury official of a quarter century prior. All of his friends saw that he had mellowed, and his quick-moving mind was now more prone to kind words than barbed attacks. Traveling with Lydia made him unusually cheerful and optimistic for a war diplomat.

Keynes hadn't worked for the government since the Macmillan Committee had issued its report in 1931. As he recovered his health, he had been dividing most of his time between Cambridge and Tilton. In July 1940, he relocated back to London to accept an unpaid position as an adviser to the Treasury, where he rapidly accumulated power, eventually becoming the functional equivalent of wartime chancellor of the Exchequer.[19] That meteoric rise within the British civil service was assisted by the improbable political resurrection of Winston Churchill, who had ascended to prime minister upon the resignation of Neville Chamberlain in May 1940. Churchill didn't hold a grudge against Keynes over his treatment in *The Economic Consequences of Mr. Churchill.* He instead blamed Bank of England governor Montagu Norman and the City pundits for talking him into the gold debacle of 1925.[20] A few positive reviews Keynes had written of Churchill's lengthy history books had helped assuage any residual angst.[21] This time around, Churchill would trust economic matters to Keynes.

For the first time since the Paris Peace Conference, Keynes had his hands on the levers of power within the British government. With Great Britain under bombardment, he suffered no qualms from his conscience over his role in the war machine. The idealistic young European leftists of 1914 had been pacifists. In the 1930s, they had called for Britain to confront the Fascists in Spain. Now there was simply no escaping war.

The delays on Lend-Lease aid were as political as they were practical. Treasury Secretary Henry Morgenthau initially refused to advance any assistance until the British Empire had liquidated its overseas assets to pay for what it could. If the Americans were to provide relief, he reasoned, the British should at least be expected to pay reasonable prices until they were unable to do so. But that simple principle could not easily be applied to the financial complexities of the British Empire. Some assets that the British held abroad—their shares of stock in Malaysian tin mines and rubber plantations, for instance—could not be quickly liquidated, and forcing them off onto the market in a fire sale would generate very little up-front revenue for the United States. Both countries, Keynes argued, would be better off if Britain held on to them, collecting revenue that it could turn over to the United States as payment.[22]

Morgenthau was also demanding that the British pay the United States in gold to the point at which "the gold reserve of the Bank of England was virtually nil." But eliminating British gold reserves would make it impossible for the British to pay for *anything* from abroad for the duration of the war—or even maintain its conventional commerce with the United States. That was obviously not practical for a nation at war, whatever its obligations to America. Morgenthau's stubbornness on the gold issue, Keynes told British diplomats, showed "every indication that the man is not merely tiresome but an ass."[23]

Keynes wasn't particularly interested in maximizing U.S. revenue, of course. He thought of Britain as a "great and independent nation"[24] and was reluctant to repeat the British government's financial mistakes from the Great War, which had ceded so much geopolitical power to the United States, diminishing his country's stature on the world stage and saddling it with insurmountable war debts that had undermined its postwar prosperity.

So Keynes went to Washington in May 1941 to negotiate more

practical terms of cooperation and promptly infuriated nearly every-one he met. Morgenthau was personally insulted by Keynes' sugges-tion that he and FDR were not doing enough to help Britain. "For them to send a person over here to put me in a position as though I wasn't trying to do everything I can, I say it is a damn outrage," he fumed shortly after Keynes' arrival. He was just as angry about Keynes' casual advice to the U.S. government that it spend more money do-mestically to increase its total economic output. "He goes to a meeting and criticizes the President of the United States for the way he is run-ning this country," Morgenthau raged. "I say that man should go home."[25]

In fact, Keynes was caught between feuding wings of the Roosevelt administration. Lauchlin Currie, the top White House economic ad-viser and an ardent Keynesian, had urged Keynes to present his "ideas" directly to the president in "the plainest possible terms,"[26] hoping that the British economist's words would sway FDR away from the advice of his well-meaning but financially unsophisticated Treasury secretary. The battle between Currie and Morgenthau went back years: Currie was the lead proponent of budget deficits when Morgenthau advo-cated balanced budgets. Keynes was baffled by the intricacies of Wash-ington power dynamics. "One wonders how decisions are ever reached at all," he wrote to British officials. "The different departments of the Government criticise one another in public and produce rival pro-grammes. There is perpetual internecine warfare between prominent personalities. . . . Members of the so-called Cabinet make public speeches containing urgent proposals which are not agreed as part of the Government policy." Equally bewildering were the reporters, who congregated outside the offices of Morgenthau and Roosevelt and "as-saulted" Keynes for details on his meetings as soon as he emerged from within.[27]

Despite these professional frustrations, Keynes was enjoying him-self. He adored Roosevelt. He even liked the Americans this time around. "One cannot exaggerate the strength of sympathy and good intention in almost every quarter here,"[28] he reported home—a state-ment that included Morgenthau, who though "almost intolerably tiresome to deal with," was genuinely trying his best to help Great Britain win the war. He dined with his old friend Felix Frankfurter, caught up with Walter Lippmann—whose book had not tarnished their long friendship—and made a quick jaunt up to Princeton to visit Albert Einstein. All were anxious about the war and eager for the United States to enter; all had thrown off the financial orthodoxy that had confounded U.S. administrations in the past. Keynes was surrounded by evidence of his intellectual triumph from the people he respected most.

Best of all was the president himself, whom Keynes sketched in a June 2 memo to the chancellor of the Exchequer, a dispatch that rivals the most colorful sections of *The Economic Consequences of the Peace* for its characterization and detail:

The president sat at his big flat-topped study desk without ever moving or getting up. We sat at each side of it, small napkins for our plates, with nowhere for our knees (in both our cases awkward objects!). The negro servants brought in a serving wagon containing the lunch which they put by the President and then finally withdrew. From this he gradually took out the courses of an excellent lunch and handed them to us with much courtesy and dexterity. I thought he was in grand form. I had heard many reports how I should find him much older and very tired compared with my memories of what is now seven years ago. He was also said to have been pulled down by his recent prolonged attack of acute diarrhoea. One is told that sometimes life and force goes out of his face and that he looks like a tired old woman with all the virility departed. But this was certainly untrue that morning. Perhaps his speech and its success had raised his spirits. I thought him calm and gay and in full possession of his own personality and of his will and purpose and clarity of mind. He still had that supreme equanimity which I have seen in him before, and I again felt an extraordinary charm in his expression and countenance, especially when it lights up with an upward glancing quizzical expression when he has used some teasing or half serious expression. I do not see how anyone can doubt in his presence that he is the outstanding American to-day, head and shoulders above everyone else.[29]

The warmth of the passage is unmistakable. In Roosevelt, Keynes saw the leader who most fully embodied his own ideals, a man he trusted as a partner and kindred spirit in the great battle for "civilisation." Yet the passage also contains complications for the war narrative Roosevelt would present to the American public of stalwart leaders leading a fight for human liberation. Keynes glided past the racial hierarchy embodied in the White House staffing arrangements and casually noted widely shared concerns about the commander in chief's health, which were being withheld from the American public on the eve of war. Even at the start of his third term, FDR's physical condition had deteriorated to the point where his top aides openly discussed it with foreign diplomats.

Keynes received assurances from most of the New Dealers that his differences with Morgenthau were technical misunderstandings, not ill will or disagreement over the broad strategic imperatives of the war. "He will do no one no harm *on purpose*," Keynes told British officials. "But how easily he might without intending it!"[30] After a few weeks, the passion within the administration for liquidating the empire's assets seemed to have cooled. A few British holdings were sold off for the sake of appearances. Keynes saw that the fate of American Viscose Corporation, the U.S. division of a British rayon manufacturer, had taken on "a symbolic, almost a mystic importance" with the Americans,[31] and the firm was sold off to investors to raise money, yielding just $54.4 million—about one-tenth of 1 percent of the total aid the United States ultimately supplied to its allies under the Lend-Lease program.[32]

But by the end of May, Keynes had a deal. He outlined the basic terms in a cable to London on May 26: Any "warlike" materials that survived the war would be returned to the United States. Those that were used up would be written off entirely. For nonwarlike items— food, raw materials, textiles—the two allies would keep an account that would be settled after the war. But the postwar account would not be cleared through traditional "economic consideration." Instead they would be settled by "politico-economic considerations taking the form of common purpose during the war and common economic policy after the war."[33] They would deal with it later, as friends and allies.

Just what would this new world order look like? "The president was emphatic that he would have no discussion at the present time of any post-war details," Keynes cabled home. "He then went on to mention some of his own post-war ideas." All of Europe would be "entirely deprived" of armaments, leaving Britain and the United States "to act as the police-men of Europe." And this time American political and economic aid would not pack up after the peace treaties were signed. "He refused to consider the possibility that America would not take her full share of responsibility for the post-war situation in Europe," Keynes reported. Germany, moreover, might be politically partitioned into smaller realms to prevent it from rearming in the future. It was an idea that Roosevelt acknowledged having lifted from an old conversation with Georges Clemenceau. No other man alive could have so easily earned Keynes' assent to the ideas of his old adversary. When FDR presented it alongside an economic agenda cribbed from *The Economic Consequences of the Peace*, Keynes was delighted.

It was classic Roosevelt, charming his guests with what he knew they wanted to hear, avoiding the differences of opinion that would offend them. Though Keynes would never fully recognize it, there were important strategic issues on which he and the American president never saw eye to eye. To Keynes, FDR seemed to be pledging to help realize the idealized imperialism Keynes had embraced as a young man. The United States and Britain would be equal partners on a crusade to save democracy and fine living from militarism and barbarism all over the world. And as America got its act together in the summer of 1941, moving money and munitions as Keynes pleaded Britain's despair, it was a comforting conclusion to draw. But to FDR, Britain and the United States were allies of convenience against a uniquely destructive threat. And he planned to use America's military and financial clout to shape a new world order in which Britain and its centuries of imperialist ambition would be wholly subjugated to the United States on the international stage. They would be partners but not equals.

Occasionally Keynes caught glimpses of the Roosevelt administration's longer-term vision. Even as he defended Britain's overseas financial assets, it did not occur to him that Americans might question the legitimacy of Britain's imperial territory. He had taken for granted that U.S. leaders would understand protecting the Suez Canal and the British trade route to India as a top military priority. Instead, he was "astonished by the extent to which nearly all responsible people over here seem to have written off Africa altogether."[34] The Americans were thinking ahead.

On a busy day at the Office of Price Administration and Civilian Supply, thirty-two-year-old John Kenneth Galbraith was grappling with plans for what he expected to be one of the most important battles in the war: the fight against inflation. Galbraith's secretary, Carol Piper, came into the office and informed her young boss that a visitor had dropped by. Galbraith asked Piper to dismiss the man. It was a politically sensitive time for the administration as it wrangled with Congress for the legal authority to implement its price agenda, and Galbraith wasn't eager for an uninvited headache. Anyone who wanted to make problems for him could make an appointment.

But Piper noted there was something unusual about the guest. "He gave me the impression that he expects to see you—and asked if you had received this," she said, handing Galbraith an academic paper. The topic—hog pricing—was not especially interesting, but he was stunned to see the author's name: John Maynard Keynes. As Galbraith recalled years later, "It was the Holy Father dropping in on the parish priest!"[35]

Galbraith was invited to dinner along with Walter Salant and a handful of other top New Deal economists, the first of many wartime colloquies in the United States at which Keynes re-created the atmosphere of the Apostles as he cultivated a generation of admirers among American policy makers. The Americans were too young to remember the way inflation had taken hold during World War I. Keynes knew this was among the most important strategic pieces of the fight, critical not only for morale on the home front but for the ability of the British and U.S. economies to produce the materiel required by the fight. Runaway inflation wasn't just a problem for consumer paychecks; it could disrupt trade patterns and throw the economic mechanism of the war out of whack, threatening the prospects for rebuilding and recovery after the war. At the dinner, Keynes detailed the phases of price increases the United States could expect to see in the coming months, based on his own observations from a quarter century earlier. The marked emphasis on inflation surprised some of the economists, who, after so many years of depression, were still focused on employment as the top national economic concern. But with the war orders coming in on a massive scale, Keynes insisted that it was only a matter of time until rapid price increases took effect. Americans would need to have a battle plan ready when they did.

First, he said, speculators anticipating an increase in production from the war would bid up the prices of key commodities—everything from cotton for uniforms to iron, coal, and cement. Next, as workers joined the military or filled positions in military manufacturing, employers would begin offering higher salaries to attract and retain talent. After that, labor unions, correctly perceiving their greater leverage with employers, would begin to demand—and receive—higher pay under collective bargaining contracts. All of this would have an impact on prices. Commodity speculation would raise the cost of raw goods for manufacturers and force them to charge retailers more, while retailers would sense the better purchasing position of their customers and raise prices themselves. The entire phenomenon would be exacerbated by the fact that enormous segments of the economy, though operating at full tilt and with essentially no unemployment, would be producing war materiel for use overseas rather than consumer goods to be purchased at home. The purchasing power created by widespread availability of good-paying jobs would face a shortage of products it could actually buy. Demand would rage far ahead of supply. Without "heavy taxation, a high pressure savings campaign or rationing on a wide scale," the United States was in store for an inflationary explosion.[36]

Governments typically battled inflation by raising interest rates. By making borrowing more expensive, businesses borrowed less, cut production, and laid off workers—all of which put downward pressure on prices. But that was a particularly bad strategy during a war, when the government needed the economy to be running at maximum output. So Keynes devised a very different anti-inflation plan for Great Britain, published in a few popular essays from 1939 and collected together as the policy pamphlet *How to Pay for the War: A Radical Plan for the Chancellor of the Exchequer.* The piece was a sensation, inspiring political cartoons and informing the government's wartime budgets. It was also the best analysis of inflation Keynes ever presented and an essential pairing for *The General Theory.* Most economists who read *The General Theory* had been looking for guidance on how to grapple with a shortage of demand. *How to Pay for the War* discussed how to deal with an excess.

In the pamphlet, Keynes called for a "mandatory savings program" to accompany the inevitable tax increases and government borrowing that would be needed in the fight. Companies, he argued, should be free to pay their workers whatever they wished, according to the demand for their skills. But the government should set aside a block of this pay—progressively larger by income—and hold it until the war was over, adding some interest to compensate workers for the inconvenience. It was a clever way, he acknowledged, of reimagining national debt as a set of "rights to deferred consumption,"[37] which allowed workers to stake a claim on the future wealth of the country that "would belong otherwise to the capitalist class."[38] Instead of relying on rich people to purchase war bonds, Keynes was essentially forcing them on workers, who would hand over money in the present in exchange for more money in the future.

During World War I, rising prices had accrued to industrialists in the form of higher profits, which were then taxed away by the government, borrowed by the government, or spent on consumer goods, further driving up their prices. When those profits were borrowed, the industrialists received an asset—bonds—that their workers did not. Workers benefited only in the form of higher pay—and that was cold comfort, since the value of their paychecks was steadily being inflated away. The most egalitarian method, of course, would have been to tax profits to the hilt—but there was a limit to how much governments could actually tax. In the United States, for instance, the tax rate on the highest incomes would eventually reach 94 percent during the war. For taxes to really do the trick, they would ultimately have to hit working people of more modest means. By forcing workers to accept a program of "deferred pay," Keynes was attempting to redistribute postwar wealth from the investor class to the working class.

The title of the piece is misleading. Compulsory savings wouldn't really "pay" for anything. By hook or by crook, the British government was going to maximize war production. When it wanted bombs, it would make them, and, since the gold standard was long gone, it could print the money to pay for them without having to yoke its printing presses to the amount of gold at the Bank of England. Mandatory savings were a way of managing inflation. By pulling demand out of the economy—reducing the purchasing power of ordinary people—Keynes wanted to limit their ability to bid up retail prices.

This was a critical observation about the way money, debt, and even taxes functioned in a post–gold standard world. In 1931, it had been possible for the British government to spend so much money that it could not meet its debt obligations, because it could print only so much money; its debts were written in pounds tied to a certain amount of gold. Under the gold standard, it was possible for a government to run out of money; there was only so much gold in the vaults. But a government that controlled its own currency, Keynes observed, could not go bankrupt. Under the fiat currency that had prevailed in Great Britain since 1931, the government could easily print its way out of excessive debt. Taken to extremes, the consequence of that strategy would be inflation, of course. And so the purpose of taxes—or deferred savings or any similar instrument—was not to "pay" for government services but to regulate the value of money.

With Keynes installed at the Treasury, the British government adopted a mandatory savings plan as part of its 1941 budget, cementing his status as a key economic policy maker of the war. But controlling inflation in the United States would require an apocalyptic political struggle.

The war was an unceasing source of ironies. After years of being tarred as an inflationist, nobody was more assertive—or creative—about fighting the upward surge of war prices than Keynes. And nobody was more hostile to the effort than the American business elite who had spent the past decade warning that deficit-financed public works would turn Great Britain or the United States into another Weimar. Now that price increases were imminent, those same experts screamed that any effort to control them—and thus crimp short-term profits—was pure communism.

The United States never implemented a forced savings program, but it also did not rely on high interest rates from the central bank to battle inflation. Beginning in 1942, the Fed publicly committed itself to maintaining a 0.375 percent interest rate on Treasury bills, a decision that helped keep down financing costs for the ballooning debt the government was issuing. But coordinating monetary and fiscal policy in this manner meant the Fed could not use interest rates as a tool to bring down prices; it instead deliberately fixed interest rates at a specific level, regardless of what happened to prices. That was for the best anyway—Keynes and many of his American admirers, including Fed chair Marriner Eccles, believed that low interest rates had been essential to the recovery and would help boost war production. So the U.S. government relied on heavy taxation, aggressive price controls, and eventually the physical rationing of consumer goods to maintain economic order. Wall Street hated all of these policies, but Wall Street was not the only source of opposition.

As the summer of 1941 turned to fall, Galbraith and his boss, Leon Henderson, were called to Capitol Hill again and again to testify on

Roosevelt's request for additional authority over U.S. prices. It was, "by a wide margin," according to Galbraith, "the most controversial" legislation of the entire war.[39] In 1941, the economy was closing in on full employment, wages were rising, and profits were soaring. After years of depression, nobody on Capitol Hill wanted to *think* about another round of economic pain, much less take active steps to crimp paychecks or the stock market. Farm prices in particular had taken on a sort of sacred status within the Democratic Party, which became increasingly dependent on southern votes as Wall Street Republicans began chipping away at northern congressional seats. Since the beginning of the Roosevelt administration, the federal government had been working relentlessly to raise crop prices. Labor unions, a key Democratic constituency in the Northeast and upper Midwest, were furious about the prospect of accepting wage concessions while industrialists locked in guaranteed profits on government contracts. Working people had waited years for a period of genuine prosperity, and now that it had arrived, a few ambitious young New Dealers were threatening enforced sacrifice. Few were eager to confront the reality of coming inflation, and many channeled their frustration into paranoia.

At a hearing before the House Banking and Currency Committee, Georgia commissioner of agriculture Tom Linder testified that the whole idea for inflation control was a Jewish plot. Henderson, Linder insisted, was secretly Jewish; he had received his job in the administration due to his connections with "Baruch, Morgenthau, Straus, Ginsburg and the Guggenheim interests." Lawmakers on the committee assailed Henderson for chairing an organization called the Washington Friends of Spanish Democracy, an anti-Franco group that raised red flags for ardent anti-Communists among both Republicans and southern Democrats.[40]

Henderson threw off his attackers by reading aloud the speech he had given on the evening he had accepted his leadership post in the organization. Without stalwart, principled opposition from democratic peoples, Henderson had warned, Hitler and Mussolini would soon begin nihilistic campaigns of military conquest far beyond Spain. With the international march of fascism proving Henderson's words prescient, the speech mollified the committee. But when lawmakers became aware that Galbraith staffer Robert Brady had written a book published by the Left Book Club in England called *The Spirit and the Structure of German Fascism*, they quickly found a new target for Red hunting. At one hearing, Galbraith incorrectly testified that the Left Book Club was like a British Book-of-the-Month Club and was pilloried for his error by Texas Democrat Martin Dies, Jr., of the House Committee on Un-American Activities.[41]

The most persistent and menacing insinuation against Galbraith and his team of aspiring price fixers was of a dangerous connection with Moscow—a malignant notion that had not yet been complicated by the U.S. government's formal alliance with Soviet Russia. It was not hard to sketch the broad outlines of a socialist conspiracy: first the New Dealers had substituted government works for private enterprise, now they wanted to implement comprehensive price controls across the entire economy.

Galbraith had hoped to tailor price controls with more specificity and nuance than Keynes had suggested in *How to Pay for the War*. Trying to keep prices down chiefly by forcing cutbacks on personal incomes could, he argued, impede total output and employment. Inflation wasn't going to happen uniformly across every sector or all at once. Different industries would see prices rise at different times. Raw materials like copper and iron, for instance, were certain to shoot up quickly, but goods unaffected by war orders would take longer. Sucking demand out of the economy by decreasing overall consumer purchasing power would bring down the price of copper, but it would also bring down the price of everything else. In lagging sectors that were not yet operating at full capacity, lower prices would send a signal to produce less, reducing wartime output.

Keynes didn't like the idea of tinkering with the prices of individual items. He preferred to think about regulating the general price level, allowing the relative prices of different goods to respond to consumer preferences wherever possible. He also had the benefit of experience. Keynes had lived through a big war before and understood exactly how hard it was to actively manage the price of *everything*. By April 1942, the Office of Price Administration had relented, issuing a General Maximum Price Regulation, rolling back all prices to their level of a month earlier. OPA continued to be flooded with work as companies applied for exceptions, but the task of price management entered the realm of bureaucratic feasibility.

It remained a political nightmare. Two days after Pearl Harbor, Galbraith ordered a freeze on all tire sales to preserve rubber for military needs. Over the coming months, he went on to ration gasoline, butter, cigarettes, sugar, nylon, shoes, canned vegetables, and fruit, all in the name of directing U.S. production to the war effort.[42] "You can't have 500 bombers a month *and* business as usual," Leon Henderson said.[43] But business leaders pressed on with demands to keep producing consumer goods at whatever price the market would bear. When *Fortune* magazine polled business executives on the rationing and price control programs, three out of four suspected there were "darker designs" at work.[44] It took an executive order from Roosevelt himself to get Detroit to stop manufacturing cars. When the auto companies maintained production for an extra two months anyway, Henderson took revenge by appropriating 200,000 cars for government use. A meeting with oil producers in San Francisco broke into a "near riot," according to Galbraith, when OPA asked them to roll back a recent price increase.[45] "At times it seemed that our war with business took precedence over the war in Europe and Asia," Galbraith later told Doris Kearns Goodwin. "There were weeks when Hitler scarcely entered our minds compared with the business types in Washington."[46]

The frustration extended well beyond the c-suite. The government was ordering significant changes in daily life for millions of families. OPA banned the production of "refrigerators, vacuum cleaners, sewing machines, electric ranges, washing machines and ironers, radios and phonographs, lawn mowers, waffle irons, and toasters. The use of stainless steel was prohibited in tableware. Shoe manufacturers were ordered to avoid double soles and overlapping tips; lingerie makers were limited to styles without ruffles, pleating, or full sleeves."[47]

Coffee was the last straw. On November 29, it was rationed to one cup per person per day. Two weeks later, Henderson was forced to resign, as congressmen threatened to withhold funding for the Office of Price Administration unless its leader was removed. Of course the problem wasn't Henderson, it was war. Almost as soon as Henderson left the job, his replacement, Galbraith, became a front-page target. The *Washington Times-Herald* and the *Chicago Tribune* began accusing Galbraith of personally attempting to subvert the American way of life. The trade journal *Food Field Reporter* even changed its masthead to include the line "GALBRAITH MUST GO."[48]

The tone on Capitol Hill was even worse, particularly after Republicans picked up forty-four House seats in the 1942 election. Congressman Everett Dirksen, a Republican from Illinois, introduced legislation that would have barred anyone who didn't have at least five years of experience in "business" from running OPA—a direct shot at Galbraith and his academic background. The top Republican on the House Appropriations Committee, John Taber, even falsely reported Galbraith to the FBI as an enthusiastic and "doctrinaire" Communist—though the FBI agent misunderstood him, causing years of confusion within the bureau about the identity of a mysterious Dr. Ware.[49]

The pressure on the Roosevelt administration was relentless. On May 31, 1943, Galbraith was ordered to resign to appease the anger on Capitol Hill. But the exhaustion of the war workload and political maneuvering around so many Red Scare antics had taken a toll on him. The next day, he collapsed on the floor of his living room. Revived by his wife and the family maid, he was taken to a doctor, who prescribed a strict regimen of bed rest. Like Keynes a few years earlier, Galbraith was on the verge of working himself to death.

After a few weeks of rest, he was back to his usual self. But though he was offered a post in the Lend-Lease office, he quickly decided to leave Washington officialdom for a writing job at *Fortune* magazine. The pay was good—Galbraith's $12,000 starting salary translates to about $170,000 today. But mostly he was tired of being a target. Dirksen—a future ally of Wisconsin senator Joseph McCarthy—followed through with the antiprofessor amendment anyway.

The war created a strange American scenario in which Keynesians began to be assailed as dangerous subversives, even as Keynesian policies were implemented with ringing success. Unemployment all but disappeared as federal spending rose nearly 50 percent in 1941 to more than $13.6 billion, more than triple its level when Herbert Hoover had left office. In 1942, the level of spending more than doubled again, to $35 billion, then doubled again in 1943. By the end of the war, the federal government was spending $92.7 billion a year. More than half of the war effort had been financed with borrowed money.[50] Economic growth, which had reached an impressive 8.0 percent after FDR renewed public works spending in 1939, shot to an unheard-of 17.7 percent in 1941, eclipsed in 1942 at 18.9 percent, followed by 17.0 percent the following year. As Keynes had predicted, few worried about the nominal size of the debt when the economy was booming.

Across the Atlantic, meanwhile, Keynes was finally being embraced by the political establishment. Parliament listened to his budget ideas, and he was now one of Great Britain's most important diplomats. He was even named to the Court of the Bank of England, the original temple of laissez-faire orthodoxy, where he could once again tangle with his old nemesis Montagu Norman. Felix Frankfurter, who had befriended Keynes at the Paris Peace Conference, offered a note of congratulation. "What rejoices all your friends," wrote Frankfurter, now a Supreme Court justice, "is that the mountain has come to Mohammed and not the other way around." Joan Robinson, ever the irreverent radical, joked, "Never mind, I will always say you were grand while you lasted."[51]

Though Lydia protested against Keynes overextending himself, he had resumed a pace of activity nearly as frenetic as that he had maintained before his collapse, editing an economic journal, attending to administrative concerns at Cambridge, and keeping up with Bloomsbury. The rift with Vanessa finally mended, Lydia and Maynard now spent Christmases with Duncan and Vanessa and made time as often as possible for the Memoir Club.[52] In June 1942, the British government honored Keynes by elevating him to the peerage, giving him a seat in the House of Lords and the title Baron Keynes of Tilton. Clive Bell recalled the countryside celebration: "When he came to Charleston with Lady Keynes for the first time after his peerage had been announced he was downright sheepish. 'We have come to be laughed at' he said."[53]

It was a different Bloomsbury from the buoyant and zealous crowd of young ambition that had weathered the Great War together. Many of its social rituals were now maintained by a younger set of admirers led by Bunny Garnett, as the old guard retired from the scene. On March 28, 1941, Virginia disappeared after going out for a walk from the third wartime country house she shared with Leonard. Her hat and cane were discovered by the banks of the Ouse River, and Leonard found a note she had written at their house: "I have a feeling I shall go mad," she had written. "I cannot go on any longer in these terrible times. I hear voices and cannot concentrate on my work. I have fought against it but cannot fight any longer. I owe all my happiness to you but cannot go on and spoil your life."

Keynes was devastated. "She had seemed so very well and normal the last time we saw her," he wrote to his mother, mourning the bond he and Lydia had shared with Leonard and Virginia for nearly two decades. "The two of them were our dearest friends."[54]

The first great shift in the Bloomsbury social order had come when its members settled into their unconventional marriages in the 1920s. Now it was going through its final metamorphosis. Woolf's last book had been a biography of Duncan's old painting ally Roger Fry, who had died unexpectedly in 1934. With Lytton and Virginia gone, Bloomsbury was down to its last bona fide genius. It was not lost on Keynes that the chief activity that now brought his old friends together was an act of collective reminiscence. The major endeavors of nearly every member of the Memoir Club were now in the past. As the war progressed, Keynes knew he was entering the twilight of his life. Alone among his remaining friends, Keynes still had great work left to be done.

And during the 1940s, his results were hard to argue with. Unemployment had been abolished, inflation was controlled, and the decline of the world's democracies had been reversed. This success shifted the debate between Keynes and his adversaries in the economics profession. The doctrine espoused by Friedrich von Hayek—austerity, tight money, letting deflation purge excess from the system—didn't have much inherent political allure. It could be maintained only if Keynesian spending remained an amorphous, abstract bogeyman. Faced with the concrete reality of the Keynesian war boom, it was extremely difficult to persuade people that deficit spending and cheap money were self-defeating. "By the end of the war the entire academic profession was Keynesian," according to Paul Samuelson, who had himself converted after some early skepticism.[55] It was only a slight exaggeration. Lionel Robbins, a conservative economist who had recruited Hayek to the London School of Economics in 1931 and tussled with Keynes on the Macmillan Committee, formally recanted his views in the face of the evidence before him, lamenting his feud with Keynes as "the greatest mistake of my professional career."[56] A young economist at the University of Chicago named Milton Friedman called for the federal government to balance its budget *only* during periods of full employment, with the government financing its deficits by issuing new money.[57] To the general public, austerity and deflation were understood as the Great Depression. To government officials on both sides of the Atlantic, the war boom was a result of Keynesian spending and inflation control. Insisting that Keynesianism couldn't work was a political dead end.

But the war had unleashed an intense spirit of American nationalism that reacted unpredictably with the long-standing antipathy to Roosevelt evident among much of the American elite. They loved

editor of the academic *Economic Journal,* and chairman of the government's new Council for the Encouragement of Music and the Arts. Lydia protested against the physical strain he shouldered, but she knew the activity helped keep his mind away from the horrors a wartime bureaucrat contemplated at the office. It also helped him avoid ruminating on his own fate. At age sixty, Keynes' health was once again in decline. No longer the "heavy," "portentous" man who had been the subject of Virginia Woolf's bitter gossip in the 1920s, he was now thin and frail. The distinguished gray hair of middle age had given way to a pure, ghostly white. Plesch prescribed wild new rounds of treatment, and Lydia spent hours applying ice packs to her husband's chest, but Maynard collapsed from another heart attack in March. He had again reached the point of total physical exhaustion.

But D-Day appeared to have turned the tide in the conflict and with it the focus of his Treasury work. President Roosevelt called an international economic conference of all forty-four Allied governments to plan for the postwar economic order. With the war still ongoing and the reconstruction needs of its victors still unclear, it was a bit premature to be marking out the financial future. Nevertheless, FDR wanted to tout a major international agreement as he campaigned for reelection that November, and any pact would have to be signed by the summer to serve a domestic political purpose.

Impatient as he was to escape from London, the situation threatened to combine two of the most unpleasant experiences of Keynes' life—the chaos of Paris in 1919 and the hellacious swelter of Washington, DC, in 1941. Keynes knew he didn't have many summers left, and he wanted to spend them in luxury. In May, he urged Harry Dexter White, the top U.S. financial diplomat, to consider hosting the conference at a Rocky Mountain resort. "For God's sake," Keynes wrote, "do not take us to Washington in July."[2]

They settled instead on the remote village of Bretton Woods in rural New Hampshire, with a week of preparatory work in the coastal resort atmosphere of Atlantic City. For Lydia and Maynard, simply getting out of London would be a holiday. As they steamed across the ocean for America, Maynard took a break from his official duties to indulge in one of his favorite leisure activities: He immersed himself in a dense work of political economy. Casually, almost by accident, he would fire off one of the most important philosophical statements of his life, a comprehensive update to the political theory he had sketched twenty years earlier in *The End of Laissez-Faire* and a new front in his intellectual struggle with Friedrich von Hayek over the course of Enlightenment liberalism.

Hayek had never wanted to be remembered as a political theorist. He considered himself an economist, a man whose great life project was the scientific study of money and the principles of its movement. But in 1944, at forty-five years of age, nobody was paying much attention to the ideas about inflation and business cycles that Hayek had developed back in the early 1930s. His latest book, *The Pure Theory of Capital*, was a flop. The Blitz had forced him to relocate from the London School of Economics to the relative safety of King's College at Cambridge, where John Maynard Keynes set the agenda. At Cambridge, every new idea seemed to either come from Keynes and his top lieutenants or emerge in response to their innovations. The man himself was a titan on campus: A public official with important duties at bastions of prestige including the Bank of England and the House of Lords, Keynes was also a cultural leader who showboated at dinners and cocktail parties with a flamboyant ballerina-actress-broadcaster wife who was nearly as famous as he himself. Hayek lived in his shadow, a minor lecturer with a strong accent whose major works were more than a decade old, unscrutinized and unloved. He was friendly with Lord Keynes, but the great man did not spend much time worrying what Hayek thought about him—the battles of the 1930s were long over, and the public, it was clear to both men, had decided the victor. They exchanged cordial letters and were on occasion assigned to fire-watch duty together atop the medieval Gothic chapel at King's, armed with shovels, tasked with pitching any stray German incendiaries from the roof, should one land unexploded during an air raid.[3]

Hayek was a little ambivalent about writing a book on political philosophy, concerned it might drive people to dismiss his monetary work as ideologically tainted. He eventually decided this was a minor risk; nobody was taking his monetary ideas seriously, anyway. So Hayek assembled a ferocious, scholarly attack on Keynes and the New Deal, not as an empirical analysis or a work of economic theory but as a political treatise. The book, titled *The Road to Serfdom*, would in time be recognized as a foundational text of modern conservatism, though Hayek resisted the label all his life. To Hayek the word *conservative* connoted the "paternalistic, nationalistic, and power-adoring tendencies"[4] of British Tories. He preferred to think of himself as a "classical liberal" inspired by Locke, Hume, and Smith—many of the same figures who animated Keynes. Keynes had tried to redefine liberalism for the twentieth century with *The End of Laissez-Faire*, sketching ideas that came to fruition in the New Deal; Hayek wanted to offer an alternative liberal vision.

Early sales of *The Road to Serfdom* were respectable. The University of Chicago Press almost immediately ran through its first run of two thousand copies thanks to strong reviews in *The New York Times* and the *New York Herald Tribune*. But the brief polemic transformed Hayek into an international right-wing celebrity when *Reader's Digest* produced a condensed edition, bringing his ideas into literally millions of homes. This sudden and unexpected fame for a British intellectual prompted an American speaking tour that put Hayek face-to-face with thousands of like-minded men and women across the country.[5] Those elements of the American upper class who had been spending the long, long Roosevelt presidency exiled from political power had finally discovered a spokesman who could channel their fears and frustrations. In Hayek, elite grievances won a new intellectual legitimacy.

Few recognized it in the spring of 1944, but Hayek's attack on the political implications of Keynesian economics would be a turning point in twentieth-century thought. Within months of his book tour, Hayek was accepting meetings with deep-pocketed donors eager to defend freedom and seeking guidance for how best to spend their money. The network of think tanks, university professorships, and book publishing houses those men established with Hayek's input rendered *The Road to Serfdom*, in the words of *Reason* magazine senior editor Brian Doherty, "an epochal work in forging the modern libertarian mind."[6] Hayek himself was a thoughtful, mild-mannered man—but the dire warnings in his book about a slippery slope from Keynesian liberalism to totalitarianism would mix potently with Cold War paranoia. His colleagues in the backlash against Keynesianism fueled—and at times even helped to finance—a McCarthyist fever in academia.

Friedrich August von Hayek was born into an aristocratic family who had supported Austro-Hungarian emperor Franz Josef in the decades before the Great War. He had enlisted with the Austrian army as a teenager and served on the Italian front before enrolling at the University of Vienna, where he began sampling rebellious ideologies, embracing socialism for a brief period before becoming enraptured by an ideal of laissez-faire liberalism proffered by Ludwig von Mises, an economist seventeen years his senior. The seminars with Mises caught Hayek at a potent moment in Austrian history. Hayek had lived through the Weimar Republic's hyperinflationary destruction in Vienna, an experience which left him terrified of inflationary policy ever after. His growing admiration for English individualists and enthusiasm for Gilded Age capitalism, meanwhile, made him sensitive about his family background, and he eventually dropped the honorific "von" from his name. He wanted to be recognized for his devotion to free markets, not hereditary prestige, though in the words of historian Angus Burgin, he "maintained the cultivated reserve and unabashed elitism of a Viennese aristocrat."[7]

Like Keynes, he looked back to the world before 1914 as a lost Golden Age of high culture. He admired the Hapsburg Empire much as Keynes had celebrated the British Empire, describing the world of his youth as a model for the world he hoped to create: a kind of federation in which ethnic groups maintained an independent political nationality, even as a central imperial power established the economic arrangements of its vassal territories. His economic work landed him a job at LSE in the early 1930s, but *The Road to Serfdom* made his career. When he was awarded the Nobel Prize in Economics in 1974, the Royal Swedish Academy of Sciences cited his "important interdisciplinary research"—an allusion to the political ideas he had advanced in the book—in addition to his "contributions to central economic theory."[8]

The Road to Serfdom is an academic overhaul of Walter Lippmann's *The Good Society*, which had been Lippmann's effort to distill the economic ideas of Hayek and Mises into a systematized political theory. And like *The Good Society*, Hayek's treatise is a book at war with itself. There are two distinct social visions competing with each other within its pages. The first, which endeared Hayek to the anti–New Deal American upper class, was an audacious rejection of the Four Freedoms.

Or at least, *one* of the Four Freedoms. By declaring "freedom from want" a human right, FDR had presented the social reforms of the New Deal as a moral imperative every bit as pressing as the military defeat of Nazism. By including it in the Atlantic Charter, he and Churchill had declared personal economic security a defining characteristic of any democracy, a bedrock guarantee that distinguished a free society from tyranny. Hayek turned this argument on its head—a daring maneuver at the height of the war that had transformed FDR and Churchill into figures of public adulation. The very idea of "economic freedom," Hayek argued, was antithetical to what true advocates of political freedom had championed for centuries. "Freedom from necessity," he claimed, was an inherently "socialist" idea. It was not a bulwark for the democracies against Nazism but an ingredient of Nazism and Soviet communism alike, which could only be effectively implemented by a violent dictatorship that crushed other political rights. As Hayek explained:

To the great apostles of political freedom the word had meant freedom from coercion, freedom from the arbitrary power of other men, release from the ties which left the individual no choice but obedience to the orders of a superior to whom he was attached. The new freedom promised, however, was to be freedom from necessity, release from the compulsion of the circumstances which inevitably limit the range of choice of all of us, although for some very much more than for others. Before man could be truly free, the "despotism of physical want" had to be broken, the "restraints of the economic system" relaxed.

Freedom in this sense is, of course, merely another name for power or wealth. . . . What the promise really amounted to was that the great existing disparities in the range of choice of different people were to disappear. . . . What was promised to us as the Road to Freedom was in fact the High Road to Servitude.[9]

He embedded his antigovernment message in a grand historical narrative that linked the economic system of the Gilded Age with Christian morality and his own intellectual heroes from classical antiquity. Europe and the United States had to choose, he insisted, between this vaunted Western individualist tradition and the new, dangerous totalitarian movements represented by Hitler and Stalin. Nazism, according to Hayek, had been misunderstood as an outgrowth of the radical political Right. In Hayek's vision, the Third Reich was just a different strain of socialism; it was merely a coincidence that Hitler happened to have made alliances in the Reichstag with conservative parties and business interests. Hayek devoted an entire chapter to "The Socialist Roots of Naziism," arguing that over the course of decades, various social welfare policies and protectionist trade strategies had gradually acclimated the German mind to Nazi ideas. It was not the Depression or deflation that had led to the Nazi takeover but creeping government intervention in the economy. However well intentioned they might be, the New Deal and Keynesian economics were setting the world's democracies on the same path.

"We are rapidly abandoning not the views merely of Cobden and Bright, of Adam Smith and Hume, or even of Locke and Milton, but one of the salient characteristics of Western civilization as it has grown from the foundations laid by Christianity and the Greeks and Romans," he warned. "Not merely nineteenth- and eighteenth-century liberalism, but the basic individualism inherited by us from Erasmus and Montaigne, from Cicero and Tacitus, Pericles and Thucydides, is progressively relinquished."[10]

Hayek's brand of antiauthoritarianism was ambivalent about democracy. "Democracy is a means, a utilitarian device for safeguarding internal peace and individual freedom," he wrote. "There has often been much more cultural and spiritual freedom under an autocratic rule than under some democracies."[11] What mattered to Hayek was liberty, and by liberty he meant the rights of an aristocracy against the central government, whatever form that government took.

The antigovernment refrain of *The Road to Serfdom* was perfectly in key with Mises' uncompromising libertarian tract *Bureaucracy*, published in the same year, in which Hayek's mentor forcefully declared New Deal liberalism a variant of authoritarian communism. "Capitalism means free enterprise, sovereignty of the consumers in economic matters, and sovereignty of the voters in political matters," he wrote. "Socialism means full government control of every sphere of the individual's life. . . . There is no compromise possible between these two systems."[12] You could have laissez-faire, or you could have Soviet Russia; there was no middle ground.

Hayek recognized that the all-or-nothing severity of his old instructor was a political dead end in an era in which every government seemed to be pursuing new Keynesian reforms. And so, like Lippmann before him, Hayek attempted to graft his laissez-faire conception of liberty onto something compatible with the emerging modern nation-state. The government might be allowed to maintain some basic minimum standard of living for everyone, after all. He drew a distinction between "regulation"—which was merely designed to solve obvious problems—and dangerous "planning"—which could only be achieved by a dictator orchestrating the lives and limiting the choices of free individuals. The size and scope of corporate enterprises, he argued, should be closely limited and monitored to prevent big firms from interfering with free competition in the marketplace.

By 1944, U.S. government expenditures accounted for no less than 40 percent of the entire American economy. Most people expected that figure to decline after the war (it is around 20 percent today), but Hayek was right to believe that much of the administrative apparatus that had been assembled over the past dozen years was here to stay. Yet with a little semantic creativity, almost anything FDR and Keynes had dreamed up in the past two decades could have been justified by these Hayekian precepts concerning regulation, competition, and the social safety net. The somewhat comprehensive socialization of investment Keynes had described in *The General Theory* might be described as the commonsense *regulation* of inflation and employment, rather than the nefarious *planning* that Hayek excoriated. Glass-Steagall's government-mandated breakup of the American investment houses was just a responsible antitrust action to restore competitive banking. Social Security and public works spending were inoffensive elements of the basic social guarantee. Hayek, of course, did not support any of those efforts. He intended his book as a frontal assault on them and never wavered in his hostility to them. As his Keynesian rival Paul Samuelson noted decades later, Hayek always "bemoaned progressive income taxation, state-provided medical care and retirement pensions" and detested "fiat currencies remote from gold."[13] Mises may have been severe, but he had at least found a governing principle—laissez-faire or bust—that was consistent with his policy views.

In the final chapter of *The Road to Serfdom,* Hayek called for a "supranational authority" to keep governments in check and block the democracies of the world from engaging in dangerous economic planning—a Hapsburg-esque economic hegemon that would prevent war by enforcing the principles of free-market capitalism. In recent years, various scholars have come to understand this vision as an intellectual predecessor of the both the European Union and the World Trade Organization.[14] But the idea of an international authority to bring peace through economic discipline was not uniquely Hayekian. Keynes read *The Road to Serfdom* on his way to a conference aimed at creating exactly that kind of entity.

Keynes responded to Hayek in a personal letter from the Claridge Hotel in Atlantic City. That he bothered to respond at all is a testament to the force of Hayek's rhetoric, the sweep of his narrative, and the great significance Keynes attached to the struggle over the liberal tradition. Hayek was not a famous man, and his book was not yet a publishing sensation.

Keynes began his letter with sincere congratulations before presenting a devastating critique. "In my opinion it is a grand book," he wrote. "We all have the greatest reason to be grateful to you for saying so well what needs so much to be said. You will not expect me to accept quite all the economic dicta in it. But morally and philosophically I find myself in agreement with virtually the whole of it; and not only in agreement with it, but in a deeply moved agreement."[15] The rise of totalitarian government was a tragedy, and the best defense against it was a reinvigorated liberalism.

But it seemed to Keynes that Hayek had not offered a serious liberal program. All of Hayek's compromises with the social safety net, regulation, and antitrust policy put him on the same slippery slope to totalitarianism which Hayek himself admonished his political opponents for treading. "You admit here and there that it is a question of knowing where to draw the line. You agree that the line has to be drawn somewhere, and that the logical extreme is not possible. But you give us no guidance whatever as to where to draw it. . . . But as soon as you admit that the extreme is not possible, and that a line has to be drawn, you are, on your own argument, done for, since you are trying to persuade us that so soon as one moves an inch in the planned direction you are necessarily launched on the slippery path which will lead you in due course over the precipice."[16]

Even Hayek's admirers have cited the weakness of the historical argument behind his chief case study, the rise of Nazi Germany. University of Chicago economist Frank Knight, who shared Hayek's politics, discouraged the University Press from publishing the book due to its "over-simplification" of German history as little more than a slow encroachment of socialism leading to Hitler. Bruce Caldwell, a contemporary economist at Duke University, argues in the most recent introduction to *The Road to Serfdom* that Hayek's history is "on very shaky ground."[17] To Keynes, that deficient history was not merely an incidental mistake that could be divorced from the book's broader vi-

sion; it was a central misunderstanding about the sources of anger and
social dysfunction that had enabled fascism.

In *The End of Laissez-Faire*, Keynes had argued that liberalism
could not stand on abstract principles alone; it had to actually deliver
the goods for the people who lived under it. Laissez-faire had led to
vast inequality and grinding depression, failing a basic test for democratic legitimacy. By shrugging off the practical shortcomings of
laissez-faire, Keynes argued, Hayek had deluded himself about the
causes of dictatorship in Germany. The economic fuel for the rise of
Hitler had been the suffering and despair generated by deflation—not
the social welfare policies Hayek decried as "socialism." The democracies of the world could not turn their backs on the economic strategies
that had rejuvenated them in the late 1930s and 1940s; doing so would
only unleash a new wave of political uncertainty, encouraging new
authoritarian social movements. Hayek's call to abandon the New
Deal and Keynesian economic management was a recipe for more
strongmen. "What we need therefore, in my opinion, is not a change
in our economic programmes, which would only lead in practice to
disillusion with the results of your philosophy," he wrote, "but perhaps
even the contrary, namely, an enlargement of them."[18]

For Keynes, economics was the critical realm that had to unite the
drive for stability with the drive for social justice. And so he believed
that most of his disagreement with Hayek was about practical questions surrounding scarcity—whether there were enough resources to
go around and whether states could effectively manage their distribution. "I think you strike the wrong note," he wrote to Hayek, "where
you deprecate all the talk about plenty just round the corner"[19]—a
point ultimately vindicated by the postwar economic boom.

But for Hayek scarcity was as much a moral question as it was a
question of results. Scarcity created "the sphere where material circumstances force a choice upon us" and was essential to his vision of a
good life. The necessity of picking some things over others, of being
unable to have it all, was the font of individual expression, "the air in
which alone moral sense grows and in which moral values are daily
re-created."[20] What was true for the individual was true for society.

Without having to choose some works and traditions over others, culture would become degraded, empty. As Corey Robin has emphasized, Hayek believed the world needed an upper class to transmit knowledge and define society's values through the generations. In a broadly egalitarian society with enough resources for all, the upper class would disappear.

This was the critical distinction between the two men. Hayek and Keynes agreed that democracy was not the fundamental organizing principle of society; it was a tool for achieving more important goals. They even agreed that the most critical function of democracy was its ability to produce a vibrant, elite culture. The value Keynes placed on Bloomsbury was in some respects very similar to Hayek's appreciation for the old Viennese aristocracy. But to Keynes, nothing was lost in guiding all the world to Bloomsbury, while for Hayek, aristocracy was inherently exclusive; the whole point was that not everyone could be an aristocrat. And so where Keynes sought to democratize the comforts and privileges of the elite, Hayek hoped to reinforce the aristocracy's social distance from the masses. What Hayek believed could be achieved only through inequality, Keynes believed could be accomplished through education.

"I should say that what we want is not no planning, or even less planning, indeed I should say that we almost certainly want more," Keynes wrote. "But the planning should take place in a community in which as many people as possible, both leaders and followers, wholly share your own moral position. Moderate planning will be safe if those carrying it out are rightly orientated in their own minds and hearts to the moral issue. . . . what we need is the restoration of right moral thinking—a return to proper moral values in our social philosophy. If only you could turn your crusade in that direction you would not look or feel quite so much like Don Quixote. I accuse you of perhaps confusing a little bit the moral and the material issues. Dangerous acts can be done safely in a community which thinks and feels rightly, which would be the way to hell if they were executed by those who think and feel wrongly."[21]

Keynes was both embracing Rousseau's conception of the state as an expression of democratic will and restating Edmund Burke's emphasis on the power of culture and tradition. He presented a vision that relied neither on the ruthless pursuit of self-interest nor a utopian generosity of spirit. Through economic planning and moral education, communities can fight off the most destabilizing elements of uncertainty, instilling their members with both the moral values and the material comforts that will protect them against militarist nationalism. As with *The End of Laissez-Faire,* Keynes was attempting to harmonize the left-wing and right-wing philosophical traditions that had defined the opposite poles of Western thought since the French Revolution: making Burke's traditionalism fit with Rousseau's radical democracy. As Keynes had told readers of *The New Statesman and Nation* in 1939, "The question is whether we are prepared to move out of the nineteenth-century *laissez-faire* state into an era of liberal socialism, by which I mean a system where we can act as an organised community for common purposes and to promote social and economic justice, whilst respecting and protecting the individual—his freedom of choice, his faith, his mind and its expression, his enterprise and his property."[22]

As a practical guide to political life, Keynes' letter to Hayek is no more useful than *The Road to Serfdom.* It says almost nothing about *how* to educate or plan. And it is very relaxed about the massive new powers the state had acquired. Hayek's warnings about the dangerous, inherent violence of government are more compelling in light of the atrocities committed by the Allied war machine itself—a point that the politics of 1944 essentially forbade Hayek from broaching. Churchill, FDR, Truman, and Keynes himself as Great Britain's functional wartime Treasury chief did not establish any meaningful principles of restraint in their conduct of the war. More than 750,000 civilians were killed by Allied bombing campaigns in Europe and the Pacific.[23] Entire cities were flattened; ancient cultural monuments were erased. And this sustained campaign of terror had almost no strategic effect on the enemy's economic production, a fact that John Kenneth Galbraith formally reported as a director of the United States Strategic Bombing Survey in the final days of the war. Democracy had the power to liberate, and it had the power to destroy.

The ideas about scarcity, equality, and democracy that Keynes shared with Hayek on his trip were more than a friendly exchange between colleagues. They revealed the intellectual backdrop for the grand economic designs Keynes would present at the United National Monetary and Financial Conference of 1944 in Bretton Woods. For Europe and the United States, the conference would be the most important diplomatic summit since the debacle at Paris in 1919. For Keynes, it was a chance at redemption, an opportunity to put into practice all of the ideas and programs he had developed since the disaster that had made him a celebrity. At age sixty, with his health failing, Keynes had reached the zenith of his intellectual and political powers. Bretton Woods would be his final, grueling test.

The Mount Washington Hotel was a lavish artifact of Gilded Age ambition nestled into a remote valley of New Hampshire's White Mountains. It was spectacular in the summer. The verandas and balconies offered breathtaking views of the six-thousand-foot peaks nearby, the rolling expanses of the resort's private golf course, and the sparkling bend of the Ammonoosuc River, where Lydia shocked delegates by bathing nude each morning.[24] Indoors, the hotel was packed with every conceivable amenity, including an indoor swimming pool, Turkish baths, a bowling alley, a gun room for sportsmen, a card room for wives and gamblers, and multiple ornate bars including the intimate Cave and the opulent Moon Room, where an orchestra entertained patrons who flowed through all day and evening, into the small hours of the morning.[25]

But the Bretton Woods conference was not a calm, peaceful getaway. Keynes called it a "monstrous monkey-house." Delegates and their families numbered 730, accentuated by 500 journalists at a hotel with just 234 rooms. The reporters were technically housed at the Twin Mountain Hotel, but it was six miles away and bereft of either running water or food when the financial talks began. White and the Americans, moreover, had decided to give the press free access to the entire event. When negotiations dragged on past dinner and even midnight, the thick crowd of journalists remained and frequently joined in the socializing afterward.[26]

Nothing in the hotel seemed to work. "The taps run all day, the windows do not close or open, the pipes mend and unmend and no one can get anywhere," Lydia wrote to Maynard's mother on July 12.[27] Almost everyone seemed to be operating at various stages of inebriation throughout the gathering. Evening negotiations would break for cocktails, and any delegation looking to soften up the opposition would host a boozy afternoon reception. Drinks at the Moon Room were just a dollar, and when formal diplomacy wrapped up—often as late as 3:30 in the morning—White would lead the revelry with an adaptation of an American drinking song that became known as "The Bretton Woods Song":

> *And when I die don't bury me at all*
> *Just cover my bones with alcohol.*
> *Put a bottle of booze at my head and feet,*
> *And pray the Lord my soul to keep.*[28]

Lydia imposed a strict ban on late-night talks, but the strain on Keynes was immense. He was bombarded by documents and proposals and sent a hundred long telegrams back to London to update the government on the status of negotiations over the course of the three-week conference. Within just a few days he was struggling to maintain his physical composure. "I don't think I have ever worked so continuously hard in all my life," he said.[29] At times he would lose his temper, wisecracking about the clever "rabbinics" from the U.S. Treasury when negotiations went poorly for Great Britain (White and some of his top deputies were Jewish).[30]

There were some moments of release. One evening Lydia and Maynard sang "The Blue Danube" to guests in the upstairs lounge as H. E. Brooks of the British delegation played piano.[31] But such moments of levity were rare. Keynes worked himself ragged because he understood the profound stakes of the moment, both personal and international. Bretton Woods was his final opportunity to breathe political life into the beautiful abstractions he had spent a quarter of a century dreaming up to save humanity from itself.

The great project of Keynes' life, from the end of the Great War to the close of the Bretton Woods conference, was to decipher the means by which money could be deployed as a weapon against war. The international investment scheme he had outlined in *The Economic Consequences of the Peace* had in time given way, step by step, to calls for flexible exchange rates, tariffs, and eventually the strategy of demand management outlined in *The General Theory*. But throughout his development as a thinker, Keynes had followed the idea that economic instability was a dangerous catalyst for international conflict. He had parted ways with the free traders of the Gilded Age, but he had not abandoned their internationalist vision.

For Norman Angell and his disciples in U.S. foreign policy, including Secretary of State Cordell Hull, economic isolation was the greatest structural threat to world peace. Free trade and the intertwining of national economic interests across borders, they believed, were essential steps toward international harmony. Trade increased understanding between peoples and bound together their mutual prosperity as a unified project. Isolation encouraged greed and belligerence by eliminating domestic economic penalties for foreign aggression.

Keynes had come to believe that the problem was really much simpler: Unemployment was a breeding ground for fascism. It created dangerous political instability and a source of anger that could easily be weaponized. The terms of trade might help or hurt efforts to establish international goodwill, but tariffs or no tariffs, the legitimacy of an international economic order depended entirely on whether it did, in fact, provide for mutual prosperity.

For Angell and Hull, the relationship between free trade and economic abundance was a bedrock belief bordering on religious faith. Keynes was familiar with the attitude. He himself had viewed free trade "almost as part of the moral law" during his youth.[32] The belief that free trade led to prosperity was rooted in the idea that it improved efficiency in a world of scarce resources. In the nineteenth century, Keynes believed, free trade had in fact encouraged peace and prosperity by enabling nations to specialize in what they did best, growing the economic pie for the whole world and thereby limiting the potential for anger and unrest.

But Keynes was also convinced that the economic problem of the twentieth century was not scarcity but mismanagement. Depressions were caused not by production shortfalls but by financial instability and uncertainty.[33] The British general strike of 1926 and the rise of Hitler had been driven by desperate people seeking radical solutions to intractable domestic misery. The cause of their suffering had not been some insufficient dedication to comparative advantages, it was deflation—a decline in prices that had forced layoffs and shuttered businesses. And Keynes now believed that deflation had been spread around the world by the very free-trading gold standard he had admired as a young man.

Because economists became the primary stewards of the Keynesian legacy, *The General Theory* has long been understood as the climactic summit of Keynes' intellectual life. But if diplomats or philosophers had claimed him instead, that great book would be recognized as just one important stage in the development of a broader political agenda for fine living and international accord. Keynes still had one more breakthrough left in him. It would not be released as a book or a magazine feature; it was instead a diplomatic proposal for a postwar international financial and trade regime, intended to resolve once and for all the myriad problems posed by the gold standard.

Keynes had initiated his attack on that "barbarous relic" in *A Tract on Monetary Reform* by calling for flexible exchange rates. The financial chaos that followed World War I had convinced him that countries needed to be able to revalue their currencies—within reason—to correct for economic imbalances or escape from some unplanned disruption. But it was hard to distinguish between an acceptable devaluation attuned to the natural order of things and a predatory attack on foreign markets. One of the few benefits of the gold standard had been the adoption of a clear, shared understanding of what constituted fair play. A nation that violated the rules of the game was understood to be either reckless or predatory. But once Keynes—and the international community more broadly—came to accept that countries often had *no choice* but to violate these rules, the question of how to evaluate fair play became much thornier.

By the time he completed *The General Theory*, Keynes had resolved the matter by simply rejecting international trade commitments as a meaningful priority. Demand management through public works, tax policy, and "socialisation of investment" would hopefully make obvious attempts at beggar-thy-neighbor policies including tariffs and currency manipulation obsolete. Boosting domestic demand would increase imports, helping other countries that depended on exports. If every government was permitted to care for its own needs, a robust system of international rules might be unnecessary. He had embraced economic nationalism as a tool for fighting economic predation.

But there were limits to that strategy, particularly for weak countries. And at the end of the war, almost every country except the United States was weak. Keynes foresaw "a financial Dunkirk" in which Great Britain would simply be unable to afford the necessary tasks ahead of it: rebuilding industry, securing the well-being of a population battered by war, and making good on the debts it had incurred in the conflict (never mind the costs of maintaining its empire).[34] Sometimes, he believed, even with robust government spending and low interest rates, protectionist measures could be necessary to give weak nations some economic breathing room. But who would determine whether such measures were fair, and how?

Keynes started by revisiting an idea from *A Treatise on Money*. That book had been an attempt to use central banks to solve all of the economic problems of the day. Central bankers conventionally tasked themselves with moving interest rates up and down to preserve their gold stocks and balance trade flows. Keynes had argued they should instead manage interest rates to guarantee full employment. To help manage the odd fluctuations in international trade that such domestic management would create, Keynes called for a new "Supernational Bank" to regulate the global money supply, currency, and trade flows.

This international central bank would issue "Supernational Bank–money" to ordinary national central banks all over the world. The Federal Reserve, the Bank of England, and their various counterparts would borrow SBM from the Supernational Bank as a matter of course as they conducted their ordinary monetary policy operations. By managing that new international currency, the Supernational Bank could allow individual nations to grapple with domestic problems without resorting to deflation. Countries would never have to worry about running out of money in an emergency, because the Supernational Bank would always be there to provide it on reasonable terms. As a result, no government would have to intentionally create unemployment to resolve a currency or trade problem.[35]

During the war, Keynes expanded this sketch—it had taken up only about three pages of the nearly seven-hundred-page *Treatise*—into an official British government proposal for what he now called an International Clearing Union.

The gold standard, he maintained, had broken down because it forced countries into deflationary corners. Countries that ran trade deficits became entirely responsible for restoring trade balance, Keynes believed, and they would eventually be placed in a position where they could only achieve competitive prices for their goods abroad by forcing down domestic wages, causing mass domestic unemployment. If Britain, for instance, ran a trade deficit with the United States by importing more than it exported, it would result in a balance-of-payments problem: Britain would be paying out more money to the United States than it was taking in. If the situation persisted long enough, Britain would run out of money with which to pay for American goods.

This problem could in theory be resolved by international lending. If Americans, flush with money earned by exporting so many goods, made loans on reasonable terms to Great Britain, then the British would have the money needed to keep buying exports. During the fifty years before the Great War, Keynes believed, the gold standard had survived precisely because Britain had been a wise and generous creditor country. London had loaned money abroad where it was needed.

But if these loans became unavailable for whatever reason—the disruption caused by war, banking instability, bad monetary policy, a stock market bubble, or a simple disinterest in foreign lending—the only way for a country running a trade deficit to fix its situation would be to force down the price of its goods in foreign markets. And ultimately it would have to resort to deflation and mass unemployment to do so.

Under the ethical norms of the gold standard, the resulting suffering was the price a country had to pay for being weak or lazy. Keynes readily accepted that many countries had ineffective economic infrastructure. But nations often ran trade deficits because they had to, not because they were any more or less reckless than countries running trade surpluses. What's more, governments that ran surpluses weren't in fact being injured by countries that ran deficits. Though the deficit country would run up large financial debts, the surplus country enjoyed a fat export trade that employed its workers and raised its standard of living. The gold standard ethic heaped shame upon countries for piling up large debts, but it was the surplus countries that benefited most from those debts—and benefited at the expense of the debtor country employment. Keynes recognized that in the international order, as in ordinary life, the real villains were rarely beggars.

The trick to making any trade regime sustainable, he believed, was to make countries running surpluses—the major international creditors—participate in the adjustment back to trade balance. The world needed an international authority that could punish countries for running a persistent trade deficit *or* a persistent trade surplus. That would mean, in essence, forcing rich countries to pay to correct their imbalances with poor countries.

Keynes would achieve this through his International Clearing Union. As in the *Treatise,* the central bank of every participating nation would open an account with the ICU. International trade payments would be made through those accounts, using a new international currency called Bancor that the ICU would be empowered to create at will. When a country ran a persistent deficit *or* a persistent surplus, the ICU would require it to revalue its currency to bring the system back toward balance. Countries running deficits would have to depreciate their currency by up to 5 percent, while countries running surpluses would have to raise the value of their currencies by up to 5 percent. The ICU would even seize particularly large surplus balances at the end of each year.

Keynes expected such confiscation to be extremely rare. The central idea was to establish an international commitment to balanced trade and provide some mechanism to enforce that commitment.

It was brilliant. Even Keynes' old adversary Lionel Robbins was intoxicated by the plan. "It would be difficult to exaggerate the electrifying effect on thought throughout the whole relevant apparatus of government," he crowed. "Nothing so imaginative and so ambitious had ever been discussed."[36] But there was a reason why both Keynes and his old nemesis liked the plan: In 1944, Great Britain was in the weakest economic position it had faced in centuries, its empire on the verge of collapse and its domestic economy dependent on foreign aid. The Keynesian plan not only created international regulators to check the power of rich nations, it forced rich nations to help poor nations solve their economic problems. In the name of free trade and international harmony, Keynes was defending the interests of the collapsing British Empire against the economic might of the American juggernaut.

The Americans wanted nothing to do with the plan. At first, Keynes believed that the resistance from Harry Dexter White and the Roosevelt administration was due to confusions about how the plan would function, and he eventually became convinced that a hostile, conservative Congress was responsible for the U.S. resistance. But in truth the U.S. government simply had no interest in creating an international order that would diminish American power. The Roosevelt administration was clear-eyed about raw-power realpolitik considerations, but

FDR and many of his top diplomats were also influenced by misunderstandings about the causes of the Great Depression and infused with a righteous Wilsonian sense of national destiny.

To FDR, the Great Depression and World War II were predictable consequences of the U.S. retreat from the international scene in the 1920s. Europe was a backwater of medieval rivalry and conflict. America was a land of progress and enlightenment free from ancient jealousies. The United States had recovered quickly from the severe inflation that had followed World War I, while Europe had mired itself in trade disputes, currency mismanagement, and military aggression. That toxic atmosphere eventually drifted across the Atlantic. Many American economists believed that the Federal Reserve had been too easy with monetary policy during the 1920s in an effort to prop up Great Britain. When the Fed finally moved to impose some discipline on the wild speculation in the stock market in 1928, the matter was already out of hand, and the bursting of the bubble had set off the Great Depression, which had been prolonged and exacerbated by Europe's tit-for-tat efforts to prop up domestic industry with tariffs. But in spite of all that, FDR believed, he had cured the Depression with the New Deal—a creative new solution—while Britain, the next strongest economy among the Allies, had resorted to crude tariffs and devaluation, sure signs of weakness and dysfunction. If the United States had played its proper role as leader of the free world instead of leaving Europe to the Europeans, the chaos of the past twenty years would have been avoided.

This story was a gross oversimplification at best, but it was true that more effective U.S. leadership would have prevented a great deal of the trouble. The Roosevelt administration just didn't understand how the United States had slipped up. Neither British backwardness nor cheap money had caused the Depression. Though there was plenty of blame to go around, the lion's share belonged to the Fed's excessively tight monetary policy from 1928 onward. Interest rates had been much too high in 1928 and 1929, and when the Fed at last reduced them after the stock market crash, it had failed to bring them down enough to make up for the rash of bank failures that were destroying the nation's money supply. As Keynes had warned in the 1920s, returning to the gold standard meant turning over the most important economic decisions in Europe to the United States; the Fed, not the Bank of England, became the conductor of the international monetary regime. It had orchestrated a disaster.

American diplomats were wrong about the causes of the Depression, but their beliefs carried tremendous political force. Whatever their other differences, Roosevelt, White, and Morgenthau all agreed that a top priority for the United States in the war was the liquidation of the British Empire and the economic subjugation of Great Britain itself. In this vision of the future, America's chief partner in the economic era to come would be the world's other innovative new superpower: the Soviet Union.[37]

After almost three weeks of negotiations in New Hampshire, Keynes collapsed on his way up the stairs on the evening of July 19. He was down for just fifteen minutes and soon seemed to regain his strength, but word spread like wildfire through the hotel that he had suffered a heart attack. The outward signs of his deterioration had been so severe that when the ubiquitous press corps caught wind of the rumor, German newspapers printed premature obituaries. Keynes tried to make light of the mistake, writing to a friend that he had in fact been feeling "exceptionally well" at the conference, which, as anyone who had actually seen him could attest, was obviously not true. "We were on the edge of a precipice," Robbins wrote in his diary. "I now feel that it is a race between exhaustion of his powers and the termination of the conference."[38]

The great struggles for which Keynes sacrificed so much of his health at Bretton Woods had almost nothing to do with economics and everything to do with diplomatic signaling games. White, the head of the U.S. delegation and the chairman of the conference, had rejected the Keynes plan before anyone had even arrived. Instead, all the nations that joined the Bretton Woods project would agree to make their currencies convertible into dollars at a fixed exchange rate.

The dollar, alone among these currencies, would be convertible into gold. Instead of a central international bank to regulate trade deficits and surpluses, an International Monetary Fund would be established to provide emergency loans in a crisis. In addition, a World Bank would be established to assist with postwar reconstruction. Keynes had imagined an international regulatory apparatus to prevent predatory trade arrangements and financial crises. What he got was the gold standard with a bailout fund.

Keynes and White haggled over details. Exchange rates, for instance, could be allowed to fluctuate by up to 1 percent in either direction. The IMF and the World Bank would be capitalized by new "quotas" assessed against each participating nation. Everyone soon recognized that a bigger quota at the IMF would mean more control over its policies and better access to future aid. A bigger quota at the World Bank, meanwhile, meant immediately flushing money away to other countries. Even if a nation planned to make use of World Bank money to rebuild factories and repair agricultural fields, it wanted to be getting that money from abroad, not laundering its own cash through a new international mechanism.

Keynes convinced himself that the final arrangement was acceptable because the United States would pay more than any other country. An essential point from his own rejected ideal scheme was for rich countries to pay a big chunk of whatever costs were required to correct international imbalances. The Bretton Woods pact, he reasoned, could at least provide some check to American power by making the United States put up substantial funding for the new order. Ultimately the United States agreed to pay $2.75 billion into the IMF—32.5 percent of its start-up finance—while Great Britain paid $1.3 billion, China $550 million, and France $450 million. Diplomats agreed to identical quotas for the World Bank.

White spent much of the conference trying to secure the cooperation of the USSR. He had initially proposed an $800 million quota for the Russians—an amount that far exceeded its share relative to the size of its overall economy—and the chief Soviet diplomat, Mikhail Stepanov, in time pushed that figure up to $1.2 billion, hoping for greater influence over the new institutions. But White's mission to forge a new future with Russia failed. The USSR never ratified the Bretton Woods agreement. The United States got what it wanted from Great Britain, but the Roosevelt administration's vision of a postwar alliance with the Soviet Union had already come to an end. For the Russian officials, Bretton Woods seemed to involve ceding too much economic independence to America.

There wasn't much Keynes could do about any of it. Britain was broke and entirely dependent upon the United States for its continued survival. The war was not over, and when it was, the United Kingdom would still need U.S. money for food and reconstruction. Just over a year after Bretton Woods broke up, Harry Truman abruptly suspended the Lend-Lease program before Japan had even surrendered. Truman came to regret the decision and later said he had been tricked by Lend-Lease administrator Leo Crowley, who had insisted that Roosevelt had planned to cut Britain off the moment the war in Europe ended.[39] Crowley hadn't told the truth, but the lie reflected a genuinely callous attitude toward Britain that permeated much of the administration.

The new British prime minister, Labour leader Clement Attlee, dispatched Keynes to Washington to salvage what he could of the situation. It was an extraordinary request made out of sheer financial desperation. In March, Keynes had written to a friend in France that "my heart is very deficient in strength . . . and I cannot walk."[40] In time he was again on his feet, but the talks in Washington caused him painful heart flutters, and he was forced to lie down for extended periods just to get through each day.[41] He retained his congenital optimism to the end, however, and believed that once the Americans understood the truly dire state of Britain's accounts, they would offer up a multibillion-dollar gift that could go toward reconstruction, which would not need to be repaid. It was a delusional attitude after Bretton Woods, but Truman's cancellation of Lend-Lease was such an extreme, abrupt decision, it was easy to chalk up to confusion. Which of course it was. The Americans had overestimated Britain's financial vigor.

After Keynes' entreaties, the United States extended Britain a $3.75 billion loan at an interest rate of 2 percent—shockingly low for international finance but a bitter disappointment to Keynes, who had hoped for an outright donation rather than a loan. For him, the negotiations were about more than money. His lifelong intellectual project had always been supported by American political will. Together, he believed, Britain and America had cured the Great Depression and defeated Adolf Hitler. It was at last evident to him that the United States had no intention of following through on the plan FDR had disclosed to him in 1941 for the two nations to "police" a disarmed Europe together. The partnership was over and with it Britain's time as a great power.

Keynes had guided his country through no fewer than three of the greatest calamities it had ever experienced. He had become disillusioned with the way his country managed its empire, but he had never stopped working toward the ideal of Great Britain that he had treasured as a young man: a strong nation leading the world to truth, liberty, and prosperity. He had done his part in saving his people from destruction. But he could not restore their glory.

He could, however, help lead them to the good life. In 1941, the British minister of labour, Ernest Bevin, set the economist William Beveridge to work on a plan to reform Great Britain's patchwork social safety net. Bevin envisioned a narrow project of simplification and consolidation, but Beveridge embarked instead on a wildly ambitious overhaul of British government into a "cradle-to-grave" welfare state. The Treasury quickly distanced itself from the project, insisting that Beveridge alone be responsible for the final product, which would be published under his own name, rather than the official stamp of any government committee.

That would eventually prove a boon to Beveridge and his personal legacy. But in March 1942, he was out on a very lonely limb. He turned to Keynes for help and found, to his surprise, an eager ally. Keynes told Beveridge that he had "wild enthusiasm" for his "vast constructive reform of real importance." Whereas Chancellor of the Exchequer Sir Kingsley Wood had already been alienated by the cost of the plan, Keynes was "relieved to find it is so financially possible."[42]

Keynes became Beveridge's champion within the Treasury, forming a committee to workshop the proposals into something that could pass both economic muster and Parliament. He recruited Sir Richard Hopkins, second in command to Wood at the Treasury, as a member of the team, ensuring that whatever final plan Beveridge produced would carry the prestige of officialdom. Keynes focused on reducing up-front costs to limit sticker shock—curbing some benefits and phasing in others over time. The result, published in December 1942, was, in Keynes' words, a "grand document"[43] charting a new course for the future of British life. Beveridge proposed a National Health Service to provide direct government health care to every British subject, a national pension system for the elderly, widows, and the disabled, a new system of unemployment insurance to replace the dole, and a weekly allowance paid to families with more than one child.

It was the most ambitious social program ever proposed in Europe—one so transformative it would lead Hayek to conclude that Great Britain had abandoned the Enlightenment liberalism of its prewar history for unmitigated socialism. And indeed it was the resurgent Labour Party that would implement the Beveridge Plan after its electoral triumph in 1945. But even had the Tories held on to power after the war, the package Beveridge devised with Keynes might still have found its way into law. British subjects took the declarations of FDR's Four Freedoms speech and the Roosevelt-Churchill Atlantic Charter more seriously than the American public did, and the daily bombardment of the country by Nazi warplanes had instilled in them a tremendous demand for peace and security. And although National Insurance, as the program came to be known, has been reviled by Hayek's disciples—among them Prime Minister Margaret Thatcher—its opponents have never been able to dismantle it, even under decades of conservative government. To this day the NHS remains a source of national pride, while the pension paid to retirees is the most ferociously defended terrain in British politics.

These were great achievements—the fulfillment of the ideas Keynes had first sketched in *The End of Laissez-Faire* two decades prior. In the twilight of his life, Keynes was designing a new structural landscape for modern democracies, mobilizing the resources and energy of the community in the national interest. But the democratic cause closest to his heart was not health care but art. Even as he had insisted to Americans during the First World War that the British Treasury was stretched to its utmost limit, he had found a few thousand pounds to splurge at the French sale of Degas' collection of paintings. He repeated the maneuver on a much larger scale at the close of World War II. While Keynes directed the full force of his moral outrage at the Americans for their stinginess with Britain in the fall of 1945, his own government was, at his encouragement, expanding the scope of the Council for the Encouragement of Music and the Arts. Keynes had helped establish the new body in 1940, placing it directly under the purview of the Treasury, which enabled him to influence its budget. True to form, Keynes had operated CEMA as both a public works agency and a performing arts philanthropy as its first chairman, embarking on plans to remodel large buildings as public performance halls. The public had endured years of sacrifice for the war effort, and Keynes believed it needed reminders of what it was fighting to preserve. But the project did much more than help citizens keep the faith.

"We soon found that we were providing what had never existed even in peace time," he told BBC listeners in the summer of 1945. "Our wartime experience has led us already to one clear discovery: the unsatisfied demand and the enormous public for serious and fine entertainment. This certainly did not exist a few years ago." BBC broadcasts brought symphonies and opera into millions of homes and "trained" the ears of working-class radio listeners, "bringing to everybody in the country the possibility of learning these new games which only the few used to play," establishing "new tastes and habits . . . enlarging the desires of the listener and his capacity for enjoyment." Productions that had once served as exclusive markers of upper-class status were becoming part of the national character. Nothing could have more surprised the Keynes of 1925, who had disparaged working people as aesthetically hopeless rubes and exalted the "quality" of the bourgeoisie. And nothing brought greater satisfaction to the Keynes of 1945. "Half the world is being taught to approach with a livelier appetite the living performer and the work of the artist," he gushed.[44] The world was closer to the utopia of "Economic Possibilities for Our Grandchildren" than he had dreamed in 1930.

His artistic ideas tracked his development as a political thinker. The people were no longer simply a dangerous variable that must be controlled to prevent militarist outrages; they were also pillars of civilizational greatness. If the common man could teach himself to appreciate a symphony, so, too, could he be taught to wield power responsibly. Democracy created a virtuous cycle in which wise economic management enabled artistic flowerings, which encouraged a generosity of spirit and further bound the political community together in the cause of shared prosperity.

With the war over, Keynes hoped to expand the democratization of fine living by transforming the CEMA into the Arts Council of Great Britain (Keynes intentionally selected "unpronounceable" initials that could not be bureaucratized into "a false, invented word"[45]) with its own budget accountable to Parliament. He planned for Scottish theaters in Glasgow, Welsh performing arts centers, and local opera houses throughout the country, featuring local playwrights, actors, dancers, and musicians wherever possible. "Nothing can be more damaging than the excessive prestige of metropolitan standards and fashions," he enthused. "Let every part of Merry England be merry in its own way. Death to Hollywood."

But Keynes still intended to transform bombed-out London into "a great artistic metropolis, a place to visit and to wonder at." The crown jewel of this dazzling new capital would be the Royal Opera House at Covent Garden, which had been stripped of its Gilded Age splendor during the war to serve as a dance hall when it was not being used for other mundane utilitarian functions.[46]

Even with its new budget, remodeling Covent Garden under the constraints of the war economy was fraught with difficulty. Acquiring fabric for lampshades, for example, was especially vexing. When funds had finally been exhausted, the usherettes hired by the Arts Council to staff the venue donated their war rationing coupons for clothing, which enabled Keynes to secure the final bolts of material, a sacrifice that moved him to tears in conversation with his family.

For the inaugural gala on February 20, 1946, Keynes hired Ninette de Valois and her company to perform Tchaikovsky's lavish *Sleeping Beauty,* the very same ballet to which an entranced Keynes had been drawn night after night to admire Lydia Lopokova in the first days of their romance. In one of the greatest honors of Keynes' life, King George VI and Queen consort Elizabeth Bowes-Lyon named him to escort them to the newly restored royal opera box and take in the pageantry. He had at last fused the once contradictory passions of his life: Bloomsbury and public affairs.

But his health was again giving way. Gripped by severe chest pains on the evening of the gala, Keynes deputized Lydia to attend the monarchs in his stead. By intermission he felt strong enough to join the king and queen for the remainder of the performance. The ballet had always stirred something within him, and the rendition by the Valois company stayed with him. When he addressed the Bretton Woods ratification conference in Savannah, Georgia, in March, he offered the assembled diplomats allusions from *Sleeping Beauty,* saying he hoped the good fairies would guide the new IMF and World Bank to practice "the virtues of Universalism, courage and wisdom," just as they had done for the sleeping Princess Aurora in Tchaikovsky's masterpiece. The parallel was lost on the U.S. delegation, whose leader, Frederick Vinson, groused at "being called a fairy."[47]

The Savannah conference was Keynes' final act on behalf of the public. He collapsed on the train back to Washington in the dining car and spent hours in agony, struggling to breathe, as Lydia and Harry Dexter White attended to him helplessly. Lydia was eventually able to pack him away on the *Queen Mary* for the voyage home and took him

to Tilton for the Easter holiday. They enjoyed a final walk through the
countryside down the heights of Firle Beacon that Saturday. He died
on the morning of Easter Sunday, 1946.[48]

No European mind since Newton had impressed himself so profoundly on both the political and intellectual development of the
world. When the *Times* wrote Keynes' obituary, it declared him "the
greatest economist since Adam Smith." But even praise so high as this
sold Keynes short, for Keynes was to Smith as Copernicus was to
Ptolemy—a thinker who replaced one paradigm with another. In his
economic work he fused psychology, history, political theory, and observed financial experience like no economist before or since. Few
lives have ever been lived to the same vibrant, eclectic excess as Keynes
lived his. He was a philosopher who rivaled Wittgenstein, a diplomat
who became the financial hero of two world wars, a historian who
uncovered peculiarities of great Enlightenment figures and ancient
currencies, a journalist who enraged and inspired the public, the patron of a famed artistic movement. He was as vain, petty, shortsighted,
and impolitic as he was generous, kindhearted, and persuasive. Few
who encountered him in his element came away from the experience
unchanged. Even his ideological adversaries left poignant remembrances of him, few more affecting than the notes left by Lionel Robbins in his diary from the Bretton Woods voyage:

> In the late afternoon we had a joint session with the Americans, at
> which Keynes expounded our views on the Bank. This went very
> well indeed. Keynes was in his most lucid and persuasive mood;
> and the effect was irresistible. At such moments, I often find my-
> self thinking that Keynes must be one of the most remarkable
> men that have ever lived—the quick logic, the birdlike swoop of
> intuition, the vivid fancy, the wide vision, above all the incompa-
> rable sense of the fitness of words, all combine to make something
> several degrees beyond the limit of ordinary human achievement.
> Certainly, in our own age, only the Prime Minister is of compa-

rable stature. He, of course, surpasses him. But the greatness of the Prime Minister is something much easier to understand than the genius of Keynes. For, in the last analysis, the special qualities of the Prime Minister are the traditional qualities of our race raised to the scale of grandeur. Whereas the special qualities of Keynes are something outside all that. He uses the classical style of our life and language, it is true, but it is shot through with something which is not traditional, a unique unearthly quality of which one can only say that it is pure genius. The Americans sat entranced as the God-like visitor sang and the golden light played around.[49]

THIRTEEN

◇

THE ARISTOCRACY STRIKES BACK

I N 1948, HOWARD BOWEN, dean of the University of Illinois College of Commerce and Business Administration, asked John Kenneth Galbraith if he would be interested in chairing the burgeoning economics department at his school. Galbraith was intrigued. He had taught at both Harvard and Princeton when between Roosevelt administration jobs, but he'd never landed a tenured position, much less a job heading an entire department. At age forty, he was still considered a young man in academia, and although UI didn't carry Ivy League prestige, Galbraith often found the aristocratic culture on elite campuses stifling. He agreed to fly out to Champaign-Urbana for an interview, carefully warning Bowen that his family wasn't quite sold on the idea of settling down in a small midwestern town: "It is conceivable that my wife believes the United States ends at the Alleghenies."[1]

Bowen liked New Dealers, and he liked Galbraith. He had served in FDR's Commerce Department during the war and performed a stint on Capitol Hill as the chief economist for the Joint Congressional Committee on Internal Revenue Taxation.[2] Like Galbraith, Bowen was a top beneficiary of the new hierarchy of Washington expertise established by the Roosevelt administration. When FDR brought Keynesian economists to the nation's capital to replace the Wall Street grandees who had dominated economic policy making in the 1920s, an entire generation of inexperienced young men were transformed into professionals armed with impressive government credentials. Now Bowen was bringing many of them back into the academic fold. The twenty appointments he had overseen at the economics department in his short tenure at Illinois included a host of Keynesians who were quickly building reputations for themselves as important scholars, most prominent among them Franco Modigliani, a future Nobel laureate.[3]

For Keynesian economists, the late 1940s and 1950s weren't just an opportunity to flex their credentials; the era seemed to vindicate their entire school of thought, as the federal government deployed the ideas of *The General Theory of Employment, Interest and Money* to manage the booms and busts of the business cycle. World War I had ended with a sharp, devastating recession, but Keynesian policy maneuvering after World War II ensured that the war boom never really ended. Soldiers who returned home from Europe and the Pacific with money in their pockets spent it on everything from new cars to new houses and all of the ingenious home appliances that had been banned during the war to make way for military production. Corporate profits surged and tax rates went down. Unemployment generally fluctuated between 2.5 and 6 percent, as first Truman and then Dwight D. Eisenhower began using Keynesian demand management to heal or head off economic downturns. It was a massive and permanent change in the scale and responsibility of the American government. During the Eisenhower years, government spending averaged over 17.5 percent of the total U.S. economy—far more than even FDR's peacetime budgets, which had peaked at 11.7 percent on the eve of World War II.[4] From 1947 to 1974, the annual unemployment rate peaked at 6.8 percent, while the monthly rate never eclipsed 8 percent—figures that those old enough to remember the Depression would have celebrated as astounding prosperity.[5]

The postwar boom also radically transformed American higher education. The 1944 GI Bill had changed the meaning of a college degree by providing unprecedented federal tuition support for World War II veterans. More than 7.8 million Americans eventually took advantage of the GI Bill's higher education benefits.[6] University classrooms that had once been small outposts of intergenerational family privilege were flooded with a wave of students seeking a foothold in the burgeoning American middle class. After decades of depression, state government budgets were suddenly flush, as the booming postwar economy raised incomes and returning soldiers bought houses and paid property taxes. There had never been so many students to teach or so much money to pay professors.

Keynes and FDR were gone, but it seemed their disciples were about to inherit a new era of personal influence and national prosperity. But when Galbraith arrived at Illinois, he instead found himself in the middle of a statewide political firestorm.

The controversy centered around Ralph Blodgett, an archconservative who had been warning his fellow economists since at least 1946 that "innocent-sounding things" such as "full employment," "a system of social security," and "higher minimum wages" would lead to the "destruction" of the U.S. economic system.[7] Bowen had little patience for Blodgett's ideas and was steadily demoting him. He stripped him of some undergraduate teaching duties and added insult to injury by replacing a Blodgett-authored textbook in the introductory curriculum with the new textbook by Paul Samuelson. When the University of Florida offered Blodgett a $500 raise to move south, Bowen decided to let him go.

What followed was chaos, according to the economic historians Winton Solberg and Robert Tomlinson. Conservative faculty went to the press, and the Champaign-Urbana *News Gazette* started bashing Bowen as a man planning a "heavy infiltration" of "leftist and ultra liberal" New Dealers opposed to "good American principles,"[8] while a university economist gave a speech accusing Bowen of trying to "pack" the faculty with radicals. An internal university committee cleared Bowen of subversive intent, but not before newspapers in Chicago and the Twin Cities started picking up on the story. University president George D. Stoddard was shocked by a *Chicago Daily News* headline blaring "Stoddard Denies Reds in Control," and both the *Champaign-Urbana Courier* and *The News-Gazette* started calling for Bowen's head. Before leaving town, an embittered Blodgett gave a farewell address declaring that although there were no "reds" currently on staff in the economics department, there were "a few pale pinkos . . . and great reds from little pinkos grow."⁹

Blodgett settled in at Florida, which he found ideologically hospitable and, much to his relief, "without the chosen people"—Jews— whom Bowen had been bringing on at Illinois. But even with Blodgett comfortably out of the picture, the controversy continued to escalate. The Illinois Republican Party made it a top political priority to secure positions for hard-line conservatives on the university board of trustees. State representative Reed Cutler decided that Blodgett had been too charitable in his assessment of the faculty: "They've got some professors over there that are so pink you can't tell them from reds." Another state legislator, Ora D. Dillavou, went further, declaring that there were about fifty "Reds, pinks and socialists" on staff. When the university president asked him for names, Dillavou responded that the "University is being used to indoctrinate youth with radical political philosophies. . . . the taxpayers of Illinois do not care to finance the cutting of our own throats."¹⁰

The school soon decided that Bowen had to go. Right or wrong, the situation had become too heated. His position as dean of the business school was allowed to lapse, though he was permitted to continue teaching while he looked for another post. He would go on to serve as president of Grinnell College and then as president of the University of Iowa. Illinois tried to make amends in 1975 by awarding him an honorary doctorate.

But the economics department was decimated. Sixteen professors resigned rather than subject themselves to further harassment. The university, wrote the outraged Modigliani, was "in the grip of a clique of faculty members interested not in scholarship but in personal power, not in the welfare of the University but in the gratification of their vindictive impulses." Yes, the university had at last ended the "strife" in its economics department. "But let us be clear about it, it is the peace of death."[11]

Galbraith did not get the job.

What came to be called McCarthyism was much more than the excesses of a single senator. It was a political movement that fused conspiracy theorists with the American corporate elite and neoliberal intellectuals, uniting conservative Democrats with aristocratic Republicans, fomenting abuses beyond government agencies and Hollywood blacklists, staining the fabric of American life. Academia became a central battleground, as McCarthyist crusaders sought to discredit New Deal intellectuals. The purge did more than damage careers; it profoundly shaped the development of Keynesian economics, as Keynesians were either forced out of work or pressured to disguise their ideas in conservative clothing to avoid drawing the fury of the new right-wing zeitgeist.

Few men personified the social intersections of McCarthyism like Merwin K. Hart. A successful corporate lawyer, Hart had been a member of FDR's graduating class at Harvard and served a brief stint in the New York State Legislature before devoting his efforts to an organization called the National Economic Council. Neither a government body nor an association of economists, the NEC distributed pamphlets decrying excessive government spending and sounded the alarm against immigrants and Jews—"issues" that often overlapped during the refugee crisis surrounding the Holocaust.[12] In 1946, he told his supporters "there is reason to suspect" that as many as "three million" immigrants had entered the country "illegally" in the prior decade, causing a "housing shortage."[13] He was a Holocaust denier who attributed the "enormous influx of Jewish refugees" to an international conspiracy backed by "huge sums of money" aimed at upending the American way of life. "It cannot be overlooked that a large number of the Communists in the United States are Jews."[14]

Hart wasn't an oddball from the freak fringe of American politics;

he had close ties with several business leaders involved in the National Association of Manufacturers, by far the most influential corporate lobbying outfit in Washington, and his NEC relied on contributions from wealthy patrons, securing funding from the du Ponts, Standard Oil, Gulf Oil, Armco Steel, Bethlehem Steel, and "very large" donations from Harold Luhnow's William Volker Fund, a key institution in the development of neoliberal economic theory.[15] In 1945, Hart hired Rose Wilder Lane, a popular fiction writer who reached hundreds of thousands of homes through serializations in *The Saturday Evening Post* and helped her mother, Laura Ingalls Wilder, write the *Little House on the Prairie* novels. Lane wrote book reviews for Hart and gave the organization a friendly, respectable public face, though her politics were every bit as right-wing as those of her boss. "The superstition that all men have a right to vote is a triumph of Old World reasoning," she wrote in 1943, arguing that "extensions of the franchise are dangerous to individual liberty." "Democracy," she claimed, "always creates an irresponsible tyrant."[16]

In 1947, Hart and Lane began to focus their attentions on a shocking new textbook by Lorie Tarshis, the economist who had studied with Keynes at Cambridge and helped bring Keynesian ideas to the United States when he arrived at Tufts University in 1936 along with his friends Robert Bryce and Paul Sweezy. After working on Allied bombing campaigns in Africa and Italy during the war, Tarshis decided to try his hand at textbook writing. By 1947, Keynesian ideas were thoroughly mainstream in academia, but professors didn't have anything to offer students but the convoluted, plodding *General Theory*. And thanks to the GI Bill, the demand for textbooks at American universities had never been stronger. When the book came out, professors at Brown, Middlebury College, Yale, and other universities eagerly picked it up. *Elements of Economics* went through about ten thousand copies in just a few months—the beginnings of an academic publishing hit. Tarshis had solved a very real teaching problem. As he recalled years later, "I thought, 'Boy, that bank account will be picking up.'"[17]

Hart and Lane were not impressed. "*The Elements of Economics* plays upon fear, shame, pity, greed, idealism, and hope to urge young Amer-

icans to act upon this theory as *citizens,*" Lane wrote to NEC subscribers. "This is not an economics text at all; it is a pagan-religious
and political tract." Calling the book "effective propaganda for the
Keynesian theory," Lane insisted that Keynesian economics had "ancient, pre-Christian theological origins" and shared an "explanation of
depressions" with Marx. "In modern economics, it represents Karl
Marx's theory of 'the inherent contradictions of capitalism.'"[18] At a
moment when most Americans had still never heard of John Maynard
Keynes, Lane and Hart fomented the idea that Tarshis and his brand
of economics were part of a dangerous subversive plot intended to
pervert the minds of impressionable students, transforming clean-cut
young men into ferocious revolutionaries.

Hart and Lane didn't just give Tarshis a bad review; they launched
letter-writing campaigns to universities urging administrators to drop
the textbook. The form letter they sent to university trustees carried
the obvious influence of Hayek's *The Road to Serfdom:* "Our country
grew great through freedom. Private enterprise—in which the individual is encouraged to produce for appropriate rewards—is freedom
in action. Such men as Tarshis are drilling at its foundations. . . . Is it
ethical tolerance, or something else, to *encourage and promote* an ideology that could destroy us? Do we want the United States to drift into
a Socialism like that of Britain,—which many of us feel is only a tran-
sitory stop on the road to State Absolutism such as that of Russia?"[19]

Hart's project was an innovative tactic in American political organization. School trustees were astonished to receive thousands of letters from concerned citizens denouncing their use of a specific
textbook. Local newspapers even picked up on the sudden controversy, and universities scrambled to respond.

Hart's campaign was an expensive, sophisticated operation that lev-
eraged his connections with some of the most prominent businessmen
in the country. Some of his donors wrote to ask for copies of the review to distribute independently. Hart and Lane worked with Leonard Read, whose Foundation for Economic Education had just
published a pamphlet by Milton Friedman inveighing against housing

rent control,[20] to set local newspaper editors against the book. Lane believed "these little towns of 100 or so population are more important than the cities,"[21] as they offered more newspapers to cultivate press clippings that could be used to document anti-Tarshis energy. Those small-town papers would have not only sympathetic editors but significant influence with their readers, who often wouldn't have access to four or five different news outlets. The NEC targeted 178 newspaper editors in Oregon alone.

The press push worked. R. C. Hoiles, publisher of the *Santa Ana Register*, wrote to Hart saying the Tarshis book "seems to us to be some sort of second edition of Karl Marx's book 'Capital.'"[22] The *Chicago Tribune* published a story in September 1947 with the ominous headline "Red Taint of Text Weighed by Coast Guard," relying on Associated Press reports from Connecticut and Washington, DC, indicating that Tarshis was being used as an economics text in the Coast Guard Academy. And the NEC's connections with big business brought influential names into the battle. Southern California Edison executive W. C. Mullendore and Phillips Gas and Oil president Thomas W. Phillips, Jr., a former Republican congressman, both leaned on the Coast Guard,[23] which promptly dropped the book.

Meanwhile, Frank Gannett of Gannett newspapers and B. F. Goodrich president John Collyer wrote to Hart saying they were trying to get the book removed from Cornell University.[24] A. F. Davis, a vice president of the Lincoln Electric Company in Cleveland, convinced his Republican congressman Clarence Brown to request that the House Committee on Un-American Activities launch an investigation into Tarshis. Davis then obtained from the NEC the names of every trustee at every university that had adopted the book and prepared to turn them over to the House Committee on Un-American Activities.[25] R. E. Woodruff of the Erie Railroad Company and Sunoco Oil president J. Howard Pew—soon to found the Pew Charitable Trusts—intervened directly with former president Herbert Hoover, trying to get the book removed from Stanford, where Hoover had donated his personal papers. Pew also pressured the trustees at

Drexel Institute of Technology, Duke, and Cornell, and brought the matter up with Ohio senator Robert Taft. "I am sure that out of this will come some fireworks," Pew reported to Hart.[26]

This flurry of elite political pressure was invisible to Tarshis. And he couldn't imagine that anyone at a university would seriously consider the NEC's accusation that his textbook was a subtle Soviet indoctrination manual. He decided not to answer the attacks. But colleges that were already having trouble keeping up with the administrative challenges of rapid expansion didn't know what to do with thousands of angry letters sent over a textbook. The campaign against Tarshis started to get results. "Before the summer was over, sales had fallen just as sharply as they had risen," he recalled.[27] Some university trustees were themselves wealthy businessmen alarmed by Keynesian ideas and sympathetic to Hart's nativism. Others just wanted to avoid controversy over something as silly as an introductory economics textbook. One by one, schools dropped Tarshis' book from their curriculum. Within a year, his publisher, Houghton Mifflin, gave up on the project. The first American textbook on Keynesian economics had been destroyed. And the American university had been established as a central battleground for conservative activism—a status it maintains today in culture wars over free speech and political correctness.

Paul Samuelson's textbook slipped in to fill the teaching void left by the Tarshis text. Samuelson had written his book "carefully and lawyer-like"[28] amid the attacks, hoping to fend off criticism, and both he and his publisher responded forcefully to attacks by McCarthyists, giving university administrators arguments to cite when defending their choice of the book. As a result, *Economics: An Introductory Analysis* emerged as one of the great academic publishing successes of the twentieth century. Over Samuelson's life, his textbook went through nineteen editions and sold millions of copies.

This early monopoly Samuelson enjoyed in the market for Keynesian textbooks had profound implications for the way Keynesian ideas came to be understood by the general public. The standard collegiate presentation of basic economics for more than half a century has been Samuelson's—either directly from his text, or from a handful of copycats that adopted his conceptual framework. As Samuelson later crowed: "I don't care who writes a nation's laws—or crafts its advanced treaties—if I can write its economics textbooks." [29]

And Samuelson's break with Tarshis was profound. In Tarshis' presentation, markets—particularly the markets for money and debt—were creatures of the state, an expression of democratic politics that citizens could manage and adjust. Samuelson, by contrast, attempted to harmonize the classical economic worldview with Keynesian policy making. For Samuelson, Keynes enabled classical ideas to work by bringing the economy to full employment—the "special case" in which markets were self-correcting and supply created its own demand. Where Tarshis had presented a warning about the limits of the market in a democracy, Samuelson revived the power of the market to order social preferences, with the help of just a little fiscal adjustment. The widespread acceptance of Samuelson's ideas—particularly his views about inflation—would have far-reaching implications for the development of Keynesian policy making in the 1960s.

But in the 1940s, Keynesian academics had been put on notice: There was an effective, organized conservative movement afoot that was willing and able to destroy careers. Whether an economist sank or swam in the postwar waters could depend entirely on his ability to avoid attacks from professional conspiracy theorists.

The attacks didn't stop. In 1951, a young protégé of Hart named William F. Buckley, Jr., brought the crusade against Keynesian economics to a broad national audience with his first book, *God and Man at Yale*. The NEC was elated, throwing a dinner in Buckley's honor in December 1951 and promoting the book for sale to everyone on its impressive mailing list, an effort that Henry Regnery, Buckley's publisher, was "sure" would "help materially"[30] with the book's sales.

God and Man at Yale is the story of a conservative Catholic's rude awakening to a world of ideas that conflicted with the rigid doctrines of his youth. Buckley was shocked by the Protestantism that circulated around campus and denounced the religious leaders at the school as promoters of "atheism" and "collectivism," which university administrators mysteriously tolerated in the name of "academic freedom."

"The institution that derives its moral and financial support from Christian individualists," he wrote in his preface, "addresses itself to the task of persuading the sons of these supporters to be atheistic socialists."[31]

The socialism Buckley discovered was Keynesian economics. In his book, he expanded Hart's campaign against Keynesian textbooks to include three new volumes—including the Samuelson edition—and continued the now-unnecessary assault on Tarshis, quoting directly from Lane's review in his attack. Buckley stitched together quotes using fragments of sentences separated by dozens of pages, enabling him to manufacture preposterous ideas and arguments and credit them to Tarshis and Samuelson in their own voices. The Keynesians, Buckley suggested, were part of a Communist plot afoot at Yale and universities across the country to quietly transition a sleepwalking America into Stalinist totalitarianism. If even an institution as resolutely conservative as Yale had been infected, what could be occurring at other schools? "It is a revolution . . . that advocates a slow but relentless transfer of power from the individual to the state, that has roots in the Department of Economics at Yale, and unquestionably in similar departments in many colleges throughout the country."[32]

Tarshis never forgave Buckley for the smear. "That bastard Buckley—I get so angry when I think of him," he raged more than thirty years later. "He's *still* parading his objectivity and concern for 'moral values,' and so on. The amount of distortion is enormous."[33]

God and Man at Yale made quite a splash, drawing reviews in *The Atlantic* and *The New York Times* and establishing its publisher Henry Regnery as a major force in conservative letters. Hart was thrilled to see his influence spread so widely. He tried unsuccessfully to get Buckley a speaking slot at the National Association of Manufacturers' annual conference and maintained a warm relationship with the young provocateur, agreeing to distribute his 1954 book, a defense of Senator Joe McCarthy called *McCarthy and His Enemies*.[34] Buckley wrote Hart to tell him "how terribly gratifying" his support was.

Conservative donors were enticed as well, helping Buckley found

National Review, which became the leading American outlet for conservative commentary and criticism. In its early years, the magazine fit neatly with Hart's newsletter, as Buckley advocated biological racism and segregation, insisting that black America was genetically incapable of democracy. When Robert Welch, Jr., founded the John Birch Society in 1958, Buckley was initially supportive of the outfit. Welch had donated $1,000 (about $9,000 today) to *National Review,* and Buckley offered to give the new organization a "little publicity."[35] But when Welch began arguing that Republican president Dwight D. Eisenhower was a Communist agent, Buckley reluctantly decided to distance himself and his publication; the Birchers were giving the entire conservative cause a bad name. Before Buckley could begin his denunciation, his old friend Hart caught wind of the pending attack and wrote to him to insist that a purge of the Birchers would be "wholly unwarranted" and bad for the conservative cause. "I have known Bob Welch for years and there is no greater American patriot."[36] Buckley went ahead with the attack, and his assault on the Birchers earned him a reputation as a thoughtful critic willing to call out extremism. But his own swift rise to fame was built on the same elite paranoia. When he died in 1962, Hart was head of the John Birch Society's Manhattan chapter.[37]

Whether he liked it or not, Friedrich August von Hayek was the intellectual godfather of Buckley's counterrevolution. When the obscure academic had penned *The Road to Serfdom* in 1944, he had not expected the book to transform him into a cause célèbre among American businessmen. But dozens of wealthy men on the right were drawn to Hayek, eager to sound trumpets of liberty against the Keynesian din, entranced by Hayek's warning that government intervention in the economy would lead to butchery and ruin. The *Reader's Digest* condensation of *The Road to Serfdom* had elided Hayek's compromises with regulation and the social safety net, and corporations began ordering reprints to distribute on their own. The management of General Motors and New Jersey Power and Light gave copies to their employees for free, and the National Association of Manufacturers had fourteen thousand copies shipped to its members.[38]

But no partnership would prove more instrumental to unwinding the Keynesian social project than Hayek's connection with a midwestern home furnishing magnate named Harold Luhnow.

Luhnow and his uncle William Volker ran William Volker & Company, a retailer of "picture moldings, picture frames, mirrors, cabinet hardware and furniture novelties" in Kansas City during the early twentieth century.[39] As the city's population swelled, so did their fortunes, and by the time the Depression hit, the family had grown rich enough to be more concerned with politics than profits. Volker deployed his wealth against poverty and incarceration, founding the Kansas City Board of Public Welfare, a hybrid public-private institution that together with the local government helped establish a local social safety net. When Volker died in 1947, he entrusted Luhnow to run his $15 million–plus estate as an ambitious philanthropy devoted to poverty relief, education, and everything in between. But when Luhnow encountered *The Road to Serfdom* at age forty-nine, he began dreaming of a world in which the clunky and corrupt apparatuses of government might be replaced by the genius and generosity of the wealthy. Under his direction, the William Volker Fund transformed into an ideological project rooted in "hostility toward Keynesian economics and communism."[40]

Luhnow met Hayek after his speech in Detroit on his tour for *The Road to Serfdom* and eventually helped convince the University of Chicago to bring on Hayek as a professor in its interdisciplinary Committee on Social Thought—a sign of both Hayek's burgeoning influence as a political theorist and the lack of enthusiasm among even the conservative Chicago economics department for his scientific work. Though Hayek was an employee of the university, Luhnow paid his salary and worked out a similar arrangement for Mises at New York University. "Hayek's position in Chicago was very important," notes one scholar, "because he acted as a bridge between various colleagues and significant sources of business finance"—particularly Luhnow, who helped turn "the Chicago School" into a world-famous economic worldview.[41]

Luhnow also helped Hayek found the Mont Pelerin Society—an international consortium of intellectuals inspired by the meeting of the Colloque Walter Lippmann that had gathered in Paris to celebrate the publication of *The Good Society*. In 1948, Hayek helped assemble many of the same luminaries at the Hotel du Parc near Mont Pèlerin in Switzerland. Luhnow agreed to take care of the travel costs for Hayek's University of Chicago friend Milton Friedman and other *Road to Serfdom* proselytizers. The Mont Pelerin Society would quickly become the world's preeminent right-wing intellectual organ, but though its members shared an affinity for nineteenth-century laissez-faire, they were divided about its application to the postwar world. At the society's first meeting, Ludwig von Mises denounced those gathered as "a bunch of socialists" for even discussing progressive taxation as a (potentially) defensible policy.[42]

In *The Road to Serfdom*, Hayek had reached back to Locke, Hume, Smith, and Burke in an effort to wrest the mantle of liberalism away from Keynes. At Mont Pèlerin, many fellow travelers on Hayek's intellectual journey adopted the moniker "neoliberal," seeing themselves not as keepers of an eighteenth-century flame but as the progenitors of an original—if historically inspired—doctrine. Keynes had been right that Smith, like many early liberals, had never adhered rigorously to laissez-faire, and it was not obvious what David Ricardo or John Stuart Mill would think about the problems of the postwar world. As Mises emphasized in an introduction to a 1952 edition of *The Wealth of Nations*, Smith "does not say anything" about "the Communist challenge."[43] Milton Friedman, who would become the most influential neoliberal economist, was troubled by various concessions to state power made by Smith in particular, including his enthusiasm for public works projects and public education.

Similarly, though the Mont Pèlerin thinkers occasionally gestured to Edmund Burke, who had emphasized the importance of political continuity and tradition, they were organizing a political movement

that called for swift, sweeping political change—the overturning of
the New Deal model, which, courtesy of the Beveridge Report, had
become standard in Euro-American politics. Their radicalism became
the intellectual currency of *National Review,* as Buckley, who had
cited both Hayek and Mises in *God and Man at Yale,*[44] now befriended
Mont Pèlerin stalwarts Milton Friedman and Wilhelm Röpke. In *The
Road to Serfdom,* Hayek had expressed an enthusiasm for Western
Christianity unusual amid the decline of British religiosity in the early
twentieth century. Buckley seized upon it, seeing an avenue through
which American churchgoers might form a coalition with enthusiasts
of nineteenth-century economics. Over time, Röpke would fuse the
economic ideas of the early Mont Pèlerin thinkers with a racial fun-
damentalism promoting the superiority of white Westerners. The result was an ideological coalition that would eventually culminate in
the presidency of Ronald Reagan.

Hayek himself was never comfortable with that political assem-
blage. He rejected Friedman's economics as an impure compromise
with Keynesianism. He couldn't stomach Röpke's virulent racism.
And he had a distaste for just about everything about Buckley, refusing to blurb *God and Man at Yale* or lend his name to the *National
Review* masthead. Nevertheless, it was through Hayek that Buckley's
conservative movement was able to envision a link between itself and
the Enlightenment past.

National Review, whose subscription base swelled to over 100,000
by the mid-1960s, was not the only popular outlet for neoliberal ideas.
Between 1943 and 1954, Mises worked for the National Association
of Manufacturers, lending the group intellectual prestige as it pursued
an aggressive—and paranoid—public relations campaign on behalf of
the American corporate elite.[45] When Harry Truman called to raise
the minimum wage, establish a national health care program, and
begin a new federal commitment to civil rights for black America in
his 1948 State of the Union address, NAM's weekly newsletter suggested this cocktail would "ultimately destroy the American business
system." NAM's president gave speeches warning of creeping "totalitarianism," and an "unremitting" "threat to American freedom."[46]

Such warnings about the latent communism of Harry Truman seem absurd in retrospect, but they were typical of the feverish McCarthyist atmosphere. In 1954, NAM even won a Peabody Award, the highest honor in broadcast journalism, for "Industry on Parade," a fifteen-minute television show the group paid TV networks to run in nearly every U.S. market. The Peabody Board concluded that the infomercial served as "a potent weapon for the American way" and offered a "valuable contribution to education, public service, and patriotism."[47]

Luhnow, meanwhile, was providing the war chest for neoliberal economics. He began helping publisher Henry Regnery finance conservative book projects and worked with Hayek on developing a new book that could function as "an American version of *The Road to Serfdom.*" After years of incubation, Luhnow paid for the lectures Friedman eventually published in 1962 as *Capitalism and Freedom*, the book that established him as the leading voice of neoliberal politics before he was widely recognized as a great economist.[48] From the 1940s into the 1960s, Luhnow deployed about $1 million a year on neoliberal intellectual causes and supported the academic research of no fewer than six future Nobel laureates in economics.[49]

Luhnow's financing changed academia. In the early postwar era, the idea of a private individual quietly supporting ideologically tailored research for university scholars wasn't just unusual; it was considered ethically dubious. "Some academics [Luhnow's fund] approached rebuffed it haughtily—I'm not *that* kind of a thinker, sir!" notes Brian Doherty, a chronicler of libertarian history.[50] But over time Luhnow's model has won out. Today, universities are accustomed to corporations and wealthy donors such as Charles and David Koch supporting everything from book research to peer-reviewed studies to basketball programs to the economics department at George Mason University. Support from deep-pocketed special interests is a common—if controversial—supplement to careers in academic economics.

As Luhnow seeded the neoliberal academic project, however, he was also flirting with madness. In February 1962, he convened a meeting in California with Hayek and other leading neoliberals to consider the course of future think-tank investments and disclosed to those assembled that he had developed a unique spiritual command over the world's political leaders. "The power I have may enter even Khrushchev," he revealed. "The step is to tune in on this power and let it work."[51] A month later, Luhnow abruptly shuttered the Volker Fund and put its resources into the Center for American Studies, a new endeavor highlighting the work of a Holocaust denier named David Leslie Hoggan. Luhnow, it turned out, had been financing Hoggan's Hitler-friendly academic research at Harvard since as early as 1957.[52]

Behind all of the outlandish charges of disloyalty and subversion was, as with much of McCarthyism, the shadow of an important truth. A lot of Keynesians were really pretty radical. Paul Sweezy, who taught unofficial seminars on *The General Theory* with Robert Bryce at Harvard in 1935 and 1936, continued to identify as a Marxist throughout his career. So for a time did Lawrence Klein, one of Samuelson's first students at MIT, who became a leading interpreter of *The General Theory* and scholar of the early developments in Keynesian theory. Keynes himself had advocated a "liberal socialism" and helped write the British plan to socialize health care. It had been young Marxists, after all, whom Keynes had chiefly hoped to convert at Cambridge during the 1930s. His economic project had not been a sterile enterprise aimed at ensuring the appropriate equations balanced; it had been an attempt to transform society slowly and peacefully, to avoid the pain and disruption of Marxist revolution.

Plenty of Marxists were in fact convinced. Lytton Strachey's cousin, the Labour politician John Strachey, had written a best-selling Marxist tract in the early 1930s arguing that violent class war was the only solution to capitalist oppression.[53] But by 1956, Strachey, a good friend of Galbraith, believed that everything he had hoped to achieve by taking up arms could now be attained—indeed, could *only* be attained—through Keynesian democratic management of the economy. "Keynesian economic policies, joined with traditional socialist measures of public ownership and social reform, have become indispensable instruments by means of which democracy can effect its purposes," he wrote in another bestseller, *Contemporary Capitalism.* "Unless democratic and socialist political parties comprehend and command these policies they will not succeed in transforming capitalism to serve their purposes."[54] And in Great Britain, at least, Keynesian disciples exercised tremendous power. After leaving the Communist Party for Labour, Strachey served as minister of food and secretary of state for war. As Red hunting kicked into high gear in the United States, however, economists with affinities for both Marx and Keynes began to identify increasingly as Keynesians to preserve their careers. By the 1950s, Sweezy joked, you could count the number of Marxists in academic economics "on the thumbs of your two hands."[55]

And so in an important respect, even the most paranoid McCarthyists were onto something. In 1957, Theodore Roosevelt's youngest son, Archibald, and Zygmund Dobbs published *Keynes at Harvard: Economic Deception as a Political Credo,* which claimed that Keynesianism was "the ideological beachhead from which leftism invaded" Harvard and then the United States, insisting that the moniker "Keynes" was typically used as a shield for a deeper left-wing intent. The point was essentially true, even if much of the book was a fantastical fever dream (in a 1969 reissue, Dobbs claimed that Keynesianism was part of a leftist movement to advance "narcotic addiction, sexual abuse and animalistic perversions.")[56]

The McCarthyist panic was a nationwide cultural phenomenon, but its nexus was in Washington, where it functioned as a simple struggle for power. If the American Right could not discredit Keynesian liberalism by pointing to its economic results, it would attempt to do so by discrediting the moral character of its practitioners. Conservative politicians in both parties shouted attacks on New Dealers in speeches and aired them in public hearings that were amplified by the political press. The lurid coverage in the nation's capital set the tone for the rest of the country and left reputational damage on individual careers long after the McCarthyist wave had been discredited by mainstream American thought. But just as there were genuine radicals in the Keynesian academic milieu, so, too, were there some New

Dealers in Washington who had on occasion done the very things the anti-Communist conspiracy theorists claimed they had—sometimes near the pinnacle of U.S. wartime diplomacy.

On October 30, 1944, John Bricker gave the most blistering American political speech of the year. Bricker was finishing his second term as governor of Ohio and had been added to the Republican presidential ticket as a sop to conservatives frustrated with the party's nomination of Thomas Dewey, a relatively liberal Republican then serving as governor of New York. With the war on, Dewey had exchanged the isolationism that dominated GOP circles after World War I for a foreign policy doctrine that sounded a lot like FDR's, only better and cheaper. Dewey's Republican Party wouldn't withdraw from the world stage; it would beat the Nazis faster than FDR would and bring soldiers home faster after securing a better and more stable peace than FDR could. Ideologically, according to Dewey, Roosevelt was all right. With a few exceptions, he had overseen a polite campaign.

And Republicans were getting crushed. So with only days to go before the election, Bricker tried something different. Speaking to a sold-out crowd of fifteen thousand at Olympia Stadium in Detroit,[57] he assailed FDR's domestic agenda as the corrupt offspring of "foreign influence," claiming that "Franklin Roosevelt and the New Deal are in the hands of the radicals and the Communists." There was an "actual working relationship," he said, among the Roosevelt administration, international communism, and the Congress of Industrial Organizations—the most racially progressive federation of American labor unions—which aimed to annihilate the American way of life. "Today, as never before," he said, "a foreign influence of the most subversive kind is trying to take over our American government by boring from within."[58]

The speech was broadcast on nationwide radio. The next day, seven names were printed in newspapers all across the country as members of "subversive organizations." Bricker had singled out Craig Vincent, Arthur Goldschmidt, Robin Kinkead, Thomas I. Emerson, Gene

Mangion, Gregory Silvermaster, and Lauchlin Currie. There were, he claimed, 1,117 more in the federal bureaucracy.

Most of these personalities have faded from history. But even in 1944, Currie was the only one of Bricker's targets who was anything close to a household name. One of the top economic diplomats of the war, Currie had negotiated with Keynes on Lend-Lease terms, worked to convince Switzerland to break its economic ties with Germany,[59] and served as FDR's personal liaison with Chiang Kai-shek's Kuomintang to keep warring factions in China allied against Imperial Japan. In 1943, the Associated Press had profiled him as one of "Six Mystery Men Behind the President" but could say little about him. "Unobtrusive, sandy-haired . . . Currie toys constantly with an ivory cigaret holder while talking, but he actually smokes few cigarets [sic]."[60]

Bricker's speech galvanized the conservative faithful and caused serious anxiety for Currie. In a December 1944 cable to London, Keynes himself had noted that singling out Currie by name as a "crypto-Communist"—despite being "contrary to the facts" and "without evidence"—had the effect of limiting Currie's negotiation room on Lend-Lease. Anything that might look overly generous to the British would be taken as a sign of disloyalty.[61]

Bricker's attacks didn't stick. He and Dewey lost badly in November, and even as anti-Communist paranoia deepened in Washington, Bricker's speech was considered an ugly outlier—an example of political desperation and undisciplined campaigning.

But four years later, Currie had a real problem. In testimony before the House Un-American Activities Committee in 1948, a former Soviet spy named Elizabeth Bentley shocked the country by naming dozens of U.S. government officials as Soviet collaborators or informants. That list included Currie. Though Bentley openly acknowledged that she had never met Currie and told the panel he "was not a Communist," she claimed he had been a source of information for her spy ring, which had included Gregory Silvermaster, another of the men Bricker had attacked in his Detroit speech. Bentley couldn't remember many specifics, but one charge sounded particularly grave to the audience in July 1948. Under questioning by a California congressman named Richard Nixon, she reported, "Mr. Silvermaster told me that one day Mr. Currie came dashing into Mr. Silverman's house, sort of out of breath, and told him that the Americans were on the verge of breaking the Soviet code."[62]

This was much more serious than Bricker's vague accusations. Bentley was accusing him of espionage, if not treason. And Currie did in fact know a handful of the men she had named as Soviet assets. He met George Silverman and Harry Dexter White when all three were studying at Harvard in the 1920s, and the trio had eventually traveled to Washington to take jobs in the Roosevelt administration. Currie and White rose quickly to positions of influence, while developing reputations for "strong" and "abrasive" personalities.[63] White became a dominant figure in the Roosevelt Treasury Department, eventually serving as lead negotiator for the U.S. delegation at Bretton Woods, where he bulldozed objections and competing proposals from one of his heroes, John Maynard Keynes. Silverman never reached the administrative heights of his friends, but he spent time as a functionary at the Treasury and a handful of other New Deal agencies. Silverman was close to the Russian-born Silvermaster. In Washington, Silvermaster, Silverman, and White had developed a relaxed social routine. They played volleyball and ping-pong together and held evening music sessions with Silvermaster on guitar and White on mandolin.[64]

Silverman and Silvermaster were members of the Communist Party of the United States of America. To most Americans in the 1930s, the CPUSA was hard to distinguish from the byzantine array of left-wing parties—socialists, Trotskyists, and others—that sprang to life as the U.S. economy crumbled. The CPUSA made its mark with aggressive outreach to black farmers, which the party viewed as a nascent proletariat, and strident advocacy for antilynching laws, which FDR had opposed in order to preserve his political coalition with white southern Democrats. Most Americans did not know that the CPUSA was an official arm of the Soviet government.

After arriving in Washington, White began passing privileged government information to Silverman—material that White was authorized to see, but not his midlevel bureaucrat friend. He had good reason to believe that it would be shared with the CPUSA, but he may not have known it was making its way to Russian intelligence. Silverman and Silvermaster, by contrast, not only understood the CPUSA's link to the Stalinist government, they were part of it. Both men worked as Soviet spies throughout their careers in Washington. As the historian Eric Rauchway has detailed, White's realization that he was cooperating not only with American Communists but indirectly with Moscow itself gave him, in the words of one KGB source, "a big scare."[65] For a while after this revelation, White stopped communicating with his Soviet friends altogether. But though his motives remain mysterious, he would intermittently provide federal documents to Silvermaster and Silverman all the way through to Bretton Woods.

The United States and the Soviet Union were, of course, allies during the war, and White was the Treasury's top liaison with the Russian Embassy in Washington. He may have considered himself to be conducting a form of back-channel diplomacy through Silverman and Silvermaster, or his early indiscretions might have been used to blackmail him into making further disclosures later in his career. Soviet intelligence in Moscow seems to have been nonplussed by the material White provided, but there is no question that he knowingly and illegally turned over secret U.S. government information and in doing so put himself in a compromised position with a foreign government as he conducted official diplomacy.

By the time Bentley testified before HUAC, White had a reputation to manage but no career. President Harry Truman had quietly forced him out of office after receiving a detailed secret memo on White's work with Silverman and Silvermaster from FBI Director J. Edgar Hoover (the memo does not mention Currie). But both Currie and White agreed to testify before HUAC to rebut Bentley's allegations. In separate appearances, both firmly denied any wrongdoing.

The HUAC hearings were the end of the drama for White. He died of a heart attack three days after his testimony. For Currie, the situation at least appeared under control. Eleanor Roosevelt, still a major force in American politics and a syndicated columnist, defended his loyalty.[66] Bentley hadn't claimed that he was aware that either Silverman or Silvermaster was a Communist, much less that he knew that they were Soviet spies. And his performance before HUAC was good enough that after several rounds of inquiry, both a Republican and a ferociously anti-Communist southern Democrat were defending his integrity. South Dakota Republican Karl Mundt declared Currie "a man in whose Americanism I believe," while Dixiecrat John Rankin mused, "It just looks to me as if we have gone pretty far afield here to smear this man by remote control." When the Truman administration appointed Currie to a World Bank mission to Colombia in 1949, the storm seemed to have passed.

And then China fell to Mao Zedong's Communists. To McCarthy and Democratic Cold Warriors, including Nevada senator Pat McCarran, the Communist victory was not just a diplomatic setback; it was a piece of deliberate sabotage by Communist agents in the Roosevelt and Truman administrations. New Dealers and Keynesians, with their flexible ideas about government management of the economy, were particularly suspect. Currie made an almost perfect target. During the war, he had been responsible for keeping Mao's Communists and Chiang Kai-shek's Kuomintang Nationalists focused on the fight against Japan, rather than the fight between each other. Like just about every American who had worked with Chiang, Currie had been frustrated by the corruption and incompetence that permeated his operation, which contained a secretive paramilitary wing styled after Benito Mussolini's blackshirts (the Kuomintang faction wore blue shirts). After Mao's victory in the civil war, every critical word Currie had ever uttered against the Kuomintang was turned against him.

"The full outlines of Currie's betrayal have yet to be traced," Senator Joseph McCarthy said in June 1951 on the Senate floor, where his words were protected against slander lawsuits. The Wisconsin demagogue declared that Currie had been secretly working to destroy Chiang since as early as 1942 and that he had personally denied the Kuomintang twenty thousand German rifles in order to help Mao win.[67]

McCarthy's narrative of a Truman administration betrayal on

China was simply wrong, and in any case, Currie had been out of government when war broke out between Mao and Chiang in 1946—and out of it for nearly four years when Mao eventually won. Whether Bentley's charges ultimately amounted to anything depends on the interpretation of an ambiguous set of decrypted Soviet intelligence cables intercepted by the FBI that were released in the 1990s.[68]

But the public had no knowledge of those decrypts in the 1940s and 1950s. What mattered for economists trying to navigate the McCarthy era—and what mattered for the development of Keynesian ideas in the United States—was how easily a thin, in some ways contradictory public case against Currie swiftly came to define his entire career. Bentley's allegations were loose. Testifying before the Senate in 1951, she changed her story about the Soviet code to say that Currie had told White, not Silverman, about the code breaking. Since White, like Currie, was a top-level diplomat, it would not have been unusual or inappropriate for Currie to discuss sensitive information with him. Bentley, moreover, had turned herself over to the FBI in 1945, while the United States hadn't actually cracked the Soviet code until 1946. Whatever else Currie might have said to White or Silvermaster, he could not have actually divulged that the United States was on the verge of cracking the Soviet code, because that simply wasn't true at the time.

Even anti-Communist hard-liners on HUAC hadn't been convinced that Currie was a problem in 1948. McCarthy had targeted him for the same reason Bricker had: Currie was a left-wing intellectual who wielded real power. If someone in Currie's position *had* served as a Soviet spy, that fact would have helped legitimize McCarthy's wider, zanier conspiracy theories. And since Currie had been mentioned, however vaguely, by Bentley and Bricker, McCarthy had a better case to press against him than he did against most of his victims.

Once McCarthy set the ball rolling, the campaign against Currie was relentless. In 1954, Buckley casually denounced Currie as a "Communist" in *McCarthy and His Enemies*.[69] That same year, the State Department refused to renew Currie's passport. Under a policy later ruled unconstitutional, State was empowered to revoke the citizenship of immigrants who later moved out of the country. With Currie spending more and more time in Colombia—first for the World Bank and then as an adviser to the Colombian government—State made him choose between the United States and Colombia. He decided to stay in Colombia, forfeiting his U.S. citizenship. When Colombia's democratic government fell to a military junta, Currie, once the most powerful economist of the New Deal, bought a plot of land in the mountains twenty miles from Bogotá and became a dairy farmer.

It is impossible to overstate the effect of the right-wing campaign against Currie on Keynesian veterans of the Roosevelt administration. Every New Dealer was friends with a Communist or two; that was just part of life on the American Left during the Great Depression. But Currie and White weren't low-level functionaries like the more famous Soviet collaborator Alger Hiss. Currie had recruited some of the best and brightest minds of the Keynesian revolution to Washington. To anti-Communist crusaders, nearly all of those recruits were suspect. The Treasury suspended the economist George Eddy, citing his friendship with Currie and White, saying that it showed a lack of judgment on Eddy's part and was an indication he could not be trusted. Though he was later cleared of wrongdoing and given full back pay, Eddy's reputation was permanently damaged. He didn't return to the economics profession until the 1980s.[70] Other New Deal economist associates of Currie and White—Mordecai Ezekiel, Leon Keyserling, Irving Friedman, and Charles Kindleberger—were all hounded by the FBI, subjected to loyalty investigations, or worse.[71]

To his friends in America, including John Kenneth Galbraith, Currie's treatment seemed a grave injustice. But the alternative—that their benefactor *was* in fact a longtime Soviet collaborator—was even worse. Either way, Currie's downfall was a threat to his friends' careers. They would spend the better part of a decade girding themselves against charges of disloyalty. Success would come at a price.

FOURTEEN

THE AFFLUENT SOCIETY
AND ITS ENEMIES

JOHN MAYNARD KEYNES HAD adored old books. When his health permitted, he and Piero Sraffa would devote their Saturday afternoons to the used-book stores in Cambridge, scouring dusty shelves for obscure pamphlets, collections of letters, or hardbound volumes penned by major and minor figures of the Enlightenment.[1] Their weekend conquests would have been more than enough to earn both men tenured positions as intellectual historians had they not already established themselves as important economic theorists. In 1933, the pair encountered a glowing review of David Hume's *A Treatise on Human Nature*, published as an anonymous pamphlet in 1740, shortly after the arrival of Hume's magnum opus. Philosophical lore had long bestowed a near-mythical status on the review. Hints in Hume's correspondence suggested that its uncredited author was the great Adam Smith. According to legend, Smith had not attached his name to the pamphlet in order to conceal the fact that he was only a seventeen-year-old student at the time. Historians had been unable to get their hands on a copy of the review itself, lending an aura of mystery to the account. *A Treatise on Human Nature* had initially flopped—in Hume's words, "it fell dead-born from the press"—and only came to be seen as a masterpiece decades later, after Hume became famous as a historian.

Smith's early enthusiasm helped validate the belated academic appreciation for the *Treatise;* surely it must be a work of genius if Adam Smith had immediately recognized it as such.

But when Keynes and Sraffa at last examined the pamphlet itself in the 1930s—the title and publisher markings made clear that it was indeed the long-sought review of Hume's *Treatise*—they soon determined that its true author was not Smith but none other than Hume himself, trying to gin up interest in his failing book. Apart from obvious similarities in style, the obscure artifact presented a series of ideas and arguments Hume would later publish in future volumes of the *Treatise.* "If a copy of the pamphlet had been available to earlier commentators, it is impossible that they could have doubted this conclusion," according to Keynes and Sraffa.[2] Today historians generally accept that Hume's first piece of good press was actually written by Hume.

There was more to these studies than the vanity of aging collectors. Keynes was preoccupied all his life with the philosophical foundations of knowledge itself—the nature of science and the limitations of its methods. He immersed himself in the minutiae left behind by great minds not only to access the wisdom of prior generations but to gain insight into the subtle differences in systems of belief that had enabled great breakthroughs—and to understand the strange contortions of history that could both elevate and suppress good ideas. He developed both a deep reverence for the ideas of his predecessors and an arrogant, fearless zeal to critique their greatest contributions. This relentless philosophical inquiry led Keynes to venerate scientists not for their quantitative mathematical prowess but for their creativity. True to his Bloomsbury creed, he elevated great science to the highest plane of human achievement: art.

"Newton was not the first of the age of reason," according to Keynes. "He was the last of the magicians."[3] Keynes meant it as a compliment. He called Newton "our greatest genius,"[4] and the "our" referred to Cambridge, which allowed Keynes to declare himself an intellectual heir to the great physicist. "He looked on the whole universe and all that is in it *as a riddle,* as a secret which could be read by applying pure thought to certain evidence, certain mystic clues which God had laid about the world."[5] And Newton's gift, Keynes believed, was like that of a poet or a painter possessed by a muse. After a frenzy of insight, he would take care to present his new knowledge in the formal language of science in order to lend persuasive force to his creative break-through. "Newton could hold a problem in his mind for hours and days and weeks until it surrendered to him its secret. Then being a supreme mathematical technician he could dress it up, how you will, for purposes of exposition, but it was his intuition which was pre-eminently extraordinary. . . . The proofs, for what they are worth, were, as I have said, dressed up afterwards—they were not the instrument of discovery."[6]

This enthusiasm for ideas over numbers was not a devaluation of empiricism. For an economist, in particular, intuition had to be grounded in lived experience. Keynes faulted mathematics for en-abling economists to become so entangled in their own abstractions that they lost track of the real world. He hailed the "philosophical" methods of Thomas Malthus for addressing human motivations and behavior and denounced the "pseudo-arithmetical doctrines" of David Ricardo, among them the quantity theory of money, whose "complete domination . . . for a period of a hundred years has been a disaster to the progress of economics."[7]

Economics was not like physics, and even physics reached its great-est heights only when it most closely resembled art. As Keynes ex-plained his own methods in *The General Theory:* "The object of our analysis is, not to provide a machine, or method of blind manipula-tion, which will furnish an infallible answer, but to provide ourselves with an organised and orderly method of thinking out particular problems. . . . Too large a proportion of recent 'mathematical' econom-ics are mere concoctions, as imprecise as the initial assumptions they rest on, which allow the author to lose sight of the complexities and interdependencies of the real world in a maze of pretentious and un-helpful symbols."[8]

This was the Keynes who mesmerized Joan Robinson: Keynes the great theorist of progress who approached the economics discipline as a philosopher, who believed, like his friends Ludwig Wittgenstein, Bertrand Russell, and G. E. Moore, that the ultimate truths were those of word and idea—not of quantification and calculation.

And yet he had also called his greatest work *The General Theory of Employment, Interest and Money*, hoping to bestow the academic prestige of physics on both his book and the economics profession itself. It was a grand rhetorical maneuver; just as Einstein had demonstrated that Newtonian physics were only a special case of a broader paradigm, so Keynes would show that the ideas of the classical economists could only hold true under special, rare conditions. And though Keynes had been deeply skeptical of the emerging discipline of "econometrics," which transformed his field into a dizzying array of sigmas and deltas, in "Economic Possibilities for Our Grandchildren" he had longed for the day when economists could be seen as "dentists"[9]—technicians who could move in to correct well-understood malfunctions. Though he downplayed statistical and mathematical economics for nearly the whole of his career, by the end of the war he informed the top economic thinkers in the British government that "theoretical economic analysis has now reached a point where it is fit to be applied. Its application only awaits the collection of the detailed facts." He foresaw a "new era of 'Joy through Statistics.' "[10]

And indeed, over the course of the 1930s, the quality of the data available to economists had improved dramatically. During the Depression, FDR's Department of Commerce had commissioned Simon Kuznets to create a new measurement of "national income," which Wassily Leontief developed further during the war. Today, it's called "gross domestic product" and is the standard measure of the overall output of an economy. By the end of the war, governments in both the United States and Europe had developed vast, stunningly accurate statistical operations compiling everything from crop prices to manufacturing output to wage growth, unemployment, and even poverty, which had been notoriously difficult to measure due to its prevalence in remote areas of the country. Economists, awed by the tools now at their disposal, wholeheartedly pursued a methodology that emphasized precise measurement and prediction over conceptual or linguistic analysis.

The greatest prophet of this "New Economics," as it would come to be known in the John F. Kennedy years, was Paul Samuelson. His wildly popular textbook offered what he called a "neoclassical synthesis" between the ideas of *The General Theory* and the economic thinkers who had dominated the era of the gold standard. In Samuelson's hands, human behavior and the economy more broadly were best understood as rational, profit-maximizing endeavors. Markets would clear themselves, and supply and demand would find their own rational equilibrium, just as David Ricardo and Adam Smith had posited long ago. But they would only do so, according to Samuelson, when the economy was operating at something close to full employment. By deploying Keynesian deficit spending or providing Keynesian tax cuts, policy makers could keep the economy from slipping "into a topsy-turvy wonderland where right seems left and left is right; up seems down; and black, white."[11] So long as unemployment did not spin out of control, the rational, profit-maximizing behavior of human beings would allow statistics to reliably predict when and where economic forces would reach equilibrium—if the data were sufficiently accurate. For Samuelson and his followers, physics was the foundation of knowledge, and mathematics was its language. Where *The General Theory* had proclaimed "uncertainty" to be the bedrock analytical concept for economic thinking, Samuelson and his protégés sought not only certainty but precision.

Samuelson led a generation of titans to intellectual battle not only with the faltering classical gods but with other interpreters of Keynes and his vision. John Hicks developed the first and most influential distillation of *The General Theory* into a mathematical model. Alvin Hansen transmitted Hicks' work from Harvard to Washington, training future bureaucrats and cabinet officials in graduate courses, as Samuelson built an entire department around it at MIT, incubating future Nobel laureates Robert Solow, Lawrence Klein, and Franco Modigliani, who developed their own innovations, transforming the

moniker "Keynesian" into a word meaning, for a time, "American economics." Without those luminaries, *The General Theory* would today
be an intellectual curiosity, the brilliant and confusing work of an
influential Englishman that had briefly animated the Roosevelt administration. Through Samuelson and his clan, Keynesian economics
became not only a new orthodoxy in American social science but integral to the very language of U.S. political power, a slate of ideas inseparable from the basic governing assumptions of the Democratic
Party.

But there was another way of understanding Keynes that continued
to develop in Cambridge, England, which viewed the entire American
development as a terrible and dangerous mistake, a sacrilege against
Keynes himself. These thinkers included the collaborators who had
helped Keynes prepare his magnum opus. "The economic theory
which was developed in America was a return to pre-Keynesian doctrines" that "smothered" everything important in Keynes, argued Joan
Robinson.[12] For Richard Kahn, the reengineering of *The General Theory* into mathematics was a Faustian bargain—a fatal turn that would
ultimately lead "to Keynes being discredited."[13]

Only a few months after Keynes released *The General Theory*, John
Hicks presented his interpretation of the book as a series of stable,
predictable relationships among money, interest rates, investment, and
economic growth. Using what became a famous graphical diagram, he
showed that as interest rates on government debt declined, the amount
of investment and savings in the economy would expand as companies
took advantage of lower rates to buy equipment and launch new ven-
tures. This would lead the overall economy to grow. But as the economy grew, the demand for money would rise, as people saw that more
investment opportunities were available and wanted to borrow money
to make investments. The higher demand for money would cause interest rates to increase. There were, in effect, two opposing forces
pushing interest rates in opposite directions: the amount of investment in the economy and the demand for money to invest. Where

those two forces intersected, the economy would be in a state of equilibrium; the trick for policy makers was to dial in the special conditions under which this equilibrium would eliminate unemployment. That, according to what became known as the IS-LM model (short for investment-savings and liquidity preference–money supply), could be achieved through one of two methods: lowering interest rates through monetary policy or running a fiscal deficit. When economists fed the new, cutting-edge statistics monitoring economic activity into this model, Hicks and his followers believed it would tell them *exactly* how much governments need to spend or cut taxes in order to lift a sluggish economy out of a slump.

Keynes reviewed a draft of Hicks' proposal and sent along a private note of encouragement: "I found it very interesting and really have next to nothing to say by way of criticism."[14] Publicly, however, he was silent about Hicks and his model, spending his energy rebutting critiques from classical economists. When Keynes himself offered a simplification of his book in *The Quarterly Journal of Economics* in February 1937, he presented a conceptual framework totally incompatible with Hicks' project.

"I am more attached to the comparatively simple fundamental ideas which underlie my theory than to the particular forms in which I have embodied them, and I have no desire that the latter should be crystallised at the present stage of the debate," he wrote before emphasizing the importance of uncertainty in his economic thought: "By 'uncertain' knowledge . . . I do not mean merely to distinguish what is known for certain from what is only probable. The game of roulette is not subject, in this sense, to uncertainty. . . . The sense in which I am using the term is that in which the prospect of a European war is uncertain, or the price of copper and the rate of interest twenty years hence, or the obsolescence of a new invention, or the position of private wealth owners in the social system in 1970. About these matters there is no scientific basis on which to form any calculable probability whatever. We simply do not know." Classical economics and its law of supply and demand were among several "pretty, polite techniques, made for a well-panelled board room and a nicely regulated market" that created the illusion of stability and predictability in economic life but that were in fact "liable to collapse" "without warning" when people changed their minds about how the future was likely to turn out. It was a lesson Keynes had been learning from financial crises and speculative bloopers since the summer of 1914.[15]

So Keynes was critical of *any* economic model that claimed to offer reliable information about the future—even the "Keynesian" models developed by Hicks, Hanson, and Samuelson. Economics was at best a field of rules of thumb, trends, and patterns that were liable to change. So his final statement on postwar employment policy differed from the fiscal therapies and stimulus agendas that are today associated with his name. Though his American followers would pursue fine-tuned tax-and-spending plans to lift demand during recessions, Keynes instead called for the government to manage future stages of overall economic scarcity through direct investment spending.

Immediately after the war, Keynes assumed, the government would need to continue its all-hands-on-deck approach to combating inflation. But after that period, he argued, the government should seek "to *prevent* large fluctuations" in employment by enacting "a stable long-term programme" that would spend money on things like infrastructure, factory equipment, and scientific research. Keynes did not expect such an investment plan to completely eliminate "fluctuations," but he did believe it could result in a "much narrower" range of ups and downs and that the government would be able to "maintain a steady level of employment" throughout. Keynes thought the government would need to control about two-thirds of all investment in the economy for his idea to work.

It was a fusion of *The General Theory* with "Economic Possibilities for Our Grandchildren." After ten or fifteen years, Keynes believed, the economy would become so "saturated" with investment that there would be no way to increase it any further without "embarking upon wasteful and unnecessary enterprises." This inability to boost investment would not lead to unemployment or misery, as it had in the Great Depression. It would instead herald a new "golden age" in which workers would be free to pursue "increased leisure," "more holidays," and "shorter hours." Without useful projects to invest in, there would be no need for workers to accumulate savings by working so many hours.[16] The trend in work-life balance over the course of the twentieth century had in fact been quite promising, though that was in part due to the inability of so many to find full-time work amid the Depression. In 1900, the average working American spent 58.5 hours each week on the job. By 1935, the workweek had declined to 41.7 hours. Keynes was simply projecting that progress into the future.[17]

From the 1940s onward, governments in both Europe and the United States took on a permanently broader role in large-scale investment. The Eisenhower administration developed the interstate highway system, created NASA, and dramatically expanded the role of the federal government in supporting medical research. But we have not, of course, entered an era of rest and relaxation—at least, not in the United States. In much of Europe, shorter workweeks are an explicit and uncontroversial public policy goal. Germans, for instance, work an average of twenty-six hours a week when vacation time is averaged out over the year.[18]

But the policies that eventually became synonymous with Keynes were not ambitious, long-term programs of government investment. When Keynesian economists came to Washington after the war, they encountered an atmosphere of paranoia and persecution in which every New Dealer was suspect and the word "Keynesian" was presumed evidence of Soviet influence. And the struggle to define the Keynesian tradition—to follow Robinson or Samuelson—was shaped by the McCarthyism raging in postwar America.

John Kenneth Galbraith understood this conservative backlash against Keynesian ideas firsthand. He had studied with Joan Robinson at Cambridge in the late 1930s and put his knowledge to work running the Office of Price Administration in the early years of the war. But his days as an inflation fighter had not earned him many admirers in corporate America. Galbraith was hounded out of Washington in 1943, as Republicans and businessmen had taken turns denouncing him as an incompetent and a traitor. It was a formative experience for Galbraith that changed the way he thought about the relationship between American government and corporate power. If even wartime patriotism couldn't protect a bureaucrat who was crimping corporate profits in the name of victory, there was no hope for any man or idea in Washington that failed to make itself amenable to at least some factions of American business.

Once the newspapers stopped printing his name in their headlines, Galbraith landed a comfortable job at *Fortune* magazine, which turned out to be a flexible employer, allowing him to take several months of leave at a time for stints on the occasional government project. *Fortune* was the first glossy business magazine, the brainchild of Henry Luce, a self-made mogul who had launched *Time* in 1923. Raised in China by Christian missionaries, Luce took a hawkishly anti-Communist approach to the political situation in the land of his youth. He loved Chiang Kai-shek and hated Franklin D. Roosevelt, and he devoted a great deal of print real estate to the musings of Whittaker Chambers, a former Soviet spy who spent the 1940s and '50s insisting that New Dealers were inexorably guiding the nation into a Soviet future. The liberal Galbraith didn't seem like a natural fit to most Time Inc. insiders, including Luce himself. "I taught Kenneth Galbraith to write," he told John F. Kennedy in 1960. "And I tell you I've certainly regretted it."[19]

But Luce believed good business required clever politics. He recognized Galbraith's pull within a Democratic Party that in the early 1940s appeared to have a permanent grip on executive power. Galbraith gave Luce a name he could drop to help open doors with liberals in Washington or at least put them at ease in conversation. He could also get scoops that Luce's more conservative writers couldn't; liberal politicians didn't want to turn over juicy details to their right-wing adversaries. American magazines were a high-profit world of cutthroat competition—television did not yet exist as a competing medium—and Galbraith's *Fortune* stories were informed by conversations about where policy was headed and the way policy makers were thinking. And he was already familiar with the novel "Keynesian" economics that now guided them.

Fortune, improbably, was the most left-wing title in Luce's empire. While *Time* followed iconic personalities in politics and the art world, Luce encouraged *Fortune* writers to pursue high concepts about the future structure of the economy. One big idea, in particular, captivated Galbraith: "The early *Fortune,* more than any other journal anywhere in the industrial world, saw the modern large corporation as a primary economic and social force."[20]

In January 1944, Galbraith published a seven-thousand-word cover story titled "Transition to Peace: Business in A.D. 194Q." It envisioned a brave new alliance between big business and the federal government in which wartime regulations and tax rates retreated and the public works agencies of the Depression—the Work Projects Administration, the Civilian Conservation Corps, and similar bureaus— would be replaced by public spending to support corporations. When the government ran deficits to keep employment high, its spending would spur business investment and increase consumer purchasing power, guaranteeing corporate profits that would "make a Midas ill with envy."[21] Galbraith was presenting a peculiar brand of Keynesianism, but he intentionally avoided any mention of Keynes. The business leaders who had run him out of Washington, Galbraith reasoned, might accept Keynesian policies if they recognized them as profitable business opportunities. If Keynes were simply a symbol of liberal big government, however, then the name of Keynes would become an ideological flash point in the Cold War. And of course the name Keynes was already viewed with grave suspicion among the business elite. After all, men like Galbraith, who had literally controlled the prices of everything during the war, were Keynesians.

The war had fused Keynesian ideas with military production and corporate supply chains; now Galbraith was promising big business an even better peacetime deal. CEOs could expect the same government-backed profits of the war years without all the price controls and tax headaches. Corporate Keynesianism had arrived.[22] Whereas Keynes himself had called for direct government investment, Galbraith was suggesting a more indirect program of economic management through state support for large corporations.

But big business remained skeptical. "194Q" "ignited several strong protests" within Time Inc., including calls for Galbraith to be dismissed. And though Luce stood by his man, Galbraith became well practiced in the art of "self-censorship" as he tried to repackage Keynesian concepts for the ultraconservative climate of the early Cold War. He was a popular manifestation of a broader trend; in academia, Samuelson was repackaging Keynes to make peace with conservative classical economists, while in Washington, Keynesian policy makers tried to avoid drawing attention to themselves with ambitious policy goals. "Self-censorship at *Fortune*," Galbraith wrote, "involved a constant calculation as to whether a particular statement—sometimes a sentence or a paragraph—was worth the predictable argument, perhaps with Luce, possibly with some frightened or zealous surrogate. Often one decided that it was not the day for a fight. Or if your conscience was compelling, you couched the favorable reference to Roosevelt or the CIO in such careful language that it would slip by, overlooking the near-certainty that it would slip by all your readers as well."[23]

The money was good, and Galbraith's family was expanding. His wife, Kitty, had given birth to two young sons and would soon deliver two more. They enjoyed a spacious apartment in Manhattan overlooking the Hudson River and had a comfortable summer cabin in Vermont. But it didn't feel right to Galbraith. He savored his time away from the city and was disappointed by the conversation at the cocktail parties he attended. Washington had buzzed with gossip about his OPA directives and political future; in New York he was just another well-heeled citizen. "I rarely encountered anyone who had read anything I had written," he remarked. *Fortune* had cachet, but it had a low circulation, especially compared to *Time*, and Luce typically did not permit authors to take credit for their work with bylines. At first, the anonymity came as a relief after his days as a very public target at

OPA. But as he mastered his new craft, he found anonymous communication with a "minuscule audience" increasingly "unrewarding."[24]

And so, after four years at *Fortune*, Galbraith abandoned the magazine world for academia—at precisely the moment academic McCarthyism erupted. His old mentor from Harvard in the 1930s, the agricultural economist John Black, lured him back to Cambridge with assistance from a plush government grant to research crop prices. Though Galbraith would receive the lowly title of lecturer at first, Black promised to pay him an acceptably high salary out of the federal pot until he landed a tenured position, which Black of course would vouch for.

So Galbraith took the plunge, only to discover that the heavy concentration of young Keynesians at Harvard had prompted a reactionary backlash in the gray-haired university administration. Paul Sweezy—the Marxist who had helped bring Keynes from Cambridge, England, to Cambridge, Massachusetts—was passed over for tenure, despite a vehement protest from Joseph Schumpeter, who cited the importance of intellectual diversity and academic freedom. Both Galbraith and Samuelson were passed over for tenure in 1948, prompting Samuelson to move down the street to MIT, where he was given charge of what would become a world-famous department.[25]

In 1949, the Harvard economics department at last approved Galbraith for a tenured job, shortly after he was denied the department chair at Illinois. But no sooner had Harvard's economics department rendered its verdict than Harvard's board of overseers intervened to block the appointment. The board was a politically formidable panel. Its members included former Republican senator Sinclair Weeks and aging J.P. Morgan magnate Thomas Lamont. As Harvard president James Conant explained with frustration, the name of Keynes had transformed into "the proverbial red rag. In the eyes of many economically illiterate but deeply patriotic (and well-to-do) citizens, to accuse a professor of being a Keynesian was almost equivalent to branding him a subversive agent."[26] Those were strong words for Conant. Like Columbia University president Dwight D. Eisenhower,

he supported a blanket ban against hiring openly Communist professors. In Galbraith's case, however, Conant put his own career on the
line, telling Harvard he would quit if the hire didn't go through. To
everyone's surprise, Galbraith ultimately got the job.

But for decades his life and work would be haunted by the specter
of McCarthyism. Galbraith knew he was exactly the kind of man the
McCarthyists hated most—not an outright Soviet collaborator but an
idealist with a grand vision of progress who hoped to use economic
reforms to break down social distinctions of rank and privilege. But
the prestige of his Harvard credentials proved enormously helpful for
Galbraith as he aspired to take up Keynes' mantle as a public intellectual. In the 1950s, Galbraith wrote three books—*American Capitalism: The Concept of Countervailing Power*; *The Great Crash, 1929*; and
The Affluent Society—all of which flew off the shelves and reestablished
a place for him in Washington not as a technocratic functionary but
as a leading man of American ideas. As many Keynesians began settling into quiet roles as specialists, Galbraith was aiming to be the big
thinker Keynes had been: journalist, professor, adviser to presidents,
and architect of a new economic era.

Galbraith never took his elite status for granted. He was always
looking over his shoulder for the next attack, and typically, one was on
the way. From the 1950s all the way through to the 1970s, everyone
from far-right fringe groups to U.S. senators and academic economists
secretly offered information on Galbraith to FBI Director J. Edgar
Hoover.[27]

But Galbraith's personal experience with paranoid Cold War persecution convinced him that neither his career ambitions nor the social
progress he envisioned could be realized without help from corporate
America. The Republicans and conservative Democrats who had
driven him out of Washington were never going to turn to him for
advice, nor were the various political organizations and magazines
flowering on the American Right. But they did listen to men like
Henry Luce. As Hayek and his disciples had drawn inspiration from
nineteenth-century Britain, Galbraith looked to the postwar industrial corporation, hoping to apply the great breakthroughs of *The Gen-*

eral Theory to what he saw as an entirely new landscape of corporate and political power, which he believed might secure a better and more egalitarian future.

The product of all this thinking was Galbraith's first publishing hit, 1953's *American Capitalism*, a tribute to the American businessman disguised as a critique. Throughout its two hundred pages, Galbraith ribs corporate leaders not for corrupting government, exploiting workers, or ripping off consumers but for failing to appreciate the wonders of shared prosperity in postwar America.

It is a book written from a defensive crouch. Both the title and the argument were a response to the McCarthyist attacks on Keynes and his followers. Galbraith wanted the world to know that he not only loved capitalism but *American* capitalism, lest anyone confuse his Cold War loyalties. As Galbraith sketched it, the great virtues of the U.S. political system everyone learns in grade school—checks and balances—were at last being extended to the American economy. Militant labor unions, the proliferation of government regulations in the 1930s, and the discovery of countercyclical fiscal policy were forces that might perturb the businessman of the 1950s but that he had no reason to fear. Just as Congress, the White House, and the judiciary checked one another's power, so, too, did government, business, and labor curb the excesses of politics and the marketplace. The government did not intrude on the businessman with the goal of taking him over but only to establish a prosperous equilibrium. Despite the apocalyptic warnings of the Hayekian elite, everything was really just fine. The unemployment rate, hovering at about 3 percent, proved it.[28]

All of this had been made possible by technological advances and the "enlightened conservatism"[29] of Keynesian thinking, which sought to preserve capitalism rather than subvert it, blessing the United States with an "opulence" almost unheard of in previous eras. Problems of inefficiency and waste still existed, but they were minor troubles. If scarcity was the real economic problem facing the country, then everyone "should without question be at work producing potatoes, beans and coal so that people might be slightly less hungry and cold."[30] Instead, entire industries were devoted to entertainments and frivolities, while another industry—advertising—had developed as a method of persuading people into parting with their excess wealth.

With the age of economic scarcity ended, Galbraith believed that many of the objections economists had raised about economic organization in the past were no longer significant. Corporate monopolies might well be wasteful, but waste was not very important. What mattered was power. And even tremendous concentrations of power such as those of the modern corporation were not necessarily a problem so long as they were "countervailed" by other great powers—other large corporations in the supply chain or distribution scheme or, more important, powerful labor unions and a powerful government.

American Capitalism was informed by Galbraith's own experience at OPA during the war. He had dealt with both large and small producers and found that it was often easier for the government to get the social results it wanted by favoring big business. Regulating prices across an entire industry was much simpler when the government had to work with only a few large producers instead of trying to address the complaints of hundreds of small players.

So the government would battle recessions with countercyclical fiscal management, and labor and business would battle each other for their respective cuts of the resulting largesse. It might not always work out perfectly, but the sheer abundance of the U.S. economy meant that getting things a little wrong—crimping profits too much here, shortchanging workers a little there—wouldn't be catastrophic. Though Galbraith talked about an equilibrium of power rather than equilibrium of supply and demand, he arrived at the same basic model of economic management that his friend Paul Samuelson had. The government should boost spending and cut taxes in a slump and raise taxes and cut spending to tame a boom. The government would provide the right environment for the market to work its magic.

"The essence of the Keynesian formula consists in leaving private decisions over production, including those involving prices and wages, to the men who now make them," Galbraith wrote. "The businessman's apparent area of discretion is in nowise narrowed. Centralized decision is brought to bear only on the climate in which those decisions are made; it insures only that the factors influencing free and intelligent decision will lead to a private action that contributes to economic stability."[31]

Both the social vision and the policy agenda Galbraith presented in *American Capitalism* were a sharp departure from what Keynes had embraced in the final years of his life. Where Keynes had called for the government to take over two-thirds of all economic investment, Galbraith celebrated the autonomy of the private corporation. Where Keynes had imagined the steady emancipation of workers from work itself, Galbraith believed that labor unions would make sure everyone got paid a reasonably fair share. Galbraith's ideas were more politically realistic in McCarthyist America precisely because they were less ambitious than what Keynes had envisioned.

The most aggressive attacks on *American Capitalism* had come from conservative classical economists, who decried Galbraith's acceptance of labor unions and his insistence that oligopolies and monopolies were a "natural" element of capitalist development. Even defenders of big business in conservative economics at the time preferred to think of large corporations as victors in a competitive market, rather than as predatory or exploitative centers of power. The economy might be dominated by big companies, but surely these were not anticompetitive.

But the criticisms that Galbraith took to heart came from his liberal and leftist friends, who saw *American Capitalism* as a paean to complacency. Joan Robinson attacked the book for "rebunking *laissez-faire*"[32] and an unwarranted contentment with corporate power. Galbraith, Robinson argued, had simply replaced the automated prosperity of the classical economists' competitive market with an automated social harmony of countervailing power. And indeed, Galbraith's embrace of the large corporation as an engine of social progress was very dangerous for the future of American liberalism. Corporate power, it would turn out, was not easily checked. Over the coming decades, it would become clear that the government did not find it easier to exert power over a few large corporate players but the reverse: a few large corporate players could bend entire wings of the federal government to their will.

Galbraith insisted that he was not promoting the idea of a self-correcting mechanism. Labor and government would have to exercise agency to check the power of big business; the process did not balance "automatically." But in truth he had not written the book to curry favor with the Left. He wanted *American Capitalism* to assuage the fears of corporate executives and a general public in the grip of a McCarthyist panic, and had deliberately sanded away the most controversial edges from Keynesian thinking. "The basic tenets of Keynesian policy have been embraced, though again without invoking the name of Keynes, by a Republican administration,"[33] he emphasized when the book was reissued—a reference to Eisenhower's reliance on a peacetime budget deficit to relieve unemployment.

American Capitalism was a hit, eventually selling over 400,000 copies and introducing an entire generation to Keynesian ideas, including readers who had never had the opportunity to experience them through Samuelson's textbook.[34] And it did in fact grab corporate America's attention. When *Harper's* ran an excerpt that included a reference to cellophane as a symbol of opulent frivolity, the DuPont chemical company's PR team sent a frantic letter to the magazine saying the firm was "somewhat disturbed by the reference to Du Pont cellophane," protesting that the chemical wrap was not "social waste" but a "low cost" improvement to food distribution that enhanced "freshness" and "efficiency."[35]

Galbraith had also clearly stated one of the most important and overlooked ideas from *The General Theory:* that most contemporary economic trouble isn't about scarcity. As a result, economic reforms aimed at improving efficiency and output are likely to matter only at the margins. Shifting the focus of economic analysis from production to power—an analysis not merely of prices and output but of the relationships among the state, corporations, organized labor, and other interest groups—was an important breakthrough, even if Galbraith's assessment of the emerging political dynamic in 1953 was overly sanguine.

Galbraith's efforts to placate big business, however, did little to quell the attacks on his loyalty. In 1955, he was called before the Senate Banking and Currency Committee to offer expert testimony on the recent jitters in the stock market. His latest book, *The Great Crash, 1929,* was a history of the stock market collapse of 1929, and lawmakers wanted his advice on how to prevent another disaster. Galbraith suggested limiting the amount of borrowed money that investors could use to place bets on stock prices. Forcing stock speculators to pony up more of their own cash would both serve to limit the amount of money moving into the stock market and reduce bank exposure to defaults on loans that had been used to finance bad bets.

This was standard fare, and Galbraith had no power to impose it as a mere expert witness at a congressional hearing. But during the course of his statement, the stock market took a dive, ultimately falling 7 percent on the day, wiping out $3 billion in paper wealth. That plunge over essentially nothing should have served to prove Galbraith's point: The stock market was clearly prone to unhealthy volatility. Instead, a McCarthyist uproar ensued. The day after the hearing, Galbraith's phone in Cambridge began ringing off the hook with angry callers. "My secretary went home in annoyance," he later recalled, as he began receiving "a mountain of mail" filled with threats of violence and death. When he broke his leg in a skiing accident two days after his testimony, he received another round of letters "from those whose belief in the existence of a just and omnipotent God had been deeply strengthened" by his misfortune.[36]

Senator Homer Capehart, a Republican from Indiana, announced on television that his committee would be calling Galbraith back to testify on the grounds that Galbraith, Capehart had learned, was a Communist sympathizer who had defended the Communist cause in a 1949 report for the National Planning Association (the paper had in fact called for further U.S. economic aid to Europe to prevent Soviet gains).

Capehart reached out to Sinclair Weeks for help in building his case. Weeks, who just a few years earlier had attempted to deny Galbraith tenure at Harvard, was now Eisenhower's commerce secretary. He asked the FBI to investigate whether Galbraith had any Soviet connections, and J. Edgar Hoover complied, asking his staff, "What do our files show on Galbraith?" The answer, he reported back to a dispirited Weeks, was generally "favorable," with the caveat that Galbraith was "conceited, egotistical and snobbish."[37]

Galbraith decided to counterpunch. He held a press conference in which he noted that the supposedly controversial NPA report had been endorsed by both Allen Dulles, who was now the director of the CIA, and the president's brother Milton Eisenhower. He had delivered this supposedly subversive report as a speech at the University of Notre Dame, which had published it as a pamphlet. Was Notre Dame under Soviet control, too? Capehart backed down.

It was time for a break. In 1956, Galbraith reconnected with the Cambridge University Keynesians, traveling to India with Joan Robinson's good friend Nicholas Kaldor before heading to Switzerland for a family vacation, where he met with Richard Kahn. He was now crafting a new book that would update the ideas of *American Capitalism* to accommodate the criticisms he had received from Robinson and incorporate some of the new ideas that were percolating in Cambridge. He honed his arguments during a trip to Cambridge itself, where he stayed at Kaldor's house and workshopped ideas with Kahn and Robinson, who were still affectionate twenty years after their romance had first blossomed.[38] "I remember walking over from the Kaldor house," Galbraith said, "and encountering Joan and Kahn just starting out to walk. I asked them where they were going, and they said, 'To London and back' or something of the sort." When he asked Robinson who the good younger economists at Cambridge were, she gave a "stern" reply: "My dear Ken, we were the last good generation."[39]

There was more to Robinson's answer than egotism. Robinson and Kahn were protective of *The General Theory*'s intellectual legacy. They had, after all, helped write it. Robinson understood Keynesian thinking as a *doctrine*—a way of thinking about the world and its problems that could compete with other great philosophies in human history, a system of thought akin to Buddhism or Marxism. Whereas Keynes had hoped that *The General Theory* would stimulate debate and clear away outdated ideas, Robinson regarded it as a kind of sacred text—a guide to human action that need only be elaborated upon and interpreted for the specific new circumstances that would arise across the decades. Whereas Keynes had hoped to convert members of his own generation, Robinson had quickly recognized the old guard as a lost cause and taken it upon herself as "chief propagandist of the revolution"[40] to train the next generation of economists. By the late 1950s, Keynesian economics had indeed conquered the world, and for the most part it had been students of the 1930s who had done the conquering. But to Robinson's horror, they had the dogma all wrong.

The whole point of *The General Theory,* she believed, was to show that economic production could not be understood as a self-sustaining set of processes independent from social norms and political realities. The mathematical relationships that Samuelson, Hicks, and Hansen had presented as "Keynesian" eliminated all human agency from economic decision making. She assailed their reliance on old classical ideas such as "general equilibrium." Their economics were internally contradictory; there was no role to be played by *time* in economic mathematics, no long run or short run in a graph charting supply and demand. Such static mathematical representations contradicted the way Samuelson and his followers claimed to "describe a *process* of accumulation that *raises* wages, *alters* technology, and *changes* a stock of inputs"[41]—ideas that all involved movement from one point in time to another. "For a world that is always in equilibrium there is no difference between the future and the past," Robinson once said. "There is no history and there is no need for Keynes."[42] Kahn agreed. The Samuelson club's "stable relationships handed down from heaven" were a dangerous illusion that elided everything Keynes had taught about the instability of financial markets and uncertain expectations about the future.

There was no escaping the political gulf that existed between Sam-

uelson and the British Keynesians. Samuelson described himself as a
"dull centrist"in politics,[43] while Robinson was a fierce critic of American empire and capitalism itself. Samuelson and his disciples believed
corporate profits were derived from productivity—a kind of just reward for creating social value; Robinson argued that they were the
result of a power struggle among owners, managers, and workers.[44] As
Robinson and Samuelson went back and forth in academic journals
about the nature of capital, time, and equilibrium, their disputes took
on an unmistakably political dimension with supporters falling into
line according to their ideological commitments.

But the American Keynesians were getting results. Unemployment
had been stubbornly low for years. Inflation, despite a few brief out-
bursts, had never soared out of control. Over the course of the 1950s,
median household income in the United States increased by 30 percent, while the purchasing power of the average family more than
tripled.[45] Galbraith viewed this record as a tremendous success and
felt some personal pride in having helped establish the regime during
the war. But his sojourn in Cambridge with the original Keynesians
helped focus his attention on the broader philosophical problems
Keynes had once concerned himself with. And in 1958, he delivered
the first—and most successful—update on Keynesian social theory.

Only a handful of economic works have captured the public imagination like *The Affluent Society*. It stands alongside *The Economic Consequences of the Peace* and *The Communist Manifesto* as the rare work that
proves both wildly popular and enormously influential on public affairs. In the sixty years since its publication, only Thomas Piketty's
Capital in the Twenty-first Century has carried so immediate an impact
on American economic attitudes, and Piketty's tome on inequality is
yet to exert anything approaching the policy impact of *The Affluent
Society*, which would eventually become an intellectual pillar of Lyndon B. Johnson's Great Society agenda.

The Affluent Society represents Galbraith's intellectual break with
Samuelson and the dominant line of Keynesian thinking in the United

States. *American Capitalism* served as an ode to the postwar economy; *The Affluent Society* was a biting critique that showed the clear influence of Robinson, along with Galbraith's increasing confidence in his own new ideas. The book was Keynesian to its core, but, unlike nearly every other Keynesian text of its generation, the book took "Economic Possibilities for Our Grandchildren," not *The General Theory*, as its chief inspiration. *The General Theory* had succeeded in vanquishing unemployment and inflation, but Galbraith believed it had failed in propagating a good life or a just society. Though the numbers all seemed to add up, the United States had entered an era of "private opulence and public squalor,"[46] which Galbraith depicted in the book's most famous passage:

The family which takes its mauve and cerise, air-conditioned, power-steered and power-braked automobile out for a tour passes through cities that are badly paved, made hideous by litter, blighted buildings, billboards, and posts for wires that should long since have been put underground. They pass on into a countryside that has been rendered largely invisible by commercial art. . . . They picnic on exquisitely packaged food from a portable icebox by a polluted stream and go on to spend the night at a park which is a menace to public health and morals. Just before dozing off on an air-mattress, beneath a nylon tent, amid the stench of decaying refuse, they may reflect vaguely on the curious unevenness of their blessings. Is this, indeed, the American genius?[47]

As the Cold War and McCarthyism had corroded U.S. politics, Americans had numbed themselves at shopping malls and before television screens. Suburbs had sprung to life around every city, as urban renters spent their burgeoning incomes on new homes with government-backed mortgages and filled them with suddenly ubiquitous staples that, like television and the mall, had not even existed only a few years earlier. It was the era of Hanna-Barbera cartoons and Disneyland, of stainless-steel kitchen appliances and plastic toys, of the corporate commute and the barbiturate. Like other liberal elites of his day, Galbraith worried that his generation had traded the material despair of the Depression for a spiritual emptiness of consumerism and conformity. There was more than a whiff of snobbery to Galbraith's indictment, but his assessment resonated with millions of Americans and continues to resonate today, when consumers no longer even need to leave their homes to shop and social existence, particularly for young people, is increasingly an online activity. We worry about becoming addicted to social media as Galbraith worried about billboards and television, a process in which we become more distant from members of our community even as we become more closely linked by commerce.

American Capitalism had celebrated the end of scarcity. Now *The Affluent Society* decried the country's increasing dependence on unnecessary production to establish the financial security of most families. The relentless postwar reliance on boosting economic output as the chief, if not only, means of improving the American standard of living had subjugated the work of democracy to the mechanics of the market. Nobody in her right mind would choose to work longer hours for dirty public parks. But that was what the logic of the market was dictating, because the market could only reward ideas that turned a profit. Nobody stood to profit from clean parks; they were just nicer to live with than dirty parks. But if nobody made the political judgment that clean parks were better, a society organized around profit incentives from production alone would almost automatically end up with dirty parks. The market was not an impartial guide to the beliefs of the public, and some of its verdicts were crazy.

Galbraith was in effect resurrecting Keynes' 1924 pamphlet *The End of Laissez-Faire*, which had declared, "The important thing for government is not to do things which individuals are doing already, and to do them a little better or a little worse; but to do those things which at present are not done at all."[48] Determining just what the market could *not* do had never been an easy task, but Galbraith believed that the advertising age had made it even harder, because people now actually *enjoyed* many of the things that cheapened their quality of life, even if they would never *choose* them as critical social priorities.

People bought fancy cars because they had the ability to make the purchase on their own; they did not have the power to buy collective goods or to trade in a Cadillac for a Chevrolet and a nice park nearby. When public goods fell into disorder or neglect, people found them unpleasant and satiated their desires with what the market had to offer.

Mass media and highway billboards didn't just convince people which luxury items to acquire with their excess cash; they created *new* wants that could be satisfied only by consumer purchases. Even if those wants were frivolous, they were very real, and they established a standard of living and set of social expectations defined by frivolities. By running the economic machine at full tilt to create fripperies, the United States was diverting resources and labor from other activities that would contribute to a better way of life—schools, parks, and better public housing. The economic organization of society was devoted not to maximizing social comfort and harmony but to satisfying the consumer desires created by advertising and production itself. And that in turn was hampering society's ability to grapple with poverty. "If such is the nature of our system that we have production only because we first create the wants that require it, we will have few resources to spare. We will be rich but never quite rich enough to spare anything much for the poor. . . . If we understand that our society creates the wants that it satisfies, we may do better." [49]

For conservative critics and Galbraith's chief Keynesian rivals, including his friend Samuelson and his ally at MIT Robert Solow, *The Affluent Society* smacked of unscientific moralism—the work of an elite thinker eager to substitute his own judgments for those of society. Which of course it was. For Galbraith, democracy was inevitably concerned with realizing a particular kind of world. But the only arena in which the government seemed to take this task seriously was national defense—and here Galbraith decried the "weapons extravaganza" [50] that had taken over Cold War policy. The insanity of the arms race only proved that the United States could *afford* whatever it wanted; it simply *chose* to organize its economic life in a particularly shallow, uncharitable, and violent way. The United States had tamed the unpredictability of the business cycle and moved past the constraints of outright resource scarcity. But the task of government was not finished once the basic material needs of society were met.

Persuading people to live otherwise was a matter of changing what Galbraith called "the conventional wisdom"—a phrase now so commonplace in political discourse that few even realize it has a specific origin. Galbraith used "conventional wisdom" to denote the class of ideas considered acceptable to right-thinking people in government. Those ideas were not necessarily directly related to the financial interests of the ruling class, but they were the ideas that elites found most comfortable and enjoyed reading about in newspapers or hearing repeated in speeches or represented in art. Such thinking was not necessarily wrong, but it was inevitably behind the times; the conventional wisdom had always been developed in response to a particular set of circumstances and was always vulnerable to political and social change. Keynes might have been right, Galbraith mused, that ideas were always sovereign in politics—but only in the immediate sense. Over time, ideas were dislodged not by rational argument but by the brute force of social change: "The enemy of the conventional wisdom is not ideas but the march of events."[51]

Conservatives were predictably cool to *The Affluent Society*, but the book's reception from liberals and the Left was almost universal admiration. Both John Strachey and Joan Robinson were ecstatic. But eventually the Swedish economist Gunnar Myrdal would publish a rejoinder, *Challenge to Affluence*, that resonated with Galbraith. To Myrdal, Galbraith's interest in affluence and the productive power of the modern corporation had blinded him to the prevalence of a broad "underclass" of the elderly, people with disabilities, and people of color, which, he surmised, constituted about a fifth of American society.[52] Poverty statistics backed up Myrdal's view. Although the unemployment rate averaged just 5.5 percent in 1959, the poverty rate was 22.4 percent. Much more alarming, the black poverty rate was a staggering 55.1 percent.[53] Galbraith's portrait of the cheerful but discontent overconsumer was a portrait not of America but of *white* America.

And even white Americans still struggled on the farm, where 40 percent of families remained impoverished.[54]

Yet Myrdal's critique only underscored Galbraith's broader point about democracy, markets, and mathematics. The economic system could run at full capacity—or at least at what politicians accepted as full capacity—while still leaving out a tremendous swath of society. A 5.5 percent unemployment rate wasn't an objective, neutral number. It was a statistic that obscured the intensity of American racism. Economists may have eliminated recessions, but the work of delivering a just democratic order could not depend on consumer demand alone.

The Affluent Society was both a coming-out party for Galbraith's leftism and a call to arms for all of the Keynesian economists who had scaled back their rhetoric and political ambition under the threat of McCarthyism. Galbraith had not abandoned the concepts he had developed in *American Capitalism;* he retained a general contentment with monopoly and oligopoly, and the idea of countervailing power would always play a starring role in his thought. But he was now calling for a much more expansive role for the state than what he had sketched in the late 1940s and early 1950s, insisting that the market could not solve the problems facing postwar America on its own.

It was a declaration of intellectual war against American Keynesianism. And in time it would be American Keynesians—not rightwing McCarthyists—who would bring about Galbraith's professional undoing.

FIFTEEN

───◇───

THE BEGINNING OF THE END

IT WAS HARD TO miss John F. Kennedy when he arrived at Harvard in the fall of 1936. "Handsome" and "gregarious," according to his tutor at Winthrop House, Kennedy bought fancy cars with his father's Wall Street money, joined the football, swimming, and sailing teams, and organized an extravagant party featuring jazz orchestras, multiple numbers by the Dancing Rhythmettes, and appearances by two major-league baseball stars.[1] Kennedy's father had just stepped down as chairman of the Securities and Exchange Commission to work for FDR's new Maritime Commission, and a few politically ambitious faculty members tried to ingratiate themselves as mentors to the Kennedy boys. But Jack, as everyone called him, was intellectually overshadowed by his older brother, Joe, and preferred to devote himself—again in the words of his tutor—"affectionately and diversely to women." Jack was "not quite serious." "One did not cultivate such students."[2]

That tutor was John Kenneth Galbraith, whose first path to power would run not through his well-connected pupils but through his fellow Harvard economist Lauchlin Currie. Galbraith had grown up on a farm and attended a one-room schoolhouse before studying animal husbandry as an undergraduate. He regarded the young scions of wealth and privilege who surrounded him at Harvard with curiosity but, for the most part, little esteem. And yet there was something about Jack. Both young men—Galbraith was only eight years Kennedy's senior—had come to Harvard with something to prove. Neither was embraced by the elite northeastern families of "Cabots, Lowells, Whitneys, Roosevelts [and] Peabodys" who held Irish families and the upwardly mobile alike in contempt. Jack had money, and his family had power. But in the aristocratic world of "Harvard before democracy," as Galbraith called it, "many at Harvard have had difficulty in believing that the Kennedy brothers are in the very first league, wholly worthy of the Harvard badge and blessing."[3] For all of Kennedy's playboy excess, Galbraith saw in him an outsider who strove, like Galbraith himself, to be accepted by arbiters of prestige who did not, in 1936, really want him.

In time Galbraith would establish a connection with the Kennedy family that would long outlive Jack himself. When Jacqueline Kennedy Onassis died in 1994, Galbraith and his wife, Kitty, were among the "tiny handful" of people outside the Kennedy family invited to gather at Jackie's Fifth Avenue apartment for an evening of private mourning the night before her public funeral.[4]

But it would not be until the late 1950s that JFK and Galbraith would forge a serious bond. His association with Camelot would return Galbraith to the center of American public power for the first time in nearly two decades, cementing his status as the most prominent American intellectual of the 1960s. At the outset of their partnership, however, Kennedy needed the economist much more than the economist needed him. Beginning with his first congressional campaign in 1946, Kennedy's reputation at Harvard had followed him into public office. Washington buzzed with rumors about his philandering, and his attendance record in the Senate was among the chamber's worst. His health frequently kept him off the Hill in surgery or under medical supervision, but he enforced a strict code of secrecy about the severity of his physical condition, and his inability to provide plausible explanations for his whereabouts contributed to his Washington image as a charming, distracted political lightweight.

And in truth, JFK didn't really like Congress. He considered even members of his own party "windbags and demagogues." To Galbraith, it seemed that JFK avoided legislating just to escape the company of other politicians.[5]

The votes he did manage to cast brought him just as much difficulty as those he missed. In 1957, the Senate took up a civil rights bill that included new voting rights protections. To archsegregationist Strom Thurmond, the 1957 bill was such a threat to white power in the South that he launched a twenty-four-hour filibuster in an attempt to prevent it from going to a vote, reading the Declaration of Independence and the voting laws of every state to delay Senate business. It was high Capitol Hill theater that achieved almost nothing for Thurmond legislatively. The bill was already toothless, and eventually passed by an overwhelming margin.

But it survived without any meaningful help from JFK. Though he voted for the final, defanged bill, Kennedy also cast procedural votes to water down the bill and appease Jim Crow Southerners. Like Thurmond's filibuster, JFK's public stand with segregationists was mostly for show—and liberals got the message.

Kennedy had money and charisma, two traits that never go out of style with political power brokers. In 1956, he very nearly secured his party's vice presidential nomination at the Democratic National Convention in San Francisco. But for many party insiders, it wasn't clear whether the handsome young man wanted to carry the mantle of FDR or a conservative like Grover Cleveland. His father, Joseph Kennedy, Sr., the source of JFK's money, had split with Roosevelt over U.S. involvement in World War II and was widely regarded as an anti-Semite. Much more damning was the Kennedy family's longtime friendship with Wisconsin senator Joseph McCarthy. In 1950, JFK, then a member of the House of Representatives, had told a Harvard graduate school seminar that McCarthy "may have something" on Communist infiltration of the government and boasted of voting for the McCarran Internal Security Act, which had created a new government board empowered to strip Americans of their citizenship if it found ample evidence of "disloyalty."[6] And when Robert Kennedy finished managing his brother's successful 1952 Senate campaign, he took his first job on Capitol Hill working for McCarthy at the height of his crusade against New Dealers. Bobby lasted only about six months in the post, but the stint left a permanent stain on his reputation among liberal Democrats. When the Senate voted to censure McCarthy in 1954, Kennedy was the only Senate Democrat who refused to support the measure, arguing that it would "have serious repercussions upon the social fabric of this country."[7]

This light touch with McCarthyism may very well have cost him the vice presidential nod in 1956. When he asked for Eleanor Roosevelt's support at the convention, she publicly scolded him for his silence on McCarthy, creating a spectacle that wounded JFK politically and emotionally for years.[8]

Galbraith, meanwhile, had become a patron saint of liberal lost causes for his work on two failed Adlai Stevenson presidential campaigns. Shortly after FDR's death, Galbraith had helped found Americans for Democratic Action with Eleanor Roosevelt, Arthur M. Schlesinger, Jr., and the theologian Reinhold Niebuhr. They intended the group to serve as an institutional redoubt for New Deal energy and idealism against an aristocratic Republican Party and hostile conservative southern Democrats. Its founders spent years busying themselves in private meetings with other liberal intellectuals developing platforms and policy agendas for Democratic administrations that never came to be. But ADA exercised real power within the party— a precursor to the think tanks that would dominate Washington a generation later, offering a prestigious seal of approval for both liberal politicians and liberal ideas.

By the waning years of the 1950s, JFK held a Senate seat in Massachusetts and Galbraith was still teaching at Harvard. With his eye on the White House, Kennedy began courting his former tutor by asking his advice on everything from the outflow of gold in Fort Knox to the function of agricultural price supports, inviting him to regular dinners at a private room in Boston's high-end Locke-Ober restaurant, where Kennedy, "never varying . . . always ordered lobster stew."[9] Galbraith could be professorial and long-winded, and the young senator developed a habit of telling him to cut to the chase. But he kept inviting the economist back. And the intimate setting—often just the two of them, sometimes a trio with their historian friend Schlesinger—created an atmosphere of high-stakes political machination that flattered Galbraith's ego and whetted his appetite for the backroom dealing that made Washington move. Galbraith had no illusions about Kennedy's ambitions or his liberal apostasies. But he saw just as clearly that his former pupil was a rising star who could restore him to public power.

By the end of 1959, everyone in Democratic Party politics knew Kennedy was planning a presidential run, and almost everyone knew Galbraith—much to the chagrin of Stevenson true believers holding out for a third run—was now a Kennedy man. That fact alone increased Kennedy's stock with the American Left and helped him clear out potential challengers. But Galbraith didn't just put his own reputation on the line; he was intent on linking JFK with Eleanor Roosevelt, the woman who continued to represent the New Deal and, to liberals, the best of FDR's legacy. Eleanor hosted a TV interview program out of Brandeis University, and Galbraith brokered an introduction between the two, securing an interview for Kennedy that would air the same day he officially announced his bid for the presidency. This early stagecraft was a sign of just how much work Kennedy recognized he needed to put in with the left wing of the party. Though Eleanor was far from ready to endorse JFK—a fact she made clear to newspaper reporters afterward—the cordial on-camera repartee between the two bolstered JFK's credibility with liberals and initiated a process of reconciliation that eventually led Eleanor to support him.[10]

Galbraith offered Kennedy more than an ideological bridge to the left. JFK's youth helped him project optimism and confidence, but it also contributed to his fluffy public image as a celebrity more interested in partying with Marilyn Monroe than poring over policy details. No living American was more famous simply for being smart than Galbraith. His support signaled even to more conservative voters that serious minds were for Kennedy—a fact campaign strategists exploited in the general election battle with Richard Nixon. "Ken's function, both at the convention and subsequently, was to lead intellectuals back to Kennedy," according to Paul Samuelson.[11]

Kennedy, of course, won. And as he looked ahead to his administration, he had to decide what to do with all the liberal intellectuals who had supported his campaign. The most feverish years of McCarthyism had ended. McCarthy had died three years earlier, and Kennedy himself had helped dent the Hollywood blacklist by publicly praising the 1960 film *Spartacus*, a film written by a Communist screenwriter. Washington was at last a safe place for Keynesians.

Franklin Delano Roosevelt had fundamentally changed the hierarchy of expertise in the nation's capital, exiling Wall Street's old guard from positions of administrative influence and replacing them with academic economists. By the Kennedy years, economists ruled the two most powerful agencies in the federal bureaucracy: the Council of Economic Advisers and the Federal Reserve.

The CEA had been created by the Employment Act of 1946, a law that Keynesians had understood as a legislative defeat, even though one of their own, Alvin Hansen, had helped write it. Keynesians had wanted not an Employment Act but a *Full* Employment Act that would *mandate* government action to eliminate unemployment, replete with specific worker protections and remedies. But as Cold War paranoia began to set in, the idea of so much government power seemed positively Soviet to Congress, so Keynesians were forced to settle for a vague legislative commitment to the federal government's "responsibility" to "promote maximum employment" and the Council of Economic Advisers.

Today, the CEA is a minor analytical outfit that publishes an annual report which almost nobody reads. But in the 1940s and '50s, it was surpassed only by the Pentagon and the State Department in its influence over public policy. Under the leadership of its early chairmen, the CEA became a permanent White House think tank tasked with everything from monitoring economic growth to recommending government budget plans and even—during the Truman years—advising on Cold War strategy. "When I was chairman of the Council, I could never conceive of my having left that job voluntarily," recalled

Leon Keyserling, who served as CEA chair under Truman, where he enjoyed "absolute and complete access to the President."[12] Both Truman and Eisenhower were staunch believers in a balanced budget, yet under pressure from CEA chairs Leon Keyserling and Arthur Burns, both presidents accepted budget deficits in the name of economic growth (for the most extreme McCarthyists, Eisenhower's willingness to run a deficit was proof that he had been compromised by the Soviets).

The role of the Federal Reserve had also changed. Under the leadership of Marriner Eccles in the 1930s, the Fed board of governors in Washington had effectively fused with the Treasury Department, allowing the United States to pursue a unified fiscal and monetary agenda. Under the arrangement, the Fed pursued a monetary policy that kept interest rates low and money cheap for both banks and the federal government. Inflation and unemployment were managed not by interest rate adjustments but by fiscal policy—government spending and taxation—and, during the war, price controls. From 1937 to 1947, the Fed kept the discount rate at 1 percent, and beginning in 1942, it publicly coordinated monetary policy with the Treasury Department to keep down the interest rate on World War II bonds. Even after the war, when inflation briefly shot up after price controls were eliminated, the United States didn't battle rising prices with high interest rates and the unemployment high interest rates created. As late as 1951, the discount rate was still just 1.75 percent, and the Fed remained formally committed to guaranteeing a specific, predictable interest rate on U.S. government debt.

With the outbreak of the Korean War, however, economists at the Fed began agitating against the dictates of the Treasury and the CEA. Inflation suddenly erupted as consumers, expecting another round of wartime price controls, went on a buying spree, forcing up the prices of everything on the shelves. By February 1951, prices were increasing at an annual rate of 21 percent. The Treasury wanted the Fed to keep guaranteeing low interest rates on government debt by purchasing bonds from U.S. banks, helping to keep down war costs for the government. But that policy, the Fed believed, would also encourage banks to issue more loans, which would put further upward pressure on prices. Appalled by what they considered the Treasury's complacency with inflation, top officials at the Fed began demanding the right to manage prices independently of the other policy makers in the administration. Truman agreed and severed the Fed's official connection to the Treasury, giving it "independent" authority over monetary policy and the power to put the brakes on the U.S. economy at will.[13]

In practice, however, the Fed continued to play a supporting role as the CEA took center stage. Monetary policy had been the chief lever of economic management during the 1920s and early 1930s, and monetary policy had neither prevented nor cured the Great Depression. Most economists agreed that fiscal policy was both more powerful and more flexible. Kennedy's choice to run the CEA would therefore be a major statement about the kind of president he wanted to be.

The president-elect recognized his debt to his old tutor from Winthrop House and felt obliged to offer Galbraith the job as CEA chair. To Kennedy it seemed like a generous proposal. Previous CEA chairs had maintained a low public profile, and Kennedy would be inviting years of headaches for himself by picking Galbraith, a bona fide celebrity who actively courted ideological conflict. But Kennedy never extended the offer. When he dispatched Schlesinger to see if Galbraith might be interested, Galbraith instead urged Kennedy to appoint Walter Heller, a Keynesian who chaired the economics department at the University of Minnesota.

Kennedy was relieved, if a little baffled. Every adviser to a presidential campaign wants to be rewarded with a dream job, but Galbraith's ambition was extraordinary: he wanted Jack's Senate seat. When Kennedy moved to the White House, there would still be four years left in the term he had won in 1958. Though Galbraith denied he was the source of rumors in "the Boston papers" and *The New York Times* that named him as a serious "prospect" to succeed JFK,[14] the idea of appointing him to the Senate wasn't *completely* crazy. The Kennedy family had controlled Boston politics for two generations, and Ken and Kitty had grown close to them over the course of the campaign. They were given seats of honor at the inauguration next to John Steinbeck and his wife, Elaine, and the president-elect leaned on Galbraith for advice on filling positions throughout the administration—at the Treasury, at the Labor Department, even foreign policy jobs.[15] He was the only economist in the administration to maintain what Samuelson described as a "social relationship" with the Kennedys. "Among the economists, there's no question that Galbraith was closer to the president and Jackie in particular," Heller later recalled. "He bought art for her over in India."[16]

But the Kennedys intended to keep their dynasty a family affair. Jack turned his seat over to his college roommate Benjamin Smith II, who vacated it for Ted in 1962, once the youngest Kennedy brother's thirtieth birthday rendered him constitutionally eligible for Senate service. Galbraith ended up accepting an appointment as ambassador to India—a prestigious diplomatic post where his ideas about poverty and democracy could be put to work as the United States reorganized its Cold War strategy in Asia. But it was lost on no one that JFK had shipped the most prominent liberal from his campaign half a world away.

Paul Samuelson never spent more than three consecutive nights in the nation's capital.[17] He hated Washington. There were too many lobbyists running around and not enough intellectuals. He enjoyed teaching and avoided confrontation—he wasn't built for the arm-twisting and backstabbing that built and broke careers in Washington. As Kennedy searched for a CEA chair, Samuelson, like Galbraith, wouldn't take the job. The move just wasn't worth it. But he couldn't turn Kennedy down outright. As he told members of the CEA in 1964, "It was too important to leave a great country of ours to the likes of universal geniuses like Walt Rostow and Ken Galbraith."[18] So instead of moving to Washington, Samuelson agreed to head a special task force that would allow him access to the president while he maintained his post as head of the economics department at MIT. Heller became CEA chair, as Galbraith had suggested.

Samuelson and Galbraith were friends who agreed about deficit spending, public works, and voting Democratic. Both had made names for themselves with brash, playful economic writing informed by *The General Theory,* and both had struggled to keep Keynesian ideas alive during the McCarthy era. But the similarities ended there. Even Galbraith's friends took note of his arrogance, while even Samuelson's detractors acknowledged his humility. Galbraith worked with linguistic concepts and social theory. Samuelson declared that all economic reasoning was mathematical and regarded even his own English-language output as substantively superfluous. He adored markets; Galbraith didn't trust them.

The ideological clash between the two men would define the economic agenda of the Kennedy and Johnson era and shape the public's idea of the economy over the next half century. For Galbraith, Keynesian demand management wasn't just about making sure the numbers added up so that unemployment could be cured; it was about realizing a particular kind of society. To Galbraith, it was terribly important *how* the government brought the economy into balance. Some choices were morally and politically superior to others, and he believed that economists had a responsibility to alert the public to economic forces that could encourage society to become chintzy, shallow, and warlike. Though Samuelson's own preferences often coincided with Galbraith's idea of progress, his more famous friend's attempt to discredit the moral authority of the market in *The Affluent Society* had been a direct challenge to what Samuelson believed economics should—or could—achieve as a discipline.

Samuelson had devoted much of his career to purging economics of moral and even linguistic content, stripping it down to bare, numerical essentials. He was reluctant to substitute his own judgment for the verdict of the market. Samuelson and his acolytes at MIT considered their work both more modest and more intellectually rigorous than Galbraith's social theory. They were doing hard science with cold data, restricting their observations and advice to their field of expertise. Samuelson was like a physicist, an impartial student of the laws of the market. Galbraith, Samuelson once said, was better suited for "writing a best seller about utopia" than engaging in serious economics.[19]

But in their own way, Samuelson, Heller, and Robert Solow, who all worked for the CEA under Kennedy and Johnson, were making even grander claims than their more popular rival. They claimed that their work reflected deep scientific truths about human behavior and organization. Whereas Galbraith viewed economics as a fragile belief system always on the verge of being displaced by a new paradigm, Samuelson saw it as a progressive science of incrementally accumulated knowledge and claimed to have unearthed mathematically binding natural laws of human behavior. Samuelson eventually developed an ambiguous relationship with the mathematization of his profession. "Like herpes, math is here to stay," he lamented to *The New Yorker* in 1996.[20] But first it would get him—and the entire Keynesian economic project—into serious trouble.

The Affluent Society dominated popular economics in 1958, but the work that commanded the most attention from Keynesian academics that year was a paper by a New Zealand economist, A. W. Phillips. Scouring nearly a century's worth of British data, Phillips uncovered a startling correlation between inflation and unemployment. A trade-off seemed to exist between the two: Where unemployment was lower, inflation was higher; where inflation was lower, unemployment was higher. Though Phillips refrained from making strong claims about the trend, Samuelson and Solow weren't so bashful when, inspired by Phillips, they discovered a similar relationship in a quarter century of U.S. data. This, they declared, was an "astonishing" and stable tool for regulating the economy.[21] Policy makers could pick and choose from a "menu" of inflation and unemployment options, just by setting aggregate demand to the desired level.[22] By accepting a slightly higher level of inflation, governments could reliably push down the unemployment rate and vice versa. If inflation was too high, the government should cut spending or increase taxes. If unemployment was too high, it should increase spending or cut taxes. Samuelson was so confident that he had uncovered a major breakthrough that he put the "Phillips Curve" into the 1961 edition of his textbook.[23] It was *science*, and Samuelson, Solow, and Heller did not hesitate to bring the latest wonder of the Atomic Age with them to the Kennedy administration, where they eventually settled on targets of 4 percent unemployment and 2 percent inflation.[24]

The Phillips Curve had enormous implications, not only for taxation and spending but for monetary policy. Following Keynes, Galbraith saw interest rate increases deployed by central banks as the most unjust and wasteful method of bringing down prices. Monetary policy functioned by throwing people out of work. Higher taxes and even direct price controls had their drawbacks, but at least they didn't directly put anyone out of a job. The Phillips Curve seemed to suggest that the pain of unemployment was the inevitable price of controlling inflation. One way or another, unemployment would have to go up if prices were going to come down. The new data reinforced Samuelson's view that many of Galbraith's ideas were irresponsible, even dangerous. "I thought it my duty to offset the influence of Ken Galbraith, who was strong in the opinion that the only good interest rate is a low interest rate," he later confided to the CEA.[25] Coupled with the growing influence of the Federal Reserve as a policy-making institution, Samuelson and his enthusiasm for the Phillips Curve helped monetary policy recover the intellectual prominence it had lost during the Depression. Taxes and spending, after all, weren't the only way to influence aggregate demand. Higher interest rates could take money out of people's pockets by forcing layoffs, and lower interest rates, under the right circumstances, might induce companies to hire more workers by making the cost of credit cheaper. It was a change in the intellectual landscape as dangerous to Keynesian thinking as it was monumental.

More than any other president of the twentieth century, Kennedy made a spectacle of soliciting input from intellectuals. This was in part a matter of genuine personal affinity; JFK didn't like congressmen, and Washington was crawling with phonies. But it was also a private way of exacting revenge against his detractors. If he was such a lightweight, why did so many brilliant minds compete for his attention? He installed Arthur Schlesinger, Jr., as a special assistant to the president, which gave the Harvard historian plenty of material he could put to use intellectualizing JFK's administration for posterity. And he relied on economists for advice on almost every aspect of his program— from forecasts on growth and unemployment to diplomacy and even military strategy. By 1961, the economics profession was nearing the peak of "a rising trend of influence which dated back to Roosevelt and his Brain Trust,"[26] and Kennedy longed to be seen not merely as a glamorous, camera-ready celebrity but one of the great minds of his day. When JFK offered Yale economist James Tobin a place on the CEA, Tobin protested that he was "only an ivory-tower economist." Kennedy replied, "That is the best kind. I am only an ivory-tower President."[27]

Galbraith, who had been advising Kennedy for years, understood this dynamic and exploited his highbrow persona to wage, in the words of his friend Schlesinger, "unremitting guerrilla warfare in support of the public sector."[28] He called for spending on public parks, education, medical care, and museums, coupled with more generous Social Security and veterans' benefits, a higher minimum wage and higher taxes on the wealthy (the top tax bracket was already 91 percent), and even direct government suppression of prices at the expense of corporate profits. When the unemployment rate briefly jumped to 8.1 percent just after Kennedy's inauguration, Galbraith urged immediate administrative action to boost public spending.[29] "He went over and browbeat the veterans administrator into an early disbursement of VA dividends," recalled CEA member Kermit Gordon.[30] He ignored State Department protocol and the pleadings of National Security Advisor McGeorge Bundy by circumventing the bureaucratic chain of command and addressing his memos directly to Kennedy. Along with Walt Rostow, Galbraith became a powerful economist voice on foreign affairs.[31]

Samuelson thought that Galbraith was abusing the prestige of their profession. Economists were not qualified to opine on war; it was a matter on which the field had little to say. He saw himself as a tactician rather than a strategist, an expert instead of an adjudicator. And his conception of the proper role of the economist carried tremendous weight with Heller, Gordon, Solow, and Tobin, who regarded him as the most eminent mind in the profession. But in practice, Schlesinger observed, Samuelson's humility meant that he "adjusted his recommendations to fit the presidential and congressional mood."[32] As Galbraith was romping through the bureaucracy trying to shove money out the door, Samuelson took note of Kennedy's desire to avoid being "tagged as a big spender"[33] and authored a "tentative"[34] report suggesting increased defense spending and, perhaps, speedier deployment of existing spending programs as the means for fighting recession. If trouble persisted, a "temporary" tax cut might help. "What is definitely not called for in the present situation is a massive program of hastily devised public works whose primary purpose is merely that of making jobs and getting money pumped into the economy."[35]

Samuelson's quantitative instincts were sound. The country didn't plunge into depression, and a moderate budget deficit of a little over $3 billion fueled by defense spending, the dispersal of unemployment benefits, and more generous Social Security payments was enough to bring unemployment down substantially. Galbraith was relieved to see the economy moving again, but he recognized a dangerous ideological drift among his Keynesian colleagues away from the peacetime public works doctrine of the 1930s. If the government kept assembling all of those bombs and battalions as a way to boost employment, Galbraith reasoned, eventually somebody might want to use them.

In 1961, that was not a uniquely liberal fear. When Dwight D. Eisenhower bid farewell to the presidency, he had warned the American public to be vigilant about the growing influence of what he called "the military-industrial complex," which now exercised "economic, political, even spiritual" influence in "every city, every State house, every office of the Federal government."[36]

Yet it was becoming difficult to discern who was taking cues from whom in the Kennedy White House. In a commencement speech at Yale on June 11, 1962, Kennedy told the graduating class that the great problems of their generation would "relate not to basic clashes of philosophy or ideology but to ways and means of reaching common goals. . . . What is at stake in our economic decisions today is not some grand warfare of rival ideologies which will sweep the country with passion but the practical management of a modern economy."[37] Here was the bloodless, harmless formulation of Keynesian thinking that Galbraith himself had propagated during the Truman and Eisenhower years as he beat back McCarthyist charges of Communist disloyalty. And Galbraith had in fact helped Kennedy write the speech.[38] But under the cover of a practical, nonideological program, Kennedy was transforming Keynesian economic tools into powerful weapons in the Cold War.

The fate of American Keynesianism had also become entangled in JFK's relationship with the barons of American business. In April 1962, after a few months of negotiation, the administration reached an agreement with major labor unions and steel company executives on wages, a move intended to keep down inflation throughout the economy. Though the Office of Price Administration was long gone, the government still cut deals with sensitive industries to fix prices on an ad hoc basis. An increase in workers' pay for the production of basic goods like steel or oil could have a ripple effect; high prices for such commodities would drive up costs for other manufacturers, which would have to pass them on to consumers. Kennedy's arrangement to control steelworkers' wages was cooperative and modest. His economic team hoped it would give him room to pursue a more aggressive fiscal policy without worrying about overshooting and running up inflation.

But only a few days after the deal was finalized, U.S. Steel chairman Roger Blough casually informed Kennedy that he would be raising prices by $6 a ton anyway. After using Washington to knock down higher pay demands from his employees, Blough intended to let his shareholders feast on profits from higher prices anyway.

Kennedy was incensed. "My father always told me that all businessmen were sons-of-bitches, but I never believed it till now," he told aides, a remark so caustic that it soon leaked to the press. Though the president spent the next few days doing damage control, privately he remained outraged. "They *are* a bunch of bastards," he told Schlesinger and Adlai Stevenson, "and I'm saying this on my own now, not just because my father told it to me."[39]

The administration coordinated with other steel companies to create competitive pressure to force down U.S. Steel's prices, and Kennedy ultimately won the steel war. But his disenchantment with the executive suites in corporate America was not a simple matter of friend versus foe. Even sitting in the White House, JFK saw himself as an underdog. It wasn't that he wanted to *defeat* the industrial magnates of the 1960s; he wanted to prove to them he wasn't just a handsome rich kid but every bit the serious man of affairs. Blough's betrayal had stung because Kennedy craved his approval.

At the end of May, the stock market took an unexpected plunge. Even when the economy seemed to be steadily strengthening, the terrors of Black Tuesday were never far from the minds of White House staffers who came of age during the Depression. Kennedy spent a week talking over his response with advisers—an unthinkable chasm of time by today's standards—and announced that the federal government would respond forcefully to the stock jitters with a major tax cut for both individuals and corporations.

Internally, Kennedy and the CEA were anxious about offending the business-class enthusiasm for balanced budgets. In the president's second year in office, the budget deficit expanded to more than $7 billion, and though the economics profession was quite comfortable with the idea, the corporate world initially screamed for fiscal discipline, longing for balanced budgets as a sign of government restraint. But those complaints were suddenly muted as the administration presented its new plan. As it turned out, wealthy people liked the idea of having their taxes cut. "By 1962 the commandment to balance the budget was a paper tiger," concluded economic historian and future Nixon adviser Herbert Stein a few years later. In 1938, 1947, and 1953, business-backed conservatives in Congress had pushed hard for tax cuts in the face of obvious budgetary red ink. The deficit had already become a fig leaf for the conservative yearning for lower taxes—and if a president would just offer up a tax cut outright, Wall Street would not complain about its effect on the national debt.[40] That same phenomenon has subsequently proved true for presidents Richard Nixon, Ronald Reagan, George W. Bush, and Donald Trump.

Conservatives hadn't actually received their big, bold tax cuts under FDR or Eisenhower; they'd voted for bills that had never been signed into law. With Kennedy, the policy was still innovative.[41] A Gallup poll revealed that 72 percent of Americans would oppose a tax cut if it increased the national debt, while only 19 percent approved of the idea.[42] If Keynesian thinking was dominant at American universities, it remained far from a consensus position even among Democrats. Kennedy himself wasn't completely on board with his own tax cut until December. In a speech to the Economic Club of New York, an elite gathering of bankers and corporate executives, JFK hailed the effect a tax cut would have on investment incentives. He promised to scale back government spending and tamp down on federal employment even as "defense and space expenditures" would increase in the name of "our own security."[43] He even adjusted his rhetoric about budget deficits. They were still bad, he argued, but the economic growth unleashed by the right tax cut would ultimately result in *higher* government tax receipts and *smaller* deficits. "Budget deficits are not caused by wild-eyed spenders but by slow economic growth and periodic recessions. . . . The soundest way to raise the revenues in the long run is to cut the rates now." And of course there was the Cold War to consider. If the United States did not pass a tax cut that would enable the nation to outproduce the centrally planned economy of the Soviet Union, "the hope of all free nations" would be jeopardized. When the audience cheered, the president was finally sold.

After the speech, a giddy Kennedy called White House counsel Ted Sorensen. "I gave them straight Keynes and Heller, and they loved it." Sorensen had a different assessment. "It sounded like Hoover, but it was actually Heller." Galbraith was withering, denouncing the talk as "the most Republican speech since McKinley."[44] Helping the rich get richer, Kennedy had argued, was the surest way to help the country. "I am not sure," Galbraith had previously told Kennedy, "what the advantage is in having a few more dollars to spend if the air is too dirty to breathe, the water too polluted to drink, the commuters are losing out on the struggle to get in and out of the cities, the streets are filthy, and the schools so bad that the young, perhaps wisely, stay away."[45]

Galbraith didn't dispute the judgment of Heller, Samuelson, and Tobin that a big tax cut would provide a jolt to economic growth and further reduce unemployment. But he was starting to think that the administration's team had become lost in their own equations. One of the great achievements of *The General Theory* had been its demonstration that economic growth and progress did not require steep levels of economic inequality; society was free to pursue more egalitarian tax policies. The Kennedy plan to boost demand through tax cuts would surely benefit the wealthy more than other sectors of society. What's more, it would just encourage the production of more consumer goods. "The addition of more and better depilatories has nothing to do with national health and vigor," he told Kennedy.[46] Historians would not attribute "the glories of the Kennedy Era" to "the rate of economic growth" but rather to "the way it tackles the infinity of problems that beset a growing population and an increasingly complex society."[47] Kennedy had put civil rights legislation, education funding, poverty relief, and health care reform on the back burner in his drive for the tax cut. Thirty-six separate bills had been introduced that would have provided medical insurance to people over sixty-five. The political will existed to pursue big, liberal projects. But they would all have to wait on JFK's tax agenda.

Kennedy sketched out his tax plan in his January 1963 State of the Union address. Individual taxes would be reduced by $11 billion by cutting tax rates across the spectrum; the lowest bracket would be reduced from 20 percent to 14 percent, while the highest would fall from 91 percent to 65 percent. Corporate taxes would fall $2.5 billion by slashing the rate on the largest firms from 52 percent to 47 percent, while closing a host of special-interest loopholes.[48]

To the president's surprise, he faced the greatest resistance not from balanced budget conservatives but from social justice liberals. Tennessee senator Albert Gore, Sr., railed against the plan as a handout for the rich, telling Kennedy that millionaires would see their take-home pay increased by 50 to 200 percent, while typical citizens would get a bump somewhere in the mid–single digits. "This simply cannot be justified—socially, economically or politically," he fumed. "And I hold these sentiments passionately! This is something that no Republican administration has dared do; it is something you must not do."[49]

Galbraith shared Gore's concerns. But his greatest frustrations with Kennedy involved foreign policy. What was the point of converting the United States into a Keynesian economic juggernaut if its economic strength was to be deployed for military adventurism?

Galbraith had recognized that his influence on domestic policy would steadily wane once he decamped for his post as ambassador, but the flip side of his exile was a tremendous degree of independence regarding foreign affairs. When the tax cut debate erupted in Washington, Galbraith was stationed in New Delhi, grappling with the unraveling political situation in Vietnam alongside one of America's most powerful allies in Asia, Indian prime minister Jawaharlal Nehru. Massive U.S. food shipments to India had purchased—within reasonable limits—loyalty to the Kennedy administration from the Indian regime.

That alliance encountered a potential crisis in the summer of 1962, when the Communist government of China launched a military offensive across the Himalayas and into India. The conflict escalated during the fall, a time when every eye in the White House became fixated on the Cuban Missile Crisis. Galbraith, acting "in the convenient absence of instructions"[50] from Washington, advised Nehru against an aggressive response to the Chinese army, calling for cool heads and limited engagement. Within a month, China had retreated—despite a series of military victories—and Americans quickly forgot the entire conflict. That the border skirmish did not escalate into a drawn-out proxy war between the United States and Communist China was a credit both to Galbraith's diplomacy and his management of the U.S. foreign policy bureaucracy.

Galbraith remembered it as one of the great achievements of his life. But the real trouble was not to India's northern border but to the country's east, across the Indochinese Peninsula. Galbraith had successfully urged Kennedy to keep out of the turmoil in Laos (he did not know about the CIA's ongoing efforts there), but Vietnam appeared with each passing day to be drawing the United States deeper into a political and military quagmire. Galbraith's plan was to use the Indian government to provide diplomatic cover for an American withdrawal. The U.S. government, he warned Kennedy, risked becoming an oppressive colonial force in a region that offered no meaningful strategic advantages against either Soviet Russia or Maoist China. South Vietnamese president Ngo Dinh Diem was an unreliable ally, Galbraith argued, a petty strongman whose commitment to democracy was purely rhetorical and whose capacity to fend off Communist militants depended almost entirely on U.S. aid. Advising Kennedy that "nothing succeeds like successors," Galbraith insisted that "almost any non-Communist change [in government] would probably be beneficial."[51] Ideally, the United States should reach an agreement with the Soviet Union to withdraw American troops in exchange for an end to guerrilla attacks by the Communist-backed Viet Cong in South Vietnam. After the withdrawal, trade relations between North and South could be reestablished, and eventually the two sides could talk of reunification. The diplomatic détente could begin with an overture from the Indian government to the Ho Chi Minh regime in Hanoi.[52]

Kennedy seemed to agree with the plan. After reading through a memo from Galbraith in April 1962, he instructed his ambassador to approach the Indian government about initiating peace talks. And then, with the order delivered, Kennedy waited. And waited. Months passed. After the botched Bay of Pigs invasion of Cuba the prior year and his public refusal to deploy ground troops in Laos, JFK wanted a politically opportune moment to draw down U.S. commitments in Vietnam to avoid looking weak. Eventually, it seemed to Galbraith that the moment might never come.[53]

Vietnam underscored just how little Keynes had achieved at Bretton Woods. For Keynes, the conference at the end of World War II had been an opportunity to eliminate the economic sources of international conflict—to forge a new global order of balanced, fair trade, regulated by international authorities. Instead, the Bretton Woods monetary system had become part of the economic administration of the Cold War, a set of financial tools the United States used to pursue its geopolitical interests. Because the system relied on the dollar, any nation that participated in the Bretton Woods system was effectively signing up for some degree of U.S. economic management. Bretton Woods facilitated cooperation, but only through hegemony. The monetary system did nothing to impede the United States from becoming a violent, hostile power to the new postcolonial nations that did not align with its Cold War interests. Keynes and his dream of eliminating economic sources of imperial conflict were irrelevant to the debacle in Vietnam, which represented no perceivable economic interest to either the United States or the Soviet Union. The U.S. military presence existed to prevent Vietnam—North and South together—from holding an election to form a national government. U.S. leaders recognized that the winner of that election would almost certainly be Ho Chi Minh. The anti-Communist rationale for intervention was also an attack on democracy and the promise of postcolonial nationalism.

So while all the top American economists were Keynesians by the 1960s, nobody thought about Keynesian economics as an international idea. Keynes and Keynesianism were strictly confined to a set of strategies that individual nation-states could pursue to climb out of recession or fine-tune unemployment and inflation. Keynes the philosopher of war and peace had given way to Keynes the fiscal therapist.

Galbraith's life in New Delhi slowly settled into a luxurious procession of superfluous dinners and commemorations. He could have secured an extension to his leave from Harvard to remain in India, but by the summer of 1963, with the border trouble with China settled and Kennedy on autopilot in Vietnam, he decided to return home. *The Affluent Society* had appeared five years earlier. It was time to resume work on a new book. After stopping for a brief visit in Washington at Kennedy's request, Galbraith assessed the continued outflow of gold from the United States under the Bretton Woods system and began teaching in Cambridge in the fall semester.

In September, the House of Representatives passed Kennedy's tax cut by a margin of 271 to 155, with 48 Republicans concentrated in the business centers of the Northeast joining 223 Democrats. Tellingly, the Democratic majority didn't need Republican support to pass the bill; the business class liked the idea of the tax cut more than it disliked the idea of handing a legislative victory to a Democratic president. Democratic opposition, meanwhile, was concentrated among balanced-budget conservatives in the South. Though few recognized it at the time, the tax-cut vote was a watershed moment for American liberalism and Keynesian thinking. The northern, urban, organized-labor Democrats who had formed the core of FDR's New Deal coalition were supporting a tax cut heavily slanted in favor of the rich. And they were backing it on the grounds that the latest economic science from Keynesian economists showed that the tax cut would be good for the workingman. Over the next thirty years, similar thinking would steadily drown out other Democratic Party priorities, culminating in the presidency of Bill Clinton and the Democratic Party's repudiation of New Deal liberalism in the name of neoliberal progress.

Galbraith was discouraged by the vote, but there would at least be an opportunity to improve the bill in the Senate. Senators might be cajoled, and if necessary, magazine articles might be written to broadcast the danger. One afternoon in November, Galbraith and Schlesinger were meeting with *Washington Post* and *Newsweek* publisher Katharine Graham in New York when the trio was interrupted with the news that the president had been shot.[54]

The following days were a haze of anguish and confusion. Galbraith hurried to the White House, where, despite holding no official post, he mourned, planned, and coordinated with an emotionally shattered sea of friends, family, and advisers. Four decades later, he told a biographer that although the hours had been "full of activity," "I can now barely recall what it was we were doing."[55]

One exchange, at least, stayed with him. The day after the assassination, he ran into Lyndon Johnson, who ushered Galbraith back into what only a day before had been his vice presidential office in the Executive Office Building. Johnson had a speech to give to Congress the following week and wanted Galbraith's help in outlining the tasks ahead for the Johnson presidency. "He was at pains to speak of his commitment to civil rights and the liberalism we had both inherited from Roosevelt," Galbraith wrote in his memoir. It was a case LBJ was making to all of the Kennedy liberals that week, including Walter Heller.[56] Whereas most Democrats were skeptical of Johnson's commitment to liberal ideals, Galbraith, who had known LBJ since the early 1940s, had always believed in the sincerity of Johnson's New Deal populism. Johnson's father had been a state legislator in Texas, but the new president had always presented his personal history as a rags-to-riches story in which the family income of his childhood seemed to decline "around fifty percent for each year" Johnson spent in Washington.[57] To Galbraith, the narrative said as much about what Johnson found admirable as it did about his flexibility with the truth. "Easily persuaded" by Johnson's insistence on civil rights, Galbraith "emphasized another concern": Vietnam. Johnson, who had come of age before the era of the economist-as-policy-sage, brushed off Galbraith's foreign policy concerns. "Our exchange was a metaphor of the Johnson years," Galbraith later recalled. "A man who was strong, innovative, confident and resourceful on domestic policy would be destroyed by a military effort which served no American purpose and which, in its political aspects, wholly misjudged the nature of power and the scope for influence in the post-colonial world."[58]

But first, there would be a tax cut. In February, Johnson signed into law a tax bill that looked much like what Kennedy had called for. The new law reduced the top rate on individuals from 91 percent to 70 percent and the lowest rate from 20 percent to 14 percent, while slashing the corporate rate from 52 percent to 48 percent. Johnson promised government spending restraint over the next fiscal year as the price of the deal, meaning that conservatives would get both lower taxes and lower spending.

But Johnson had grander designs than the unfinished business of the Kennedy administration. He intended the tax cut to anchor a domestic agenda unmatched since FDR's in its ambition. It would juice the economy and guarantee the availability of jobs to everyone able and willing to work. For everyone else, there would be a War on Poverty. With Keynesian experts steering the ship to ensure steady economic expansion, poverty would become the result of personal and local inadequacies: shortcomings in education or infrastructure or a culture that had become accustomed to intergenerational joblessness. "Very often a lack of jobs and money is not the cause of poverty but the symptom," Johnson said in his first State of the Union address, a line directly inspired by Heller. "The cause may lie deeper in our failure to give our fellow citizens a fair chance to develop their own capacities, in a lack of education and training, in a lack of medical care and housing, in a lack of decent communities in which to live and bring up their children."[59] And so Johnson created the Job Corps to help young people who lacked marketable skills, the National Teachers Corps to improve the quality of teaching in public schools, the Volunteers in Service to America (VISTA) program to put socially conscious young people to work refurbishing poor neighborhoods. He created the Office of Economic Opportunity, a new agency with $1 billion to dole out for "community action" programs conceived of and implemented by small, local organizations across the country. A new federal legal aid program would help protect the poor from predators, while food stamps would guarantee that no family had to go hungry.

Johnson looked back to FDR and saw himself engaged in a vast project of energy and experimentation, armed with advantages his hero had not enjoyed: a thorough understanding of a modern economy and the best economic advisers the country had to offer.

But although the War on Poverty achieved a great deal of good, the agglomeration of plans and programs failed to eliminate poverty for a simple reason Galbraith later pinpointed: "One possible remedy for poverty would be to give the poor income; this alone was excluded."[60] By conceiving of poverty as a kind of personal affliction rather than a simple lack of resources, the Keynesian macro experts who had appointed themselves managers of the national economic machine had also absolved themselves of responsibility for many of the country's most pressing economic problems. Improving education, for instance, probably helped at the margins by creating more jobs for teachers. But the ultimate result was a better-educated underclass just as poor as the one that preceded it. Even programs such as Head Start, which enabled young children to go to school at an earlier age, weren't conceived of as a way to lower child care bills or free up time for parents to work. Heller always took for granted that society's basic economic unit consisted of a single-earner family in which wives didn't work.[61]

After the tax cut, Galbraith became increasingly peripheral to the administration's policy making. When Johnson appointed him president of the Office of Economic Opportunity, Galbraith treated the position as an honorific, focusing his energies on writing his next book and waging an increasingly vocal public campaign against the Vietnam War. Galbraith didn't even step down from his teaching post at Harvard to oversee the grant-making process. In 1964, the $1 billion allotted for OEO was real money, but still less than 1 percent of the federal budget. The former Kennedy whisperer was accustomed to greater things.

Galbraith was angry—with Johnson, with the war, and with the change in the economics profession that was taking place before his eyes. The Johnson administration was, in important respects, the most liberal the country had ever known. But its liberal energy did not come from its top economists, who were sitting out debates over the war, offering fundamentally conservative advice on taxes, and misdiagnosing the nature of poverty.

Galbraith began publicly attacking not only the war but his fellow liberal economists. Both in private conversation and in public testimony before Congress, he denounced the Kennedy-Johnson tax cut as a new "reactionary Keynesianism" that posed a grave danger to the future course of U.S. politics. Keynesian economists had offered a great gift to the political Right. Post-McCarthyists who wished to privilege the interests of wealthy warmongers above the needs of society at large could now rely on liberal science to certify the legitimacy of their programs.

To Samuelson, Heller, and Solow, this was an act of staggering hypocrisy. Where had Galbraith's antiwar conscience been during the conflict in Korea? Galbraith, who had found so many opportunities to praise the Eisenhower administration as enlightened Keynesian technocrats, was now attacking the most liberal presidency in a generation as the naive abettors of an irresponsible corporate aristocracy. It was too much. When Galbraith eventually published his next book, *The New Industrial State,* Solow savaged it in a review fueled as much by personal vitriol as by scientific disagreement. Calling Galbraith a "moralist" who wished to cloak his own "values" with "an elaborate theory" that "simply does not stand up," Solow issued a blistering attack on the glitz and glamour Camelot had bestowed on Galbraith.

"Galbraith is, after all, something special," Solow wrote. "His books are not only widely read, but actually enjoyed. He is a public figure of some significance; he shares with [Federal Reserve chairman] William McChesney Martin the power to shake stock prices by simply uttering nonsense. He is known and attended to all over the world. He mingles with the Beautiful People; for all I know, he may actually be a Beautiful Person himself. It is no wonder that the pedestrian economist feels for him an uneasy mixture of envy and disdain."[62]

Galbraith was not particularly beautiful. And his long-standing contentment with corporate monopoly power became a target for intellectual opponents eager to prove their own liberal bona fides in the face of Galbraith's attacks from the left. Samuelson made speeches ripping Galbraith's antitrust views as a "reactionary and conservative"[63] heresy against the New Deal tradition Galbraith sought to embody. Even Galbraith's affinity for price controls over monetary policy was just another expression of his elite vanity, a tribute to his own tenure at OPA.

It was a dangerous dynamic for Galbraith and his stature as a towering twentieth-century intellectual. The Galbraith persona was the delicate product of two mutually reinforcing phenomena: the prestige of the economics profession made him desirable to politicians, while his influence with the political elite enhanced his prestige within the economics profession. If either turned decisively against him, the foundation of his influence would crumble.

And the attacks by Samuelson and Solow stung because they were, in some respects, true. After a decade spent at the height of Democratic Party politics, Galbraith's ego was slipping from arrogance into delusion. When the chairman of Americans for Democratic Action resigned, Galbraith jumped at the opportunity to resume the leadership of the lefty organization he had founded with Eleanor Roosevelt. He planned to use it as a stepping-stone to greater things. Touring the country, giving speeches against the war, he began making plans to challenge Johnson in the 1968 presidential election on an anti-Vietnam platform. He abandoned the scheme only after his son Alan, a lawyer, insisted that the constitutional ban on foreign-born presidents would bar him from taking office.

Galbraith's grip on public power was weakening, but the Democratic Party elite remained entranced by his social vision throughout the 1960s. Even Johnson, increasingly frustrated with the great thinker's constant attacks on the Vietnam War, still wanted his help in articulating the domestic aspirations of his presidency. As Johnson prepared a speech laying out what he called "The Great Society," he quietly called in Galbraith, then vacationing in his Vermont country home, to make a "confidential" trip to the West Wing to help him write the speech. Johnson did not want to be seen enlisting the services of a war critic.[64]

Galbraith agreed, boarding a government plane from the nearest airport in Keene, New Hampshire, before stopping to pick up White House counsel Joseph Califano in New Jersey and decamping to Washington. Galbraith spent the day banging out a condensed version of *The Affluent Society*, and by the evening, LBJ was ecstatic: "I'm not going to change a word. That's great."[65]

The speech Johnson gave later that week at the University of Michigan was part economic history, part social diagnosis, and pure Galbraith:

For a century we labored to settle and to subdue a continent. For half a century we called upon unbounded invention and untiring industry to create an order of plenty for all of our people. The challenge of the next half century is whether we have the wisdom to use that wealth to enrich and elevate our national life, and to advance the quality of our American civilization. . . . The catalog of ills is long: there is the decay of the centers and the despoiling of the suburbs. There is not enough housing for our people or transportation for our traffic. Open land is vanishing and old landmarks are violated. Worst of all expansion is eroding the precious and time honored values of community with neighbors and communion with nature. The loss of these values breeds loneliness and boredom and indifference. Our society will never be great until our cities are great. Today the frontier of imagination and innovation is inside those cities and not beyond their borders. New experiments are already going on. It will be the task of your generation to make the American city a place where future generations will come, not only to live but to live the good life. . . . So, will you join in the battle to give every citizen the full equality which God enjoins and the law requires, whatever his belief, or race, or the color of his skin? Will you join in the battle to give every citizen an escape from the crushing weight of poverty?[66]

In practice, the Great Society became a massive civil rights and antipoverty agenda. The Civil Rights Act of 1964 banned employment discrimination based on race and outlawed segregation, while the Voting Rights Act put an end to poll taxes, literacy tests, and other tactics designed to deny black citizens the right to vote. Just as important, it established a system of federal enforcement to ensure that southern states abided by the new rules. Johnson created Medicare as a new socialized health insurance program for the elderly, and Medicaid as a complementary program for the poor. He vastly expanded both the scope of Social Security—which had initially excluded agricultural workers in order to deny benefits to black workers in rural America—and the size of benefit payments. Other existing antipoverty programs, including FDR's Aid to Families with Dependent Children (better known by the Clinton years as "welfare"), were dramatically expanded, while the Elementary and Secondary Education Act began delivering more than $1 billion a year in federal funding to public schools. Johnson established both the National Endowment for the Arts and the National Endowment for the Humanities, along with the Corporation for Public Broadcasting, which created PBS and National Public Radio. A barrage of environmental legislation, including the Clean Air Act, the Water Quality Act, the Motor Vehicle Air Pollution Control Act, the Wilderness Act, and the Wild and Scenic Rivers Act followed suit.

It was nothing short of a second New Deal—a vast expansion of the state through the provision of new public goods to meet the needs of a democracy that even a full-employment economy could not fulfill.

And for the most part, it worked. LBJ's War on Poverty programs had been small, piecemeal attempts to help people learn how to participate in the labor market. They had failed to eliminate poverty because poverty was not, for the most part, a result of personal confusion about how to get and hold down a job. There simply weren't enough job opportunities for much of the population, and many of the jobs available paid only poverty-level wages. The broader agenda of the Great Society, by contrast, succeeded in permanently lowering the American poverty rate by turbocharging the labor market and taking care of household expenses that drove families into destitution. The tax cut, as much as Galbraith maligned it, really did release a lot of spending power, which in turn pushed corporations to ramp up production and increase hiring. By creating Medicare and expanding food stamps, welfare, and Social Security, the Great Society not only helped families meet major expenses, it increased their purchasing power, which further juiced the labor market. By 1969, the year Johnson left office, the poverty rate was down to 12.1 percent—a reduction of more than 12 million people and more than one-third of the impoverished population at the time Johnson had taken office.

But like FDR's before him, Johnson's economic triumphs were incomplete. The Great Society's civil rights agenda did help spread the gains of the roaring economy more equally. The black poverty rate dropped to 32.2 percent, a dramatic improvement from the rate of 55 percent that had prevailed when Galbraith had published *The Affluent Society*. But the statistical chasm between black and white poverty remained an unresolved crisis in American democracy. The black poverty rate would not drop below 30 percent until 1995. It is 21.8 percent today, compared to 8.8 percent among white households. The Civil Rights Act banned racial discrimination in hiring and wages, but its enforcement has always been uneven, and subsequent legislative battles to improve upon it—particularly the 1978 struggle for a true Full Employment Law—were stymied by conservative opposition and a lack of interest on the part of Democratic Party leaders.

And there were danger signs piling up for Johnson's version of the Keynesian economic system. Overall economic inequality plummeted during the 1940s and 1950s, according to every metric scrutinized by the economists Emmanuel Saez and Gabriel Zucman. But over the course of the 1960s, that progress flatlined.[67] Inflation, which had barely been a factor during the 1950s and most of the 1960s, began to rise. Though by no means a crisis, price increases had moved from just over 1 percent a year in 1965 to over 5 percent when Richard Nixon took office. Though Johnson, Heller, and Samuelson were notching staggering annual GDP numbers, this growth was much more modest once inflation was factored in. In 1969, the economy expanded by more than 7 percent, a number that would have been cause to rejoice during the deflationary 1930s. But that gain translated to just over 2 percent when the upward pressure on prices was factored in—respectable, but nothing to write home about.[68] These troubles with inflation would continue into the 1970s and jeopardize what was remained of the Keynesian project.

By the end of the 1960s, Keynesian economics had become a dry and technocratic field divorced from the philosophical ideas of its namesake. In Washington and academia, the word *Keynesian* no longer carried the subversive connotation it had during the heyday of McCarthyism. There were now liberal Keynesians and conservative Keynesians and reactionary Keynesians who recognized that the tools created by Paul Samuelson, John Hicks, and Alvin Hansen could be deployed for a variety of political ends. But the liberal achievements of the Great Society were nevertheless supported by the economic engine Keynesian economists had built by stimulating aggregate demand. If Keynesianism lost its intellectual credibility, liberal efforts to fight poverty and advance civil rights would surely go down with it.

SIXTEEN

———— ◊ ————

THE RETURN OF THE NINETEENTH CENTURY

"KEYNES' PLEASANT DAYDREAM," DECLARED Joan Robinson, "was turned into a nightmare of terror."

It was December 1971, and Robinson was speaking from the podium in the opulent presidential salon of the Jung Hotel in New Orleans. She had been invited to give the Richard T. Ely keynote address to the annual meeting of the American Economic Association—a rare professional honor for Robinson, who seized her moment in the limelight to castigate the leading minds of her field. Economists, she declared, had to take responsibility for forty years of sustained poverty, brutal violence, and ecological catastrophe that had been inflicted in the name of "growth." It was a blistering, unrelenting rhetorical assault. She began by describing the audience as a "throng of superfluous economists" and closed by indicting "the evident bankruptcy of economic theory which . . . has nothing to say on the questions that, to everyone except economists, appear to be most in need of an answer."[1]

Robinson had a score to settle, and the crowd knew it. One of the most accomplished economists of her generation, she had nevertheless been clawing for professional respectability all her life. When she and Edward Chamberlin had independently discovered new problems with the accepted theory of monopoly and competition in 1933, the economics faculty at Harvard had publicly dismissed her half of the discovery. Everyone who worked in economic theory knew that she and Richard Kahn had been critical to the development of *The General Theory;* Joseph Schumpeter even referred to her as an uncredited "coauthor" of the book. But she had been feuding with Samuelson and Solow over the Keynesian mantle in the decades since, and in 1970 the Royal Swedish Academy of Sciences seemed to side with the MIT boys, naming Paul Samuelson the first Keynesian recipient of the Nobel Prize in Economics. Robinson would never receive the award, but the Nobel Committee was only the most recent major intellectual institution to snub her. Cambridge hadn't even bothered to make her a full professor until 1965. Like Rosalind Franklin, who had codiscovered the molecular structure of DNA with James Watson and Francis Crick, Robinson was a brilliant woman persistently sidelined by a profession hostile to women. At the time of her AEA lecture, women constituted just 11 percent of the students in graduate economics programs and a mere 6 percent of the faculty.[2]

Robinson also had a mean streak. She pursued conflict as a strategy to draw attention to her ideas, goading other prominent economists into debate by bludgeoning them with criticism, forcing them to defend themselves. Even her intellectual allies could be stunned by her vitriol. When her former student Amartya Sen accepted the Nobel Prize in 1998, he described her as "totally brilliant but vigorously intolerant."[3] "She was a terrible woman in that sense," according to her friend Paul Davidson. "She had no qualms about being rude if she wanted to be." Her professional rivalries frequently escalated into personal grudges. The evening of her AEA speech, Robinson and Davidson had been dining together in an empty restaurant when Samuelson and his wife, Marion, had walked in. The two parties shared the room uninterrupted for forty minutes without so much as acknowledging each other.[4]

The list of Ely lecturers is littered with Federal Reserve governors and Treasury secretaries. Backed for one night with the prestige of the AEA, Robinson was ruthless. The orthodox economists of the 1920s and '30s, she said, had been incapable of grappling with a world in which economic problems would not work themselves out. What they called "equilibrium analysis" put a scientific veneer on a quasi-religious faith in automatic progress that foreclosed "free will" in favor of "predestination." Economists preferred to live in textbooks, where they were not confronted with the ugly tragedies of the real world. They simply could not cope with a debacle like the Great Depression, which had shown that the universe didn't naturally trend toward social harmony.

Once they got over the shock, these men—and they were almost all men—had embraced Keynes for the wrong reasons. Instead of seeing *The General Theory* as a new doctrine with its own social and political implications, they believed Keynes had discovered the "one simple device" that could restore the easy progress of the nineteenth century—a new incantation to realign the stars. By managing aggregate demand to ensure full employment, the world could get back to normal, and economists could fall back on their neat, predictive models with rational actors maximizing their profits.

This was a dangerous delusion. "There is no such thing as a normal period of history," Robinson said. "Normality is a fiction of economic textbooks. . . . If the world of the nineteenth century had been normal, 1914 would not have happened."

Keynes had shown the economics profession the way out of its first great crisis, the Great Depression. But a quarter century of Keynesian economic management had led the world into a second crisis—one filled with choking pollution, mass poverty, a cold war, "and several hot wars." That was bad enough, but leading economists now alternately believed they had actually solved these problems or insisted they were not economic problems at all. Pollution was just a question of pricing the social costs of "externalities"—costs that businesses imposed on the world around them as by-products of production. But how, Robinson demanded, could anyone set an appropriate price for flooding a community with cancer? How could money equate a certain number of human lives with a certain level of corporate profit? "Where is the pricing system that offers the consumer a fair choice between air to breathe and motor cars to drive about in?"

Poverty, the economists now said, was just a question of "growth." Keep the economy out of recession, and poverty would eventually disappear. Twenty-five years after the war, Robinson was still waiting.

And war? One way of spending money to boost demand was as good as another. The Keynesians, she said, had governed as if Keynes' thought experiments had been a serious policy agenda, treating the production of "armaments" as though they were no different from bottles to be buried in the ground. Robinson couldn't believe she had to say it: "Keynes did not *want* anyone to dig holes and fill them."

To Robinson the point of *The General Theory* had been to restore human agency to economic theory. Keynes, she argued, forced economists to grapple with "life lived in time." Systems didn't immediately snap to equilibrium. People made choices based on expectations about an uncertain future. Decisions like whether to save or spend, or whether to buy new factory equipment or lay off workers, were never obviously rational or irrational in the moment, because long-term consequences could not be predicted. This made government inescapable, since the job market wouldn't automatically correct to full employment. But the Keynesians, led astray by Samuelson, had taken Keynes' theory and constructed a system that, just like the orthodoxy of the 1920s, dismissed the significance of human agency. One government spending choice was as good as another as long as the result was full employment. And so the economics profession and the Keynesian tradition had lent their prestige to horrific political choices: the Cold War and ecological destruction.

"I do not regard the Keynesian revolution as a great intellectual triumph," she concluded. "On the contrary, it was a tragedy."

After thirty minutes of unstinting abuse, however, a curious thing happened. As Robinson drew her narrative to a close, John Kenneth Galbraith, seated behind her on the dais, rose to his feet and began to applaud. The crowd assembled before her stood in appreciation, the full auditorium offering a "vigorous" and "sustained" standing ovation.[5]

By 1971, the crisis facing the economics profession was not a secret. Reporting on the previous year's AEA meeting, *The New York Times* concluded that economics as a discipline had peaked in 1965. In 1968, a crop of dissidents had formed a new official caucus within the AEA, calling themselves the Union for Radical Political Economics and demanding representation at AEA events, frustrated by the rightward drift in academia. In three years, their ranks had swelled to 1,500 members. But it wasn't just the young radicals from URPE who were eager for Robinson's discipline. "The targets of her indictment loved every word," according to James Tobin, a Samuelson devotee who had advised both Kennedy and Johnson. It was a relief to have the problem stated so plainly.[6]

And in truth Robinson had offered the establishment an easy way out. It didn't need to start from scratch or burn any heroes in effigy; the answers were all right there in Keynes.

Economics had one final indignity in store for Robinson. Offered a clear and coherent path to save the Keynesian project that had survived for thirty-six years, her fellow economists would choose instead to abandon it. Robinson would not be surprised.

Milton Friedman had been waiting for the 1970s his entire professional life. Born to Hungarian Jewish immigrants in Brooklyn, he grew up in Rahway, New Jersey, where his parents ran a dry-goods store. A Keynesian New Dealer during the late 1930s, Friedman worked for the Roosevelt administration during the war, but eventually fell under the sway of the laissez-faire advocates at the University of Chicago, where he accepted a job in the economics department in 1946. Like Keynes, Friedman was a relentless optimist, enchanted all his life with an idea of progress that, paradoxically, he believed to have been embodied by the American past.

"The closest approach that the United States has had to true free enterprise capitalism was in the nineteenth century," Friedman once said. "Anybody was free to put up an enterprise, anybody was free to come to this country: it was a period in which the motto on the Statue of Liberty meant what it said. It was a period in which the ordinary man experienced the greatest rise in his standard of life that was probably ever experienced in a comparable period in any country at any time."[7]

Friedman was a founding member of Hayek's Mont Pelerin Society but began his tenure in the neoliberal movement as a junior partner with a tainted ideological history. Many of his colleagues viewed him with skepticism, even hostility. It wasn't just his recent conversion from Keynesianism. He was thirteen years younger than Hayek and more than thirty years younger than Mises. He had no memory of the lost Eden before 1914. For Friedman the era was shrouded in the mists of a vast unknowable past, imbued with a romantic glow by his family history and American national mythology, rather than any longing for the cultural achievements of the Austro-Hungarian Empire. Friedman wanted not a new European aristocracy but the energy and enthusiasm of John Wayne's American frontier.

The clashes between Friedman and his mentors were about much more than style. His ideas about the nature of economics were infected with both an American sense of progress and a deep, quantitative scientific rationalism. Hayek and Mises aggressively opposed the mathematical turn in the economics profession led by Samuelson after the war. Hayek, in particular, preached a radical skepticism regarding human economic knowledge. For Hayek, the principal virtue of the price system in a free market was its ability to process a vast array of information about individual preferences that no single person could comprehend, let alone calculate. The inevitability of human ignorance, Hayek believed, made government intervention a fool's errand that no set of statistics could overcome.

But like Samuelson, Friedman saw economics as something very close to a pure science that could drive social progress through empirical observation and statistical analysis. Where people appeared to have ideological disputes, economics could adjudicate by revealing the real-world consequences of different policies. In Friedman's happy worldview, "differences about economic policy among disinterested citizens derive predominantly from different predictions about the economic consequences of taking action—differences that in principle can be eliminated by the progress of positive economics—rather than from fundamental differences in basic values, differences about which men can ultimately only fight."[8] Seeing the facts clearly—with enough data—people of goodwill would come to agreement. To Hayek, Friedman's data-driven thinking made his ideology "every bit as dangerous as that of Keynes."[9]

Hayek had spent the postwar years struggling to reconcile his enthusiasm for laissez-faire with some semblance of the New Deal nation-state. By 1962, he had been unable to come up with an elegant solution to the problem, and none of his attempts had generated anything like the public response that *The Road to Serfdom* had almost two decades prior. *The Constitution of Liberty*, which Hayek regarded as his most important political statement, had flopped upon publication in 1960, the same year the election of John F. Kennedy seemed to doom once and for all the political viability of his intellectual movement. As Hayek's public celebrity subsided, Keynesian ideas grew more influential and prestigious, and Hayek's chief financial supporter in the intellectual resistance, Harold Luhnow, lost his mind. Exhausted and defeated, Hayek retreated from the American scene to the University of Freiburg, a medieval institution founded by the Habsburgs, where his academic output slowed considerably.

Hayek's departure created an opening for Milton Friedman at the top of the Mont Pelerin Society and the broader—but never more politically marginalized—neoliberal community. And unlike Hayek, Friedman felt no need to compromise with post–New Deal modernity. Instead, he espoused a cheerful, uncompromising celebration of laissez-faire that took free markets to be almost wholly incompatible with state action. For Friedman, nothing could stand in the way of hard work and good ideas—not racism, class distinction, or even the monopoly power of large corporations. Possessed with a supremely benevolent vision of humanity, he believed there was no problem the market could not solve—even war.

"If a chemist feels it is immoral to make napalm, he can solve his problem by getting a job where he doesn't have to," Friedman told a journalist for *Business and Society Review* in 1972. "He will pay a price. But the ultimate effect will be that if many, many people feel that way, the cost of hiring people to make napalm will be high, napalm will be expensive, and less of it will be used. This is another way in which the free market does provide a much more sensitive and subtle voting mechanism than does the political system."[10]

Friedman had labored away in relative obscurity through the 1940s and '50s, making the occasional academic splash by arguing against rent control (he concluded it ultimately raised rents) and medical licensing for doctors (again, increased costs for consumers). He turned down an offer to join Eisenhower's CEA, predicting that the job would require too much "compromise" with his antigovernment views, quipping "I think society needs a few kooks, a few extremists."[11]

Like Hayek, Friedman always insisted he was not a conservative, believing he professed a doctrine of progressive innovation. "Good God, don't call me that. The conservatives are the New Dealers like Galbraith who want to keep things the way they are. They want to conserve the programs of the New Deal."[12] His rhetoric combined strains of populism—the market was the voice of the people, which the government sought to suppress—with a celebration of heroic genius. "Newton and Leibnitz; Einstein and Bohr; Shakespeare, Milton, and Pasternak; Whitney, McCormick, Edison, and Ford; Jane Addams, Florence Nightingale, and Albert Schweitzer"—all had provided "individual" impetus for social change that "government can never duplicate."[13]

But he became a household name in 1964 for his association with the most uncompromising conservative political movement in America: the presidential campaign of Arizona senator Barry Goldwater. Whatever Friedman said about his own views, in practice his work—like that of Mises and Hayek before him—generated a sense of intellectual legitimacy for hard-right politics.

No "respectable intellectual in New York . . . was willing to defend Goldwater"[14] in 1964. "In academic circles, admitting to Goldwater leanings has come close to wearing the scarlet letter," *The Wall Street Journal* reported. "Even many parts of the more-Republican business and professional community have tended to look down their noses at Goldwater fans."[15] This was not a divide born of abstractions about rent control and medical licensing. Goldwater's path to the Republican presidential nomination rested on uniting southern and western states against northern Republicans led by Nelson Rockefeller, a civil rights supporter who provided financial backing to Dr. Martin Luther King, Jr. "As Goldwater took the nomination, black Republicans became an endangered species," one historian has noted. "In Georgia, the triumph of the Goldwater supporters at the state convention led to the virtual elimination of blacks from leadership positions."[16] The conservative newspaper columnist Robert Novak observed that the party had been taken over by "Republicans [who] want to unmistakably establish the Party of Lincoln as the white man's party."[17]

Goldwater insisted his campaign was about government overreach, not racial animus, and he recruited Friedman as an economic adviser. But civil rights were the central issue of both the GOP primary and the general election. Goldwater voted against the 1964 Civil Rights Act and gave speeches opposing the Supreme Court's 1954 *Brown v. Board of Education of Topeka* decision, which had ruled that segregated public schools were unconstitutional. Though he personally agreed "with the *objectives* of the Supreme Court as stated in the *Brown* decision," Goldwater refused "to impose that judgment of mine on the people of Mississippi or South Carolina."[18] It was "their business, not mine," he said. Friedman declared Goldwater's position "excellent," an ideal expression of the principle of "equal treatment of all, regardless of race."[19] For Friedman, the market was a cure-all; it would price out war and napalm and racism without any clumsy directives from politicians.

As public school districts began grudgingly integrating after *Brown*, Friedman had opposed the busing programs that brought black and white students from different neighborhoods into the same schools. As an alternative, Friedman argued, the government should provide families with vouchers that could buy their children slots at either public or private schools. The resulting competitive market for education would surely liberate black America more thoroughly and efficiently than any government mandate.

Of course the Republican faithful who pulled the lever for Goldwater in 1964 didn't believe a word of this. Goldwater's base didn't think *Brown* and the Civil Rights Act were just too slow and clumsy about putting an end to segregation; they flocked to Goldwater precisely *because* they expected him to maintain the Jim Crow social order. This was not a mystery during the campaign, as political commentators within and without the party decried the segregationist turn taken by the Party of Lincoln. But even after Goldwater's landslide loss to Johnson, Friedman said he had no regrets about the racial politics of the campaign. "The defeat of the hitherto dominant Rockefeller Republicans was a crucial step in the gradual shift of public opinion away from liberalism as popularly understood and toward free-market conservatism,"[20] he recalled. Not everyone in his intellectual circle agreed. Hayek supported the Civil Rights Act from his increasingly irrelevant perch in German academia.

Friedman believed that freedom was to be found not in humanity's capacity for self-government but in the ability of each individual to participate in a market. The only legitimate role for government was to establish the institutions necessary for free-market capitalism: a military to defend against foreign aggression, a police force to protect against theft, and a central bank to ensure an adequate monetary system to facilitate exchange. He detailed these ideas in *Capitalism and Freedom*, which he wrote with financial support from the addled Luhnow and published in 1962.

"Underlying most arguments against the free market is a lack of belief in freedom itself," Friedman wrote. "A free market" was "a system of economic freedom and a necessary condition for political freedom."[21] Despite all of his differences with Hayek, this conceit linked Friedman with the ideas about the Depression and the rise of totalitarianism that his mentor had expressed in *The Road to Serfdom*. Totalitarian regimes come to power, according to this doctrine, when governments break the faith with laissez-faire. It was a clear rejection of the narrative Keynes had presented, in which the Nazis and Bolsheviks capitalized on the material despair caused by market dysfunction. But Friedman was not alone in his belief in a link between "economic freedom" and "political freedom"; Keynes had believed in one, too. The two men just defined freedom in very different ways. For Keynes, economic freedom included a guarantee of material security and the basic ingredients of the Bloomsbury good life. For Friedman, it meant only the ability to participate in a market economy. And so when critics assailed Friedman for his decision to advise Chilean dictator Augusto Pinochet amid his campaign of political assassinations and repression, Friedman argued that he was trying to bring Chileans political freedom through economic freedom. As China adopted more market-friendly reforms in the late twentieth century, Friedman said the changes confirmed his "faith in the power of free markets," that the citizens of China were now "freer and more prosperous than they were under Mao," and that economic reform had ensured that Chinese politics were "moving in the right direction."[22] A quarter of a century later, the Chinese government continues to jail, torture, and kill political dissidents.

Capitalism and Freedom, the historian Daniel Stedman Jones has noted, was a late entry in a "Cold War of ideas." It "consistently identifies New Deal liberalism with socialism and even communism," a "guilt-by-association" tactic emblematic of the very "McCarthyism" that Friedman "tepidly" rebuked within the book's pages.[23] For Friedman, the differences between New Deal liberalism and Soviet totalitarianism were superficial. Like Mises, he believed that no philosophical middle ground could exist between them, and he readily identified the income tax, Social Security, and public education as "socialist" policies.

In the meantime, Friedman worked to put the antidemocratic implications of his worldview into practice. When the debate over U.S. complicity in South Africa's apartheid system began to boil over in the 1970s, Friedman traveled to Cape Town, where he gave a speech arguing against universal suffrage for black South Africans. The "political market" of voting, he insisted, would unfairly weight South African politics toward "special interests." The free economic market, however, was "a system of effective, proportional representation" that offered true freedom for all South Africans. Progress under apartheid would come not from the expansion of voting rights in a political democracy but from increased foreign investment and unregulated commerce.[24] Friedman recognized "the extraordinary inequality of wealth" in South Africa, with its "great scarcity of Black entrepreneurship" and "Black capital." He was under no illusions about the practices of its corporate magnates. He described the chairman of Mobil Oil South Africa as a "bigoted" man with "hardboiled attitudes." But he told political leaders on the trip that "a laissez-faire policy was the only kind of policy that would make it possible for a society like the South African to have a peaceful multiracial society," because it was the only arrangement that "would make it possible for people to cooperate economically without having to make it a matter of legislative action."[25]

Such forthright antipathy to democracy was remarkable during the Cold War, when even ardent anti-Communist conservatives pointed to American democracy as a political ideal superior to Soviet dictatorship. And yet, as Galbraith observed, by the 1970s, democracy or no, "the age of John Maynard Keynes gave way to the era of Milton Friedman."[26]

In the spring of 1967, the Keynesian economic managers of the Kennedy and Johnson years seemed invincible. The unemployment rate had fallen from 7.1 percent in Kennedy's first year in office to just 3.8 percent, while every measure of inflation had remained below 3 percent. The tax cut that Galbraith had railed against had delivered years of strong economic growth. Adjusted for inflation, the economy had grown by 6.5 percent in both 1965 and 1966, the best two-year performance since the Korean War boomlet of 1950–1951.[27] Speaking to an economics symposium, Samuelson declared the Phillips Curve— the direct, statistically robust trade-off between inflation and unemployment—to be "one of the most important concepts of our time,"[28] a tool that had revolutionized both economic theory and practice.

And so Friedman must have seemed a little quixotic that December, when, at the AEA annual meeting, he condemned the economic record of the Kennedy-Johnson years as a dangerous mirage that would lead to runaway inflation. It was an audacious claim. Friedman did not content himself with accusations of mismanagement or poor judgment. The entire theoretical consensus of the economics profession dating back to the Great Depression would, he insisted, have to be thrown out. It was not merely a political attack on the Johnson administration; it was a scientific assault on John Maynard Keynes himself. Whatever his ideological opponents thought of Friedman's political views, nobody could pretend he didn't have guts.

He began his attack in the 1930s. Keynes, Friedman argued, had wrongly dismissed the power of monetary policy in his assessment of the crisis. To Keynes, "money did not matter." Cheap money had not ended the Depression, and so fiscal policy had to be the primary conduit of economic management. But Friedman and the economist Anna Schwartz had assembled an impressive array of data in *A Monetary History of the United States* suggesting that monetary policy had been much too tight during the early years of the Depression, largely because the Fed had not rescued the banking system, and the resulting bank failures had destroyed customer deposits and choked off credit to businesses. That regulatory failure by the Fed, Friedman said, had kick-started the Depression, which had then been aggravated by New Deal policies of the 1930s. Contrary to the prevailing Keynesian wisdom, the Depression had not been a failure of capitalism, but rather the catastrophic result of government mismanagement.

In Friedman's narrative, Keynesianism had not simply misdiagnosed the Depression; it had predicted a world that never came to be. After the war, Keynesians had anticipated depression. Europe and America had instead experienced an economic boom accompanied by price inflation, which had eventually been controlled by monetary policy—a fact, Friedman said, that disproved the Keynesian insistence upon the "impotency" of monetary policy.

Keynesianism had failed twice: it was based on insufficient data about the 1930s and had not predicted the real economic movement of postwar America. Friedman presented a grand theory to replace it. The prime mover of economic activity, he argued, was the money supply. When it expanded, people spent more, received bigger paychecks, and paid higher prices. But crucially, rising prices created the *expecta-*

tion of higher prices—and that could lead to a vicious inflationary cycle. The belief that prices would go up would cause retailers to charge more and inspire labor unions to demand pay raises. When those increases were realized, they would again generate expectations of further price hikes. Inflation could take on a life of its own, even when policy makers least expected it. The tiny price increases manifesting themselves in the Johnson economy were a canary in the coal mine.

What, then, was a central banker to do with this dangerous threat of an inflationary spiral always around the bend? According to Friedman, there was a "natural rate" of unemployment below which no policy maker, fiscal or monetary, could push the economy without causing inflation. It was hard to pinpoint just what this "natural rate" was; it depended on technology, productivity, unionization rates, and regulatory policies. But tinkering with fiscal or monetary policy to boost employment was a fool's errand. Over the long term, there was no trade-off between inflation and unemployment; there was only the natural rate of unemployment, which the economy would eventually, stubbornly settle upon. The Phillips Curve that Samuelson and Solow put so much stock in simply wasn't true. And the ever-present specter of self-reinforcing inflation made the idea of tolerating "contained" or "limited" inflation for the sake of slightly lower unemployment a very dangerous game. Friedman suggested instead that the Fed adopt a general rule of steadily increasing the money supply at all times— enough to accommodate natural economic growth but not enough to generate expectations of substantially increased prices. That strategy, he argued, should be pursued in both booms and slumps. The key was to maintain steady price expectations and allow "natural" economic forces to work their magic and restore economic harmony whenever disruptions occurred. Friedman called this doctrine *monetarism*[29] and consciously presented it as a "counter-revolution" against Keynes in his subsequent work.[30]

It was a rhetorically deft presentation, delivered by a master storyteller. But there were problems with the story. Keynes himself had predicted a postwar boom, not a depression (so had Galbraith, in "194Q"). He had never claimed that monetary policy didn't matter.

He had opposed using high interest rates as a policy device because they were the most socially destructive method available for bringing down prices. He never claimed it didn't work. And although it was true that Keynes had strongly preferred fiscal policy to monetary policy for fighting economic downturns, he had believed there were some circumstances in which loose monetary policy would boost employment; it would just depend on what changing, uncertain attitudes about the future were prevalent.

In his zeal to present himself as an Anti-Keynes, Friedman skated over just how much his own ideas relied on Keynesian thinking. His monetarism was essentially a rehabilitation of an idea Keynes had presented all the way back in 1923, updated with help from a key insight from *The General Theory*. In *A Tract on Monetary Reform*, Keynes had argued that the proper goal of economic policy making was for central bankers to ensure a stable price level—a point he shared with other early monetarists including Irving Fisher, whom Friedman now cited as his sole inspiration. In *The General Theory*, Keynes had broken down the traditional distinction economists had made between "the real economy" of resources and production and the "monetary economy" of wages and prices. To Keynes, money wasn't a neutral device that simply measured what was going on in the real world. Beliefs and expectations about money, he'd argued, had repercussions in the world of production. Friedman was taking those ideas about expectations and applying them selectively to price and wage inflation. It was a Keynesian framework—just one that turned over responsibility for economic management exclusively to central bankers instead of elected governments.

Harry Johnson, Friedman's colleague at the University of Chicago, recognized the similarities, telling Friedman that his monetarism "does manage quite skillfully to avoid mentioning Keynes' contribution to the theory of demand for money, and any suggestion even that he existed." Johnson saw Friedman as being engaged in a politicized intellectual proxy war of "liberal-Keynesian-Democrats versus the radical-anti-Keynesian Republicans,"[31] playing with words and labels to make his position sound more revolutionary than it was. And indeed, adherents of the radical Right who could identify the Keynesian scaffolding in Friedman's framework were uncomfortable with his new line of attack, seeing it as Keynes in sheep's clothing. A nonplussed Hayek told an interviewer, "Milton's monetarism and Keynesianism have more in common with each other than I have with either."[32] For Hayek, who believed that depressions simply had to burn themselves out, even monetary therapy was dangerous.

Then there were the technical problems. Friedman couldn't settle on a single consistent definition of either money or the money supply. He dodged empirical questions about the correlation among interest rates, unemployment, and the quantity of money by insisting that time lags in central banking operations made such observations difficult. Low interest rates, he said, were "a sign that monetary policy *has been* tight"—rather than a sign that it was tight at any given moment.

There was a harmony between Republican Party political strategy and Friedman's focus on inflation. In 1966, Richard Nixon had started campaigning across the country, attacking Johnson as a weak and irresponsible inflationist. The charge made no sense, as Democratic economists were quick to note; the inflation Nixon was railing against was a figment of his imagination. But it gave Nixon a polite, technical issue that demonstrated an attention to serious policy beyond the demagoguery on racial integration that Republicans were using to win white defections from the Democratic Party. By talking up inflation in 1967, Friedman was lending expert academic seriousness to the political attack, much as a generation of Keynesians had provided academic prestige to Democratic Party priorities.

Time was on Friedman's side. Even in 1966, Johnson's CEA had been warning him that the pace of war spending in Vietnam was making the price level difficult to maintain. The government had needed price controls and rationing to keep prices down during World War II. And the Federal Reserve was now raising interest rates to tamp down the inflationary pressure caused by Vietnam War spending. Despite the Fed's efforts, prices began to creep up in 1968 and accelerated in 1969. And then in 1970, something truly shocking occurred: the unemployment rate began to increase as inflation rose still faster. Growth turned negative, marking the formal onset of a recession. By 1971, the unemployment rate was at 6 percent, the highest sustained level in a decade, while inflation was approaching 5 percent, more than enough for people to feel the diminishing purchasing power of their paychecks.

These were not crisis conditions by the standards of the Great Depression. But they sent the economics profession into a panic. The simultaneous rise of both unemployment and inflation undermined the scientific legitimacy of the Phillips Curve; if there was a trade-off between unemployment and inflation, how could they rise at the same time? And for a decade, the Phillips Curve had been virtually synonymous with Keynesianism. The profession, led from the left by Paul Samuelson and from the right by Milton Friedman, had insisted upon mathematical rigor and predictive accuracy as the hallmarks of theoretical virtue. Now the numbers weren't adding up. Federal Reserve chairman Arthur Burns warned Congress that "the rules of economics are not working the way they used to."[33]

And by the early 1970s, the sheer dominance of Keynesian thinking across the profession had made it vulnerable to shifting political winds. Keynesian economics was not the vaguely utopian set of ideas that Keynes had presented to the British government as a reason to establish the National Health Service and a golden age of short workweeks and community theater. Burns was no starry-eyed liberal, and neither was the typical Keynesian economist. President Nixon's economic advisers featured politically conservative Keynesian economists who had embraced the doctrine *despite* the politically liberal connotations of its adherents in the Johnson administration, overwhelmed by its apparent empirical power. Herbert Stein, who would eventually chair Nixon's CEA, had published a book in 1969 called *The Fiscal Revolution in America* that praised Keynesianism for its scientific rigor and its ability to implement long-standing conservative policy goals including the Kennedy-Johnson tax cut. For such men, the collapse of the Phillips Curve made it easy to wonder if Friedman might just be onto something—not only about Samuelson and the Kennedy-Johnson era but about Keynes himself.

Thirty-five years of Keynesian policy making could not be unwound by a year of unusual price activity, however. Galbraith's push to win over corporate America in the 1940s and '50s had won plenty of converts beyond academia who did not consider themselves hippies; even Johnson had grown accustomed to receiving riotous applause from speeches to American businessmen.

The strangest and most unpredictable figure in this milieu was the president himself. Richard Nixon had won his first political race all the way back in 1946 by bashing the Office of Price Administration as a breeding ground for capital-C Communism. Once in office, he'd made himself a household name by almost single-handedly taking down the Soviet spy Alger Hiss, using his perch on the House Un-American Activities Committee to set an example envied by Joe McCarthy himself. Chronically paranoid, Nixon interlaced his years in the White House with long, private rants about his "enemies," Jewish conspiracies, and the soft younger generation that was making America weak.

He nursed a special hatred for Galbraith. Back in 1956, Galbraith had written a speech for Adlai Stevenson attacking Eisenhower for sharing the Republican ticket with Nixon. "Nixonland," in Galbraith's words, was "a land of slander and scare; the land of sly innuendo, the poison pen, the anonymous phone call and the hustling, pushing, shoving; the land of smash and grab and anything to win."[34] As Nixon presented himself as the commonsense champion of regular Americans, Stevenson and Galbraith understood him as a servant of the superrich, a con man attempting to dismantle the programs the Democratic Party had implemented to create the very middle class Nixon now claimed to represent. With war hero Ike recovering from a heart attack, Stevenson and Galbraith had tried to make the 1956 election a referendum on Nixon. Stevenson had lost in a landslide, but Nixon remembered the beating his reputation had taken. As Galbraith's biographer Richard Parker has detailed, in closed-door meetings with White House advisers, Nixon fantasized about punishing Galbraith in the press, of turning him into "a terrible goblin" and making his very name a political lightning rod that would make "the Democratic candidates and spokesmen repudiate him."[35]

Nixon blamed Eisenhower's CEA for the economic weakness in 1960 and blamed the sagging 1960 economy for his loss to JFK. When the economy had looked sluggish in 1958, Eisenhower had run a huge deficit. When it was stronger in 1959 and 1960, Eisenhower had cut spending to tamp down on inflation, but the result had been to cool off the economy. Nixon's electoral defeat by a razor-thin margin had resulted in years of shame and frustration. As vice president, Nixon had worked with the CIA to overthrow leftist governments in Iran and Guatemala. In the early 1960s, he was reduced to picking up political consulting gigs and writing books about politics—cash-out work for a has-been. His route back to the White House had depended on the Republican Party's implosion around Goldwater in 1964 and the Democratic Party's splintering over Vietnam—and even then Nixon had devoted years of his life to struggle and strategy to get over the hump.

All of this because Eisenhower's people had been a little too tight with federal money in 1960. Nixon was determined to prevent that history from repeating itself in 1972. But as 1970 turned to 1971, reelection seemed a Herculean task. Nixon's Vietnam War was just as unpopular as Johnson's, and it didn't pair well with rising unemployment. In one poll, just 27 percent of the country said it wanted to see a second Nixon term.[36]

On January 4, 1971, after two years of balanced budgets, Nixon dropped a bombshell on a team of television reporters when he casually disclosed off camera, "I am now a Keynesian in economics." The remark made its way into *The New York Times* within a few days, and within a few weeks, the president was defending a federal budget that would "balance at full employment"—a gentle way of saying that he would be running a deficit of $23 billion. Not since Eisenhower had the government run a deficit so large. Liberals in Washington didn't quite know how to react. Here was a conservative president from the McCarthy wing of the Republican Party praising Keynes and pushing for deficit spending to help the economy. Was it—could it be?—good?

In testimony before the congressional Joint Economic Committee on July 20, Galbraith offered committed Democratic partisans a way out, telling lawmakers, "Mr. Nixon has proclaimed himself a Keynesian at the moment in history when Keynes has become obsolete." Coming from the most prominent American Keynesian, it was a startling declaration. And it was accompanied by an equally startling policy remedy: Galbraith said the government should impose direct price controls on every firm with at least five thousand employees—the two thousand largest companies in the United States.[37]

To Galbraith, the scramble of inflation and unemployment numbers that had discredited the Phillips Curve was a product of corporate monopoly and powerful unions. "There has been a diminishing conflict between management and labor, an increasing tendency to resolve difficulties not by the traditional conflict but, after some ceremonial insult, for the corporation to concede the more urgent demands of the unions and pass the cost along, in higher prices, to the public."

Galbraith's rhetoric sounded more extreme than it was. In 1971, the United States had been at war in Vietnam for eight years. The conflict was not a minor undertaking; more than 2.5 million Americans were deployed to Vietnam over the course of the war, which ultimately cost $141 billion to prosecute, excluding veterans' benefits paid out after soldiers returned home.[38] The entire government budget of 1966— Great Society and all—had reached only $134 billion. The country had imposed wartime price controls in the 1940s, and it wasn't wild to contemplate such policies again during a conflict on the scale of the Vietnam War. And Galbraith's theoretical explanation for his proposal was thin. He'd been preaching the same line about big business and big labor fundamentally changing the economic scene for twenty years, but the Phillips Curve had fallen apart only in 1970. The break with Keynes had more to do with Galbraith's vanity than with a close reading of his predecessor. If the new era required a great new theorist, Galbraith suggested, he was ready to serve.

But Galbraith's announcement that the Age of Keynes had ended reflected the damage the Keynesian legacy had sustained in just a few short years. Friedman's attempt to use a problem with an economic theory from Samuelson and Solow—the Phillips Curve—to discredit Keynes was working. Even Galbraith no longer wanted to be tainted by association with the dread Keynes.

Nixon hated being mocked, particularly by a Harvard-Kennedy-Camelot-know-it-all such as Galbraith. Eight days after his testimony, the president held four hours of meetings in the Oval Office in which he ranted to cabinet members about the political nightmare constructed by his "enemies": "the Negroes and the Jews" who wouldn't vote Republican, the CEOs who acted like "sad damn sacks," the "uneducated Irish Catholics" who passed for union leaders. Somebody needed to be blamed for this mess. He told Treasury Secretary John Connally, a conservative Democrat from Texas, "I know you often use your principle 'It's nice to have an enemy'—well, one of the best ones I can think of is John Kenneth Galbraith." The recent testimony from "this son-of-a-bitch" had "unmasked what these bastards, all these bright New Dealers, want. They want another OPA, they want to control the economy, they want to control wages and prices." Nixon growled to Connally, "You get out there and make an issue of it—and destroy him on it."[39]

But the intellectual crisis of the Phillips Curve was giving way to a crisis in international affairs. Two weeks after the president told Connally to go off on Galbraith, the British Treasury informed the Nixon administration that it was about to shore up the pound by redeeming $3 billion in U.S. assets—dollars and Treasury securities—for gold. It was, in essence, a vote of no confidence against American inflation management. The United States was the only country in the Bretton Woods system with a currency convertible into gold. For the British, there was no difference between holding a dollar bill and holding the dollar's exchange weight in gold—unless they expected the value of those dollars to decline. The United States had been leaking gold for years thanks to inflationary pressures and the new phenomenon of an American trade deficit. And so U.S. trading partners increasingly pre-

ferred holding gold to holding dollars. Great Britain's decision was
sure to rattle financial markets all over the world. A bold, multibillion-
dollar gesture from a close diplomatic ally might even spark a run on
the dollar. No one could guess what that might mean for an international trade and finance order anchored in dollars. The United States
and the world stood at the precipice of the first acute, ruinous economic crisis since the Great Depression.

That Friday, Nixon helicoptered to Camp David with his economic
team, his closest aides and speechwriters, and Fed chair Arthur Burns
(though the Fed had been formally independent of the administration
since 1951, Burns was a committed Republican partisan who wanted
to bolster Nixon's reelection prospects). There, many learned for the
first time that the president and his Treasury secretary had been secretly meeting for months, developing a sweeping economic program
to replace Bretton Woods and save the Republican Party's dwindling
electoral hopes for 1972.

Nixon would abandon the last vestige of the gold standard, refusing
to honor international commitments to exchange dollars and Treasury
bonds for gold. There would be a massive monetary and fiscal stimulus
program—low interest rates and business-friendly tax cuts, accompanied by a 10 percent tariff on all imports to improve the competitive
position of domestic manufacturers. The administration would tamp
down the inevitable resulting inflation by doing something that no
Republican president in the twentieth century had dreamed of doing:
On Sunday night, Nixon would announce a nationwide wage and price
freeze and the beginning of a new price control program that would
last through election day.

Nixon's aides were stunned. Stein recalled a "suspension of realism"
that pervaded the remainder of the meeting, as aides hammered out
price, spending, and interest rate plans in a frenzied daze. "After only
a few hours," according to the economic historian Richard Parker, "the
group adjourned," leaving Nixon's speechwriters and political aides to
iron out the Sunday-night address.[40]

There was a certain right-wing logic to Nixon's about-face on price controls. The president's real passion was for war, not economic policy. He had been elected by promising to bring the conflict in Vietnam to a swift, honorable end. But in almost every respect he had in fact escalated the violence. He had authorized the secret expansion of the war into Cambodia and dramatically intensified the CIA's operations in Laos with a program that had killed tens of thousands of civilians. In Vietnam itself, Nixon had recently begun to draw down troop levels—burned by antiwar protests at home, embarrassed by the Kent State massacre in 1970 and the publication of the Pentagon Papers in early 1971. But fewer American boots on the ground made it politically easier for Nixon to amplify the Vietnamese body count. He authorized massive bombing raids that included attacks on essential civilian infrastructure. By 1972, he was seriously considering using "the nuclear bomb," pushing Secretary of State Henry Kissinger to "think big, for Christ's sake."[41]

Nixon thought of his economic plan in similar terms, telling advisers he wanted "total war on all economic fronts," something bold and tough that would show "these symps, these crawling bastards like Galbraith and Kennedy"[42] who had the guts to do what it took to restore American resolve. If that meant making a few casualties out of conservative economics totems, so be it.

The night after the staff briefing, Chief of Staff H. R. Haldeman encountered Nixon alone in his Camp David cabin, gazing into a roaring fireplace in the dark, "in one of his sort of mystic moods." The president told Haldeman that the real purpose of his economic plan was to "change the spirit" of the country. "Let America never accept being second best," he said.[43] "You must have a goal greater than the self, either a nation or a person, or you can't be great."[44] Like Keynes, Nixon understood economic policy was concerned with much more than statistics, and sought to revitalize the country with aggressive economic action. Unlike Keynes, he was in love with war.

Two days later, the country found itself nearly as shocked as Nixon's inner circle had been. Galbraith's phone began ringing while Nixon was still speaking to the camera, and he didn't stop talking to reporters until after midnight. As massive government programs go, Nixon's program was not terribly liberal. He slipped $5 billion in domestic spending cuts into the package, and the tax cuts were weighted heavily in favor of large corporations and the wealthy. Bretton Woods was a hard-fought diplomatic arrangement that Galbraith strongly disapproved of dismantling, but he was almost delirious from Nixon's abrupt conversion on price controls, telling *The Washington Post* he felt "like the streetwalker who had just learned that the profession was not only legal, but the highest form of municipal service."[45] It was a remarkably generous assessment from a man who had attacked Johnson's Vietnam War–era tax cut as "Reactionary Keynesianism." Nixon was turning up the dial on all the reactionary parts of Johnson's agenda, from the tax code to napalm delivery tonnage.

The consensus of economists slightly to Galbraith's right was even more supportive. Samuelson told *The New York Times* that "he approved of everything" Nixon had outlined except the spending cuts, while Arthur Okun, a Samuelsonian CEA chair under Johnson, told the paper that Republicans had made "a leap forward into realism."[46] In her AEA address a few months later, Joan Robinson was more cautious, noting that even a "successful" price freeze would at best "keep everyone in the position where he happened to be when the scramble for relative gains was brought to a halt." Nixon's plan, she said, was designed not to improve the social power of working people but to "perpetuate the division of income between work and property that happened to exist when it set in." Robinson suggested that wage bargaining would become more explicitly political under Nixon's system—a prospect that might or might not be good for working people.

Friedman was beside himself over the price freeze, writing in *Newsweek:* "Sooner or later . . . it will end as all previous attempts to freeze prices and wages have ended, from the time of the Roman emperor Diocletian to the present, in utter failure and the emergence into the open of the suppressed inflation."[47] AFL-CIO president George Meany complained that the wage freeze didn't include a complementary freeze on dividends or corporate profits, meaning that executives and shareholders would reap the lion's share of the benefits from Nixon's bold plan. It didn't matter; the country had been waiting for Nixon to do something big and bold on the economy, and to most people, Nixon's "New Economic Program" fit the bill. And it worked, at least for a while. Over the next two years, inflation declined from around 5 percent to below 3 percent as the unemployment rate fell from 6 percent to 5 percent and growth jumped back above 5 percent. And it was wildly popular. A whopping 73 percent of the country had disapproved of Nixon's handling of the economy in the summer of 1971. A White House poll conducted the week after Nixon's speech found that 75 percent of the country approved of his new plan. "In all the years I've been doing this business," the pollster remarked, "I've never seen anything this unanimous, unless it was Pearl Harbor."[48]

The rest of the world was horrified. Nixon's abrupt break with the Bretton Woods agreement signaled a complete breakdown of American economic leadership. The United States had blown up the very international system it had insisted upon creating at the end of World War II, and it had done so in part to avoid bringing an end to the brutal war in Vietnam. Nixon had essentially flown blind, making no preparations for how international financial markets might respond to his announcement or how the global monetary order would adjust. It was amazing that financial markets had not spun into panic or broken down.

And another wave of economic trauma was rolling toward American shores. Nixon lifted the price controls following his landslide victory over South Dakota senator George McGovern in 1972. Prices soared over the course of 1973 and received another jolt in the fall when the Organization of Arab Petroleum Exporting Countries (OAPEC) declared an oil embargo in an effort to punish the United States for supporting Israel in the Yom Kippur War. Oil prices quadrupled, hammering consumers at the pump and driving up the price of everything that relied on oil to be transported—which in practice meant just about everything. The Consumer Price Index soared by 11 percent in 1974 and 9 percent in 1975. To fight this raging inflation, the Federal Reserve raised interest rates to a high of nearly 13 percent in July 1974, slamming the economy into recession. Unemployment climbed steadily to a high of 8.9 percent in the second quarter of 1975. If policy makers were to rely on the conventional tools of Samuelsonian economic management—interest rates and budget deficits— they would be stuck between a rock and a hard place: Low interest rates and big budget deficits would improve employment, but the subsequent inflation would eat away at worker paychecks; high interest rates and government spending cuts would stabilize paychecks but force layoffs.

Galbraith argued that Nixon had mishandled the price controls. They should have been a permanent part of the policy mix, not something to be turned on and off like a light switch. But his protestations had almost no effect on public opinion. Economists now had a name for the twin phenomenon of rising unemployment and rising inflation: "stagflation." The public had a villain to blame—Nixon—and a policy to denounce—price controls.

On August 9, 1974, Richard Nixon resigned as president of the United States. The Watergate investigation revealed that he and his top aides had abused campaign funds to illegally sabotage the 1972 Democratic Party primary—and then repeatedly lied to the public and obstructed justice in a failed effort to cover up the crime. Every policy Nixon had pursued was now tainted with his disgrace.

The most influential political theories to arise out of the Depression were Keynesian economics and Friedrich Hayek's neoliberalism. Both had been devised as protective measures intended to shield society against the twin evils of authoritarianism and war. Yet by the mid-1970s, both were being deployed in defense of mass violence. The Kennedy, Johnson, and Nixon administrations made use of Keynesian fiscal maneuvers and price controls to prosecute the Vietnam War, a fruitless conflict that ultimately cost over a million lives, most of them civilian. Hayek and Friedman, meanwhile, were advising Pinochet in Chile after the dictator's violent overthrow of the nation's democratically elected government, the murder of thousands of political prisoners, and the imprisonment and torture of tens of thousands more. Hayek's work became concerned not only with the restraints that must be placed on democracy but with the methods by which it would be appropriate for dictators to oust democratic regimes. He defended Pinochet by declaring that he would personally "prefer a liberal dictator to a democratic government lacking liberalism,"[49] and wrote in *Law, Legislation and Liberty* that once New Deal–style social democracy was implemented, it created "a wholly rigid economic structure which . . . only the force of some dictatorial power could break."[50] Even Joan Robinson, who had articulated the most promising left-wing formulation of Keynesianism, had stained her reputation with fulsome praise for both North Korea and the Cultural Revolution in China. Her attachment to democracy was more flexible than her commitments to ending poverty and war.

When the Keynesian system came apart, none of the alternatives immediately present to the economics profession and the U.S. political establishment had clean hands. Vietnam and Watergate, meanwhile, had done tremendous damage to popular faith in American government. For the first time in decades, an aggressively antigovernment message could plausibly carry progressive promise. The government was dishonest. Democrats and Republicans alike had sent people to die for lies. Keynesianism was bound up in a cynical attempt to rig the 1972 elections by rigging the 1972 economy. And Democratic Party leaders could see that prominent Keynesians had praised Nixon's economic agenda, while Friedman had made the case that it was an inflationary illusion. Whatever his politics, the man seemed to have had a point.

When Jimmy Carter was elected in 1976, he installed an economic team broadly sympathetic to neoliberal ideas and began pursuing a deregulation agenda that garnered support on some measures from both Ted Kennedy—who would eventually challenge Carter from the left in the 1980 Democratic primary—and the ultraliberal consumer advocate Ralph Nader. Government regulation, they mused, often served to protect big players by raising the cost of doing business for entire industries—costs that big, established firms could more easily bear. Many of Carter's advisers blamed labor unions for the persistent inflation, arguing that collective bargaining contracts for some workers ultimately raised prices for others—an argument that had its roots in both Mises' and Galbraith's work.

"I'd love the Teamsters to be worse off," said Alfred Kahn, a Cornell University economist whom Carter appointed to head the Civil Aeronautics Board and begin lifting government airline regulations. "I'd love the automobile workers to be worse off. You may say that's inhumane; I'm putting it rather baldly but I want to eliminate a situation in which certain protected workers in industries insulated from competition can increase their wages much more rapidly than the average without regard to their merit or to what a free market would do."[51]

But the most dramatic change came at the Federal Reserve. Milton Friedman described monetarism as a free-market theory that got the government out of the business of actively managing the economy. It wasn't really true; Friedman just shifted the locus of power from the legislature and the presidency to the central bank, the government agency where Wall Street exercised the greatest degree of influence. But Friedman had long been associated in the public mind with Barry Goldwater's antigovernment message. And when a second oil shock after the Iranian Revolution began in 1979, a decade of high inflation entered a new crisis phase, with consumer costs rising more than 11.25 percent. Friedman's 1967 speech about self-reinforcing inflation expectations seemed prophetic.

In July 1979, Carter nominated former Nixon Treasury official Paul Volcker to serve as chairman of the Federal Reserve. Monetary policy had slowly accumulated legitimacy in Washington from the end of the Treasury-Fed Accord in 1951 through to Samuelson's feud with Galbraith in the Kennedy years. Under Volcker, monetary policy executed a complete takeover of the government's economic policy apparatus. The Fed raised interest rates to an astronomical 17.81 percent in February 1980, in a no-holds-barred effort to crush inflation. Unemployment surged to 7.8 percent, but prices would not abate until 1981, much too late for Carter's reelection prospects. After Ronald Reagan's inauguration, Volcker resumed the pain, bringing the federal funds rate over 19 percent.

Volcker did in fact dismantle inflation, as sufficiently tight monetary policy always does. In the process, he also destroyed just about everything else. Businesses that relied on debt failed. The mortgage market collapsed. Reagan's first term became mired in the worst recession since the Great Depression, with unemployment peaking at 10.8 percent in December 1982. Coupled with Reagan's staunch anti–organized labor views, Volcker's recession devastated U.S. labor unions, forcing them to make political concessions in Washington and wage concessions in collective bargaining contracts. That was the idea. By deliberately causing unemployment, Volcker was trying to bring down wages and with them inflation. Unions, which created upward pressure on wages, were a welcome casualty.

By withdrawing the Democratic Party's political support for Keynesian economists of any variety, Carter all but demolished the academic legitimacy of Keynesian thinking for more than two decades. Without a patron in Washington, up-and-coming economists pursued other ideas. The dwindling few who continued to hold out against the storm—Paul Krugman, Joseph Stiglitz—were Samuelson disciples from MIT who treated Galbraith with professional disdain. "Galbraith broke important new ground in the relationship between politics and economics," wrote Krugman. "He was the first celebrity economist (where the definition of a celebrity is the usual one: someone who is famous for being famous). His rise as a policy entrepreneur was one marker of the growing dominance of style (which he has in abundance) over substance in American political discourse."[52] As Galbraith was essentially exiled from the club of serious economists, Samuelson continued to enjoy success with his textbook, but only by making greater concessions to conservative thinking—tax cuts, the virtues of financial markets, even Friedman's monetarism—with each new edition.[53]

Academic economics became dominated by conservative ideas. Monetarism quickly faded once Volcker found he couldn't accurately or effectively target the precise supply of money in the economy. It was replaced by the rational expectations hypothesis, formulated by future Nobel laureate Robert Lucas. The rational expectations school essentially took Friedman's ideas about price expectations and applied them to government policy. Rational people, according to Lucas, would factor the future effects of any change in tax rates or regulatory arrangements into their economic decisions. Increasing government spending to boost the economy was futile, according to this thinking, because people would recognize that the resulting budget deficit would eventually have to be cured through higher taxes and would therefore save any money they received in anticipation of future tax bills. As a result, it was impossible for policy makers to make any lasting improvement in the lives of citizens through macroeconomic management; the market would quickly adjust and subsequently overrule the government meddlers. It was as if Keynes had never existed; uncertainty had given way to hyperrationality and the ability to see the future. Lucas even went so far as to claim that his work had rendered the entire field of macroeconomics superfluous.

But though the intellectual tide had abandoned Keynes, Reagan never quite could. Throughout his administration, he relied on heavy military spending and tax reductions to counter the devastating effects of Volcker's interest rates (and when Volcker was too stubborn about the need to fight inflation over unemployment, Reagan sacked him for Alan Greenspan). In Reagan's first year in office, he ran a $79 billion deficit—more than double Nixon's gambit from 1971, even adjusted for inflation. By 1986, the deficit was over $221 billion. Government spending remained well over 20 percent of GDP in every year of Reagan's presidency—higher than in Johnson's tenure and more than double the rate during the prewar New Deal years under FDR. Initially, Friedman celebrated the budget deficits. By "starving the beast," he said, the government would eventually be forced to cut spending. But more than a decade later, when pressing for a tax cut package that heavily favored the wealthy, Vice President Dick Cheney had learned a different lesson. "Reagan proved deficits don't matter," he told Treasury Secretary Paul O'Neill. The Iraq War would be funded with debt, following a well-established tradition of Reactionary Keynesianism.

In moments of candor, leading neoliberals acknowledged economic reality. Reagan's rhetoric about small government didn't match his policy agenda. He was running a reactionary Keynesian government alongside an incredibly powerful and historically ruthless Federal Reserve. Friedman, who viewed Reagan as a Goldwater clone, calling them "two men with essentially the same program and the same message,"[54] acknowledged his disappointment by the end of the Reagan presidency. Reagan "talked about cutting down the size of government," Friedman said. "He did not succeed."[55] It would take a Democrat to finish the job.

SEVENTEEN

THE SECOND GILDED AGE

On January 7, 1993, the best and brightest economic minds in the Democratic Party assembled at the Governor's Mansion in Little Rock, Arkansas. The meeting had been called by Robert Rubin, a former Goldman Sachs chairman who was now responsible for shepherding the incoming president's economic recovery package through Congress. Rubin's deadline for passage was Bill Clinton's hundredth day in office, a traditional benchmark for presidential achievement ever since FDR's first term. With inauguration day still two weeks away, Rubin was already behind schedule.

Presidential transitions are inevitably hectic, but Rubin's new boss, Bill Clinton, had overseen two months of near chaos. Just a week after the election, NBC News reporter Andrea Mitchell had asked the president-elect if he planned to fulfill his campaign promise to allow gays and lesbians to serve openly in the military. When Clinton innocently replied in the affirmative, a massive political battle had opened up in which Clinton, yet to take office, had wielded no official power. His insistence on appointing a cabinet that "looks like America" had been met with hostility even by the ostensibly liberal *New Republic*, which sniped that Clinton was "rigging certain departments for a single gender or race." When feminist organizations argued that

Clinton should be appointing more women to his administration, the president shot back that they were playing "quota games" and acting like "bean counters."[1] In a few days, *The New York Times* would torpedo his nominee for attorney general by revealing that she had once employed undocumented workers from Peru as a nanny and driver. New faces in town, the Clintons were clumsy with the Washington press corps, which became a mouthpiece for the Republican opposition and the old hands of elite Washington, who regarded the incoming first family as a batch of guileless rednecks unfit for the worldly sophistication of life in the nation's capital.

The Clintons were, in fact, unprepared. With even cabinet appointments in limbo, some of the people Rubin brought to Little Rock weren't sure exactly what their position in the new administration would be. Rubin himself would be serving as chairman of the National Economic Council, a new panel established specifically for Rubin that would function as the central White House economic policy hub, relegating the existing Council of Economic Advisers to second-class status. The CEA was for economists, and Rubin's degree was from Yale Law School, so naturally something had to be done.

But at least everyone had arrived at the Governor's Mansion on time. CEA chair Laura Tyson and her deputy, Princeton University economist Alan Blinder, were there, along with Vice President Al Gore, Treasury Secretary Lloyd Bentsen, Budget Director Leon Panetta, Chief of Staff Mack McLarty, campaign policy hand Gene Sperling, and soon-to-be Treasury leaders Roger Altman and Larry Summers.

The president-elect, however, was late. It was a moment of reckoning he had been delaying for his entire campaign, if not the whole of his political life. He had secured the Democratic Party's nomination and the presidency with pledges to cut middle-class taxes by 10 percent, oversee "a burst" of public works spending, and devote $60 billion to annual "investments" in education and child care—commitments he didn't think should count as typical government spending, because they would pay off later in the form of bigger social benefits (the way advocates of any government project feel about their policy priorities).

But he had also campaigned on balancing the budget by 1997, and on January 6, the day before the meeting Rubin assembled in Little Rock, the outgoing Bush administration had left Clinton with an unwelcome surprise: Budget deficits were now running $290 billion a year. According to the latest forecast, the deficit would be a third higher by 1997 than previous estimates had indicated.[2] Unemployment, which had peaked at 7.8 percent over the summer, remained stubbornly high at 7.1 percent.[3] It was ugly out there.

Traditional Keynesians would have presented Clinton with an obvious dose of reality: He couldn't tackle unemployment aggressively and bring down the budget deficit at the same time. But by the 1990s, even top Democratic Party advisers put only limited stock in the ideas of John Maynard Keynes. Summers drew as much if not more inspiration from Milton Friedman and Joseph Schumpeter, while Panetta was a former Republican who referred to himself as a "deficit hawk." McLarty was a natural gas executive. Back in 1970, John Kenneth Galbraith had urged Texas liberals to vote for Bentsen's Republican opponent in the Senate elections that November, since the two men were "equally conservative" and "equally bad"[4] and electing a conservative Republican wouldn't alter the liberal bent of the Democratic Party. Bentsen won without Galbraith's support. His opponent, George H. W. Bush, had taken the defeat in stride.

Rubin and his fellow experts shared a faith in the power of financial markets to deliver the prosperity that New Dealers had once entrusted to the federal government. Over the course of a grueling six-hour meeting, they told Clinton that the shackles that had held the economy back during the Bush years could be unlocked if he built credibility with Wall Street on the national debt. Lower deficits could convince bankers and bond traders to bring interest rates down—if the government was paying its bills, the thinking went, people investing in government debt wouldn't fret about the potential for default or inflation, and this would make them more willing to buy debt at lower interest rates. Those lower interest rates would reverberate through the economy, making the cost of credit cheaper and encouraging businesses to invest in new equipment. The savings on consumer loans induced by lower interest rates would give people more spending money than they'd get from a tax cut. Of course, the bond markets were unpredictable, and the Fed would have to go along—always a delicate proposition, particularly under the current archconservative chairman, Alan Greenspan. But the incoming Democratic economic team urged Clinton to make a calculated gamble: If he could tame the bond markets—the world of Wall Street investment houses that bought and sold government debt—he could bring down unemployment and the deficit at the same time.

Clinton was visibly upset, according to the recounting of the meeting by veteran Washington journalist Bob Woodward. "You mean to tell me that the success of my program and my re-election hinges on the Federal Reserve and a bunch of fucking bond traders?" Clinton wanted to be a president of bold initiatives and big ideas. The Cold War was over. He was the first president from the baby-boom generation. He had an opportunity to define the challenges of the next century, to guide the United States into an exciting new future. And his top people were talking about interest rates.

Gore, the son of a liberal senator who inherited his father's love for politics and served fourteen years in Congress, tried to reframe the discussion. Going after the deficit *was* going big. Clinton had an opportunity to govern as a second FDR. "Look at the 1930s," he said. FDR had done some politically unpopular things, but his "boldness" had inspired the whole country. People had supported Clinton in 1992 because he'd talked realistically about the economy and what it would take to build a better tomorrow. Clinton could scale back government in ways that even Republicans hadn't dared. He could be tough, maybe even cut Social Security. These things looked unpopular in polling data, but as part of a big, assertive agenda, voters would recognize that Clinton was doing the right thing. "If you're bold," he said, "people will come around."

"Roosevelt was trying to help people," Clinton countered. "Here we help the bond market, and we hurt the people who voted us in."[5]

Clinton felt protective of the people he understood to be his political base. He began his career in politics as an unabashed Southern populist. In 1974, at just twenty-eight years of age, he challenged a Republican incumbent in a conservative Arkansas district by calling for selective wage and price controls, an assault on corporate welfare, and greater congressional oversight of the Fed—a major issue for farmers whose debts were becoming untenable with the high interest rates that the central bank had implemented to keep down inflation.[6] Clinton narrowly lost that congressional race, but a similar message carried him into the state attorney general's office in 1976 and the Governor's Mansion in 1978. When he was ousted in 1980 after a single two-year term, he had recalibrated his strategy, allying himself with the state's biggest corporate interests, Tyson Foods and Wal-Mart, pitching himself not to farmers but to suburban white voters. It proved to be a winning combination; his second stint as governor lasted a decade.

Clinton maintained a self-image as a progressive, though doing so often required some mental gymnastics. He named more black appointees to top posts in state government than any other governor in Arkansas history, but he also presided over racist voting restrictions that prompted three lawsuits from the Legal Defense Fund, a civil rights group. When an electronics factory and a shirtmaker announced plans to close up shop in Arkansas, Clinton kept them open by brokering deals with Wal-Mart to have the retailer market their wares in its stores. Yet his wife, Hillary Rodham Clinton, joined Wal-Mart's board of directors, and organized labor leaders complained that Clinton let the retail giant's executives dictate his policy on labor rights. As one union man had summarized: "Bill Clinton is the kind of man who'll pat you on the back and piss on your leg."[7]

By the late 1980s, Clinton's record had drawn the attention of the Democratic Leadership Council, a new alliance of conservative Democrats from the South and Mountain West. The DLC believed that winning back white working-class voters who had drifted to Ronald Reagan's Republican Party was essential for the Democratic Party's survival. This observation was not terribly controversial among political professionals, but the DLC's strategy was; it wanted to get tough on crime, more militant on foreign policy, and tighter with the public purse, while avoiding feminist issues and gay rights altogether. To old-line liberals, the DLC represented a betrayal of core principles. Arthur M. Schlesinger, Jr., warned that the DLC's "Me-too Reaganism" would lead to electoral disaster.[8] Reverend Jesse Jackson was more blunt, alternately dismissing the DLC as the "Southern White Boys' Caucus" or "Democrats for the Leisure Class."[9]

Clinton agreed to serve as DLC chairman in 1990 and burst onto the national stage as a presidential contender with his keynote address to the 1991 DLC convention in Cleveland. "Too many of the people who used to vote for us, the very burdened middle class we are talking about, have not trusted us in national elections to defend our national interests abroad, to put their values into our social policy at home, or to take their tax money and spend it with discipline," he told a rapt audience. "We've got to turn these perceptions around or we can't continue as a national party."

But even as the face of the DLC, Clinton never fully committed to the organization or its ideals. He dithered about accepting the job for so long that the group's founder, Al From, almost picked another candidate. Once Clinton finally accepted, From frequently complained about getting sidelined by the governor. Clinton made scheduling room for From only during car rides between airports and hotels and seemed uninterested in acting on much of From's agenda. "I really hate writing memos like this one, but I'm afraid if I don't, we'll have another one of those sessions where you'll charm my pants off and then nothing changes," the DLC founder wrote after one particularly fruitless exchange with Clinton.

Clinton remained extremely popular with black voters. He consistently won over 95 percent of the black vote in Arkansas and did almost as well with black voters in his presidential run. He even tried to name Lani Guinier, the very woman who had spearheaded the Legal Defense Fund's voting rights lawsuits against his Little Rock administration, to the top civil rights job at the Department of Justice (Clinton eventually withdrew Guinier's nomination after an outcry from conservatives).

In January 1993, it wasn't obvious what kind of president Bill Clinton wanted to be. While his economic advisers were urging a shotgun marriage between the White House and Wall Street, his political team was talking about the kinds of issues Clinton had campaigned on: universal health care, federal education funding, child care, and family leave. When Clinton began discussions with Congress and Fed chairman Alan Greenspan, it immediately became clear that all of those ambitions were far beyond the scope of what he could hope to achieve in an economic recovery bill if he was going to take the deficit seriously.

And so just a week after the economic team held its meeting in Little Rock, Democratic pollster Stan Greenberg, one of the most reliable liberals in Clinton's orbit, concluded that "the presidency has been hijacked." What was the point of being a Democrat if you were just going to govern like a Republican? "Why did we run?" he asked a group of similarly dispirited campaign aides.[10] James Carville, the president's chief campaign strategist in 1992, agreed. The administration, he said, had been taken over by "experts and schoolmarms."[11]

Clinton responded to these frustrations by marrying a big deficit reduction bill with at least a few progressive priorities; his "investments" in education and child care might be offset by other spending cuts on things that didn't really matter—requiring White House officials to fly coach instead of first class, for instance. And he could get more tax revenue by raising taxes on the very wealthy. But as the package wound through Congress, just about everything except the tax hike was stripped out in the name of deficit reduction. "I know this thing is a turkey," Clinton confided to Paul Begala, another campaign veteran, over Memorial Day weekend. Rubin even warned Clinton against talking up the tax increases too much; he was alienating businessmen. "They're running the economy," Rubin said. "If you attack them, you wind up hurting the economy." Even the word *rich* was verboten.[12]

The Clinton team was united in horror, however, by the fate of the debt reduction package in Congress. The bill was being held up by brick-wall Republican opposition and holdouts from conservative Democrats. The votes didn't look good. The Clinton administration had to wrestle liberal Democrats into voting for a conservative bill just to help a Democratic president avoid a humiliating defeat on his first major legislative initiative. "Where are the Democrats?" an embittered Clinton roared to his inner circle, according to Woodward. "I hope you're all aware we're all Eisenhower Republicans," he said. "We're Eisenhower Republicans here, and we are fighting the Reagan Republicans. We stand for lower deficits and free trade and the bond market. Isn't that great?"[13]

Bill Clinton eventually won the budget battle of 1993. The deficit reduction bill passed the House by two votes, and Gore cast the tiebreaking vote to secure Senate passage 51 to 50. Five of the six Democratic holdouts in the Senate were conservatives from the South or the West who wanted even bigger spending cuts than what Clinton had on offer, even though the bill slashed the deficit by nearly $500 billion over five years through a combination of tax hikes and spending cuts. "It's too little to match the greatness needed from Americans now, at this critical moment in this world's history," complained Bob Kerrey, a Nebraska senator who had reluctantly sided with Clinton at the last minute.[14]

The bill had been a mess from start to finish. But by the end of Clinton's presidency, the administration had recast the event as a turning point in American history. The final report of Clinton's Council of Economic Advisers in 2000 concluded that the decision to make the deficit the administration's top priority upon entering office had laid the groundwork for a "New Economy" in which low interest rates, expanded foreign trade, and "deregulation in finance and telecommunications" had created a "virtuous circle" of low interest rates, increased corporate investment, and technological innovation.[15] Vice President Gore's comparison to FDR at the January 7, 1993, meeting—caustically dismissed by the president himself—had become the official narrative of the Clinton presidency. By unleashing the innovative potential of financial markets and globalization, the administration had overseen an era of sweeping social change and unmatched prosperity.

The budget battle established the governing philosophy of the Clinton presidency. Afterward, Clinton relentlessly pursued a single, unified economic vision on every policy front, from taxes to trade to poverty and financial regulation. At every opening, the Clinton administration transferred power from the government to financial markets, a Wall Street–friendly agenda that would have been right at home in a Mont Pelerin Society meeting in the 1950s.

It was a thorough renunciation of Keynesian thinking. At its core, *The General Theory of Employment, Interest and Money* was a book about the dangers and limitations of financial markets. Given uncertainty about the future, it was impossible for markets to accurately price the full slate of risks attached to any financial asset. Investors were constantly processing new, unexpected information and attitudes, including their own. If a society relied excessively on financial markets to allocate resources, develop research, and improve industry, Keynes believed, it was destined for underperformance, instability, and unemployment. He had designed a theory and a policy agenda in which financial markets were subjugated to the authority of the state, believing the coordinated action of a government was capable of meeting the investment needs of society which financial markets could only secure through fleeting accidents. The Clinton administration was doing the opposite of what Keynes had prescribed: subjugating both the governing agenda of American democracy and the direction of global economic development to the currents of international capital markets.

The story the Clinton economists told about their stewardship was at most half true. There was no clear relationship between deficits and interest rates during the Clinton years. The conclusion of the 1993 budget battle did not spur a sudden, dramatic plunge in interest rates, and the interest rate on U.S. government debt gyrated up and down throughout the presidency—a very different pattern of activity from the federal budget deficit, which declined steadily on its way to a surplus. Treasury bond rates didn't track government spending patterns, and neither did interest rates on consumer loans. The interest rate on a typical thirty-year home mortgage had fluctuated, beginning the

Clinton years at about 8 percent and closing them out around 7 percent.

Few critics paid attention to such details when the economy was performing well. And compared to the economic records of his four immediate predecessors, Clinton's stewardship looked very good. By the time he left office, median household income had increased by $6,000, the unemployment rate had been nearly halved, inflation was all but nonexistent, and the poverty rate had declined. But the roaring nineties, as Nobel laureate Joseph Stiglitz came to call them, were fundamentally unstable. The prosperity Americans enjoyed for a few brief years was dependent on a volatile, unregulated financial sector overflowing with capital it could not control. Income inequality exploded in the 1990s, and by the time of the Enron scandal and the dot-com bust, the gains of the Clinton years had already been erased for everyone outside the top 1 percent of the American income distribution. Less than a decade after Clinton left office, the masters of the universe his economic program had empowered would blow up their own banks and the global economy, launching the United States and the world into the worst recession since the Great Depression. We are still paying the price today.

Clinton hadn't said much about international trade on the campaign trail. He had refused to take a position on the North American Free Trade Agreement when George H. W. Bush had completed negotiations for it in 1992,[16] and in campaign brochures he had vowed to enact "tough, effective trade laws" and "open up new markets"—commitments that both archprotectionists and free traders could support.[17]

Five weeks after his budget bill passed, however, Clinton walked down the red carpet to the East Room of the White House flanked by three former presidents—Bush, Carter, and Ford—to deliver a message to Congress and the country: His administration would be putting its full political weight behind NAFTA. Clinton was making a political gamble, especially after the near defeat of his previous legislative initiative. NAFTA was controversial. Even Republicans were divided over it, and Democrats were overwhelmingly opposed. In an address that was part Norman Angell, part Milton Friedman, Clinton took Gore's early advice to go bold and dare the country to follow his lead. He linked the trade pact to the fall of the Berlin Wall and the Oslo peace accords, which had just been signed by Israeli and Palestinian leaders. He presented market forces and technological innovation as "winds of change" that no government could hope to counter. There was "an old world dying" and "a new one being born in hope and a spirit of peace." NAFTA would "provide an impetus to freedom and democracy in Latin America and create new jobs for America as well." It offered American workers an opportunity to "compete and win," "to face the future with confidence" instead of clinging to the jobs and industries of the past.[18]

NAFTA was the first of three trade policy changes Clinton pursued that would transform the global economy. Alongside the creation of the World Trade Organization and the establishment of permanent normalized trade relations with China, NAFTA embodied a conscious attempt to forge a new international trading order to replace the Bretton Woods system that had collapsed in the 1970s. Bretton Woods had relied on fixed exchange rates to prevent countries from manipulating the value of their currencies to secure unfair advantages in trade. Whatever its merits, the arrangement hadn't worked; the United States had blown up the very system it had created. So the Clinton administration took a different tack: Instead of focusing on money, Clinton would focus on just about everything else.

Inspired by decades of work by neoliberal theorists, Clinton tried to implement a vision of free trade in which international markets—particularly financial markets—rather than a single, dominant central bank would call the tune. To ensure that markets would be able to function smoothly, identifying profitable opportunities and adjusting to changing international conditions, the United States would write new trade agreements and help establish a new international trade regulator, the World Trade Organization, to prohibit national governments from establishing unfair barriers to trade. Unfair barriers included tariffs—the age-old bugbear of free traders everywhere—but also a vast array of once mundane government responsibilities. Everything from environmental protection regulations to the duration of patents to restrictions against excessive financial speculation would be subject to international review.

What Clinton and his neoliberal admirers were advancing was new. Nothing like it had ever been attempted before. Prior to 1914, the concept of free trade had been inseparable from the gold standard. Under Bretton Woods, it had been contiguous with the U.S. side of the Cold War. Now it was a detailed system of international law telling countries what was—and was not—governable. A few years after NAFTA became law, Milton Friedman observed that "ever since Adam Smith there has been virtual unanimity among economists, whatever their ideological position on other issues, that international free trade is in the best interests of trading countries and of the world."[19] He was right, but only because of the adaptability of the term "free trade," which in practice denotes whatever international political order the economics profession prefers at a given historical moment.

And the economics profession overwhelmingly approved of Clinton's globalization initiative. As Clinton made his case for NAFTA in front of White House reporters, he pointed to that consensus. Of the nineteen "serious" studies of NAFTA that economists had performed, eighteen had concluded that the deal would not result in any net job loss for the United States. In the first few months after the treaty was implemented, most economists reasoned, a lot of high-wage jobs in the United States would go to Mexico, as corporations sought to cut costs by taking advantage of lower wages. But the increased demand for labor in Mexico would quickly drive up wages, and higher pay for Mexican workers would increase the demand for goods produced in both the United States and Mexico. Ultimately, lower tariffs would lead to expanded, balanced trade—more jobs and better pay for everyone. NAFTA would be a win-win.

A similar expert consensus had coalesced around the prospect of establishing the WTO. As *New York Times* reporter Thomas L. Friedman explained to his readers, "few economists" believed that the WTO treaties threatened American workers.[20] Eliminating tariffs would serve as "the world's biggest tax cut"[21] and "stimulate some $5 trillion in new trade."[22] Senators who objected to the treaty were "rambling" old men, "ideologically" out of step with the world and the state of the art in economics.[23]

Like Milton Friedman before him, Clinton portrayed the neoliberalization of trade as a step toward political freedom for oppressed peoples everywhere, the logical next phase in America's liberation of the world now that the Cold War had come to an end. With global economic organization set by financial markets rather than arbitrary governments, peace and prosperity would bloom. It was Norman Angell with a touch of the rational expectations hypothesis. "NAFTA was essential," Clinton wrote later, "not just to our relationships with Mexico and Latin America but also to our commitment to building a more integrated, cooperative world."[24]

In 2000, Clinton put the finishing touches on both his presidency and the WTO project with a bill to permanently normalize U.S. trade relations with China—a Communist bogeyman in American politics since the days of Joseph McCarthy. Bringing China into the WTO system was a gamble—even WTO officials regarded the country as a "nonmarket economy," meaning China would have to overhaul the entire relationship between its government and commercial life in order to abide by WTO rules. But Clinton was confident that the China trade bill was "likely to have a profound impact on human rights and political liberty," creating pressure for Chinese leaders to "choose political reform." Bringing China into the global economic community wouldn't guarantee that it would adopt democratic government, but Clinton counseled his doubters that "the process of economic change will force China to confront that choice sooner, and it will make the imperative for the right choice stronger." "By joining the W.T.O.," he said, "China is not simply agreeing to import more of our products; it is agreeing to import one of democracy's most cherished values: economic freedom."[25]

These high principles were supported by economic calculations predicting modest, positive benefits from trade with China. The United States International Trade Commission projected that the deal would boost U.S. economic growth by a mere $1.7 billion— almost nothing relative to the $10 trillion U.S. economy.[26] The Peterson Institute for International Economics said it would improve U.S. exports by about $3.0 billion.[27] Paul Krugman, soon to win a Nobel Prize for his empirical work on trade patterns in the 1970s, told *New York Times* readers that "the trade arithmetic suggests that union members as a group would if anything benefit from China's offered concessions." He dismissed arguments that China should demonstrate democratic reforms before being rewarded with permanent access to the U.S. market and spoke for most of the economics profession when he said that labor unions would use "anything short of political perfection" in China "as an excuse" to oppose any future trade expansion.[28]

As the historian Quinn Slobodian has chronicled, there were sophisticated neoliberal theorists who understood the Clinton trade project as a specific form of international *political* organization—a rearrangement of the rights and powers between the global elite and national democracies. But the arguments used to advance the agenda in the United States were more simplistic; they presented politics as something artificial that interfered with a natural, inevitable process in which the market harmonized world affairs. "We cannot stop global change," Clinton said in December 1993. "We cannot repeal the international economic competition that is everywhere. We can only harness the energy to our benefit."[29] But the rosy promises and predictions surrounding NAFTA, WTO, and China would break apart due to their inability to grapple with political reality. As Keynes had written decades earlier, markets and even money itself were fundamentally political creatures. There was no ideal market process floating in the ether, waiting to be realized when government disappeared.

This was obvious when the rules of the WTO treaties came under scrutiny. Intellectual property regulations served as a glaring example. WTO treaties required all countries to grant patent rights to new inventions for twenty years. That extended the duration of patents in the United States, which had been set at seventeen years. A patent is a government-granted monopoly on a new product that allows the patent holder to charge essentially whatever she wants for her innovation. So while most free-trade advocates were emphasizing the power of increased global competition to bring down prices for consumers, the WTO was intentionally elevating prices by extending the length of monopolies on new products.

More important, those longer monopolies applied to pharmaceutical products, a decision with deadly consequences when exported to the postcolonial world. The same year the WTO treaty on patents was signed, a fully franchised South Africa elected Nelson Mandela as its first president. Mandela took office in the middle of a public health crisis. The HIV rate was rapidly spiraling out of control, with about 10 percent of the country's 39 million citizens already infected.[30] U.S. pharmaceutical companies had developed effective new drugs to treat HIV that could extend the lives of patients by years, even decades. But they were expensive. Bolstered by patent rights, AIDS and HIV medication cost $12,000 per patient per year in South Africa, a country with an average annual income of around $2,600.[31] Since South Africa's economy generated about $140 billion a year,[32] treating every AIDS and HIV patient would have required shipping a third of the nation's entire annual wealth to overseas pharmaceutical companies every year.

The Clinton administration argued that WTO intellectual property rules gave those pharmaceutical companies the clear right to charge what they wanted without interference from Mandela's government. When Mandela signed a law authorizing his government to shop around for cheaper drugs in other countries, the United States threatened to retaliate with trade sanctions, claiming that Mandela's action would "abrogate patent rights."[33] So Mandela put implementation of the law on hold as the AIDS crisis spread. By 2000, more than 22 percent of his country's population would be infected. In the meantime, Cipla, a pharmaceutical firm in India, began producing generic versions of the U.S. HIV drugs for the "humanitarian" price of $1 a day, but the Clinton administration continued to hold the line against South Africa on its "international commitments," pressuring the country against importing generics until protesters disrupted a campaign rally for Vice President Al Gore in 2000, unveiling a banner for the cameras reading GORE'S GREED KILLS; AIDS DRUGS FOR AFRICA.[34] Millions of people died in South Africa while Clinton fought Mandela on AIDS medication. It was not a fight that anyone who read Thomas Friedman's coverage in the *Times* would have recognized as a trade dispute, which were presented as questions about tariffs, economic growth, and jobs.

Economists, meanwhile, were stunned by the ultimate results of NAFTA and the new U.S. trade agreement with China. The United States quickly slipped into a chronic trade deficit with both Mexico and China. Absent strong labor unions and the political will to develop national infrastructure and establish worker protections, Mexico couldn't deliver the prosperity NAFTA's enthusiasts had promised. When a unionized manufacturing job went to Mexico, a position that secured a middle-class lifestyle in the United States was converted into a position that, as late as 2018, still paid just $1 an hour south of the border.[35] Mexican farmers, meanwhile, found themselves unable to compete with U.S. agribusiness conglomerates that, despite the treaty, remained subsidized by the federal government. In Mexico, 4.9 million family farmers were displaced by NAFTA, while wages barely budged, and economic growth limped along at a meager 1 percent. By some measures, poverty actually increased over the two decades after the pact was signed.[36] Instead of a win-win, the pact delivered a lose-shrug.

The China results were even worse. Since the mid-1980s, total U.S. manufacturing employment had held roughly even at around 17 million jobs. In the fall of 2000, when the China bill was approved, manufacturing employment suddenly went off a cliff, plunging from 17.3 million to 14.3 million, where it held steady until the onset of the Great Recession in 2007, when another 3 million jobs disappeared. Only about 1.5 million of these were recovered over the subsequent eight years.[37]

This was not a hostile robot takeover, fueled by technological innovation and advanced automation. Productivity metrics reflect the pace of automation, and overall U.S. productivity advanced smoothly from the 1970s right through to 2008. What changed abruptly in 2000 was U.S. trade policy toward China. During the depths of the Great Recession, many of the most ardent supporters of globalization from the 1990s came to recognize that the trade deficit with China was forcing the United States into a deeper recession, with Krugman, among others, advocating a U.S. tariff against China to counter the hemorrhage of domestic manufacturing jobs.

Not all of those manufacturing job losses were China driven. Work by the economists David H. Autor, David Dorn, and Gordon H. Hansen put the China manufacturing tally at about 985,000.[38] Factoring in the effects on local communities where unemployed former factory workers were no longer spending their money on retail and restaurants, Autor and his coauthors pegged the total job fallout from "the China Shock" at somewhere between 2.0 million and 2.4 million. Most economic analyses of the China trade deal had assumed that if jobs in one U.S. community became scarce because a factory closed, people would maximize their paychecks by moving to a town where jobs were more plentiful. Losers in the manufacturing economy would become winners in the service economy. But human beings aren't disembodied profit maximizers. People value their family, friends, and local haunts. When the jobs disappeared, they stuck around.

The political reform in China that Clinton envisioned in 2000 never materialized either. In 2018, China's president, Xi Jinping, abolished presidential term limits, opening the door for permanent, personal autocratic rule, as the government rounded up hundreds of thousands of Uighur Muslims and sent them to detention camps. In richer countries, including the United States and members of the European Union, globalization exacerbated economic inequality, driving up corporate profits and stock prices while putting downward pressure on wages. As Joseph Stiglitz concluded in 2017, globalization "was an agenda that was driven by large corporations at the expense of workers, consumers, [and] citizens in both the developed and developing world."[39] The social milieus of citizens and shareholders became increasingly divergent, leading to disparities not only in wealth but in education and physical health, with those further down the income ladder registering lower test scores and shorter life expectancies, according to the OECD.[40] The result has been heightened political tension not only between different countries but within individual nation-states as economically insecure populations question whether they do in fact belong to the same political project as their more affluent neighbors. "I think globalization has contributed to tearing societies apart," argues economist Dani Rodrik.[41]

In the face of these political debacles, more sophisticated champions of globalization have reframed the argument for its success. Instead of claiming that free trade is a rising tide that lifts all boats, they acknowledge setbacks for the American middle class but argue that these troubles are more than compensated for by gains in the developing world. But the actual story for the global poor has been uneven at best. In 2000, the World Bank concluded that the number of people living on less than $2 a day had actually increased over the course of the 1990s.[42] By 2012, things looked a little better; the World Bank declared that it had met its goal of reducing "extreme poverty" in the world's poorest countries by one-half over the previous dozen years.[43] The number of people living on less than $1.90 a day—the bank's updated benchmark for extreme poverty—fell from about 1.8 billion in 1990 to around 800 million today. But adjust the metric just slightly, and progress seems much less impressive. Much of globalization's purported success has simply involved moving people out of extreme poverty and into garden-variety poverty: 1.8 billion people still live on less than $2.50 a day.[44] And about half of the reduction in $1.90-a-day poverty comes from China, where improvements in the standard of living have been the result not of free exchange between democratic peoples but of a protectionist industrial policy tightly and effectively managed by a one-party government. The improvement in living standards, meanwhile, has come at a steep cost. China's industrial boom has turned it into the world's largest producer of greenhouse gases.[45] Most of its carbon dioxide emissions, moreover, are produced by coal-fired power plants that provide electricity to factories making goods for export to the United States and Europe, indicating that the United

States improved its carbon footprint during the twenty-first century largely by offshoring its dirty work to China.[46] Life expectancy for Chinese families living in the smog-choked northern cities has declined by 3.1 years as a result of chronic long-term exposure to air pollution.[47]

The economics profession botched trade in the 1990s by attempting to substitute a world of cleanly adjusting rational markets for the complicated, often brutal realities of international politics. The adjustment to globalization has proceeded through negotiation, protest, and political struggle—not a swift, smooth transition to wage and price equilibrium.

By the time Clinton took office, a few voices in the economics profession had been speaking out against the burgeoning free-trade consensus. In 1979, a few years before her death, Joan Robinson published an article in *Journal of Post-Keynesian Economics* highlighting the risks posed to both the United States and Great Britain by persistent trade deficits. Manufacturing, she argued, appeared particularly vulnerable, and the most prominent remedy proposed by free trade enthusiasts— floating exchange rates—didn't seem to have worked in the United Kingdom. "It is plain that the international economy is not a self-balancing system and that both Britain and the United States are exceptionally vulnerable," she wrote, arguing that most economists were courting ruin by "arguing on the basis of idealized assumptions" instead of conditions on the ground. Robinson believed that a trade shock could be just as disruptive as the oil shock of the 1970s had been, and warned that "new forms of regulation of trade will be required" and that "carefully devised protection might be a necessary part of any solution to recession." This was an international application of Keynes. Insisting that the economy—global or national— would naturally work out its problems on its own was never good economics. Just as a nation could settle into equilibrium with high unemployment, so, too, could international trade slip into chronic imbalance and dysfunction.

But Robinson was writing in an obscure specialty publication for academics who had been exiled from the professional mainstream. For

Clinton, the overwhelming consensus among the economics profession on trade was akin to the scientific judgment on global warming or the ozone layer. And it was that verdict of prestigious scholars that both convinced Clinton that he needed to overcome the political headwinds his trade agenda faced and enabled him to do so. Labor unions, environmental groups, consumer advocates, and public health experts lined up to oppose NAFTA—a united front of traditionally liberal, Democratic Party allies. Most of corporate America wanted to see the trade deal implemented, but it wasn't obvious in 1993 that siding with big business was a smart political play for Clinton. He had been elected with just 43 percent of the vote and been greeted with universal Republican opposition in Congress. The billionaire Ross Perot, who won over millions of swing voters in the 1992 election, had been running a one-man campaign against NAFTA all year, turning it into one of the highest-profile issues on cable news. For Clinton, opposing the pact would have both shored up his party's traditional constituency and extended an olive branch to people who hadn't voted for him but couldn't bring themselves to vote Republican. The Democrats who opposed NAFTA were not limited to the liberal redoubts of the Northeast and upper Midwest. Sixty-five of the House Democrats who ultimately voted against the pact hailed from the South and West, while nearly a third of those who sided with Clinton on NAFTA would be replaced by Republicans in the midterm elections. "Politically," concluded *Washington Post* reporter John Harris, "it was agony for him."[48]

Appropriating much of the old Republican Party economic platform—NAFTA had originally been negotiated by George H. W. Bush—was one example of a political strategy Clinton dubbed "triangulation," in which he presented his policy ideas both as a compromise between liberal and conservative poles of debate, and simultaneously above the fray of partisan squalor. Clinton was not merely a centrist but a centrist operating on a higher intellectual and moral plane than his critics. After the Democratic Party's thumping in the 1994 midterm elections, Clinton believed that triangulation was good branding. But he also imagined it putting him in good historical company. A

fanatical devotee of Arthur Schlesinger, Jr., Clinton had been powerfully influenced by his account of the Kennedy administration, *A
Thousand Days: John F. Kennedy in the White House*, which had been an
effort to link Camelot to the legacy of FDR and the New Deal. In
1949, Schlesinger had published *The Vital Center: The Politics of Freedom*, a book celebrating the New Deal as a middle ground that had
saved a country set adrift by sweeping technological change. But
Schlesinger had understood FDR to be operating in a "center" between fascism and authoritarian communism. Clinton was staking out
terrain somewhere between Goldman Sachs and Wal-Mart.

Shortly after the Republican takeover in Congress, Clinton gave a
speech at FDR's cottage in Warm Springs, Georgia, intended to link
his own administration with the administration that had brought the
country out of the Great Depression. Both Schlesinger and Galbraith
were invited to attend. Neither was impressed. "FDR enjoyed his enemies," Galbraith told *The Washington Post*. "I'd like to see Bill Clinton
enjoy them more." Schlesinger accused Clinton of "appeasement" with
Republicans. FDR, by contrast, had "loved a good fight." When Clinton read the story, he "exploded" with fury, dashing off an acid letter to
Schlesinger in his own hand. "Those who fought me tooth and nail
the last two years know well that I believed in and relished the battles,"
Clinton said.[49] The president was genuinely wounded at the rejection
by his heroes. There were more disappointments to come.

Clinton's trade agenda was a consistent source of public controversy.
Passing NAFTA proved to be almost as grueling as moving his first
budget through Congress. When WTO delegates gathered in Seattle
at the end of November 1999, tens of thousands of protestors descended on the meeting and effectively shut down the city.[50] The public response to Clinton's domestic financial agenda, by contrast, was
almost nonexistent, though its consequences would prove to be no less
pyrotechnic.

It was not as if the world hadn't provided ample warnings about the
risks associated with unregulated finance. In 1995, years of financial

liberalization in Mexico had culminated in a peso crisis and financial collapse that had required emergency aid from both the United States and the International Monetary Fund. In 1997, a financial crisis in Thailand had quickly spread through much of Southeast Asia, again spurring the IMF to action.

But by 1997, U.S. markets seemed to have weathered the Clinton years quite nicely. The Standard & Poor's 500 stock index more than doubled between Clinton's inaugurations, as did the NASDAQ index, which had become a benchmark for hot new Silicon Valley tech stocks. Clinton and the Republican Congress responded by urging investors to let the good times roll, slashing taxes on capital gains from 28 percent to 20 percent. Since more than half of all capital gains between 1991 and 2011 accrued to the wealthiest one-tenth of 1 percent of households, the move helped funnel money to the wealthy and encouraged them to put more money into the stock market.[51]

That December, the Royal Swedish Academy of Sciences awarded the Nobel Prize in Economics to Myron Scholes and Robert Merton, academics who had developed a groundbreaking tool for Wall Street traders.[52] The two economists had worked out an equation to determine the precise value of a stock option, taking into account mathematical probability, swings in the value of the stock price, and the duration of the option. A stock option gives an investor the right to buy stock at a specific price on a specific date. For investors, it's essentially a bet that the price of a stock will either go up or down. By establishing a way to value that bet—without knowing whether or not it would pay off—Merton and Scholes helped fuel an explosion in the market for derivatives. Simple varieties of derivatives had been around for centuries; futures contracts allowed farmers to hedge the price of their crops or helped airlines lock in the price of fuel months in advance. But suddenly derivatives were being created that allowed people to bet on all sorts of things, including the likelihood that a company would default on its debts. By some measures the derivatives market quintupled in the early 1990s, but the sheer scope of new products made it hard to even define the market, much less put a reliable figure on its explosive growth.[53]

Scholes and Merton, meanwhile, put their mathematical minds to work as cofounders of the world's biggest hedge fund, Long-Term Capital Management. Started with $1.25 billion in 1994, LTCM more than quadrupled its investors' money in just a few years by finding small price mismatches in government bonds and currencies and placing enormous bets on them. LTCM borrowed huge sums of money, leveraging its own funds to drastically amplify the payout for relatively small price changes. So long as markets behaved rationally, and so long as prices didn't swing well outside the norms dictated by probability metrics, the hedge fund earned incredible returns. In both 1995 and 1996, the fund popped 40 percent, wildly outperforming even the roaring stock market.

But mathematical models couldn't predict the future. When the Russian financial crisis hit in August 1998, the firm's trading models were devastated. LTCM abruptly lost $4.6 billion—an astronomical sum for a hedge fund. Although the company had started 1998 with $4.8 billion in equity, it was also carrying more than $120 billion in debt. If LTCM went under, its creditors—which included every major firm on Wall Street—could have gone down with it. Nobody in Washington wanted to think about what the fallout might be.

In response, Rubin, Greenspan, and Summers organized an industry-funded bailout, cobbling together $3.6 billion so that LTCM could be unwound in a safe and orderly manner. Wall Street breathed a collective sigh of relief.

The collapse of LTCM should have been a wake-up call to economists and policy makers alike. LTCM's Nobel-caliber trades hadn't seemed reckless; the firm had executed careful, meticulously researched bets and hedged itself against an array of calculated risks. It was LTCM's massive debt—what financial professionals referred to as "leverage"—that had steered it into trouble; just as leverage had magnified profits during the company's boom years, so it had magnified its losses into terrifying dimensions in 1998. The firm's mathematical models lulled LTCM management into a false sense of security.

It was not a new problem. Scholes and Merton were experts at quantifying risk and hedging against it. They had been brought down by something else: uncertainty. Keynes had published an entire book on probability and uncertainty in 1921, and the concept had formed the basis for much of *The General Theory*. Financial markets, Keynes had emphasized, seemed rational only during periods of stability. The risk metrics that LTCM deployed were extrapolations from past experience. As soon as a new or unexpected factor emerged—a war, a natural disaster, an unexpected election outcome, an unusually bad harvest—all of the firm's advanced calculations lost their meaning. Financial markets only functioned reliably when the world did not change, and even during periods of stability the judgments that formed the basis for buying and selling assets were based on expectations and assumptions as much as on any hard facts and economic fundamentals.

The fall of LTCM was a breathtaking reminder of Keynes' insights, one that carried obvious implications not only for American banking but for the Clinton economic team's entire economic project, both at home and abroad. The neoliberal version of free markets and free trade was transmitting financial instability all over the world. If important social functions—industrial investment, scientific research, or social welfare services—were organized around financial markets, those institutions would become as fragile as financial markets themselves.

Rather than heed this warning, Clinton's economic team took the opportunity to further empower high finance at home. The LTCM crisis was front-page news. Rubin, Summers, and Greenspan made a laudatory cover of *Time* magazine, where the trio were dubbed "The Committee to Save the World." But as they were orchestrating the hedge fund rescue, these men were also waging a much quieter war within the Washington bureaucracy. Brooksley Born, head of the Commodity Futures Trading Commission, warned that the runaway growth in the market for financial derivatives was becoming dangerous. One particular strain, credit default swaps, seemed to offer endless avenues for speculative excess.

Credit default swaps had emerged in the early 1990s as an insurance product. An investor who bought risky corporate debt could take out a credit default swap to insure that debt against default; if whoever issued the debt went bankrupt, the credit default swap would pay out. But there was no requirement that anybody who took out a credit default swap had to actually own the asset they were insuring. As a result, credit default swaps transformed into a vehicle for speculation: By purchasing a credit default swap, banks, hedge funds, and other speculators could essentially gamble that other companies would go bankrupt.

The CFTC was not a powerful agency in the social hierarchy of Washington bureaucracy, and Born was almost immediately shut down by Rubin, Summers, Greenspan, and Securities and Exchange Commission chair Arthur Levitt. "Regulation of derivatives transactions that are privately negotiated by professionals is unnecessary," Greenspan told Congress. It would serve "no useful purpose" and impede "the efficiency of markets to enlarge standards of living." Rubin accused Born, the only woman in charge of a financial oversight body, of being too "strident" and refusing to engage with her critics "in a constructive way." "The parties to these kinds of contract," Summers insisted, "appear to be eminently capable of protecting themselves."[54] And so Congress passed a law banning federal regulation of credit default swaps and even exempted them from state antigambling statutes. Clinton signed it into law, thinking almost nothing of it.

Nor did he waste much mental energy on a bill to repeal Glass-Steagall, the Depression-era law that had forbidden banks that accepted deposits to trade securities. Glass-Steagall had been designed to prevent conflicts of interests—a banker betting against his clients, for instance—and to prevent government-guaranteed deposits, a cheap source of funding for banks, from fueling risky activity. But regulators had been chipping away at the New Deal landmark for several years, and when Citibank announced its intention to acquire the insurance giant Travelers, Congress and the administration eagerly broke down the final barriers to mergers between different types of financial institutions. Banks had been on a merger binge since 1994, when Clinton had signed a law permitting them to open branches across state lines and merge with banks in other states. Now the mania could expand into securities, insurance, and even hedge funds like Long-Term Capital Management. Economists enraptured by the promise of rational market progress argued that larger firms with more diverse lines of business would be more stable, better able to hedge against risks and compensate for losses in isolated lines of business. They did not worry about the management difficulties posed by overseeing firms with hundreds of billions of dollars in assets across dozens of different lines of business or the prospect of an unforeseen shock in one sector taking down an entire conglomerate.

Citigroup signed its megamerger. When Rubin left the Treasury, he accepted a position at Citi, where he would collect $126 million in total compensation over the next decade.[55] In his 2004 memoir, Clinton joked about the Wall Street payout for his adviser: "After he supported the 1993 economic plan, with its tax increase for the highest-income Americans, I used to joke that 'Bob Rubin came to Washington to help me save the middle class, and when he leaves, he'll be one of them.' Now that Bob was moving back into private life, I didn't think I'd have to worry about that anymore."[56]

It would not end well. In 2010, the official Financial Crisis Inquiry Commission would refer Rubin to the Department of Justice for criminal prosecution, saying he may have been " 'directly or indirectly' culpable in failing to disclose material information" about the banking behemoth's subprime mortgage exposure.[57] After the crash of 2008, Citigroup received more federal assistance than any other U.S. financial institution.

But in 1999 and 2000, nobody seemed to care. The repeal of Glass-Steagall didn't make the front page of any major American newspapers, and nightly news broadcasts devoted no more than twenty seconds of airtime to it. A poll conducted shortly afterward revealed that more than half of the country had never heard of the repeal bill. No major general-audience newspaper even assigned a reporter to cover the derivatives bill.[58] When John Harris published a revealing biography of Clinton's White House years in 2005, he didn't mention any of the financial controversy in Washington over Long-Term Capital Management, Glass-Steagall, or derivatives, because there hadn't been any.[59] Clinton himself didn't even find room to talk up his bipartisan achievements on banking in his 969-page autobiography.[60]

By 2014, however, the economic record Clinton had championed at the end of his presidency had become a sore spot. At a deficit reduction conference hosted by private equity billionaire Peter G. Peterson, Clinton insisted that "not one" bank had failed as a result of the repeal of Glass-Steagall. It was technically true; the banks hadn't failed, they'd been bailed out by the federal government. But his defense included a reminder about the political and intellectual climate at the time: "If I had known that we basically would see the end of banking and SEC oversight, would I have signed it? Probably not. Would it have passed? Yes. Let me remind you, that bill passed 90 to 8."[61] Like Winston Churchill in the 1920s, Clinton had been led into disaster by an expert consensus that had attempted to substitute the clamor of the real world for a set of harmonious abstractions.

In August 2000, Clinton invited John Kenneth Galbraith to the White House, where he bestowed the ninety-one-year-old economist with the nation's highest civilian honor, the Presidential Medal of Freedom. As Galbraith was feted alongside liberal luminaries Jesse Jackson, George McGovern, and Sargent Shriver, the ceremony seemed to celebrate a distant past, a generation of idealists whose energy and imagination belonged to another time. The Cold War had given way to the Information Age; technology and innovation had replaced the Depression and authoritarianism as the great affairs dominating the minds of statesmen. Privately, Clinton proposed coauthoring a book with Galbraith on "enduring liberal values"—a project that made sense only as a bridge between disparate eras that had addressed different concerns. Galbraith declined, citing the impediments of age and ill health.[62]

It was not just Galbraith who seemed out of date but his entire intellectual tradition. In academia, discussion and debate of Keynesian themes were relegated to specialty journals maintained by intellectuals who wielded no political influence and were tolerated by their more prestigious colleagues as harmless eccentrics. And who could blame them? Bill Clinton had overseen the best eight years of economic life the country had experienced in more than three decades. Unemployment had plunged while inflation had barely budged and new fortunes had been raised by fascinating new technologies. Innovation on both Wall Street and Silicon Valley, from the internet to credit default swaps, seemed to have rendered the risks and concerns of the twentieth century obsolete. Though Galbraith warned that the speculative craze in dot-com stocks threatened another great crash, his fears seemed exaggerated when the resulting recession proved to be a brief, mild disruption.

At a retreat for Federal Reserve officials in Jackson Hole, Wyoming, in 2001, Summers and his former deputy at the Treasury Department Brad DeLong argued that "modern data processing and data communications technologies" were "seismic innovations" that had changed the nature of the economy itself. Technological revolution would wreak "profound microeconomic effects" upon the future humanity now faced. "The new economy is 'Schumpeterian,'"[63] they concluded—an era that would be defined by the process of "creative destruction" that the conservative Austrian economist Joseph Schumpeter had described in the 1930s, in which new innovations would wreak havoc upon the techniques and traditions of the old order and transform the economic underpinnings of society. The framework of economic competition, Summers and DeLong believed, would likely give way to a world of "natural monopoly," in which high-octane data processing and instantaneous information distribution would enable the production of new goods at tiny marginal costs. It was a new era that called for new legal structures and norms to meet the changing economic landscape. The problems of the future were about intellectual property rights, education, and who yet knew what else.

The presentation was more than a little overheated. But it entranced the audience at Jackson Hole because much of it was true. We have indeed witnessed the emergence of new digital monopolies in the twenty-first century, and our government's failure to grapple with the legal challenges Summers and DeLong sketched in 2001 has resulted in grave social and economic problems—from the decimation of the news and music industries to the disruption of U.S. elections by foreign governments to rising levels of anxiety, depression, and suicide among young people.

But the Jackson Hole speech also sketched an economic history and a theory of social change that were fundamentally at odds with the work of John Maynard Keynes and his disciples. *The General Theory* was a book about, among other things, inequality and social progress. The central problems of the twentieth century, Keynes argued, were best solved by alleviating inequality. Enterprise and economic growth were driven not by the unique genius and vast fortunes of the very rich but by the purchasing power of the masses, which created markets for new ideas. To put people to work, governments needed to create systems of support for the poor and the middle class, not new favors for the rich. Summers and DeLong offered a contrasting narrative going all the way back to the seventeenth century in which inequality was an engine for social improvement. Cautiously, they compared the turn of the millennium to the Gilded Age of a century prior—a period in which, they argued, great technological change had given way to extraordinary inequality and rampant capitalist abuses even as it had supported a high standard of living for "the average American." The Chicago meatpacking houses that had inspired Upton Sinclair to write *The Jungle* had also made a better, healthier diet available on a massive scale. So, too, would the dawning age of the microprocessor deliver new wonders at a previously unthinkable scale, bringing great gains for some and a new way of life for all.

Against this coming age of transformation, the simple goal of full employment, managed by familiar tools like deficit spending—which had dominated so much of twentieth-century economics—appeared quaint, insufficient for the bold new "replacement paradigm" already being born. The Age of Keynes, it seemed, had come to an end.

CONCLUSION

———— ◊ ————

WHEN DONNA EDWARDS ARRIVED on Capitol Hill in June 2008, her new colleagues told her to expect a lazy summer. She'd earned the break. Edwards was arriving in Washington at an unusual time for a House freshman, in a class of exactly one, after winning the most difficult congressional election of the cycle not once but twice. She had challenged Albert Wynn, a fellow Democrat who had represented one of the most reliably liberal districts in the country for fifteen years. Wynn enjoyed the backing of several major labor unions and a constellation of powerful corporate interests, including the American Bankers Association, AT&T, and Lockheed Martin.[1] But Wynn had supported the Iraq War and backed a 2005 bankruptcy bill that the progressive blogosphere—a new force in American politics—viewed as a handout to abusive credit card companies. Edwards was the head of the Arca Foundation, one of the most prominent funders of liberal and progressive causes in the nation's capital. She'd been around Washington long enough to recognize that Wynn would be vulnerable to a challenge from a progressive reformer, and she was politically capable enough to build the organization that could take him down. After a bitter, grueling primary, Edwards secured the Democratic nomination in February.

But her ordeal wasn't quite done. Wynn was so eager to embark on a new career as a lobbyist that he decided to resign from office early instead of serving out the remainder of his term as a lame duck. His departure triggered a new special general election to fill his suddenly vacated seat. So Edwards ran again and won that race, too. She was finally sworn into office about six weeks ahead of the August recess, a time when lawmakers traditionally return to their districts to escape the Washington heat. And it was a presidential election year—a notoriously unproductive time for legislators—meaning that Edwards could expect a gentle introduction to the rituals and customs of life as a member of Congress.

Instead, the global financial system collapsed. On June 9, Lehman Brothers reported its second-quarter results, posting a $2.8 billion loss and—equally concerning—plans to sell $6 billion in fresh stock to shore up its finances.[2] Hedge fund managers and private equity magnates began telling officials at the Federal Reserve that it was just a matter of time before Lehman faced an electronic bank run similar to the panic that had brought down Bear Stearns a few months earlier.[3] The early stages of the worst financial crisis in a century had begun.

The crash of 2008 was the denouement of a massive international credit bubble built on the U.S. housing market. Between 1996 and 2006, U.S. home prices experienced an unprecedented boom. Even adjusted for inflation, nationwide home values had soared by more than two-thirds, with prices in some markets, including California and Las Vegas, doubling or even tripling.[4] Those soaring home prices were both an invitation for and the product of a fanatic expansion of the mortgage business fueled by Wall Street credit. As home values rose, a greater percentage of conventional homeowners were progressively priced out of the housing market. The price of middle-class living went up, and since middle-class incomes hadn't budged, the middle class became a riskier bet for lenders. To keep business moving, banks offered subprime loans and other exotic mortgage products designed for borrowers with risky credit profiles to families who just a few years back would have qualified for a traditional, plain-vanilla thirty-year mortgage. As a result, even as the total size of the mortgage market nearly quadrupled between 2000 and 2003, the overall U.S. home ownership rate barely budged, inching from 67.1 percent of households to just 68.6 percent.[5]

A lot of subprime lending was nakedly predatory, with shady operators simply taking borrowers for everything they could. A lot of it was overtly fraudulent, as banks offered loans that didn't even bother to document a borrower's income, letting everyone pretend that a loan that made no sense was a reasonable transaction. But an even more common scenario was a straightforward risk-reward calculation of the kind that banks make all the time. When borrowers represented a higher risk of default, lenders would charge them more to cover for higher potential losses. The whole reason that subprime borrowers were considered risky, of course, was that they had relatively low incomes for the amount of housing debt they were taking on. This meant they couldn't really afford to make the higher payments lenders were demanding in exchange for taking on extra risk. So the subprime architects stuffed the higher costs of the loan later in the repayment schedule. At first, borrower payments were low, but after a few years, the loans would reset to a higher interest rate or trigger a wave of big fees. As early as the late 1990s, consumer advocates began warning federal regulators that the subprime flood would drown borrowers in loans they did not understand and could not afford to repay. But regulators, trusting to the wisdom of financial markets to accurately price risk and allocate capital, shrugged off those warnings, allowing the subprime sector to eventually take over a quarter of the entire market.[6]

The explosion in risky mortgage lending began at private-sector lenders, but housing giants Fannie Mae and Freddie Mac—private institutions tasked with a public mission to promote home ownership—began chasing the subprime dragon in 2003 and grew to control nearly one-fifth of the more than $1-trillion-a-year exotic mortgage business at the top of the bubble.[7]

Even so, actual mortgages accounted for only a fraction of the debt explosion that would eventually break global finance. Home loans were packaged into complex securities en masse and sold to investors. These securities, in turn, were often sliced and diced into even more complex debt products. And speculators could place bets on the performance of all those securities by taking out credit default swaps against them. Or against the investment banks that created them. Or the investors who purchased them. By the end of 2007, U.S. banks had over $14.4 trillion in credit default swaps outstanding, roughly equal to the entirety of U.S. economic output for one year, while the international CDS market had swelled to a face value of $61.2 trillion, larger than the annual economic output of the entire world.[8] Financial markets had not helped reallocate risk to safer corners of the economy; they had created a ludicrous casino of paper debts that could not possibly all be paid.

All it would take for the entire pyramid of debt to collapse was a slight downturn in home prices. The logic of subprime mortgages could be sustained only if borrowers were able to refinance out of their loans before they reset to higher, unaffordable payment levels. So long as home prices kept going up, most borrowers had an escape hatch: taking out another loan. But as soon as home prices fell—even a small amount—they would owe more on their loans than their homes were worth, making them ineligible to refinance. The inevitable foreclosures would radiate through the system as losses for investment houses across the globe.

In May 2006, U.S. home prices finally leveled off, then began to decline. Mortgage defaults accelerated. Banks started recording heavy losses on real estate. In August 2007, two hedge funds controlled by the investment bank Bear Stearns collapsed, and in March 2008, the Federal Reserve committed $29 billion to help JPMorgan acquire Bear in an emergency merger. Every major American financial institution was exposed, and Wall Street immediately began to wonder which domino would be the next to fall. Pension funds in the United States and central banks in Asia began reducing their exposure to Lehman Brothers, in particular, and Citigroup demanded that Lehman hand over billions of dollars as a "comfort deposit" in order to continue doing business with Citi.[9] Lehman's stock price, which had started the year at over $60 a share, slipped below $20.

The Fed responded by lending money to embattled banks at a furious pace. By June 2008, the central bank had initiated three separate emergency lending programs and was already issuing a record volume of overnight loans to banks that couldn't obtain short-term funds elsewhere. It expanded all of those programs after Lehman's troubling earnings report, moving billions of dollars a day simply to keep banks from running out of money. As long as a bank owned decent collateral—stocks, bonds, or other financial assets—it could go to the Fed, offer up its assets, and receive a short-term loan to meet any pressing obligations. After a few days or weeks, the bank could pay back the loan and get back its collateral—or roll over the loan for another term. Banks that possessed fundamentally valuable assets, the thinking went, shouldn't go under just because they couldn't sell those assets at reasonable prices during a panic.

But emergency lending alone wasn't going to stop what was beginning to look like an institutional run on several banks, especially Lehman. With home prices falling, massive losses were inevitable, even on conventional mortgages. So Treasury Secretary Hank Paulson went to Congress and asked for a new regulatory regime for Fannie Mae and Freddie Mac. Though he carefully presented the legislation as a precautionary measure, the new oversight system gave the Bush administration power to nationalize Fannie and Freddie if things really turned south. If banks wanted to sell off deteriorating assets at optimistic prices, the government could make Fannie and Freddie serve as willing buyers, putting the losses on the public balance sheet. By turning the housing giants into wards of the state, moreover, the government could ensure that the basic nuts and bolts of the housing market wouldn't simply disappear in a crash; banks that would otherwise be reluctant to lend would keep issuing mortgages if Fannie and Freddie were standing by to purchase them. Edwards voted for the bill in one of her first votes cast as a member of Congress. Soon after, on Saturday, September 6, Paulson pulled the trigger, nationalizing Fannie and Freddie.

But the fear pulsing through trading desks around the world did not abate. Creditors continued to withdraw funds from Lehman, and on Tuesday, September 9, the bank's stock price fell 55 percent to close at $7.79.[10]

According to Lehman's official accounting, none of its difficulties made any sense. It had been profitable the prior quarter, and even with the recent loss the bank was sitting on $26 billion in equity, enough to absorb nine straight quarters of bad news on the scale it had just delivered.

The trouble was, nobody believed Lehman's accounting. Lehman Brothers had purchased five different mortgage lenders in 2003 and 2004. At first, it had used them to generate mortgages that Lehman could package into securities for sale to outside investors who wanted to bet on the housing market. But in 2006, with home prices at their highest level on record, Lehman began acquiring and keeping real estate assets on its own books, hoping to directly capitalize on housing profits for itself. By November 2007, the bank had more than doubled its total real estate exposure from $52 billion to $111 billion.[11]

Or so Lehman's books claimed. But everyone knew that real estate prices were on their way down. Never mind what Lehman reported to the SEC; what were those assets *really* worth? And what were they worth *to Lehman Brothers* if potential buyers knew the bank had to dump them in a hurry to raise money to pay its bills? Later, when investigators asked JPMorgan Chase CEO Jamie Dimon whether he believed his competitors at Lehman had been solvent during the crash, he offered a philosophical response: "What does solvent mean?"[12]

Dimon wasn't being evasive. Lehman's viability—like that of every other major bank over the course of 2008—depended on a series of judgments not only about the near-term trajectory of land and property values but about enormously complex securities tied to loan payments on that land and the prospects for government support that might or might not come to financial houses that were heavily invested in them. These were not questions that could be answered with better information about real estate sales or mortgage default patterns or job market data. Nobody knew what was going to happen six weeks or six months hence. Everyone knew that Lehman had been reckless, but the market was powerless to determine whether it was solvent. Just as in the London financial system in 1914, the global financial system was being governed by acute, irreducible *uncertainty*. And just as in 1914, when the outbreak of war had thrown the international payment system of the gold standard into chaos, political authority alone could resolve the crisis.

But top officials in the Bush administration and the Fed had decided it was time for market discipline to take over and public support to retreat. In March 2008, when the Fed had helped rescue Bear Stearns, the bailout had not only prompted public outrage but established the expectation of government support for other faltering banks among investors and even bank executives themselves. The Bush administration knew the economy was in trouble—in February the president had signed a bill providing $600 tax rebates to American families, a straightforward effort at Keynesian stimulus—but the idea of bailing out every big bank in the country seemed absurd in the summer of 2008. Like most top officials in the Bush administration, Hank Paulson, Fed chairman Ben Bernanke, and New York Fed president Timothy Geithner believed in financial markets. They were skeptical of government actions that might distort incentives and expectations and thought they had to draw the line on public support somewhere. After Bear, Fannie, and Freddie, they picked Lehman as the place to make their stand. Lehman might not have been the *most* reckless of American banks,[13] but its problems were grave,[14] and the bank was now borrowing tens of billions of dollars from the Fed's emergency facilities as a matter of course.

On Friday, September 12, Paulson assembled the heads of the major Wall Street banks at the headquarters of the New York Fed, hoping to broker a rescue package akin to the 1998 deal to shore up Long-Term Capital Management. Like Robert Rubin and Alan Greenspan before him, Paulson was willing to assemble the saviors and bless the deal, but he insisted that "not a penny" of public funds would be involved. By the end of the night, he had a deal to sell Lehman to the British bank Barclays, but on Saturday morning, Chancellor of the Exchequer Alistair Darling vetoed the arrangement. The British government couldn't stomach putting British money into a collapsing U.S. bank. Sticking to their guns on the need for market discipline, the U.S. officials continued to refuse aid to Lehman, forcing it to file for bankruptcy early on the morning of Monday, September 15.[15]

According to the minutes of the Federal Reserve's Open Market Committee meeting the next day, top officials at the central bank were on high alert but generally approved of the plan to let Lehman fail. Richmond Fed president Jeffrey Lacker, St. Louis Fed president Sam Bullard, and Kansas City Fed president Thomas Hoenig all said the government had done the right thing by steering Lehman into bankruptcy rather than providing it with a bailout.[16] But the chaos that enveloped the financial system that morning forced the Fed to reverse its judgment within hours. It became clear that Lehman's collapse was too much for the already strained insurance titan AIG, which had billions of dollars in contracts outstanding with Lehman that were now contingent on the outcome of what would become a years-long bankruptcy case. AIG, in turn, had hundreds of billions of dollars' worth of contracts with major banks all over the world. If AIG collapsed, there was no telling what else might go down with it. At 9:00 P.M. on September 16, the Fed announced that it would extend an $85 billion emergency loan to AIG in exchange for a 79.9 percent ownership stake in the company.

But the panic on Wall Street was no longer restricted to individual institutions. The entire dollar-denominated monetary system was breaking down. The trillions of dollars staked on housing could not possibly be repaid, and financial institutions withdrew money from all over, fearing that it might end up locked away in a failed bank within a few days or hours. Money market mutual funds—investments so safe that investors used them interchangeably with cash or checking accounts—came under severe pressure, and one prominent fund, the Reserve Primary Fund, had to be liquidated at a loss. Major corporations found themselves unable to access the commercial paper market, the standard source of cheap, reliable, short-term loans that they used to meet routine expenses. And the panicked withdrawals from major banks continued. With Lehman down, investors began guessing which bank would be next to fall and pulled funds out of Morgan Stanley. The Fed started a new program to support the commercial paper market and allowed Morgan Stanley and Goldman Sachs to convert to bank holding companies, changing their federal charters so they could access a wider array of emergency funds from the central bank.

The Fed was now taking every step it could imagine to print new money and funnel it into the faltering international banking system. The U.S. central bank would ultimately provide more than $16 trillion in emergency liquidity to combat the crisis, including $5.5 trillion to foreign central banks to help overseas institutions meet their dollar-denominated obligations. Whatever happened, the Fed ensured that no institution would collapse due to a shortage of cash on hand. With the gold standard long gone, there was no need to worry about re-serves running dry.

But the financial crisis was operating outside the realm of balance sheets and debt obligations. Faith in the viability of the global financial system had been broken. The only way to restore it was with a political statement—a persuasive signal that the world's governments would not let the banking system destroy itself. So Paulson and Bernanke began making conference calls with lawmakers on Capitol Hill, explaining the severity of the situation and asking for congressional aid.

For Donna Edwards, it was a baptism of fire. At age fifty, she'd already had a serious professional career in Washington, helping to pass the Violence Against Women Act in the 1990s as the executive director of the National Network to End Domestic Violence before moving on to the Arca Foundation. She'd lived through plenty of high-stakes legislative drama and was comfortable operating in an environment of intense political pressure. But this was different.

"It was actually scary," she recalls, thinking back on the conversation with Paulson. "There was one point where I actually wondered whether I would be able to go to the ATM and get a couple hundred dollars out."[17]

"I just remember thinking, you know, Armageddon," Congressman Mel Martinez, a Florida Republican, told the Financial Crisis Inquiry Commission.[18] According to Pennsylvania Democrat Paul Kanjorski, Paulson had convinced him that the country was perilously near "the end of our economic system and our political system as we know it."[19] After hesitating to use its authority to salvage Lehman, the Bush administration was running out of methods to bolster confidence on its own. It would need congressional help to put an end to the chaos.

But lawmakers were insulted by the legislation Paulson sent to Capitol Hill. Brief and simple, the law would have given the Treasury secretary $700 billion to spend as he pleased, with no oversight mechanisms to ensure accountability and no metrics to gauge success or failure. Edwards was incredulous. "We got three pieces of paper," she says. "For $700 billion."

Paulson did not suffer from an excess of tact. Before serving in Treasury, he had been the CEO of Goldman Sachs, where he had been accustomed to giving orders and having them obeyed. He couldn't imagine that elected officials wouldn't trust him with the same unquestioned authority his board of directors once had. And time was short. Every day that passed, the crisis deepened. There was no time to write the perfect bill or cut individual deals with every skeptical lawmaker. House Speaker Nancy Pelosi and her Republican counterpart, John Boehner, had twisted as many arms as they could, but they simply had no choice but to put the bill on the floor for a vote and hope the pressure of the moment would bring critics around. As the yeas and nays were counted, the Dow Jones Industrial Average began to fall. In a matter of minutes, it crashed over 700 points. The bailout vote had failed. Without it, the banking system would be destroyed. A second Great Depression seemed to be on the horizon.

The Senate calmed the markets by making a few cosmetic changes to Paulson's original bill, adding two new oversight entities and clearing the revised legislation by a broad margin two days later. But the House remained a problem. Leaders began cajoling reluctant members of Congress. Democrats had supplied 140 of the bill's 205 favorable House votes, but liberal Democrats remained among its most vehement opponents.[20] "The poor—poor blacks, poor whites, Native Americans, Latinos—get little help, little assistance," Congressman John Lewis of Georgia, a civil rights icon, explained at the time. "And then they come in here and ask us to bail out Wall Street. I'm not prepared to do that."[21] The feeling was strong throughout much of the Congressional Black Caucus. Elijah Cummings, a liberal stalwart from Baltimore, held a press conference with Edwards laying out similar objections, insisting that any bailout for Wall Street should include help for struggling homeowners.

Lawmakers were inundated with phone calls from constituents alternately outraged by the idea of bailing out Wall Street and terrified of their own bankruptcy. "After that first vote failed there was a lot of pressure on people," says Edwards, who voted against the bailout. "What happened over the course of that next week and weekend was like cold water being thrown on you. There was an absolute tailspin in the market. I remember getting calls from small business owners in my district. There was a guy who ran a used book store who said that his line of credit was completely shut down and he was worried about being able to meet payroll that week."

The messenger who carried the most credibility with liberal skeptics like Edwards was the Democratic Party's presidential candidate, a young senator from Illinois named Barack Obama. A shrewd politician, Obama recognized that the liberal reluctance didn't stem from ideological opposition to government intervention or fear of electoral blowback. Edwards, Lewis, and Cummings all hailed from safely Democratic districts and had nothing to gain politically by changing their votes. They wanted liberal changes to the terms of the bailout—or no bailout at all. And after several phone calls, Obama got the job done. The bailout passed on October 3. The banks were saved.

Obama helped salvage the bailout with a private promise: If liberal Democrats would support the bank rescue, he would enact a sweeping antiforeclosure agenda once he entered the White House. Cummings and Edwards had specifically called for a new bankruptcy law that would allow financially stressed families to shed excessive mortgage debt if the value of their home dropped below the amount they owed on their mortgage. If banks were getting bailed out for risky housing bubble bets, liberals wanted to make sure that families got a piece of the pie. In talks with Edwards, Obama agreed to make the bankruptcy change once in office. She and Cummings switched their votes. After the election, the White House made Obama's private vow a public one.

"We will implement smart, aggressive policies to reduce the number of preventable foreclosures by helping to reduce mortgage payments for economically stressed but responsible homeowners, while also reforming our bankruptcy laws and strengthening existing housing initiatives," Obama's economic adviser Larry Summers wrote to every member of Congress on January 15, 2009.[22] In February, Obama announced a $75 billion program—funded with money set aside under the bank bailout authorization—designed to save up to 4 million homes from foreclosure by reducing borrowers' monthly payments and writing off the amounts they owed on their mortgages.

None of it happened. Obama quietly abandoned the promises he made to Edwards and millions of families in financial distress. When the mortgage bankruptcy bill went to the Senate floor in May, it came up fifteen votes short of the sixty needed to clear a filibuster. Dick Durbin, the number two–ranking Democrat in the Senate, raged about the failed vote on Illinois talk radio. "The banks," he said, "are still the most powerful lobby on Capitol Hill. And they frankly own the place."

A popular new president equipped with hundreds of billions of dollars in bailout money to use as political leverage over a crumbling financial system might well have been able to beat the banks in Congress, but we will never know for certain. Obama put zero political capital behind Durbin's bill: no phone calls, no meetings, no letters, nothing. The apathy on housing was pervasive. Obama and Treasury Secretary Timothy Geithner didn't need congressional help to implement their $75 billion antiforeclosure fund; the money had already been allocated. But nobody in the administration took the initiative seriously, allowing it to become the rare government program that failed to spend the money allotted to it (the administration ultimately spent about $19.9 billion on the project[23]). Geithner turned over the program's implementation to big banks, which used it to squeeze households even further by deploying illegal tricks, only to eventually foreclose anyway. In 2012, the administration inked a massive $25 billion settlement with the nation's largest banks over a wave of fraudulent foreclosures that had swept the country.[24] It was a damning indictment of the administration's housing agenda, but only a fraction of the settlement ever made its way to families wronged during the foreclosure blight, typically in small payments that arrived much too late to be of any help averting eviction.[25] Between 2006 and 2014, 9.3 million families lost their homes,[26] and a large volume of economic research has concluded that the demolition of housing wealth from foreclosure contributed substantially to the increase in unemployment during the Great Recession.[27] Families strained themselves to keep making payments until they were financially exhausted; by the time they were evicted, their savings were gone and their spending plummeted, devastating consumer demand, encouraging producers to reduce their payrolls.

"For the life of me, I can't figure out why a community organizer who says he cares about families, who says he cares about communities, has just turned his back on one of the biggest problems in America," California Democrat Dennis Cardoza told the press in June 2011. "The way they get defensive when you point out it's been a failure just underscores to me they don't have a clue about what to do."[28]

The bailouts of 2008 and 2009 saved the global financial system. But they did not save the American middle class.

Both the Bush and Obama administrations used Keynesian tools to mitigate the disaster that began to unfold in 2008. Starting with Bush's $600 stimulus checks, the two administrations repeatedly spent money and drove up deficits to salvage the monetary system, increase aggregate demand, and boost employment. But neither administration was ever enthusiastic about this agenda. Such tactics might be necessary, but they were unseemly, vaguely embarrassing, an unfortunate detour from the important business of (for the Bush administration) streamlining government or (for the Obama administration) lowering the long-term federal debt burden.

There is a palpable ambivalence about Keynesian ideas evident in the reports of Obama's Council of Economic Advisers. In 2010, the year unemployment reached its annual peak during the Great Recession, the CEA emphasized "taming the federal budget deficit" as a top government priority, warning that "deficits drive up interest rates, discouraging private investment" and claiming that "greater personal saving will tend to encourage investment"—a flat contradiction of the argument Keynes had presented in *The General Theory* in which spending, not saving, encourages investment by stimulating demand.[29] In the following year, with unemployment at or above 9 percent for all but three months, the CEA devoted nearly twenty pages of its annual report to an argument that "increasing demand for high-skilled workers is outstripping their supply,"[30] suggesting that unemployment was being driven by inadequate technical education—a problem that just happened to have emerged at the very moment Lehman Brothers collapsed. As late as 2013, the Obama CEA was still pressing for an additional $1.5 trillion in deficit reduction in the name of economic growth and boasting of the $2.5 trillion in deficit cutting that had been secured since 2009.[31] Even the Affordable Care Act (better known as "Obamacare") received its highest praise from the CEA not for easing the burden of poverty but for helping reduce long-term government spending. Not until Jason Furman took over as CEA chair in late 2013 did the council's reports embrace an openly liberal philosophical approach, with Furman presenting the Obama administration as a warrior against inequality and heir to the domestic legacies of Franklin Delano Roosevelt and Lyndon B. Johnson.

But the administration's key economic policy decisions were decidedly more conservative. Despite its $784 billion price tag, Obama's 2009 stimulus bill featured very little in the way of direct investment. Tax breaks for individuals and businesses accounted for $194 billion of the package, while $271 billion came in the form of direct financial aid to individuals, mostly in the form of unemployment benefits, while another $174 billion helped fill the health care and education budgets of state governments. All of that money helped prevent things from getting worse; paying teachers, treating the sick, and giving people spending money ultimately resulted in more money being spent and more people being hired. But the main event for Keynesian stimulus is always direct government investment, things such as infrastructure spending, which accounted for only $147 billion of the total. The tax breaks for businesses may have helped streamline the bill's path politically but probably did little to bolster employment or economic growth. Companies are taxed based on profits, and a key problem during a recession is that companies don't have much in the way of profits.

This didn't mean that the stimulus didn't work. A study by the nonpartisan Congressional Budget Office concluded that the legislation reduced the unemployment rate, which had peaked at 10.0 percent,[32] by between 0.6 percent and 1.8 percentage points, while economists Alan S. Blinder and Mark Zandi found that the stimulus had saved about 2.7 million jobs.[33] By the close of Obama's presidency, unemployment had returned to a healthy 4.8 percentage points, economic growth was a respectable 1.5 percent, and the financial system—though riddled with abusive activity from Wells Fargo and other banks—was able to meet the routine credit demands of the economy.

But the recovery also exacerbated worrying trends in the U.S. economy that had been developing since the Carter years. According to research by University of California, Berkeley, economist Emmanuel Saez, households in the top 1 percent of all incomes captured 49 percent of the economic gains during the recovery.[34] The incomes of the top 10 percent accounted for a greater share of annual national wealth than at any other time on record, while the gap between the richest 0.1 percent and everyone else had reached a level not seen since the Roaring Twenties, according to Saez's colleague Gabriel Zucman.[35] This was a reflection of the recovery strategy that Bush, Obama, Congress, and the Fed had delivered. The bailout salvaged the financial sector, the stimulus boosted consumer spending, and the Federal Reserve kept interest rates low in a quest to increase the value of financial assets. With the profits from loans suppressed by low interest rates, investors would put their money into the stock market, bidding up prices. All of it was helpful. Higher asset prices boosted confidence and raised the prospect of future profits, encouraging further economic activity. But today, 80 percent of all financial stock is owned by the wealthiest 10 percent of all households.[36] Ever since the New Deal, the most important financial asset for the American middle class has been a home, and houses were the one financial asset the government had elected not to rescue. Fannie, Freddie, and the Fed had ensured that the mortgage pipeline continued to function, but homeowners facing foreclosure were left to twist in the wind, and their neighborhood property values with them. Keynes had closed *The General Theory* with a call to euthanize the rentier; Obama had instead delivered a blow to the American homeowner and the primary source of American middle-class wealth. The toll was especially hard on families of color. In 2010, median white household wealth, including home equity, was $136,375, according to Federal Reserve data, while the median black household had just $17,210. By 2016, white wealth had climbed to $162,770, while black wealth had actually declined over the course of the recovery to $16,600.[37]

In 2008, Donna Edwards had urged Obama to choose a different path: If Wall Street needed to be saved, save it—but show the same commitment to the families caught up in the same calamity. Obama's rejection of this plan was a political choice. The national tragedy that ensued was not the inevitable culmination of ruthless economic forces beyond the power of democratic government to contain.

In one sense of the term, the Obama administration was inescapably Keynesian. It managed the economy by relying on a few concepts established by Keynes himself and by manipulating time-tested policy levers developed by his disciples. The financial crisis of 2008 revived the intellectual authority of that version of Keynesianism by discrediting its neoliberal and neoclassical competitors in academia. The chief policy prescription of neoliberalism—let financial markets organize the distribution of resources and capital—had failed very publicly. Financial markets were obviously not rational—banks had blown themselves up—nor could they claim to offer a predictable, stable route to prosperity. The crash-induced recession had caused mass suffering.

In truth, the political dominance of Keynesian policy tools in the United States had wavered only during the Clinton administration. Even as Paul Volcker imposed the monetarist recession of the 1980s, Ronald Reagan was pursuing the classic Reactionary Keynesian agenda developed by John F. Kennedy, stimulating demand through tax cuts for the wealthy and amplified military spending. When George W. Bush told people to go shopping after September 11, 2001, he was offering the same advice Keynes had proffered to British housewives during the Great Depression. The $600 tax rebates Bush delivered in 2008 were straightforward Keynesian economic stimulus. The world of serious American economics in the twenty-first century—the variety that people in power actually rely on—is divided into different strains of Keynesianism, whether or not the field's most conservative practitioners find it politically convenient to acknowledge. The U.S. government almost always spends money and runs deficits to support its economy; the question is who and what it spends that money on.

But the school of thought that has come to be associated with the name of Keynes no longer has much to do with the moral and political ideals Keynes himself prized. Keynesianism in this broader sense was for a time synonymous with liberal internationalism—the idea that shrewd, humane economic management could protect democracies from the siren songs of authoritarian demagogues and spread peace and prosperity around the globe. *That* Keynesianism had its roots in a particular, historically blinkered strain of nineteenth-century European imperialism and a conception of the good life that, unlike its imperialist origin, remains as compelling today as it was a century ago. As a child, Keynes celebrated the British Empire as a humanitarian, democratic force in world affairs. When the Great War and the Paris Peace Conference taught him an uglier truth, he began an intellectual project to create a new global order that would fulfill the ideals of his youth, hoping to transform an international system founded on predation into a scheme of justice, stability, and aesthetic brilliance—

without resorting to war. If nineteenth-century empire couldn't do it, Keynes would devise a system that would.

The key to realizing that international vision was domestic economic policy making. International political stability would be achieved—or at least encouraged—by alleviating domestic economic inequality. State spending on public works and public health could be combined with redistributive taxation to boost consumer demand, while establishing an environment in which great art could thrive. In his maturity, Keynes offered radicals a deal: They could realize the cultural and moral aims of liberationist revolution—a more equal society and a democratically accountable political leadership—while avoiding the risks and tragedies inherent to violent conflict. He claimed that the social order established by nineteenth-century imperialism and nineteenth-century capitalism was not so rigid that it could not be reformed rather than overthrown.

After nearly a century on trial, this Keynesianism has not embarrassed itself, but neither has it been vindicated. The New Deal, the Beveridge Plan, and the Great Society fundamentally reordered British and American life, making both societies more equal, more democratic, and more prosperous. In the 1930s, black poverty in the United States was so high that nobody bothered to measure it. By the 1950s, it was over 50 percent. Today it is about 20 percent. This is progress. But it is decidedly not the world promised by the Communist Party in the 1930s, when it denounced Franklin Delano Roosevelt as a tool of the business elite. It cannot compete with the dreams of liberation presented by Black Power revolutionaries of the 1960s.

The gains for white America have been greater but also unequal and unstable. American life expectancy declined in 2016 and 2017, according to the Centers for Disease Control and Prevention, driven by causes of death among white men that reflect deep despair: opioid overdoses, alcohol-related fatalities, and suicide.[38] The wealthiest nation in the world is rotting from within, its political dysfunction a reflection of deep internal social discord. All of this has taken place while the world's economic engine—as Keynes prophesied in 1930—has become so powerful that poverty could be eliminated around the globe by redistribution of private wealth and corporate profit. In 2008, Joseph Stiglitz calculated that if the $48 trillion global economy were simply divided among every one of its inhabitants, a family of four would receive $28,000, high enough to end poverty in every country, including the United States, with its relatively high cost of living.[39] In 2018, with an $85.8 trillion economy and 7.5 billion people, the global economy produces $11,440 per person, more than $45,000 for a family of four. The economic problem of humanity is no longer a problem of production but of distribution—inequality.

There is no single cause or simple explanation behind any of these misfortunes. And Keynesians can persuasively argue that today's tragedies are the product of a failure to fully implement Keynesian ideas rather than a failure of Keynesian policies. Instead of the Keynesian international monetary system, the postwar world received U.S. hegemony through the Bretton Woods agreement. Liberal internationalism has become associated with imperialist projects such as the Iraq War and the Obama administration's drone program, rather than cooperative economic diplomacy. NAFTA and the World Trade Organization have established rules of international exchange that prioritize the economic interests of a global elite. And for the past thirty-five years, the United States and Great Britain have mixed Keynesian disaster management—bailouts and stimulus programs—with the aristocratic deregulatory agenda of Hayekian neoliberalism.

It is appropriate for neoliberalism to take most of the blame for the political upheavals of the twenty-first century. The neoliberal faith in the power of financial markets bequeathed us the financial crisis of 2008, and the fallout from that disaster has fueled dozens of hateful movements around the world. While the American commitment to Keynesian stimulus after the crash was inconstant, Keynesian ideas were simply abandoned throughout most of Europe. The European Central Bank and the IMF, in cooperation with the government of German chancellor Angela Merkel, demanded that countries in crisis reduce their budget deficits through fiscal austerity, inducing devastating recessions in Spain, Italy, Portugal, and most famously Greece. The economic ruin brought about by that project—the destruction of local

industry, soaring unemployment, stingier social safety nets—has ener-
gized neofascist political parties, which now threaten the political establishment in some countries and have been effectively absorbed into
mainstream conservatism in others. From Hungary's Viktor Orbán to
Italy's Matteo Salvini to France's Marine Le Pen to the United Kingdom's Boris Johnson to America's Donald Trump, this is an era of
far-right demagoguery unseen since the 1930s.

But pointing the finger at neoliberalism raises uncomfortable questions for Keynes and his defenders. Why has Keynesianism proven to
be so politically weak, even among ostensibly liberal political parties
and nations? The Keynesian bargain of peace, equality, and prosperity
ought to be irresistible in a democracy. It has instead been fleeting and
fragile. Keynes believed that democracies slipped into tyranny when
they were denied economic sustenance. Why, then, have so many democracies elected to deny themselves economic sustenance?

I do not have satisfying answers to these questions. Larry Summers
once dismissed the idea that markets function as an expression of rational individual self-interest with the observation "There are idiots.
Look around."[40] His axiom cuts not only against efforts to organize
society through markets but against democracy itself. Keynes believed
that good ideas would eventually triumph over bad ideas, that people
could ultimately recognize good arguments and change their minds.
At times, his faith seems admirable. At others, it is hard to disagree
with Joan Robinson's assessment from the 1970s that Keynes was
tragically naive. Perhaps the type of social change he envisioned can
be achieved only through the moral quagmire of revolution that he
ardently hoped to avoid. Certainly the American experience does not
inspire confidence. The greatest American victories for democracy and
equality—the end of slavery in the nineteenth century and the defeat
of fascism in the twentieth—came at the end of a gun.

This is a dark time for democracy—a statement that would have
been unthinkable to U.S. and European leaders only a few short years
ago. It took decades of mismanagement and unlearning to manufacture this global crisis, and it cannot be undone with a few new laws or
elections.

But all over the world, people are acting as if even this frightening global slide into authoritarianism might be reversed through the mechanisms John Maynard Keynes proposed three-quarters of a century ago. They are organizing, planning, and voting as if they really can improve society for themselves and their children by changing the economic arrangements that currently divert so much of the world's wealth into the hands of so few. In the United States, activists and politicians are promoting a Green New Deal, reviving the legacy of FDR to combat climate change through public investment. Mainstream economists now speak openly of moving "beyond neoliberalism,"[41] and there is talk in academic circles of a new Bretton Woods conference that might replace the global order erected in the 1990s with a new harmony of international economic interests.

These optimists may succeed, and they may fail. But they are pursuing a vision that sustained Keynes through three world crises and demonstrated beyond any doubt that a better world was possible on the other side. Keynesianism in this purest, simplest form is not so much a school of economic thought as a spirit of radical optimism, unjustified by most of human history and extremely difficult to conjure up precisely when it is most needed: during the depths of a depression or amid the fevers of war.

Yet such optimism is a vital and necessary element of everyday life. It is the spirit that propels us to go on living in the face of unavoidable suffering, that compels us to fall in love when our hearts have been broken, and that gives us the courage to bring children into the world, believing that even in times such as these we are surrounded by enough beauty to fill lifetime after lifetime.

"Down with those who declare we are dumped and damned," the twenty-one-year-old Keynes cried in 1903. "Away with all schemes of redemption and retaliation!"[42] A better future was *not* beyond our control if the different peoples of the world worked together, leading one another to prosperity. Twenty-seven years later, Keynes had reconsidered the economic strategies of his youth, but not his bet on tomorrow. We would build for the future not through Victorian self-denial or by waiting for deliverance but by taking action today. "Were the Seven Wonders of the world built by Thrift?" he asked readers of *A Treatise on Money*. "I deem it doubtful."[43]

And so it is today. Despite everything, we find ourselves back with Keynes—not merely because deficits can enable sustained growth, or because the rate of interest is determined by liquidity preference, but because we are here, now, with nowhere to go but the future. In the long run, we are all dead. But in the long run, almost anything is possible.

ACKNOWLEDGMENTS

◇

THIS BOOK EXISTS BECAUSE my wife, Jia Lynn Yang, put me up to it in the spring of 2016. After I had worked for a decade as a financial and political journalist, she told me it was time for me to try my hand at something longer. This was not a typical case of spousal encouragement. My wife is a professional editor, trained to get the most out of her writers, and she knew what she was doing. Over the past three years, she has not merely been a source of support but an intellectual partner who sharpened arguments, tightened prose, and shot down bad ideas. She's been through these chapters with a fine-tooth comb and argued with me about liquidity preference and the Treaty of Versailles over dinner more times than either of us can count. As she began work on a very different book of her own, our projects became entwined, and we traveled together, doing our research side by side at the John F. Kennedy Presidential Library in Boston; the Harry S. Truman Presidential Library in Independence, Missouri; session after session at the Library of Congress in Washington, D.C.; and too many vacations-turned-writing-retreats to count. My love, it has been the thrill of a lifetime to share this with you.

Every book begins as an idea, but the concept changes over the course of the project—at least, if the book is any good. I'm particularly indebted to Neil Irwin for helping me develop the ideas in this book from the beginning, and for serving as a kind of coach in the life of the journalist-author, from finding the right agent to identifying the right way to celebrate the completion of a draft. My agent—the brilliant, indomitable Howard Yoon—has been a partner through every step of this process, a steady, experienced hand whose creative advice has proved at least as important to me as his well-established professional acumen.

Molly Turpin, my editor at Random House, has been a revelation, seeing connections that were invisible to me, developing themes that once seemed insignificant into major narratives, discarding cherished but ultimately expendable detours, and maintaining a relentless focus on the essentials. Her insistence on clarity and character development has not always been easy to live up to, but it has made a book about one hundred years of economic policy into a literary endeavor I had not imagined when I sold her the proposal in the spring of 2017. If better book editors exist, they must be very good indeed.

I am compelled to voice a special note of appreciation for Dr. Patricia McGuire and Peter Monteith at the archives of King's College, Cambridge, whose guidance through what can only be described as an overwhelming collection of material from the life of John Maynard Keynes made my time there more fruitful than I could have imagined.

All modern Keynes scholars begin their journey with the work of Lord Robert Skidelsky, whose three-volume biography established an interpretive foundation for everyone who has written after him—both those who agree with him and those who do not. I am grateful for his conversation, his patience, and his intellectual versatility in our discussions concerning this project. Where I have differed with him, I often felt as if I took my life in my hands, but not for any lack of generosity of spirit on his part. I am similarly indebted to James K. Galbraith for his passionate but clear-eyed guidance on the life and work of his father, whose own interpretations and modifications of Keynes have informed so much of my own understanding. This manuscript was markedly improved by the penetrating comments of New Deal historian Eric Rauchway, whose scholarship in *The Money Makers* and *Winter War*, is, to use an unfortunate metaphor, the gold standard for work on the relationship between high intellectual theory and realpolitik maneuvering in the age of Franklin D. Roosevelt. I am also indebted to John Milton Cooper, Jr., for his time and insight on Woodrow Wilson and the Treaty of Versailles. Greg Veis and Richard Kim—two of the most gifted journalists working in the field today—offered invaluable feedback on this manuscript and its narrative structure.

No work of history is written in a vacuum, and while I have relied on dozens of scholars in the research for this project, there are a handful whose work has exercised a particularly potent influence through no knowledge of their own. Adam Tooze and his masterful *The Deluge* is as exciting as 500-plus-page economic history gets, a searing portrait of the connections among power, politics, resources, and markets between the World Wars. Richard Parker's stunning biography of John Kenneth Galbraith is a remarkable document not only for its narrative grace but for its continued argumentative power a decade and a half since its publication. Daniel Stedman Jones' *Masters of the Universe*, Angus Burgin's *The Great Persuasion*, and Quinn Slobodian's *Globalists* are essential guides to the neoliberal order that challenged and replaced Keynesian thinking in the twentieth century, while Judith Mackrell's *Bloomsbury Ballerina* is not only a revelatory biography of Lydia Lopokova but an insightful portrait of her husband.

I lost my father, Lawrence D. Carter, before this book was released, and in many respects it is the product of his investments in time and tutelage. He fostered my earliest interest in economics in grade school, and his feedback on early drafts of this manuscript was essential to the development of the argument. He bestowed on me at an early age his passion for the scientific method and rigorous scholarship, with his guidance on science fair entries, history papers, and art exhibits. This is our last project together as father and son, and, I think, our best.

My mother, Bonnie Bell, taught me to write—from the alphabet through undergraduate term papers. This book is the fruit of her labors, as well.

This book would not have been completed without the support of my in-laws, Ed and Mei Shin Yang, as career advisors, babysitters, and literary critics. Ed's invaluable insight as an economist with decades of experience at the Department of Commerce has shaped not only the argumentation of this book but my own worldview.

Finally, I want to thank my loyal and persistent research assistant Pepper, who has always recognized that the best way through a rough patch of writing is usually a long walk in the woods. Or, at least, a short walk with plenty of treats.

NOTES

————————— ◇ —————————

ABBREVIATIONS

CW: Elizabeth Johnson, Donald Moggridge, and Austin Robinson, eds., *The Collected Writings of John Maynard Keynes, Vols. 1–30* (New York: Cambridge University Press for the Royal Economic Society, 1971–1982).

JMK: John Maynard Keynes

LL: Lydia Lopokova

JKG: John Kenneth Galbraith

INTRODUCTION

1. Quoted in Robert Skidelsky, *John Maynard Keynes*, vol. 2: *The Economist as Savior, 1920–1937* (New York: Allen Lane, 1994), 93.

2. Lytton Strachey to Virginia Woolf, February 6, 1922, in Lytton Strachey, *The Letters of Lytton Strachey*, ed. Paul Levy (New York: Farrar, Straus and Giroux, 2005), 501.

3. Virginia Woolf, *The Letters of Virginia Woolf*, vol. 2: *1912–1922*, ed. Nigel Nicolson and Joanne Trautmann (New York: Harcourt Brace Jovanovich, 1976), 8.

4. Quoted in Judith Mackrell, *Bloomsbury Ballerina: Lydia Lopokova, Imperial Dancer and Mrs. John Maynard Keynes* (London: Phoenix, 2009 [2008]), 181.

5. Quoted in ibid., xviii.

6. Quoted in Skidelsky, *John Maynard Keynes*, vol. 2, 93.

7. Quoted in Alison Light, "Lady Talky," *London Review of Books*, December 18, 2008.

8. S. P. Rosenbaum, ed., *The Bloomsbury Group: A Collection of Memoirs and Commentary* (Toronto: University of Toronto Press, 1995), 120; "The Art of Bloomsbury," Tate Modern, 2017, https://www.tate.org.uk/art/art-terms/b/bloomsbury/art-bloomsbury.

9. Keynes received £300 from *The Manchester Guardian*, £350 from the *New York World*, and £25 from the *Neue Freie Presse* of Vienna. *CW*, vol. 17, 354. Current value calculated using the average 1922 exchange rate of $4.43 to the pound; see "Foreign Exchange Rates, 1922–1928," *Federal Reserve Bulletin*, January 1929, https://fraser.stlouisfed.org/files/docs/publications/FRB/pages/1925 -1929/28191_1925-1929.pdf; and "CPI Inflation Calculator," Bureau of Labor Statistics, https://data.bls.gov/cgi-bin/cpicalc.pl.

10. JMK to LL, May 3, 1924, JMK/PP/45/190/1/122.

11. LL to JMK, April 19, 1922, JMK/PP/45/190/9/32.

12. LL to JMK, April 24, 1922, JMK/PP/45/190/9/46.

13. John Maynard Keynes, "On the Way to Genoa: What Can the Conference Discuss and with What Hope?," *The Manchester Guardian*, April 10, 1922; in *CW*, vol. 17, 372.

14. Quoted in Adam Tooze, *The Deluge: The Great War, America and the Remaking of the Global Order 1916–1931* (New York: Penguin, 2014), 433.

15. JMK to Henry de Peyster, February 25, 1921, in *CW*, vol. 17, 219.

16. Russia owed nearly $3.5 billion to Great Britain and another $4 billion to France, accounting for a quarter of all French foreign investment. See Tooze, *The Deluge*, 425.

17. John Maynard Keynes, "Reconstruction in Europe," *The Manchester Guardian*, April 18, 1922; *CW*, vol. 17, 388.

18. John Maynard Keynes, "On the Way to Genoa: What Can the Conference Discuss and with What Hope?," *The Manchester Guardian*, April 10, 1922; *CW*, vol. 17, 373.

19. John Maynard Keynes, *A Tract on Monetary Reform* (London: Macmillan, 1923).

20. Ibid., 172–73.

21. For more on Keynes and his ideal of "civilisation," see Geoff Mann, *In the Long Run We Are All Dead: Keynesianism, Political Economy and Revolution* (New York: Verso, 2017).

22. Quoted in Alan Brinkley, *American History: A Survey* (New York: McGraw-Hill, 1995).

23. See, e.g., John Maynard Keynes, "British Foreign Policy," *The New Statesman and Nation*, July 10, 1937, in *CW*, vol. 28, 61–65.

24. John Maynard Keynes, *The General Theory of Employment, Interest and Money* (New York: Prometheus, 1997 [1936]), 382.

25. D. M. Bensusan-Butt, *On Economic Knowledge: A Sceptical Miscellany* (Canberra: Australian National University, 1980), 34–35.

26. Rosenbaum, *The Bloomsbury Group*, 272–75.

ONE: AFTER THE GOLD RUSH

1. Bertrand Russell, *The Autobiography of Bertrand Russell, 1872–1914* (Boston: Little, Brown, 1967), 96.

2. Mark Twain and Charles Dudley Warner coined the term "Gilded Age" in their 1873 novel *The Gilded Age: A Tale of Today* to mock the opulence of the era as a thin veneer covering a dysfunctional social order. The term did not become widely used until decades later, by which time it had lost much of its venom.

3. Georges Auguste Escoffier, *Le Guide Culinaire* (Paris: Imprimerie de Lagny,

1903); Escoffier, *A Guide to Modern Cookery* (London: William Heinemann, 1907).

4. John Maynard Keynes, *The Economic Consequences of the Peace* (London: Macmillan, 1919), 8–9.

5. In early 1908, the India Office assigned Keynes the task of editing a 197-page report titled "Statement Exhibiting the Moral and Material Progress and Condition of India," which drew the ire of his superior, Sir Thomas Holderness, for portraying a "coldblooded" British response as "the country has been terribly ravaged by plague." See *CW*, vol. 15, 11.

6. Keynes, *The Economic Consequences of the Peace*, 10.

7. Robert Skidelsky, *John Maynard Keynes*, vol. 1: *Hopes Betrayed, 1883–1920* (New York: Penguin, 1994 [1983]), 290.

8. Liaquat Ahamed, *Lords of Finance: The Bankers Who Broke the World* (New York: Penguin, 2009), 29.

9. "A Population History of London: The Demography of Urban Growth," The Proceedings of the Old Bailey: London's Central Criminal Court 1674 to 1913, https://www.oldbaileyonline.org/static/Population-history-of-london.jsp#a1860-1913.

10. Keynes, *The Economic Consequences of the Peace*, 9.

11. Norman Angell, *The Great Illusion* (New York: G. P. Putnam Sons, 1913 [1910]).

12. Barbara Tuchman, *The Guns of August: The Outbreak of World War I* (New York: Random House, 2014 [1962]), 13.

13. Thomas L. Friedman, *The World Is Flat: A Brief History of the Twenty-First Century* (New York: Farrar, Straus and Giroux, 2005), 421.

14. Charles Kindleberger, *A Financial History of Western Europe* (London: George Allen & Unwin, 1984), 291.

15. John Maynard Keynes, "War and the Financial System," *The Economic Journal*, September 1914, in *CW*, vol. 11, 238–71. See 246–48 for details on foreign payment difficulties.

16. John Maynard Keynes, *A Treatise on Money: The Pure Theory of Money and the Applied Theory of Money. Complete Set*, vol. 2 (Mansfield Center, CT: Martino Fine Books, 2011 [1930]), 306–7.

17. Keynes wrote about this process in an October 22, 1917, letter to Professor Charles Rist, JMK/L/17/8.

18. E. Victor Morgan, *Studies in British Financial Policy 1914–25* (London: Macmillan, 1952), 4–7.

19. Morgan, *Studies in British Financial Policy*, 4–30.

20. John Maynard Keynes, "War and the Financial System," *The Economic Journal*, September 1914, in *CW*, vol. 11, 254.

21. Ahamed, *Lords of Finance*, 30–31.

22. Lippmann's thoughts are described in Ronald Steel, *Walter Lippmann and the American Century* (Boston: Little, Brown, 1980), 306.

23. John Maynard Keynes, *Indian Currency and Finance* (London: Macmillan, 1913).

24. Skidelsky, *John Maynard Keynes*, vol. 1, 277; Russell, *The Autobiography of Bertrand Russell*, 96.

25. Russell, *The Autobiography of Bertrand Russell*, 97.

26. Basil Blackett to JMK, August 1, 1914, in *CW*, vol. 16, 3.

27. David Lloyd George, *War Memoirs of David Lloyd George, 1915–1916* (Boston: Little, Brown, 1933), 61–75.

28. Ibid., 64–67.
29. Quoted in Tuchman, *The Guns of August*, 129.
30. John Maynard Keynes, "Memorandum Against the Suspension of Gold," August 3, 1914, in *CW*, vol. 16, 10.
31. Morgan, *Studies in British Financial Policy*, 11.
32. JMK to John Neville Keynes, August 6, 1914, in *CW*, vol. 16, 15.
33. John Maynard Keynes, "Memorandum Against the Suspension of Gold," memorandum for David Lloyd George, August 3, 1914, in *CW*, vol. 16, 12.
34. JMK to Basil Blackett, June 24, 1914, in *CW*, vol. 16, 5.
35. JMK to Alfred Marshall, October 10, 1914, in *CW*, vol. 16, 30–31.
36. John Maynard Keynes, "War and the Financial System," *The Economic Journal*, September 1914, in *CW*, vol. 11, 252, 255.
37. John Maynard Keynes, "The Proper Means for Enabling Discount Operations to be Resumed," memorandum for David Lloyd George, in *CW*, vol. 16, 16.
38. "The Longest Bank Holiday," Royal Bank of Scotland, November 11, 2014, http://www.rbsremembers.com/banking-in-wartime/supporting-the-nation/the-longest-bank-holiday.html.
39. Morgan, *Studies in British Financial Policy*, 14.
40. The Federal Reserve did not formally suspend specie payments but did so in effect. See ibid., 20.
41. John Maynard Keynes, *The General Theory of Employment, Interest and Money* (New York: Prometheus, 1997 [1936]), 161–62.
42. Quoted in Virginia Woolf, *The Diary of Virginia Woolf*, vol. 1: *1915–1919*, ed. Anne Olivier Bell (New York: Harcourt Brace Jovanovich, 1977), xxv.
43. JMK to John Neville Keynes, January 29, 1915, in *CW*, vol. 16, 66.

TWO: BLOOD MONEY

1. Virginia Woolf in S. P. Rosenbaum, ed., *Bloomsbury on Bloomsbury* (Toronto: University of Toronto Press, 1995), 48.
2. Virginia Woolf in ibid., 56.
3. Virginia Woolf in ibid., 44.
4. Virginia Woolf in ibid., 55.
5. Leonard Woolf, *Beginning Again: An Autobiography of the Years 1911 to 1918* (New York: Harcourt Brace Jovanovich, 1964), 34–35.
6. Virginia Woolf, quoted in Rosenbaum, *Bloomsbury on Bloomsbury*, 50.
7. Quoted in ibid., 110.
8. L. Woolf, *Beginning Again*, 34–35.
9. Quoted in Rosenbaum, *Bloomsbury on Bloomsbury*, 105–6.
10. Grace Brockington, "'Tending the Lamp' or 'Minding Their Own Business'? Bloomsbury Art and Pacifism During World War I," *Immediations*, January 2004, 9.
11. Quoted in Rosenbaum, *Bloomsbury on Bloomsbury*, 58.
12. Quoted in ibid., 111.
13. John Maynard Keynes, quoted in *CW*, vol. 16, 3.
14. Quoted in David Garnett, *The Flowers of the Forest* (New York: Harcourt, Brace and Company, 1956), 148–49.
15. Michael Holroyd, *Lytton Strachey: A Biography* (New York: Holt, Rinehart and Winston, 1980 [1971]), 244.

16. John Maynard Keynes, "My Early Beliefs," September 9, 1938, in *CW*, vol. 10, 433–50.

17. Ibid., 435.

18. G. E. Moore, *Principia Ethica* (Cambridge, UK: Cambridge University Press, 1922 [1903]), 21.

19. Ibid., 188–99.

20. Bertrand Russell, *The Autobiography of Bertrand Russell, 1872–1914* (Boston: Little, Brown, 1967), 94–95.

21. Wittgenstein would join the Apostles and resign quickly, only to rejoin much later in 1929; see Bertrand Russell to JMK, November 11, 1912, JMK/PP/45/349/1:

> Dear Keynes,
>
> All the difficulties I anticipated have arisen with Wittgenstein. I persuaded him at last to come to the first meeting and see how he could stand it. Obviously from his point of view the society is a mere waste of time. But perhaps from a philanthropic point of view he might be made to feel it worth going on with. I feel, on reflection, very doubtful whether I did well to persuade him to come next Saturday, as I feel sure he will retire in disgust. But I feel it is the business of the active brethren to settle this before next Saturday.
>
> If he is going to retire, it would be better it should be before election.
>
> Yours fraternally,
>
> B Russell

22. Robert Skidelsky, *John Maynard Keynes*, vol. 1: *Hopes Betrayed, 1883–1920* (New York: Penguin, 1994 [1983]), 19, 51.

23. Quoted in Frances Spalding, *Duncan Grant: A Biography* (London: Pimlico, 1998), 67.

24. Quoted in Rosenbaum, *Bloomsbury on Bloomsbury*, 51.

25. JMK to Duncan Grant, February 16, 1909, quoted in Spalding, *Duncan Grant*, 77.

26. Ibid. As Duncan Grant once observed, "These Apostolic young men found to their amazement that they could be shocked by the boldness and skepticism of two young women"—namely, Vanessa and Virginia. See Rosenbaum, *Bloomsbury on Bloomsbury*, 101.

27. Quoted in Holroyd, *Lytton Strachey*, 253.

28. JMK/PP/20A.

29. Russell, *The Autobiography of Bertrand Russell*, 95.

30. Quoted in Skidelsky, *John Maynard Keynes*, vol. 1, 122.

31. Carlo Cristiano, *The Political and Economic Thought of the Young Keynes* (London: Routledge, 2014), sec. 2.3.

32. Lytton Strachey, *The Letters of Lytton Strachey*, ed. Paul Levy (New York: Farrar, Straus and Giroux, 2006), 110.

33. Virginia Woolf, *The Diary of Virginia Woolf*, vol. 1: *1915–1919*, ed. Anne Olivier Bell (New York: Harcourt Brace Jovanovich, 1977), 24.

34. Woolf, *Beginning Again*, 36, 184.

35. JMK to Lytton Strachey, November 27, 1914, in Strachey, *The Letters of Lytton Strachey*, 241.

36. Skidelsky, *John Maynard Keynes*, vol. 1, 302. One was Rupert Brooke, a famous poet and close friend of the Woolfs who enlisted with the British army and fought at Antwerp before dying of disease on his way to battle at Gallipoli.

See Julia Briggs, *Virginia Woolf: An Inner Life* (New York: Harvest Books, 2006), 87.

37. Barbara Tuchman, *The Guns of August: The Outbreak of World War I* (New York: Random House, 2014 [1962]), 247–48.

38. "Laws of War: Laws and Customs of War on Land (Hague II); July 29, 1899," Lillian Goldman Law Library, Yale Law School, http://avalon.law.yale.edu/19th_century/hague02.asp.

39. "Laws of War: Laws and Customs of War on Land (Hague IV); October 18, 1907," Lillian Goldman Law Library, Yale Law School, http://avalon.law.yale.edu/20th_century/hague04.asp.

40. Woolf, *Beginning Again*, 184.

41. Ian Kershaw, *To Hell and Back: Europe, 1914–1949* (New York: Penguin, 2016), 48.

42. JMK to John Neville Keynes, June 1, 1915, in *CW*, vol. 16, 108.

43. David Lloyd George, *War Memoirs of David Lloyd George, 1915–1916* (Boston: Little, Brown, 1933), 410.

44. JMK, "The Financial Prospects of This Financial Year," Treasury memorandum, September 9, 1915, in *CW*, vol. 16, 117–25; JMK, "The Meaning of Inflation," Treasury memorandum, September 15, 1915, in *CW*, vol. 16, 125–28.

45. The Cambridge War Thrift Committee, "An Urgent Appeal," November 1915, in *CW*, vol. 16, 141–42.

46. Hermione Lee, *Virginia Woolf* (New York: Alfred A. Knopf, 1997), 339.

47. David Garnett to JMK, November 15, 1915, JMK/PP/45/116/3.

48. David Garnett to JMK, December 6, 1915, JMK/PP/45/116/6.

49. David Garnett to JMK, October 6, 1916, JMK/PP/45/116/9.

50. David Garnett to JMK, JMK/PP/45/116/13.

51. David Garnett to JMK, JMK/PP/45/116/33.

52. JMK, Treasury memorandum, September 9, 1915, in *CW*, vol. 16, 117–25.

53. Quoted in Martin Horn, *Britain, France, and the Financing of the First World War* (Montreal and Kingston, Canada: McGill–Queen's University Press, 2002), 105–7.

54. John Maynard Keynes, untitled memorandum, August 23, 1915, in *CW*, vol. 16, 110–25.

55. Stephen Broadberry and Mark Harrison, "The Economics of World War I: A Comparative Quantitative Analysis," *Journal of Economic History* 66, no. 2 (June 2006), https://warwick.ac.uk/fac/soc/economics/staff/mharrison/papers/ww1toronto2.pdf, 26.

56. "Loos Memorial," Commonwealth War Graves Commission, http://www.cwgc.org/find-a-cemetery/cemetery/79500/LOOS%20MEMORIAL.

57. Lee, *Virginia Woolf*, 340; Brockington, "'Tending the Lamp,'" 11.

58. JMK as Politicus, letter to the editor, *Daily Chronicle*, January 6, 1916, in *CW*, vol. 16, 157–61.

59. JMK to Florence Keynes, January 13, 1916, in *CW*, vol. 16, 161–62.

60. Strachey, *The Letters of Lytton Strachey*, 259–67.

61. JMK to LK, November 16, 1924, JMK/PP/45/190/2.

62. PP/45/316/5/36.

63. Keynes wrote at least one letter back to Wittgenstein, on January 10, 1915: "I am astonished to have got a letter from you. Do you think it proves that you existed within a short time of my getting it? I think so. I hope you have been safely taken

prisoner by now. . . . Your dear friend Bekassy is in your army and your very dear friend Bliss is a *private* in ours. It must be much pleasanter to be at war than to think about [philosophical] propositions in Norway. But I hope you will stop such self-indulgence soon." JMK/PP/45/349/99.

64. JMK to "the Tribunal," February 28, 1916, in *CW*, vol. 16, 178.

65. Quoted in Skidelsky, *John Maynard Keynes*, vol. 2, 327.

66. JMK to Florence Keynes, September 8, 1915, JMK/PP/45/168/8/105.

67. JMK to Florence Keynes, June 6, 1916, JMK/PP/45/168/8/145.

68. Florence Keynes to JMK, June 6, 1916, JMK/PP/45/168/8/147.

69. Virginia Woolf, *The Letters of Virginia Woolf*, vol. 2: *1912–1922*, ed. Nigel Nicolson and Joanne Trautmann (New York: Harcourt Brace Jovanovich, 1976), 133.

70. John Maynard Keynes, "The Financial Dependence of the United Kingdom on the United States of America," Treasury memorandum, October 10, 1916, in *CW*, vol. 16, 197.

71. Ron Chernow, *The House of Morgan: An American Banking Dynasty and the Rise of Modern Finance* (New York: Grove Press, 2001 [1990]), 188–89. Among other achievements, Morgan had backed Thomas Edison's electricity venture, created the U.S. Steel monopoly, and single-handedly bailed out the entire U.S. financial system in 1907.

72. Adam Tooze, *The Deluge: The Great War, America and the Remaking of the Global Order, 1916–1931* (New York: Viking, 2014), 38.

73. John Maynard Keynes, "Report to the Chancellor of the Exchequer of the British Members of the Joint Anglo-French Financial Committee," October 24, 1916, in *CW*, vol. 16, 201–6.

74. John Maynard Keynes, "The Financial Dependence of the United Kingdom on the United States of America," Treasury memorandum, October 10, 1916, in *CW*, vol. 16, 197–98.

75. In what follows I draw heavily from John Milton Cooper, Jr., *Woodrow Wilson: A Biography* (New York: Vintage Books, 2009).

76. Woodrow Wilson, *A History of the American People*, vol. 5: *Reunion and Nationalization* (New York: Harper and Brothers, 1902), 212.

77. Woodrow Wilson, *The Papers of Woodrow Wilson*, vol. 24: *January–August 1912*, ed. Arthur S. Link (Princeton, NJ: Princeton University Press, 1978), 252.

78. See Don Wolfensberger, "Woodrow Wilson, Congress and Anti-Immigrant Sentiment in America: An Introductory Essay," Woodrow Wilson International Center for Scholars, March 12, 2007, https://www.wilsoncenter.org/sites/default/files/immigration-essay-intro.pdf.

79. John Maynard Keynes, "Note for Mr McAdoo," Treasury memorandum, July 20, 1917, in *CW*, vol. 16, 245–52.

80. JMK to Florence Keynes, March 23, 1918, JMK/PP/45/168/9/85.

81. JMK to Vanessa Bell, March 23, 1918, CHA/1/341/3/1.

82. JMK to Florence Keynes, March 29, 1918, JMK/PP/45/168/9/87; Garnett, *The Flowers of the Forest*, 146–47.

83. JMK to Florence Keynes, March 23, 1918, PP/45/168/9/85.

84. Virginia Woolf to Nicholas Bagenal, April 15, 1918, in Virginia Woolf, *The Letters of Virginia Woolf*, vol. 2, 230.

85. Quoted in Garnett, *The Flowers of the Forest*, 148.

86. Quoted in ibid., 40.

87. Virginia Woolf to Vanessa Bell, May 15, 1927, Virginia Woolf, *The Letters of Vir-*

ginia Woolf, vol. 3: *1923–1928*, ed. Nigel Nicolson and Joanne Trautmann (New York: Harcourt Brace Jovanovich, 1977), 376.

88. JMK to Florence Keynes, December 24, 1917, in *CW*, vol. 16, 265.

89. JMK to Florence Keynes, March 29, 1918, JMK/PP/45/168/9/87.

90. Basil Blackett to H. P. Hamilton, January 1, 1918, in *CW*, vol. 16, 264.

91. JMK to Florence Keynes, December 24, 1917, *CW*, vol. 16, 265–66.

92. JMK to Duncan Grant, December 15, 1917, in Jonathan Atkin, *A War of Individuals: Bloomsbury Attitudes to the Great War* (New York: Manchester University Press, 2002), 24.

93. JMK to Florence Keynes, October 25, 1918, JMK/PP/45/168/9/131.

94. Virginia Woolf, January 14, 1918, *The Diary of Virginia Woolf*, vol. 1, 106.

95. JMK to Florence Keynes, October 13, 1918, JMK/PP/45/168/9/129.

THREE: PARIS AND ITS DISCONTENTS

1. Quoted in A. Scott Berg, *Wilson* (New York: Berkley, 2013), 18–19.

2. Quoted in ibid., 521.

3. Margaret MacMillan, *Paris 1919: Six Months That Changed the World* (New York: Random House, 2003 [2001]), 15.

4. Quoted in Sarah Gertrude Millin, *General Smuts*, vol. 2 (London: Faber & Faber, 1936), 172–75.

5. John Maynard Keynes, *The Economic Consequences of the Peace* (London: Macmillan, 1919), 34.

6. Berg, *Wilson*, 18.

7. JMK to Florence Keynes, December 23, 1918, JMK/PP/45/168/9/141.

8. JMK to Florence Keynes, October 25, 1918, JMK/PP/45/168/9/131, "I think the prospects of peace good"; the rest is from JMK to Florence Keynes, December 23, 1918, JMK/PP/45/168/9/141.

9. JMK to Neville Keynes, January 14, 1919, JMK/PP/45/168/9/145.

10. See Keynes' biographical sketches of Winston Churchill and the German banker Carl Melchior in his 1933 book *Essays in Biography*, in *CW*, vol. 10, 53, 390, where Keynes noted the distinction between "dining-room diners" and "restaurant diners."

11. Paul Cravath to JMK, December 20, 1918, JMK/RT/1/8.

12. Henry Wickham Steed, *Through Thirty Years: 1892–1922* (London: William Heinemann, 1924), vol. 2, 266.

13. Charles G. Fenwick, "Organization and Procedure of the Peace Conference," *American Political Science Review* 13, no. 2 (May 1919): 199–212.

14. JMK to Neville Keynes, January 14, 1919, JMK/PP/45/168/9/145.

15. Quoted in Edward Mandell House and Charles Seymour, eds., *What Really Happened at Paris: The Story of the Peace Conference, 1918–1919* (New York: Charles Scribner's Sons, 1921), 336.

16. Mark Sykes, the thirty-nine-year-old author of the infamous Sykes-Picot treaty in which Britain and France had secretly agreed to divide up the Ottoman Empire between them, was killed by the flu in February. See Harold Nicolson, *Peacemaking, 1919* (London: Constable & Co. Ltd., 1943 [1937]), 214. Lloyd George was still recovering from the flu when he arrived. Keynes would fall ill in February, Wilson would contract the flu in the spring, and Clemenceau battled several weeks of "colds" in March and April—most likely a prolonged bout with the flu.

See Laura Spinney, *Pale Rider: The Spanish Flu of 1918 and How It Changed the World* (New York: PublicAffairs, 2017). On William Stang's death and the atmosphere at the Hotel Majestic, see Clifford R. Lovin, *A School for Diplomats: The Paris Peace Conference of 1919* (Lanham, MD: University Press of America, 1997), 12–17.

17. Keynes, *The Economic Consequences of the Peace*, 3–4.

18. John Maynard Keynes, "Dr Melchoir: A Defeated Enemy," February 2, 1921, in *CW*, vol. 10, 390.

19. Keynes, *The Economic Consequences of the Peace*, 26.

20. *CW*, vol. 16, 387.

21. John Maynard Keynes, "Notes on an Indemnity," Treasury memorandum, October 31, 1918, in CW, vol. 16, 337–43; and John Maynard Keynes, "Memorandum by the Treasury on the Indemnity Payable by the Enemy Powers for Reparation and Other Claims," undated Treasury memorandum, in *CW*, vol. 16, 344–86.

22. John Maynard Keynes, "Memorandum by the Treasury on the Indemnity Payable by the Enemy Powers for Reparation and Other Claims," undated Treasury memorandum, in *CW*, vol. 16, 375.

23. See Marc Trachtenberg, "Reparation at the Paris Peace Conference," *The Journal of Modern History* 51, no. 1 (March 1979): 33.

24. Adam Tooze, *The Deluge: The Great War, America and the Remaking of the Global Order, 1916–1931* (New York: Viking, 2014), 293.

25. Quoted in House and Seymour, *What Really Happened at Paris*, 275–76.

26. Quoted in ibid., 259.

27. Woodrow Wilson, "Wilson's War Message to Congress," April 2, 1917, World War I Document Archive, Brigham Young University, https://wwi.lib.byu.edu/index.php/Wilson%27s_War_Message_to_Congress.

28. Ibid.

29. JMK to Allyn Young, February 29, 1920, JMK/EC/2/3/62.

30. JMK to Norman Davis, April 18, 1920, JMK/EC/2/4/27.

31. Memo from JMK to Sir John Bradbury, January 14, 1919, JMK/RT/9/1/32.

32. Nadège Mougel, "World War I Casualties," Centre Européen Robert Schuman, http://www.centre-robert-schuman.org/userfiles/files/REPERES%20%E2%80%93%20module%201-1-1%20-%20explanatory%20notes%20%E2%80%93%20World%20War%20I%20casualties%20%E2%80%93%20EN.pdf.

33. Amos Crosby to JMK, January 7, 1919, JMK/RT/1/24.

34. MacMillan, *Paris 1919*, 10.

35. "World War I Casualties," Centre Européen Robert Schuman.

36. "Redrawing the Map: How the First World War Reshaped Europe," *The Economist*, August 2, 2014.

37. Derek Howard Aldcroft, *From Versailles to Wall Street, 1919–1929* (Berkeley: University of California Press, 1977), 19.

38. JMK to Florence Keynes, October 25, 1918, JMK/PP/45/168/9/131; JMK to Florence Keynes, November 3, 1918, JMK/PP/45/168/9/134.

39. Robert Nye, *Masculinity and Male Codes of Honor in Modern France* (Berkeley: University of California Press, 1998 [1993]), 185.

40. Richard J. Evans, *The Pursuit of Power: Europe, 1815–1914* (New York: Viking, 2016), 598. See also Gregor Dallas, *At the Heart of a Tiger: Clemenceau and His World, 1841–1929* (New York: Carroll and Graf, 1993), 302–3.

41. Quoted in Dallas, *At the Heart of a Tiger,* 561.
42. Quoted in George Riddell, *Lord Riddell's Intimate Diary of the Peace Conference and After, 1918–1923* (London: Victor Gollancz, 1933), 41.
43. Keynes, *The Economic Consequences of the Peace,* 29.
44. Tooze, *The Deluge,* 175.
45. Dallas, *At the Heart of a Tiger,* 566.
46. Keynes, *The Economic Consequences of the Peace,* 26.
47. Keith Laybourn, *Modern Britain Since 1906* (London: I. B. Taurus, 1999), 20.
48. Quoted in MacMillan, *Paris 1919,* 33.
49. Quoted in Trachtenberg, "Reparation at the Paris Peace Conference," 32.
50. Quoted in Stephen Bonsal, *Unfinished Business* (New York: Doubleday, 1944), 69.
51. N. P. Howard, "The Social and Political Consequences of the Allied Food Blockade of Germany, 1918–19," *German History* 11, no. 2 (April 1, 1993): 162.
52. JMK, memorandum to Sir John Bradbury, January 11, 1919, JMK/RT/9/1.
53. Quoted in House and Seymour, *What Really Happened at Paris,* 338.
54. John Maynard Keynes, "Dr Melchoir," in *CW,* vol. 10, 397.
55. Ibid., 395.
56. House and Seymour, *What Really Happened at Paris,* 343.
57. Herbert Hoover, dispatch to Italian food minister Silvio Crespi, December 31, 1918, in *Papers Relating to the Foreign Relations of the United States 1919: The Paris Peace Conference* (Washington, D.C.: U.S. Government Printing Office, 1942), vol. 2, 688–89.
58. JMK, memorandum to Sir John Bradbury, January 14, 1919, JMK/RT/1/36–40.
59. John Maynard Keynes, "Dr Melchoir," in *CW,* vol. 10, 401.
60. Riddell, *Lord Riddell's Intimate Diary of the Peace Conference and After,* 42.
61. John Maynard Keynes, "Dr Melchoir," in *CW,* vol. 10, 405.
62. Lovin, *A School for Diplomats,* 13.
63. JMK to Florence Keynes, January 25, 1919, JMK/PP/45/168/9/149.
64. "I wrote to Walter to ask him if he advised inoculation against influenza; but he answered that he hadn't *yet* any vaccine that he could recommend," Keynes wrote to his mother on November 3, 1918. "Sheppard hasn't left the house at all this week for fear of the plague." JMK/PP/45/168/9/131.
65. Clive Bell to JMK, February 2, 1919, JMK/PP/45/25/32.
66. JMK to Florence Keynes, March 16, 1919, JMK/PP/45/168/9/157.
67. John Maynard Keynes, "Dr Melchoir," in *CW,* vol. 10, 416–24.
68. Cunliffe returned the favor by mocking his Treasury adversary as "Herr von K"—accusing him of pro-German sympathies. See Antony Lentin, *Lloyd George and the Lost Peace: From Versailles to Hitler, 1919–1940* (New York: Palgrave Macmillan, 2001), 24.
69. Quoted by Keynes in a March 25, 1919, memo, JMK/RT/1/71.
70. JMK to Philip Kerr, March 25, 1919, JMK/RT/1/71.
71. Quoted in House and Seymour, *What Really Happened at Paris,* 272.
72. Reproduced in Philip Mason Burnett, *Reparation at the Paris Peace Conference from the Standpoint of the American Delegation* (New York: Columbia University Press, 1940), 776.
73. Quoted in House and Seymour, *What Really Happened at Paris,* 262.
74. Amos T. Crosby to JMK, January 7, 1919, JMK/RT/1/24.
75. JMK, memorandum to Woodrow Wilson, "The Treatment of Inter-Ally Debt Arising Out of the War," March 1919, *CW,* vol. 16, 427–28.

76. Quoted in House and Seymour, *What Really Happened at Paris,* 289.

77. JMK to Florence Keynes, April 12, 1919, JMK/PP/45/168/9/164.

78. John Maynard Keynes, "Scheme for the Rehabilitation of European Credit and for Financing Relief and Reconstruction," Treasury memo for Woodrow Wilson, April 1919, in *CW,* vol. 16, 433–35.

79. Woodrow Wilson to David Lloyd George, May 3, 1919, JMK/RT/16/33.

80. Quoted in Robert Skidelsky, *John Maynard Keynes,* vol. 1: *Hopes Betrayed, 1883–1920* (New York: Penguin, 1994 [1983]), 372.

81. Ron Chernow, *The House of Morgan: An American Banking Dynasty and the Rise of Modern Finance* (New York: Grove Press, 2001 [1990]), 370–73.

82. Ibid., 280–86.

83. Quoted in Noam Chomsky, *Deterring Democracy* (New York: Hill and Wang, 1992), 39.

84. Chernow, *The House of Morgan,* 336–43.

85. Keynes, *The Economic Consequences of the Peace,* 41.

86. Eric Rauchway, *The Money Makers: How Roosevelt and Keynes Ended the Depression, Defeated Fascism, and Secured a Prosperous Peace* (New York: Basic Books, 2015), 16.

87. JMK to Florence Keynes, May 14, 1919, JMK/PP/45/168/9/168.

88. JMK to Norman Davis, June 5, 1919, in *CW,* vol. 16, 471.

89. JMK to David Lloyd George, June 5, 1919, in *CW,* vol. 16, 469.

FOUR: CONSEQUENCES

1. John Milton Cooper, Jr., *Woodrow Wilson: A Biography* (New York: Vintage, 2009), 502–4; A. Scott Berg, *Wilson* (New York: Berkley, 2013), 600–602.

2. Woodrow Wilson, *The Papers of Woodrow Wilson,* ed. Arthur S. Link, vol. 61 (Princeton, NJ: Princeton University Press, 1990), 292–93.

3. The two men had much in common. Wilson was the first son of the American South to reach the presidency after the Civil War, while Smuts was an Afrikaner who became prime minister of South Africa under British rule. Both held paternalistic views about nonwhite peoples while proclaiming high democratic ideals. See Sarah Gertrude Millin, *General Smuts,* vol. 2 (London: Faber & Faber, 1936), 172–73.

4. Cooper, *Woodrow Wilson: A Biography,* 502–4; Berg, *Wilson,* 600–602.

5. Robert Skidelsky, *John Maynard Keynes,* vol. 1: *Hopes Betrayed, 1883–1920* (New York: Allen Lane, 1983), 379–80. Keynes was in Charleston from June 20 to July 9, 1919. The Treaty of Versailles was signed on June 28.

6. David Garnett, *The Flowers of the Forest* (New York: Harcourt, Brace and Company, 1956), 145.

7. JMK/L/19.

8. Lord Robert Cecil to JMK, July 31, 1919, JMK/L/19.

9. JMK to Florence Keynes, December 23, 1918, JMK/PP/45/168/9/141.

10. JMK/L/19.

11. Jan Smuts to JMK, in Millin, *General Smuts,* vol. 2, 255–56.

12. Quoted in Tom Regan, *Bloomsbury's Prophet: G. E. Moore and the Development of His Moral Philosophy* (Philadelphia: Temple University Press, 1986), 154.

13. Lytton Strachey, *Eminent Victorians: Cardinal Manning, Florence Nightingale, Dr. Arnold, General Gordon* (London: G. P. Putnam Sons, 1918).

14. John Maynard Keynes, *The Economic Consequences of the Peace* (London: Macmillan, 1919), 18.

15. Ibid., 19.

16. Ibid., 251.

17. Herbert Hoover, *The Ordeal of Woodrow Wilson* (Washington, D.C.: Woodrow Wilson Center Press, 1992 [1958]), 152.

18. Keynes, *The Economic Consequences of the Peace*, 220.

19. Michael V. White and Kurt Schuler, "Retrospectives: Who Said 'Debauch the Currency': Keynes or Lenin?," *Journal of Economic Perspectives* 23, no. 2 (2009): 213–22.

20. Edmund Burke, *Reflections on the Revolution in France* (London: John Sharpe, 1820), 138.

21. Leonard Woolf, *Downhill All the Way: An Autobiography of the Years 1919 to 1939* (New York: Harvest, 1967), 139.

22. John Maynard Keynes, *The Political Doctrines of Edmund Burke* (unpublished thesis, 1904), 57–58, JMK/UA/20/3/61–2.

23. Keynes, *The Economic Consequences of the Peace*, 11.

24. John Maynard Keynes, "My Early Beliefs," September 9, 1938, in *CW*, vol. 10, 447.

25. Keynes, *The Economic Consequences of the Peace*, 38.

26. Lytton Strachey to JMK, October 4, 1919, JMK/PP/45/316/5/61.

27. Florence Keynes to JMK, JMK/EC/1/9.

28. JMK to Arthur Salter, October 18, 1919, JMK/EC/1/21.

29. Skidelsky, *John Maynard Keynes*, vol. 1, 381.

30. Julia Briggs, *Virginia Woolf: An Inner Life* (New York: Harvest Books, 2006), 22–28.

31. John Maynard Keynes, "Mr. Lloyd George's General Election" (London: The Liberal Publication Department, 1920), JMK/EC/2/5/21.

32. Adam Tooze, *The Deluge: The Great War, America and the Remaking of the Global Order, 1916–1931* (New York: Viking, 2014), 295.

33. Austen Chamberlain to JMK, December 8, 1919, JMK/EC/2/1/8.

34. JMK to Austen Chamberlain, December 28, 1919, JMK/EC/2/1/12.

35. Reginald McKenna to JMK, December 27, 1919, JMK/EC/2/1/129.

36. Allyn Young to JMK, February 11, 1920, JMK/EC/2/3/58.

37. Paul Cravath to JMK, February 4, 1920, JMK/EC/2/3/37.

38. Amos T. Crosby to JMK, March 8, 1920, JMK/EC/2/2/7.

39. Ronald Steel, *Walter Lippmann and the American Century* (Boston: Little, Brown, 1980), 162. Keynes' American publisher, Harcourt, wrote about the decision to publish *The Economic Consequences of the Peace* in his memoir *Some Experiences*, excerpted by the publisher in a January 27, 1965, letter to John Kenneth Galbraith, available at JKG, Series 9.4, Box 941.

40. Keynes, *The Economic Consequences of the Peace*, 28–29.

41. Ibid., 36.

42. Allyn Young to JMK, June 10, 1920, JMK/EC/2/4/76.

43. Norman Davis to JMK, March 19, 1920, JMK/EC/2/4/23.

44. JMK to Norman Davis, April 18, 1920, JMK/EC/2/4/27.

45. Quoted in Miller, *General Smuts*, vol. 2, 174–75.

46. Bernard Baruch, *The Making of the Reparation and Economic Sections of the Treaty* (New York: Harper and Brothers, 1921).

47. Ibid., 5–8.

48. André Tardieu, "The Treaty and Its Critic," *Everybody's Magazine,* November 1920, JMK/EC/2/5/12.

49. Charles Homer Haskins, cited in Edward Mandell House and Charles Seymour, eds., *What Really Happened at Paris: The Story of the Peace Conference, 1918–1919* (New York: Charles Scribner's Sons, 1921), 65.

50. Paul Mantoux to the League of Nations, September 13, 1924, JMK/EC/2/6/48; Philip Mason Burnett, *Reparation at the Paris Peace Conference from the Standpoint of the American Delegation* (New York: Columbia University Press, 1940), 847, 1000.

FIVE: FROM METAPHYSICS TO MONEY

1. *CW,* vol. 15, 13–15.

2. David Felix, *Keynes: A Critical Life* (Westport, CT: Greenwood Press, 1999), 141.

3. Piero V. Mini, *John Maynard Keynes: A Study in the Psychology of Original Work* (New York: St. Martin's Press, 1994), 86.

4. Roberta Allbert Dayer, *Finance and Empire: Sir Charles Addis, 1861–1945* (London: Macmillan, 1988), 81.

5. JMK to Ludwig Wittgenstein, January 10, 1915, JMK/PP/45/349.

6. Bertrand Russell to JMK, March 23, 1919, JMK/PP/45/349/18.

7. Ludwig Wittgenstein to Bertrand Russell, March 13, 1919, JMK/PP/45/349/19.

8. John Coates, *The Claims of Common Sense: Moore, Wittgenstein, Keynes and the Social Sciences* (Cambridge, UK: Cambridge University Press, 1996), 129.

9. JMK to Ludwig Wittgenstein, May 13, 1919, JMK/PP/45/349/101.

10. JMK to Ludwig Wittgenstein, June 28, 1919, JMK/PP/45/349/102.

11. Ludwig Wittgenstein, *Tractatus Logico-Philosophicus* (London: Kegan Paul, Trench, Trübner, 1922), 23.

12. Bertrand Russell, *The Selected Letters of Bertrand Russell: The Public Years, 1914–1970,* ed. Nicholas Griffin (London: Routledge, 2001), 441.

13. Quoted in Robert Skidelsky, *John Maynard Keynes,* vol. 2: *The Economist as Savior, 1920–1937* (New York: Allen Lane, 1994), 56.

14. John Rawls' "original position" in *A Theory of Justice* is another similar attempt by philosophers to smuggle their conclusions into the basic construction of their system. Much of Rawls' work, including the difference principle, is an attempt to construct the foundations of a broadly liberal, egalitarian philosophy using Keynesian concepts.

15. Wittgenstein, *Tractatus Logico-Philosophicus,* 90.

16. The personal wealth and investment numbers that follow in this section are from Mini, *John Maynard Keynes,* 84–86, and David Felix, *Biography of an Idea: John Maynard Keynes and the General Theory of Employment, Interest and Money* (New York: Routledge, 2017 [1995]).

17. John Maynard Keynes, statement to the Royal Commission on Lotteries and Betting, December 15, 1932, in *CW,* vol. 18, 399.

18. JMK to LL, September 16, 1923, JMK/PP/45/190/1/10.

19. JMK to LL, September 19, 1923, JMK/PP/45/190/1/14.

20. Alison Light, "Lady Talky," *London Review of Books,* December 18, 2008.

21. Light, "Lady Talky."

22. Judith Mackrell, *Bloomsbury Ballerina: Lydia Lopokova, Imperial Dancer and Mrs. John Maynard Keynes* (London: Phoenix, 2009 [2008]), 108.

23. Ibid., 169–72.

24. Ibid., 192.

25. LL to JMK, JMK/PP/45/190/8.

26. Mackrell, *Bloomsbury Ballerina*, 196.

27. Ibid., 1–37.

28. Virginia Woolf mocked Lydia's intellectual claims and her accent by repeating Lydia's "seerious wooman" pronunciation behind her back. See Virginia Woolf to Jacques Raverat, November 4, 1923, in Virginia Woolf, *The Letters of Virginia Woolf,* vol. 3: *1923–1928*, ed. Nigel Nicolson and Joanne Trautmann (New York: Harcourt Brace Jovanovich, 1978), 76.

29. LL to JMK, March 10, 1922, PP/45/190/9/5.

30. LL to JMK, undated, located between letters sent on April 21, 1922, and April 28, 1922, PP/45/190/9/37.

31. LL to JMK, June 26, 1922, PP/45/190/10/30.

32. Mackrell, *Bloomsbury Ballerina*, 196.

33. JMK to LL, January 20, 1926, JMK/PP/45/190/1/62.

34. LL to JMK, April 26, 1922, JMK/PP/45/190/9/53.

35. LL to JMK, April 19, 1922, JMK/PP/45/190/9/32.

36. LL to JMK, undated, JMK/PP/45/190/12/23.

37. Virginia Woolf to Jacques Raverat, June 8, 1924, in Virginia Woolf, *The Letters of Virginia Woolf,* vol. 3, 115.

38. Virginia Woolf to Jacques Raverat, November 4, 1923, in ibid., 76.

39. Virginia Woolf to Vanessa Bell, December 22, 1922, in Virginia Woolf, *The Letters of Virginia Woolf,* vol. 2: *1912–1922*, ed. Nigel Nicolson and Joanne Trautmann (New York: Harcourt Brace Jovanovich, 1977), 594–95.

40. LL to JMK, April 17, 1922, JMK/PP/45/190/9/26.

41. LL to JMK, April 12, 1922, JMK/PP/45/190/9/12.

42. LL to JMK, April 20, 1922, JMK/PP/45/190/9/34.

43. LL to JMK April 22, 1922, JMK/PP/45/190/9/40.

44. Mackrell, *Bloomsbury Ballerina*, 202.

45. Ibid., 181–203.

46. Ibid., 201.

47. John Maynard Keynes, *The Economic Consequences of the Peace* (London: Macmillan, 1919), 278–79.

48. Keynes received £300 from *The Manchester Guardian,* £350 from the *New York World,* and £25 from the *Neue Freie Presse* of Vienna; see *CW,* vol. 17, 354. Current value calculated using the average 1922 exchange rate of $4.43 to the pound, according to the Federal Reserve Bank of St. Louis, https://fraser.stlouisfed.org/files/docs/publications/FRB/pages/1925-1929/28191_1925-1929.pdf, and the Bureau of Labor Statistics' "CPI Inflation Calculator," https://data.bls.gov/cgi-bin/cpicalc.pl.

49. And when the United States formally entered the conflict in 1917, it used tricks of its own to effectively suspend the gold standard, as well. The Wilson administration required everyone who wanted to export gold to apply for a special license to do so from the Treasury Department, and nearly all of these applications were denied.

50. Liaquat Ahamed, *Lords of Finance: The Bankers Who Broke the World* (New York: Penguin, 2009), 155–56.

51. Ibid., 158–59.

52. "U.S./U.K. Foreign Exchange Rate in the United Kingdom," Federal Reserve Bank of St. Louis, https://fred.stlouisfed.org/series/USUKFXUKA#0; Adam Tooze, *The Deluge: The Great War, America and the Remaking of the Global Order, 1916–1931* (New York: Viking, 2014), 355.

53. Albert O. Hirschman, *The Passions and the Interests: Political Arguments for Capitalism Before Its Triumph* (Princeton, NJ: Princeton University Press, 1997), 60.

54. John Maynard Keynes, "The Stabilisation of the European Exchanges: A Plan for Genoa," April 20, 1922, *Manchester Guardian Commercial Supplement*, April 20, 1922, in *CW*, vol. 17, 355–57.

55. Ahamed, *Lords of Finance*, 161.

56. "Unemployment Statistics from 1881 to the Present Day," Government Statistical Service, UK Statistics Authority, January 1996, http://www.ons.gov.uk/ons/rel/lms/labour-market-trends--discontinued-/january-1996/unemployment-since-1881.pdf.

57. Tooze, *The Deluge*, 359.

58. John Maynard Keynes, "The Consequences to Society of Changes in the Value of Money," *The Manchester Guardian Commercial Supplement*, July 27, 1922 in *CW*, vol. 9, 67–75.

59. JMK, Treasury memorandum, February 15, 1920, in *CW*, vol. 17, 184.

60. JMK to LL, April 28, 1922, PP/45/190/9/60.

61. JMK to LL, April 27, 1922, PP/45/190/9/57.

62. JMK to LL, April 17, 1922, PP/45/190/9/26.

63. It was not, however, exclusively Keynes' innovation. Other monetary reformers included in particular the Yale economist Irving Fisher.

64. John Maynard Keynes, *A Tract on Monetary Reform* (London: Macmillan, 1924), 80.

65. JMK to Charles Addis, July 25, 1924, JMK/L/24/77.

66. Virginia Woolf to Ottoline Morrell, January 1923, in Virginia Woolf, *The Letters of Virginia Woolf*, vol. 3, 8.

67. Leonard Woolf, *Downhill All the Way*, 142–43.

68. Virginia Woolf to JMK, February 12, 1923, in Virginia Woolf, *The Letters of Virginia Woolf*, vol. 3, 11–12.

69. Harold Bloom, *T. S. Eliot's The Waste Land (Bloom's Modern Critical Interpretations)* (New York: Infobase, 2007), 77–82.

70. Donald Gallup, *T. S. Eliot: A Bibliography* (New York: Harcourt Brace, 1969).

71. Virginia Woolf to Lytton Strachey, February 23, 1923, in Virginia Woolf, *The Letters of Virginia Woolf*, vol. 3, 14–15.

72. Virginia Woolf to JMK, March 13, 1923, in Virginia Woolf, *The Letters of Virginia Woolf*, vol. 3, 20.

73. JMK to LL, June 15, 1924, JMK/PP/45/190/2.

74. Leonard Woolf, *Downhill All the Way*, 97.

75. Ibid., 142–43.

76. A 1925 essay on the gold standard and Winston Churchill quickly went through seven thousand copies, generating profits that were recycled through Hogarth to pay for poetry and fiction. See Leonard Woolf, *Downhill All the Way*, 162.

77. Quoted in S. P. Rosenbaum, ed., *The Bloomsbury Group: A Collection of Memoirs and Commentary* (Toronto: University of Toronto Press, 1995), 281.

78. John Maynard Keynes, "Editorial Forward," *The Nation and Athenaeum*, May 5, 1923, in *CW*, vol. 18, 123–26.

79. JMK to LL, December 4, 1923, JMK/PP/45/190/1/147.
80. Ibid.
81. JMK to LL, December 5, 1923, JMK/PP/45/190/1/49.
82. Ibid.
83. JMK to LL, December 9, 1923, JMK/PP/45/190/1/55.
84. Winston Churchill, letter to *The Times*, January 18, 1924.
85. Quoted in Chris Cook, *The Age of Alignment: Electoral Politics in Britain: 1922–1929* (London: Macmillan, 1975), 188.
86. Sally Marks, "The Myths of Reparations," *Central European History* 11, no. 3 (September 1978): 234.
87. As a wealthy conservative, Stinnes generally opposed seeing his tax rate go up, and the Weimar government was as reluctant to alienate the rich as it was to alienate the poor—either group could bolt to support an authoritarian alternative. See Fritz K. Ringer, ed., *The German Inflation of 1923* (London: Oxford University Press, 1969), 92.
88. Ringer, *The German Inflation of 1923*, 91.
89. JMK to Rudolf Havenstein, January 17, 1923, in *CW*, vol. 18, 68.
90. Quoted in Tooze, *The Deluge*, 456.
91. Niall Ferguson, *The Ascent of Money: A Financial History of the World* (New York: Penguin, 2008), 104.
92. Tooze, *The Deluge*, 442–43.
93. Ibid., 439.
94. Josiah Stamp to JMK, *CW*, vol. 18, 235.
95. John Maynard Keynes, "The Experts' Reports," *The Nation and Athenaeum*, April 12, 1924, in *CW*, vol. 18, 241.
96. Carolyn K. Kitching, "Prime Minister and Foreign Secretary: the Dual Role of James Ramsay MacDonald in 1924," *Review of International Studies* 37, no. 3 (July 2011): 1412.
97. John Maynard Keynes, "The Progress of the Dawes Scheme," *The Nation and Athenaeum*, September 11, 1926, in *CW*, vol. 18, 281.

SIX: PROLEGOMENA TO A NEW SOCIALISM

1. David A. Andelman, *A Shattered Peace: Versailles 1919 and the Price We Pay Today* (Hoboken, NJ: John Wiley & Sons, 2008), 232.
2. JMK to LL, May 28, 1924, JMK/PP/45/190/1/161.
3. JMK to LL, May 27, 1924, JMK/PP/45/190/1/159.
4. "It was naughty of you to read out my letter about the banquet." JMK to LL, May 30, 1924, JMK/PP/45/190/1/161.
5. JMK to LL, May 30, 1924JMK/PP/45/190/1/166.
6. Quoted in Michele Barrett, ed., *Virginia Woolf: Women and Writing* (New York: Harcourt, 1997), 193–97.
7. Quoted in Richard Kahn, *The Making of Keynes' General Theory* (Cambridge, UK: Cambridge University Press, 1984), 203.
8. Ibid., 204.
9. Carnegie Endowment for International Peace, *Report of the International Commission to Inquire into the Causes and Conduct of the Balkan Wars*, 1914, https://archive.org/details/reportofinternat00inteuoft.
10. JMK to H. N. Brailsford, December 3, 1925, JMK/CO/1/98.

11. John Maynard Keynes, "Editorial Forward," *The Nation and Athenaeum*, May 5, 1923, in *CW*, vol. 18, 126.
12. John Maynard Keynes, "The End of Laissez-Faire" (London: Hogarth Press, 1926) based on the Sidney Ball Lecture, November 1924, in *CW*, vol. 9, 294.
13. See Jean-Jacques Rousseau, *The Basic Political Writings* (Indianapolis: Hackett, 1987).
14. John Maynard Keynes, "The End of Laissez-Faire," in *CW*, vol. 9, 291–92.
15. Ibid., 287.
16. Ibid., 287–88.
17. Ibid., 291.
18. Ibid., 288.
19. Ibid., 289.
20. Ibid., 290.
21. Ibid., 288.
22. Keynes believed Burke's most convincing arguments for laissez-faire turned entirely on empirical fact of economic scarcity. See John Maynard Keynes, "The Political Doctrines of Edmund Burke" (unpublished, 1904), JMK/UA/20/3/1.
23. Robert Skidelsky, *John Maynard Keynes*, vol. 2: *The Economist as Savior, 1920–1937* (New York: Allen Lane, 1994), 207–8; Judith Mackrell, *Bloomsbury Ballerina: Lydia Lopokova, Imperial Dancer and Mrs. John Maynard Keynes* (London: Phoenix, 2009 [2008]), 266.
24. Quoted in Mackrell, *Bloomsbury Ballerina*, 266.
25. Ibid., 267.
26. Kahn, *The Making of Keynes' General Theory*, 169.
27. Michael Holroyd, *Lytton Strachey: A Biography* (New York: Holt, Rinehart and Winston, 1980 [1971]), 902–3.
28. JMK to LL, November 9, 1923, JMK/PP/45/190/1/33; JMK to LL, December 9, 1923, JMK/PP/45/190/1/57.
29. Lytton Strachey, *The Letters of Lytton Strachey*, ed. Paul Levy (New York: Farrar, Straus and Giroux, 2005), 478, 483, 497–98.
30. Leonard Woolf's biographer Victoria Glendenning argued that some of Virginia's attraction to Leonard was a product of his Jewishness, as it inspired in her a sense of rebellion against Victorian conventions. See Victoria Glendenning, *Leonard Woolf: A Biography* (New York: Free Press, 2006), 142.
31. See, e.g., LL to JMK, April 22, 1922, in which Lydia exults "and jews are jews very funny!" PP/45/190/9/57.
32. Quoted in Mackrell, *Bloomsbury Ballerina*, 280.
33. Virginia Woolf, *The Diary of Virginia Woolf*, vol. 3: *1925–1930*, ed. Anne Olivier Bell and Andrew McNeillie (New York: Harcourt Brace Jovanovich, 1981), 43.
34. Mackrell, *Bloomsbury Ballerina*, 272.
35. John Maynard Keynes, "A Short View of Russia," in *CW*, vol. 9, 253–71.
36. Ibid., 270.
37. Ibid., 271.
38. Ibid., 258.
39. Ibid., 271.
40. Ibid., 267.
41. Ibid., 268.
42. John Maynard Keynes, "Am I a Liberal?," *The Nation and Athenaeum*, August 8 and 15, 1925, in *CW*, vol. 9, 306.

43. Ibid., 297.

44. Ibid., 311.

45. Ibid., 309.

46. Ibid., 311.

47. "Unemployment Statistics from 1881 to the Present Day," Government Statistical Service, UK Statistics Authority, January 1996, https://www.ons.gov.uk/ons/rel/lms/labour-market-trends--discontinued-/january-1996/unemployment-since-1881.pdf.

48. Nicholas Crafts, "Walking Wounded: The British Economy in the Aftermath of World War I," Vox, August 27, 2014, https://voxeu.org/article/walking-wounded-british-economy-aftermath-world-war-i.

49. John Maynard Keynes, "The Speeches of the Bank Chairmen," *The Nation and Athenaeum,* February 23, 1924, in *CW,* vol. 9, 199.

50. Ludwig von Mises, *Socialism: An Economic and Sociological Analysis* (New Haven, CT: Yale University Press, 1951 [1927]), 485, https://mises-media.s3.amazonaws.com/Socialism%20An%20Economic%20and%20Sociological%20Analysis_3.pdf.

51. John Maynard Keynes, "The Economic Consequences of Mr Churchill," *Evening Standard,* July 22–24, 1925, in *CW,* vol. 9, 207.

52. Ibid., 220.

53. Ibid., 211.

54. JMK to Charles Addis, July 25, 1924, JMK/L/24/77.

55. Quoted in P. J. Grigg, *Prejudice and Judgment* (London: Jonathan Cape, 1948), 182–83.

56. Winston Churchill, "Return to Gold Standard," speech to Parliament, April 28, 1925, https://api.parliament.uk/historic-hansard/commons/1925/apr/28/return-to-gold-standard.

57. Quoted in Grigg, *Prejudice and Judgment,* 184.

58. John Maynard Keynes, "The Economic Consequences of Mr Churchill," *Evening Standard,* July 22–24, 1925, in *CW,* vol. 9, 223.

59. Stanley Baldwin, "Message from the Prime Minister," *The British Gazette,* May 6, 1926, Warwick Digital Collections, http://contentdm.warwick.ac.uk/cdm/compoundobject/collection/strike/id/378/rec/33.

60. Skidelsky, *John Maynard Keynes,* vol. 2, 250; Leonard Woolf, *Downhill All the Way: An Autobiography of the Years 1919 to 1939* (New York: Harvest, 1967), 217.

61. Keynes issued a statement for *The New Republic* and *The Nation,* which never ran in either. When he gave *The End of Laissez-Faire* as a lecture at the University of Berlin on June 24, 1926, he also prepared some notes on the General Strike. In the notes he described the conflict as "essentially senseless" rather than "a revolution," adding that "after a few days war atmosphere intensified." "Military mind gaining control which means in England—I expect everywhere—complete collapse not only of intellect but of ordinary intelligence and of daily common sense. All the people who are too stupid to be of any value or importance in peacetime began to feel themselves essential and even to find themselves in charge." *CW,* vol. 19, 534, 543–46.

62. Leonard Woolf, *Downhill All the Way,* 162.

63. These comments are from Keynes' notes from his lecture at the University of Berlin on June 24, 1926, *CW,* vol. 19, 545.

64. "Chancellor Winston Churchill on Gold and the Exchequer," *Finest Hour* 153

(Winter 2011–12), https://www.winstonchurchill.org/publications/finest-hour/finest-hour-153/chancellor-winston-churchill-on-gold-and-the-exchequer.

65. Margot Asquith to JMK, June 1, 1926, JMK/PP/45/190/3/104.

66. JMK to Margot Asquith, JMK/PP/45/190/3/100.

67. John Maynard Keynes, letter to the editor, *The Nation and Athenaeum,* June 12, 1926, in *CW,* vol. 19, 538–41.

68. JMK to LK, June 1, 1926, JMK/PP/45/190/3/104.

69. In *We Can Conquer Unemployment,* the Liberals put the roadbuilding jobs numbers at 850,000 in year one, of which 350,000 would be directly created by the program. In *Can Lloyd George Do It?,* Keynes and Henderson wrote, "We are satisfied on this matter that the estimates given in 'We Can Conquer Unemployment,' taken as a whole, understate rather than overstate the case." *CW,* vol. 9, 106.

70. John Maynard Keynes, "Can Lloyd George Do It?—The Pledge Examined," Hogarth Press, May 10, 1929, in *CW,* vol. 9, 99.

71. Ibid., 98.

72. "There is the far greater loss to the unemployed themselves, represented by the difference between the dole and a full working wage, and by the loss of strength and morale. There is the loss in profits to employers and in taxation to the Chancellor of the Exchequer. There is the incalculable loss of retarding for a decade the economic progress of the whole country." *CW,* vol. 9, 93.

73. Ibid.

74. Ibid., 92.

75. Ibid., 113.

76. Ibid., 125.

77. Virginia Woolf to Quentin Bell, May 11, 1929, in Virginia Woolf, *The Letters of Virginia Woolf,* vol. 4: *1929–1932,* ed. Nigel Nicolson and Joanne Trautmann (New York: Harcourt Brace Jovanovich, 1979), 56–57.

78. Virginia Woolf to Quentin Bell, May 30, 1929, in ibid., 63.

79. JMK to LK, June 3, 1929, JMK/PP/45/190/4/158.

SEVEN: THE GREAT CRASH

1. Liaquat Ahamed, *Lords of Finance: The Bankers Who Broke the World* (New York: Penguin, 2009), 358.

2. Churchill's visit to the New York Stock Exchange on Black Thursday is recorded in Arthur M. Schlesinger, Jr., *The Age of Roosevelt,* vol. 1: *The Crisis of the Old Order, 1919–1933* (New York: Mariner Books, 2003 [1957]), 158; Ron Chernow, *The House of Morgan: An American Banking Dynasty and the Rise of Modern Finance* (New York: Grove Press, 2001 [1990]), 315; John Kenneth Galbraith, *The Great Crash, 1929* (Boston: Houghton Mifflin, 1961), 105. His dinner with Baruch on the evening of Black Thursday is in Martin Gilbert, *Winston Churchill,* vol. 5: *The Prophet of Truth: 1922–1939* (London: Minerva, 1990 [1976]), 349–50. Gilbert cites Churchill's recollection that "I happened to be walking down Wall Street at the worst moment of the panic and a perfect stranger who recognised me invited me to enter the gallery of the Stock Exchange."

3. Quoted in Chernow, *The House of Morgan,* 314.

4. Galbraith, *The Great Crash, 1929,* 26–36.

5. Schlesinger, *The Age of Roosevelt,* vol. 1, 158.

6. Galbraith, *The Great Crash, 1929*, 104.
7. Chernow, *The House of Morgan*, 315.
8. Quoted in Matthew Josephson, *The Money Lords: The Great Finance Capitalists, 1925–1950* (New York: Weybright and Tally, 1972), 90.
9. Chernow, *The House of Morgan*, 315.
10. Galbraith, *The Great Crash, 1929*, 104.
11. Ahamed, *Lords of Finance*, 211–12.
12. Chernow, *The House of Morgan*, 322.
13. Ibid., 221.
14. Ibid., 312.
15. Quoted in ibid., 317.
16. Quoted in ibid., 314–15.
17. Herbert Hoover, *The Memoirs of Herbert Hoover: The Great Depression, 1929–1941* (New York: Macmillan, 1952), 17.
18. Quoted in Ahamed, *Lords of Finance*, 354.
19. Hoover, *The Memoirs of Herbert Hoover: The Great Depression, 1929–1941*, 127.
20. Chernow, *The House of Morgan*, 315.
21. Josephson, *The Money Lords*, 93.
22. Galbraith, *The Great Crash, 1929*, 108.
23. "Bankers Halt Stock Debacle," *The Wall Street Journal*, October 25, 1929.
24. JMK to LL, October 25, 1929, in *CW*, vol. 20, 1.
25. Schlesinger, *The Age of Roosevelt*, vol. 1, 157.
26. Quoted in Maury Klein, "The Stock Market Crash of 1929: A Review Article," *The Business History Review* 75, no. 2 (Summer 2001): 329.
27. Charles P. Kindleberger, *The World in Depression, 1929–1939* (Berkeley: University of California Press, 2013 [1973]), 116.
28. John Maynard Keynes, "A British View of the Wall Street Slump," *New-York Evening Post*, October 25, 1929, *CW*, vol. 20, 2–4.
29. Kindleberger, *The World in Depression*, 113.
30. Ibid., 124–27.
31. Quoted in Robert Skidelsky, *John Maynard Keynes*, vol. 2: *The Economist as Savior, 1920–1937* (New York: Allen Lane, 1994), 343.
32. Quoted in ibid., 314.
33. John Maynard Keynes, *A Treatise on Money: The Pure Theory of Money and the Applied Theory of Money. Complete Set*, vol. 2 (Mansfield Center, CT: Martino Fine Books, 2011 [1930]), 175.
34. Ibid., 376.
35. JMK to LL, January 18, 1924, JMK/PP/45/190/1/60.
36. JMK to LK, November 29, 1925, JMK/PP/45/190/3/35.
37. JMK to LK, November 30, 1925, JMK/PP/45/190/3/37.
38. JMK to LK, December 3, 1925, JMK/PP/45/190/3/39.
39. JMK to LK, December 6, 1925, JMK/PP/45/190/3/42.
40. Thomas Hobbes, *Leviathan, with Selected Variants from the Latin Edition of 1688*, ed. Edwin Curley (Indianapolis: Hackett, 1994), 76.
41. *CW*, vol. 28, 253.
42. Ibid., 254.
43. Ibid., 226.
44. Ibid.
45. Keynes, *A Treatise on Money*, vol. 1, 4.

46. Keynes referenced Georg Friedrich Knapp as a kindred spirit who developed some of these ideas in Germany. Knapp published *The State Theory of Money* in 1905, but the book probably appeared on Keynes' radar only after it was translated into English in 1924.

47. Hearing of the Macmillan Committee, February 21, 1930, in *CW*, vol. 20, 84.

48. Keynes, *A Treatise on Money*, vol. 2, 152–53. This point was based on early work by Earl J. Hamilton, who eventually published the results as *American Treasure and the Price Revolution in Spain, 1501–1650* in 1934.

49. Ibid., 159.

50. Ibid., 154.

51. Ibid., 156, n. 1.

52. Niall Ferguson, *The Cash Nexus: Money and Power in the Modern World, 1700–2000* (New York: Basic Books, 2001), 23.

53. Hearing of the Macmillan Committee, February 20, 1930, in *CW*, vol. 20, 64.

54. Keynes, *A Treatise on Money*, vol. 2, 148–49.

55. Ibid., 150.

56. "Memorandum by Mr. J.M. Keynes to the Committee of Economists of the Economic Advisory Council," September 21, 1930, in *CW*, vol. 13, 186.

57. Keynes, *A Treatise on Money*, vol. 2, 291.

58. Ibid., 376.

59. "The friends of gold will have to be extremely wise and moderate if they are to avoid a Revolution." Ibid., 292.

60. Hearing of the Macmillan Committee, March 6, 1930, in *CW*, vol. 20, 126.

61. *CW*, ibid., 146–47.

62. F. A. Hayek, "Reflections on the Pure Theory of Mr. J. M. Keynes," *Economica*, no. 35 (February 1932), 44.

63. Quoted in Angus Burgin, *The Great Persuasion: Reinventing Free Markets Since the Depression* (Cambridge, MA: Harvard University Press, 2012), 30.

64. John Maynard Keynes, "The Pure Theory of Money. A Reply to Dr Hayek," *Economica*, November 1931, in *CW*, vol. 13, 252.

65. See, e.g., Nicholas Wapshott, *Keynes Hayek: The Clash That Defined Modern Economics* (New York: W. W. Norton, 2011).

66. Milton Friedman and Anna Jacobson Schwartz, *A Monetary History of the United States, 1867–1960* (Princeton, NJ: Princeton University Press, 1971 [1963]), 306, 308–10.

67. Robert S. McElvaine, *The Great Depression: America, 1929–1941* (New York: Three Rivers Press, 2009 [1984]), 79–80, 92.

68. "Unemployment Statistics from 1881 to the Present Day," Government Statistical Service, UK Statistics Authority, http://www.ons.gov.uk/ons/rel/lms/labour-market-trends--discontinued-/january-1996/unemployment-since-1881.pdf.

69. Barry Eichengreen, "The British Economy Between the Wars," April 2002, https://eml.berkeley.edu/~eichengr/research/floudjohnsonchaptersep16-03.pdf, 55.

70. "Schact Demands War Debt Respite" and "Schact Here, Sees Warning in Fascism, Ridicules Fear of Hitler," *The New York Times*, October 3, 1930, quoted in John Weitz, *Hitler's Banker* (New York: Warner Books, 2001 [1999]), 111–12.

71. John Maynard Keynes, "Economic Possibilities for Our Grandchildren," *The Nation and Athenaeum*, October 11 and 18, 1930, *CW*, vol. 9, 322.

72. John Maynard Keynes, "Economy," *The Listener*, January 14, 1931, in *CW*, vol. 9, 138.

73. John Maynard Keynes, "Economic Possibilities for Our Grandchildren," October 1930, in *CW,* vol. 9, 329.
74. Ibid., 323.
75. Ibid., 325–26.
76. Ibid., 326.
77. Ibid., 329.
78. Ibid., 330–31.
79. Karl Marx, *The German Ideology,* in *The Marx-Engels Reader,* ed. Robert C. Tucker, (New York: Norton, 1978 [1932]), 160.
80. Ibid., 146.
81. Joseph Stiglitz, "Toward a General Theory of Consumerism: Reflections on Keynes's Economic Possibilities for Our Grandchildren," in Lorenzo Pecchi and Gustavo Piga, eds., *Revisiting Keynes: Economic Possibilities for Our Grandchildren* (Cambridge, MA: MIT Press, 2008), 41.
82. Benjamin M. Friedman, "Work and Consumption in an Era of Unbalanced Technological Advance," *Journal of Evolutionary Economics* 27, no. 2 (April 2017): 221–37.
83. Robert Solow, "Whose Grandchildren?," in Pecchi and Piga, *Revisiting Keynes,* 88.
84. Keynes, "Economic Possibilities for Our Grandchildren," 326.
85. Leonard Woolf, *Downhill All the Way: An Autobiography of the Years 1919 to 1939* (New York: Harvest, 1975 [1971]), 141, 206–9.
86. Virginia Woolf to Margaret Llewelyn Davies, September 14, 1930, Virginia Woolf, *The Letters of Virginia Woolf,* vol. 4: *1929–1932,* ed. Nigel Nicolson and Joanne Trautmann (New York: Harcourt Brace Jovanovich: 1979), 213.
87. John Maynard Keynes, "Proposals for a Revenue Tariff," *New Statesman and Nation,* March 7, 1931, in *CW,* vol. 9, 238.
88. *CW,* vol. 20, 492.
89. Ethel Snowden to JMK, March 7, 1931, in *CW,* vol. 20, 489.
90. Hubert Henderson to JMK, February 14, 1931, *CW,* vol. 20, 483–84.
91. John Maynard Keynes, "Economic Notes on Free Trade," *New Statesman and Nation,* March 28, April 4, and April 11, 1931, in *CW,* vol. 20, 500.
92. John Maynard Keynes, letter to *The Times,* March 26, 1931, in *CW,* vol. 20, 509.
93. John Maynard Keynes, "Put the Budget on a Sound Basis: A Plea to Lifelong Free Traders," *Daily Mail,* March 13, 1931, in *CW,* vol. 20, 491–92.
94. John Maynard Keynes, "Economic Notes on Free Trade," *New Statesman and Nation,* March 28, April 4, and April 11, 1931, in *CW,* vol. 20, 505.
95. David Ricardo, *On the Principles of Political Economy* (London: John Murray, 1817), chap. 7.
96. John Maynard Keynes, "National Self-Sufficiency," *The New Statesman and Nation,* July 8 and 15, 1933, in *CW,* vol. 21, 235.
97. Ibid., 236.
98. Ahamed, *Lords of Finance,* 404.
99. Barry Eichengreen, *Golden Fetters: The Gold Standard and the Great Depression, 1919–1939* (Oxford, UK: Oxford University Press, 1992), 268.
100. *CW,* vol. 20, 529, 561.
101. John Maynard Keynes, memorandum for the Economic Advisory Council, July 1931, in *CW,* vol. 20, 568.
102. Friedman and Schwartz, *A Monetary History of the United States,* 308.

103. John Maynard Keynes, "A Note on Economic Conditions in the United States," memorandum for the Economic Advisory Council, July 1931, in *CW*, vol. 20, 587.

104. Quoted in Chernow, *The House of Morgan*, 328.

105. Ahamed, *Lords of Finance*, 416–19.

106. JMK to R. F. Kahn May 29, 1931, in *CW*, vol. 20, 310; and JMK to Walter Gardner, September 16, 1931, in *CW*, vol. 20, 311.

107. Skidelsky, *John Maynard Keynes*, vol. 2, 393.

108. Ahamed, *Lords of Finance*, 424.

109. Charles Loch Mowat, *Britain Between the Wars, 1918–1940* (Boston: Beacon Press, 1971 [1955]), 382.

110. JMK to Ramsay MacDonald, August 5, 1931, in *CW*, vol. 20, 590–91.

111. Quoted in Chernow, *The House of Morgan*, 331.

112. Quoted in ibid., 330.

113. JMK to Ramsay MacDonald, August 12, 1931, in *CW*, vol. 20, 594.

114. *CW*, vol. 20, 596.

115. Virginia Woolf, *The Diary of Virginia Woolf*, vol. 4: *1931–1935*, ed. Anne Olivier Bell and Andrew McNeillie (New York: Harvest, 1983), 39.

116. Chernow, *The House of Morgan*, 332.

117. Ibid., 332–33.

118. Ahamed, *Lords of Finance*, 428.

119. JMK to F. A. Keynes, August 28, 1931, in *CW*, vol. 20, 596.

120. JMK to Walter Case, September 14, 1931, in *CW*, vol. 20, 603.

121. John Maynard Keynes, "A Gold Conference," *The New Statesman and Nation*, September 12, 1931, in *CW*, vol. 20, 600.

122. John Maynard Keynes, notes for a speech to members of Parliament, September 16, 1931, in *CW*, vol. 20, 608.

123. Ibid., 609–11.

124. Ibid., 611.

125. Virginia Woolf, *The Diary of Virginia Woolf*, vol. 4, 45.

EIGHT: PHOENIX

1. JMK to Alexander Shaw, January 13, 1932, in *CW*, vol. 18, 364.

2. John Maynard Keynes, "An End of Reparations?," *The New Statesman and Nation*, January 16, 1932, in *CW*, vol. 18, 366.

3. Ibid., 365–66.

4. These accounts of Hitler's supposed moderation appear in Matthew Dessem, "You Know Who Else Was Always Impressing Journalists with His Newfound Maturity and Pragmatism?," *Slate*, September 10, 2017.

5. Quoted in Ronald Steel, *Walter Lippmann and the American Century* (Boston: Little, Brown, 1980), 331.

6. John Maynard Keynes, "Two Years Off Gold: How Far Are We From Prosperity Now?," *Daily Mail*, September 19, 1933, in *CW*, vol. 21, 285.

7. JMK to Ottoline Morrell, May 2, 1928, quoted in Robert Skidelsky, *John Maynard Keynes*, vol. 2: *The Economist as Savior, 1920–1937* (New York: Allen Lane, 1994), 236.

8. David C. Colander and Harry Landreth, eds., *The Coming of Keynesianism to America: Conversations with the Founders of Keynesian Economics* (Brookfield, IL: Edward Elgar, 1996), 61–62.

9. John Strachey, *The Coming Struggle for Power* (New York: Modern Library, 1935 [1932]).

10. Quoted in Skidelsky, *John Maynard Keynes*, vol. 2, 515–16.

11. John Maynard Keynes, Letter to the Editor, *The New Statesman and Nation*, November 24, 1934, in *CW*, vol. 28, 35–36.

12. John Maynard Keynes, "Farewell to the World Conference," *Daily Mail*, July 27, 1933, in *CW*, vol. 21, 281.

13. JMK to R. H. Brand, November 29, 1934, in *CW*, vol. 21, 344.

14. JMK to George Bernard Shaw, January 1, 1935, in *CW*, vol. 13, 492–93.

15. Jerome E. Edwards, *Pat McCarran: Political Boss of Nevada* (Reno: University of Nevada Press, 1982), 33–41.

16. Quoted in ibid., 49–50.

17. Quoted in Arthur M. Schlesinger, Jr., *The Age of Roosevelt*, vol. 1: *The Crisis of the Old Order, 1919–1933* (New York: Mariner Books, 2003 [1957]), 475–76.

18. Herbert Hoover, *The Memoirs of Herbert Hoover: The Great Depression, 1929–1941* (Eastford, CT: Martino Fine Books, 2016 [1952]), 30.

19. Quoted in Milton Friedman and Anna Jacobson Schwartz, *A Monetary History of the United States, 1867–1960* (Princeton, NJ: Princeton University Press, 1993 [1964]), 341.

20. Roger Sandilands, *The Life and Political Economy of Lauchlin Currie: New Dealer, Presidential Adviser, and Development Economist* (Durham, NC: Duke University Press, 1990), 31–38.

21. Ibid., 50.

22. Friedman and Schwartz, *A Monetary History of the United States*, 352.

23. Gerald D. Nash, "Herbert Hoover and the Origins of the Reconstruction Finance Corporation," *The Mississippi Valley Historical Review* 46, no. 3 (December 1959): 455–68.

24. Quoted in Glen Jeansonne, *The Life of Herbert Hoover: Fighting Quaker, 1928–1933* (New York: Palgrave Macmillan, 2012), 199.

25. Hoover, *The Memoirs of Herbert Hoover*, 203–4.

26. Quoted in Schlesinger, *The Age of Roosevelt*, vol. 1, 476–77.

27. Ibid., 475.

28. Friedman and Schwartz, *A Monetary History of the United States*, 326.

29. Hoover, *The Memoirs of Herbert Hoover*, 212–17.

30. Schlesinger, *The Age of Roosevelt*, vol. 1, 481.

31. For more on the assembly of the early New Deal program during the 1932 election, see Eric Rauchway, *Winter War: Hoover, Roosevelt, and the First Clash over the New Deal* (New York: Basic Books, 2018).

32. Franklin Delano Roosevelt, "First Inaugural Address of Franklin D. Roosevelt," March 4, 1933, Lillian Goldman Law Library, Yale Law School, http://avalon.law.yale.edu/20th_century/froos1.asp.

33. Friedman and Schwartz, *A Monetary History of the United States*, 422–27.

34. Franklin D. Roosevelt, "On the Bank Crisis," March 12, 1933, Franklin D. Roosevelt Presidential Library and Museum, http://docs.fdrlibrary.marist.edu/031233.html.

35. Ibid.

36. Quoted in Ron Chernow, *The House of Morgan: An American Banking Dynasty and the Rise of Modern Finance* (New York: Grove Press, 2001 [1990]), 357.

37. *The New York Times*, April 21, 1933.

38. Richard Parker, *John Kenneth Galbraith: His Life, His Politics, His Economics* (Chicago: University of Chicago Press, 2005), 55–57.

39. Quoted in Eric Rauchway, *The Money Makers: How Roosevelt and Keynes Ended the Depression, Defeated Fascism, and Secured a Prosperous Peace* (New York: Basic Books, 2015), 80.

40. Rodney D. Karr, "Farmer Rebels in Plymouth County, Iowa, 1932–1933," *The Annals of Iowa* 47, no. 7, State Historical Society of Iowa, 1985, 638.

41. Franklin D. Roosevelt to Edward M. House, April 5, 1933, quoted in Helen M. Burns, *The American Banking Community and New Deal Banking Reforms, 1933–1935* (Westport, CT: Greenwood Press, 1974), 78.

42. John Maynard Keynes, Open letter to FDR, *The New York Times*, December 31, 1933, in *CW*, vol. 21, 295.

43. John Kenneth Galbraith, *Money: Whence It Came, Where It Went* (Princeton, NJ: Princeton University Press, 2017 [1974]), 245.

44. "Consumer Price Index: All Items in U.S. City Average, All Urban Consumers," Federal Reserve Bank of St. Louis, https://fred.stlouisfed.org/series/cpiaucns.

45. Ferdinand Pecora, *Wall Street Under Oath: The Story of Our Modern Money Changers* (New York: Graymalkin Media, 1939), Kindle edition, chap. 1, loc. 60.

46. Peter Grossman, *American Express: The Unofficial History of the People Who Built the Great Financial Empire* (New York: Random House, 1987), 236–38.

47. Chernow, *The House of Morgan*, 369–71.

48. Burns, *The American Banking Community and New Deal Banking Reforms*, 89–90.

49. Quoted in ibid., 80.

50. Quoted in ibid., 65–66.

51. Ibid., 68.

52. John Kenneth Galbraith, *The Great Crash, 1929* (Boston: Houghton Mifflin, 1961 [1955]), 196–97.

53. JMK to Alexander Shaw, January 13, 1932, in *CW*, vol. 18, 364.

54. John Maynard Keynes, "President Roosevelt Is Magnificently Right," *Daily Mail*, July 4, 1933, in *CW*, vol. 21, 276.

55. Charles Kindleberger, *The World in Depression, 1929–1939* (Berkeley: University of California Press, 2013 [1975]), 224.

56. JMK to FDR, in *CW*, vol. 21, 289.

57. Ibid., 293.

58. Ibid., 294.

59. Ibid., 295.

60. JMK to Franklin D. Roosevelt, February 1, 1938, in *CW*, vol. 21, 435.

61. Walter Lippmann to JMK, April 17, 1934, in *CW*, vol. 21, 305.

62. Quoted in Arthur M. Schlesinger, Jr., "The 'Hundred Days' of F.D.R.," *The New York Times*, April 10, 1983.

63. Edwards, *Pat McCarran*, 105–6.

64. Frances Perkins, *The Roosevelt I Knew* (New York: Penguin, 2011 [1946]), 215–16.

65. *CW*, vol. 21, 321.

66. Quoted in Robert Dallek, *Franklin D. Roosevelt: A Political Life* (New York: Viking, 2017), 177.

67. Quoted in Arthur M. Schlesinger, Jr., *The Politics of Upheaval* (Boston: Houghton Mifflin, 1960), 298.

68. Hansen uttered this phrase to the Keynesian economist Walter Salant, claiming to have heard it from Harvard University president James Conant; see Don Paninkin and J. Clark Leith, eds., *Keynes, Cambridge and the General Theory* (New York: Macmillan, 1977), 46, and Walter Salant and Francis H. Heller, *Economics and the Truman Administration* (Lawrence: Regents Press of Kansas, 1981), 107.

NINE: THE END OF SCARCITY

1. Quoted in Marjorie S. Turner, *Joan Robinson and the Americans* (Armonk, NY: M. E. Sharpe, 1989), 18.
2. Quoted in ibid., 12.
3. Quoted in ibid., 55.
4. Quoted in ibid., 56.
5. Quoted in ibid., 55.
6. Straight claimed in his memoir that he was a reluctant spy who only passed unimportant economic reports to a Soviet agent. He went on to work in both the Kennedy and Nixon administrations, in addition to working as publisher of *The New Republic*. See Michael Straight, *After Long Silence* (New York: W. W. Norton & Co., 1983).
7. John Maynard Keynes interview with Kingsley Martin, "Democracy and Efficiency," *New Statesman and Nation*, January 28, 1939, in *CW*, vol. 21, 494–96.
8. Quoted in David C. Colander and Harry Landreth, eds., *The Coming of Keynesianism to America: Conversations with the Founders of Keynesian Economics* (Brookfield, IL: Edward Elgar, 1996), 204.
9. Joan Robinson, *The Economics of Imperfect Competition* (London: Macmillan, 1948 [1933]), 307–27.
10. Ibid., 218–34.
11. Quoted in Turner, *Joan Robinson and the Americans*, 166.
12. Mary Paley Marshall to Joan Robinson in ibid., 12–13.
13. Quoted in Colander and Landreth, *The Coming of Keynesianism to America*, 54–55.
14. Quoted in Peter Clarke, *Keynes: The Rise, Fall, and Return of the 20th Century's Most Influential Economist* (New York: Bloomsbury, 2009), 141.
15. Quoted in Colander and Landreth, *The Coming of Keynesianism to America*, 101.
16. JMK to Susan Lawrence, January 15, 1935, in *CW*, vol. 21, 348.
17. JMK to Joan Robinson, March 29, 1934, in *CW*, vol. 13, 422.
18. Roger E. Backhouse, *Founder of Modern Economics: Paul A. Samuelson*, vol. 1: *Becoming Samuelson, 1915–1948* (New York: Oxford University Press, 2017), 518–19.
19. Quoted in Turner, *Joan Robinson and the Americans*, 51–52.
20. Nahid Aslanbeigui and Guy Oakes, *The Provocative Joan Robinson: The Making of a Cambridge Economist* (Durham, NC: Duke University Press, 2009), 177.
21. Quoted in Turner, *Joan Robinson and the Americans*, 53.
22. *CW*, vol. 13, 268–69, 376–80, 638–52; *CW*, vol. 14, 134–50.
23. Joan Robinson to JMK, December 2, 1935, in *CW*, vol. 13, 612.
24. Quoted in Aslanbeigui and Oakes, *The Provocative Joan Robinson*, 55–56.
25. Ibid., 56.
26. Ibid.
27. Quoted in ibid., 57.

28. Quoted in ibid., 65.
29. Ibid., 67–87.
30. John Maynard Keynes, *The General Theory of Employment, Interest and Money* (New York: Prometheus, 1997 [1936]), x.
31. Ibid., 3n.
32. Ibid., 9.
33. John Kenneth Galbraith, *A Life in Our Times* (Boston: Houghton Mifflin, 1981), 65.
34. Jean-Baptiste Say, *Traité d'économie politique*, trans. R. R. Palmer, 1997, 76, quoted in Allin Cottrell, "Keynes, Ricardo, Malthus and Say's Law," http://users.wfu.edu/cottrell/says_law.pdf, 3.
35. Keynes, *The General Theory of Employment, Interest and Money*, 21.
36. Ibid., xi.
37. Ibid., 293.
38. Ibid., 104.
39. Ibid., 156.
40. Ibid., 157.
41. Ibid., 149–50.
42. Ibid., 155.
43. Ibid., 129.
44. Ibid., 159.
45. Ibid., 378.
46. Ibid., 375–76.
47. Ibid., 164.
48. Ibid., 373.
49. Ibid., 376.
50. Ibid., 374.
51. John Maynard Keynes, "Art and the State," *The Listener*, August 26, 1936, in *CW*, vol. 28, 342–43.
52. Ibid., 344.
53. Ibid., 348.
54. Keynes, *The General Theory of Employment, Interest and Money*, 382–83.
55. Ibid., 383–84.
56. Quoted in Hyman Minsky, *John Maynard Keynes* (New York: McGraw-Hill, 2008 [1975]), 3.
57. Lorie Tarshis, "The Keynesian Revolution: What It Meant in the 1930s," unpublished, quoted in Robert Skidelsky, *John Maynard Keynes*, vol. 2: *The Economist as Savior, 1920–1937* (New York: Allen Lane, New York, 1994), 574.

TEN: CAME THE REVOLUTION

1. Michael Holroyd, *Lytton Strachey: A Biography* (New York: Holt, Rinehart and Winston, 1980 [1971]), 1051.
2. Virginia Woolf, *The Diary of Virginia Woolf*, vol. 4: *1931–1935*, ed. Anne Olivier Bell and Andrew McNeillie (New York: Harvest, 1983 [1982]), 64–65.
3. Leonard Woolf, *Downhill All the Way: An Autobiography of the Years 1919 to 1939* (New York: Harvest, 1975 [1967]), 146.
4. Virginia Woolf, *The Diary of Virginia Woolf*, vol. 4, 78.
5. JMK to James Strachey, November 19, 1933, in Judith Mackrell, *Bloomsbury Bal-*

lerina: Lydia Lopokova, Imperial Dancer and Mrs. John Maynard Keynes (London: Phoenix, 2009 [2008]), 330.

6. Robert Skidelsky, *John Maynard Keynes*, vol. 2: *The Economist as Savior, 1920–1937* (New York: Allen Lane, 1994), 633–34.

7. Duncan Grant to JMK, April 21, 1937, JMK/PP/45/109/125/9.

8. Diary entry, May 25, 1937, in Virginia Woolf, *The Diary of Virginia Woolf*, vol. 5: *1936–1941*, ed. Anne Olivier Bell and Andrew McNeillie (San Diego, CA: Harcourt Brace Jovanovich, 1984), 90.

9. LK to Florence Keynes, July 19, 1937, quoted in Mackrell, *Bloomsbury Ballerina*, 356.

10. Quoted in Skidelsky, *John Maynard Keynes*, vol. 2, 635.

11. LK to Florence Keynes, February 12, 1938, quoted in Mackrell, *Bloomsbury Ballerina*, 355.

12. Skidelsky, *John Maynard Keynes*, vol. 2, 633–35.

13. John Maynard Keynes, "King's College: Annual Report," November 13, 1937, in *CW*, vol. 10, 358–60.

14. Duncan Grant to JMK, July 21, 1937, in JMK/PP/45/109/125/9.

15. Quoted in Frances Spalding, *Vanessa Bell: Portrait of the Bloomsbury Artist* (London: Tauris Parke Paperbacks, 2016 [1983]), 299.

16. Vanessa Bell to JMK, November 30, 1937, JMK/PP/45/27/7.

17. Quoted in Keynes, "King's College: Annual Report," 358–60.

18. John Maynard Keynes, "British Foreign Policy," *The New Statesman and Nation*, July 10, 1937, in *CW*, vol. 28, 61–65.

19. Ibid.

20. Robert Solow, "Whose Grandchildren?," in Lorenzo Pecchi and Gustavo Piga, eds., *Revisiting Keynes: Economic Possibilities for Our Grandchildren* (Cambridge, MA: MIT Press, 2008), 90.

21. John Maynard Keynes, "Einstein," unpublished, June 22, 1926, in *CW*, vol. 10, 383–34.

22. Quoted in Skidelsky, *John Maynard Keynes*, vol. 2, 486.

23. Quoted in ibid., 486.

24. Ludwig Wittgenstein to JMK, March 18, 1938, JMK/PP/45/349/81; and Ludwig Wittgenstein to JMK, February 1, 1939, JMK/PP/45/349/88.

25. Ludwig Wittgenstein to JMK, February 11, 1939, JMK/PP/45/349/93.

26. This was a generous interpretation of Roosevelt's as-ever obscure motivations. In any case, America was all but useless on the refugee problem. A 1924 law had severely restricted immigration, and those who opposed admitting Jewish refugees successfully invoked the law to prevent them from coming to America.

27. JMK to Archibald Sinclair, April 4, 1938, in *CW*, vol. 28, 107.

28. R. F. Harrod, *The Life of John Maynard Keynes* (London: Macmillan, 1951), 497.

29. Ludo Cuyvers, "Erwin Rothbart's Life and Work," *Journal of Post-Keynesian Economics* 6, no. 2 (Winter 1983–84): 305–12.

30. Quoted in Robert Skidelsky, *John Maynard Keynes*, vol. 3: *Fighting for Freedom, 1937–1946* (New York: Viking, 2000), 13.

31. Quoted in Mackrell, *Bloomsbury Ballerina*, 358.

32. John Kenneth Galbraith, *A Life in Our Times* (Boston: Houghton Mifflin, 1981), 35.

33. Ibid., 39.

34. Ibid., 40.

35. Real GDP grew at 10.8 percent, 8.9 percent, and 12.9 percent during 1934, 1935, and 1936, respectively, according to data from the Federal Reserve Bank of St. Louis; 1934 was the first full year of FDR's presidency.

36. Historical Statistics of the United States Millennial Edition, Table Ba470-477, "Labor force, employment and unemployment 1890–1990," Cambridge, UK: Cambridge University Press, 2006.

37. Office of Management and Budget, *Budget of the U.S. Government, Fiscal Year 2016, Historical Tables,* 2015, https://www.gpo.gov/fdsys/pkg/BUDGET-2016 -TAB/pdf/BUDGET-2016-TAB.pdf.

38. Ron Chernow, *The House of Morgan: An American Banking Dynasty and the Rise of Modern Finance* (New York: Grove Press, 2001 [1990]), 390.

39. Richard V. Gilbert, George H. Hildebrand, Arthur W. Stuart, et al., *An Economic Program for American Democracy* (New York: Vanguard Press, 1938), 70–71.

40. Chernow, *The House of Morgan,* 380.

41. Ferdinand Pecora, *Wall Street Under Oath: The Story of Our Modern Money Changers* (New York: Graymalkin Media, 1939), chap. 1.

42. Quoted in Arthur M. Schlesinger, Jr., *The Age of Roosevelt,* vol. 2: *The Coming of the New Deal, 1933–1935* (Boston: Houghton Mifflin, 1959), 567.

43. Quoted in Josephine Young Case and Everett Needham Case, *Owen D. Young and American Enterprise* (Boston: David R. Godine, 1982), 702.

44. *Time,* April 27, 1936, quoted in Schlesinger, *The Age of Roosevelt,* vol. 2, 567.

45. Franklin D. Roosevelt speech at Madison Square Garden, October 31, 1936. Transcript available from the American Presidency Project at The University of California, Santa Barbara, https://www.presidency.ucsb.edu/documents/address -madison-square-garden-new-york-city-1.

46. Charles D. Ellis, *The Partnership: The Making of Goldman Sachs* (New York: Penguin, 2008), 1–38.

47. Case and Case, *Owen D. Young and American Enterprise,* 716.

48. Galbraith, *A Life in Our Times,* 40.

49. Larry DeWitt, Social Security Administration, "The Development of Social Security in America," *Social Security Bulletin* 70, no. 3 (2010), https://www.ssa.gov/ policy/docs/ssb/v70n3/v70n3p1.html.

50. Office of Management and Budget, *Budget of the U.S. Government, Fiscal Year 2016, Historical Tables,* 2015, https://www.gpo.gov/fdsys/pkg/BUDGET-2016 -TAB/pdf/BUDGET-2016-TAB.pdf, 26.

51. H. W. Brands, *Traitor to His Class: The Privileged Life and Radical Presidency of Franklin Delano Roosevelt* (New York: Anchor Books, 2008), 486.

52. Bureau of Labor Statistics, "Technical Note," 1948, https://www.bls.gov/opub/ mlr/1948/article/pdf/labor-force-employment-and-unemployment-1929-39 -estimating-methods.pdf.

53. Quoted in Brands, *Traitor to His Class,* 486.

54. Quoted in ibid., 487.

55. Quoted in ibid., 487.

56. Quoted in ibid., 487.

57. Quoted in Robert Dallek, *Franklin D. Roosevelt: A Political Life* (New York: Viking, 2017), 288.

58. Brands, *Traitor to His Class,* 491.

59. See "G.C. M'Guire Dies; Accused of 'Plot,'" *The New York Times,* March 26,

1935, https://timesmachine.nytimes.com/timesmachine/1935/03/26/93463252 .html?pageNumber=13.

60. JMK to Franklin D. Roosevelt, February 1, 1938, in *CW,* vol. 21, 438.

61. Dallek, *Franklin D. Roosevelt,* 288.

62. Quoted in Schlesinger, *The Age of Roosevelt,* vol. 2, 482–87.

63. JMK to Franklin D. Roosevelt, February 1, 1938, in *CW,* vol. 21, 438–39.

64. Franklin D. Roosevelt to JMK, March 3, 1938, in *CW,* 439.

65. Quoted in Brands, *Traitor to His Class,* 494.

66. David C. Colander and Harry Landreth, eds., *The Coming of Keynesianism to America: Conversations with the Founders of Keynesian Economics* (Brookfield, IL: Edward Elgar, 1996), 40.

67. Quoted in ibid., 56.

68. Paul Sweezy, quoted in ibid., 84.

69. Paul Sweezy, quoted in ibid., 78–79.

70. Robert L. Bradley, *Capitalism at Work: Business, Government and Energy* (Salem, MA: M&M Scrivener Press, 2009), 144, n. 2.

71. Richard Parker, *John Kenneth Galbraith: His Life, His Politics, His Economics* (Chicago: University of Chicago Press, 2007), 106, n.

72. Douglass V. Brown, Edward Chamberlin, Seymour Edwin Harris, et al., *The Economics of the Recovery Program* (New York: Whittelsey House, 1934).

73. Quoted in Galbraith, *A Life in Our Times,* 90.

74. John Kenneth Galbraith, "Came the Revolution," *The New York Times Book Review,* May 16, 1965, JKG, Series 9.2, Box 798.

75. John Kenneth Galbraith, "Joan Robinson: A Word of Appreciation," *Cambridge Journal of Economics,* September 1, 1983, JKG, Series 9.2, Box 831.

76. Quoted in Colander and Landreth, *The Coming of Keynesianism to America,* 80–81.

77. Gilbert et al., *An Economic Program for American Democracy,* ix.

78. Ibid., 90–91.

79. Parker, *John Kenneth Galbraith,* 95.

80. Henry Morgenthau, Jr., testimony before the House Ways and Means Committee, May 29, 1939. See *The Congressional Record: Proceedings and Debates of the 76th Congress, First Session, Appendix: Volume 84, Part 13* (Washington, D.C.: United States Government Printing Office, 1939), 2297.

81. Ibid., 104–6.

82. Walter Lippmann, *The Good Society* (Boston: Little, Brown, 1938), vii, 123, 329–30.

83. Ronald Steel, *Walter Lippmann and the American Century* (Boston: Little, Brown, 1980), 324.

84. Ibid., 315, 393–94.

85. Historical Statistics of the United States Millennial Edition, Table Ba47-477: "Labor Force, Employment, and Unemployment 1890–1990," Cambridge, UK: Cambridge University Press, 2006.

ELEVEN: WAR AND COUNTERREVOLUTION

1. Richard V. Gilbert, George H. Hildebrand, Arthur W. Stuart, et al., *An Economic Program for American Democracy* (New York: Vanguard Press, 1938), 90–91.

2. Open letter from JMK to Franklin D. Roosevelt, *The New York Times,* December 31, 1933, 1934, in *CW,* vol. 21, 293.

3. For U.S. military casualties in Iraq, see "Iraq Coalition Casualty Count," http://icasualties.org/App/Fatalities. For World War I and Vietnam War statistics, see "U.S. Military Casualties, Missing in Action, and Prisoners of War from the Era of the Vietnam War," National Archives, Defense Casualty Analysis System, https://www.archives.gov/research/military/vietnam-war/electronic-records.html.

4. Ronald Steel, *Walter Lippmann and the American Century* (Boston: Little, Brown, 1980), 165.

5. Franklin Delano Roosevelt, State of the Union Address, January 6, 1941, https://millercenter.org/the-presidency/presidential-speeches/january-6-1941-state-union-four-freedoms.

6. Quoted in Elizabeth Borgwardt, *A New Deal for the World: America's Vision for Human Rights* (Cambridge, MA: Belknap Press, 2005), 21.

7. Roosevelt, State of the Union Address, January 6, 1941.

8. Ibid., 5.

9. John Kenneth Galbraith, *A Life in Our Times* (Boston: Houghton Mifflin, 1982), 149–50.

10. David Lilienthal, a stout New Dealer who had chaired the Tennessee Valley Authority, would eventually be named head of the new U.S. Atomic Energy Commission, putting him in charge of the nation's nuclear arsenal. See Ira Katznelson, *Fear Itself: The New Deal and the Origins of Our Time* (New York: Liveright Publishing, 2013), 432.

11. Ibid., 186.

12. Alan Brinkley, *The End of Reform: New Deal Liberalism in Recession and War* (New York: Vintage, 1996), 168, 170.

13. Ed Conway, *The Summit: Bretton Woods, 1944: J. M. Keynes and the Reshaping of the Global Economy* (New York: Pegasus, 2015), 92–93.

14. John Stevenson and Chris Cook, *The Slump: Britain in the Great Depression* (London: Routledge, 2013), 20.

15. Barry Eichengreen, "The British Economy Between the Wars," April 2002, https://eml.berkeley.edu/~eichengr/research/floudjohnsonchaptersep16-03.pdf, 37.

16. John Maynard Keynes and Kingsley Martin, "Democracy and Efficiency," *The New Statesman and Nation*, January 28, 1939, in *CW*, vol. 11, 497–500.

17. Quoted in Mark Seidl, "The Lend-Lease Program, 1941–1945," Franklin Delano Roosevelt Presidential Library and Museum, https://fdrlibrary.org/lend-lease.

18. Virginia Woolf, diary entry, August 26, 1940, in Woolf, *The Diary of Virginia Woolf*, vol. 5: *1936–1941*, ed. Anne Olivier Bell and Andrew McNeillie (San Diego, CA: Harcourt Brace Jovanovich, 1984), 311.

19. A point emphasized by Robert Skidelsky in *John Maynard Keynes*, vol. 3: *Fighting for Freedom, 1937–1946* (New York: Viking, 2000), xvii.

20. Liaquat Ahamed, *Lords of Finance: The Bankers Who Broke the World* (New York: Penguin, 2009), 432.

21. Martin Gilbert, *Winston Churchill*, vol. 5: *The Prophet of Truth, 1922–1939* (London: Minerva, 1990 [1976]), 229, 318–19.

22. JMK to Sir Richard Hopkins, October 27, 1940, in *CW*, vol. 23, 13–21.

23. JMK, memorandum to Nigel Bruce Ronald, March 11, 1941, in *CW*, vol. 23, 45–46.

24. "Maynard thinks we are a great and independent nation, which on the financial side is patently not true," wrote Edward Playfair, an official at the British Treasury, to S. D. Waley in the spring of 1941. *CW*, vol. 23, 79.

25. Quoted in Conway, *The Summit: Bretton Woods, 1944*, 114–15.

26. JMK, memorandum to Sir Horace Wilson, May 19, 1941, in *CW*, vol. 23, 79–91.

27. JMK, memorandum to Sir Kingsley Wood, June 2, 1941, in *CW*, vol. 23, 106–7.

28. JMK, memorandum to Sir Horace Wilson, May 25, 1941, in *CW*, vol. 23, 94–101.

29. JMK, memorandum to Chancellor of the Exchequer Sir Kingsley Wood, June 2, 1941, in *CW*, vol. 23, 108.

30. JMK, memorandum to Sir Horace Wilson, May 19, 1941, in *CW*, vol. 23, 91.

31. JMK to Sir Edward Peacock, May 12, 1941, in *CW*, vol. 23, 72n4.

32. "Lend-Lease and Military Aid to the Allies in the Early Years of World War II," Office of the Historian, United States Department of State, https://history.state .gov/milestones/1937-1945/lend-lease.

33. JMK, cable to Treasury, May 26, 1941, in *CW*, vol. 23, 101–2.

34. JMK, memorandum to Sir Kingsley Wood, June 2, 1941, in *CW*, 112.

35. Quoted in David C. Colander and Harry Landreth, eds., *The Coming of Keynesianism to America: Conversations with the Founders of Keynesian Economics* (Brookfield, IL: Edward Elgar, 1996), 141–42.

36. Walter Salant, notes from the dinner, in *CW*, vol. 23, 182–84.

37. John Maynard Keynes, *How to Pay for the War: A Radical Plan for the Chancellor of the Exchequer*, in *CW*, vol. 9, 379.

38. Ibid., 375.

39. Galbraith, *A Life in Our Times*, 139.

40. Ibid., 143.

41. Ibid., 141.

42. Richard Parker, *John Kenneth Galbraith: His Life, His Politics, His Economics* (Chicago: University of Chicago Press, 2007), 146.

43. Quoted in ibid., 140.

44. Ibid., 147.

45. Ibid., 147.

46. Doris Kearns Goodwin, *No Ordinary Time: Franklin and Eleanor Roosevelt: The Home Front in World War II* (New York: Simon & Schuster, 1994), 56.

47. Ibid., 394–95.

48. Galbraith, *A Life in Our Times*, 181.

49. Ibid., 182–83.

50. Office of Management and Budget, *Budget of the U.S. Government, Fiscal Year 2016, Historical Tables*, 2015, https://www.gpo.gov/fdsys/pkg/BUDGET-2016 -TAB/pdf/BUDGET-2016-TAB.pdf.

51. Quoted in Robert Skidelsky, *John Maynard Keynes*, vol. 3, 203.

52. Ibid., 167.

53. Quoted in S. P. Rosenbaum, ed., *The Bloomsbury Group: A Collection of Memoirs and Commentary* (Toronto: University of Toronto Press, 1995), 281.

54. Quoted in Skidelsky, *John Maynard Keynes*, vol. 3, 86–87.

55. Quoted in Colander and Landreth, *The Coming of Keynesianism to America*, 169.

56. Lionel Robbins, *Autobiography of an Economist* (London: Macmillan, 1971), 154.

57. Milton Friedman, "A Monetary and Fiscal Framework for Economic Stability," *The American Economic Review* 38, no. 3 (June 1948): 245–64. This article of Friedman's was essentially erased from the economic historical record until 2002, when it was uncovered by L. Randall Wray, one of the most influential proponents of Modern Monetary Theory, a strain of radical Keynesian economics.

TWELVE: MARTYR TO THE GOOD LIFE

1. Betsy Mason, "Bomb-Damage Maps Reveal London's World War II Devastation," *National Geographic*, May 18, 2016, https://www.nationalgeographic.com/science/phenomena/2016/05/18/bomb-damage-maps-reveal-londons-world-war-ii-devastation/.

2. JMK to Harry Dexter White, May 24, 1944, in *CW*, vol. 26, 27.

3. Nicholas Wapshott, *Keynes Hayek: The Clash That Defined Modern Economics* (New York: Norton, 2011), xi.

4. F. A. Hayek, *The Road to Serfdom: Text and Documents, The Definitive Edition* (London: University of Chicago Press, 2007 [1944]), 45.

5. Ibid., 18–19.

6. Brian Doherty, *Radicals for Capitalism: A Freewheeling History of the Modern American Libertarian Movement* (New York: PublicAffairs, 2008), 108.

7. Angus Burgin, *The Great Persuasion: Reinventing Free Markets Since the Depression* (Cambridge, MA: Harvard University Press, 2012), 88.

8. Royal Swedish Academy of Sciences Press Release, October 9, 1974, https://www.nobelprize.org/prizes/economic-sciences/1974/press-release/.

9. Hayek, *The Road to Serfdom*, 77–78.

10. Ibid., 67–68.

11. Ibid., 110.

12. Ludwig von Mises, *Bureaucracy* (New Rochelle, NY: Arlington House, 1969 [1944]), 10.

13. Robert Samuelson, "A Few Remembrances of Friedrich von Hayek (1899–1992)," *Journal of Economic Behavior & Organization* 69, no. 1 (January 2009): 1–4.

14. Quinn Slobodian, *Globalists: The End of Empire and the Birth of Neoliberalism* (Cambridge, MA: Harvard University Press, 2018), 105.

15. JMK to Friedrich von Hayek, June 28, 1944, JMK/PP/CO/3/173.

16. JMK to Friedrich von Hayek, June 28, 1944, JMK/PP/CO/3/175.

17. Bruce Caldwell, introduction to Hayek, *The Road to Serfdom*, 23. Frank Knight to University of Chicago Press, December 10, 1943, appendix to *The Road to Serfdom*, 250.

18. JMK to Friedrich von Hayek, June 28, 1944, JMK/CO/3/173.

19. JMK to Friedrich von Hayek, June 28, 1944,, JMK/CO/3/176.

20. Hayek, *The Road to Serfdom*, 216–17. The connection between scarcity and aristocracy is from Corey Robin, *The Reactionary Mind*, 2nd ed. (New York: Oxford University Press, 2018), 151–58.

21. JMK to Friedrich von Hayek, June 28, 1944, JMK/CO/3/175-7.

22. John Maynard Keynes, "Democracy and Efficiency," *The New Statesman and Nation*, January 28, 1939, in *CW*, vol. 11, 500.

23. Ira Katznelson, *Fear Itself: The New Deal and the Origins of Our Time* (Liveright Publishing, 2013), 351.

24. Conway, *Summit*, 205.

25. Ibid., xxvi, 4.

26. Ibid., 3, 201–3.

27. LK to Frances Keynes, July 12, 1944, quoted in Judith Mackrell, *Bloomsbury Ballerina: Lydia Lopokova, Imperial Dancer and Mrs. John Maynard Keynes* (London: Phoenix, 2008), 386.

28. Conway, *Summit*, 212, 254.

29. Quoted in ibid., 214–15.
30. James Buchan, "When Keynes Went to America," *The New Statesman,* November 6, 2008.
31. Conway, *Summit,* 254.
32. John Maynard Keynes, "National Self-Sufficiency," *The New Statesman and Nation,* July 8, 1933, in *CW,* vol. 21, 233.
33. Ibid., 238.
34. John Maynard Keynes, "The Present Overseas Financial Position of U.K.," memorandum, August 13, 1945, in *CW,* vol. 24, 410.
35. John Maynard Keynes, *A Treatise on Money: The Pure Theory of Money and the Applied Theory of Money. Complete Set,* vol. 2 (Mansfield Center, CT: Martino Fine Books, 2011 [1930]), 399–402.
36. Quoted in George Monbiot, "Keynes Is Innocent: The Toxic Spawn of Bretton Woods Was No Plan of His," *The Guardian,* November 18, 2008.
37. For more on this ill-fated effort at geopolitical realignment, see Benn Steil, *The Marshall Plan: Dawn of the Cold War* (New York: Simon & Schuster, 2018).
38. Quoted in Robert Skidelsky, *John Maynard Keynes,* vol. 3: *Fighting for Freedom, 1937–1946* (New York: Viking, 2001), 355.
39. Harry Truman, *Memoirs,* vol. 1: *Year of Decisions* (New York: Doubleday, 1955), 227–28.
40. JMK to Marcel Labordère, March 28, 1945, in Skidelsky, *John Maynard Keynes,* vol. 3, 378.
41. Mackrell, *Bloomsbury Ballerina,* 394.
42. Quoted in Skidelsky, *John Maynard Keynes,* vol. 3, 267.
43. Quoted in ibid., 269.
44. John Maynard Keynes, "The Arts Council: Its Policy and Hopes," *The Listener,* July 12, 1945, in *CW,* vol. 28, 369.
45. Ibid., 367.
46. Ibid., 371.
47. Quoted in Mackrell, *Bloomsbury Ballerina,* 396.
48. Ibid., 394–97.
49. Lionel Robbins, journal, June 24, 1944, in R. F. Harrod, *The Life of John Maynard Keynes* (London: Macmillan, 1951), 576.

THIRTEEN: THE ARISTOCRACY STRIKES BACK

1. John Kenneth Galbraith to Howard Bowen, October 13, 1948, in John Kenneth Galbraith, *The Selected Letters of John Kenneth Galbraith,* ed. Richard P. F. Holt (New York: Cambridge University Press, 2017), 76.
2. Winton U. Solberg and Robert W. Tomlinson, "Academic McCarthyism and Keynesian Economics: The Bowen Controversy at the University of Illinois," *History of Political Economy* 29, no. 1 (1997): 59.
3. Ibid., 60.
4. Office of Management and Budget, *Budget of the U.S. Government, Fiscal Year 2016, Historical Tables,* 2015, https://www.gpo.gov/fdsys/pkg/BUDGET-2016-TAB/pdf/BUDGET-2016-TAB.pdf.
5. "Civilian Unemployment Rate (UNRATE)," Federal Reserve Bank of St. Louis, https://fred.stlouisfed.org/series/UNRATE#0.

6. Joshua Zeitz, *Building the Great Society: Inside Lyndon Johnson's White House* (New York: Viking, 2018), 43.

7. Richard Parker, *John Kenneth Galbraith: His Life, His Politics, His Economics* (Chicago: University of Chicago Press, 2005), 196–99.

8. Solberg and Tomlinson, "Academic McCarthyism and Keynesian Economics," 63.

9. Ibid., 64–67.

10. Ibid., 67–68.

11. Quoted in ibid., 80.

12. "Merwin K. Hart of Birch Society: Controversial Lawyer Was Head of Chapter Here," *The New York Times*, December 2, 1962.

13. Merwin K. Hart, *National Economic Council Letter,* December 6, 1946. Housing was in fact in short supply at the end of World War II. The government-directed wartime economy hadn't prioritized domestic homebuilding.

14. Merwin K. Hart, "Let's Talk Plainly," *National Economic Council Letter,* December 1, 1946, https://archive.org/details/1946NEC156.

15. *Hearings Before the House Select Committee on Lobbying Activities,* June 6, 20, 21, and 28, 1950, pt. 4 (Washington, D.C.: Government Printing Office, 1950), 132–33. See also Ralph M. Goldman, *The Future Catches Up: Selected Writings of Ralph M. Goldman,* vol. 2: *American Political Parties and Politics* (Lincoln, NE: Writers Club Press, 2002), 95.

16. Rose Wilder Lane, *The Discovery of Freedom: Man's Struggle Against Authority* (New York: John Day, 1943), 208, 211, https://mises-media.s3.amazonaws.com/The%20Discovery%20of%20Freedom_2.pdf.

17. Quoted in David C. Colander and Harry Landreth, eds., *The Coming of Keynesianism to America: Conversations with the Founders of Keynesian Economics* (Brookfield, IL: Edward Elgar, 1996), 67–68.

18. Roger E. Backhouse, *Founder of Modern Economics: Paul A. Samuelson,* vol. 1: *Becoming Samuelson, 1915–1948* (New York: Oxford University Press, 2017), 568.

19. Papers of Merwin K. Hart, University of Oregon Archives, Box 5, Folder 1.

20. Milton Friedman and George J. Stigler, *Roofs or Ceilings? The Current Housing Problem* (Irving-on-Hudson, NY: Foundation for Economic Education, 1946).

21. Rose Wilder Lane to Merwin K. Hart, September 29, 1947, Papers of Merwin K. Hart, University of Oregon Archives, Box 5, Folder 1.

22. R. C. Hoiles to Merwin K. Hart, August 30, 1947, Papers of Merwin K. Hart, University of Oregon Archives, Box 5, Folder 1.

23. W. C. Mullendore to Joseph F. Farley, September 4, 1947, and Thomas W. Phillips, Jr., to Joseph F. Farley, August 28, 1947, Papers of Merwin K. Hart, University of Oregon Archives, Box 5, Folder 1.

24. John Collyer to Merwin K. Hart, October 1, 1947, and Frank Gannett to Merwin K. Hart, September 29, 1947, Papers of Merwin K. Hart, University of Oregon Archives, Box 5, Folder 1.

25. A. F. Davis to Rose Wilder Lane, September 16, 1947, and A. F. Davis to Constance Dall, September 12, 1947, Papers of Merwin K. Hart, University of Oregon Archives, Box 5, Folder 1.

26. R. E. Woodruff to Rose Wilder Lane, August 25, 1947, and J. Howard Pew to Hattie De Witt, September 11, 1947, Papers of Merwin K. Hart, University of Oregon Archives, Box 5, Folder 1.

27. Colander and Landreth, *The Coming of Keynesianism to America*, 66–68.
28. Ibid., 172.
29. Quoted in Michael M. Weinstein, "Paul A. Samuelson, Economist, Dies at 94," *The New York Times*, December 13, 2009.
30. Henry Regnery to Merwin K. Hart, October 4, 1951, Papers of Merwin K. Hart, University of Oregon Archives, Box 2, Folder 34.
31. William F. Buckley, Jr., *God and Man at Yale* (Washington, D.C.: Regnery Publishing, 2001 [1951]), lxv.
32. Ibid., 42–43.
33. Quoted in Colander and Landreth, *The Coming of Keynesianism to America*, 69–70.
34. William F. Buckley, Jr., to Merwin K. Hart, April 8, 1954, and Earl Bunting to Merwin K. Hart, November 8, 1951, Papers of Merwin K. Hart, University of Oregon Archives, Box 2, Folder 34.
35. Quoted in Alvin Felzenberg, "The Inside Story of William F. Buckley Jr.'s Crusade Against the John Birch Society," *National Review*, June 20, 2017.
36. Merwin K. Hart to William F. Buckley, Jr., March 24, 1961, Papers of Merwin K. Hart, University of Oregon Archives, Box 2, Folder 34.
37. "Merwin K. Hart of Birch Society; Controversial Lawyer Was Head of Chapter Here, Target of Ickes," *The New York Times*, December 2, 1962.
38. Angus Burgin, *The Great Persuasion: Reinventing Free Markets Since the Depression* (Cambridge, MA: Harvard University Press, 2012), 89.
39. David Boutros, "The William Volker and Company," State Historical Society of Missouri, 2004.
40. Michael J. McVicar, "Aggressive Philanthropy: Progressivism, Conservatism, and the William Volker Charities Fund," *Missouri Historical Review*, 2011, http://diginole.lib.fsu.edu/islandora/object/fsu:209940/datastream/PDF/view, 198.
41. Daniel Stedman Jones, *Masters of the Universe: Hayek, Friedman, and the Birth of Neoliberal Politics* (Princeton, NJ: Princeton University Press, 2012), 91.
42. Brian Doherty, "Best of Both Worlds: An Interview with Milton Friedman," *Reason*, June 1995.
43. Quoted in Jones, *Masters of the Universe*, 114–15.
44. Buckley, *God and Man at Yale*, 62, n. 72.
45. Quinn Slobodian, *Globalists: The End of Empire and the Birth of Neoliberalism* (Cambridge, MA: Harvard University Press, 2018), 298, n. 13.
46. John Kenneth Galbraith, *American Capitalism* (Boston: Houghton Mifflin, 1956 [1952]), 2–3.
47. "Industry on Parade," Peabody Awards, http://www.peabodyawards.com/award-profile/industry-on-parade.
48. Jones, *Masters of the Universe*, 91–92.
49. The Nobel Prize winners were Hayek, Friedman, Ronald Coase, James Buchanan, Gary Becker, and George Stigler. See Brian Doherty, *Radicals for Capitalism: A Freewheeling History of the Modern American Libertarian Movement* (New York: PublicAffairs, 2007), 183–86.
50. Doherty, *Radicals for Capitalism*, 185.
51. Ibid., 291–93.
52. McVicar, "Aggressive Philanthropy: Progressivism, Conservatism, and the William Volker Charities Fund," 211, n. 77.

53. John Strachey, *The Coming Struggle for Power* (New York: Modern Library, 1935 [1932]), vii–xx.

54. John Strachey, *Contemporary Capitalism* (New York: Random House, 1956), 294.

55. John Bellamy Foster, "Remarks of Paul Sweezy on the Occasion of His Receipt of the Veblen-Commons Award," *Monthly Review*, September 1, 1999.

56. Zygmund Dobbs, *Keynes at Harvard: Economic Deception as a Political Credo* (West Sayville, NY: Probe Publishers, 1969 [1958]), https://www.bigskyworld view.org/content/docs/Library/Keynes_At_Harvard.pdf.

57. *Oakland Tribune,* October 31, 1944.

58. *Los Angeles Times,* October 31, 1944; and *New York Daily News,* October 31, 1944.

59. [York, PA.] *Gazette and Daily,* March 20, 1945.

60. *Moline* [IL] *Daily Dispatch,* January 2, 1943.

61. JMK, cable to Sir John Anderson, December 12, 1944, in *CW,* vol. 24, 208–9.

62. Quoted in "Hearings Regarding Espionage in the United States Government," July 31, 1948, https://archive.org/stream/hearingsregardin1948unit/mode/2up.

63. Roger Sandilands and James Boughton, "Politics and the Attack on FDR's Economists: From the Grand Alliance to the Cold War," *Intelligence and National Security* 18, no. 3 (Autumn 2003): 73–99.

64. Eric Rauchway, *The Money Makers: How Roosevelt and Keynes Ended the Depression, Defeated Fascism, and Secured a Prosperous Peace* (New York: Basic Books, 2015), 116.

65. Quoted in ibid., 119.

66. Eleanor Roosevelt, "My Day," August 16, 1948, https://www2.gwu.edu/~erpapers/ myday/displaydocedits.cfm?_y=1948&_f=md001046. ER also defended Alger Hiss in the same column.

67. William F. Buckley, Jr., and L. Brent Bozell, *McCarthy and His Enemies: The Record and Its Meaning* (New Rochelle, NY: Arlington House, 1970 [1954]), 366.

68. Currie is mentioned only nine times in the mass of cables that were released in 1995, in fragments that are at times incomplete and generally ambiguous. The case for his innocence rests largely on a piece of one March 20, 1945, KGB cable from Moscow that states, "Currie trusts Silvermaster, informs him not only orally, but also by handing over documents. Up to now Currie's relations with Silvermaster were expressed, from our point of view, only in common feelings and personal sympathies [material missing] question of more profound relations and an understanding by Currie of Silvermaster's role." This suggests that Currie didn't know Silvermaster was working for the Soviets. And as Currie's biographer Roger Sandilands has noted, there is no evidence that Currie ever turned over anything illegal to Silvermaster; friends in the federal bureaucracy share documents all the time. See Roger Sandilands, "Guilt by Association? Lauchlin Currie's Alleged Involvement with Washington Economists in Soviet Espionage," *History of Political Economy* 32, no. 3 (September 2000): 473–515.

69. Buckley and Bozell, *McCarthy and His Enemies,* 52, 110.

70. Papers of George A. Eddy, Harvard University Law School Library, https:// hollisarchives.lib.harvard.edu/repositories/5/resources/6480.

71. Sandilands and Boughton, "Politics and the Attack on FDR's Economists."

FOURTEEN: THE AFFLUENT SOCIETY AND ITS ENEMIES

1. Richard F. Kahn, *The Making of Keynes' General Theory* (London: Cambridge University Press, 1984), 171.
2. John Maynard Keynes and Pierro Sraffa, "An Abstract of A Treatise on Human Nature 1740: *A Pamphlet Hitherto Unknown by David Hume*," Cambridge University Press, 1938, in *CW*, vol. 28, 373–90; the quote is from 384.
3. John Maynard Keynes, "Newton, The Man," unpublished, in *CW*, vol. 10, 363–64.
4. Ibid., 368.
5. Ibid., 366.
6. Ibid., 365.
7. John Maynard Keynes, "Thomas Robert Malthus," 1933, in *CW*, vol. 10, 88, 98.
8. John Maynard Keynes, *The General Theory of Employment, Interest and Money* (New York Prometheus, 1997 [1936]), 297–98.
9. John Maynard Keynes, "Economic Possibilities for Our Grandchildren," *The Nation and Athenaeum*, October 11 and 18, 1930, in *CW*, vol. 9, 332.
10. JMK, memorandum to Steering Committee on Post-War Employment, February 14, 1944, in *CW*, vol. 27, 371.
11. Paul Samuelson, *Economics* (New York: McGraw-Hill, 1997 [1948]), 10.
12. Quoted in Kahn, *The Making of Keynes' General Theory*, 203.
13. Ibid., 159.
14. JMK to John Hicks, March 31, 1937, in *CW*, vol. 14, 79.
15. John Maynard Keynes, "The General Theory of Employment," *The Quarterly Journal of Economics*, February 1937, in *CW*, vol. 14, 111, 113–15.
16. JMK, memorandum to Treasury, May 25, 1943, in *CW*, vol. 27, 320–24.
17. This decline represented the actual number of hours paid by firms based on the number of workers employed, showing that even during the Depression with employer bargaining power exceptionally high due to the severe levels of unemployment, the amount of time expected from each worker each week continued to drop. See Thomas J. Kniesner, "The Full-Time Workweek in the United States, 1900–1970," *Industrial and Labor Relations Review* 30, no. 1 (October 1976): 4.
18. Organisation for Economic Co-operation and Development, "Average Annual Hours Actually Worked per Worker," https://stats.oecd.org/Index.aspx?DataSet Code=ANHRS.
19. John Kenneth Galbraith, *A Life in Our Times* (Boston: Houghton Mifflin, 1981), 264.
20. Ibid., 268.
21. Richard Parker, *John Kenneth Galbraith: His Life, His Politics, His Economics* (Chicago: University of Chicago Press, 2005), 161–62.
22. Ibid., 163.
23. Galbraith, *A Life in Our Times*, 262.
24. Ibid., 261.
25. Roger E. Backhouse, *Founder of Modern Economics: Paul A. Samuelson* (New York: Oxford University Press, 2017), 570–73.
26. James Bryant Conant, *My Several Lives* (New York: Harper & Row, 1970), 440.
27. John Kenneth Galbraith, "My Forty Years with the FBI," in Galbraith, *Annals of an Abiding Liberal* (Boston: Houghton Mifflin, 1979), 155–81.
28. "Databases, Tables, & Calculators by Subject," Bureau of Labor Statistics, https://data.bls.gov/timeseries/LNU04000000?periods=Annual+Data&periods_option =specific_periods&years_option=all_years.

29. John Kenneth Galbraith, *American Capitalism* (Boston: Houghton Mifflin, 1956 [1952]), 180.
30. Ibid., 97.
31. Ibid., 178.
32. Marjorie S. Turner, *Joan Robinson and the Americans* (Armonk, NY: M. E. Sharpe, 1989), 166.
33. Galbraith, *American Capitalism*, 180.
34. Parker, *John Kenneth Galbraith*, 234.
35. Robert J. Buckley, Jr., to Frederick Lewis Allen and J. K. Galbraith, January 28, 1952, JKG, Series 3, Box 10.
36. John Kenneth Galbraith, *The Great Crash, 1929* (Boston: Houghton Mifflin, 1961 [1954]), xii–xvi.
37. Galbraith, "My Forty Years with the FBI," 170.
38. Galbraith, *A Life in Our Times*, 335. Turner, *Joan Robinson and the Americans*, 164.
39. Quoted in Turner, *Joan Robinson and the Americans*, 164.
40. Quoted in Nahid Aslanbeigui and Guy Oakes, *The Provocative Joan Robinson: The Making of a Cambridge Economist* (Durham, NC: Duke University Press, 2009), 212.
41. Quoted in Turner, *Joan Robinson and the Americans*, 109.
42. Quoted in ibid., 112.
43. "Economics Focus: Paul Samuelson," *The Economist*, December 17, 2009.
44. Soma Golden, "Economist Joan Robinson, 72, Is Full of Fight," *The New York Times*, March 23, 1976.
45. Joshua Zeitz, *Building the Great Society: Inside Lyndon Johnson's White House* (New York: Viking, 2018), 41.
46. John Kenneth Galbraith, *The Affluent Society: 40th Anniversary Edition* (Boston: Houghton Mifflin, 1998 [1958]), 191.
47. Ibid., 187–88.
48. John Maynard Keynes, "The End of Laissez-Faire," 1924, in *CW*, vol. 9, 291.
49. Galbraith, *The Affluent Society: 40th Anniversary Edition*, 258.
50. Ibid.
51. Ibid., 11.
52. Gunnar Myrdal, *Challenge to Affluence* (New York: Pantheon Books, 1963), 60.
53. Unemployment data from "Databases, Tables & Calculators by Subject," Bureau of Labor Statistics, https://data.bls.gov/timeseries/LNU04000000?periods =Annual+Data&periods_option=specific_periods&years_option=all_years. Poverty data from "Historical Poverty Tables: People and Families—1959 to 2018," United States Census Bureau, https://www.census.gov/data/tables/time-series/demo/income-poverty/historical-poverty-people.html.
54. Zeitz, *Building the Great Society*, 54.

FIFTEEN: THE BEGINNING OF THE END

1. Kevin Hartnett, "JFK the Party Planner," *The Boston Globe*, November 7, 2013.
2. John Kenneth Galbraith, *A Life in Our Times* (Boston: Houghton Mifflin, 1981), 53.
3. Ibid., 53–55, 355.
4. Richard Parker, *John Kenneth Galbraith: His Life, His Politics, His Economics* (Chicago: University of Chicago Press, 2005), 408.

5. Galbraith, *A Life in Our Times*, 373–74.
6. Robert Dallek, *An Unfinished Life: John F. Kennedy, 1917–1963* (New York: Little, Brown, 2003), 162–63.
7. "McCarthy, Joseph R., undated," Papers of John F. Kennedy, JFKPOF-031-024, John F. Kennedy Presidential Library and Museum, https://www.jfklibrary.org/Asset-Viewer/Archives/JFKPOF-031-024.aspx.
8. Eleanor Roosevelt, "On My Own," *The Saturday Evening Post*, March 8, 1958.
9. Galbraith, *A Life in Our Times*, 357.
10. Ibid., 375–76. Parker, *John Kenneth Galbraith*, 332.
11. "Council of Economic Advisers: Oral History Interview—JFK #1, 8/1/1964," John F. Kennedy Presidential Library and Museum, August 1, 1964, https://www.jfklibrary.org/Asset-Viewer/Archives/JFKOH-CEA-01.aspx.

    A confidential internal memo from August 1960 detailed the JFK campaign's problems with "a large and vocal faction" of "Kennedy doubters"—liberal voters generally, including "the Jews" and "some Negro elements"—who viewed JFK's liberal convictions as "emotionally thin." This coterie harbored "an unrelenting sense of indignation over Kennedy's past reluctance to speak out on the McCarthy censure." Kennedy staffers worried these voters would stay home on election day or—particularly if Nixon was able to exploit anti-Catholic feeling—even convert to the Republican ticket. The memo called for the committee to reach out to these doubters through special events where they would be "addressed by the persons they most respect," including top-tier politicians "Adlai Stevenson, Eleanor Roosevelt and Herbert Lehman" and top-tier intellectuals including Galbraith. These figures would "stress that Nixon is a dangerous demagogue with a most immoral history . . . whereas Kennedy is an intellectual, a scholar, a committed liberal . . . a man in sympathy with the views of Stevenson, Bowles, Reuther and Galbraith." See Lisa Howard, campaign memo to Robert Kennedy, August 4, 1960, John F. Kennedy Presidential Library and Museum, Meyer Feldman Personal Papers, Series 2, Box 8.

12. Jerry N. Hess, "Oral History Interview with Leon H. Keyserling," May 3, 1971, Harry S. Truman Library & Museum, https://www.trumanlibrary.org/oralhist/keyserl1.htm.
13. Robert L. Hetzel and Ralph F. Leach, "The Treasury-Fed Accord: A New Narrative Account," Federal Reserve Bank of Richmond *Economic Quarterly* 87, no. 1 (Winter 2001): 33–55, https://www.richmondfed.org/~/media/richmondfedorg/publications/research/economic_quarterly/2001/winter/pdf/hetzel.pdf.
14. John Kenneth Galbraith to John F. Kennedy, November 10, 1960, JKG, Series 6, Box 529.
15. Parker, *John Kenneth Galbraith*, 339.
16. "Council of Economic Advisers: Oral History Interview—JFK #1, 8/1/1964."
17. Lawrence H. Summers, "In Memory of Paul Samuelson," April 10, 2010, http://larrysummers.com/wp-content/uploads/2015/07/In-Memory-of-Paul-Samuelson_4.10.10.pdf.
18. "Council of Economic Advisers: Oral History Interview—JFK #1, 8/1/1964."
19. Quoted in Israel Shenker, "Samuelson Backs New Economics," *The New York Times*, March 6, 1971.
20. John Cassidy, "Postscript: Paul Samuelson," *The New Yorker*, December 14, 2009.
21. Parker, *John Kenneth Galbraith*, 345.
22. "The Natural Rate of Unemployment," *The Economist*, April 26, 2017.

23. Daniel T. Rodgers, *Age of Fracture* (Cambridge, MA: Belknap Press, 2011), 48.

24. Parker, *John Kenneth Galbraith*, 345.

25. "Council of Economic Advisers: Oral History Interview—JFK #1, 8/1/1964."

26. Herbert Stein, *The Fiscal Revolution in America* (Chicago: University of Chicago Press, 1969), 379.

27. Arthur M. Schlesinger, Jr., *A Thousand Days: John F. Kennedy in the White House* (Boston: Houghton Mifflin, 2002 [1965]), 138.

28. Ibid., 1010.

29. Subsequent work downgraded the severity of the increase. The unemployment rate for February 1961 was now officially 6.9 percent. But the Kennedy team didn't know this at the time.

30. "Council of Economic Advisers: Oral History Interview—JFK #1, 8/1/1964."

31. John Kenneth Galbraith, *Letters to Kennedy*, ed. James Goodman (Cambridge, MA: Harvard University Press, 1998), 3–4.

32. Schlesinger, *A Thousand Days*, 628.

33. Ibid., 629.

34. Stein, *The Fiscal Revolution in America*, 386.

35. Quoted in Joseph Thorndike, "Paul Samuelson and Tax Policy in the Kennedy Administration," Tax Analysts, December 29, 2009, http://www.taxhistory.org/thp/readings.nsf/ArtWeb/AAFB5F763226FD37852576A80075F253?OpenDocument.

36. Dwight D. Eisenhower, "Military-Industrial Complex Speech, Dwight D. Eisenhower, 1961," Lillian Goldman Law Library, Yale Law School, http://avalon.law.yale.edu/20th_century/eisenhower001.asp.

37. John F. Kennedy, "Commencement Address at Yale University," June 11, 1962, John F. Kennedy Presidential Library and Museum, https://www.jfklibrary.org/archives/other-resources/john-f-kennedy-speeches/yale-university-19620611.

38. Schlesinger, *A Thousand Days*, 644–66.

39. Ibid., 636.

40. Stein, *The Fiscal Revolution in America*, 413.

41. FDR had agreed to reduce corporate taxes in 1938 in the face of his recession, but had reversed them in 1940 as the country prepared for war.

42. Dallek, *An Unfinished Life*, 507.

43. John F. Kennedy, "Address to the Economic Club of New York," December 14, 1962, John F. Kennedy Presidential Library and Museum, https://www.jfklibrary.org/Asset-Viewer/Archives/JFKWHA-148.aspx.

44. Stein, *The Fiscal Revolution in America*, 420–21.

45. Schlesinger, *A Thousand Days*, 649.

46. Quoted in Joshua Zeitz, *Building the Great Society: Inside Lyndon Johnson's White House* (New York: Viking, 2018), 56.

47. Galbraith, *Letters to Kennedy*, 53.

48. Dallek, *An Unfinished Life*, 585.

49. Quoted in ibid., 584.

50. Galbraith, *Letters to Kennedy*, 112.

51. Quoted in Dallek, *An Unfinished Life*, 456.

52. Galbraith, *Letters to Kennedy*, 100–103.

53. Dallek, *An Unfinished Life*, 456–61.

54. Galbraith, *A Life in Our Times*, 445.

55. Parker, *John Kenneth Galbraith*, 408.

56. Zeitz, *Building the Great Society*, 40.
57. Galbraith, *A Life in Our Times*, 449.
58. Ibid., 445.
59. Zeitz, *Building the Great Society*, 54.
60. Galbraith, *A Life in Our Times*, 452.
61. Zeitz, *Building the Great Society*, 51.
62. Robert Solow, "Son of Affluence," *National Affairs*, Fall 1967, 100–108.
63. Shenker, "Samuelson Backs New Economics."
64. Galbraith, *A Life in Our Times*, 449–50.
65. Holcomb B. Noble and Douglas Martin, "John Kenneth Galbraith, 97, Dies; Economist Held a Mirror to Society," *The New York Times*, April 30, 2006.
66. Lyndon B. Johnson, "Remarks at the University of Michigan," May 22, 1964.
67. Emmanuel Saez and Gabriel Zucman, "Wealth Inequality in the United States Since 1913: Evidence from Capitalized Income Tax Data," *The Quarterly Journal of Economics* 131, no. 2 (May 2016): 519–78, http://gabriel-zucman.eu/files/SaezZucman2016QJE.pdf.
68. "Percent Change of Gross Domestic Product," Federal Reserve Bank of St. Louis, https://fred.stlouisfed.org/series/CPGDPAI#0.

SIXTEEN: THE RETURN OF THE NINETEENTH CENTURY

1. Joan Robinson, "The Second Crisis of Economic Theory," *The American Economic Review* 62, nos. 1–2 (March 1972): 1–10.
2. "Combatting Role Prejudice and Sex Discrimination: Findings of the American Economic Association Committee on the Status of Women in the Economics Profession," *The American Economic Review* 63, no. 5 (December 1973): 1049–61, https://www.jstor.org/stable/1813937?seq=1#page_scan_tab_contents.
3. "Amartya Sen: Biographical," Nobel Prize, https://www.nobelprize.org/prizes/economic-sciences/1998/sen/biographical.
4. Marjorie S. Turner, *Joan Robinson and the Americans* (Armonk, NY: M. E. Sharpe, 1989), 183.
5. Richard Parker, *John Kenneth Galbraith: His Life, His Politics, His Economics* (Chicago: University of Chicago Press, 2005), 484.
6. Ibid., 481–85.
7. Quoted in Angus Burgin, *The Great Persuasion: Reinventing Free Markets Since the Depression* (Cambridge, MA: Harvard University Press, 2012), 177.
8. Ibid., 160.
9. Quoted in Quinn Slobodian, *Globalists: The End of Empire and the Birth of Neoliberalism* (Cambridge, MA: Harvard University Press, 2018), 269.
10. Quoted in Burgin, *The Great Persuasion*, 190.
11. Quoted in ibid., 177.
12. Quoted in ibid., 175–76.
13. Milton Friedman, *Capitalism and Freedom: Fortieth Anniversary Edition* (Chicago: University of Chicago Press, 2002 [1962]), 3–4.
14. Burgin, *The Great Persuasion*, 201.
15. Ibid.
16. Jeremy D. Mayer, "LBJ Fights the White Backlash: The Racial Politics of the 1964 Presidential Campaign," *Prologue* 33, no. 1 (Spring 2001), https://www.archives.gov/publications/prologue/2001/spring/lbj-and-white-backlash-1.html.

17. Rowland Evans and Robert Novak, "Inside Report: The White Man's Party," *The Washington Post*, June 25, 1963.

18. Barry Goldwater, *The Conscience of a Conservative* (Princeton, NJ: Princeton University Press, 2007 [1960]), 31.

19. Quoted in Burgin, *The Great Persuasion*, 202.

20. Quoted in ibid., 201–2.

21. Friedman, *Capitalism and Freedom: Fortieth Anniversary Edition*, 15, 4.

22. Ibid., viii–ix.

23. Daniel Stedman Jones, *Masters of the Universe: Hayek, Friedman, and the Birth of Neoliberal Politics* (Princeton, NJ: Princeton University Press, 2012), 119–20.

24. In the pages of *Newsweek*, Friedman made similar arguments against enfranchising the black population of Rhodesia (modern Zimbabwe). See Slobodian, *Globalists*, 178–79.

25. "With Rose Friedman. 'Record of a Trip to Southern Africa, March 20–April 9, 1976.' Unpublished typescript transcribed from a tape, dictated April 7–9, 1976. Excerpts published in *Two Lucky People: Memoirs*, by Milton and Rose Friedman, 435–40. Chicago: University of Chicago, 1998," https://miltonfriedman .hoover.org/friedman_images/Collections/2016c21/1976TRipToSouthAfrica .pdf.

26. John Kenneth Galbraith, *Economics in Perspective* (Boston: Houghton Mifflin, 1987), 274.

27. "Real Gross Domestic Product," Federal Reserve Bank of St. Louis, https://fred .stlouisfed.org/series/GDPC1#0; "Consumer Price Index: All Items in U.S. City Average, All Urban Consumers," Federal Reserve Bank of St. Louis, https://fred .stlouisfed.org/series/CPIAUCSL#0; "Unemployment Rate," Federal Reserve Bank of St. Louis, https://fred.stlouisfed.org/series/UNRATE.

28. Quoted in Parker, *John Kenneth Galbraith*, 438.

29. Milton Friedman, "The Role of Monetary Policy," *American Economic Review* 58 (March 1968): 1–17, https://miltonfriedman.hoover.org/friedman_images/ Collections/2016c21/AEA-AER_03_01_1968.pdf.

30. Milton Friedman, "The Counter-Revolution in Monetary Theory," Institute of Economic Affairs, occasional paper no. 33, 1970, https://miltonfriedman .hoover.org/friedman_images/Collections/2016c21/IEA_1970.pdf.

31. Jones, *Masters of the Universe*, 208–9.

32. Thomas W. Hazlett, "The Road from Serfdom: An Interview with F. A. Hayek," *Reason*, July 1992.

33. John A. Farrell, *Richard Nixon: The Life* (New York: Vintage, 2017), 446.

34. Quoted in ibid., 243.

35. Parker, *John Kenneth Galbraith*, 492.

36. Rick Perlstein, *Nixonland: The Rise of a President and the Fracturing of America* (New York: Scribner, 2008), 603.

37. "Galbraith Urges Wage-Price Curb," *The New York Times*, July 21, 1971.

38. "U.S. Spent $141-Billion in Vietnam in 14 Years," *The New York Times*, May 1, 1975.

39. Parker, *John Kenneth Galbraith*, 491–92.

40. Ibid., 495.

41. Daniel Ellsberg, *Secrets: A Memoir of Vietnam and the Pentagon Papers* (New York: Penguin, 2003), 418.

42. Parker, *John Kenneth Galbraith*, 493.

43. Perlstein, *Nixonland*, 601.

44. Parker, *John Kenneth Galbraith*, 495.

45. Quoted in ibid., 497.

46. Quoted in ibid.

47. Milton Friedman, "Why the Freeze Is a Mistake," *Newsweek*, August 30, 1971, https://miltonfriedman.hoover.org/objects/57976/why-the-freeze-is-a-mistake.

48. Perlstein, *Nixonland*, 598, 603.

49. Slobodian, *Globalists*, 277.

50. F. A. Hayek, *Law, Legislation and Liberty, Vols. 1–3: A New Statement of the Liberal Principles of Justice and Political Economy* (New York: Routledge, 2013 [1982]), 430.

51. Quoted in Thomas Frank, *Listen, Liberal: Or, Whatever Happened to the Party of the People?* (New York: Metropolitan Books, 2016), 54.

52. Paul Krugman, *Peddling Prosperity* (New York: W. W. Norton, 1994), 14.

53. Mark Skousen, "The Perseverance of Paul Samuelson's Economics," *Journal of Economic Perspectives* 11, no. 2 (Spring 1997): 137–52.

54. Quoted in Burgin, *The Great Persuasion*, 207.

55. Ibid.

SEVENTEEN: THE SECOND GILDED AGE

1. John Harris, *The Survivor: Bill Clinton in the White House* (New York: Random House, 2005), xxvii.

2. Bob Woodward, *The Agenda: Inside the Clinton White House* (New York: Simon & Schuster, 1995), 70–72.

3. "Unemployment Rate," Federal Reserve Bank of St. Louis, https://fred.stlouisfed.org/series/UNRATE#0.

4. Patrick Cockburn, "Profile: Mr Right for Wall Street: Lloyd Bentsen: The Next US Treasury Secretary Is a Wily Old Pro Who Doesn't Make Many Mistakes," *The Independent*, December 13, 1992.

5. Woodward, *The Agenda: Inside the Clinton White House*, 73–81.

6. Patrick J. Maney, *Bill Clinton: New Gilded Age President* (Lawrence: University of Kansas Press, 2016), 18.

7. Ibid., 25–27.

8. Ibid., 31.

9. Quoted in Harris, *The Survivor*, xvi.

10. Woodward, *The Agenda*, 84.

11. Ibid., 84, 91.

12. Ibid., 213, 240.

13. Ibid., 160–61.

14. Karen Tumulty and William J. Eaton, "Clinton Budget Triumphs, 51–50: Gore Casts a Tie-Breaking Vote in the Senate," *Los Angeles Times*, August 7, 1993.

15. *Annual Report of the Council of Economic Advisers*, December 29, 2000, https://www.govinfo.gov/content/pkg/ERP-2001/pdf/ERP-2001.pdf.

16. "The NAFTA Debate," *Larry King Live*, CNN, November 9, 1993.

17. "Bill Clinton for President 1992 Campaign Brochures: 'Fighting for the Forgotten Middle Class,'" 4President.org, http://www.4president.org/brochures/billclinton1992brochure.htm.

18. William J. Clinton, "Remarks at the Signing Ceremony for the Supplemental

Agreements to the North American Free Trade Agreement," September 14, 1993, https://www.gpo.gov/fdsys/pkg/PPP-1993-book2/pdf/PPP-1993-book2-doc-pg1485-2.pdf.

19. Milton Friedman and Rose D. Friedman, "The Case for Free Trade," Hoover Institution, October 30, 1997, https://www.hoover.org/research/case-free-trade.

20. Thomas L. Friedman, "President Vows Victory on Trade," *The New York Times*, September 29, 1994.

21. Thomas L. Friedman, "Congress Briefed on Funds for GATT," *The New York Times*, July 15, 1994.

22. Thomas L. Friedman, "Congress Loath to Finance GATT Treaty's Tariff Losses," *The New York Times*, April 14, 1994.

23. Thomas L. Friedman, "President Vows Victory on Trade," *The New York Times*, September 29, 1994.

24. Bill Clinton, *My Life* (New York: Vintage, 2005), 547.

25. "Full Text of Clinton's Speech on China Trade Bill," *The New York Times*, March 9, 2000.

26. "Assessment of the Economic Effects on the United States of China's Accession to the WTO," U.S. International Trade Commission, September 1999, xix, https://www.usitc.gov/publications/docs/pubs/332/PUB3229.PDF.

27. Gary Clyde Hufbauer and Daniel H. Rosen, "American Access to China's Market," *International Economic Policy Briefs*, no. 00-3, April 2000, 5, https://piie.com/publications/pb/pb00-3.pdf.

28. Paul Krugman, "Reckonings; A Symbol Issue," *The New York Times*, May 10, 2000.

29. William J. Clinton, "Remarks on Signing the North American Free Trade Agreement Implementation Act," December 8, 1993.

30. Quarraisha Abdool Karim and Salim S. Abdool Karim, "The Evolving HIV Epidemic in South Africa," *International Journal of Epidemiology* 31, no. 1 (February 2002): 37–40, https://academic.oup.com/ije/article/31/1/37/655915.

31. William W. Fisher III and Cyrill P. Rigamonti, "The South Africa AIDS Controversy: A Case Study in Patent Law and Policy," Harvard Law School, February 10, 2005, https://cyber.harvard.edu/people/tfisher/South%20Africa.pdf.

32. "South Africa," World Bank Data, https://data.worldbank.org/country/south-africa.

33. "USTR Announces Results of Special 301 Annual Review," Office of the United States Trade Representative, May 1, 1998, https://ustr.gov/sites/default/files/1998%20Special%20301%20Report.pdf; "USTR Announces Results of Special 301 Annual Review," Office of the United States Trade Representative, April 30, 1999, https://ustr.gov/sites/default/files/1999%20Special%20301%20Report.pdf.

34. Zach Carter, "How Rachel Maddow Helped Force Bill Clinton's Support for Mandela's AIDS Plan," *Huffington Post*, December 6, 2013.

35. Dudley Althaus, "NAFTA Talks Target Stubbornly Low Mexican Wages," *The Wall Street Journal*, August 29, 2017.

36. Mark Weisbrot, Lara Merling, Vitor Mello, et al., "Did NAFTA Help Mexico? An Update After 23 Years," Center for Economic and Policy Research, March 2017, http://cepr.net/images/stories/reports/nafta-mexico-update-2017-03.pdf?v=2.

37. "All Employees: Manufacturing," Federal Reserve Bank of St. Louis, https://fred .stlouisfed.org/series/MANEMP.

38. David H. Autor, David Dorn, and Gordon H. Hanson, "The China Shock: Learning from Labor-Market Adjustment to Large Changes in Trade," *Annual Review of Economics* 8 (October 2016): 205–40, http://www.ddorn.net/papers/ Autor-Dorn-Hanson-ChinaShock.pdf.

39. David Brancaccio, "How to Make Globalization Fair, According to Economist Joseph Stiglitz," *Marketplace,* December 1, 2017.

40. OECD Centre for Opportunity and Equality, "Understanding the Socio-Economic Divide in Europe," January 26, 2017, https://www.oecd.org/els/soc/ cope-divide-europe-2017-background-report.pdf.

41. Asher Schechter, "Globalization Has Contributed to Tearing Societies Apart," ProMarket, March 29, 2018, https://promarket.org/globalization-contributed -tearing-societies-apart/.

42. World Bank, "Global Economic Prospects and the Developing Countries 2000," http://documents.worldbank.org/curated/en/589561468126281885/pdf/multi -page.pdf; and World Bank, "Entering the 21st Century: World Development Report 1999/2000," https://openknowledge.worldbank.org/bitstream/handle/ 10986/5982/WDR%201999_2000%20-%20English.pdf?sequence=1.

43. Lesley Wroughton, "UN Reducing Extreme Poverty Goal Met, World Bank Says," *Huffington Post,* April 29, 2012.

44. "Goal 1: No Poverty," United Nations Conference on Trade and Development, http://stats.unctad.org/Dgff2016/people/goal1/index.html.

45. Lucy Hornby and Leslie Hook, "China's Carbon Emissions Set for Fastest Growth in 7 Years," *Financial Times,* May 29, 2018, https://www.ft.com/ content/98839504-6334-11e8-90c2-9563a0613e56.

46. "West Cuts Pollution—by Exporting It to China," University of Leeds, http:// www.leeds.ac.uk/news/article/423/west_cuts_pollution__by_exporting_it_to_ china.

47. Avraham Ebenstein, Maoyong Fan, Michael Greenstone, et al., "New Evidence on the Impact of Sustained Exposure to Air Pollution on Life Expectancy from China's Huai River Policy," *Proceedings of the National Academy of Sciences of the United States of America,* September 11, 2017, http://www.pnas.org/content/ early/2017/09/05/1616784114.full.

48. John Harris, *The Survivor: Bill Clinton in the White House* (New York: Random House, 2005), 95.

49. Ibid., 176–77.

50. John Burgess and Steven Pearlstein, "Protests Delay WTO Opening," *The Washington Post,* December 1, 1999; Lynsi Burton, "WTO Riots in Seattle: 15 Years Ago," *Seattle Post-Intelligencer,* November 29, 2014.

51. Jia Lynn Yang and Steven Mufson, "Capital Gains Tax Rates Benefitting Wealthy Are Protected by Both Parties," *The Washington Post,* September 11, 2011.

52. Their colleague Fischer Black had helped Merton and Scholes develop the model but died before the Nobel Committee presented the award for the work that had gone into the model, and the Nobel Prize is not given posthumously.

53. Saul S. Cohen, "The Challenge of Derivatives," *Fordham Law Review* 63, no. 6, article 2 (1995), https://ir.lawnet.fordham.edu/cgi/viewcontent.cgi?article=3169 &context=flr.

54. Maney, *Bill Clinton,* 230, 228.

55. William D. Cohan, "Rethinking Robert Rubin," *Bloomberg Businessweek*, September 30, 2012.

56. Clinton, *My Life*, 857.

57. Stephen Gandel, "Robert Rubin Was Targeted for DOJ Investigation by Financial Crisis Commission," *Fortune*, March 13, 2016; Aruna Viswanatha and Ryan Tracy, "Financial-Crisis Panel Suggested Criminal Cases Against Stan O'Neal, Charles Prince, AIG Bosses," *The Wall Street Journal*, March 30, 2016.

58. Maney, *Bill Clinton*, 225, 235.

59. Harris, *The Survivor*.

60. Clinton, *My Life*.

61. Zach Carter, "Austerity Fetishists Are Finally Giving Up," *Huffington Post*, May 14, 2014.

62. Parker, *John Kenneth Galbraith*, 647–51.

63. J. Bradford DeLong and Lawrence H. Summers, "The 'New Economy': Background, Historical Perspective, Questions, and Speculations," Federal Reserve Bank of Kansas City, August 30, 2001, https://www.kansascityfed.org/Publicat/econrev/Pdf/4q01delo.pdf.

CONCLUSION

1. "Rep. Albert R. Wynn–Maryland," Center for Responsive Politics, https://www.opensecrets.org/members-of-congress/summary?cid=N00001849&cycle=CAREER&type=I.

2. Lehman Brothers Holdings Inc., Form 8-K, June 9, 2008, U.S. Securities and Exchange Commission, https://www.sec.gov/Archives/edgar/data/806085/000110465908038647/0001104659-08-038647-index.htm.

3. The Financial Crisis Inquiry Commission, *The Financial Crisis Inquiry Report: Final Report of the National Commission on the Causes of the Financial and Economic Crisis in the United States*, January 2011, http://fcic-static.law.stanford.edu/cdn_media/fcic-reports/fcic_final_report_full.pdf, 325.

4. "S&P/Case-Shiller U.S. National Home Price Index/Consumer Price Index: Owners' Equivalent Rent of Residences in U.S. City Average, All Urban Consumers," Federal Reserve Bank of St. Louis, https://fred.stlouisfed.org/graph/?g=786h#0; "All-Transactions House Price Index for California," Federal Reserve Bank of St. Louis, https://fred.stlouisfed.org/series/CASTHPI; "S&P/Case-Shiller NV-Las Vegas Home Price Index," Federal Reserve Bank of St. Louis, https://fred.stlouisfed.org/series/LVXRNSA.

5. "Homeownership Rate for the United States," Federal Reserve Bank of St. Louis, https://fred.stlouisfed.org/series/RHORUSQ156N.

6. "I think this house of cards may tumble some day, and it will mean great losses for the investors who own stock in those companies," William Brennan, director of the Home Defense Program at the Atlanta Legal Aid Society, told the Senate Special Committee on Aging in 1998. Quoted in Kat Aaron, "Predatory Lending: A Decade of Warnings," Center for Public Integrity, May 6, 2009, https://publicintegrity.org/business/predatory-lending-a-decade-of-warnings/. For data on the size of the subprime market, see Gene Amronmin and Anna Paulson, "Default Rates on Prime and Subprime Mortgages: Differences and Similarities," Federal Reserve Bank of Chicago, September 2010, https://www.chicagofed.org/publications/profitwise-news-and-views/2010/pnv-september2010.

7. The real explosion in subprime lending took place in 2003, when subprime mortgages nearly quadrupled as a share of the total mortgage market. See "Where Should I Look to Find Statistics on the Share of Subprime Mortgages to Total Mortgages?," Federal Reserve Bank of San Francisco, December 2009, https://www.frbsf.org/education/publications/doctor-econ/2009/december/subprime-mortgage-statistics/.

   In 2000, the total value of subprime mortgage-backed securities purchased by Fannie Mae and Freddie Mac was negligible. By 2003, it had eclipsed $100 billion, and in 2005 it was over $200 billion. But this accounted for only a small fraction of the broader market. In 2003, Wall Street issued roughly $300 billion in exotic mortgage-backed securities, and roughly $800 billion in 2005. Including the market for private-label jumbo loans, Fannie and Freddie accounted for less than a fifth of the overall exotic mortgage activity at the height of the bubble. See Mark Calabria, "Fannie, Freddie, and the Subprime Mortgage Market," Cato Institute Briefing Papers, no. 120, March 7, 2011, https://object.cato.org/pubs/bp/bp120.pdf, 8; Laurie Goodman, "A Progress Report on the Private-Label Securities Market," Urban Institute, March 2016, https://www.urban.org/sites/default/files/publication/78436/2000647-A-Progress-Report-on-the-Private-Label-Securities-Market.pdf, 1.

8. See "OCC's Quarterly Report on Bank Trading and Derivative Activities, Fourth Quarter 2007," Comptroller of the Currency, https://www.occ.treas.gov/publications-and-resources/publications/quarterly-report-on-bank-trading-and-derivatives-activities/files/pub-derivatives-quarterly-qtr4-2007.pdf; Iñaki Aldasoro and Torsten Ehlers, "The Credit Default Swap Market: What a Difference a Decade Makes," *BIS Quarterly Review,* June 5, 2018, https://www.bis.org/publ/qtrpdf/r_qt1806b.htm; "GDP (Current US$)," World Bank, https://data.worldbank.org/indicator/ny.gdp.mktp.cd.

9. The Financial Crisis Inquiry Commission, *The Financial Crisis Inquiry Report,* 328.

10. Ibid., 330.

11. Rosalind Z. Wiggins, Thomas Piontek, and Andrew Metrick, "The Lehman Brothers Bankruptcy A: Overview," Yale Program on Financial Stability Case Study 2014-3A-V1, Yale School of Management, October 1, 2014, https://som.yale.edu/sites/default/files/files/001-2014-3A-V1-LehmanBrothers-A-REVA.pdf, 5.

12. The Financial Crisis Inquiry Commission, *The Financial Crisis Inquiry Report,* 325.

13. The U.S. government eventually committed $182 billion in emergency support for AIG, $331 billion for Bank of America, and $472 billion for Citigroup. See Congressional Oversight Panel, *The Final Report of the Congressional Oversight Panel,* March 16, 2011, https://www.govinfo.gov/content/pkg/CHRG-112shrg64832/pdf/CHRG-112shrg64832.pdf.

14. In addition to its bad real estate assets, Lehman Brothers was extremely dependent on short-term funding, and the lousy quality of its assets made it hard to summon up the collateral for Federal Reserve loans, since the Fed wouldn't accept junk bonds at its emergency lending facilities.

15. The Financial Crisis Inquiry Commission, *The Financial Crisis Inquiry Report,* 334.

16. "Meeting of the Federal Open Market Committee on September 16, 2008,"

https://www.federalreserve.gov/monetarypolicy/files/FOMC20080916meeting
.pdf, 36, 48, 51.

17. Donna Edwards, interview with author, June 2017.

18. The Financial Crisis Inquiry Commission, *The Financial Crisis Inquiry Report*, 372.

19. Interview with Paul Kanjorski, C-SPAN, January 27, 2009, https://www.c-span .org/video/?c4508252/rep-paul-kanjorski.

20. "Final Vote Results for Roll Call 674," September 29, 2008, http://clerk.house .gov/evs/2008/roll674.xml.

21. Zach Carter and Ryan Grim, "The Congressional Black Caucus Is at War with Itself over Wall Street," *The New Republic*, May 27, 2014.

22. Only half of the $700 billion bailout fund was released by the October 3 vote. In January 2009, Obama needed congressional approval to deploy the second batch. Summers' letter was intended to win over liberal skeptics—if they backed the second $350 billion tranche, Obama would throw the book at the foreclosure epidemic. See Lawrence H. Summers, letter to congressional leaders, January 15, 2009, https://www.realclearpolitics.com/articles/summers%20letter%20to%20 congressional%20leadership%201-15-09.pdf.

23. See "Bailout Tracker," *ProPublica*, updated February 25, 2019, https://projects. propublica.org/bailout/.

24. David Dayen, *Chain of Title: How Three Ordinary Americans Uncovered Wall Street's Great Foreclosure Fraud* (New York: New Press, 2016).

25. Journalist David Dayen chronicled the problems of the National Mortgage Settlement in a series of magazine articles and a book. See David Dayen, "A Needless Default," *The American Prospect*, February 9, 2015, https://prospect.org/article/ needless-default; Dayen, "Special Investigation: How America's Biggest Bank Paid Its Fine for the 2008 Mortgage Crisis—with Phony Mortgages!," *The Nation*, October 23, 2017; Dayen, *Chain of Title*.

26. Laura Kusisto, "Many Who Lost Homes to Foreclosure in Last Decade Won't Return—NAR," *The Wall Street Journal*, April 20, 2015.

27. Atif Mian and Amir Sufi, "What Explains the 2007–2009 Drop in Employment?," February 2014, http://www.umass.edu/preferen/You%20Must%20Read %20This/Mian%20Sufi%20NBER%202014.pdf; Atif Mian and Amir Sufi, *House of Debt: How They (And You) Caused the Great Recession, and How We Can Prevent It from Happening Again* (Chicago: University of Chicago Press, 2014); International Monetary Fund, "United States: Selected Issues Paper," July 2010, https://www.imf.org/external/pubs/ft/scr/2010/cr10248.pdf.

28. Zach Carter and Jennifer Bendery, "How Failed Obama Foreclosure Relief Plan Contributes to Jobs Crisis," *Huffington Post*, August 3, 2011.

29. *Economic Report of the President*, February 2010, https://obamawhitehouse. archives.gov/sites/default/files/microsites/economic-report-president.pdf, 31, 146, 30.

30. *Economic Report of the President*, February 2011, https://www.govinfo.gov/ content/pkg/ERP-2011/pdf/ERP-2011.pdf, 70.

31. *Economic Report of the President*, March 2013, https://www.govinfo.gov/content/ pkg/ERP-2013/pdf/ERP-2013.pdf, 30.

32. Bureau of Labor Statistics, "The Recession of 2007–2009," https://www.bls.gov/ spotlight/2012/recession/pdf/recession_bls_spotlight.pdf.

33. Congressional Budget Office, "Estimated Impact of the American Recovery and

Reinvestment Act on Employment and Economic Output from January 2011 Through March 2011," May 2011, https://www.cbo.gov/sites/default/files/112th -congress-2011-2012/reports/05-25-arra.pdf; Alan S. Blinder and Mark Zandi, "How the Great Recession Was Brought to an End," July 27, 2010, https://www .economy.com/mark-zandi/documents/End-of-Great-Recession.pdf.

34. Emmanuel Saez, "Striking It Richer: The Evolution of Top Incomes in the United States," March 2, 2019, https://eml.berkeley.edu/~saez/saez-UStopincomes-2017 .pdf.

35. Gabriel Zucman, "Global Wealth Inequality," *Annual Review of Economics* 11 (2019): 109–38, http://gabriel-zucman.eu/files/Zucman2019.pdf.

36. Edward N. Wolff, "Household Wealth Trends in the United States, 1962 to 2016: Has Middle Class Wealth Recovered?," National Bureau of Economic Research Working Paper no. 24085, November 2017, https://www.nber.org/papers/w24085.

37. "Survey of Consumer Finances (SCF)," Board of Governors of the Federal Reserve System, October 31, 2017, https://www.federalreserve.gov/econres/ scfindex.htm.

38. "Life Expectancy," Centers for Disease Control and Prevention, National Center for Health Statistics, https://www.cdc.gov/nchs/fastats/life-expectancy.htm. See also Lenny Bernstein, "U.S. Life Expectancy Declines Again, a Dismal Trend Not Seen Since World War I," *The Washington Post*, November 29, 2018.

39. Joseph Stiglitz, "Toward a General Theory of Consumerism: Reflections on Keynes's Economic Possibilities for Our Grandchildren," in Lorenzo Pecchi and Gustavo Piga, eds., *Revisiting Keynes: Economic Possibilities for Our Grandchildren* (Cambridge, MA: MIT Press, 2008), 41.

40. Ryan Lizza, "Inside the Crisis: Larry Summers and the White House Economic Team," *The New Yorker*, October 12, 2009.

41. Suresh Naidu, Dani Rodrik, and Gabriel Zucman, "Economics After Neoliberalism," *Boston Review*, February 15, 2019, http://bostonreview.net/forum/suresh -naidu-dani-rodrik-gabriel-zucman-economics-after-neoliberalism.

42. Quoted in Robert Skidelsky, *John Maynard Keynes*, vol. 1: *Hopes Betrayed, 1883– 1920* (New York: Penguin, 1994 [1983]), 122.

43. John Maynard Keynes, *A Treatise on Money: The Pure Theory of Money and the Applied Theory of Money. Complete Set* (Mansfield Center, CT: Martino Fine Books, 2011 [1930]), vol. 2, 150.

SELECTED BIBLIOGRAPHY

———— ◊ ————

M UCH OF THE PRIMARY source research for this book was culled from the personal papers of the figures who appear most prominently in it. They include, in order of importance:

The Papers of John Maynard Keynes in the Archives of King's College at the University of Cambridge in Cambridge, England.

The Papers of John Kenneth Galbraith at the John F. Kennedy Presidential Library in Boston, Massachusetts.

The Papers of Paul A. Samuelson at the Rubenstein Library at Duke University in Durham, North Carolina.

The Collected Works of Milton Friedman, available digitally from the Hoover Institution at Stanford University in Palo Alto, California.

The Papers of Merwin K. Hart at the Special Collections and University Archives of the University of Oregon Libraries in Eugene, Oregon.

The Papers of Leon H. Keyserling at the Harry S. Truman Presidential Library in Independence, Missouri.

The Papers of Walter S. Salant at the Harry S. Truman Presidential Library in Independence, Missouri.

This bibliography includes key and critical sources used for this book. For a comprehensive list of sources, please see the notes to each chapter.

Ahamed, Liaquat. *Lords of Finance: The Bankers Who Broke the World*. New York: Penguin, 2009.

Angell, Norman. *The Great Illusion*. New York: G. P. Putnam Sons, 1913 [1910].

Aslanbeigui, Nahid, and Guy Oakes. *The Provocative Joan Robinson: The Making of a Cambridge Economist*. Durham, NC: Duke University Press, 2009.

Backhouse, Roger E. *Founder of Modern Economics: Paul A. Samuelson*. New York: Oxford University Press, 2017.

Baruch, Bernard. *The Making of the Reparation and Economic Sections of the Treaty*. New York: Harper and Brothers, 1921.

Bell, Anne Olivier, and Andrew McNeillie, eds. *The Diary of Virginia Woolf, Vols. 1–5*. New York: Harcourt Brace Jovanovich, 1977–1984.

Bensusan-Butt, D. M. *On Economic Knowledge: A Sceptical Miscellany*. Canberra, Australia: Australian National University Press, 1980.

Berg, A. Scott. *Wilson*. New York: Berkley, 2013.

Borgwardt, Elizabeth. *A New Deal for the World: America's Vision for Human Rights*. Cambridge, MA: The Belknap Press of Harvard University Press, 2005.

Brands, H. W. *Traitor to His Class: The Privileged Life and Radical Presidency of Franklin Delano Roosevelt*. New York: Anchor Books, 2008.

Brinkley, Alan. *The End of Reform: New Deal Liberalism in Recession and War*. New York: Vintage, 1996.

Broadberry, Stephen, and Mark Harrison. "The Economics of World War I: A Comparative Quantitative Analysis." *Journal of Economic History* 66, no. 2 (June 2006).

Brockington, Grace. " 'Tending the Lamp' or 'Minding Their Own Business'? Bloomsbury Art and Pacifism During World War I." *Immediations* #1 (January 2004).

Buckley, William F. *God and Man at Yale*. Washington, D.C.: Regnery Publishing, 2001 [1951].

Buckley, William F., and L. Brent Bozell, *McCarthy and His Enemies: The Record and Its Meaning*. New Rochelle, NY: Arlington House, 1970 [1954].

Burgin, Angus. *The Great Persuasion: Reinventing Free Markets Since the Depression*. Cambridge, MA: Harvard University Press, 2012.

Burke, Edmund. *Reflections on the Revolution in France*. London: John Sharpe, 1820 [1790].

Burnett, Philip Mason. *Reparation at the Paris Peace Conference from the Standpoint of the American Delegation*. New York: Columbia University Press, 1940.

Burns, Helen M. *The American Banking Community and New Deal Banking Reforms, 1933–1935*. Westport, CT: Greenwood Press, 1974.

Case, Josephine Young, and Everett Needham Case. *Owen D. Young and American Banking Enterprise*. Boston: David R. Godine, 1982.

Chernow, Ron. *The House of Morgan: An American Banking Dynasty and the Rise of Modern Finance*. New York: Grove Press, 2001 [1990].

Churchill, Winston. *The World Crisis Volume IV: The Aftermath, 1918–1922*. New York: Bloomsbury Academic, 2015 [1929].

Clinton, Bill. *My Life*. New York: Vintage, 2005.

Colander, David C., and Harry Landreth, eds. *The Coming of Keynesianism to America: Conversations with the Founders of Keynesian Economics*. Brookfield, IL: Edward Elgar, 1996.

Conway, Ed. *The Summit: Bretton Woods, 1944: J. M. Keynes and the Reshaping of the Global Economy*. New York: Pegasus Books, 2015.

Cook, Chris. *The Age of Alignment: Electoral Politics in Britain: 1922–1929*. London: Macmillan, 1975.

Cook, Chris, and John Stevenson. *The Slump: Britain in the Great Depression*. London: Routledge, 2013 [1977].

Cooper, John Milton Jr., *Woodrow Wilson: A Biography*. New York: Vintage, 2009.

Cristiano, Carlo. *The Political and Economic Thought of the Young Keynes*. London: Routledge, 2014.

Currie, Lauchlin. *Supply and Control of Money in the United States.* Cambridge, MA: Harvard University Press, 1934.

Dallas, Gregor. *At the Heart of a Tiger: Clemenceau and His World, 1841–1929.* New York: Carroll and Graf, 1993.

Dallek, Robert. *Franklin D. Roosevelt: A Political Life.* New York: Viking, 2017.

———. *An Unfinished Life: John F. Kennedy, 1917–1963.* New York: Little, Brown, 2003.

Davenport-Hines, Richard. *Universal Man: The Lives of John Maynard Keynes.* New York: Basic Books, 2015.

Doherty, Brian. *Radicals for Capitalism: A Freewheeling History of the Modern American Libertarian Movement.* New York: PublicAffairs, 2008.

Edwards, Jerome E. *Pat McCarran: Political Boss of Nevada.* Reno: University of Nevada Press, 1982.

Evans, Richard J. *The Pursuit of Power: Europe, 1815–1914.* New York: Viking, 2016.

Farrell, John A. *Richard Nixon: The Life.* New York: Vintage, 2017.

Friedman, Milton. *Capitalism and Freedom: Fortieth Anniversary Edition.* Chicago: University of Chicago Press, 2002 [1962].

———. "The Counter-Revolution in Monetary Theory." Institute of Economic Affairs, occasional paper no. 33 (1970).

———. *Essays in Positive Economics.* Chicago: University of Chicago Press, 1966 [1953].

———. "The Role of Monetary Policy." *American Economic Review* 58 (March 1968).

Friedman, Milton, and Rose Friedman. "Record of a Trip to Southern Africa, March 20–April 9, 1976." The Collected Works of Milton Friedman at the Hoover Institution at Stanford University.

Friedman, Milton, and Anna Schwartz. *A Monetary History of the United States, 1867–1960.* Princeton, NJ: Princeton University Press, 1971 [1963].

Friedman, Milton, and George J. Stigler. *Roofs or Ceilings? The Current Housing Problem.* Irving-on-Hudson, NY: Foundation for Economic Education, 1946.

Galbraith, John Kenneth. *The Affluent Society: 40th Anniversary Edition.* Boston: Houghton Mifflin, 1998 [1958].

———. *American Capitalism.* Boston: Houghton Mifflin, 1961 [1953].

———. *Annals of an Abiding Liberal.* Boston: Houghton Mifflin, 1979.

———. *Economics in Perspective.* Boston: Houghton Mifflin, 1987.

———. *The Great Crash, 1929.* Boston: Houghton Mifflin, 1961 [1954].

———. *A Life in Our Times.* Boston: Houghton Mifflin, 1981.

———. *Money: Whence It Came, Where It Went.* Princeton, NJ: Princeton University Press, 2017 [1974].

———. *The New Industrial State.* Boston: Houghton Mifflin, 1967.

Garnett, David. *The Flowers of the Forest.* New York: Harcourt Brace and Company, 1956.

Gilbert, Martin. *Prophet of Truth: Winston Churchill, 1922–1939.* London: Minerva, 1990 [1976].

Gilbert, Richard V., et al. *An Economic Program for American Democracy.* New York: Vanguard Press, 1938.

Glendenning, Victoria. *Leonard Woolf: A Biography.* New York: Free Press, 2006.

Goldwater, Barry. *The Conscience of a Conservative.* Princeton, NJ: Princeton University Press, 2007 [1960].

Goodman, James, ed. *Letters to Kennedy: John Kenneth Galbraith.* Cambridge, MA: Harvard University Press, 1998.

Goodwin, Doris Kearns. *No Ordinary Time: Franklin and Eleanor Roosevelt: The Home Front in World War II.* New York: Simon & Schuster, 1994.

Griffin, Nicholas, ed. *The Selected Letters of Bertrand Russell: The Public Years 1914–1970.* London: Routledge, 2001.

Hall, Peter A., ed. *The Political Power of Economic Ideas: Keynesianism Across Nations.* Princeton, NJ: Princeton University Press, 1989.

Hamilton, Earl J. *American Treasure and the Price Revolution in Spain, 1501–1650.* Cambridge, MA: Harvard University Press, 1934.

Harris, John. *The Survivor: Bill Clinton in the White House.* New York: Random House, 2005.

Harrod, Roy F. *The Life of John Maynard Keynes.* London: Macmillan, 1951.

Hayek, F. A. *The Constitution of Liberty: Definitive Edition.* Chicago: University of Chicago Press, 2011 [1960].

———. *Law, Legislation and Liberty, Vols. 1–3: A New Statement of the Liberal Principles of Justice and Political Economy.* New York: Routledge, 2013 [1982].

———. *Prices and Production and Other Works: F. A. Hayek on Money, The Business Cycle, and the Gold Standard.* Auburn, AL: Ludwig von Mises Institute, 2008.

———. *The Road to Serfdom: The Definitive Edition.* Chicago: University of Chicago Press, 2007 [1944].

Heller, Francis H. *Economics and the Truman Administration.* Lawrence: Regents Press of Kansas, 1981.

Hobbes, Thomas. *Leviathan, with Selected Variants from the Latin Edition of 1688.* Indianapolis, IN: Hackett, 1994.

Holroyd, Michael. *Lytton Strachey: A Biography.* New York: Holt, Rinehart and Winston, 1980 [1971].

Holt, Richard P. F., ed. *The Selected Letters of John Kenneth Galbraith.* New York: Cambridge University Press, 2017.

Hoover, Herbert. *The Memoirs of Herbert Hoover: The Great Depression, 1929–1941.* Eastford, CT: Martino Fine Books, 2016 [1952].

———. *The Ordeal of Woodrow Wilson.* Washington, D.C.: Woodrow Wilson Center Press/Baltimore: Johns Hopkins University Press, 1992 [1958].

Horn, Martin. *Britain, France, and the Financing of the First World War.* Montreal and Kingston, Canada: McGill–Queen's University Press, 2002.

House, Edward Mandell, and Charles Seymour, eds. *What Really Happened at Paris: The Story of the Peace Conference, 1918–1919.* New York: Charles Scribner's Sons, 1921.

Johnson, Elizabeth, Donald Moggridge, and Austin Robinson, eds. *The Collected Writings of John Maynard Keynes, Vols. 1–30.* New York: Cambridge University Press for the Royal Economic Society, 1971–1982.

Jones, Daniel Stedman. *Masters of the Universe: Hayek, Friedman, and the Birth of Neoliberal Politics.* Princeton, NJ: Princeton University Press, 2012.

Kahn, Richard. *The Making of Keynes' General Theory.* Cambridge, UK: Cambridge University Press, 1984.

Katznelson, Ira. *Fear Itself: The New Deal and the Origins of Our Time.* New York: Liveright Publishing, 2013.

Keynes, John Maynard. *The Economic Consequences of the Peace.* London: Macmillan, 1919.

———. *The General Theory of Employment, Interest and Money.* New York: Prometheus Books, 1997 [1936].

———. *Indian Currency and Finance*. London: Macmillan, 1913.

———. *A Tract on Monetary Reform*. London: Macmillan, 1923.

———. *A Treatise on Money, Vols. I and II*. Mansfield Center, CT: Martino Publishing, 2011 [1930].

———. *A Treatise on Probability*. London: Macmillan, 1921.

Kindleberger, Charles. *A Financial History of Western Europe*. London: George Allen & Unwin, 1984.

———. *The World in Depression, 1929–1939: 40th Anniversary Edition*. Berkeley: University of California Press, 2013 [1973].

Lane, Rose Wilder. *The Discovery of Freedom: Man's Struggle Against Authority*. New York: John Day, 1943.

Lee, Hermione. *Virginia Woolf*. New York: Alfred A. Knopf, 1997.

Levy, Paul, ed. *The Letters of Lytton Strachey*. New York: Farrar, Straus and Giroux, 2006.

Link, Arthur, ed. *The Papers of Woodrow Wilson, Vol. 24: January–August 1912*. Princeton, NJ: Princeton University Press, 1978.

Lippmann, Walter. *The Good Society*. Boston: Little, Brown, 1938.

Lovin, Clifford R. *A School for Diplomats: The Paris Peace Conference of 1919*. Lanham, MD: The University Press of America, 1997.

Mackrell, Judith. *Bloomsbury Ballerina: Lydia Lopokova, Imperial Dancer and Mrs. John Maynard Keynes*. London: Phoenix, 2009 [2008].

MacMillan, Margaret. *Paris 1919: Six Months That Changed the World*. New York: Random House, 2003 [2001].

Maney, Patrick J. *Bill Clinton: New Gilded Age President*. Lawrence: University of Kansas Press, 2016.

Mann, Geoff. *In the Long Run We Are All Dead: Keynesianism, Political Economy and Revolution*. New York: Verso, 2017.

McElvaine, Robert S. *The Great Depression: America, 1929–1941*. New York: Three Rivers Press, 2009 [1984].

McGuinness, Brian. *Wittgenstein: A Life: Young Ludwig, 1889–1921*. Berkeley, CA: University of California Press, 1988.

Millin, Sarah Gertrude. *General Smuts, Vols. I and II*. London: Faber & Faber, 1936.

Mini, Piero V. *John Maynard Keynes: A Study in the Psychology of Original Work*. New York: St. Martin's Press, 1994.

Minsky, Hyman. *John Maynard Keynes*. New York: McGraw-Hill, 2008 [1975].

Mises, Ludwig von. *Bureaucracy*. New Rochelle, NY: Arlington House, 1969 [1944].

———. *Socialism: An Economic and Sociological Analysis*. New Haven, CT: Yale University Press, 1951 [1927].

Moore, G. E. *Principia Ethica*. Cambridge, UK: Cambridge University Press, 1922 [1903].

Morgan, E. Victor. *Studies in British Financial Policy, 1914–25*. London: Macmillan, 1952.

Mowat, Charles Loch. *Britain Between the Wars, 1918–1940*. Boston: Beacon Press, 1971 [1955].

Nicolson, Nigel, and Joanne Trautmann, eds. *The Letters of Virginia Woolf, Vols. 1–5*. New York: Harcourt Brace Jovanovich, 1976–1979.

Paninkin, Don, and J. Clark Leith, eds. *Keynes, Cambridge and the General Theory*. New York: Macmillan, 1977.

Parker, Richard. *John Kenneth Galbraith: His Life, His Politics, His Economics*. Chicago: University of Chicago Press, 2005.

Pecchi, Lorenzo, and Gustavo Piga, eds. *Revisiting Keynes: Economic Possibilities for Our Grandchildren*. Cambridge, MA: MIT Press, 2008.

Pecora, Ferdinand. *Wall Street Under Oath: The Story of Our Modern Money Changers.* New York: Graymalkin Media, 1939.

Perkins, Frances. *The Roosevelt I Knew.* New York: Penguin, 2011 [1946].

Perlstein, Rick. *Nixonland: The Rise of a President and the Fracturing of America.* New York: Scribner, 2008.

Rauchway, Eric. *The Money Makers: How Roosevelt and Keynes Ended the Depression, Defeated Fascism, and Secured a Prosperous Peace.* New York: Basic Books, 2015.

———. *Winter War: Hoover, Roosevelt, and the First Clash over the New Deal.* New York: Basic Books, 2018.

Regan, Tom. *Bloomsbury's Prophet: G. E. Moore and the Development of His Moral Philosophy.* Philadelphia: Temple University Press, 1986.

Ricardo, David. *On the Principles of Political Economy.* London: John Murray, 1817.

Riddell, George. *Lord Riddell's Intimate Diary of the Peace Conference and After: 1918– 23.* London: Victor Gollancz, 1933.

Ringer, Fritz K., ed. *The German Inflation of 1923.* London: Oxford University Press, 1969.

Robin, Corey. *The Reactionary Mind,* 2nd ed. New York: Oxford University Press, 2018.

Robbins, Lionel. *Autobiography of an Economist.* London: Macmillan, 1971.

Robinson, Joan. *The Economics of Imperfect Competition.* London: Macmillan 1938 [1933].

———. "The Second Crisis of Economic Theory." *The American Economic Review* 62, no. 1/2 (March 1972).

Robinson, Joan, and Francis Cripps. "Keynes Today." *Journal of Post-Keynesian Economics* 2, no. 1 (1979).

Rodgers, Daniel T. *Age of Fracture.* Cambridge, MA: The Belknap Press of Harvard University Press, 2011.

Rosenbaum, S. P., ed. *The Bloomsbury Group: A Collection of Memoirs and Commentary.* Toronto: University of Toronto Press, 1995.

Rousseau, Jean-Jacques. *The Basic Political Writings.* Indianapolis, IN: Hackett, 1987.

Russell, Bertrand. *The Autobiography of Bertrand Russell, 1872–1914.* Boston: Little, Brown, 1967.

Samuelson, Paul. *Economics: The Original 1948 Edition.* New York: McGraw-Hill, 1997 [1948].

Sandilands, Roger. "Guilt by Association? Lauchlin Currie's Alleged Involvement with Washington Economists in Soviet Espionage." *History of Political Economy* 32, no. 3 (Fall 2000).

Schlesinger, Arthur M., Jr. *The Coming of the New Deal.* Boston: Houghton Mifflin, 1959.

———. *The Crisis of the Old Order.* Boston: Houghton Mifflin, 2002 [1957].

———. *The Life and Political Economy of Lauchlin Currie: New Dealer, Presidential Adviser and Developmental Economist.* Durham, NC: Duke University Press, 1990.

———. *The Politics of Upheaval.* Boston: Houghton Mifflin, 1960.

———. *A Thousand Days: John F. Kennedy in the White House.* Boston: Houghton Mifflin, 2002 [1965].

———. *The Vital Center.* Boston: Houghton Mifflin, 1949.

Schumpeter, Joseph, et al. *The Economics of the Recovery Program.* New York: Whittlesey House, 1934.

Skidelsky, Robert. *John Maynard Keynes,* vol. 1: *Hopes Betrayed, 1883–1920.* New York: Penguin, 1994 [1983].

————. *John Maynard Keynes*, vol. 2: *The Economist as Savior, 1920–1937*. New York: Allen Lane, 1994.

————. *John Maynard Keynes*, vol. 3: *Fighting for Freedom, 1937–1946*. New York: Viking, 2001.

Slobodian, Quinn. *Globalists: The End of Empire and the Birth of Neoliberalism*. Cambridge, MA: Harvard University Press, 2018.

Solberg, Winton U., and Robert W. Tomlinson. "Academic McCarthyism and Keynesian Economics: The Bowen Controversy at the University of Illinois," *History of Political Economy* 29, no. 1 (1997).

Spalding, Frances. *Duncan Grant: A Biography*. London: Pimlico, 1998.

————. *Vanessa Bell: Portrait of the Bloomsbury Artist*. New York: Tauris Parke Paperbacks, 2016 [1983].

Steel, Ronald. *Walter Lippmann and the American Century*. Boston: Little, Brown, 1980.

Stein, Herbert. *The Fiscal Revolution in America*. Chicago: University of Chicago Press, 1969.

Stiglitz, Joseph. *Globalization and Its Discontents*. New York: W. W. Norton & Co., 2003.

————. *The Roaring Nineties: A New History of the World's Most Prosperous Decade*. New York: W. W. Norton & Co., 2004.

Strachey, John. *The Coming Struggle for Power*. New York: Modern Library, 1935 [1932].

————. *Contemporary Capitalism*. New York: Random House, 1956.

Strachey, Lytton. *Eminent Victorians: Cardinal Manning, Florence Nightingale, Dr. Arnold, General Gordon*. London: G. P. Putnam Sons, 1918.

Tarshis, Lorie. *The Elements of Economics*. Boston: Houghton Mifflin, 1947.

Tooze, Adam. *The Deluge: The Great War, America and the Remaking of the Global Order, 1916–1931*. New York: Penguin, 2006; Viking, 2014.

Trachtenberg, Marc. "Reparation at the Paris Peace Conference." *The Journal of Modern History* 51, no. 1 (March 1979).

Truman, Harry. *Memoirs: Year of Decisions*. New York: Doubleday, 1955.

Tuchman, Barbara. *The Guns of August: The Outbreak of World War I*. New York: Random House, 2014 [1962].

Turner, Marjorie S. *Joan Robinson and the Americans*. Armonk, NY: M. E. Sharpe, 1989.

Wilson, Woodrow. *A History of the American People, Volume V: Reunion and Nationalization*. New York: Harper and Brothers, 1902.

Wittgenstein, Ludwig. *Tractatus Logico-Philosophicus*. London: Kegan Paul, Trench, Trübner, 1922.

Wolfensberger, Don. "Woodrow Wilson, Congress and Anti-Immigrant Sentiment in America: An Introductory Essay." Woodrow Wilson Center International Center for Scholars, March 12, 2007.

Woodward, Bob. *The Agenda: Inside the Clinton White House*. New York: Simon & Schuster, 1995.

Woolf, Leonard. *Beginning Again: An Autobiography of the Years 1911 to 1918*. New York: Harcourt Brace Jovanovich, 1964.

————. *Downhill All The Way: An Autobiography of the Years 1919 to 1939*. New York: Harcourt Brace Jovanovich, 1967.

Zeitz, Joshua. *Building the Great Society: Inside Lyndon Johnson's White House*. New York: Viking, 2018.

INDEX

◊

Zachary D. Carter is a senior reporter at *HuffPost,* where he covers Congress, the White House, and economic policy. He is a frequent guest on cable news and news radio, and his written work has also appeared in *The New Republic, The Nation,* and *The American Prospect,* among other outlets. His story "Swiped: Banks, Merchants, and Why Washington Doesn't Work for You" was included in the *Columbia Journalism Review*'s anthology *Best Business Writing.* He lives in Brooklyn with his wife, Jia Lynn Yang; their daughter, Ming; and their dog, Pepper. This is his first book.